A VELVET EMPIRE

HISTORIES OF ECONOMIC LIFE

Jeremy Adelman, Sunil Amrith,
Emma Rothschild, and Francesca Trivellato, Series Editors

A Velvet Empire: French Informal Imperialism in the Nineteenth Century
by David Todd

Making It Count: Statistics and Statecraft in the Early People's Republic of China
by Arunabh Ghosh

Empires of Vice: The Rise of Opium Prohibition across Southeast Asia
by Diana S. Kim

Pirates and Publishers: A Social History of Copyright in Modern China
by Fei-Hsien Wang

Sorting Out the Mixed Economy: The Rise and Fall of Welfare and Developmental States in the Americas by Amy C. Offner

Red Meat Republic: A Hoof-to-Table History of How Beef Changed America
by Joshua Specht

The Promise and Peril of Credit: What a Forgotten Legend about Jews and Finance Tells Us about the Making of European Commercial Society
by Francesca Trivellato

A People's Constitution: The Everyday Life of Law in the Indian Republic
by Rohit De

A Local History of Global Capital: Jute and Peasant Life in the Bengal Delta
by Tariq Omar Ali

A Velvet Empire

FRENCH INFORMAL IMPERIALISM IN
THE NINETEENTH CENTURY

DAVID TODD

PRINCETON UNIVERSITY PRESS

PRINCETON & OXFORD

Published by Princeton University Press
41 William Street, Princeton, New Jersey 08540
6 Oxford Street, Woodstock, Oxfordshire OX20 1TR

press.princeton.edu

Library of Congress Cataloging-in-Publication Data

Names: Todd, David, 1978– author.
Title: A velvet empire : French informal imperialism in the nineteenth century /
David Todd.
Description: Princeton ; Oxford : Princeton University Press, [2021] |
    Series: Histories of economic life | Includes bibliographical references and index.
Identifiers: LCCN 2020022660 (print) | LCCN 2020022661 (ebook) |
    ISBN 9780691171838 (hardback) | ISBN 9780691205342 (ebook)
Subjects: LCSH: France—Foreign relations—19th century. | France—Politics and
    government—19th century. | France—Colonies—History—19th century. |
    France—Foreign economic relations—19th century. |
    France—Commerce—History—19th century.
Classification: LCC DC252 .T63 2021 (print) | LCC DC252 (ebook) |
    DDC 325/.32094409034—dc23
LC record available at https://lccn.loc.gov/2020022660
LC ebook record available at https://lccn.loc.gov/2020022661

British Library Cataloging-in-Publication Data is available

Editorial: Eric Crahan, Priya Nelson, and Thalia Leaf
Production Editorial: Natalie Baan
Jacket Design: Karl Spurzem
Production: Jacquie Poirier
Publicity: Kate Farquhar-Thomson and Alyssa Sanford

Jacket art: (top) Shutterstock; (bottom) Opening of the Suez Canal on Nov. 17, 1869.
At the invitation of the Khedive Ismail, the French empress Eugénie's imperial yacht
led the procession of ships opening the canal. 1869 engraving with 2011 color /
Everett Collection Inc. / Alamy Stock Photo

This book has been composed in Arno

Printed on acid-free paper. ∞

Printed in the United States of America

10 9 8 7 6 5 4 3 2 1

For my mother

CONTENTS

Acknowledgements   ix

List of Abbreviations   xi

Introduction   1

Forgotten Empire   4

Counter-Revolutionary Empire   10

Collaborative Empire   16

1   Empire without Sovereignty: The Political Economy of
    French Informal Imperialism   25

   Talleyrand's Imperial Vision   30

   The Invention of Neo-Colonialism   37

   Celebrating European Civilization   44

   Saint-Simonian Economics and Empire   51

   A French Imperialism of Free Trade   58

   A Turn to Formal Empire   66

2   Algeria, Informal Empire Manqué   72

   The Ideological Origins of French Algeria   78

   The Bourbon Restoration's Colonial Scheme   84

   The Politics and Geopolitics of the 1830 Expedition   89

   Collaboration with 'Abd al-Qadir   96

   Economic Failure   104

   The Arab Kingdom, a Failed Revival of Informal Empire   110

3 Champagne Capitalism: The Commodification of
  Luxury and the French Empire of Taste   123

  The Acceleration of Globalization in France   127

  The Banality of Luxury   134

  Foundations of Neo-Courtly Economic Growth   142

  The Global Commodification of French Taste   151

  The Imperialism of the Empire of Taste   160

4 Conquest by Money: The Geopolitics and Logistics of
  Investment Colonization   175

  The Global Scale of French Foreign Lending   179

  Debt and Empire in French Political Economy   186

  The Haitian Origins of French Capital Exports   196

  Conquest by Money in the Middle East   206

  Financial Imperial Overreach in Mexico   218

5 Agents of Informal Empire: French Expatriates and
  Extraterritorial Jurisdiction in Egypt   227

  French Imperial Expatriates   231

  The Colony's Influence   237

  A French Legal Borderland   245

  The Imperial Profits of Extraterritoriality   254

  The Crisis of French Extraterritoriality in Egypt   260

  End of French Ascendancy   266

  Conclusion   277

  Bibliography 287

  Index 331

ACKNOWLEDGEMENTS

THIS BOOK originates in a conversation with the late Christopher Bayly, who, around ten years ago, asked me a series of stimulating questions about the place of France in the world in the nineteenth century. I am still deeply grateful for the way in which his insightful suggestions redirected my research interests towards the global and imperial dimension of French history. The book also owes a lot, more than I could express here, to the pioneering scholarship and warm encouragement of Emma Rothschild.

As the project developed, it benefited from the suggestions and criticisms of too many scholars for me to recall, let alone list here. Still, I would especially like to thank Jeremy Adelman, Sunil Amrith, David Armitage, Andrew Arsan, David Bell, Maxine Berg, Hélène Blais, John Brewer, Martin Daunton, Nicolas Delalande, Quentin Deluermoz, James Fichter, Michael Goebel, Jerome Greenfield, Jean Hébrard, Simon Jackson, Harold James, François Jarrige, Colin Jones, Michael Kwass, Michael Ledger-Lomas, Claire Lemercier, Renaud Morieux, William Nelson, Patrick O'Brien, Ozan Ozavci, Gabriel Paquette, Jennifer Pitts, Lucy Riall, Anne-Isabelle Richard, Pernille Røge, Stephen Sawyer, John Shovlin, Pierre Singaravélou, Melissa Teixeira, Frank Trentmann, Francesca Trivellato, Alexia Yates, and the late Donald Winch, because I can still associate each of them with distinct major or minor points I make in the book. I am also very grateful to the organizers of several seminars and conferences where I presented aspects of the project—at the Casa de Velasquez in Madrid, the University of Cambridge, the Conservatoire National des Arts et Métiers, the École Normale Supérieure, the École des Hautes Études en Sciences Sociales, the European University Institute in Florence, the Freie Universität in Berlin, Harvard University, the Institute of Historical Research in London, Johns Hopkins University, Princeton University, Utrecht University and Warwick University. The enthusiasm and skepticism I encountered at these presentations inspired me, in equal measure, to complete the project.

I would also like to thank my students at King's College London for having put up with me for the past nine years and for having often served as the first, semi-captive audience of several aspects of the book's argument. I am especially grateful to two PhD students, Laura Forster and Leonard Hodges, whose research influenced my own understanding of nineteenth-century France. I cannot thank my colleagues in King's History Department warmly enough for making it such an exciting and friendly environment in which to research and teach.

All historical research owes more to the help of librarians and archivists than meets the eye, and this work is no exception. I feel especially indebted to Sylvie Prudon from the Archives Diplomatiques in La Courneuve, who helped me navigate the archival series of French consulates in the Middle East. The finished product of historical research owes an enormous deal to publishers, and I was very impressed by the professionalism and kindness of all those I have worked with at Princeton University Press, especially Brigitta van Rheinberg, Amanda Peery and Eric Crahan. I also wish to thank the Leverhulme Trust for funding an extended sabbatical leave, from 2013 to 2015, during which time a great deal of the original research for the project was completed.

This book is, in addition, the product of many influences from outside the academic world. Among these I must single out the vision of nineteenth-century France of one of its great *connaisseurs*, Georges Liébert, including an especially stimulating discussion with him and Alice d'Andigné, in 2016, about nineteenth-century Paris. A more diffuse but very decisive influence was that of spending most of my adult life in Britain, having grown up in France. I hope the book reflects my understanding of how the French see themselves, but it has hugely benefited from the opportunity I have had of learning to see France from the world outside. Translations of quotations originally in French are my own, although I have consulted and often followed contemporary translations where available.

My own Anglo-French nuclear family has been a constant source of emotional support. I am more than ever in awe of my wife, Victoria Moul, an amazing scholar and wonderful mother, who still found the time to be my first reader and expunge remaining Gallicisms from the manuscript. My young sons, Joseph and Felix, have contributed in their own mischievous ways to the endeavour, not least by helping me to take seriously the advantages of the Malthusian model of French economic development in the nineteenth century. The book is dedicated to my mother, whose love never failed me, which made everything else possible.

ABBREVIATIONS

ADM   Archives Départementales de la Marne

ADV   Archives Départementales du Var

AAE   Archives des Affaires Étrangères

AN   Archives Nationales

ANOM   Archives Nationales d'Outre-Mer, Aix-en-Provence

BNF   Bibliothèque Nationale de France

CCC   Correspondance Consulaire et Commerciale

CAEF   Centre des Archives Économiques et Financères

CAMT   Centre des Archives du Monde du Travail

HSP   Historical Society of Pennsylvania

M&D   Mémoires & Documents

TNA   The National Archives

TRA   The Rothschild Archive

WS   Worms Stadtarchiv

A VELVET EMPIRE

Introduction

IT OUGHT to be a commonplace that, for most of the nineteenth century, France expanded chiefly by means of informal empire. After the fall of Napoleon's European empire, the formal, sovereign authority of the French state became confined almost exactly to the boundaries of modern metropolitan France and a handful of secondary islands and trading posts. Between 1815 and 1880, France acquired a few more *comptoirs*, but its sole significant territorial conquest was what is today the temperate part of Algeria, an outlying province of the Ottoman Empire. Yet throughout this period France is almost unanimously recognized as a major crucible of modern European imperialism, alongside Britain. This perception is not an illusion. Contemporary French society and politics made decisive contributions to the Orientalist and pseudo-scientific racist discourses that served to justify the colonial subjugation of Asians and Africans. Thanks to its economic, scientific and military wherewithal, France remained Britain's main rival overseas. France was the world's second imperial power, but without a colonial empire.

The main purpose of this book is to resolve this paradox, showing that mid-nineteenth century France acquired a vast empire while hardly expanding its territorial jurisdiction. Looking back on Britain's imperial experience in the era of decolonization, Ronald Robinson and John Gallagher claimed that neglecting the informal dimension of British imperialism was "rather like judging the size and character of icebergs solely from the parts above the water-line."[1]

---

1. John Gallagher and Ronald Robinson, "The Imperialism of Free Trade," *Economic History Review*, 2nd ser., 6 (1953): 1. On the early impact of the informal empire paradigm on British imperial studies, see *Imperialism: The Robinson and Gallagher Controversy*, ed. Wm Roger Louis (New York: New Viewpoints, 1976); on later debates about the concept's validity and usefulness, especially in the case of Latin America, see for example the exchange between Andrew

If anything, the proportion of the nineteenth-century French imperial iceberg that lay below the waterline was even greater. France's informal empire was also more sophisticated than Britain's, because it drew to a greater extent on "soft" cultural power, and used it in combination with conventional "hard" economic and military power. This sophistication prefigured, in some respects, the global projection of American "smart power" after 1945.[2] But France's informal empire upheld an aristocratic rather than a democratic ethos. It exported silk textiles and the comedy of manners rather than blue jeans and sentimental movies. Since velvet denotes softness and refinement, and was usually made out of silk in the nineteenth century, "velvet empire" seems an apt phrase to describe this cunning but courtly imperial strategy, and a fitting title.

This emphasis on the informal deployment of French power does not seek to diminish the significance of formal manifestations of French imperialism in the nineteenth century. It is especially not my intention to downplay the extraordinary violence employed by France in conquering Algeria after 1830. Not only did this violence profoundly affect later Franco-Algerian interactions, perhaps to this day, but French Algeria also proved to be the crucible of several significant features of France's system of colonial rule as its territorial empire expanded rapidly after 1880.[3] Instead, the book seeks to reappraise the informal dimension of French imperialism between the downfall of Napoleon's

---

Thompson, "Informal Empire? An Exploration in the History of Anglo-Argentine Relations, 1810–1914," *Journal of Latin American Studies*, 24, 2 (1992) and Anthony G. Hopkins, "Informal Empire in Argentina: An Alternative View," *Journal of Latin American Studies*, 26, 2 (1994), and *Informal Empire in Latin America: Culture, Commerce and Capital*, ed. Matthew Brown (Oxford: Blackwell, 2008). On the early use of this paradigm to highlight the imperial dimension of modern US foreign policy, see William Appleman Wiliams, *The Tragedy of American Diplomacy* (Cleveland: World Publishing, 1959), and for a more recent appraisal of the achievements of Williams and the so-called Wisconsin school, see *Redefining the Past: Essays in Diplomatic History in Honor of William Appleman Williams*, ed. Lloyd Gardner (Corvallis: Oregon State University Press, 1986).

2. On the concept of soft power and its articulation with hard power, see Joseph Nye, *Soft Power: The Means to Success in World Politics* (New York: Public Affairs, 2004), and Ernest J. Wilson III, "Hard Power, Soft Power, Smart Power," *Annals of the American Academy of Political and Social Science*, 616 (2008).

3. On the violence of the French conquest, see among others William Gallois, *A History of Violence in the Early Algerian Colony* (Basingstoke: Palgrave Macmillan, 2013) and Abdelmajid Hannoum, *Violent Modernity: France in Algeria* (Cambridge, MA: Harvard University Press, 2010); on Algeria as a laboratory of French colonial rule, see for instance Emmanuelle Saada,

European empire and the rise of the Third Republic's colonial empire. During this period, it claims, France's resurgent imperial status relied far more on the global projection of its influence than on the expansion of its sovereignty. I hope that such an approach will help to draw a more comprehensive picture of the nature and scope of French imperial power by redressing the balance of a historiography that is still mainly preoccupied by the official aspects of French imperialism. Empires in world history have tended to rely not on a single mode of domination, but rather on "repertoires of rules", or combinations of various methods to assert their authority.[4] The French repertoire in the nineteenth century included a formal component which prevailed in Algeria and became the main form of French expansion after 1880. Yet by several political, economic and cultural measures, this informal component may be considered to have had an even greater impact on the world and on metropolitan France, at least until the colonial frenzy of the late nineteenth century.

As several historians of empire have noted, the very dichotomy between formal and informal can be as problematic as it is "seductive."[5] There are different types of formal rule, ranging from full annexation to protectorate regimes: recent histories of the concept and practice of sovereignty have dispelled the illusion that it was ever one and indivisible, especially in a colonial context.[6] If anything, informal rule was even more multifarious, as it relied on extremely varied combinations of cultural, economic, legal and even military elements. When we think theoretically about empire, it may be more accurate to speak of a spectrum or gradients of imperial rule.[7] At the same time, such sophisticated modelling risks detracting attention from the informal side of

Les enfants de la colonie: Les métis de l'empire français entre sujétion et citoyenneté (Paris: La Découverte, 2007), esp. 111–25.

4. Jane Burbank and Frederick Cooper, *Empires in World History: Power and the Politics of Difference* (Princeton, NJ: Princeton University Press, 2010), 3–17.

5. Paul A. Kramer, "Power and Connection: Histories of the United States in the World," *American Historical Review*, 116, 5 (2011): 1374–76.

6. See, among others, Lauren Benton, *Law and Colonial Culture: Legal Regimes in World History, 1400–1900* (Cambridge: Cambridge University Press, 2002) and Andrew Fitzmaurice, *Sovereignty, Property and Empire, 1500–2000* (Cambridge: Cambridge University Press, 2015); on the slipperiness of sovereignty in a French imperial context, see Mary Lewis, *Divided Rule: Sovereignty and Empire in French Tunisia, 1881–1938* (Berkeley: University of California Press, 2014).

7. Ann L. Stoler, "On Degrees of Imperial Sovereignty," *Public Culture* 18, 1 (2006); on efforts by political scientists to define informal imperial power, see Michael Doyle, *Empires* (Ithaca, NY: Cornell University Press, 1986), esp. 32–39, 135–36.

the spectrum, because it is by nature more elusive than the formal side. Crucially for the historian, it leaves fainter archival traces than colonial administrations. Even critiques of the dichotomy between formal and informal empire have lately found it necessary to recall that the "narrow definition of empire as territorial control" could result in dangerous elisions.[8] When we consider the dynamics of a specific imperial formation, dispensing with informal empire can cause more problems than it solves. This book seeks instead to address some of this concept's limitations, especially the mechanistic equation it often assumed between economic and imperial power. Drawing on new approaches towards the history of economic life, it pays due attention to the roles played by ideas, culture and laws, alongside those of trade and finance, in shaping informal imperial power and the effects it had.

For the sake of a clear argument, this book mostly treats the French informal imperial repertoire as a distinct form of imperialism, or another empire. Edward W. Fox, in his classic work, did not deny the existence of the centripetal forces emphasized by most historians of the French nation-state, but also sought to discern another, outward-looking France. The echo here of this approach is deliberate. There are noteworthy overlaps between Fox's "other France" and the other empire examined in this book, not least the role of transnational connections in moulding modern French economics, politics and society.[9] France's other empire in the nineteenth century may be less immediately visible than its colonial ventures. Yet it was global in scope, and although exploitative in subtler ways, imbued with a similar cultural and racial arrogance.

Forgotten Empire

There is a widespread notion that, after the fall of Napoleon, France withdrew into itself and renounced empire for the next seventy years. Historical surveys of French colonialism concede that the period saw the first tentative steps towards the constitution of what would become France's "second colonial empire" after 1880, with the conquest of Algeria and the acquisition of small territorial footholds in Africa and Indochina. But most stress the hesitations and

8. Paul Kramer, "How Not to Write the History of U.S. Empire," *Diplomatic History* 42, 5 (2018): 913–14.

9. Edward J. Fox, *History in Geographic Perspective: The Other France* (New York: Norton, 1971).

incoherence of French empire building in those decades.[10] Such views, this book claims, rely on a narrow conception of empire as an exclusively territorial enterprise and on the teleological premise that the colonial empire of the Third Republic should have been the goal pursued by French empire builders before 1880.

The main lesson drawn by the regimes that succeeded Napoleon's empire was arguably not that imperial pursuits should be forsaken, but that imperial grandeur was crucial to the preservation of domestic stability. This lesson was frequently articulated by French political elites and found validation in the cult of Napoleon that spread across France after 1815.[11] Post–revolutionary governments frequently turned to imperial ventures as a means of healing domestic divisions. Such ventures could be formal, as in the case of Algeria.[12] Yet they could also be informal, as demonstrated by the erection of the Luxor Obelisk in 1836, on the renamed Place de la Concorde—formerly Place de la Révolution, where Louis XVI was executed in 1793. The Obelisk served as a souvenir of France's brief occupation of Egypt in 1798–1801, but this gift from the Egyptian pasha Muhammad 'Ali also symbolized the renewal of French domination by economic, cultural and scientific means over what remained, formally, a province of the Ottoman Empire.[13]

Another vivid illustration of how contemporaries hoped to revive French imperial grandeur by informal means was the pompous painting by Jean-Léon Gérôme, *The Reception of Siamese Ambassadors* (see figure 0.1). Completed in 1864, the work represented a ceremony held in 1861, during which representatives of King Mongkut (or Rama IV) of Siam (modern Thailand) presented several sumptuous gifts to the French emperor Napoleon III and the empress

10. Instances of this teleological neglect include Denise Bouche and Pierre Pluchon, *Histoire de la colonisation française*, 2 vols. (Paris: Fayard, 1991), esp. vol. 2: *Flux et reflux (1815–1962)*; Bernard Lauzanne (ed.), *L'aventure coloniale de la France*, 5 vols. (Paris: Denoël, 1987–97), esp. vol. 2: Jean Martin, *L'empire renaissant, 1789–1870*; Catherine Coquery-Vidrovitch, Jean Meyer, Jacques Thobie et al., *Histoire de la France coloniale*, 2nd edn., 3 vols. (Paris: Armand Colin, 1996), esp. vol. 1: *La conquête*; and Robert Aldrich, *Greater France: A History of French Overseas Expansion* (Basingstoke: Palgrave, 1996).

11. Sudir Hazareesingh, *The Legend of Napoleon* (London: Granta, 2005).

12. On hopes that the capture of Algiers in 1830 or the conquest of the rest of the Regency under the July Monarchy would sustain domestic stability, see Jennifer Sessions, *By Sword and Plow: France and the Conquest of Algeria* (Ithaca, NY: Cornell University Press, 2011).

13. Todd Porterfield, *The Allure of Empire: Art in the Service of French Imperialism, 1798–1836* (Princeton, NJ: Princeton University Press, 1998), 13–41.

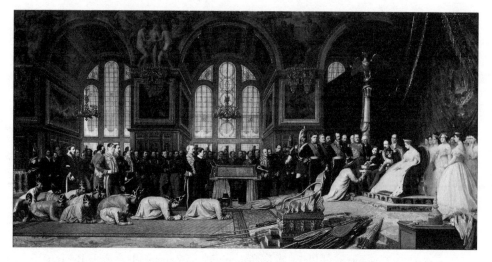

FIGURE 0.1. Jean-Léon Gérôme, *The Reception of Siamese Ambassadors by the Emperor Napoleon III at the Palace of Fontainebleau, 27 June 1861* (1864). *Source:* Château de Versailles, MV 5004; © RMN-Grand Palais. Reproduced by permission of RMN-GP (Château de Versailles).

Eugénie, in their summer residence of Fontainebleau. It also deliberately echoed the best-known pictorial representation of the first Napoleon's achievement of imperial status, Louis David's *Coronation of Napoleon* (1807).[14] Gérôme's works have often been derided as emblematic of the degeneration of neoclassical purity into a mediocre academic style, more concerned with the commercial potential of reproductions. Émile Zola argued that a painting by Gérôme was not a work of art, but "a fashionable commodity". The novelist claimed that "every living room in the provinces" contained a printed or engraved reproduction of a Gérôme.[15] *The Reception*, an official commission, cost the French state twenty thousand francs, but much smaller photomechanical prints could be purchased by any member of the public for just twenty francs.[16]

14. Meredith Martin, "History Repeats Itself in Jean-Léon Gérôme's *Reception of the Siamese Ambassadors,*" *Art Bulletin,* 99, 1 (2017).

15. Émile Zola, "Nos peintres au Champ-de-Mars," *La Situation,* 1 July 1867; repr. in *Jean-Léon Gérôme (1824–1904). L'histoire en spectacle,* eds. Laurence des Cars, Dominique de Font-Réaulx and Édouard Papet (Paris: Flammarion, 2010), 357.

16. Reproductions (27 × 43cm) of *The Reception* were sold until the end of the century; see *Gérôme et Goupil. Art & entreprise,* ed. Hélène Lafont-Couturier (Paris: Réunion des musées nationaux and Bordeaux: Musée Goupil, 2000), 154.

According to Zola, the subject in Gérôme's works was "everything", while the art of painting was "nothing". The subject of *The Reception* deserves a close analysis, because it encapsulated several major features of the French project of informal empire.[17] This project was economic, and the gift-giving ceremony represented by Gérôme was designed to seal a treaty of commerce between Siam and France that was typical of nineteenth-century "free trade imperialism". Concluded under the threat of French gunboats in 1856, the treaty limited Siamese customs duties to 3 percent *ad valorem* and granted extraterritorial jurisdiction to French nationals in Siam.[18] This project was also cultural, as suggested by the central position in the painting of the figure of Abbé Larnaurdie, a Catholic missionary who served as interpreter during the treaty's negotiation and the Siamese delegation's visit to France.[19] This project had distinctly racial and orientalizing undertones, as did Gérôme's painting—and indeed, a great deal of his oeuvre.[20] The chronicler and novelist Prosper Mérimée, who attended the original ceremony, compared the Siamese diplomats to "monkeys" and "cockchafers,"[21] because of their deportment and features. A caricature of the painting by the popular cartoonist Cham (real name Amédée de Noé, a friend of Gérôme) also represented the Siamese ambassadors as monkeys leapfrogging over each other in the midst of a bemused Bonapartist court.[22]

France's informal empire was not merely an instrument of propaganda. By the mid-1860s, not least thanks to an aggressive commercial diplomacy, the export of French commodities almost caught up with export from Britain, despite the latter's reputation as the workshop of the world. In the same period, the government's encouragement to save helped French foreign investment

17. Zola, "Nos peintres."

18. Dominique Le Bas, "La venue de l'ambassade siamoise en France," *Aséanie. Sciences humaines en Asie du Sud-Est*, 3 (1999).

19. Adrien Launay, *Siam et les missionnaires français* (Tours: Alfred Mame, 1866), 191; on French Catholicism and empire building, see *In God's Empire: French Missionaries and the Modern World*, eds. Owen White and J. P. Daughton (Oxford: Oxford University Press, 2012).

20. On Gérôme, whose *Snake Charmer*, also painted in the 1860s, was used by Edward Said for the original dustjacket of *Orientalism* (1978), as the quintessential Orientalist painter, see Linda Nochlin, *The Politics of Vision: Essays on Nineteenth-Century Art and Society* (New York: Harper & Row, 1989), 33–59.

21. Prosper Mérimée, *Lettres à une inconnue*, 2 vols. (Paris: Michel Lévy, 1874), vol. 2, 163–65.

22. Cartoon repr. in *Jean-Léon Gérôme*, 344.

surpass British capital export, despite the famed supremacy of the City of London. In the late eighteenth century, French was an international language only among Europe's courtly aristocracies. But by the 1870s it had become the lingua franca of old and new elites in Europe, the Middle East and Latin America. Restored French imperial grandeur in the mid-nineteenth century was almost certainly more profitable than the Third Republic's formal empire, the benefits of which have often appeared dubious to economic historians.[23] Colonial expansion after 1880 did little to prevent the decline of French as the language of international diplomacy, which began in the interwar period with the 1919 Peace Conference, in recognition of the American contribution to the Allies' victory during World War I.[24] So why has this informal empire—at least as profitable as the old Bourbon monarchy's colonial possessions in America and India, longer lasting than Napoleon's European empire, and a more evident source of power than the Third Republic's Empire in Africa and Indochina—been almost entirely forgotten by the public and historians alike?[25]

23. Henri Brunschwig, *Mythes et réalités de l'impérialisme colonial français, 1871–1914* (Paris: Armand Colin, 1960); Jacques Marseille, *Empire colonial et capitalisme français: histoire d'un divorce*, 2nd edn (Paris: Albin Michel, 2005). This is not to suggest that this formal empire was a significant burden for metropolitan France, or that its effects on economic development were benign; see Elise Huillery, "The Black Man's Burden: The Cost of Colonization of West Africa," *Journal of Economic History*, 74, 1 (2014), and the important ongoing research programme, "Public Finance and Investment in the French Colonial Empire," led by Denis Cogneau, Yannick Dupraz and Sandrine Meslé-Somps at the Paris School of Economics.

24. Vincent Laniol, "Langue et relations internationales: le monopole perdu de la langue française à la Conférence de la Paix de 1919," in *Histoire culturelle des relations internationales. Carrefour méthodologique*, ed. Denis Rolland (Paris: L'Harmattan, 2004), 79–116.

25. For calls to reappraise the informal dimension of French imperialism, see J. P. Daughton, "When Argentina Was 'French': Rethinking Cultural Politics and European Imperialism in Belle-Époque Buenos Aires," *Journal of Modern History*, 80, 4 (2008) and David Todd, "A French Imperial Meridian, 1814–1870," *Past & Present*, 210 (2011). Some French historians of international relations invoked the concept of informal empire, but mostly in an attempt to test the validity of the Marxist conception of imperialism for the period after 1880; see Jean Bouvier, René Girault and Jacques Thobie, *La France impériale, 1880–1914* (Paris: Megrelis, 1982) and *L'impérialisme à la française, 1914–1960* (Paris: La Découverte, 1986). Conversely, hostility to dogmatic Marxism led Raymond Aron to condemn the notion of "empire clandestin" as a conspiratorial view, in *Guerre et paix entre les nations* (Paris: Calman-Levy, 1962), 263–79, but Jean-Baptiste Duroselle took a more balanced view, although still focused on the period after 1880, in *Tout empire périra: une vision théorique des relations internationales* (Paris: Université Paris 1, 1982), 347.

A general cause of this neglect is the limited attention that has been accorded to the transnational and imperial dimension of French history.[26] France is still primarily viewed as a nation-state, even *the* original nation-state, in some accounts. In this traditional view, imperial ventures were a peripheral aspect of French history: distractions from its national and European destiny, or misguided aberrations that do not help us to understand the making of modern France. Since the 1990s, historians have reappraised the contributions of empire building (and unravelling) to the fashioning of modern French culture, society and politics. Yet such efforts have met with resistance, and few historians would yet subscribe to Frederic Cooper's pronouncement that France ceased to be an empire and became a nation-state only when Algeria gained independence in 1962.[27] Recent efforts at synthesis still tend to portray France as the least imperial, and the most national, of empires—as an "imperial nation-state", in a phrase that has gained in popularity.[28]

A limitation of this work of reappraisal has been its focus on the democratic phases of French history, the Revolution (1789–1799) and the Third Republic (1870–1940). The apparent contradiction between French revolutionary ideology on the one hand and the inequities of colonial rule on the other make this focus understandable, because a paradox needed explaining. Yet despite the global significance of the first abolition of slavery, following a successful slave insurrection in Saint-Domingue (modern-day Haiti), endeavours to reframe the founding event of modern France as a product of global rather than national forces continue to meet with skepticism.[29] Efforts to underline the Third

26. On this relative neglect, see Nancy L. Green, "French History and the Transnational Turn," *French Historical Studies* 37, 4 (2014) and Stephen Sawyer, "Ces nations façonnées par les empires et la globalisation. Réécrire le récit national du XIXe siècle aujourd'hui," *Annales. Histoire, Sciences Sociales*, 69, 1 (2014). However, some more recent grand narratives of French national history have begun to incorporate this transnational dimension; see for instance Aurélien Lignereux, *L'Empire des Français, 1799–1815* (Paris: Le Seuil, 2012) and Quentin Deluermoz, *Le crépuscule des révolutions, 1848–1871* (Paris: Le Seuil, 2012).

27. Frederick Cooper, "Alternatives to Empire: France and Africa after World War II," in *The State of Sovereignty: Territories, Laws, Populations*, eds. Douglas Howland and Luise White (Bloomington: Indiana University Press, 2009), 94–123.

28. Krishan Kumar, *Visions of Empire: How Five Imperial Regimes Shaped the World* (Princeton, NJ: Princeton University Press, 2017), 387–464.

29. On the global significance of the Haitian Revolution, see Laurent Dubois, *Avengers of the New World: The Story of the Haitian Revolution* (Cambridge, MA: Belknap Press of Harvard University Press, 2004) and on broader efforts to globalize the history of the French Revolution, see *The French Revolution in Global Perspective*, eds. Suzanne Desan, Lynn Hunt and

Republic's commitment to colonialism, including the emergence of a genuine imperial consciousness after the First World War, have encountered less resistance.[30] Yet it seems unlikely that this republican colonial empire, with around one million settlers and fifty million subjects in 1914, can ever serve to globalize the history of France as persuasively as the way in which the British Empire, with its over fifteen million settlers and four hundred million subjects, has been used to globalize the history of Britain.[31]

Repairing the neglect of France's informal imperial past therefore not only fills a significant gap in the history of French and European imperialism, but also contributes to ongoing efforts to understand how the world created France and Europe. France after Napoleon did not renounce empire. Instead, it became less interested in formal conquest and experimented with novel techniques of imperial domination. Yet, disturbingly for historians who tend to see democratic republicanism as the natural—if delayed—conclusion of the 1789 Revolution, this empire was far from an attempt to export revolutionary ideals. French proponents of informal empire usually looked back on the Revolution with a mixture of disillusion and dismay, while its collaborators outside France were mostly conservatives bent on reconciling economic modernization with the defence of their privileges. This informal civilizing mission was, in many respects, counter-revolutionary.

Counter-Revolutionary Empire

Being counter-revolutionary does not imply a reactionary longing for past institutions, or a blind adhesion to traditions. As noted by Christopher Bayly, the autocratic regimes that emerged from the age of global revolutions and

William Nelson (Ithaca, NY: Cornell University Press, 2013); on skepticism towards such approaches, see David Bell, "Questioning the Global Turn: The Case of the French Revolution," *French Historical Studies*, 37, 1 (2014).

30. See for instance Gary Wilder, *The French Imperial Nation-State: Négritude and Colonial Humanism between the Two World Wars* (Chicago: University of Chicago Press, 2005); on the penetration of colonial culture in France, especially in the interwar period, see *Culture coloniale en France: de la Révolution française à nos jours*, eds. Pascal Blanchard, Sandrine Lemaire and Nicolas Bancel (Paris: CNRS, 2008).

31. On the significance of Britain's large number of settlers, see John Darwin, *The Empire Project: The Rise and Fall of the British World-System, 1830–1970* (Cambridge: Cambridge University Press, 2009), esp. 41–44, and James Belich, *Replenishing the Earth: The Settler Revolution and the Rise of the Anglo-World, 1783–1939* (Oxford: Oxford University Press, 2009).

dominated the politics of Europe and the world between 1815 and 1865 were not resurrections, but "revamped" versions of old regime monarchies, which incorporated many innovations of the revolutionary era.[32] Christopher Clark made a similar point in his reappraisal of the decade that followed the failure of the 1848 Revolutions: far from constituting a "decade of reaction," as has often been asserted, the 1850s were a "high-water mark in political and administrative innovation across the [European] continent."[33] This phenomenon was transnational, global even, in some respects.[34] But because it had been so affected by the revolutionary turmoil, France may be seen as a key laboratory of counter-revolutionary modernity, and this exemplary role inspired and facilitated the spread of informal French imperial power by making France a protector of choice for modernizing conservative regimes.

This vision runs against the common perception of nineteenth-century France as being dominated by revolutionary outbursts, concluding with the advent of a democratic republican regime in the 1870s. Such a view has understandably appealed to historians of a republican persuasion, because it affirmed France's republican essence or destiny. It may also find support in a superficial reading of François Furet's conception of the Revolution as a one-hundred-year process and of the Third Republic as consecrating "a lasting victory of the French Revolution."[35] But the global and transnational perspectives cited above suggest another, less teleological interpretation. In reality, between 1799 and 1875, France remained almost continuously a monarchical regime, mostly de jure (First Empire, Bourbon Restoration and July Monarchy of 1804–1848, Second Napoleonic Empire of 1852–1870), sometimes de facto (Bonaparte's consulate of 1799–1804, his nephew's stint as prince-president in 1851–1852) and sometimes in absentia (royalist governments during most of the Second Republic, 1848–1851, and at the beginning of the Third Republic, 1871–1876). During this period, sincere republicans only governed the country twice, for ten months in 1848 and for five months in 1870–1871.[36]

<hr/>

32. Christopher A. Bayly, *The Birth of the Modern World: Global Connections and Comparisons, 1780–1914* (Oxford: Blackwell, 2004), 125.

33. Christopher Clark, "After 1848: The European Revolution in Government," *Transactions of the Royal Historical Society*, 22 (2012): 174.

34. Miles Taylor, "The 1848 Revolutions and the British Empire," *Past & Present*, 166 (2000).

35. François Furet, *La Révolution*, 2 vols. (Paris: Hachette, 1988), vol. 1, 9.

36. On the significance and limits of monarchical solutions to the problem of post-revolutionary political stability, see Pierre Rosanvallon, *Le moment Guizot* (Paris: Gallimard, 1985) and *La monarchie impossible: les Chartes de 1814 et 1830* (Paris: Fayard, 1994).

If one ceases to view the Third Republic as the inevitable outcome of the French Revolution, the major requirement for historians of nineteenth-century France is to understand the enduring prevalence of the monarchical model: seventy-five years is a very long time in French politics. The contingencies of domestic politics no doubt played a part, but the ceaseless reinvention of the monarchy—by Napoleon, the Bourbons, Louis-Philippe d'Orléans and Napoleon III—calls for a more structural explanation. Domestically, the fear of revolutionary disorder was almost certainly the primary factor, but this book contends that the monarchical form also survived for as long as it did in France because the latter managed to maintain its status as great global power, which it chiefly did by informal imperial means. It is probably not a coincidence that the decline of this informal empire, from the collapse of a French-backed monarchy in Mexico in 1867 until the waning of French influence in Egypt in the 1870s, went together with a faltering of domestic support for monarchical institutions. This influence of the global on the domestic would mirror the better-known role played by international humiliation during the crisis of the old pre-1789 monarchy, or the role of decolonization in bringing down parliamentary republicanism in the 1950s.[37]

Because the nineteenth-century informal empire was essentially built by monarchies, the republican teleology of modern French history has significantly contributed to its neglect. One of the more striking features of Gérôme's *Reception* is its courtly setting, which echoed not only David's *Coronation* of the first Napoleon, but also representations of a Siamese embassy at the court of Louis XIV in 1686, which Gérôme consulted.[38] This is not to suggest that the reinvented French monarchies were replicas of the pre-revolutionary order, but they did succeed in reviving those instruments of government that historians tend to associate with the early modern era, and they redeployed them to great effect. A case in point is that of the court itself, whose function was not only symbolic or political, but also economic. Historians of early mod-

37. On the geopolitical causes of the 1789 Revolution, see Timothy Blanning, *The Origins of the French Revolutionary Wars* (London: Longman, 1986), 36–68, and Bailey Stone, *Reinterpreting the French Revolution: A Global-Historical Perspective* (Cambridge: Cambridge University Press, 2002), 14–61; on the impact of decolonization on French political culture in the 1950s, see Todd Shepard, *The Invention of Decolonization: The Algerian War and the Remaking of France* (Ithaca, NY: Cornell University Press, 2006), and Frederick Cooper, *Citizenship between Empire and Nation: Remaking France and French West Africa, 1945–1960* (Princeton, NJ: Princeton University Press, 2014).

38. Martin, "History Repeats Itself": 97.

ern France have long acknowledged the important role played by the court and associated institutions in stimulating demand, especially for luxury goods.[39] After 1800 this function was amplified as the court, relocated from Versailles to Paris, saw its influence on the stimulation of consumer desire multiplied by new commercial infrastructures in the capital city—from arcaded passages, to department stores and universal exhibitions. This neo-courtly complex underlay a commercial boom that turned France into the great procurer of semi-luxury commodities for the global bourgeoisie, a socio-economic function that facilitated the recruitment of foreign collaborators of French power.[40]

One should neither paint too simple a picture nor exaggerate the monarchical proclivities of nineteenth-century France. *Légitimisme*, Orléanism and Bonapartism were not one and the same thing, and there were republicans in France before 1871. This book only claims that national historiography has not paid sufficient attention to the resistance to republicanism, nor to its contribution to the creation of modern France. The emphasis on the neo-courtly features of nineteenth-century France's economic development is not meant to suggest that there was a consensus around economic specialization along such lines—in an earlier work I underlined the intensity of political tensions between support for free trade, which became dominant only among the national elites and certain export-oriented regions, and the prevalence of protectionist sentiment among local notabilities and large swathes of public opinion.[41] Economic openness and democracy do not always go hand in hand, as the protectionist direction of the democratic Third Republic would confirm at the end of the century.

Conversely, distrust of democracy is compatible with the adhesion to modern capitalism, and the latter should not be equated with British-style large-scale manufacturing. The courtly foundations of French economic power were no more archaic than the dependence of Britain's exportation of cotton textiles

---

39. William H. Sewell, "The Empire of Fashion and the Rise of Capitalism in Eighteenth-Century France," *Past & Present*, 206 (2010).

40. On the global aspects of the emergence of a "middle class" or bourgeoisie after 1800, see *The Global Bourgeoisie: The Rise of the Middle Classes in the Age of Empire*, eds. Christof Dejung, David Motadel and Jürgen Osterhammel (Princeton, NJ: Princeton University Press, 2019)

41. David Todd, *Free Trade and Its Enemies in France, 1814–1851* (Cambridge: Cambridge University Press, 2015).

on slave labour in the American South until the 1860s.[42] From a twenty-first-century perspective, many strengths of the mid-nineteenth-century French economy, from the preeminent role of immaterial commodities to highly flexible modes of production, seem to foreshadow the post-industrial age. French economic prowess did not rely on steam power or the bundling together of hundreds of spinning jennies under the same roof, but science and technology played an important part in the extraordinary French propensity to commodify and export, albeit in a more diverse and incremental fashion.[43] The most significant example of this technological sophistication was undoubtedly the Jacquard loom (1804) and its ingenious card-punch system, that powered the phenomenal resurgence of the French silk industry after its severe decline in the 1790s.[44] From the 1820s until the 1870s, silk textiles became France's leading export item, making up a fourth of the total value of French exports around 1860.

The finest silk textiles were velvet, fabrics obtained through the simultaneous weaving of two thicknesses of fibre, mostly silk, until synthetic fibres became more commonly used in the late nineteenth century. It is therefore tempting to think of France's other informal empire as the product of what may be termed *velvet imperialism*, a phrase that simultaneously denotes France's preference for a soft and concealed style of domination and its specialization in the procurement of conspicuous commodities. A vivid illustration of the connections between France's neo-courtly model of economic growth and the resurgence of its imperial status in the nineteenth century was the crafting of scenes or portraits, woven in silk by the most skilled French silk manufacturers, to celebrate the glory of French rulers. Few specimens of such silk *tableaux* have survived in good condition, owing to the fabric's fragility and the discontinuing of this tradition after 1870, but several examples can be found in the rich collections of the Musée des Tissus in Lyon, including two imperial portraits of Napoleon I and Napoleon III, which were made for the universal exhibition held in Paris in 1855.[45] The neo-courtly model of French

42. Sven Beckert, *Empire of Cotton: A New History of Global Capitalism* (London: Allen Lane, 2014), esp. 83–135.

43. Charles Sabel and Jonathan Zeitlin, "Historical Alternatives to Mass Production: Politics, Markets and Technology in Nineteenth-Century Industrialization," *Past & Present*, 108 (1985).

44. James Essinger, *Jacquard's Web: How a Hand-loom Led to the Birth of the Information Age* (Oxford: Oxford University Press, 2004), 27–43.

45. Maison Furnion père et fils aîné, *Portrait de l'empereur Napoléon* and *Portrait de l'empereur Napoléon III*, in chiselled quadruple velvet, 1855, Lyon, Musée des Tissus, MT 42745 and MT 42746, http://www.mtmad.fr (accessed 10 Jan. 2019).

development generated large profits but required limited domestic capital investment, which helps account for the rapid growth of French foreign investment, especially in the form of loans to friendly or client states in Europe, Latin America or the Middle East. Since the work of John A. Hobson gave "imperialism" its modern meaning in the early twentieth century, capital exports are commonly seen as a crucial feature of modern-style imperial expansion.[46] In this respect, France's informal empire also comes across as uncannily modern—all the more so as foreign lending to protected states, via the commodification and dissemination among the French public of foreign states' bonds, attached hundreds of thousands of middle-class savers to the fortunes of France's expansion. French statesmen and writers on political economy explicitly viewed transnational lending as a means of consolidating a new kind of domination based on asymmetric connections, rather than the exercise of sovereignty. During his American exile in the 1790s, Charles-Maurice de Talleyrand, the mastermind of French diplomacy up until the 1830s, formed the opinion that extensive credit, especially to former colonies, was an essential means of maintaining quasi-colonial domination.[47] Twenty years before Hobson denounced modern finance as "the taproot of imperialism," Paul Leroy-Beaulieu, France's most influential economist post-1870, came up with the concept of "colonisation des capitaux" (investment colonization) as an ingenious means of levying "a tribute" on the rest of the world without incurring the costs of sovereign rule or the demographic losses of settler emigration.[48]

Talleyrand, Leroy-Beaulieu and most other advocates of this politico-economic model were skeptical, if not frankly hostile, when it came to democratic republicanism. Instead, they favoured a monarchical system of rule, although they were relatively indifferent to whichever dynasty would sit on the throne. But their ideal monarchy was one strongly committed to capitalism,

46. Richard Koebner and Helmut Dan Schmidt, *The Story and Significance of Imperialism: A Political Word, 1840–1960* (Cambridge: Cambridge University Press, 1965), 221–49.

47. Doina Pasca Harsanyi, *Lessons from America: Liberal French Nobles in Exile, 1793–1798* (University Park: University of Pennsylvania Press, 2010), 84–105; on British informal domination in the early American republic, see Hopkins, *American Empire*, 158–85.

48. Dan Warshaw, *Paul Leroy-Beaulieu and Established Liberalism in France* (DeKalb: Northern Illinois University Press, 1991), 78–105; the late Donald Winch pointed out to me the significance of this contribution of Leroy-Beaulieu and other French economists during the discussion of his paper "The Political Economy of Empire," given at the Institute of Historical Research, London, 5 November 2014.

devoid of nostalgia for feudal paternalism and ardent in its defence of private property rights. This politico-economic project was not only an attempt to heal the domestic divides inherited from the 1790s, but also a shrewd strategy for taking advantage of global economic integration. Partly by design and partly as a result of changes in the rest of the world, it tended to turn France into the centre of a global web of regimes which were committed to an authoritarian and counter-revolutionary style of modernity.

Collaborative Empire

Counter-revolutionary commitment to capitalism went hand in hand with a collaborative style of imperialism. Associating capitalism with imperialism runs the risk of evoking Leninist tropes, but the only intellectual debt to the Marxist view of empire that needs to be recorded here is Karl Kautsky's intuition, much vilified by Lenin, that empire was a collective endeavour of European capitalism and that greater significance should be attached to trans-imperial collaboration.[49] This association should not be seen as a denigration of capitalism. The words "empire", and even "imperialism", are not used here pejoratively. They merely serve to designate a mode of political organization, viewed by many scholars as alternative, and by some as preferable, to the nation-state.[50] However, creating markets requires political agency. Nation-states have long been recognized as creators of national markets, but historians of empire have reappraised their role, especially the British Empire's, in the acceleration of global economic integration.[51] This book's claim is merely that France's largely informal empire also made a significant contribution to nineteenth-century globalization, even if it employed subtler mechanisms of coercion and collaboration than the more formal British empire ever did.[52]

49. Karl Kautsky, "Ultra-Imperialismus," *Die Neue Zeit*, 11 Sep. 1914; on Kautsky's ideas and their afterlife, see Holm A. Leonhardt, *Kartelltheorie und Internationale Beziehungen. Theoriegeschichtliche Studien* (Hildesheim: Olms, 2009), 408–77.

50. See for instance Burbank and Cooper, *Empires in World History*, 1–3.

51. Niall Ferguson, *Empire: How Britain Made the Modern World* (London: Allen Lane, 2003); Gary B. Magee and Andrew S. Thompson, *Empire and Globalisation: Networks of People, Goods and Capital in the British World, c. 1850–1914* (Cambridge: Cambridge University Press, 2010).

52. Jürgen Osterhammel, *The Transformation of the World: A Global History of the Nineteenth Century* (Princeton, NJ: Princeton University Press, 2014), 436–41, 450–61.

Empires are rarely, if ever, entirely coercive. Even the most formal of colonial ventures, the British Raj in India, relied extensively on indigenous collaboration, while British settler colonists have been described as "pre-fabricated collaborators" of imperial rule.[53] From this perspective, informal empire is merely a system of collaboration that leaves intact the external layer of sovereignty of foreign, colonized states.[54] Robinson and Gallagher contended that British officials favoured this mode of domination because it was more economical: "paramountcy" was upheld "by informal means if possible" and "by formal annexations when necessary."[55] In the case of France, the preference for informal expansion was reinforced by two specific constraints. The first was Britain's global naval supremacy that rendered quixotic the notion of a new territorial challenge to the old imperial rival. The second was France's quasi demographic stagnation after 1815, which reduced its capacity for settlement emigration. France's imperial expansion therefore required two complementary kinds of collaboration: one a tacit partnership with Britain overseas, somewhat obscured in existing scholarship by a sensationalist focus on rhetorical outbursts of Anglophobia in France (and Francophobia in Britain); the other an original effort, based on the appeal of the French modernizing monarchical model, to create collaborators among the foreign elite.

The notion that British and French imperial policies were inspired by deep mutual animosity in the nineteenth century remains widespread. It cannot be denied that Britain and France's ambitions overseas sometimes collided between 1815 and 1880, most notably in the Middle East and the Pacific. However, too much attention has been paid to these clashes. Claims that Britain and France were on the brink of war in 1840 (in a dispute over Egyptian expansion) or in 1844 (in a quarrel about Tahiti) are grounded for the most part in the bellicose speeches of opposition newspapers and MPs and should be treated

53. Ronald Robinson, "Non-European Foundations of European Imperialism: Sketch for a Theory of Collaboration," in *Studies in the Theory of Imperialism*, eds. Roger Owen and Bob Sutcliffe (London: Longman, 1972), 117–42; and on collaboration in informal colonies, see Ronald Robinson, "The Excentric Idea of Empire, with or without Colonies," in *Imperialism and After: Continuities and Discontinuities*, eds. Wolfgang J. Mommsen and Jürgen Osterhammel (London: Allen & Unwin, 1986), 267–89.

54. On the layering of sovereignty as a chief characteristic of imperial formations, see Burbank and Cooper, *Empires*, 16–17.

55. Gallagher and Robinson, "The Imperialism of Free Trade": 3.

with skepticism.[56] In practice, the French government, mindful of its inferior strategic position overseas, could be relied upon to pull back from the brink. This remained true even after territorial rivalry intensified after 1880, for instance in the famous case of Fashoda in 1898, when the French government merely sought to save face and never seriously contemplated going to war with Britain.[57] Given that between 1689 and 1815 Britain and France were at war with each other for a total of fifty-six years, in a series of eight military conflicts in which colonial issues loomed very large, it seems more pertinent to try and explain how the two imperial powers succeeded in avoiding another war after 1815.[58]

We could go further and note that after Waterloo, Britain and France frequently embarked on military expeditions or full-scale wars overseas, but always as allies: in support of Greek independence against the Ottoman Empire (1827–1828); to prevent the annexation of Uruguay by Argentina through the blockade of the Rio de la Plata (1845–1847); to assert their supremacy in the Ottoman world against Russian encroachments during the Crimean War (1853–1856); to confirm the opening of China to Western trade and missionaries during the Arrow or Second Opium War (1856–1860); in a military occupation of Lebanon to protect Eastern Christians (1860–1861); and in the initial stage of a European intervention in Mexico (1861–1862) that resulted in the creation of a French-client Mexican monarchy. Other instances of significant geopolitical cooperation included the joint patrolling of the Atlantic to repress the slave trade in the 1830s or the adoption—after mutual consultation—of a policy of non-intervention in the American Civil War (1861–1865).[59] Cooperation even extended to each other's colonial possessions, as in the efforts of the

---

56. On France's bluff during the crisis of 1840 and the lack of real damages to Anglo-French relations, see Paul W. Schroeder, *The Transformation of European Politics, 1763–1848* (Oxford: Oxford University Press, 1994), 736–56.

57. Martin Thomas and Richard Toye, *Arguing about Empire: Imperial Rhetoric in Britain and France, 1882–1956* (Oxford: Oxford University Press, 2017), 65–80.

58. François Crouzet, "The Second Hundred Years War: Some Reflections," *French History*, 10, 4 (1996).

59. Paul Michael Kielstra, *The Politics of Slave Trade Suppression in Britain and France, 1814–1848: Diplomacy, Morality and Economics* (Houndmills: MacMillan, 2000), 163–206; Howard Jones, "Wrapping the World in Fire: The Interventionist Crisis in the Civil War," in *American Civil Wars: The United States, Latin America, Europe, and the Crisis of the 1860s*, ed. Don. H. Doyle (Chapel Hill: University of North Carolina Press, 2017), 34–57.

British government to suppress the smuggling of weapons to 'Abd al-Qadir, France's leading adversary during its war of conquest in Algeria (1839–1847).[60] Against this backdrop, the curious death of the Bonapartist pretender Louis-Napoléon, son of Napoleon III, as a British officer during the Anglo-Zulu war (1879) may be construed as the tail end of nineteenth-century military cooperation overseas between the two western European monarchies.[61]

Anglo-French imperial collaboration was neither perfectly balanced nor stable. Thanks to its naval and economic superiority, Britain remained the stronger of the two partners throughout this period, although the steam and iron cladding revolutions of the mid-century enabled France to reduce the gap in maritime power by the 1860s.[62] Even proponents of "realism" in International Relations Theory, who tend to uphold "balancing" models of state behaviour (that is to say, a propensity to form coalitions against potential hegemons), admit that states may opt for "bandwagonning" in relation to greater powers in special circumstances. The three main circumstances favouring such outcomes—a significant gap in raw power, the lack of potential allies against the greater power, and the perception of the latter as pursuing moderate goals—can be identified in the case of France vis-à-vis Britain after 1815: Britain's naval supremacy was uncontested, other major European powers remained wary of French ambitions, and Britain did not seek to undermine French continental security.[63] This configuration encouraged France tacitly to hitch its imperial wagon to Britain's rather than confront British power, while the preference for informal domination reduced tensions by enabling the co-existence of British and French imperial interests in informally colonized

60. Raphael Danziger, *Abd al-Qadir and the Algerians: Resistance to the French and Internal Consolidation* (New York: Homes & Meier, 1977), 230.

61. Ian Knight, *With His Face to the Foe: The Life and Death of Louis Napoleon, the Prince Impérial, Zululand 1879* (Staplehurst: Spellmount, 2001).

62. Michèle Battesti, *La marine de Napoléon III: une politique navale*, 2 vols. (Chambéry and Vincennes: Université de Savoie and Service Historique de la Marine, 1997), vol. 1, 246–7, and vol. 2, 765.

63. Additional contributory factors include ideological affinities, which may be discerned between the two capitalist monarchies between 1815 and 1870, and economic aid, which Britain provided under the form of large-scale investment in France's public debt and railways between 1815 and 1850; Stephen M. Walt, *The Origins of Alliances* (Ithaca: Cornell University Press, 1987), 29–49, 173.

territories.[64] What rivalry remained can often be better understood as emulation. For instance, the actual result of the Anglo-French naval "arms race" between 1840 and 1870 was to increase the two countries' capacity to project their
power overseas, at the expense of extra-European countries.[65]

French collaboration with the indigenous elite of territories which were
under informal influence bore a resemblance to Anglo-French imperial cooperation, not least in the way tensions occasionally flared up during attempts
to modify the terms of the partnership. The foreign elite who collaborated with
French (or British) imperial power retained their own agenda. The reception
of Mongkut's emissaries, orientalized by Gérôme, was also a Siamese diplomatic success, as close relations with France helped stave off British supremacy
and weaken a regional rival, Cambodia. Tellingly, Mongkut had a copy of
Gérôme's painting made that still hangs in the Thai royal palace.[66] As the growing technological gap meant that military confrontations with European powers were doomed to failure, many extra-European polities in the mid-
nineteenth century adopted strategies of collaboration.[67] Although Britain
may have seemed the most natural imperial protector, a large number of foreign governments favoured collaboration with France. This may have been in
part because France represented a lesser threat for their autonomy; in Egypt,
Muhammad 'Ali actively sought to develop ties with France only after the fall
of Napoleon had confirmed British hegemony in the Mediterranean.[68] Yet
ideological affinities also played a part. The conservative and authoritarian
version of modernity propounded by France often appealed more to the governing classes than the aggressively liberal version promoted by Britain. A
case in point was the troublesome question of coerced labour. Britain's virulent abolitionism alienated many potential collaborators among elites whose
economic and social status depended on the exploitation of servile or semi-
servile labour, while the relative French indifference to the persistence of

64. Conversely, in the eighteenth century the relative balance between British and French
power prevented effective cooperation between the two countries; see John Shovlin, *Trading
with the Enemy: Britain, France, and the Eighteenth-Century Quest for a Global Order* (New Haven,
CT: Yale University Press, forthcoming in June 2021)

65. C. I. Hamilton, *Anglo-French Naval Rivalry, 1840–1870* (Oxford: Clarendon Press, 1993).

66. Martin, "History Repeats Itself":121–4.

67. Daniel R. Headrick, *Power over Peoples: Technology, Environments, and Western Imperialism, 1400 to the Present* (Princeton, NJ: Princeton University Press, 2010), 177–225.

68. Khaled Fahmy, "The Era of Muhammad 'Ali Pasha," in *The Cambridge History of Egypt*,
ed. M. W. Daly, 2 vols. (Cambridge: Cambridge University Press, 1998), vol. 2, 152–53.

slavery and *corvée* facilitated cordial relations with the Brazilian and Egyptian governments.[69]

Although France's imperial allure relied on ideological factors until the 1870s, it had little to do with its revolutionary or republican political culture. Even in Britain, the Tories were far more inclined than the Whigs or Liberals to endorse a cooperation with France, while British radicals forged the word "imperialism" to decry the authoritarian and militaristic style of the French Bonapartist monarchy.[70] In the Americas and the Ottoman world, and as far as Japan, it was the least liberal faction of the elite who proved the most susceptible to French influence, from slave plantation owners to conservative Tokugawa shoguns.[71] This web of global conservative connections echoed France's specialization in luxury and semi-luxury commodities—its informal imperial power can be construed as the external facet of the domestic, counterrevolutionary modernizing project.

Despite these positive (from a conservative perspective) incentives, this global project can still be deemed an empire because coercion, or the threat of coercion, was frequently employed, in combination with persuasion. Informal empire also requires a powerful military, and French informal imperialism often proved compatible with the pursuit—if not always the attainment—of military glory on an unprecedented global scale. French influence in the Middle East owed a great deal to memories of the occupation of Egypt between 1798

69. On the contrast between British and French attitudes towards slavery, see Seymour Drescher, "British Way, French Way: Opinion Building and Revolution in the Second French Slave Emancipation," *American Historical Review*, 96, 3 (1991); on the Francophilia of the Brazilian conservative elites, see Jeffrey Needell, *The Conservatives, The State, and Slavery in the Brazilian Monarchy, 1831–1871* (Stanford, CA: Stanford University Press, 2006), 77–80, 167–22, and on its cultural imprint see Jeffrey Needell, *A Tropical Belle Époque: Elite Culture and Society in Turn-of-the-Century Rio de Janeiro* (Cambridge: Cambridge University Press, 1987); on the dispute between Britain, France and Egypt on the use of *corvée* labour, especially in relation to the construction of the Suez Canal, see Nathan J. Brown, "Who Abolished Corvée Labour in Egypt and Why?," *Past & Present*, 144 (1994).

70. Koebner and Schmidt, *The Story and Significance of Imperialism*, 1–26; Jon H. Parry, "The Impact of Napoleon III on British Politics, 1851–1880," *Transactions of the Royal Historical Society*, 11 (2001).

71. On the appeal of the French conservative and authoritarian model beyond slave-owning elites in the Americas, see Edward Shawcross, *France, Mexico and Informal Empire in Latin America, 1820–1867: Equilibrium in the New World* (Basingstoke: Palgrave MacMillan, 2018), 157–95; on French support for the conservative Bakufu in Japan in the 1860s, see Marius B. Jansen, *The Making of Modern Japan* (Cambridge, MA: Belknap Press, 2000), 306–8.

and 1801, while military interventions in Latin America culminated with the French invasion of Mexico between 1861 and 1866. French gunboats served to impose treaties that conceded special privileges, both legal and economic, from Haiti in the Caribbean in the 1820s to several East Asian states in the 1850s. And the rapid waning of French influence after 1870 was in large part a product of France's defeat against Prussia, which dented its military reputation and diminished its capacity to coerce overseas. The case of Algeria confirms that collaboration and coercion were complementary, rather than mutually exclusive, aspects of French expansion, since it was only after hope of collaborating with 'Abd al-Qadir's regime collapsed in 1840 that the French resorted to territorial conquest, the most extreme form of coercion.

Such French international *rayonnement* should be considered imperial because it was conceived as such by contemporary French intellectuals and statesmen (chapter 1, on the political economy of informal empire), because it could relapse into formal colonization (chapter 2, on the failure of informal domination in Algeria) and because the commercial, financial and legal connections drawn with Europe, Latin America and the Middle East enhanced the leverage of the French government in the domestic and foreign affairs of other countries (chapters 3, 4 and 5, on French commodities, capital and law as instruments of domination). French domination often met many of the ten features of the ideal type of informal empire listed by Jürgen Osterhammel in reference to the British experience in *fin-de-siècle* East Asia; in the case of Egypt and Mexico in the 1860s, it arguably met all of them.[72] In some important ways, the French model of informal empire also foreshadowed what Victoria de Grazia identified as the five chief features of the United States' "irresistible" empire in twentieth-century Europe: free trade in cultural as well as material commodities; the forging of direct ties between the imperial and dominated civil societies; the power of making the norms that governed exchanges; a consumer ethos that enlarged access to new, often conspicuous

72. The features are the existence of a "power differential," a "veto" over domestic policy-making, the imposition of "basic guidelines for foreign-policy orientation," "some sort of military establishment," "a substantial economic establishment," a monopoly or quasi monopoly in the most dynamic sectors of the economy, control of public finances by foreign banks, significant imports of foreign capital, "collaboration of indigenous rulers and comprador groups," and adhesion of the collaborators to the "cosmology" of the dominant power's elites; see Jürgen Osterhammel, "Semi-Colonialism and Informal Empire in Twentieth-Century China: Towards a Framework of Analysis," in *Imperialism and After*, eds. Mommsen and Osterhammel, 290–314.

commodities; and a claim to peacefulness that masked the crucial role played by military force. Yet France's irresistible empire relied on the narrower "bourgeois regime of consumption" that American mass consumerism displaced in the twentieth century.[73]

This emphasis on the mechanisms of domination, notably those made possible by an asymmetric economic development, helps make the concept of informal empire feel less elusive. However, an even greater challenge than elusiveness, when studying informal imperialism, is the diffuseness of sources. Relevant evidence ranges from diplomatic ultimatums, backed up by naval or air power, to advertisements for commodities that convey an adhesion to certain imperial values, such as champagne or Coca Cola. We need to consult state archives for this, because informal empires are, in part, political constructs. While conducting research for this book, I found the rich archives of the French ministry of foreign affairs in La Courneuve to possess the most crucial government papers—from the dispatches of plenipotentiaries to extensive documentation on extraterritorial jurisdiction. Yet nation-state officials were not the only builders of informal empires. This book takes a close look at the role of economic actors, from silk or champagne merchants within France to expatriate adventurers who sought to make a quick fortune in regions under French influence. Information on these agents of informal empire is more widely scattered, but much can be gleaned in the economic and social archives of Roubaix. Perish the cynical thought that historians have always preferred to study French formal imperialism solely because the archives of French colonies are located in beautiful, sunny Aix-en-Provence, whereas the grey Parisian *banlieue* of La Courneuve and Roubaix in the northern rustbelt offer more melancholy settings for archival research.

The book places an emphasis on the economics of France's informal empire, because economic motivation and asymmetric relations have underpinned our understanding of imperialism since the beginning of the twentieth century.[74] An analysis of velvet imperialism confined to its political or cultural

73. Victoria de Grazia, *Irresistible Empire: America's Advance through Twentieth-Century Europe* (Cambridge, MA: Belknap Press, 2005), 6–9, 11; for a systematic comparison between twentieth-century American imperial power and another nineteenth-century empire, Britain's, see Julian Go, *Patterns of Empire: The British and American Empires, 1688 to the Present* (Cambridge: Cambridge University Press, 2011).

74. Jeremy Adelman, "Introduction," in *Empire and the Social Sciences: Global Histories of Knowledge*, ed. Jeremy Adelman (New York: Bloomsbury, 2019).

aspects risked reducing it to a rhetorical enterprise, or dismissing it as the vaguest type of influence. It deserves to be considered as an empire, I contend, because it combined wealth-extracting practices with claims to universal dominion, and because it affected the economic life of millions of men and women, in France itself and in parts of the world subjected to informal French colonialism.[75] This economic thread takes several forms in the book, including the conceptual framework and conventional tools of economic history, such as statistics. In addition, however, it borrows the instruments of intellectual history to reconstruct the political economy of informal imperialism, those of cultural history to highlight the intensity of commodification processes in mid-nineteenth century France, and those of legal history to examine how such influence distorted markets in favour of French agents. The book is far from an exhaustive investigation of French informal imperialism—for want of space and linguistic aptitude it rarely considers this empire from the perspective of its many non-French collaborators and victims, although I hope it will inspire others to do so. It remains first and foremost a book about France, but one which seeks to contribute to a new, global history of France, as both an instigator and a product of nineteenth-century globalization.

75. On political ideas and law as constituents of economic life, see Jeremy Adelman, *The Republic of Capital: Buenos Aires and the Legal Transformation of the Atlantic World* (Stanford, CA: Stanford University Press, 1999), 1–15; on economic life in France, from the 1760s until the late nineteenth century, see Emma Rothschild, *An Infinite History: The Story of a Family in France over Three Centuries* (Princeton, NJ: Princeton University Press, forthcoming in January 2021).

1

Empire without Sovereignty

THE POLITICAL ECONOMY OF FRENCH
INFORMAL IMPERIALISM

FEW WORKS have denounced territorial expansionism as eloquently as Benjamin Constant's *On the Spirit of Conquest*, a pamphlet published just as Napoleon's empire was crumbling, in early 1814. For Constant, the armies of conquering nations were "turning the progresses of civilization against civilization itself;" by "taking murder as a means, debauchery as a pastime, derision for gaiety, and pillage as their end," they became "separated by a moral gulf from the rest of mankind, and united among themselves only like wild animals that hurl themselves in packs upon the flocks on which they prey."[1] The pamphlet's multiple editions captured a widely shared aspiration for an end to bellicose expansionism, in both France and Europe. Even an otherwise critical response applauded Constant's lucid exposition of "the current inclination of minds."[2] And it was because the pamphlet turned Constant into a public symbol of the repudiation of conquest that Napoleon, during his brief return to power in 1815 (the Hundred Days), entrusted his erstwhile adversary with the

---

1. Benjamin Constant, "The Spirit of Conquest and Usurpation and Their Relation to European Civilization," in *Political Writings*, ed. Biancamaria Fontana (Cambridge: Cambridge University Press, 1988), 57.

2. Guillaume Coëssin, *De l'esprit de conquête et de l'usurpation dans le système mercantile* (Paris: Le Normant, 1814), 4; on Coëssin, the founder of an ephemeral religious sect ("familles spirituelles") committed to industrial progress that prefigured Saint-Simonianism, see Pierre Bénichou, *Le Temps des Prophètes. Doctrines de l'âge romantique* (Paris: Gallimard, 1977), 269–74, and Pierre Riberette, "Un réformateur du XIXe siècle et ses disciples: François-Guillaume Coëssin," in *1848, les utopismes sociaux. Utopie et action à la veille des journées de février*, eds. John Bartier and Jacques Valette (Paris: CDU-SEDES, 1981), 161–179.

drafting of a new constitution, in a vain attempt to persuade European powers that he too no longer harboured dreams of territorial expansion.[3]

On the Spirit of Conquest has sometimes been cast as the culmination of a liberal rejection of empire, rooted in late Enlightenment criticisms of the inequity and violence of European colonization in the New World. Although the pamphlet predominantly discussed Napoleonic conquests in Europe, Constant's use of expressions, such as a desire to "conquer the world," "acquire remote countries" or reach "the far ends of the earth," has been interpreted as denoting "the global scope of the phenomenon he warns against."[4] Yet words such as "world" and "earth," especially in a nineteenth-century context, do not always refer to the entire globe. In fact, Constant's preface to *On the Spirit of Conquest* described "England" and "Russia" as "the two extremities of the earth." The casting of Constant as an adversary of imperial expansion everywhere pays insufficient attention to the work's full title, which restricted his analysis of the spirit of conquest (and of usurpation) to "their relation to European civilization."[5] The very phrase "European civilization," in contradistinction to other civilizations, was a neologism, if not invented then almost certainly popularized by Constant's pamphlet.[6] It departed from the tradi-

3. On the political thought of Benjamin Constant, see Biancamaria Fontana, *Benjamin Constant and the Post-Revolutionary Mind* (New Haven, CT: Yale University Press, 1991); on *The Spirit of Conquest*, see Stephen Holmes, *Benjamin Constant and the Making of Modern Liberalism* (New Haven, CT: Yale University Press, 1984), 207–19, and Helena Rosenblatt, *Liberal Values: Benjamin Constant and the Politics of Religion* (Cambridge: Cambridge University Press, 2008), 149–57; on Napoleon's concern with proving that he was "no longer a conqueror," see Constant's relation of their conversation on 14 April 1815 in his *Mémoires sur les Cent Jours*, 2 vols. (Paris, 1820), vol. 2, 22–4.

4. Jennifer Pitts, *A Turn to Empire: The Rise of Imperial Liberalism in Britain and France* (Princeton, NJ: Princeton University Press, 2005), 173–74; on Constant as an adversary of empire, see also Anthony Pagden, *Lords of All the World: Ideologies of Empire in Spain, Britain and France, c. 1500–1800* (New Haven, CT: Yale University Press, 1995), 156, and Jennifer Pitts, "Republicanism, Liberalism, and Empire in Post-Revolutionary France," in *Empire and Modern Political Thought*, ed. Sankar Muthu (Cambridge: Cambridge University Press, 2012), 268–71. On the anti-imperialism of the late French Enlightenment, see Sankar Muthu, *Enlightenment against Empire* (Princeton, NJ: Princeton University Press, 2003), 72–121.

5. Constant, "The Spirit of Conquest," 45.

6. In the holdings of the Bibliothèque nationale de France and the British Library, Constant's *De l'esprit de conquête* appears to have been the earliest title that included "civilisation européenne" or "European civilization" or "European civilization" in France and Britain; based on searches of the online catalogues http://catalogue.bnf.fr, accessed 7 Oct. 2016, and http://explore.bl.uk, accessed 7 Oct. 2016.

tional Enlightenment usage of "civilization," becoming a word to denote a process that was common to all of humankind and that did not admit the plural, and heralding a radicalization of European ethnocentrism that informed most nineteenth-century ideologies of empire.[7] *On the Spirit of Conquest* only referred to the world outside Europe, alongside pre-modern Europe, to make a contrast with modern European commercial norms of behaviour.[8]

Constant's pamphlet did not explicitly call for the resumption of Europe's expansion overseas, but it left the door open to the possibility. A cynical reader, unmoved by Constant's moral lamentations, may still have concurred that "even a successful war always costs more than it brings in" and that, especially in Europe, international trade had cancelled out the economic benefits of territorial sovereignty: "The infinite and complex ramifications of commerce have placed the interests of societies beyond the frontiers of their own territories."[9] The same reader might conclude that new, more profitable ways to dominate foreign countries should be adopted and that territorial conquest should be restricted to commercially undeveloped societies. Demonstrating the ambivalence of his own condemnation of conquest, Constant himself later supported the creation of European colonial settlements in North Africa.[10] This chapter's aim is to show that a cynical interpretation such as this was common in post-Napoleonic France and that the popularity of *De l'esprit de conquête* should not be seen to demonstrate a widespread renunciation of empire.

Significant cynics included the Prince of Talleyrand-Périgord and several members of his circle, including the Abbé Dominique de Pradt, a former dig-

---

7. Lucien Febvre, "Civilisation: évolution d'un mot et d'un groupe d'idées," in Lucien Febvre et al., *Civilisation: le mot et l'idée* (Paris: La renaissance du livre, 1930), 10–59; Reuel Lochore, *History of the Idea of Civilization in France, 1830–1870* (Bonn: Röhrscheid, 1935), 9–17; Brett Bowden, *The Empire of Civilization: The Evolution of an Imperial Idea* (Chicago: University of Chicago Press, 2009), 23–46; special issue on "Civilisations. Retour sur le mot et les idées," *Revue de Synthèse*, 129, 1 (2008).

8. A brief passage in "The Spirit of Conquest," 99–100, condemned France's invasion of Egypt in 1798, but as an attempt by Napoleon to school his soldiers in Oriental "barbarism and ignorance" and to "make Europe go backwards" to a pre-commercial age rather than as an iniquitous conquest.

9. Constant, "The Spirit of Conquest," 54.

10. "Alger et les élections," *Le Temps*, 20 June 1830, in Benjamin Constant, *Recueil d'articles, 1829–1830*, ed. Ephraïm Harpaz (Paris: Honoré Champion, 1989), 481–3; on Constant and other liberals' ambiguities about the colonization of the Algiers Regency in 1830, see chapter 2 in this book.

nitary of the Napoleonic regime, who gained fame as a prolific commentator on international affairs after 1815.[11] Pradt has frequently been referred to as an early defender of the Americas' emancipation from European rule. But as this chapter will show, he endorsed the American colonies' independence as a means of maintaining the supremacy of White Europeans and increasing French influence in the New World. The American statesman John Quincy Adams was probably correct in his assessment that "the unprincipled loose-ness of [Pradt's] morals" in politics exceeded even that of his mentor Talley-rand.[12] Another major source of informal imperial ideas was Saint-Simonianism, a politico-religious creed dedicated to the promotion of industrial capitalism from the late 1820s. The early romantic impulses of the Saint-Simonians soon gave way to a hard-headed promotion of French global interests by economic means, a turn to informal empire illustrated in this chap-ter by the career and ideas of Michel Chevalier. An enthusiastic leader of the sect in his youth, Chevalier soon became a major advocate of the economic subjugation of the Orient by Western industrial powers. As holder of the chair of political economy at the Collège de France from 1840 until 1879, and the self-proclaimed "architect" of the Second Napoleonic Empire's economic and foreign policy, he also played a crucial part in the execution of projects of in-formal imperial domination.[13]

Scholarly debates about attitudes to empire in France after 1815 have tended to focus on canonical liberal figures such as Constant or Alexis de Toc-

---

11. In the vein of Duff Cooper's classic *Talleyrand* (London: Penguin, 2010; first published in 1932), the extensive biographical literature on the diplomatist focuses on his crafty manoeu-vring and sarcastic wit rather than his political and economic ideas; see for instance Emmanuel de Waresquiel, *Talleyrand: le prince immobile* (Paris: Fayard, 2003) and Philip G. Dwyer, *Talley-rand* (London: Routledge, 2016).

12. John Quincy Adam to Thomas Jefferson, quoted in Laura Bornholt, "The Abbé de Pradt and the Monroe Doctrine," *Hispanic American Historical Review*, 24, 2 (1944): 217–18. On Pradt, see Émile Dousset, *Abbé de Pradt, grand aumônier de Napoléon, 1759–1837* (Rennes: Nouvelles éditions latines, 1959), a special issue on Pradt of *Cahiers d'histoire*, 7, 2 (1962), and Claire Lejeune, "L'abbé de Pradt (1759–1837)," unpublished PhD dissertation (University of Paris 4, 1996).

13. Chevalier to the Comte de Persigny, 22 Apr. 1856, cited in Michael Drolet, "Industry, Class and Society: A Historiographic Reinterpretation of Michel Chevalier," *English Historical Review*, 123, 504 (2008): 1236. On Chevalier, see Jean Walch, *Michel Chevalier, économiste saint-simonien* (Paris: Vrin, 1975) and Fiorenza Taricone, *Il Sansimoniano Michel Chevalier: Industrialismo e liberalismo* (Florence: Centro editoriale toscano, 2006).

queville.[14] Shifting the emphasis towards lesser known thinkers, who nonetheless enjoyed a vast audience at the time, not only improves our understanding of the discursive context in which these well-known figures expressed their views, but also helps recover what the prevailing attitudes of the informed liberal-leaning public towards empire actually were. Political scientists may question the liberal credentials of Talleyrand and Pradt, who served Napoleon's dictatorship, and of Chevalier, a foremost supporter of the regime of Napoleon III. Yet sinners may still be believers. At least after 1815, once the word "liberal" entered the political lexicon, all three described themselves as liberals—with some justification, since they admired Britain's balanced constitution and were stalwart advocates of free trade.[15] Recovering their views on empire therefore helps to suggest that French liberals did not become imperialistic in the mid-nineteenth century, but instead consistently harboured imperial ambitions, even if, for pragmatic reasons, they tended to shun territorial expansion after 1815.

Focusing on these neglected but influential figures also helps correct the common perception of France as having withdrawn from the international stage after the fall of Napoleon. Pradt and Chevalier, in particular, demonstrated an extraordinarily precocious consciousness of the global scale of human affairs.[16] Well before the global became a fashionable genre in historical scholarship, one study singled out Pradt as demonstrating an unusal awareness of "the intensification of world-political connections" at the turn of the

14. Pitts, *A Turn to Empire*, 163–239; for an overview of the debate about empire and liberalism in the nineteenth century, and the limitations of canonical approaches, see Duncan Bell, *Reordering the World: Essays on Liberalism and Empire* (Princeton, NJ: Princeton University Press, 2016), esp. 19–61. Notable contributions besides Pitts's include Uday Singh Mehta, *Liberalism and Empire: A Study in Nineteenth-Century British Liberal Thought* (Chicago: University of Chicago Press, 1999) and Andrew Sartori, *Liberalism in Empire: An Alternative History* (Oakland: University of California Press, 2014).

15. On the capaciousness of the concept of liberalism, see Duncan Bell, "What Is Liberalism?," *Political Theory*, 42, 6 (2014); on the liberal origins of Realist thinking in international relations, see John Bew, *Realpolitik: A History* (Oxford: Oxford University Press, 2016), 17–81.

16. On the emerging consciousness of the global, see David Armitage, *Foundations of Modern International Thought* (Cambridge: Cambridge University Press, 2013), 37–8; on empire and global consciousness in the nineteenth century, see Duncan Bell, *The Idea of Greater Britain: Empire and the Future of the World Order, 1860–1900* (Princeton, NJ: Princeton University Press, 2007).

nineteenth century.[17] Similarly, more than a decade before globalization or *mondialisation* became common parlance in English and French, the author of Chevalier's major biography felt the need to forge the neologism "planétarisation" to describe the importance that Chevalier accorded to the multiplication of connections across borders.[18] Investigating the political economy of French informal imperialism therefore also reveals a little-known facet of the intellectual origins of globalization, and confirms that the pursuit of empire and the emergence of global consciousness were inextricably linked.

Talleyrand's Imperial Vision

The move away from territorial imperialism in France after 1815 was first and foremost a response to a series of imperial catastrophes: the disintegration of Napoleon's empire in Europe, of course, but also France's loss of all its overseas colonies—to rebel slaves in Haiti; to British occupation in the rest of the West Indies and the Indian Ocean; and, more broadly, the waning of European sovereignty in the New World, from the independence of the United States in the 1780s until the transformation of most of Iberian America into self-governing polities in the 1810s.[19] Previous imperial catastrophes, in particular France's loss of its North American possessions and the drastic reduction of its political influence in India at the end of the Seven Years' War (1756–1763), had already generated a virulent critique of traditional colonial methods.[20] The colonial anxieties expressed by Abbé Raynal and his collaborators in the *Histoire des*

17. Heinz Gollwitzer, "Der Abbé de Pradt als weltpolitischer Denker," *Saeculum*, 22 (1971); see also Heinz Gollwitzer, *Geschichte des Weltpolitischen Denkens*, 2 vols. (Göttingen: Vandenhoeck & Ruprecht, 1972–1982), vol. 2, 375–403.

18. Walch, *Michel Chevalier*, 101.

19. Jeremy Adelman, "An Age of Imperial Revolutions," *American Historical Review*, 113, 2 (2008); *The Age of Revolutions in Global Context, c. 1760–1840*, eds. David Armitage and Sanjay Subrahmannyam (Houndmills: Palgrave Macmillan, 2010).

20. See especially Pernille Røge, *Économistes and the Reinvention of Empire: France in the Americas and Africa, c. 1750–1802* (Cambridge: Cambridge University Press, 2019), and also Richard Drayton, *Nature's Government: Science, Imperial Britain and the Improvement of the World* (New Haven, CT: Yale University Press, 2000), 67–78; François-Joseph Ruggiu, "India and the Reshaping of French Colonial Policy (1759–1789)," *Itinerario*, 35, 2 (2011); and Christian Donath, "Persuasion's Empire: French Imperial Reformism, 1763–1801," unpublished Ph.D. dissertation (University of California San Diego, 2012).

Deux Indes (first edition in 1772), a major bestseller of the late Old Régime, were not forgotten after 1815.[21]

Debates after the fall of Napoleon were also indebted to another intense controversy about the means and ends of empire, which took place around 1800, when war weariness led the main protagonists of the conflict caused by the Revolution to opt for peace (short-lived though it was) at Lunéville in 1801 and at Amiens in 1802. The best-known contribution to this controversy remains *De l'état de la France à la fin de l'an VIII* (1800), a work authored by Alexandre d'Hauterive, a senior official at the French Ministry of Foreign Affairs (although it was rumoured to have been co-written by Hauterive's minister and patron, Talleyrand). *De l'état de la France* expounded the principles upon which the new French government, led by Bonaparte, hoped to establish a just and durable peace. Taking a long-term view of the causes of the French Revolution and the European turmoil that ensued, Hauterive attributed these events to the decay of the Westphalian order brought about by the rise of two new northern powers, Prussia and Russia, and above all by the fast growth and monopolistic tendencies of British commerce. France's aggrandizement as a result of the revolutionary wars, Hauterive implied, had been necessary and sufficient to compensate for these imbalances. No longer wishing to expand territorially, France should now seek to ally with Continental powers in order to force Britain to renounce its commercial monopoly and guarantee the freedom of the seas. *De l'état de la France* elicited a furious response, most notably by Friedrich von Gentz, the German translator of Edmund Burke's *Reflections on the Revolution in France* and an agent of the British government, who underlined instead how the whole of Europe had benefited from the natural expansion of British commercial power.[22]

It is sometimes said that *De l'état de la France* foreshadowed Napoleon's Continental Blockade of 1806–1813, which was designed to stifle British commerce. However, the book used extremely liberal language on the subject of trade, and Hauterive and Talleyrand's opposition to the Blockade contributed

---

21. On the colonial ambiguities of Raynal's *Histoire*, see Ann Thomson, "Colonialism, Race and Slavery in Raynal's *Histoire des Deux Indes*," *Global Intellectual History*, 2, 3 (2017); on the *Histoire*'s origins and dissemination, see Gilles Bancarel, *Raynal et ses réseaux* (Paris: Honoré Champion, 2011) and *Raynal's "Histoire des Deux Indes": Colonialism, Networks and Global Exchange*, eds. Cecil P. Courtney and Jenny Mander (Oxford: Voltaire Foundation, 2015).

22. Murray Forsyth, "The Old European States-System: Gentz versus Hauterive," *Historical Journal*, 23, 3 (1980).

to their semi-disgrace in 1806–1808. We should therefore give the book's portrayal of a new, immaterial French empire of universal laws and language some credence, rather than dismiss it as propaganda, and acknowledge the contrast it drew with the sordid, mercantile and colonial empire of Britain.[23] The rationale behind this new imperial vision can even be traced to the two memoirs on imperial and colonial relations that Talleyrand read at the Académie des Sciences Morales et Politiques in 1797, on his return from enforced exile in the United States. The first of these memoirs, on "the commercial relations of the United States with England," pointed to the robust growth of Britain's commercial exchanges with its former American colonies as evidence that "the independence of the United States, far from being of disadvantage to England, has benefited her in many respects." To explain the reassertion of British commercial domination after 1783, and the failure of French merchants to supersede their British rivals despite Franco-American political friendship, Talleyrand acknowledged the impact of the low price of British manufactured goods. He also appealed for other, more subtle factors, such as the dependence of American retailers on British commercial credit, and the persistence of a cultural "inclination" generated by an identity of language, laws and religion: the colonial relationship was a "connection difficult to break off," meaning that the Americans, who were still devoid of an authentic "national character," submitted to a "voluntary monopoly" in their commercial relations with Britain. "The independence of colonies," Talleyrand concluded, "was an advantage to their mother-countries," provided that the preservation of acquired "commercial habits" was not disrupted by unwise restrictions on trade.[24]

Such advocacy of independence, confined to the American context and intended to maintain an asymmetrical relationship, should not be seen as a condemnation of empire. As if to prove the point, Talleyrand's second memoir, which he read before the Académie des Science Morales et Politiques three months later, proposed the creation of new French colonies in northern or western Africa. These colonies would replace France's doomed colonial demesne in the Caribbean—although Saint-Domingue, its most precious possession, remained nominally French in 1797, it was de facto independent under the leadership of Toussaint Louverture—as a supplier of tropical commodities

23. Emma Rothschild, "Language and Empire, c. 1800," *Historical Research*, 78 (2005).

24. Charles-Maurice de Talleyrand-Périgord, *Mémoire sur les relations commerciales des Etats-Unis avec l'Angleterre; suivi d'un essai sur les avantages à retirer de colonies nouvelles dans les circonstances présentes* (London: J. de Boffe, 1808; first published in Paris, 1797), 9, 20–22, 29–30.

and raw materials. To prevent a repetition of the insurrection that had devastated Saint-Domingue since 1791, the new colonies should be slave free. They should also, Talleyrand asserted, enjoy an "independent" government, in the manner of ancient Greek colonies: the connection between a mother country and its colony should exclusively reside in "the well-understood interest of the two countries." Such a bond was very strong when combined with a "common origin," as proved by the inhabitants of Louisiana and Canada, who retained "an obvious bias" towards France.[25] Talleyrand's two memoirs therefore expounded on a novel conception of European domination as relying on informal links rather than legal subjection, which in the Americas required the recognition of formal independence, but in the rest of the world did not preclude the foundation of new autonomous colonies. It is telling that Talleyrand's vision made a powerful impression on Henry Brougham, a publicist often described as an early British advocate of free trade imperialism, who reviewed and probably translated the two memoirs into English himself a few years later.[26]

There was also an undeniable resemblance between Talleyrand's ideas about the new modalities of European domination (or the immaterial empire advocated by Hauterive in 1800) and the views expressed by Abbé Dominique de Pradt in his first published work, an early contribution to the controversy over the means of restoring order after the revolutionary upheaval, entitled *Antidote au congrès de Rasdtadt* (1798). This intellectual affinity probably owed much to Talleyrand and Pradt's acquaintanceship. They may have met while representing the clergy at the Estates General and then Constituent Assembly of 1789–1791. They almost certainly met again in Hamburg in 1796, where Pradt had emigrated to after 1792 and where Talleyrand attended French émigré circles on his return from the United States.[27] At the beginning of the Consulate, Talleyrand arranged for Pradt to become the personal chaplain of the First Consul and to receive the archbishopric of Malines (now Mechelen, in

---

25. Ibid., 42–3.

26. Three new editions of the two memoirs were published in London (in French in 1805 and 1808, and in an English translation in 1806) and in Boston (in the same English translation, in 1809); see Brougham's review of the memoirs in *Edinburgh Review*, 6, 11 (1805): 63–79, and, on Brougham's free-trade imperialist ideas, Bernard Semmel, *The Rise of Free Trade Imperialism: Classical Political Economy, the Empire of Free Trade and Imperialism, 1750–1850* (Cambridge: Cambridge University Press, 1970), 44–47.

27. On Talleyrand's years in the United States, see Harsanyi, *Lessons from America*, 84–105.

Belgium). Despite some vicissitudes (Pradt did not immediately follow Talleyrand into disgrace in 1808, and resented not being offered a position in Talleyrand's ministry during the First Restoration in 1814), the men's relationship remained close over subsequent years. When Talleyrand represented the French government at the London conference of 1830–1831, which determined the conditions of Belgium's independence and neutrality, he found the time "to look after [Pradt's] affairs," "so that [Pradt] loses nothing [in the Malines archdiocese] in the changes that will take place."[28]

When Pradt anonymously published his *Antidote*, he was still an émigré and had some harsh words for France's revolutionary regime. The publisher of an unauthorized edition even attributed the book, probably for commercial reasons, to the arch-counter-revolutionary Joseph de Maistre. In reality, the work revealed the influence of Edmund Burke, cited three times in the first chapter, whose *Reflections* had been warmly received in Germany, where Pradt wrote the *Antidote*.[29] The book's chief objective was to persuade "the European republic" not to renounce its efforts to contain revolutionary fanaticism. However, one of its more original aspects was its concern with the global origins and repercussions of the revolutionary upheaval. In particular, Pradt condemned the ill-conceived policy of Louis XVI, who had "paved the way for the revolution [in France] through the war in America [in 1778–1783]." In his opinion, France's intervention in the American war of independence had been unnecessary, because as colonies grew, they tended to become emancipated in much the same way as children naturally grow up and leave home. European mother countries should therefore not battle against the independence of their colonies. Nor should they fear it, because it does not

---

28. Talleyrand to the Duc de Dalberg, 10 Jan. 1831, in *Talleyrand und der Herzog von Dalberg: unveröffentlichte Briefe 1816–1832*, ed. Eberhard Ernst (Frankfurt am Main: Lang, 1987), 122.

29. Joseph-Marie Quérard, *Une question d'histoire littéraire résolue. Réfutation du paradoxe bibliographique de M. R. Chantelauze: le comte Joseph de Maistre auteur de l'Antidote au Congrès de Rasdadt* (Paris: the author, 1859); on the broader context of émigré publishing, see Simon Burrows, *French Exile Journalism and European Politics* (Woodbridge: The Royal Historical Society, 2000), esp. 56–94, and on the reception of Burke's *Reflections* in Germany, see László Kontler, "Varieties of Old Regime Europe: Thoughts and Details on the Reception of Burke's *Reflections* in Germany," in *The Reception of Burke in Europe*, eds. Martin Fitzpatrick and Peter Jones (London: Bloomsbury, 2017), 313–30; on Burke's conservative reinterpretation of liberal economics and its impact in Germany, see Emma Rothschild, *Economic Sentiments: Adam Smith, Condorcet, and the Enlightenment* (Cambridge, MA: Harvard University Press, 2001), 52–71.

reduce commercial exchange, as demonstrated by Britain, who "by losing the sovereignty of America, lost nothing," since its trade with the United States continued to "grow and follow the degrees of prosperity of this country." European mother countries should remain indifferent to the issue of colonial sovereignty: "The only preoccupation of the metropole should be that colonies consume a lot."[30]

These liberal views were tempered by Pradt's defence of African slavery and his lamentations over its abolition, brought about by the success of the slave insurrection in Saint-Domingue in 1794. Using the same language as French reactionary planters, he blamed the ruin of the French West Indies on "the declamations of Abbé Raynal [in the *Histoire des Deux Indes*], the precursor of all the sycophants, who under the name of *Amis des Noirs* [France's abolitionist society, founded in 1788] flooded the two worlds with their philanthropic diatribes."[31] Pradt's concern with race and slavery even led him to qualify his optimistic teleology of colonial independence by making it conditional on the "type of population" of each colony: the smaller the White European population, the less inclined it was to become independent, for fear of indigenous or slave revolts, and the less desirable independence was for European mother countries, because such revolts annihilated civilization and trade. Emancipated slaves in French islands had abandoned agriculture for soldiery and, he predicted in an allusion to the prevalence of piracy in the North African Bar-

30. [Dominique de Pradt], *Antidote au congrès de Rastadt* (London: the author, 1798), 34, 142, 234. All references relate to the edition which led to this work's misattribution to de Maistre (it bears "par l'auteur des *Considérations sur la France*" on the cover), with a London imprint, although it was printed in France or Switzerland. This edition has been chosen because it is easier to identify than the other three editions, which also bore a false 1798 London imprint, although they were probably printed in northern Germany; see Quérard, *Une question d'histoire littéraire*, 8–11.

31. [Pradt], *Antidote*, 236; colonial racism was common among royalist émigrés, but Pradt may also have been influenced by the wave of indignation against the atrocities, allegedly committed by Saint-Domingue insurgents, that swept Germany, where he lived in the 1790s; see Karin Schüller, *Die deutsche Rezeption haitianischer Geschichte in der ersten Hälfte des 19. Jahrhunderts. Ein Beitrag zum deutschen Bild vom Schwarzen* (Cologne: Böhlau, 1992), esp. 183–86 on Pradt's collaboration with the *Europäischen Annalen*, a journal that loudly condemned the "Verwüstung" (devastation) caused by the slave insurrection in Saint-Domingue, and Karin Schüller, "From Liberalism to Racism: German Historians, Journalists, and the Haitian Revolution from the Late Eighteenth to the Early Twentieth Centuries," in *The Impact of the Haitian Revolution in the Atlantic World*, ed. David P. Geggus (Columbia: University of South Carolina Press, 2001), 23–43.

bary states, would soon found "several new Algiers" on Saint-Domingue's shores. In Pradt's view, preventing the propagation of racial warfare to other European possessions was a major reason why Europe should keep fighting against the French revolution, lest Europeans be exterminated in Iberian America, British India, and the Dutch colonies of the Cape and Java, "just as the massacre of the whites followed the emancipation of the blacks in Saint-Domingue."[32]

After the positive reception of the *Antidote* (four editions in a single year), Pradt published *La Prusse et sa neutralité* (1800), which discussed the means of remedying the decay of the Westphalian order in much the same terms as Hauterive's *De l'État de la France*, although Pradt took a less favourable view of France's territorial aggrandizement since 1792.[33] In 1801, Pradt also published *Les trois âges des colonies*, a two-volume treatise on the fate of European colonization. Historians have sometimes hailed this work as the earliest metropolitan call for the recognition of Saint-Domingue's independence.[34] Yet they failed to notice that if Pradt was now reconciled with colonial independence in the Caribbean, under the form of a confederacy of British, French, Dutch, Spanish, Danish and Swedish islands, the new state he envisaged would only be established after a combined intervention of European powers had restored African slavery in Saint-Domingue and other French islands. This aspect of his proposal is easy to overlook, because the text advocated the restoration of slavery obliquely, at a time when the French government sought not to alarm its Black citizens in the Caribbean.[35] Pradt's proposed solution therefore prefigured France's disastrous attempt at regaining control of Saint-Domingue in 1802–1803, the final and most violent episode of the Haitian Revolution, and not the kind of independence, conceived as a means of guar-

---

32. [Pradt], *Antidote*, 233, 244, 254.

33. Dominique de Pradt, *La Prusse et sa neutralité* (London: the author, 1800), 1–13.

34. Yves Benot, "La réception de l'indépendance noire de Haïti en France, de l'abbé de Pradt (1801) à l'abbé Grégoire (1827)," in Yves Benot, *Les Lumières, l'esclavage, la colonisation* (Paris: La découverte, 2005), 264–72; Pitts, "Republicanism, Liberalism and Empire," 266.

35. Pradt merely advocated the "restoration" of "the colonial order" as a prerequisite of independence, but three hundred pages earlier he had described slavery as "the essential basis of the colonial order," and its restoration was designed to bring down "the empire of the blacks," in Dominique de Pradt, *Les trois âges des colonies; ou, de leur état passé, présent et à venir*, 2 vols. (Paris: Giguet, year X [1801]), vol. 2, 122, 426–35.

anteeing the abolition of slavery, which was proclaimed by Haiti's Black insurgents in 1804.[36]

At the turn of the nineteenth century Talleyrand and his entourage adhered to colonial emancipation as a means of maintaining European domination over formally independent colonies, and even White racial domination within colonial societies, in the case of Pradt. At first sight, this reinvention of empire by informal means may appear unrelated to the condemnation of territorial conquest by Constant, an adversary of slavery.[37] Yet it is not impossible that the shared premise of a depreciation of the benefits of territorial sovereignty resulted from direct intellectual exchanges. Thanks to their close, mutual friendship with Germaine de Staël, Constant was also part of Talleyrand's entourage in the late 1790s. At Constant's request in 1797, Talleyrand, who was minister of external relations, even sought to entrust him with "the organization of the Italic Republics," the satellite regimes created after French revolutionary armies overran the peninsula (Bonaparte declined the offer of Constant's services, preferring to manage his conquests himself).[38] Large sections of *On the Spirit of Conquest* were written in the early 1800s, shortly after the Hauterive-Gentz controversy.[39] These connections help to explain why Constant's condemnation of conquest in Europe was sometimes interpreted as a justification for the renewal of overseas expansion, but preferably by informal means.

The Invention of Neo-Colonialism

In *Du congrès de Vienne* (1815), his first publication on the post-Napoleonic order, Pradt paid homage to Constant, "a writer as judicious as he is elegant," for having demonstrated a fundamental truth: "However military Europe may

---

36. Philippe R. Girard, *The Slaves Who Defeated Napoleon* (Tuscaloosa: University of Alabama Press, 2011); on the significance of the proclamation of Haiti's independence, see *The Haitian Declaration of Independence: Creation, Context, and Legacy*, ed. Julia Gaffield (Charlottesville: University of Virginia Press, 2016).

37. Pitts, *A Turn to Empire*, 181–5.

38. Talleyrand to Bonaparte, 1 Brumaire year 6 [22 oct. 1797], repr. in *La Renommée*, 4 July 1819 and in Benjamin Constant, *Recueil d'Articles. Le Mercure, La Minerve et La Renommée*, ed. Ephraïm Harpaz, 2 vols. (Geneva: Droz, 1972), vol. 2., 1244–5; on the 1819 controversy about this correspondence, see Dennis Wood, *Benjamin Constant: A Biography* (London: Routledge, 1993), 147.

39. Holmes, *Benjamin Constant*, 211–13.

have been, it has now become commercial." Yet according to Pradt, in order to prevent a relapse in internal warfare, Europe needed to dedicate itself to the spread of commerce in the rest of the globe. This meant assisting the creation of stable independent states in Iberian America, still in the throes of revolutionary turmoil, and "bring[ing] civilization to all the countries where it has not yet penetrated." The connection made by Pradt between commerce and civilization was conventional in French Enlightened thought, but unlike Montesquieu or Raynal, he showed little interest in what the rest of the world might bring to Europe. Instead, he adopted an acutely Eurocentric definition of civilization as "the taste for the enjoyments that Europe offers by the products of its territory and its industry." Because the Ottoman world was just across the Mediterranean, Pradt singled it out as a particularly well-suited region in which to exert European influence to replace "languor," "ignorance," "poverty" and "abjection" with "the tastes, the industry, the needs and the activity of Europe," although he was careful to recommend merely "a moral conquest"— in other words, it was not an attack on the state of "Turkey", but on "its pitiful civilization."[40]

After losing many of his positions and honours in 1815, Pradt reinvented himself as a fashionable, liberal publicist who commented on a wide array of political affairs and, most particularly, on international politics.[41] Contemporaries frequently mocked the opportunism he showed by constantly switching allegiance after 1789, the superficiality of his analyses, and the repetitiousness of his bombastic writing style. In 1820, a compendium of texts by and about Pradt, entitled *Pradtiana*, derided him as the most eminent of the "little modern Grotiuses" [after Hugo Grotius, the Dutch seventeenth-century thinker and tutelary figure of international law] who gave "lectures to the universe from their study"—located, in Pradt's case, in his family castle in Auvergne, where he settled after 1815. Yet the author of the *Pradtiana* admitted that his works—no less than "25 to 30 in-octavo volumes", most of them published in the six years since the fall of Napoleon—had met with a "a prodigious success." His writings earned him "celebrity", which he prized greatly—"obscurity" was for him "a torment"—and a great deal of "hard cash". Indeed, they earned him "even more profit than his archbishopric [of Malines] or his embassy in War-

---

40. Dominique de Pradt, *Du congrès de Vienne*, 2 vols. (Paris: Deterville and Delaunay, 1815), vol. 2, 185–96.

41. Hervé Favier, "Un émule de Talleyrand: l'abbé de Pradt sous l'oeil de la police (1816)," *Revue d'histoire diplomatique*, 93, 1–2 (1979).

saw [in 1812]," during which time he was rumoured to have embezzled large sums of money.[42] A rigorous study has shown that Pradt's impact on geopolitical thinking in the early years of the American republic was very limited—in Thomas Jefferson's opinion, Pradt's style had "too much amphibology to be suited to the sober precision of Politics"—and surmised, probably correctly, that his "unoriginal" thought drew on material "almost invariably available to anyone who took the trouble to read two or three Parisian papers."[43]

However, Pradt's allegiance to liberalism—in 1815, he celebrated the triumph of "liberal ideas" and predicted that all European countries would henceforth seek "to imitate the constitution of England"—was less incoherent than it seemed, and not necessarily insincere.[44] At least, it conformed to the preference for a constitutional monarchy of the *monarchien* faction, to which he belonged in the Constituent Assembly, and reflected his admiration for Burke in the 1790s. Given the commercial success of his publications, it is therefore possible to see them as offering an insight into an unsophisticated but widespread French liberal view of world politics. To begin with, an acute consciousness of the global scale of politics was the trademark of Pradt's literary output, and its wide dissemination suggests that French public opinion remained interested in global affairs after 1815. For instance, his pedestrian *Petit catéchisme* (1820), designed to help Frenchmen understand "the affairs of their own country" under the format of simple questions and answers, began by asking, rhetorically, whether France was "part of the world". Pradt's answer was that, "in order to judge France, one must take into account the state of the world," which was one of "general perturbation," and that the Revolution should be construed as the culmination of a three-hundred-year process of "profound change" brought about by printing, gunpowder, commerce, the discovery of America and the Reformation. One was bound to be struck, the author of *Pradtiana* commented sarcastically, after he reproduced this passage of the *Catéchisme*, by "the novel views" and "profound insights on political subjects, which until now had been barely touched upon" that it contained.[45]

42. Cousin d'Avallon, *Pradtiana, ou recueil des pensées, réflexions et opinions politiques de M. l'abbé de Pradt* (Paris: Plancher, 1820), 1–2, 4–5, 26; on Pradt's contemporary reputation for opportunism, see also [Alexis Eymery et al.], *Dictionnaire des girouettes, ou nos contemporains peints par eux-mêmes* (Paris: Alexis Eymery, 1815), 360

43. Bornholt, "The abbé de Pradt": 211–12.

44. Pradt, *Du congrès de Vienne*, vol. 1, 57–8, 65.

45. Dominique de Pradt, *Petit catéchisme à l'usage des français, sur les affaires de leur pays* (Paris: Béchet aîné, 1820), 9–10; Cousin d'Avallon, *Pradtiana*, 103.

The global consciousness often associated with Raynal's *Histoire des Deux Indes*, such attacks suggest, was not eradicated by the revolutionary and Napoleonic era, and Pradt became one of its standard-bearers.[46]

Drawing extensively on his earlier *Antidote*, *Du Congrès de Vienne* enabled Pradt to reprise his role as a commentator on international affairs (there were three editions in two years, and a translation in English).[47] Yet it was his stringent advocacy of the independence of Spanish America in *Des colonies et de la révolution actuelle de l'Amérique* (1817), a book almost immediately translated into English and Spanish, which established his reputation as a major polemicist.[48] *Des colonies* elicited at least five responses in France, including an anonymous work entitled *Anti-Pradt* that lambasted the archbishop's "metropolicide doctrines."[49] Even Pradt's critics acknowledged that the work had been "a very great success in France" and enjoyed "one of those triumphs" that public opinion only rarely accorded political writings.[50] Undoubtedly, the reason *Des colonies et de la révolution* was so warmly received by liberal opinion, irking the mostly royalist authors who responded, was because it embarrassed a French Bourbon regime committed to supporting the Spanish Bourbons' attempts at restoring their authority in America.[51] Yet it also offered Pradt an opportunity to popularize the views he had earlier expounded on the creation

46. On the conservative reappropriation of Raynal's *Histoire* after 1815, see also the publication of a fourth posthumous edition, expurgated of most of its abolitionist content, discussed in Yves Benot, "L'esclavagisme dans la quatrième édition de l'*Histoire des Deux Indes* (1820–1821)," in Benot, *Les Lumières*, 154–63.

47. *The Congress of Vienna* (London: Samuel Leigh, 1816); several passages were also reproduced word for word in Pradt's *Congrès de Carlsbad*, 2 vols. (Paris: F. Béchet aîné, 1819–1820).

48. *The Colonies, and the Present American Revolutions* (London: Baldwin, Cradock and Joy, 1817); *De las Colonias, y de la revolución actual de la America*, 2 vols. (Bordeaux: J. Pinard, 1817).

49. Anon. *Anti-Pradt, ou considérations générales sur les colonies et sur l'Amérique, pour servir d'antidote aux doctines métropolicides de M. l'archévêque de Malines* (Paris: Anthelme Boucher, 1822).

50. Nicolas Fauchat, *Observations sur les ouvrages de M. Pradt relatifs aux colonies* (Paris: E. Gide & A. Egron, 1817), 7, and Joseph Noël de La Morinière, *L'Amérique espagnole, ou Lettres civiques à M. de Pradt* (Paris: E. Gide, 1817), i.

51. Rafe Blaufarb, "The Western Question: The Geopolitics of Latin American Independence," *American Historical Review*, 112, 3 (2007); on the crisis of the Spanish American empire, see Jeremy Adelman, *Sovereignty and Revolution in the Iberian Atlantic* (Princeton, NJ: Princeton University Press, 2006) and Gabriel Paquette, "The Dissolution of the Spanish Atlantic Monarchy," *Historical Journal*, 52, 1 (2009).

of a new kind of colonial subjection that did not rely on the exercise of sovereignty.

Unlike traditional critiques of Spanish colonialism, Pradt did not challenge the legitimacy of Spain's American conquests or the morality of its treatment of indigenous populations: "Convenience and strength," he asserted, "have always formed the legal basis of relations between nations." In his view, Spain should merely concede independence to its colonies on the pragmatic grounds that upholding its sovereignty had become too costly, while a very profitable trade could resume once the new states had been recognized: "One only possesses colonies in order to make a profit, and whether the latter derives . . . from sovereignty or from commerce, is a matter of indifference."[52] Pradt was confident that even after their formal independence, there could be "no equality" between the mother countries and their former colonies, because "for many years still the colonies will not have the industry which could set them free from the tribute they pay to Europe." As shown by the United States' relations with Britain, independence can result in "an empire all the more powerful that it is voluntary."[53]

Another major concern informing Pradt's support for the independence of Spanish colonies was a fear rooted in the Haitian Revolution that prolonged warfare would undermine European racial supremacy. Pradt did not defend African slavery as forcefully as in Les trois âges. He maintained that slavery had been "indispensable" to the exploitation of the Americas, but now conceded that it was "horrible." He approved of the abolition of the slave trade by the Congress of Vienna in 1815, although chiefly as a means of preventing new "Toussaint Louvertures" from stirring up slave revolts. He even reconciled himself to the eventual abolition of slavery, because it would constitute "a monument dedicated to the superiority of the new Europe."[54] Yet Pradt placed abolition in the distant future. For the moment, he deemed the recent decision of Simon Bolivar, the most illustrious rebel leader, to emancipate and arm slaves in Venezuela a "terrible remedy," since it risked further eroding the superior status of Europeans in the New World. His racial analysis of the conditions of colonial emancipation also led him to oppose the independence of colonies outside the Americas, where Europeans were vastly outnumbered. In

52. Dominique de Pradt, Des colonies et de la révolution actuelle de l'Amérique, 2 vols. (Paris: F. Béchet and A. Egron, 1817), vol. 1, 9, 363.
53. Ibid., vol. 1, 189 and vol. 2, 308.
54. Ibid., vol. 1, 257–92.

India for instance, he applauded to the progress of British rule, which he saw as a "European empire" rather than an "English empire," because "England rule[d] there on behalf of Europe."[55]

If Pradt's main preoccupation was the preservation of White European supremacy, even under Creole or British sovereignty, he also contended that France stood to become one of the main beneficiaries of general independence in the Americas.[56] France had already lost most of its colonies and, "in return for abandoning two or three trading posts, it will gain the colonies of the entire world."[57] Due to its intellectual and cultural eminence, France was called to play a special role in educating newly independent countries. In *Les trois âges*, Pradt had already proposed converting the monasteries that had been abandoned during the Revolution into schools for the children of the newly independent countries' elites: these would create "solid links between France and all the known colonies." He also favoured the resumption of French emigration to Canada and Spanish America as a means of cultivating the taste of local consumers for French products. Reiterating these proposals in *Des colonies*, he thought that France's role should consist in "cultivating the mind" of "the Peruvians, the Mexicans and the Creoles from the Antilles." Here as in most of his works, Pradt used the word *créole* to designate colonists of European descent, suggesting that the cultural collaboration he envisaged should be limited to the new countries' White elites.[58] One of the responses to *Des colonies*, by a Spanish colonial administrator who claimed to be of indigenous American descent, accused Pradt of propounding the advent of unrestrained creole supremacy over the indigenous, Black and mixed-race inhabitants of Spanish America.[59]

Until the mid-1820s, Pradt managed to publish a new book almost every year on the progress of Spanish American revolutions, in which he claimed vindication for his vision of a New World where Europe's domination would

55. Ibid., vol. 2, 145, 336.

56. Pradt's hopes were almost certainly inspired by memories of the dominant position of French merchants in Spanish colonial trade before the collapse of Spain's empire; see Michael Zylberberg, *Une si douce domination. Les milieu d'affaire français et l'Espagne vers 1780–1808* (Paris: Comité pour l'histoire économique et financière de la France, 1993).

57. Pradt, *Des colonies*, vol. 1, xxvi and vol. 2, 314.

58. Pradt, *Les trois âges*, vol. 2, 530–2; Pradt, *Des colonies*, vol. 2, 371–4.

59. [Santiago Jonama y Bellsolá], *Lettres à M. l'abbé de Pradt, par un indigène de l'Amérique du Sud* (Paris: Rodriguez, 1818).

survive the loss of sovereignty.[60] He also made a significant *volte-face* on the acceptability of Haitian independence. In *Des colonies* in 1817, he continued to lament the failure of the 1802 expedition to crush the rebel Black government of Saint-Domingue as "one of the greatest misfortunes that has afflicted France", and recommended once again a joint intervention of European powers to restore rule by White settlers.[61] However, in a pamphlet on Saint-Domingue the following year, these laments turned into praise for the former slaves of Haiti, who had accomplished "twenty centuries of moral and political improvement" in just twenty years. Expecting "the immense exports that constituted Saint-Domingue's wealth" to shortly resume, Pradt now advocated a recognition of Haiti's independence, combined with a commercial agreement which would enable the former colony "to yield more to Europe, and France, than when [France] had to pay for the costs of its administration."[62]

This abrupt reappraisal may be due to the alliance recently forged between the Haitian Republic and the leading Spanish American revolutionist Bolivar, whose actions Pradt was keen to defend in the face of French opinion. In any event, it anticipated the Bourbon Restoration's own change of policy regarding Saint-Domingue by several years. At the Treaty of Paris in 1814, France had obtained the recognition of its sovereign rights over the colony by European powers, before vainly attempting to negotiate the recognition of its authority by Haitian leaders. In 1825, it finally recognized Haiti's independence, but in return for significant economic concessions (preferential customs duties and a 150 million franc indemnity for expropriated White settlers) wrested under the threat of naval blockade.[63] Ange de Mackau, the naval officer who imposed the settlement on Haiti (and later, as minister of colonies between 1843 and 1848, resisted calls for the abolition of slavery), boasted that it would turn Haiti into "a Province of France that yields a lot and costs nothing," a language

60. *Des trois derniers mois de l'Amérique méridionale et du Brésil* (Paris: F. Béchet, 1817); *Les six derniers mois de l'Amérique et du Brésil* (Paris: F. Béchet, 1818); *L'Europe et l'Amérique depuis le congrès d'Aix-la-Chapelle*, 2 vols. (Paris: F. Béchet, 1821); *Examen du plan présenté aux Cortès pour la reconnaissance de l'indépendance de l'Amérique espagnole* (Paris: F. Béchet, 1822); *L'Europe et l'Amérique en 1821*, 2 vols. (Paris: F. Béchet, 1822); *L'Europe et l'Amérique en 1822 et 1823* (Paris: F. Béchet, 1824); *Congrès de Panama* (Paris: F. Béchet, 1825).

61. Pradt, *Des colonies*, vol. 1, 292–318.

62. Dominique de Pradt, *Pièces relatives à Saint-Domingue et à l'Amérique* (Paris: F. Béchet, 1818), v–vi, 1–24.

63. Jean-François Brière, *Haïti et la France, 1804–1848: le rêve brisé* (Paris: Karthala, 2008), 47–157.

suggesting that Pradt's conception of profitable domination, divorced from sovereignty, was gaining adherents among French officials. [64]

Pradt's advocacy of Haitian independence did not signal much of a decline in his preoccupation with race. Divergent views on the political implications of racial diversity were at the heart of a polemical exchange between Pradt and Constant concerning the authoritarian drift of the new Spanish American republics in the late 1820s. In 1829, Pradt applauded the increase in Bolivar's powers as President of Gran Columbia, on the grounds that a parliament made up of "an awful mixture of negroes, mullatoes, *llaneros* [Columbians of indigenous descent] and creoles" was unfit to rule. In response, Constant maintained that "nothing could legitimize unlimited power," and that just as Pradt claimed that "the incapacity of ignorant tribes" stood in the way of political liberty, the advocates of despotism in Europe said the same of "the corruption of civilized nations." Constant did not, therefore, subscribe to Pradt's vision of the post-Napoleonic global order, and especially not to his insistence on the importance of race. Yet in his response Constant also insisted that Pradt and himself, in a political context of liberal struggle against reactionary royalism, nevertheless agreed on "fundamental principles." [65] Constant and Pradt were also sufficiently close in contemporary politics for the latter to succeed the former as political chronicler of the liberal daily *Le Temps* on Constant's death in 1830.[66] The condemnation of conquest did not mechanically imply an aspiration to informal empire. But it facilitated its emergence and the boundary between the two strands of ideas remained porous.

Celebrating European Civilization

The French liberals' ambivalence towards empire was closely connected to their fascination with Britain, whose balanced constitution they admired, despite the fact that it possessed the largest European colonial demesne after 1815. Not only did Britain's extensive empire pose the question of the compatibility

64. "Extrait du rapport de M. de Mackau sur sa mission à St Domingue," [1825], La Courneuve, Archives des Affaires Étrangères (henceforth AAE), Correspondance Politique, Haiti, 1, fols. 24–7.

65. *Le Courrier français*, 1, 15 and 27 Jan. 1829, repr. in Benjamin Constant, *Recueil d'articles, 1825–1830*, ed. Ephraïm Harpaz, 2 vols. (Paris: Honoré Champion, 1992), vol. 1, 161–6, 187–201.

66. Talleyrand to the Duc de Dalberg, 24 Feb. 1831, in *Talleyrand und der Herzog von Dalberg*, 138–39.

of liberal domestic institutions with imperial expansion, but its naval supremacy and global hegemony, acquired in large part at France's expense, seemed
to preclude any attempt at a French colonial revival. Between 1815 and 1830,
many French liberals resolved these contradictions by acknowledging Britain's
colonizing aptitudes while stressing the fundamental unity of European civilization, of which France could still be portrayed as the intellectual and cultural summit. These arguments implied that France should no longer compete
for global colonial dominance with Britain, but collaborate with its former foe
and spread European civilization by other, informal means.

The bicameral monarchy and limited franchise, established by the constitutional Charter of 1814, demonstrated deep admiration for the British political model under the Bourbon Restoration.[67] Among French liberals, the
contrast between the reformist tendencies of Lord Liverpool's administration
in Britain (tariff reform, Catholic emancipation) and the reactionary policies
of French royalist governments after 1820 (tariff increases, indemnification of
émigrés, death penalty for acts of religious sacrileges) helped to dispel distrust
of revolutionary France's foremost enemy.[68] A significant demonstration of
this reappraisal of Britain was the keen interest of French liberal intellectuals
in British history and, in particular, England's revolutions in the seventeenth
century, best illustrated by François Guizot's acclaimed *Histoire de la Révolution d'Angleterre* (1826–1827). These scholarly endeavours also served as a warning to the Bourbons that they risked the same fate as the Stuarts if they continued to pursue reactionary policies. This historical parallel culminated with
the official dubbing of the three-day insurrection which replaced Charles X
with his more liberal cousin Louis-Philippe in 1830 as the "Trois Glorieuses,"
an explicit homage to England's Glorious Revolution of 1689.[69]

This new liberal appreciation of France's old rival even extended to the mer-
its of the British empire, as shown by the spectacular conversion of Jean-
Baptiste Say, the leading French writer on political economy, to Anglophilia.
Say's republican political economy was designed to educate virtuous citizens

67. John A. W. Gunn, *When the French Tried to Be British: Party, Opposition and the Quest for
Civil Disagreement, 1814–1848* (Montreal: McGill-Queen's University Press, 2009).

68. Boyd Hilton, *A Mad, Bad, and Dangerous People? England, 1783–1846* (Oxford: Clarendon
Press, 2006), 264–371; Francis Démier, *La France de la Restauration (1814–1830). L'impossible
retour du passé* (Paris: Gallimard, 2012), 617–787.

69. Geoffrey Cubbit, "The Political Uses of Seventeenth-Century English History in Bourbon Restoration France," *Historical Journal*, 50, 1 (2007).

as well as maximize wealth. The pamphlet he published following a visit across the Channel in the aftermath of the Napoleonic Wars, *De l'Angleterre et des Anglais* (1815), paid tribute to the industriousness of Britons, but it remained scathing about the inequities of British aristocratic society and its mercantile economic system. In particular, the pamphlet derided the expansion of British colonial rule, in India and elsewhere, as an economically senseless endeavour, driven by the martial spirit and greed of the British aristocracy: "Sovereignty," he asserted, "does not compel a people to buy what they cannot pay for, or what is not suited to their customs," and he confidently predicted that "the old colonial system [would] fall apart everywhere during the nineteenth century."[70]

Yet the liberal course of British politics, especially Britain's first steps towards free trade in the mid-1820s, led Say to revise his views.[71] In a review of the first volumes of the utilitarian James Mill's *History of India* in 1824 (a landmark work in the rise of negative perceptions of extra-European cultures by European progressive thinkers), Say acknowledged that thanks to its "English administration," improved by recent reforms, "never has the condition of Hindustan been happier." Say now even looked forward to the not too distant time when Europeans would "subjugate the world," although by less violent means than in the Americas, and when "Islamism" would give way to "civilization" in Africa and Asia, in the same way as "the magi's religion [Zoroastrianism in Persia] gave way to Islamism."[72] He also began to defend the virtues of

70. Jean-Baptiste Say, *De l'Angleterre et des Anglais* (Paris: Arthus Bertrand, 1815), 53, 55; see also Gareth Stedman Jones's analysis of the pamphlet in "National Bankruptcy and Social Revolution: European Observers on Britain, 1813–1844," in *The Political Economy of British Historical Experience 1688–1914*, eds. Donald Winch and Patrick K. O'Brien (Oxford: Oxford University Press, 2002), 61–92, and, on Say's republican politics, Richard Whatmore, *Republicanism and the French Revolution: An Intellectual History of Jean-Baptiste Say's Political Economy* (Oxford: Oxford University Press, 2000).

71. Todd, *Free Trade and Its Enemies*, 62.

72. Jean-Baptiste Say, *Essai historique sur les origines, les progrès et les résultats probables de la souveraineté des Anglais aux Indes* (Paris: Rignoux, 1824), 15–16, 18–19; originally published in the *Revue des Deux Mondes*, the text can also be found in Jean-Baptiste Say, *Cours complet d'économie politique pratique*, 6 vols. (Paris: Rapilly, 1828–9), vol. 4, 12–54; and see also Say's claim that European sovereignty will need to persist longer in Asia than in America in his *Cours complet*, vol. 5, 209–15. On Say's views on colonization, see Philippe Steiner, "J.-B. Say et les colonies ou comment se débarasser d'un héritage intempestif," *Cahiers d'économie politique*, 27–28 (1996) and Anna Plassart, "'Un impérialiste libéral?' Jean-Baptiste Say on Colonies and the Extra-European World," *French Historical Studies*, 32, 2 (2009).

settler colonialism in less densely populated parts of the world, where "new colonies" would accelerate "the progress of mankind." However, an important caveat was that European settlers should be endowed with "a firm and persevering character" and be able to manage without the "entertainment" provided by modern urban life. Of Huguenot descent himself, Say thought that such qualities were most abundant among the Scots, the Swiss and, above all, "the Americans of the United States." By contrast, European nations "which distinguish themselves by talent in society rather than talents useful to society"—a transparent allusion to a common construction of the French national character—were "not fit to found colonies."[73] After 1820, Say had become reconciled with colonial expansion, but only by Britons and colonists of British descent.

Say's views may have been extreme, but they reflected a growing equanimity among French liberals towards the rise of British global power. Another symptom was a blunt intervention by Abbé de Pradt, who called on France to accept Britain's "protectorate" in his *Parallèle de la puissance anglaise et russe* (1823). According to Pradt, such was the disproportion in demographic, military and economic resources between the British and the Russian empires on the one hand, and other European states on the other, that only these two powers enjoyed "effective independence." The forms of national independence may still be respected for other countries, including France, but their last real remaining freedom lay in "the choice of protector." In this description of the post-1815 world, which eerily foreshadowed Cold War geopolitics, Pradt exhorted France to opt for British protection, because Britain favoured constitutional government and commercial development, while "despotic and Asiatic" Russia was "the born enemy of Europe's liberties."[74] Only five years later, however, Pradt reappraised the civilizing virtues of the Russian empire, contrasting them with the backwardness of the Ottoman administration, in order to justify the 1827 Anglo-Franco-Russian intervention in favour of Greek independence—if Britain should exercise a protectorate over France, all European powers were, in his view, entitled to a "protectorate of mankind" that

73. Say, *Cours complet*, vol. 4, 453–60.
74. Dominique de Pradt, *Parallèle de la puissance anglaise et russe relativement à l'Europe* (Paris: Béchet, 1823), 1–3, 169; for an invocation of Pradt's world view in the context of the Cold War, see Bertrand de Jouvenel, "L'abbé de Pradt et l'Europe constitutionnelle," *Commentaire*, 7, 3 (1979).

extended "to all places, to all peoples, to all human miseries."[75] Although there
were two editions of Pradt's *Parallèle*, it elicited only one scandalized liberal
response, by Charles Dupin, who protested against his proposal of turning
France into a "vassal" of Britain—and Dupin was an atypical liberal, since after
1830 he became a staunch adversary of free trade and a defender of slavery.[76]

How could this admiration of British global and colonial power be reconciled with the exigencies of patriotism, especially in the aftermath of the Napoleonic Wars? Liberal writers did not explicitly address this potential contradiction, but geopolitical Anglophilia probably played a significant part in the
contemporary emergence of a discourse that stressed the commonalities of
European civilization and its superiority over other cultures. Given the enduring predominance of French high culture among the European elite, this European civilization could be seen as a largely French product, and any form of
European expansion—even Britain's colonial conquests—could be seen to
affirm French global eminence. If not Europe's civilization itself, the rhetoric
of European civilization was indeed very French, as the online Google Ngram
search engine suggests: the phrase "civilisation européenne" began to spread
earlier (c. 1810) and was more frequent—around ten times more frequent
c. 1830 and still three times more frequent c. 1850—in works published in
French than "European civilization" or "European civilisation" in works published in British English. After 1850, the phrase's popularity declined slightly
in French and plateaued in English, although it was still at least twice as frequent in French as in English in the 1890s (see figures 1.1 and 1.2; note the
different scale of the frequency on the vertical axis of each chart).[77]

75. Dominique de Pradt, *De l'intervention armée pour la pacification de la Grèce* (Paris:
Pichon-Béchet, 1828), 12; on the emergence of the right of intervention, see Davide Rodogno,
Against Massacre: Humanitarian Interventions in the Ottoman Empire, 1815–1914 (Princeton, NJ:
Princeton University Press, 2012), esp. 63–90 on the Greek War of Independence, and *Humani-
tarian Intervention: A History*, eds. Brendan Simms and David J. B. Trim (Cambridge: Cam-
bridge University Press, 2011).

76. Charles Dupin, *Observations sur la puissance de l'Angleterre et sur celle de la Russie* (Paris:
Plassan, 1824), 6; on Dupin, see *Charles Dupin (1784–1873). Ingénieur, savant, économiste, péda-
gogue et parlementaire du Premier au Second Empire*, eds. Carole Christen and François Vatin
(Rennes: Presses universitaires de Rennes, 2009).

77. Google Ngram frequency of "civilisation européenne" in works published in French,
1800–1899 and of "European civilization + European civilization" in works published in British
English, 1800–1899, https://books.google.com/ngrams, accessed 15 July 2017.

FIGURE 1.1. Frequency of the phrase *civilisation européenne* in works published in French, 1800–1899. *Source:* Search for "civilisation européenne" in Google Books Ngrams, works in French, moving average of 7, https://books.google.com/ngrams, accessed 15 July 2017.

FIGURE 1.2. Frequency of the phrase "European civilization" or "European civilisation" in works published in English, 1800–1899. *Source:* Search for "European civilization + European civilisation" in Google Books Ngrams, works in British English, moving average of 7, https://books.google.com/ngrams, accessed 15 July 2017.

This language of a superior French-inspired European civilization may have ultimately derived from the radical identification of western Europe as the main engine of global progress by late Enlightenment thinkers such as Condorcet or Volney. It also benefited from the efforts of Catholic writers such as François-René de Chateaubriand, whose *Génie du Christianisme* (1802) sought to rehabilitate Christianity as a major factor of Europe's civilizational superiority.[78] Yet it was in the post-Napoleonic era that the concept of European civilization came to occupy a central place in French political and intellectual life. The very pluralization of the word "civilization"—even if, as seen above, it was already implicit in the subtitle of Constant's *On the Spirit of Conquest*—has often been credited to the philosopher Théodore Jouffroy, the author of an immensely popular manifesto against the Restoration's reactionary tendencies, *Comment les dogmes finissent* (1825). In a series of lectures at the Sorbonne in 1826, Jouffroy discerned three "systems of civilization," which dominated the globe, apart from the regions still peopled by "savages": Christianity, Islam and Brahmanism, the latter term encompassing Chinese and Japanese as well as Indian culture. Jouffroy was a skeptic, but religion, he argued, generated "a specific civil order, specific politics and specific customs . . . In a word, every religion gives birth to a civilization." Christian civilization being "the truest, and as a result the most powerful," it would eventually "absorb the other two," and within the "majestic and holy" Christian civilization, France, being more scientific than England and more practical than Germany, held the eminent part of "pivot."[79]

Such a radical conception of European civilizational superiority percolated through another, more widely acclaimed series of lectures given by Guizot, a fellow liberal and Jouffroy's Sorbonne professor, on "the history of civilization in Europe" in 1828. The philosophy of history expounded by Guizot in these lectures, at once providentialist and attuned to the role of socio-economic change, was acknowledged as a significant influence by numerous European thinkers, including Alexis de Tocqueville, John Stuart Mill and Karl Marx. This common influence may have contributed to what is now often perceived as the Eurocentrism of these three writers, who otherwise upheld very different political, social and economic convictions.[80] A little-noted feature of Guizot's lectures in modern scholarship was their strident proclamation of the superi-

78. David Todd, "Transnational Projects of Empire, c. 1815–c. 1870," *Modern Intellectual History*, 12, 2 (2015): 271.

79. Théodore Jouffroy, "De l'état actuel de l'humanité," in *Mélanges philosophiques*, 2nd edn (Paris: Ladrange, 1838), 97, 102, 120–21, 129.

80. Larry Siedentop, "Introduction," in François Guizot, *The History of Civilization in Europe* (London: Penguin, 1997), vii–xxxvii; on Guizot's significance in the history of French liberalism, see Rosanvallon, *Le Moment Guizot*; Michael Drolet, "Carrying the Banner of the Bourgeoisie: Democracy, Self and the Philosophical Foundations to François Guizot's Historical and Political Thought," *History of Political Thought*, 32, 4 (2011); and Laurent Theis, *Guizot, la traversée d'un siècle* (Paris: CNRS, 2014).

ority of "European and Christian civilization" over "the other civilizations which have developed themselves in the world." According to Guizot, this European superiority was grounded in the continuous dynamism engendered by cultural diversity along national lines. By contrast, reliance on a single "social principle" accounted for the rapid decline of ancient Greece and the stagnation of ancient Egypt, modern Asia and Islam, with the latter also suffering from a propensity to "tyranny . . . inherent in Arab civilization."[81] In a series of lectures on "the history of civilization in France" the following year, Guizot also claimed, in the manner of Jouffroy, a special place for France within European civilization. Britain excelled at "material progress" and Germany at "intellectual progress," but France excelled at combining both harmoniously: "its civilization has reproduced more faithfully than any other the general type and fundamental idea of civilization. It is the most complete, the most veritable, and, so to speak, the most civilized of civilizations."[82]

It is noteworthy that the most influential paean to French-inspired European civilization was the work of a figure closely identified with nineteenth-century Anglophilia. Not only was Guizot a celebrated historian of England in the 1820s, but as a politician in the 1830s and 1840s he also became the chief architect of a policy of Entente Cordiale, which earned him the sobriquet (in French) of *Lord Guizot*.[83] The French celebration of European civilization had more than a single root or purpose, but it benefited from the liberal reappraisal of Britain since 1815 and would offer new justifications for the development of French collaboration with British imperial expansion after liberals gained power with the Revolution of 1830.

Saint-Simonian Economics and Empire

Fears that France's latest revolution would erupt into a new major European conflict were quashed by the conservative direction of the new July Monarchy in 1831 and the skilful diplomacy of Talleyrand who, as ambassador in London between 1830 and 1834, helped resolve the thorny Belgian question—the

81. François Guizot, *Histoire de la civilisation en Europe* (Paris: Robert Laffont, 1985), 61, 74–76, 103.

82. François Guizot, *Histoire de la civilisation en France*, 2nd edn., 4 vols. (Paris: Didier, 1840), vol. 1, 8–12, 21.

83. On Guizot's Anglophilia and its unpopularity, see Laurent Theis, *François Guizot* (Paris: Fayard, 2008), 263–76, 390–416.

French government had given up hope of annexing the provinces that had revolted against Dutch rule, but matrimonial and electoral devices (the marriage of the king of the Belgians to an Orléans princess, and a franchise system that favoured the Francophone industrial bourgeoisie) guaranteed France's influence in the newly independent state.[84] Yet worries about the risk of another Anglo-French war helped bring about the formulation of an alternative project of informal economic empire by Michel Chevalier, a leading light of the Saint-Simonian sect and the editor of their journal, *Le Globe*. The Saint-Simonians faced ridicule, abuse and scandal in their early years—Chevalier and several other leaders even spent a few months in prison, thanks to their immoral advocacy of free love. Nevertheless, historians have since demonstrated their extraordinarily pervasive influence on nineteenth-century French (and European) politics and economics.[85] This influence extended to the adoption of new informal means of reviving France's imperial status, without risking a conflict with Britain.

At the end of the Napoleonic Wars, Henri de Saint-Simon, the sect's founder, had already proposed the merging of Britain and France into a single state. In recognition of Britain's greater economic and political clout, the new state's capital would be London and a majority of members of parliament would be elected by Britons. Peace in Europe would be assured, and tangible economic gains would more than compensate for the French loss of sovereignty: "The empire of the sea will also be France's and extend [its] commerce, increase [its] industry."[86] In a similar vein, after the 1830 Revolution Chevalier advocated forging "an intimate political alliance" between Britain and France, seeing it as the best safeguard against the renewal of war in Europe. All European wars from Hastings in 1066 until Waterloo in 1815, he claimed, had had

84. Raymond Guyot, *La première entente cordiale* (Paris: Rieder, 1926), 52–88; Schroeder, *The Transformation of European Politics*, 670–91; and Linda Kelly, *Talleyrand in London* (London: Tauris, 2017).

85. On Saint-Simonianism and its influence, see Robert B. Carlisle, *The Proffered Crown: Saint-Simonianism and the Doctrine of Hope* (Baltimore, MD: Johns Hopkins University Press, 1987); Pierre Musso, *Télécommunications et philosophie des réseaux. La postérité paradoxale de Saint-Simon* (Paris: PUF, 1997); and Antoine Picon, *Les Saint-Simoniens: raison, imaginaire, utopie* (Paris: Belin, 2002). On the debt of Chevalier's ideas to the Saint-Simonian doctrine, see Drolet, "Industry, Class and Society."

86. Henri de Saint-Simon and Augustin Thierry, *De la réorganisation de la société européenne* (1814), repr. in *Le Saint-Simonisme, L'Europe et la Méditerranée*, ed. Pierre Musso (Houilles: Manucius, 2008), 64.

Anglo-French rivalry at their root. Conversely, the reconciliation of the two foes, only achieved previously by the Papacy during the Crusades, would herald a new era in the history of mankind: "For once France and England embrace each other; once the two nations who between them possess the riches of the world and the torch of science, who are the regulators of the feelings, thoughts and acts of the universe, unite to proceed towards the same goal, carrying along with them the peoples accustomed to follow in their steps; who will be able to stand in the way of this majestic procession?"[87]

Chevalier's reflections on the venting of European energies overseas as the best means of preserving peace in Europe led him to propose, in 1832, a grandiose "System of the Mediterranean": a network of sixty thousand kilometers of railways and hundreds of steamship lines connecting the European, African and Asian banks of that sea, at a time when barely one hundred kilometers of rail tracks had been laid in France. This project has been described as a "cosmopolitan" utopia, as well as a product of Chevalier's fascination for modern transport technologies (he was an engineer by training).[88] Yet Chevalier's cosmopolitanism was of a singularly asymmetric, imperial type. The Mediterranean, he claimed, should serve as a "nuptial bed" between a male "material" West and a female "spiritual" East. The new transport links would allow Britain and France to lead new "crusades", designed to "rebuild an Orient half buried under heaps of ruins" and enable Europe to "extend itself" over Asia and Africa by "pushing civilization forward."[89] When he first expounded on his "Mediterranean System," Chevalier did not explicitly call for the use of coercion as a way of fulfilling his vision, though he did so frequently in his later writings— for example, during the diplomatic crisis of 1840, when he called upon France to renounce its European quarrels and instead emulate Britain's efforts to open up China to Western trade. His support for Britain in the ongoing Opium war (1839–1842) was unflinching: "ruling over the world by words and by force . . . in some places with diplomatic negotiations, and in others with canon shots, is a compelling need of the European nature."[90]

---

87. "Loi des 80,000 hommes. La France et l'Angleterre," *Le Globe*, 8 Dec. 1830, repr. in *Politique européenne* (Paris: Le Globe, 1831), 13, 17.

88. Michael Drolet, "A Nineteenth-Century Mediterranean Union: Michel Chevalier's *Système de la Méditerranée*," *Mediterranean Historical Review*, 30, 2 (2015): 158–9.

89. "Politique générale: la paix est aujourd'hui la condition de l'émancipation des peoples," *Le Globe*, 5 and 12 Feb. 1832, repr. in Musso, *Le Saint-Simonisme*, 116, 123, 129.

90. Michel Chevalier, "L'Europe et la Chine, l'occident et l'orient," *Revue des Deux Mondes*, 23 (1840): 242.

Spreading European industrial civilization across the globe, and ensuring that France played a major role in this process, remained a paramount concern behind Chevalier's two-year journey across the United States, Canada, Mexico and Cuba in 1834–1835. The ostensible purpose of the journey, commissioned by the French government, was to study the construction of railways in North America. But in the same way as the study of American prisons provided Alexis de Tocqueville with a pretext for analyzing American democracy, Chevalier's real goal was to compare the dynamics of different models of imperial expansion in the New World before Europe conquered Asia and Africa. The preface of his *Lettres sur l'Amérique du Nord* (1836), a selection of chronicles previously published in the liberal daily *Le Journal des Débats*, explained that his letters should be read as an analysis of the spread of "Western civilization", before its imminent propagation to the Orient, which would constitute "the greatest event in the history of the human species."[91]

In the *Lettres*, Chevalier occasionally expressed nostalgia for "the empire of New France." Before the 1763 Treaty of Paris, Chevalier recalled from Pittsburgh (Fort Duquesne, before the Seven Years' War), that France possessed "the two largest and richest basins of northern America, those of the Saint-Lawrence and the Mississippi." The French, he added in another letter, may have appeared destined to become "the kings of the New World." Yet Chevalier invoked such memories in part to dispel their illusory character. Due to its extremely sparse settlement, France's North American empire "only ever existed on paper." In the Ohio valley, Chevalier could not even find "a stone or brick which proved that France used to be sovereign there."[92] Ultimately, Chevalier justified the disappearance of this American empire by endorsing the common view that the French were poor settlers, because they were excessively "sociable." He even applauded their replacement by the "Anglo-Americans," because the latter's aptitude for agricultural colonization, grounded in the harsh individualistic ethic of Protestantism, had accelerated the "the progress of civilization" in the New World. Chevalier didn't lament the downfall of Napoleon's European empire, because domination over other civilized European peoples was senseless. But successive French imperial failures left him anxious about France's future place in the world: "One more step

91. Michel Chevalier, *Lettres sur l'Amérique du Nord*, 2 vols. (Paris: Charles Gosselin, 1836), vol. 1, vi–viii.

92. Chevalier, *Lettres*, vol. 1, 276–8 and vol. 2, 111.

backward, and we shall be for ever relegated among secondary peoples, aged peoples, fallen peoples."[93]

Chevalier's fears about French imperial decline formed part of a broader preoccupation with the waning contribution of "the Latin race" to the global dissemination of Europe's civilization, in contrast to the triumphant colonizing success of "Teutonic" nations exemplified by the Anglo-Americans and even the rapid progress of Slavic Orthodox colonization in the Russian empire. At the same time, this diagnosis suggested a solution to the French imperial conundrum. Instead of seeking new territorial conquests, Chevalier contended, France should reassert its role as the *sommité* (leader) of Latin nations, in Europe and the Americas: "It is [France's] duty to shake [the Latin peoples] from the slumber in which they have sunk in both hemispheres, to bring them to the level of other nations, and to enable them to cut a figure in the world."[94] If the French made poor settlers on the virgin soils of relatively uninhabited regions, their sociability made them, in Chevalier's eyes, useful migrants in established societies. In his letters from Mexico (not included in the published book), he contended that the immigration of French entrepreneurs and artisans would revive the progress of civilization there.[95] In the Old World, France should similarly aim at "encouraging the development of the vigour which seems to be rekindling among the Arabs" and use its growing ascendancy in the Arab world "to shake the Far East."[96] Chevalier was alluding here to the growth of French influence in Muhammad 'Ali's Egypt, where many of his Saint-Simonian friends settled as engineers, teachers and administrators in the 1830s, rather than the colonization of Algeria, the merits of which still appeared doubtful to him.[97]

In the *Lettres*, Chevalier often used the word "race" in a relatively benign cultural sense: the characteristics of the Latin, Teutonic and Slavic races chiefly derived in his account from Catholicism, Protestantism and Orthodoxy. He also justified his proposal of French tutelage over the Arab world by highlighting a

93. Chevalier, *Lettres*, vol. 1, 169–75 and vol. 2, 109–13.

94. Chevalier, *Lettres*, vol. 1, xii–xiii.

95. "De l'état actual du Mexique," *Le Journal des Débats*, 7 Aug. 1837.

96. Chevalier, *Lettres*, vol. 1, xiii.

97. He initially suggested that France should hand over its new possessions in North Africa to Britain, in "Alger", *Le Globe*, 10 Nov. 1831, repr. in *Politique européenne*, 119–27, although in his later writings he expressed cautious optimism about France's capacity to colonize Algeria. On Saint-Simonian emigration to Egypt, see Philippe Régnier, *Les Saint-simoniens en Egypte* (Cairo: Banque de l'Union Européenne, 1989).

common aspiration to universalism in Catholicism and Islam. Yet Chevalier sometimes invoked more sinister and biological conceptions of race.[98] For instance, he considered that the French settlers' propensity for intermarrying with Native Americans, by giving birth to "a slender, anxious and indolent race," had contributed to the slow development of French settlements. By contrast, the Anglo-Americans' careful avoidance of miscegenation had permitted the growth of "an industrious and energetic population."[99] Chevalier criticized the exaggerations of the Anglo-Americans' "exclusive feeling of race" in relation to Blacks, free or enslaved, but he insisted that abolition, wherever slavery subsisted in the Americas, should take place gradually: "The bloody experience of Saint-Domingue and the miserable results it has had for the majority of the Blacks themselves, do not recommend an immediate emancipation."[100] The project of joint European "tutelage" over the Caribbean that he mooted in a letter about Cuba (not included in the published selection), in order to prevent emancipated slaves from relapsing in "idleness and barbarism," closely resembled Pradt's recommendations on how to limit the economic damages of abolition.[101]

Chevalier's enthusiasm for European expansion and his belief in the racial inferiority of Native Americans and Africans show that an abhorrence for wars of conquest in Europe should not be equated with a hostility to empire. Still, Chevalier's vision of empire was cooperative, at least among Europeans— Alexander von Humboldt praised his *Lettres* as a "treatise of the civilization of the peoples of the West."[102] And this vision assigned France a special, global but informal role among European civilizers, as the tutor of the Latin and Arab worlds. Chevalier's *Lettres* were well received, with a second edition in 1838 and a third in 1844. Together with his other publications, especially those on the development of transport infrastructures, they helped him to become a regular contributor to the most influential liberal periodicals of mid-nineteenth century France, the daily *Journal des Débats* and the monthly *Revue des Deux Mondes*, and in 1840 the government appointed him to Jean-Baptiste Say's

98. On the role of Saint-Simonians in the emergence of new, pseudo-scientific conceptions of race, see Martin S. Staum, *Labeling People: French Scholars on Society, Race, and Empire, 1815–1848* (Montreal: McGill-Queen's University Press, 2003), esp. 17–22, 136–41.

99. Chevalier, *Lettres*, vol. 2, 6.

100. Chevalier, *Lettres*, vol. 1, 253–4 and vol. 2, 278–83.

101. "De l'esclavage aux Antilles," *Journal des Débats*, 27 Feb. 1838.

102. Moncure Robinson, "Orbituary Notice of Michel Chevalier," *Proceedings of the American Philosophical Society*, 19 (1880): 30.

former chair of political economy at the Collège de France. From these positions of influence, he further disseminated an imperial vision that was more
concerned with economic domination than political sovereignty. In his inaugural lecture at the Collège de France, he redefined political economy as the
branch of knowledge most useful to guide Europe's "civilizing invasion" of the
world: "In every corner of the globe productive work is establishing itself
today, and industry is planting its banner, above those of war or barbarity. Europe submits everything to its law: its children people or govern the rest of the
earth more and more." [103]

The price attached by Chevalier to Anglo-French friendship and his preference for an informal style of French expansionism were a perfect match for the
July Monarchy's foreign policy, especially after Guizot took the reins of the
government in 1840. For reasons that will be analysed in the next chapter, the
liberal conservative monarchy felt the need to embrace a policy of conquest
in Algeria. But elsewhere, the official policy of Entente Cordiale with Britain
was combined with efforts to project French influence, but without acquiring
substantial territories. Guizot eschewed projects of annexation, such as Madagascar's, on the grounds that the French lacked the skills for "large territorial
and colonial settlements."[104] France, he claimed, should "play its part and
spread its own genius" in all the regions of the world, but without acquiring
more than "point d'appuis," or points of support, for the promotion of its political, commercial and religious interests.[105] Hence the July Monarch's frequent diplomatic and military interventions in Latin America, the Ottoman
world, the Pacific and China, mostly resulting in treaties granting the French
government, or French nationals and protégés, special rights, rather than an
expansion of French sovereignty.[106] This logic of imperial deployment intensified

103. Michel Chevalier, *Cours d'économie politique*, 3 vols. (Paris: Capelle, 1842–1850), vol. 1
(1842), 27.

104. François Guizot, *Mémoires pour servir à l'histoire de mon temps*, 8 vols. (Paris: Michel
Lévy, 1858–1867), vol. 6, 272–5.

105. See Guizot's speech in parliament on 29 Feb. 1844, repr. in François Guizot, *Histoire
parlementaire de France*, 5 vols. (Paris: Michel Lévy, 1863–1864), vol. 4, 259–60.

106. On French aspirations to informal domination in Ottoman Syria, see Andrew Arsan,
"'There is, in the Heart of Asia . . . an Entirely French Population': France, Mount Lebanon, and
the Workings of Affective Empire in the Mediterranean, 1830–1920," in *French Mediterraneans:
Transnational and Imperial Histories*, eds. Patricia M. E. Lorcin and Todd Shepard (Lincoln:
University of Nebraska Press, 2016), 76–100; on the extension of French extra-territoriality in
China after 1840, see Pär Kristoffer Cassel, *Grounds of Judgment: Extraterritoriality and Imperial*

after Louis-Napoleon Bonaparte rose to power and restored a Bonapartist monarchy in 1852, and Chevalier became the main herald of a French style of free trade imperialism.

A French Imperialism of Free Trade

Chevalier's commitment to the coup of 2 December 1851, which replaced the Second Republic with an authoritarian regime, tainted his reputation, especially in his role as a liberal thinker. Not only did Chevalier organize demonstrations of support in the Hérault department, where he presided over the local council, but his own brother Auguste, a private secretary of Louis-Napoleon, was directly involved in the coup's planning and execution. Reclaiming the significance of Chevalier's contribution to nineteenth-century debates about France's politics and economy therefore requires us to overcome the black legend of the Second Napoleonic Empire, established by Republican intellectuals and historians after the regime's fall in 1870.[107]

Liberalism in post-revolutionary France was not incompatible with occasional support for the suspension of liberal institutions, when circumstances required it. Few historians would contest that Talleyrand harboured a strong preference for a representative style of government, yet he had a hand in several anti-parliamentary coups under the Directory, and had few qualms about serving Napoleon's dictatorship. Benjamin Constant, a paragon of liberalism, supported the coups of 18 Fructidor in 1795 and 18 Brumaire in 1799. Even some British liberals, especially after the revolutions of 1848, accepted that a British-style parliamentary system was ill suited to Continental *moeurs*.[108] A case in point was the editor of *The Economist* Walter Bagehot, one of the most eloquent defenders of Britain's balanced constitution, but who endorsed

Power in Nineteenth-Century China and Japan (Oxford: Oxford University Press, 2012), 54, 63–84.

107. Sudhir Hazareesingh, *From Subject to Citizen: The Second Empire and the Emergence of Modern French Democracy* (Princeton, NJ: Princeton University Press, 1998); Roger Price, *The Second French Empire: An Anatomy of Political Power* (Cambridge: Cambridge University Press, 2001); Xavier Mauduit and Corinne Ergasse, *Flamboyant Second Empire! Et la France entra dans la modernité* (Paris: Armand Colin, 2016).

108. Georgios Varouxakis, *Victorian Political Thought on France and the French* (Basingstoke: Palgrave, 2002), 86–99, 119–22; Jonathan Parry, *The Politics of Patriotism: English Liberalism, National Identity and Europe, 1830–1886* (Cambridge: Cambridge University Press, 2006), 172–220.

Louis-Napoleon's coup on the grounds that the French national character was incompatible with "self-government": in order to maintain "the order and tranquillity which are (all agree) the essential and primary prerequisites of industry and civilisation," France needed "a really strong, a reputedly strong, a continually strong executive power." Bagehot even contended that the French would never become capable of acclimatizing to parliamentary government, in the same way that "the Jews of to-day" remained "the Jews of Moses" and "the negro" remained "the negro of a thousand years ago."[109]

Chevalier's political liberalism was similarly limited by cultural and racial relativism. Although he expressed admiration for British and American representative institutions in his *Lettres*, he considered that in Latin Catholic countries "republican principles" led to social disorder and the regression of civilization. "The anarchy that prevails in the former Spanish colonies", he wrote, "sufficiently proves the grief Catholic peoples expose themselves to when they seek to adopt the political forms of Protestant populations."[110] If anything, Chevalier was more amenable than Bagehot to the eventual transposition of representative institutions to countries other than Britain and the United States. In a review of Bagehot's *The English Constitution* (1867), Chevalier endorsed the liberal reforms, especially the increase in the powers of parliamentary assemblies, conducted by the Second Empire after 1860. He still believed that "questions of origin and race have a considerable influence on the constitution that befits a people." Yet he also thought that "personal government" or "dictatorship" was only useful "at certain times and temporarily." The greater economic efficiency of representative institutions implied that "nations wishing to preserve their influence and authority" in the world needed to adopt at least in part "the English system," or else they would become "second- or third-order states." This geopolitical justification for liberalism did not apply, in Chevalier's opinion, to "Orientals," whose long habituation to despotism rendered them forever unsuited to "the mechanisms of deliberative assemblies."[111]

---

109. Walter Bagehot, "On the new constitution of France, and the aptitude of the French character for national freedom" and "On the constitution of the Prince-President," first published in *The Inquirer* in 1852, repr. in *The Collected Works of Walter Bagehot*, 9 vols., ed. Norman St John-Stevas (London: The Economist, 1968), vol. 4, 45–53, 63–70 (quotations at pp. 50, 64).

110. Chevalier, *Lettres*, vol. 2, 291.

111. Michel Chevalier, "La constitution de l'Angleterre," *Revue des Deux Mondes*, 72 (1867): 533, 554.

At least, there can be little doubt that Chevalier thought of himself as a liberal, because in his view, authentic liberty lay in its practical and economic aspects, such as secure property rights and the freedom to purchase and sell commodities, rather than abstract constitutional arrangements. In his main theoretical work in defence of free trade, published only a few months after Louis-Napoleon's coup, he could therefore claim: "Every institution that has the misfortune of diminishing liberty . . . is destined to perish." In his opinion, "civil liberty," of which the freedoms of industry and trade were the main constituents, were the true foundations of Europe's "modern civilization." In an allusion to Constant's famous distinction between ancient and modern liberty, but somewhat exaggerating Constant's disdain for the former, Chevalier dismissed fanatical advocates of "political liberty" as enthralled to the obsolete ideas of "the philosophers of Greece and Rome." His chief concession to the need for political liberty was already grounded in its positive influence on economic development and political power: he hoped that France would eventually become governed by representative institutions, because "nations that will not learn to be worthy of [political liberty] will be relegated far from the first ranks."[112]

Proving that his concern with the practical dimension of liberty was not merely rhetorical, Chevalier played an active part in the Bonapartist state's effort to accelerate French capitalist development. As president of the "Travaux Publics" section of the Conseil d'Etat from 1852 and imperial senator from 1860, he helped devise a legal framework for numerous instruments designed to boost investment—from the creation of new joint stock banks to the guaranteeing of railway companies' loans by the state and the issuance of very small bond denominations for small savers.[113] Yet he is best remembered for his crucial role in the liberalization of French trade policies. In 1860, he secured the conclusion of a "free trade treaty" with Britain, and the following year he steered through the Senate the abolition of the *Exclusif*, a set of restrictions on

112. Michel Chevalier, *Examen du système commercial connu sous le nom de système protecteur* (Paris: Guillaumin, 1852), 3, 11–12, 16; compare with Constant, "The liberty of the Ancients compared with that of the Moderns," in Constant, *Political Writings*, 309–28.

113. Walch, *Michel Chevalier*, 258–353; on these policies' connections with French geopolitical ambitions, see chapter 4 in this book.

the trade of French colonies that had been the object of fierce controversies since the 1760s.[114]

Chevalier's commitment to free trade was grounded in an aspiration to consolidate peace in Europe and promote French influence around the globe, rather than laissez-faire economics. His enthusiasm for government intervention as a means of fostering economic development in his Collège de France lectures had drawn acerbic criticisms from orthodox economists.[115] His belated conversion to free trade owed little to the theoretical arguments of Jean-Baptiste Say or David Ricardo. In the 1830s, he continued to condemn "the theories of an absolute liberty of commerce" as "monstrous" and insisted that "commerce" needed "regulations" by the state as much as other "social relations."[116] Although he did not explicitly account for his change of views, the fact that it came about in the early 1840s suggests that it resulted from his admiration for the successes of British gunboat diplomacy in the Middle East and East Asia, and for Robert Peel's daring abolition of the Corn Laws in 1846. Protectionism may have been a sensible policy in the past, Chevalier admitted, but Britain's policies showed that "the seclusion of nations" had become "an absurdity in the times we live in."[117]

By the time Chevalier imposed himself as the leading advocate of free trade in the 1850s, he appealed for neither absolute nor comparative advantages, but more prosaically declaimed the practical benefits of cheaper, imported raw materials, the stimulation of foreign competition, and an alternative to the decaying power that resulted from protectionist policies: although formerly the greatest power in the world, China demonstrated "by the state of its industry

114. See *Documents officiels relatifs à la loi sur le régime douanier des colonies* (Paris: Challamel, 1861), 106–8; on controversies about the Exclusif, see Jean Tarrade, *Le commerce colonial de la France à la fin de l'Ancien Régime: l'évolution du régime de l'Exclusif, 1763–1789*, 2 vols. (Paris: Presses Universitaires de France, 1972) and Todd, *Free Trade*, 40–45, 171–83.

115. See for instance the critical review of his lectures in the main journal of political economy, "Cours d'économie politique du Collège de France par M. Michel Chevalier," *Journal des économistes*, 1 (1842): 204–8; upon learning that Chevalier would succeed him as professor at the Collège de France, Pelegrino Rossi, an orthodox defender of laissez-faire, allegedly quipped that "it will give [Chevalier] an opportunity to learn political economy," in Alphonse Courtois, *Notice sur la vie et les travaux de Michel Chevalier* (Paris: Guillaumin, 1889), 14.

116. Chevalier, *Lettres*, vol. 2, 209.

117. *Le Journal des Débats*, 8 Apr. 1846; on his support for gunboat diplomacy, see Chevalier, "L'Europe et la Chine"; see also the discussion of Chevalier's about-turn on free trade in Jean-Baptiste Duroselle, "Michel Chevalier et le libre-échange avant 1860," *Bulletin de la société d'histoire moderne*, 5 (1956).

as much as its sciences, its arts and its civil, political and military institutions, the fate of nations that isolate themselves."[118] Chevalier stated that global economic integration would result in an international division of labour. Yet the only significant division in his view would be between a manufacturing Western civilization on the one hand and all the other civilizations that would increasingly dedicate themselves to the production of raw materials on the other. After visiting the Great Exhibition of London in 1851, he welcomed the formidable progress of British industries because it would soon be emulated by the rest of European civilization. Despite their variety, Europeans shared "the same genius" and rapidly acquired each other's innovations. Europeans were similarly "invested with empire" over the world. Between Britain and France in particular, "the distance" in industrial capacity was "not great" and France retained a considerable advantage in all the industries where "taste plays a large part." Only its "customs tariff," he concluded, prevented France from sharing economic domination of the world with Britain.[119]

Therefore, Chevalier's conception of free trade was in stark contrast to that of Richard Cobden, the utopian adversary of realpolitik and British signatory of the 1860 treaty. Instead, it resembled—and in some respects radicalized— the instrumental case for trade liberalization propounded by British free trade imperialists. On meeting Cobden and his ally John Bright, Chevalier was bemused by the two Britons' tendency to treat free trade as "a religion," leaving us to infer that, for the French economist, it remained first and foremost an instrument of statecraft.[120] The 1860 treaty was a French initiative, imagined by Chevalier and other advisors of Napoleon III as a means of bypassing the opposition of the elected legislative chamber to tariff reduction. Over the following six years, France concluded similar free trade treaties with eleven other European powers (Britain only with four), establishing what some historians have described as Europe's "First Common Market."[121]

118. Michel Chevalier, *Cours d'économie politique*, 2nd edn., 3 vols. (Paris: Capelle, 1855–1866), vol. 2 (1858), 524.

119. Michel Chevalier, *L'exposition universelle de Londres considérée sous les rapports philosophique, technique, commercial et administratif au point de vue français* (Paris: Mathias, 1851), 14–17, 28–9.

120. Arthur L. Dunham, *The Anglo-French Treaty of Commerce and the Industrial Revolution in France* (Ann Arbor: University of Michigan Press, 1930), 3, 29–63.

121. Peter T. Marsh, *Bargaining on Europe: Britain and the First Common Market* (New Haven, CT: Yale University Press, 1999), 28–61; on the significance of the 1860 treaty in French commercial policy and Anglo-French commercial relations, see J. V. Nye, *War, Wine, and Taxes: The*

French free trade activism wasn't limited to Europe either, with the Second Empire allying itself with Britain to impose further commercial concessions on China during the Second Opium War (1856–1860), and concluding new asymmetric commercial treaties—with Siam in 1858, as seen in this book's introduction, and also Madagascar, Japan, Korea and other African and Asian polities after 1860.[122]

Another imperial aspect of France's global commercial strategy in that period was the prominent French involvement in the construction of interoceanic canals. The allegedly "universal" company that completed the Suez Canal in 1869 was primarily a French venture, whose success owed a great deal to the informal patronage of Napoleon III and the lobbying of Saint-Simonians, including Chevalier. It was designed to consolidate French dominance in Egypt and facilitate French enterprises in Asia.[123] Another canal project that would have connected the Atlantic to the Pacific and opened a new commercial route from Europe to Asia also played a significant part in the invasion of Mexico by French forces in 1862, a venture often described as puzzling by historians who have ignored or been unaware of France's informal imperial strategy.[124] Since his youthful fascination with Saint-Simonian ideas, even Napoleon III had expressed interest in the economic potential of a canal across the central American isthmus.[125] Since his journey across North America in the 1830s, Chevalier had also been promoting the idea of a canal as a means of regenerating Mexico's languishing economy.[126] In response to a series of monetary

Political Economy of Anglo-French Trade, 1689–1900 (Princeton, NJ: Princeton University Press, 2007), 1–19.

122. J. Y. Wong, *Deadly Dreams: Opium, Imperialism and the 'Arrow' War (1856–60) in China* (Cambridge: Cambridge University Press, 1998); Harry Gelber, *Battle for Beijing: Franco-British Conflict in China, 1858–1860* (Basingstoke: Palgrave Macmillan, 2016).

123. Caroline Piquet, *Histoire du Canal de Suez* (Paris: Perrin, 2009).

124. Edward Shawcross, *France, Mexico and Informal Empire*; see also Christian Schefer, *La grande pensée de Napoléon III: les origines de l'expédition du Mexique* (Paris: M. Rivière, 1939) and Michelle Cunningham, *Mexico and the Foreign Policy of Napoleon III* (Basingstoke: Palgrave, 2001). On contemporary French perceptions of Mexico, see Nancy Nichols Barker, *The French Experience in Mexico 1821–1861: A History of Constant Misunderstanding* (Chapel Hill: University of North Carolina Press, 1979) and Guy-Alain Dugast, *La tentation mexicaine en France au XIXe siècle: L'image du Mexique et l'intervention française*, 2 vols. (Paris: L'Harmattan, 2008).

125. Napoleon Louis Bonaparte, *Canal of Nicaragua* (1846), repr. in *Œuvres de Napoléon III*, 5 vols. (Paris: Amyot, 1854–1869), vol. 2, 475–543.

126. See his letters on Mexico in *Journal des Débats*, 20 July, 1 Aug., 7 Aug. and 15 Aug. 1837, and Michel Chevalier, *Du Mexique avant et pendant la conquête* (Paris: Fournier, 1845) and *Le*

shocks, including the Californian and Australian gold rushes and the growing Asian demand for silver, after 1850 Chevalier began to put forward a second, complementary economic argument to promote French intervention in Mexico: the decline of Mexican silver ore production, which threatened to undermine the stability of France's bimetallic gold-silver standard. Enforcing political stability in the chaotic former Spanish colony and providing the technical assistance of French mining engineers would help restore global monetary stability and preserve Paris's role as a major financial centre.[127]

Chevalier was not the only advocate of an intervention in Mexico in the early 1860s, and other considerations, including the manoeuvres of the Swiss financier Jean-Baptiste Jecker and a desire to take advantage of the American Civil War, inspired the project. But Chevalier's early enthusiasm and strident support for the expedition when it was launched in 1862 are significant. France's venture to Mexico between 1862 and 1866 corresponds closely with existing models of informal empire: it was designed to establish control and put collaborators in power without formally extending French sovereignty. Chevalier was one of the first writers to suggest that the expedition should replace Mexico's republican institutions with a monarchy and that the new crown should be offered to Maximilian of Habsburg. After independence a misguided attempt to emulate the "Anglo-Saxon" United States had led to the adoption of a republican form of government, but the results had been "insecurity for properties and lives, violation of the government's [financial] commitments, industry languishing or annihilated, roads regularly ransomed by bandits, declining morality of the nation, waning of science and disorganisation of public education, [and] a hideous corruption in the administration and the judiciary." By contrast, a "liberal" monarchy would enable Mexico to become again "the first country of the earth for precious metals" and to take advantage of its exceptional situation between Europe and "the great and populous empires of Asia." France, the "protector" and "elder sister" of all

Mexique (Paris: Maulde et Renou, 1851); for his interest in an interoceanic canal in central America, see Michel Chevalier, *L'isthme de Panama. Examen historique et géographique des différentes directions suivant lesquelles on pourrait le percer et des moyens à y employer. Suivi d'un aperçu de l'isthme de Suez* (Paris: C. Gosselin, 1844).

127. On Chevalier's growing concern about the future of bimetallism, see his *Des mines d'argent et d'or du nouveau-monde* (Paris: Gerdès, 1846), *Question de l'or. Métaux précieux et monnaie* (Paris: Guillaumin, 1853) and *De la Baisse probable de l'or, des conséquences commerciales et sociales qu'elle peut avoir et des mesures qu'elle provoque* (Paris: Claye, 1857), and his lectures at the Collège de France in the 1850s in *Cours d'économie politique*, 2nd edn., vol. 3 (1866).

Latin nations, was expected to encourage the endeavour, even by military means. Yet it should refrain from acquiring territory and the new Mexican monarchy would be "perfectly independent."[128]

Chevalier's stress on the predilection of Latin nations for monarchical institutions, echoed by the regime's propaganda for the expedition, helped render it anathema among contemporary and later French republicans. Equally if not more troubling from a modern perspective is the emphasis that Chevalier placed on Mexico's racial makeup as a guarantee of its immense economic potential. In his view, "the near complete absence of negroes" ensured the "superiority of the average intelligence of the Mexican people, by comparison with the situation in several other parts of Spanish America." Half of the population were native Amerindians and the other half of mixed European-indigenous descent, and as shown by the achievements of the Aztec civilization, "[Mexican] Indians had a more spontaneous taste than blacks for hard work, and obviously surpassed them for the faculties of the mind." Chevalier also considered encouraging the immigration of Indian and Chinese coolies across the Pacific Ocean.[129] His vision for Mexico demonstrates that an opposition to formal conquest did not preclude racial determinism and the sort of imperial hubris often associated after 1880 with the age of high imperialism.

With the benefit of hindsight, historians have often dismissed the Mexican expedition as an adventure doomed to failure. But at the time it elicited appreciation beyond the ranks of paid sycophants of the Bonapartist regime. Bagehot congratulated Napoleon III on having obtained for France "a splendid position upon the American continent," destined to become as profitable as Britain's possessions in India, and on having done so "without incurring all the responsibility a colony would have imposed."[130] The British Liberal prime minister, Palmerston, also expressed his admiration.[131] Until the mid-1860s, the project of a French empire of free trade seemed like, if not a triumph exactly, at least a reasonable gamble.

128. Michel Chevalier, L'expédition du Mexique (Paris: E. Dentu, 1862), 43, 60, 65, 87–88; the work was previously published in La Revue des Deux Mondes, 38 (1862), 513–61 and 879–918, and an extended version was published the following year as Le Mexique ancien et moderne (Paris: Hachette, 1863).

129. Chevalier, L'expédition du Mexique, 70–4.

130. Walter Bagehot, "The New Mexican Empire," The Economist, 22 Aug 1863.

131. Shawcross, France, Mexico and Informal Empire, 183.

A Turn to Formal Empire

After 1865, the global projection of French influence met with a succession of significant setbacks. In Mexico, there was greater opposition to the French intervention than anticipated, and pressures from the United States at the end of the Civil War forced an evacuation by French forces in 1866, quickly followed by the overthrow and execution of Emperor Maximilian. In Algeria, efforts to encourage the development of indigenous society under French tutelage, instead of settler immigration, were discredited by a catastrophic famine in 1867 and republican propaganda: the fiasco of the so-called Arab Kingdom policy can also be interpreted as the failure of an attempt to reduce the formal character of French domination in North Africa.[132] In Europe, the rise of Prussia, illustrated by its crushing victory over the Habsburg monarchy in 1866, jeopardized the Second Napoleonic Empire's dominant position. France's defeat to Prussia in 1870 not only confirmed its demotion in Europe, but also reduced its intellectual and cultural wherewithal overseas. This global geopolitical context accounts for the rapidly declining popularity of ideas of informal empire between 1865 and 1880.

Chevalier acknowledged the revival of a bellicose spirit within Europe itself, but initially wished it away as "one of those accidents that are ordinary in human affairs."[133] After France's defeat by Prussia, he adopted a more sombre tone, lamenting the decline and fearing the end of "European civilization," but his prominent role in the Bonapartist regime relegated him to the margins of political life.[134] Even before the Franco-Prussian war, new liberal writers such as Anatole Prévost-Paradol urged a return to a more territorial strategy, focused on the expansion of France's colonial demesne and settler population in North Africa, as a means of staving off relative decline. A publishing sensation with ten editions in the years 1868 and 1869, Prévost-Paradol's *La France nouvelle* captured this change of mood very well.[135] Not unlike the earlier

132. On the connections between the Second Empire's Mexican and Algerian policies, see Christina Carroll, "Imperial Ideologies in the Second Empire: The Mexican Expedition and the *Royaume Arabe*," *French Historical Studies*, 42, 1 (2019); on the Arab Kingdom as a project of informal colonization, see chapter 2 in this book.

133. Michel Chevalier, *La guerre et la crise européenne* (Paris: Claye, 1866), 10.

134. Michel Chevalier, *Du droit international, de ses vicissitudes et de ses échecs dans le temps présent* (Paris: Claye, 1873), esp. 16–19.

135. Pierre Guiral, *Prévost-Paradol: 1829–1870: pensée et action d'un libéral sous le Second Empire* (Paris: Presses Universitaires de France, 1955), 568–80.

works of Pradt and Chevalier, *La France nouvelle* called on contemporaries to attentively observe changes in "the map of our globe" since the beginning of our century, but he reached a more troublesome conclusion: while a soon-to-be united Germany threatened to dominate Europe and Russia spread across Asia, "the Anglo-Saxon race" had irremediably secured its hold over the Americas and Oceania. Belittling France's economic achievements and anticipating the decline of French as a medium of communication across the world, he implicitly denounced the policy of global influence as a delusion. Instead, the last remedy to France's imminent *déchéance*, he concluded, lay in an "increase in population" and an "increase in territory" in a French North Africa enlarged by the addition of Morocco and Tunisia to Algeria. By such means, "eighty to one hundred million Frenchmen, solidly established on both banks of the Mediterranean, in the heart of the old continent, will maintain in the future the name, the language and the legitimate consideration of France."[136]

The liberal conversion to the necessity of formal empire was not always as abrupt, and the potential impact of Prévost-Paradol's views was cut short in August 1870 when he took his own life while serving as ambassador in Washington. A more significant, if tortuous, case of conversion was that of the economist Paul Leroy-Beaulieu. The author of a reference treatise on colonial expansion under the Third Republic, *De la colonisation chez les peuples modernes* (1874; new editions in 1882, 1886, 1891, 1902 and 1908), Leroy-Beaulieu has often been considered the most important ideologist of modern French colonialism.[137] Yet his commitment to territorial expansionism came late and remained hesitant until the 1880s. Leroy-Beaulieu even had strong personal connections to the main proponents of informal expansion, having been a protégé of Guizot in his youth and having married Chevalier's daughter Cordelia in 1870—he succeeded his father-in-law at the chair of political economy at the Collège de France, upon Chevalier's death in 1879. Leroy-Beaulieu shared his patrons' abhorrence for intra-European warfare. His first publication, in 1868, was a denunciation of the losses in human lives and capital caused by wars between 1853 and 1866, which he placed at 1,750,000 and forty-eight billion francs respectively. However, his publication *Les guerres contemporaines* failed to mention the losses caused by wars between non-Europeans and, in

136. Anatole Prévost-Paradol, *La France nouvelle* (Paris: Perrin, 2012), 301–5.

137. Agnes Murphy, *The Ideology of French Imperialism, 1871–1881* (Washington, DC: Catholic University of America Press, 1948), 103–75 and Raoul Girardet, *L'idée coloniale en France de 1871 à 1962* (Paris: Hachette, 2005; first published in 1972), 53–7.

the case of wars between Europeans and non-Europeans, only included the losses in lives and capital suffered by the former.[138] Leroy-Beaulieu's strident pacifism was combined with a disturbing degree of Eurocentrism, as in the earlier moving pleas for peace of Constant, Pradt, Guizot and Chevalier.[139]

Scholarly attention has focused on the second (1882) and later editions of Leroy-Beaulieu's famous *De la colonisation*, published at the height of the Third Republic's colonial expansion. However, the first edition, published in 1874, was anything but an unambiguous call for the resumption of French territorial expansion overseas. In typical French liberal fashion, the bulk of the work was a condemnation of the mercantile style of European colonization that had prevailed until 1800, combined with an homage to the economic merits of Anglo-American settlerism. Leroy-Beaulieu's main sources of inspiration, frequently acknowledged, were British free trade imperialist authors—John Stuart Mill, Edward Gibbon Wakefield, Herman Merrivale—and Michel Chevalier. Only the chapter dedicated to Algeria alluded to the possibility of further expansion on the African continent ("by joining Algeria to Senegal, we shall one day dominate and civilize all the north-west of Africa"), but without stating whether this expansion should be formal or informal.[140] Tellingly, this chapter is also the only one that was altered after Leroy-Beaulieu completed the original manuscript in 1867 and submitted it for a prize competition organized by the Académie des Sciences Morales et Politiques.[141] The disdain for formal conquests, other than settler colonies, that pervades this first edition continued to reflect the optimism of an earlier age for the possibilities of in-

138. Paul Leroy-Beaulieu, *Les guerres contemporaines (1853–1866): recherches statistiques sur les pertes d'hommes et de capitaux* (Paris: Guillaumin, 1868), 92.

139. The same combination can be observed in Norman Angell's famous pacifist manifesto on the eve of the First World War, which endorsed the partitioning of the extra-European world as a means of reducing tensions between European powers; see Norman Angell, *The Great Illusion: A Study of the Relation of Military Power to National Advantage* (Memphis, TN: Bottom of the Hill, 2012; first published in 1909), 68–89. On the connections between racialist thinking and the new academic subject of international relations, see Robert Vitalis, *White World Order, Black Power Politics: The Birth of American International Relations* (Ithaca, NY: Cornell University Press, 2015).

140. Paul Leroy-Beaulieu, *De la colonisation chez les peuples modernes* (Paris: Guillaumin, 1874), 355.

141. Dan Warshaw, *Paul Leroy-Beaulieu*, 84–5; the chapter on Algeria in *De la colonisation*'s first edition includes a discussion of the 1873 law on land property in the colony, proving that it had been altered since 1867, but in the rest of the book, no later date than 1866 is mentioned, suggesting that the original text was not extensively revised.

formal empire. As will be shown in a later chapter on finance as an instrument of informal control, the work's insistence on the beneficial effects of capital exports for exporting countries, its main original feature, did not imply—and even implicitly discouraged—formal colonization.[142]

Leroy-Beaulieu's gradual adhesion to formal expansion was probably inspired by defeat in the war of 1870–1871, which he expected France to win on account of its more powerful navy and larger economic resources than backward, "Spartan" Prussia.[143] However, for an author whose reputation relied on systematic rigour rather than sparkling originality, his pronouncements in the 1870s show a remarkable inconsistency. For instance, in 1873 he asserted that in the future "the power and influence of a people will be proportionate to the quantity of territory it will be able to occupy, exploit, and civilize in countries that are now barbaric." But in 1879 he expressed a preference for the colonization of Africa by a "moral and civilizing influence" rather than by "conquest."[144] It was only after 1880 that he came to advocate colonial expansion consistently, perhaps out of fear that the increasingly radical republican government would otherwise seek a war of revenge against Germany (Leroy-Beaulieu distrusted the new regime and unsuccessfully ran as an *orléaniste* candidate in 1877). Hence the substantial alterations to the second edition of *De la colonisation* (1882), which now referred to existing French colonies as "embryos of territorial empires" and defined a new category, "colonies of exploitation," to describe the modern expansion of formal rule without significant European emigration.[145] At the root of the liberal conversion to formal empire, Leroy-Beaulieu's evolution suggests, lay a disillusion with informal empire, rather than a radical shift in perceptions of the extra-European world.

The aversion of French liberal thinkers to military conquest in the wake of Napoleon's fall can therefore not be equated with a condemnation of empire. Benjamin Constant's own stance was ambiguous as regards conquest beyond the pale of European civilization, while Pradt and Chevalier used Constant's celebration of commerce to justify the expansion of European domination over the rest of the world. Even outside Europe, Pradt, Chevalier and their

142. See chapter 4 in this book.

143. Paul Leroy-Beaulieu, "Les ressources de la France et de la Prusse," *Revue des Deux Mondes*, 89 (1870): 146.

144. *Journal des Débats*, 27 Feb. 1873 and *L'économiste français*, 1 Feb. 1879, quoted in Warshaw, *Paul Leroy-Beaulieu*, 54, 93.

145. Leroy-Beaulieu, *De la colonisation*, 2nd edn (1882), 249, 577–8.

followers were wary of the costs of territorial rule, thereby favouring an economical form of imperial dominance by cultural and economic means: local
elites, of European descent or brought to heel by European gunboats, would
encourage or tolerate an admiration for European civilization that would in
turn facilitate asymmetrical commercial exchanges between European manufactured goods and local primary products. By such means, France would
continue to play a prominent role in European expansion—thanks to its prestigious culture rather than its limited capacity for settlement colonization—
especially in parts of the world where it had strong historical or cultural ties,
such as Latin America or the Ottoman world.

The most disturbing aspect of this political economy of French expansion
was the emphasis placed by Pradt and Chevalier on European racial or civilizational superiority as a fundamental principle of the post-Napoleonic global
order. This trumpeting of Europe's superior merits and unity of interests
served to justify not only projects of domination outside Europe, but also
collaboration with Britain, France's former imperial rival. Such a strident ra-
cialism was unusual among liberals in the age of abolitions, even in France.[146]
Together with the enthusiasm of Pradt and Chevalier for military interventions outside Europe, it warrants the inclusion of these thinkers in the history
of European ideas about empires, and helps to bridge a gap between racial
justifications of slavery in the age of mercantile empires and the pseudo-
scientific racism of high imperialism in the late nineteenth century. The dis-
paragement of conquest did not entail the end of aspirations to European
global domination over other races or civilizations. By reducing the risk of
territorial collision between European empires, or the chances for non-
European polities to play European imperial formations against each other, it
may even have intensified them.

Although the racialist conceptions of Pradt and Chevalier may have been
extreme, they cannot be dismissed as stray or marginal aberrations. It is no
coincidence that the liberal thinkers with the most pronounced interest in the
global scale of human affairs were the most inclined to think in racial terms.
Unlike the racist theories of Arthur de Gobineau, to which contemporaries
gave scant attention, the works of Pradt were avidly read, while those of Che-

146. Jan E. Goldstein, "Toward an Empirical History of Moral Thinking: The Case of Racial
Theory in Mid-Nineteenth-Century France," *American Historical Review*, 120, 1 (2015).

valier also brought him considerable honours.[147] The exceptional access to the corridors of power enjoyed by both—but also by Talleyrand before them, and by Leroy-Beaulieu after them—suggests that their advocacy of informal empire influenced official thinking about France's position in the post-Napoleonic world. Their ideas offer a compelling rationale for France's policy in most parts of the world between 1820 and 1870, from Haiti and Mexico in the Americas, to Egypt in the Middle East. The one significant exception to this pattern was the extremely brutal and formal colonization of Algeria in the mid-century. However, as the following next chapter will argue, Algeria can also be construed as the unintended product of a failed project of informal colonialism.

147. Steven Kale, "Gobineau, Racism, and Legitimism: A Royalist Heretic in Nineteenth-Century France," *Modern Intellectual History*, 7, 1 (2010).

2

Algeria, Informal Empire Manqué

SHIPWRECKED ON THE COAST near Algiers in 1876, Joseph Loubon went on to reconnoitre the area. Having walked through a double alley of orange and lemon trees, he reached an elegant belvedere at the top of a small hill. From there, he saw a vast plain, divided between large fields of wheat and "a considerable mass of cotton plants, which seemed to be yielding plentifully." Loubon then followed an alley of mulberry trees that led to a farm, before which stood an extraordinary *bosquet*: "there were gathered the cochineal-rich nopal and low-yield lemon tree, the palm tree and the breadfruit, the fig tree and the coffee tree, the pear tree and the cacao tree, the apricot tree and the clove tree, the plum tree, the peach tree, the orange tree and an infinity of other trees that were unknown to [him]." In the *bosquet*, a beautiful young woman, upon learning that he had been shipwrecked and that he was French, invited him inside the farm, where she introduced him to her grandfather, a venerable old "Moor" (an indigenous Muslim from the coast). At dinner, Loubon and his hosts were joined by the young woman's father, who was a "Frenchman," and two neighbouring farmers, the one a "Kabyle" (Berber speaker) and the other an "Arab" (indigenous Muslim from the interior). The "pleasant, interesting and instructive" conversation of his fellow diners proved that "the civilization of the former inhabitants of the Regency [of Algiers] had become complete," and exploring the rest of the country he found that "a most complete union" reigned among them. Loubon then regained consciousness, in 1836, realizing he had experienced a "hallucination." Yet he was confident that forty years hence, his dream would become "truth itself."[1]

Loubon's dream was a pedestrian work of literature, but it is noteworthy for the contrast it offers with the actual course of French colonization of Algeria

1. Joseph Loubon, *Alger en 1876* (Marseille: Feissat aîné et Demonchy, 1837), 11–20.

over the next four decades. Even by the low moral standards of modern colonial conquest, the violence deployed by France's army, especially during the fierce war against the resistance led by 'Abd al-Qadir between 1839 and 1847, was extraordinary.[2] New words such as *enfumade* and *emmurade* were forged to describe the "smoking-in" or "walling-in" of indigenous civilians who had sought refuge in deep caves, and historians have legitimately asked whether French counter-insurgency tactics should be considered genocidal.[3] Once conquered, French Algeria also proved one of the most viciously segregated modern colonial societies, with sharp tensions between a sizeable minority of European citizens (and Jews, elevated to French citizenship in 1870) and a majority of Muslim Arabic- or Berber-speaking subjects. And far from becoming a large producer of raw materials needed by French manufacturers, such as cotton, Algeria's economy languished, at least until a boom in vine cultivation after 1880 turned it into a major exporter of wine—hardly a scarce commodity in metropolitan France, although imports of Algerian wines may have facilitated the release of labour from agriculture to services and industry in southern France.[4] The good standard of living enjoyed by European settlers relied on fiscal inequities at the expense of Muslim subjects and large subsidies from the French state, and paled in comparison with the startling economic success of other settler societies such as the United States, Australia or Argentina.[5]

How should we account for the discrepancy between Joseph Loubon's dream and the reality of what French Algeria became? Loubon's vision was not idiosyncratic. A banker and member of the Marseille municipal council, Loubon himself was typical of the milieu of Marseillais *notables* who lobbied relentlessly for the establishment of French domination in Algeria.[6] His vision

2. Gallois, *A History of Violence*; Olivier Le Cour Grandmaison, *Coloniser, exterminer: sur la guerre et l'État colonial* (Paris: Fayard, 2005); Benjamin C. Brower, *A Desert Named Peace: The Violence of France's Empire in the Algerian Sahara, 1844–1902*. (New York: Columbia University Press, 2009).

3. William Gallois, "Genocide in Nineteenth-Century Algeria," *Journal of Genocide Research*, 15, 1 (2013).

4. Charles Issawi, *An Economic History of the Middle East and North Africa* (New York: Columbia University Press, 1982), 33–4.

5. For a comparison with "Anglo" settler colonies, see Belich, *Replenishing the Earth*, 502–4.

6. Pierre Guiral, *Marseille et l'Algérie* (Gap: Ophrys, 1956), 173; Ian Coller, "The Republic of Marseille and the Making of Imperial France," in *Place and Locality in Modern France*, eds. Philip Whalen and Patrick Young (London: Bloomsbury, 2014), 3–14

of communal harmony and commercial prosperity echoed several projects of
Enlightened colonization in the late eighteenth century, and until 1840 it was
shared by many members of the French political elites. This idyllic future can
be construed as a project of informal empire combined with limited French
settlement. Loubon did not specify the political status of the former Regency
of Algiers in his dream. Yet he called it "a civilized nation," "a civilized kingdom" or "a new kingdom," suggesting that it was not under French sovereignty,
although it was under "French domination." At any rate it was not annexed by
France, as it would be in 1848, before being turned into three *départements* in
1870.[7] So why did this project of informal empire flounder, and why did Algeria become one of the most brutal instances of formal colonization
instead?

The question is important because the historiography has tended to treat
the invasion of Algeria as the fount of France's modern colonial empire in a
way that distorts our perceptions of French aspirations in the mid-nineteenth
century. This conception dates back at least to the era when most Western
historians sang the praises of European colonialism. A particularly eloquent
statement was the work of Gabriel Esquer on the capture of Algiers in 1830,
published in 1923 and tellingly entitled *Les commencements d'un empire* (The
beginnings of an empire). Esquer was an ardent republican as well as an influential bigwig, and his book, like much academic colonial history at the time,
was intended to celebrate the colonial genius of the Third Republic. It was a
tale of origins, which focused on what appeared to predict the future republican empire and left discordant elements in the shade. It was particularly careful
not to credit French monarchical regimes with much colonial foresight, and
to discredit alternatives to settler colonialism, considering them dead ends.[8]

7. Loubon, *Alger en 1876*, 9, 11, 17.

8. Gabriel Esquer, *Les commencements d'un empire. La prise d'Alger. 1830* (Algiers: L'Afrique
latine, 1923). Esquer was the director of the Bibliothèque Nationale in Algiers, the head of the
Algerian Gouvernement Général's archives and the long-time editor of the *Revue africaine*, a
major review in French colonial history. A second edition of *Les commencements d'un empire*
came out in 1929 and inspired several works, published to coincide with the celebration of
French Algeria's centenary in 1930, including Christian Schefer, *L'Algérie et l'évolution de la colonisation française* (Paris: Honoré Champion, 1928), François Charles-Roux, *France et Afrique du
Nord avant 1830. Les précurseurs de la conquête* (Paris: Félix Alcan, 1932), and Augustin Bernard,
L'Algérie, the second volume in the *Histoire des colonies françaises et de l'expansion de la France
dans le monde*, eds. Gabriel Hanotaux and Alfred Martineau, 6 vols. (Paris: Société de l'histoire
nationale et Librairie Plon, 1929–1934). On Esquer's career, see Germaine Lebel, "Gabriel Esquer,"

This narrative therefore paradoxically stressed both the colonial innocence of France's invasion, which it attributed to the provocations of uncivilized Turkish officials, and the inevitability of harsh formal rule, seen as the only means of maintaining French domination.

Historians who were critical of the French colonial regime in Algeria, such as Charles-André Julien and his disciple Charles-Robert Ageron, have debunked some of the myths that underlay this colonialist narrative.[9] In particular, they demonstrated that the *coup d'éventail*—the three blows of a fly swatter inflicted by Hussein Dey of Algiers upon the French consul Pierre Deval—should not be seen as the real or main cause of the Franco-Algerian conflict of 1827–1830. However they replaced this interpretation with an emphasis on the role of French domestic politics—especially a royalist plot to overturn France's constitutional charter, which was supposed to be facilitated by the military glory of the capture of Algiers—that revived colonial innocence under a new guise. In their view, France's largest overseas military operation since the failed reconquest of Saint-Domingue in 1802 was "a makeshift expedient for domestic political consumption."[10] Julien and Ageron also subjected the official discourse of republican colonialism on the benefits of French rule to a well-deserved and devastating critique.[11] However, perhaps because

---

Bibliothèque de l'École des chartes, 119, 1 (1961) and Xavier Yacono, "Gabriel Esquer (1876–1961)," *Revue africaine*, 105 (1961). On the celebration of French Algeria's one hundredth anniversary and its place in colonialist propaganda in the interwar period, see Jean-Robert Henry, "Le centenaire de l'Algérie, triomphe éphémère de la pensée algérianiste," in *Histoire de l'Algérie à la période coloniale*, eds. Abderrahmane Bouchêne, Jean-Pierre Peyroulou, Ouanassa Siari Tengour and Sylvie Thénault (Paris: La Découverte, 2014), 369–75.

9. See the influential account by Charles-André Julien and Charles-Robert Ageron, *Histoire de l'Algérie contemporaine*, 2 vols. (Paris: Presses universitaires de France, 1964–1979), esp. vol. 1, *La conquête et les débuts de la colonisation* (1964). On Julien and his disciple, see André Raymond, "Une conscience de notre siècle: Charles-André Julien, 1891–1991," *Revue du monde musulman et de la Méditerranée*, 59, 1 (1991) and Guy Pervillé, "In Memoriam: Charles-André Julien (1891–1991)," *Outre-Mers. Revue d'histoire*, 360–361 (2008); see also Charles-Robert Ageron, "Charles-André Julien (1891–1991)," *Revue française d'histoire d'outre-mer*, 79, 296 (1992).

10. Charles-Robert Ageron, *Modern Algeria: A History from 1830 to the Present*, trans. Michael Brett (London: Hurst & Co, 1991), 5; the original French, "un expédient improvisé et un geste de politique intérieur," is hardly less vigorous, in Charles-Robert Ageron, *Histoire de l'Algérie contemporaine*, 8th edn (Paris: Presses Universitaires de France, 1983), 6.

11. See especially the voluminous doctoral thesis supervised by Julien of Charles-Robert Ageron, *Les Algériens musulmans et la France, 1871–1918*, 2nd edn., 2 vols. (Saint-Denis: Bouchene, 2005; first published in 1968).

their main object of investigation remained republican colonialism, they were far less critical of French domination before 1870, taking at face value proclamations of imperial ingenuity by French liberals in the 1830s or dismissing projects to roll back settler colonialism under the Second Napoleonic Empire as chimerical. Under their pen, the exploitative and oppressive nature of the French regime became regrettable, but it remained inevitable.

There is much to admire in the erudite scholarship of Julien, Ageron and even Esquer.[12] Their interpretations were persuasive in different ways, and they continue to influence historical scholarship on the early years of French domination in Algeria. Yet like every interpretation, theirs relied on a selective use of the evidence, often governed by a political imperative: the celebration of colonialism in Esquer's case, the acceptance of decolonization in Julien and Ageron's. There is therefore room for alternative interpretations that would revisit certain pieces of evidence and highlight the significance of others. In this chapter I wish to sketch out one possible alternative, more concerned with what the French invaders sought and failed to achieve than what Algeria eventually became.[13] This book is more concerned with the place of Algeria within French global aspirations in the mid-nineteenth century than the idea of re-tracing the origins of modern colonial Algeria or France's republican colonial empire in the twentieth-century empire.

This perspective is inspired by the work of Christopher Bayly, who warned against the teleological temptation to reduce European expansion in the age of global revolutions to "a precursor of the 'real' imperialism of the later-nineteenth century."[14] First, the chapter aims to show that the expedition of Algiers in 1830 was neither fully innocent of colonial aspirations nor set on full territorial domination. Instead, it was in part inspired by a project of small coastal settlement, combined with a vague aspiration to informal domination over the Algerian hinterland. This project was rooted in Enlightened and lib-

12. Even Fernand Braudel, the grand adversary of *histoire évènementielle* but a former student of Esquer, commended *Les commencements d'un empire* as "beautiful," in Fernand Braudel, "Gabriel Esquer (1876–1961)," *Annales. Économies, Sociétés, Civilisations*, 18, 3 (1963): 607. On the colonial ambiguities of the Annales school, see Pierre Singaravélou, *Professer l'Empire: "les sciences coloniales" en France sous la IIIe République* (Paris: Publications de la Sorbonne, 2011), 280–1.

13. This interpretation draws on David Todd, "Retour sur l'expédition d'Alger: les faux-semblants d'un tournant colonialiste français," *Monde(s)*, 10, 3 (2016), 205–22.

14. Christopher Bayly, "The First Age of Global Imperialism, c. 1760–1830," *Journal of Imperial and Commonwealth History*, 26, 2 (1998): 29.

eral thought about empire and continued to inform French policy after the Revolution of 1830, as shown by the official motto of *occupation restreinte* (limited occupation) and efforts to turn 'Abd al-Qadir's new Arab emirate into a client state. The failure of this policy may have been inevitable. But it was precipitated by contingent factors, including a territorial tussle between the French and 'Abd al-Qadir in the eastern Constantine province and the great European war scare of 1840, which highlighted the precariousness of French settlements on the North African coast. Only then did the French government embark on a deliberate policy of territorial conquest. However, the mediocre economic returns of territorial rule led the Second Napoleonic Empire to try to adopt a less formal style of domination by transforming the French colony into an "Arab Kingdom." The failure of this attempt at a partial return to informal rule may, too, have been inevitable, but it was certainly accelerated by a series of droughts that discredited its supposed economic virtues in the late 1860s and the abrupt downfall of the Bonapartist regime in 1870.

This emphasis on hopes of informal domination is not intended to elide the existence of another aspiration, frequently voiced by some French soldiers and settlers, to a more formal and brutal type of rule. In fact, I hope that a serious examination of the enduring appeal of this informal project will contribute to a better understanding of the dynamics of colonial violence in Algeria. The paradigm forged by Robinson and Gallagher did not preclude formal conquest. Instead, it made it conditional on the failure of informal domination: paramountcy was to be achieved "by informal means if possible," but also "by formal annexations when necessary."[15] The formulation recalls the melancholy condoning of French atrocities as "unfortunate necessities" by Tocqueville, after he renounced his own hopes for a milder kind of French domination.[16] It helps explain the about-face of other members of the French elite, such as François Guizot and General Bugeaud, who warmly endorsed cooperation with 'Abd al-Qadir in the 1830s before becoming the chief artisans of the most savage phase of the conquest between 1840 and 1847. But it is also a reminder that hostility to conquest should not be equated with opposition to empire, or even with violence: Ismaÿl Urbain, the chief advocate of an Arab Kingdom after 1850, did not object to French methods while he served in the military in the 1840s, and the Arab Kingdom aimed to entrench French su-

15. Gallagher and Robinson, "The Imperialism of Free Trade": 3.

16. "Essay on Algeria (October 1841)," in Alexis de Tocqueville, *Writings on Empire and Slavery*, ed. Jennifer Pitts (Baltimore, MD: Johns Hopkins University Press, 2001), 59–116: 70.

premacy by subtler means, rather than abolish it. Algeria did not only become a very formal type of colony by design; it can also be construed as a case of informal empire manqué.

The Ideological Origins of French Algeria

The view that France harboured no serious imperial designs on North Africa when a thirty-five-thousand-strong military expedition stormed Algiers on 7 July 1830 remains widespread. Undeniably, contingent events played an important part in bringing about the invasion. On 28 April 1827, Hussein Dey hit Pierre Deval, the French consul, as part of a dispute over an obscure debt contracted by France with a Jewish Algerian merchant house in return for grain deliveries in the 1790s. France retaliated by blockading Algerian ports, but the blockade was ineffective and failed to bring the Ottoman Regency to heel. The last government of the Bourbon Restoration therefore decided upon a military intervention that would not only avenge the affront, it would also topple a regime that was infamous across Europe for its endorsement of privateering and Christian slavery. The success of France's expedition coincided almost exactly with the liberal revolution of 1830, and the new July Monarchy was not committed to colonization. Only in 1834 did it decide not to evacuate areas occupied by the French army, before gradually embarking upon a policy of full territorial conquest and intensive colonial settlement.

This narrative is factually accurate. However, such a close focus on events arguably exaggerates the part played by contingency. Taking into consideration the broader Mediterranean and global context suggests that factors other than chance played a significant role in bringing about the French invasion. First comes the crisis of the Ottoman world during the age of global revolutions. The growing fiscal and military threat posed by European states— illustrated by Ottoman difficulties during the Russo-Turkish wars of 1787–1792 and 1806–1812, but also by France's occupation of Egypt in 1798–1801 and the Anglo-Turkish war of 1807–1809—put Ottoman imperial structures under serious strain. The crisis culminated in the Greek War of Independence (1821–1830), which resulted in the destruction of the Ottoman fleet by Anglo-French-Russian naval forces at Navarino on 20 October 1827 and another Russian invasion in 1828–1829.[17] Such disarray in the heart of the Ottoman Empire left it

17. Şükrü Hanioğlu, *A Brief History of the Late Ottoman Empire* (Princeton, NJ: Princeton University Press, 2008), 6–71; Ali Yaycioglu, *Partners of the Empire: The Crisis of the Ottoman Order in the Age of Revolutions* (Standford, CA: Stanford University Press, 2016).

unable to provide much assistance to the outlying Regency of Algiers.[18] This was certainly as important a consideration regarding France's expedition as Algerian privateering and enslavement of Christian captives, both of which were in sharp decline due to British naval hegemony in the Mediterranean since the 1810s.

A second crucial factor was an enduring French aspiration to found a new type of colony, based on free White labour, which would be unencumbered by mercantilist regulations and politically autonomous. This aspiration dated back to efforts to reinvent colonization in the aftermath of France's catastrophic defeat during the Seven Years' War (1756–1763), notably by the liberal Physiocrats.[19] Its most spectacular manifestation was the Enlightened scheme of Guyana between 1763 and 1765.[20] The scheme ended in failure as most of the fifteen thousand European settlers quickly perished, but the aspiration endured and, along with French geopolitical interests, turned to the Mediterranean and Africa. There were several new colony projects in Raynal's influential *Histoire des Deux Indes* (1772). One of them can be found in the *Histoire's* section on the "Barbary States" (Morocco and the Regencies of Algiers, Tunis and Tripoli), where a passage, most probably written by Raynal himself, envisaged an expedition that would eradicate piracy and turn the existing Muslim polities into European "possessions." Raynal had a very limited form of colonization in mind: "merchants from Europe", established in North African towns, would suffice to encourage the indigenous inhabitants to cultivate a wide variety of crops on a soil "so fertile."[21]

Raynal's interest in the region's economic possibilities was sincere and long lasting. While living in Marseille between 1786 and 1790, he collected further information on North Africa's agriculture and commerce from the Compagnie d'Afrique, which had its seat in the Mediterranean port and enjoyed a monopoly on French trade with the Regencies of Algiers and Tunis. Raynal's studies reinforced his conviction that the arbitrary and despotic

---

18. Jamil M. Abun-Nasr, *A History of the Maghrib in the Islamic Period* (Cambridge: Cambridge University Press, 1987), 151–68; Tal Shuval, "The Peripheralization of the Ottoman Algerian Elite," in *The Ottoman World*, ed. Christine Woodhead (London: Routledge, 2012), 264–75.

19. Røge, *Économistes and the Reinvention of Empire*.

20. Emma Rothschild, "A Horrible Tragedy in the French Atlantic," *Past & Present*, 192 (2006); see also Marion Godfroy, *Kourou, 1763: le dernier rêve de l'Amérique française* (Paris: Vendémiaire, 2011).

21. Raynal, *Histoire* (1772 edn), vol. 4, 113–16; the passage was left unmodified in the 1774 and 1780 editions.

forms of these countries' "Turkish" mode of government was the sole cause of their economic stagnation.[22] Raynal's hopes that a military intervention would sweep away Ottoman domination in North Africa is not incompatible with this book's emphasis on the informal dimension of French imperialism—he did not specify that the intervention should be carried out by France, and the project implied neither full territorial conquest nor large-scale European immigration. Raynal's main concern was the advent of new institutions that would aid economic development for the benefit of indigenous inhabitants, as well as European and in particular French trade. Due to the enormous impact of the *Histoire* on French opinion and intellectual life, this project can be considered an important ideological factor behind efforts to assert French dominance in North Africa.

During the Revolution, the collapse of effective French rule in the West Indies rekindled interest in "colonisation nouvelle."[23] The ideas of the influential Talleyrand provide a compelling example. As seen in the previous chapter, in the first of two memoirs, which Talleyrand read at the Paris Institut in 1797, he had highlighted the possibility of keeping former colonies under a new kind of economic and cultural subjection. In the second memoir, he also endorsed the creation of new colonies, to be located "in warm countries" so that they could replace France's doomed Caribbean possessions for the supply of tropical commodities. Informal imperialism and new colonial settlements were, in his view, complementary strategies, especially as these new settlements, based on the model of ancient Greek colonies, should become "independent." Talleyrand did not pronounce himself on the most desirable location for such new settlements, although he mentioned "the coast of Africa" and Egypt as possibilities.[24] In 1798, as minister of external relations, he warmly supported the invasion of Egypt. But after the fall of the Napoleonic empire,

22. See the two manuscripts written by Raynal in the late 1780s, "Mémoire sur Alger," in Paris, Bibliothèque Nationale de France (henceforth BNF), Fonds français, Ms 6429 and "Mémoire sur la Compagnie royale d'Afrique," in BNF, Fonds français, Ms 6431; on Raynal's stay in Marseille, see Gilles Bancarel, *Raynal ou le devoir de vérité* (Paris: Honoré Champion, 2004), 368–409, and on his interest in the Maghreb, see Ann Thomson, "Raynal, Venture de Paradis et la Barbarie," *Dix-Huitième Siècle*, 15 (1983).

23. Bernard Gainot, "*La Décade* et la 'colonisation nouvelle'," *Annales historiques de la Révolution française*, 339 (2005); see also Jean-Louis Marçot, *Comment est née l'Algérie française (1830–1850)* (Paris: La différence, 2012), 21–96.

24. Charles-Maurice de Talleyrand-Périgord, *Essai sur les avantages à retirer de colonies nouvelles dans les circonstances présentes* (Paris: Baudouin, Year V [1797]), 11–16.

he regretted that the ill-fated expedition of Saint-Domingue in 1802–1803 had not instead been directed to the Barbary states: there, "philosophy would have been put into practice" and enabled France to obtain new and vast supplies of tropical goods "on the African coast of the Mediterranean."[25] This was the philosophical aspiration of Raynal, combined with a greater concern for national interest and power.

Following the end of the Napoleonic Wars and interventions by the American, British and Dutch navies to rein in privateering between 1815 and 1817, there was a proliferation of calls for the eradication of the North African Regencies.[26] Two examples are noteworthy here, because they illustrate what these projects owed to Raynal's vision and because they originated from figures who, although they are almost forgotten, were well connected in French official circles: Jacques Peuchet and William Shaler. Peuchet was a former collaborator of Abbé Morellet, a major advocate of colonial free trade at the end of the Old Regime.[27] Between 1819 and 1821, Peuchet issued a posthumous edition of Raynal's *Histoire*, from which abolitionist and other progressive passages were removed, and in 1826 he published a separate edition of the *Histoire*'s chapters on "Septentrional Africa."[28] This edition combined the original text of 1772 with some of the information collected by Raynal on the economic potential of the Regencies in the late 1780s, showing that Peuchet had access to these manuscripts. Some additional notes by Peuchet himself unambiguously called for the creation of "military and agricultural settlements" on the North African coast, in order to "spread civilization there."[29] One should not exaggerate the significance of this publication, yet it is enough

25. "Le domaine de la France est la Méditerranée," 1816, in Charles-Maurice de Talleyrand-Périgord, *Mémoires: 1754–1815*, eds. Paul-Louis Couchoud and Jean-Paul Couchoud, 2nd edn (Paris: Plon, 1982), 82–6.

26. Ann Thomson, *Barbary and Enlightenment: European Attitudes towards the Maghreb in the Eighteenth Century* (Leiden: Brill, 1987), 123–42; Gilian Weiss, *Captives and Corsairs: France and Slavery in the Early Modern Mediterranean* (Stanford, CA: Stanford University Press, 2011), 131–55.

27. René Maunier, "Un économiste oublié: Peuchet (1758–1830)," *Revue d'histoire des doctrines économiques et sociales*, 4 (1911), and Ethel Groffier-Kilbansky, *Un encyclopédiste réformateur. Jacques Peuchet (1758–1830)* (Laval, Canada: Presses universitaires de Laval, 2009), esp. 325–41.

28. Benot, "L'esclavagisme dans la quatrième édition de l'*Histoire des Deux Indes*."

29. Guillaume-Thomas Raynal, *Histoire philosophique et politique des établissements et du commerce des européens dans l'Afrique septentrionale*, ed. Jacques Peuchet, 2 vols. (Paris, 1826), vol. 1, 160–1.

to show that neither Raynal nor the potential colonization of North Africa had been entirely forgotten by French officialdom: Peuchet worked for the Ministry of the Interior under the Bourbons, and Karl Marx remarked that he was someone "not without influence, both directly [in the French governement] and as a writer" on French politics.[30]

A second notable call for the colonization of North Africa was William Shaler's *Sketches of Algiers*, also published in 1826. Shaler was the United States' consul in Algiers between 1815 and 1827. It is natural to overlook his book's impact on French designs, because Shaler was American and his work advocated colonization by Britain. Yet Shaler's career and ideas were closely intertwined with the economic and intellectual life of French global ambitions. In the 1790s, while sailing ships for an American merchant house in Bordeaux that specialized in trade with French colonies, he learned French and became well versed in French political and economic debates. In the early 1800s, he conducted commercial operations with Île de France (Mauritius), France's main possession in the Indian Ocean, and in 1812, the Spanish colonial government expelled him from Cuba on account of his French sympathies.[31] When he served as a member of the American delegation that negotiated the end of the war of 1812–1815, he still extolled France, due to its "democratic" tendencies, as the United States' "only natural ally" in Europe.[32]

After 1815, Shaler remained a supporter of democracy, critical of Britain's aristocratic tendencies.[33] Yet his abhorrence for the reactionary course

30. Karl Marx, "Peuchet: On Suicide" (1846), in Karl Marx and Frederick Engels, *Collected Works*, 50 vols. (London: Lawrence and Wishart, 1975–2004), vol. 4 (1975), 597–612.

31. On Shaler's career, see Roy F. Nichols, "William Shaler: New England Apostle of Rational Liberty," *New England Quarterly*, 9, 1 (1936) and "Diplomacy in Barbary," *Pennsylvania Magazine of History*, 74, 1 (1950); on his involvement in French colonial trade in the 1790s, see Silvia Marzagalli, *Bordeaux et les Etats-Unis, 1776–1815: politique et stratégies négociantes dans la genèse d'un réseau commercial* (Geneva: Droz, 2015), 381–2. The Navigocorpus database of commercial maritime voyages in the eighteenth and nineteenth centuries records two departures of ships captained by William Shaler (or Shaller) from Bordeaux in the 1790s, the *Two Sisters*, bound for New York in June 1795 and the *Mary*, bound for Senegal in September 1798, at http://navigocorpus.org (accessed 13 Dec. 2016); the *Two Sisters*, still commissioned by the same merchant house in Bordeaux, John Bernard's, is mentioned as bound to "Cape Nicola Mole & Jeremie" in Saint-Domingue in Isaac Roger to Nathaniel Shaler, 1 Nov. 1797, Historical Society of Pennsylvania, Philadelphia (henceforth HSP), Shaler MSS, 589/1.

32. Draft letter, Shaler to unamed recipient, Nov. 1814, HSP, Shaler MSS, 1172/1.

33. See several draft letters critical of British political and colonial hypocrisy by Shaler to an unnamed American recipient, 1825, HSP, Shaler MSS, 1172/2.

taken by the Bourbon Restoration and its commitment to the "Holy Alliance" trumped these feelings, and this is probably why he recommended Britain as the best possible colonizer of North Africa.[34] The conception of colonization he described in *Sketches* nonetheless retained a strong French flavour. He completed the book's manuscript in Marseille, where he spent most of his leaves from Algiers. His insistence that the colonizers of North Africa should emulate "the principles upon which the Ancients founded colonies" closely resembled the ideas and language of French advocates of *colonisation nouvelle*, who systematically opposed the virtuous model of independent Greek colonies to "modern" exploitative schemes of colonization.[35] After all, as seen in the previous chapter, French advocates of settler colonialism themselves sometimes supported British colonial expansion, even as they continued to condemn French attempts to found settlements overseas.

The French origins of Shaler's ideas on the future of the Regency help understand why the *Sketches* attracted significant attention in France. Deval, the French consul in Algiers, enclosed translated extracts from the book in the same dispatch in which he recounted his altercation with Hussein Dey in April 1827.[36] The dissemination of *Sketches* in France would have also benefited from Shaler's extensive network of French friends. These included Guillaume Hyde de Neuville, a former French consul in New York and the minister of the navy and colonies who supervised the blockade of Algiers in 1828–1829.[37] An official translation of *Sketches*, by an Orientalist "secretary interpreter" of King Charles X, was published in Paris at the beginning of 1830.[38] A pamphlet giving an overview of the Algiers Regency, aimed at members of the French expeditionary corps, reproduced several passages translated from

34. William Shaler, *Sketches of Algiers, Political, Historical, and Civil* (Boston, MA: Cummings, Hilliard and Company, 1826), 168–9.

35. Shaler, *Sketches*, 170–73.

36. The consul general to the minister of foreign affairs, 30 Apr. 1827, AAE, Mémoires & Documents (henceforth M&D), Algérie, 2.

37. Nichols, "Diplomacy in Barbary," 139.

38. William Shaler, *Esquisse de l'État d'Alger, considéré sous les rapports politique, historique et civil*, trans. Xavier Bianchi (Paris: Ladvocat, 1830); Bianchi, a translator specializing in Ottoman Turkish, served as an interpreter in French negotiations with the Regency in 1829, as reported in his own *Relation de l'arrivée dans la rade d'Alger du vaisseau de S. M. La Provence* (Paris: the author, 1830).

Shaler's work.[39] References to *Sketches* in the correspondence of French colonial officials after 1830 suggest that Shaler's ideas, such as his insistence on
commerce as the means of gaining indigenous consent to foreign rule, or his
conviction that the Berber-speaking Kabyles were more amenable to civilization than Arab speakers, continued to influence France's early Algerian
policies.[40]

It was not Peuchet and Shaler's works alone that determined France's decision to invade and colonize the Ottoman Regency of Algiers. But they are
useful reminders of the broader geopolitical and ideological context in which
the Franco-Algerian war of 1827–1830 took place. This context, in turn, suggests
that the causal chain of events that resulted in invasion and colonization was
not the sole product of contingency. Projects of domination, combined with
limited settlement in North Africa, were in the air in the 1820s. In fact, careful
reconsideration of evidence shows that one such project entertained by
French officials played a very direct role in the breakdown of Franco-Algerian
relations in the mid-1820s.

The Bourbon Restoration's Colonial Scheme

The colonialist historiography of Algeria, by emphasizing the role of the *coup
d'éventail* in the outbreak of the Franco-Algerian conflict, insisted that France
was not intent on colonizing Algeria. Hussein lost his temper, it claimed, over
the French government's reluctance to settle the *créances Bacri*, a debt contracted with the Algiers Jewish merchant house of Bacri, in return for grain
deliveries in the 1790s, and of which seven million francs remained unpaid in

39. Hélène Blais, *Mirages de la carte: l'invention de l'Algérie coloniale* (Paris: Fayard, 2014),
37–8.

40. Léon Blondel, director of finance, to Jean-Baptiste Drouet d'Erlon, governor general, 22
Nov. 1834, in *Correspondance du general Drouet d'Erlon*, ed. Gabriel Esquer (Paris: Champion,
1926), 129, 133–4, and Blondel to Maréchal Clauzel, governor general, 17 Aug. 1835, in *Correspondance du Maréchal Clauzel, gouverneur général des possessions françaises dans le nord de l'Afrique,
1835–1837*, ed. Gabriel Esquer, 2 vols. (Paris: Larose, 1948), vol. 1, 24; Shaler himself described
his identification of the Kabyles as the original, only superficially Islamicized inhabitants of
North Africa, in the *Sketches'* fourth chapter, as the book's most significant contribution, in a
letter to the French-born American philologist Pierre-Etienne du Ponceau, draft, [1824], HSP,
Shaler MSS, 1172/2. On French illusions about the Kabyles in early colonial Algeria, see Patricia
Lorcin, *Imperial Identities: Stereotyping, Prejudice and Race in Colonial Algeria* (London: Tauris,
1995), 146–66.

1827. This account conveniently blamed the conflict on the uncouth manners of Algiers's Turkish rulers and their inability to comprehend the sophistication of French commercial law: the house of Bacri had gone bankrupt in the late 1810s, and French courts had to consider multiple claims before allowing the settlement of the Regency's. Conforming to a colonialist trope that attributed Franco-Muslim quarrels in Algeria to the manoeuvres of indigenous Jews, this account also pointed to the responsibility of Jewish merchants, "the true sovereigns of Algiers," who allegedly abetted Hussein's anger.[41] More recent scholarship has dismissed this interpretation, placing the emphasis instead upon the domestic political motives of France's intervention. Yet reviewing the incident in more detail shows that Hussein's anger was not only due to the *créances Bacri*: it was also inspired by a French attempt to turn a set of commercial privileges dating from the seventeenth century into a small territorial settlement, or what French officials described as "the possible seed of a colony," in the eastern province of Constantine.[42]

The scheme's origins lay in a failed attempt after 1815 to restore France's commercial exchanges with the Regency to their prosperous pre-revolutionary footing. In 1817, the dey's government handed the "Concessions d'Afrique" back to France. This was a set of commercial privileges enjoyed by the Compagnie d'Afrique until the Revolution and purchased by Britain in 1807. The *Concessions* consisted of a monopoly on coral fishing and external trade in the region of Bona (Annaba) in the Constantine province, near the border with the Tunis Regency. However, the economic returns of France's diplomatic success proved disappointing: although the dey had trebled the dues for the *Concessions*, Franco-Algerian trade stagnated well below its pre-revolutionary level.[43] In 1824, a report by the Ministry of Foreign Affairs acknowledged the

41. Esquer, *Les commencements d'un empire*. ch 1: "Les créances Bacri," 7–68: 18; on the debt and litigation surrounding it, see Morton Rosenstock, "The House of Bacri and Busnach: A Chapter from Algeria's Commercial History," *Jewish Social Studies*, 14, 4 (1952). On the French colonial discourse about Algerian Jews, see Lorcin, *Imperial Identities*, 173–86; Joshua Schreier, *Arabs of the Jewish Faith: The Civilizing Mission in Colonial Algeria* (New Brunswick, NJ: Rutgers Press, 2010); and Julie Kalman, *Orientalizing the Jew: Religion, Culture and Imperialism in Nineteenth-Century France* (Bloomington: Indiana University Press, 2017).

42. Minutes of the Conseil Supérieur du Commerce et des Colonies, 18 Oct. 1825, AN, F12* 193/4, fols. 288–313.

43. Laurent Féraud, *La Calle: et documents pour servir à l'histoire des anciennes concessions françaises d'Afrique* (Algiers: Aillaud et Cie, 1877); Paul Masson, *A la veille d'une conquête: concessions et compagnies d'Afrique (1800–1830)* (Paris: Imprimerie nationale, 1909).

failure of French policy and proposed transforming the *Concessions,* around the old disused warehouse of La Calle (el Kala), into "a kind of colonial regime." Rejecting the conclusions of an earlier ministerial commission that had deemed La Calle a mere "foothold . . . tolerated by the power that commanded the surrounding country," the report argued that the designation of the old Company as the "owners" of the shores over ten *lieues* (c. 40km) entitled France to treat the region as "[its] own territory."[44]

As a preliminary step towards the foundation of a settlement, the report recommended the rehabilitation of the abandoned fort of La Calle and its garrisoning with a permanent force of fifty. The settlement's main purpose would be tropical agriculture, including the cultivation of cotton:

> One must here note that on the Concessions' shores, the land, for a large part uncultivated and covered with a population which will easily be encouraged to work, can, according to the observations of the consul general [Deval] . . . contain and bring to their level of perfection a large number of crops from the old and the new world; that these crops include cotton, the attempted cultivation of which has met with complete success; and that therefore, it would not be impossible, given some time, to imitate the enterprises of this kind undertaken by the Pasha of Egypt.[45]

Pierre Deval's observations on the soil's suitability for the cultivation of cotton were credible—after his dismissal from the consular service due to his "counter-revolutionary" opinions in the 1790s, he had become a merchant between 1803 and 1814, specializing in the Levantine cotton trade. Talleyrand had a keen interest in the cultivation of tropical crops in North Africa, and his decision to appoint Deval as consul in Algiers in 1815 was probably influenced by the latter's commercial expertise.[46] The report advocating the transformation

---

44. "Rapport sur les Concessions d'Afrique," Apr. 1824 [day unknown], AAE, Correspondance consulaire et commerciale (henceforth CCC), Alger, 46; see also another copy of the report, dated 2 Sep. 1825 and addressed to Conseil Supérieur du Commerce et des Colonies in Pierrefitte-sur-Seine, Archives Nationales (henceforth AN), F12 6220. On debates about sovereignty in the Mediterranean, see Guillaume Calafat, *Une mer jalousée: contribution à l'histoire de la souveraineté, Méditerranée, XVIIe siècle* (Paris: Le Seuil, 2019).

45. "Rapport sur les Concessions d'Afrique," Apr. 1824, AAE, CCC, Alger, 46

46. The son of a first dragoman (interpreter) at France's embassy in Constantinople, Pierre Deval had served as dragoman in Syria and vice-consul in Bagdad in the 1780s; see report on Deval's dismissal, 27 pluviôse Year III [15 Feb. 1795], Deval to Talleyrand, 20 thermidor year X [8 Aug. 1802] and 21 May 1814, and a recommendation by Comte Choiseul-Gouffier, a close

of the *Concessions* into a colonial settlement also reflected the strong impression made in France by the successful cultivation of a new type of long-staple cotton in Muhammad ʿAliʾs Egypt, where it had been introduced by the French industrialist Louis Alexis Jumel. French officials estimated that Egyptʾs output of "Jumel" (or "Maho") cotton had risen from two hundred tons in 1821 to twenty thousand tons in 1824.[47] This success inspired hopes that cotton cultivation might expand into other Mediterranean countries, showing a limited awareness of the plantʾs need for humidity as well as warmth: cultivation in Egypt relied on the Nileʾs waters and remained confined to the riverʾs delta.[48] Yet this confusion is understandable in an era when the global geography of cotton cultivation was in flux. It was also around 1820 that the introduction of a new hybrid variety, "Petit Gulf," unlocked the Mississippi Valley to cotton planters and their slaves, enabling the emergence of the American Cotton Kingdom.[49]

Europeʾs archives teem with nineteenth-century colonial fantasies, but the implementation of the 1824 proposal to turn La Calle into a colonial settlement played an easily traceable and direct role in the outbreak of the Franco-Algerian conflict in 1827. In 1825 the Conseil Supérieur du Commerce et des Colonies, a body inaugurated the previous year and which enjoyed considerable influence over colonial policy (a few months earlier, it had sanctioned the recognition of Haitian independence), endorsed the conclusions of the 1824 report on the *Concessions* and granted 150,000 francs for the rebuilding of La Calle. The works would establish that France held "a veritable territorial

friend of Talleyrand and former French ambassador in Constantinople, to Talleyrand, 8 May 1814, in AAE, Personnel, folder 1309. See also Anne Mézin, *Les Consuls de France au siècle des Lumières* (Paris: Direction des archives et de la documentation du ministère des affaires étrangères, 1997), 237–8.

47. Report to the Bureau du commerce et des colonies, "Commerce des cotons: des compagnies de commerce se proposent pour faire ce commerce avec l'Egypte," June 1825, AN, F12 8893.

48. Roger Owen, *Cotton and the Egyptian Economy, 1820–1914: A Study in Trade and Development* (Oxford: Clarendon, 1969), 28–57; François Charles-Roux, *La production du coton en Egypte* (Paris: Armand Colin, 1908), 21–40.

49. Walter Johnson, *River of Dark Dreams: Slavery and Empire in the Cotton Kingdom* (Cambridge, MA: Belknap, 2013), 8–9, 151–2; Giorgio Riello, *Cotton: The Fabric That Made the Modern World* (Cambridge: Cambridge University Press, 2013), 204–6. On cotton cultivation as a major inspiration of colonization projects, see Beckert, *Empire of Cotton*, esp. 340–78.

property" on the Barbary Coast, constituting "the possible seed of a colony."[50] Accounting documents show that the works began in 1826 and that in 1827 La Calle had a garrison of around thirty-five European soldiers, most of whom had Italian names, and ten indigenous servants.[51]

The fort's rehabilitation elicited furious objections from the dey's government. In retaliation, Deval reported, the Regency discouraged the population in the Bona region from trading with French merchants and threatened to hand over the *Concessions* to another European power. It was also in response to the construction of fortifications, the consul stated in a dispatch from October 1826, that the old "Algerian debts" (the *créances Bacri*) were "stirred up again" (*remises sur le tapis*).[52] It was only in his dispatch about the fly swatter incident, in April 1827, that Deval put the emphasis on the *créances Bacri*, although he still mentioned that, after hitting him, Hussein demanded the removal of all French "cannon-guns" from La Calle.[53] According to William Shaler, still the American consul in Algiers and an eyewitness to the incident, the first and main object of the dispute was the new French fortification: "The passion of H[is] Highness [Hussein Dey] had been excited, by a discussion relative to the French bastion at La Cala, . . . H[is] Highness was indignant at the conduct of the French Government, in enlarging that fortification, upon his own territory, without express stipulation, or his previous consent." Only after this conversation did a briefer exchange take place over the Bacri debt: "the rage of H[is] Highness became so indomitable, that he committed this outrage of personal violence."[54] A tribal leader from the Constantine province

50. Minutes of the Conseil Supérieur du Commerce et des Colonies, 18 Oct. 1825, AN, F12* 193/4, fols. 288–313; the decision of the Conseil Supérieur was communicated to Deval, in the minister of foreign affairs to Deval, 15 Nov. 1825, AAE, CCC, Alger, 47.

51. "Montant des frais faits au fort de la Calle, pour les réparations concernant cet établissement et les dépenses y relatives" in the winter of 1825–1826 and "État général des recettes et dépenses pour les réparations et la restauration des propriétés françaises dans les Concessions d'Afrique et dépendances" in the summer of 1826 and the winter of 1826–1827, in Archives Nationales d'Outre-Mer, Aix-en-Provence (henceforth ANOM), GGA, 3 B 33; see also "État des dépenses pour nourriture & solde de la garnison" at the beginning of 1827 in ANOM, GGA, 5 B 19. A later report claims that the works had in fact cost 329,000 francs; see Lieutenant Colonel Prétot, "Notice sur la Calle et sur la pêche au Corail," 17 Jan. 1834, in ANOM, GGA, E 103, folder 2.

52. Deval to the minister of foreign affairs, 18 Oct. 1826, AAE, M&D, Algérie, 1.

53. Deval to the minister of foreign affairs, 30 April 1827, AAE, M&D, Algérie, 2.

54. Shaler to secretary of state, 27 June 1827, United States National Archives, College Park, MD, Record Group 59, M23, roll 13.

and a German doctor at the court of the dey also attributed the quarrel to the French fortifications in La Calle.[55]

A dispatch from Hussein to the Ottoman government pointed to "the sums which the French owe the victorious *Ocak* [Turkish garrison]" as the dispute's main cause. Yet it also cited the construction of a new fort in La Calle as evidence that the French "manifestly nourished hostile designs."[56] Only five days after France's declaration of war to the Regency on 13 June 1827, the dey had the fortifications "destroyed and burnt to the ground." [57] It is not possible to determine with certainty the respective part played by Hussein's various grievances against the French government in bringing about his outbreak of anger—and the outbreak of war. But on balance it remains likely that Deval and the French government—as well as the colonialist historians who came in their wake—deliberately sought to exaggerate the significance of the *créances Bacri* and downplay that of the Le Calle settlement.[58] The Bourbon Restoration did not intend the territorial conquest of the entire Algiers Regency, but it harboured a limited colonial design in its eastern province that contributed to the outbreak of war. This project harked back to Raynal's aspirations and would inspire French policies until the late 1830s.

The Politics and Geopolitics of the 1830 Expedition

In the era of decolonization, historians repudiated the colonialists' insistence that the Bacri debts were the main cause of the French invasion. But they focused instead on the role of domestic politics, which also tended to obscure French imperial designs. France's military expedition and capture of Algiers

---

55. Laurent Féraud, "La prise d'Alger en 1830 d'après un écrivain musulman," *Recueil des notices et mémoires de la Société archéologique de Constantine*, 3 (1865); Alfred Michiels, "La prise d'Alger, raconté par un captif," *Revue contemporaine*, 17 (1854).

56. "Report of the Dey Hüseyini paşa to the Ottoman Grand Vezir, 19 December 1827," in *The Middle East and North Africa in World Politics: A Documentary Record*, ed. Jacob C. Hurewitz, 2 vols. (New Haven, CT: Yale University Press, 1975–1979), vol. 1, 228–31.

57. Prétot, "Notice sur la Calle," in ANOM, GGA, E 103, folder 2.

58. Esquer, *Les commencements d'un Empire*, 61 even dismissed Algerian anxieties about the "cannon-guns" of La Calle as the product of a false "rumour" spread by "imbecile" Turkish officials unfamiliar with the sophistication of European commercial warehouses; but payments for items of weaponry in the accounts of the construction works, including one for "lead bullets for the use of the artillery," suggest that the dey's officials were right to worry, in "État général des dépenses pour les réparations du fort de la Calle," 30 Sep. 1826, ANOM, GGA, 5 B 18.

in 1830, they claimed, was chiefly intended to bolster the Restoration's military prestige and facilitate a reassertation of the Crown's prerogative at the expense of parliamentary chambers. By contrast, liberal opponents of the regime resisted the expedition out of hostility to colonial conquest. When the revolution of 1830 defeated the royalist machination and substituted the July Monarchy to the Restoration, the liberals, now in power, found themselves embarrassed by the conquest of Algiers, and it wasn't until the mid-1830s that they resolved to colonize the former Regency.

This political interpretation remains extremely influential, in large part because it is true that the Bourbon regime hoped to draw benefits from the capture of Algiers on the domestic stage, and that liberals fiercely opposed the expedition. [59] However, there are two caveats that must be mentioned. First, French royalists were not always guided by an obsession to restore the Old Regime, and we should not dismiss geopolitical and imperial considerations in the decision to launch an expedition against Algiers in 1830. Official proclamations that were meant to reassure the major European powers may have claimed that the opposite was true, but confidential documents show that the Restoration continued to envisage the creation of a colonial settlement in the east of the Regency, along with the subordination of the rest of the country to French influence. Second, French liberals also had ulterior political motives. Many of them opposed the expedition because they feared its domestic political consequences, rather than because of some principled hostility towards colonization. Major liberal figures even opposed the expedition on the opposite grounds that it would fail to result in colonization.

The expedition to capture Algiers was a response to the situation in North Africa and the Mediterranean, as well as a product of French domestic political quarrels. Contrary to the hopes of Deval and other French officials, the blockade of Algerian ports from June 1827 failed to cow the dey's regime, while a recrudescence of Algerian privateering inflicted significant damage on French Mediterranean trade. The new royalist ministry, led by Jules de Polignac from July 1829, had to find a solution to the Algerian conundrum. At first it encouraged an invasion of the Regency by Muhammad 'Ali, the ruler of Egypt and a close ally of France. This plan was suggestive of the French preference for establishing domination in North Africa by indirect means. But it was abandoned as a result of British opposition, and also because 'Ali made exorbitant

59. See for instance Bouchène et al., *Histoire de l'Algérie coloniale*, 24 and Sessions, *By Sword and Plow*, 25.

demands, including the gift of several French ships of the line to the Egyptian navy, in return for his assistance.[60] It was this scheme's failure, alongside worsening domestic political tensions, which led Polignac's government to decide upon a large-scale military expedition in January 1830 to resolve the Algerian question.

Advocates of an interpretation that puts the onus on domestic politics have noted that as early as October 1827, a report by the Comte de Clermont-Tonnerre, the minister of war, proposed an expedition as a means of reminding French opinion that "military glory survived the Revolution."[61] However, his memorandum also waxed lyrical about the strategic and economic benefits that lasting French domination would bring: Algerian forests and mines would facilitate shipbuilding and the strengthening of the French navy, while the Regency's fertile soil "naturally [grew] a large number of colonial plants" and would "lend itself to the cultivation of all those that we may wish to transpose there." What the report really demonstrated was that domestic political calculations and imperial aspirations were not mutually exclusive. Rather, they reinforced one another, even if the hope that North Africa could become a major supplier of tropical commodities—Clermont-Tonnerre was especially sanguine about the prospects of cane sugar and indigo—still betrayed a poor understanding of the natural conditions required for their cultivation and of those prevailing in the Maghreb. The report was extremely vague in terms of the political status of this potential new "possession." Clermont-Tonnerre proposed the creation of French "military settlements," but insisted on the need for cooperation in a way that suggested an informal type of domination: indigenous inhabitants "will be very useful for us if we succeed in establishing with them relations that will guarantee them advantages and security."[62]

Historians who have put emphasis on the domestic political origins of the Algiers expedition have also pointed to the lack of declared colonial objectives in the official proclamations of King Charles X, which instead described the extirpation of piracy and Christian slavery as its main objective.[63] However,

60. Muhammad Sabri, L'empire égyptien sous Mohammed Ali et la question d'Orient (1811–1849) (Paris: P. Geuthner, 1930), 169–81.

61. See for instance Julien, La conquête, 30–1; for the quotation from the report, see Paul Azan, "Le rapport du comte de Clermont-Tonnerre, ministre de la guerre (1827)," Revue africaine, 338–39 (1929): 216.

62. Azan, "Le rapport du comte de Clermont-Tonnerre": 223–4, 239–41.

63. Julien, La conquête, 36–8; see also Esquer, Les commencements, 163.

these proclamations were addressed to European governments and designed to assuage any anxieties other powers may have had when it came to French expansionism. At least this is what Polignac claimed in his memoirs published in 1845, and politicians' recollections are not always entirely inaccurate.[64] The claim is made all the more credible by a memorandum written in 1814, in which Polignac had advocated the creation of French "settlements" on the North African coast that would provide "immense commercial resources."[65] Seasoned European diplomats were unconvinced by the proclamations of Charles X. Lord Aberdeen, the British foreign secretary, declared himself "persuaded" that France would "establish itself in Africa," and considered French assurances to the contrary "worthless."[66] Klemens von Metternich, his Austrian counterpart, was similarly unimpressed: "That's a colony founded there [in the Regency of Algiers]," he commented, "you can count on it."[67]

Several confidential reports addressed to Polignac in the months preceding the expedition show that imperial designs remained an important consideration, and that the scheme of limited settlement in eastern Algeria had not been forgotten. "Of all the projects" on the future of Regency, one of the reports asserted, "the one which would certainly suit France best would be that it keeps Algiers," or at least "the easternmost part of the country," in order "to colonize it." Another report argued that France should aim to retain possession of the coast from Stora to La Calle (about one hundred kilometers, including the *Concessions* shores), a "tract of land renowned . . . for its fertility"; in particular, "cotton could be advantageously cultivated."[68] Polignac himself, in a report to the King's Council in May 1830, endorsed the project of founding settlements on the North African coastline: these would become "our *natural colonies*, much more profitable than those [in the Antilles] that the climate prevents us from cultivating ourselves."[69] The French government's instruc-

64. Jules de Polignac, *Etudes historiques, politiques et européennes* (Paris: Dentu, 1845), 227–35.

65. Jules de Polignac [to King Louis XVIII], 19 Sep. 1814, AAE, M&D, Afrique, 6.

66. The French ambassador in London to Polignac, 10 May 1830, AAE, Correspondance Politique, Angleterre, 627; see also Aberdeen to the British ambassador in Paris, 4 May 1830, Kew, The National Archives (henceforth TNA), FO 27/405.

67. Reported by W. Chad, a British diplomat in Germany, to the Duke of Wellington, Prime Minister, 18 June 1830, Hartley Library, Southampton, Wellington Papers, 1/1120/13.

68. "Affaire d'Alger," May 1830 and "Note sur les cessions territoriales à demander en Afrique," May 1830, AAE, M&D, Algérie, 7.

69. "Note pour le conseil," 26 May 1830, AAE, M&D, Algérie, 6.

tions to the expedition's commander-in-chief have sometimes been cited as evidence of the Bourbon regime's lack of imperial ambitions, because they recommended the restoration of the Ottoman Sultan's formal authority over the Regency after France's probable military victory.[70] Yet these instructions included two significant caveats: first, the extension of France's "territorial concessions from the Cape Bujaroni [Bougaroni] to the border of the Tunis Regency" (about 120km of coastline, including the *Concessions* shores), and second, the French government's right to appoint local officials in the eastern and central provinces of the Regency.[71] The Bourbon Restoration had imperial ambitions in Algeria, although they consisted in a limited coastal settlement and informal rule, rather than full territorial conquest.

Conversely, liberal opponents of the Restoration did not resist the expedition only out of hostility towards colonial conquest.[72] Fear that a successful expedition would weaken their hand on the domestic political stage was another significant factor. In fact, several luminaries of the liberal party criticized Polignac's ministry for lacking colonial ambitions and falsely accused Polignac of having promised Britain the prompt evacuation of the Regency after the likely victory of French forces. A pamphlet by Alexandre de Laborde, a leading adversary of the expedition, expressed fear that a permanent "conquest" would not compensate France for the expenses of the expedition: "colonization," Laborde lamented, "is not permitted to us."[73] Similarly, it is dubious whether the attack against the expedition by Benjamin Constant, a major figure of the liberal party, should be interpreted as showing his hostility to imperial conquest.[74] In reality, Constant only condemned the venture because it was an "affair of honour", used by the royalist government to promote its electoral interests. Yet if "an undisputed, indisputable colonization should be the prize

70. Charles-Roux, *France et Afrique du Nord*, 702.

71. Polignac to Bourmont, 26 June 1830, AAE, M&D, Algérie, 6; see also "Projet de Traité avec la Porte Ottomane relativement à Alger," [July 1830], AAE, M&D, Algérie, 7.

72. See the early studies by Charles-André Julien, *L'opposition et la guerre d'Alger à la veille de la conquête* (Oran: Fouque, 1921), *La question d'Alger devant l'opinion, de 1827 à 1830* (Oran: Fouque, 1922), and *La question d'Alger devant les chambres sous la Restauration* (Alger: J. Carbonel, 1922), the conclusions of which informed his later standard account, *La conquête*.

73. Alexandre de Laborde, *Sur les véritables causes de la rupture avec Alger et sur l'expédition qui se prépare*, 2nd edn (Paris: Truchy, 1830), iii–iv. After 1830, Laborde, a former owner of plantations in Saint-Domingue, unsurprisingly proved a warm supporter of colonization in North Africa; see Marçot, *Comment est née l'Algérie française*, 361–2.

74. Pitts, *A Turn to Empire*, 184–5.

of victory," Constant asserted that he would then support such "a national affair."[75]

The hostility of liberals to colonization in the early nineteenth century has often been attributed to the influence of political economists. One old but influential study even claimed, in relation to the future of the Algiers Regency in 1830, that "following [Jean-Baptiste] Say, most economists proclaimed the uselessness of colonies."[76] In support of this assertion, the study gave the example of two pamphlets by little-known figures, who have more often been described as, respectively, a geographer and a naval officer than as economists.[77] As for Jean-Baptiste Say, it is true that he had many disciples among French economists, but as seen in the previous chapter, he endorsed settler colonies. In the second edition of his *Treatise on Political Economy* (1814), Say even recommended the foundation of "independent colonies" in the countries with a warm climate "closest to Europe"; and in a footnote added five years later, he suggested as a possible location, "the coasts of Barbary."[78] One illustrious liberal economist, Jean-Charles Simonde de Sismondi, intervened in the debate about the expedition of Algiers in *La Revue encyclopédique*, the leading liberal monthly of the Restoration. Far from condemning a possible colonization as useless, Sismondi supported it enthusiastically, even claiming that "Saint-Domingue . . . was not worth a tenth of what Algiers may be worth," because the latter combined "the most beautiful climates of Provence, Italy and Spain" with "the climates and the sky of the Antilles."[79] Political economists rejected mercantilist commercial restrictions and slavery, but they did not discourage imperial projects in North Africa.

75. "Alger et les élections," *Le Temps*, 20 June 1830, in Benjamin Constant, *Recueil d'articles, 1829–1830*, ed. Ephraïm Harpaz (Paris: Honoré Champion, 1989), 481–3.

76. Charles-André Julien, *L'avenir d'Alger et l'opposition des libéraux et des économistes en 1830* (Oran: Fouque, 1922), 22; see also Julien, *La conquête*, 45; Pitts, *A Turn to Empire*, 185, and Marçot, *Comment est née l'Algérie française*, 351–3.

77. Maurice Allart, *Considérations sur la difficulté de coloniser la Régence d'Alger* (Paris: Selligue, 1830) and Jean-Chrysostôme Lacuée-Saint-Just, *Économie politique. Des colonies: d'Alger, de sa possession, du système colonial* (Paris: Vve Béchet, 1830).

78. Jean-Baptiste Say, *Traité d'économie politique. Édition variorum des six éditions (1803–1814–1817–1819–1826–1841)*, eds. Emmanuel Blanc, Pierre-Henri Goutte, Gilles Jacoud et al., 2 vols. (Paris: Economica, 2006), vol. 2, 646–7.

79. Jean-Charles Simonde de Sismondi, *De l'expédition contre Alger* (Paris: Bureau de la Revue encyclopédique, 1830), 12–13; first published in *Revue encylopédique*, 46 (1830).

Once in power after 1830, liberals hesitated less about the future of the Algiers Regency than has been claimed.[80] Only in 1834 did a parliamentary commission formally decide against evacuation and in favour of colonization. Yet as in the case of the Restoration's proclamations on the goals of the expedition, we must look at official statements in the light of geopolitical tensions. European fears about French expansionism worsened with the 1830 Revolution and France's military intervention in favour of Belgian insurgents in 1831–1832.[81] Only after Talleyrand, serving as ambassador in London between 1830 and 1834, succeeded in defusing Anglo-French tensions did it become possible to avow projects of domination in the former Regency.[82] On the domestic stage, liberals were not quite so coy. Almost immediately after the July Revolution, the liberal press appropriated the capture of Algiers as a victory for the cause of liberty and civilization, and began to clamour for colonization.[83] Instructions from the July Monarchy's first governments to commanders of French forces in North Africa were unequivocal. In November 1830, the progressive ministry headed by Jacques Lafitte stated: "the French government intends to maintain its possession of Algiers," where French manufactured goods could be usefully exchanged with "other products alien to our soil and our climate."[84] In June 1831, the more conservative government headed by Casimir Perier confirmed: "The occupation of this country is determined. Colonization will be continued and encouraged."[85]

The conclusions of the 1834 parliamentary commission were, in this respect, foregone. "We are all or nearly all agreed on the need to keep Algiers," a member commented during the proceedings, and the commission's recommendation that France "should retain its possessions on the northern coast of

80. Julien, *La conquête*, ch. 2: "La période d'incertitude," 64–105; seel also Hélène Blais, "Qu'est-ce qu'Alger ? Le débat colonial sous la Monarchie de Juillet," *Romantisme*, 139 (2008), and Bouchène et al., *Histoire de l'Algérie*, 52–7.

81. Schroeder, *The Transformation of European Politics*, 666–711.

82. Talleyrand in London also worked to obtain British acquiescence to French supremacy in Algiers; see Charles-Maurice de Talleyrand-Périgord, *Mémoires et correspondance du Prince de Talleyrand*, ed. Emmanuel de Waresquiel (Paris: Laffont 2007), 1138–41, 1147–9.

83. Sessions, *By Sword and Plow*, 61–6.

84. Maréchal Gérard to Maréchal Sebastiani, minister of foreign affairs, 12 Nov. 1830, quoted in Charles-Roux, *France et Afrique du Nord*, 724.

85. Maréchal Soult to General Berthezène, commander-in-chief of French forces in North Africa, 5 June 1831, quoted in Charles-Robert Ageron, *Le gouvernement du general Berthezène à Alger en 1831* (Saint-Denis: Bouchène, 2005), 50, 175–6.

Africa" was practically unanimous (seventeen votes for, two against). Of perhaps greater significance was its other recommendation, also passed almost unanimously, that France should eschew full territorial conquest. Instead, it proposed that France should evacuate the small ports of Arzew and Mostaganem and only retain direct control of the four largest port-cities (Algiers, Oran, Bugia and Bona), while agricultural settlements should be confined to the immediate vicinity of Algiers and Bona. In yet another echo of the project entertained since 1824, the commission described the latter eastern location as the most promising for colonization due to its "fertile soil."[86]

The fierceness of domestic struggles should therefore not conceal a broad agreement among the political elite concerning the desirability of French domination in North Africa and a remarkable continuity regarding the best way to proceed. From the mid-1820s until the 1830s, the Restoration and July Monarchy only envisaged limited colonial settlements, more modest in scale than contemporary British or American settlerism in the Pacific and North America. The natural complement of this scheme was informal domination over the vast Algerian hinterland through willing indigenous collaborators.

Collaboration with ʿAbd al-Qadir

The most compelling evidence that, beyond its colonial settlements, France favoured informal rule in Algeria was its pursuit of collaboration with ʿAbd al-Qadir in the 1830s. Historians—especially defenders of the French colonial regime—have often dismissed this policy as proof of French indecision or a serious error, because it aided the emergence of a formidable rival for supremacy in the former Regency. Yet it is only with the benefit of hindsight that we can see how this cooperation with ʿAbd al-Qadir would break down. Collaboration was a deliberate policy, inspired by awareness of the enormous costs of a potential formal conquest, rather than the fruit of indecision. Whether it was an error in the sense that it was doomed to failure should be open to discussion. It is possible to argue that the French thirst for military glory, the dehumanizing of indigenous Algerians by European settlers, or even ʿAbd al-Qadir's hopes of expelling the French invaders rendered confrontation ultimately inevitable. Yet at least two contingent factors played a significant part in the unravelling of a collaboration: a dispute over the future of the Constantine

---

86. *Procès-verbaux et rapports de la commission d'Afrique instituée par ordonnance du Roi du 12 décembre 1833* (Paris: Imprimerie royale, 1834), 152, 405, 428–30.

province, where the French tried and failed to establish domination by informal means; and the major diplomatic crisis of 1840, which altered French perceptions of the relative costs of informal and formal rule in North Africa.

After the capture of Algiers and other coastal towns in 1830, French officials
sought to obtain recognition of their supremacy in the Algerian interior by
appointing indigenous beys who, in return for a modest tribute, would enjoy
extensive autonomy. However, in the east, Ottoman officials like Ahmad, bey
of Constantine, rebuffed French offers of protection, while in central and western Algeria, the collapse of the Ottoman system of government prevented
French-appointed officials from exercising much control. It was out of this
chaotic situation that 'Abd al-Qadir, the son of a prestigious marabout,
emerged as the most effective power in western Algeria. His success owed
much to his skilful invocation of Islam to legitimize his state-building efforts,
including the raising of new taxes and formal conscription. But it was also
aided by the French garrison in Oran, which from 1832 provided him with light
weapons and military instructors.[87] This early collaboration culminated in
the Desmichels Convention, or Treaty of 26 February 1834: 'Abd al-Qadir acknowledged French power in coastal towns, while the French recognized him
as emir and de facto ruler of the rest of the Oran province.[88]

This entente soon broke down as 'Abd al-Qadir expanded his dominion
into central Algeria. The French eventually gained the upper hand in military
operations, but the war, which began with a serious French defeat at La Macta
on 28 June 1835, also demonstrated the extent of the emir's state-building
achievements, and enhanced his worth as a potential collaborator in the eyes
of many French observers. This is why, instead of curtailing 'Abd al-Qadir's
authority, the Tafna treaty, concluded on 30 May 1837, extended the area under
his effective government to include most of central Algeria, as well as the western Oran Province. This treaty can be interpreted as the most serious French
effort to dominate the bulk of Algeria by informal means. The French version
of the treaty invoked the concept of sovereignty. Yet article 1 merely stipulated
that 'Abd al-Qadir "recognizes the sovereignty of France in Africa" in a way that
did not imply acceptance of French sovereignty over the entire Regency. The

---

87. Marcel Emerit, *L'Algérie à l'époque d'Abd el-Kader* (Paris: Bouchène, 2002; first edn in
1951), 23–36; Danziger, *Abd al-Qadir and the Algerians: Resistance to the French and Internal Consolidation* (New York: Holmes and Meier, 1977), 88–113.

88. "Treaty of Peace and Friendship: The French Military Governor of Oran and 'Abd al-
Qadir," in Hurewitz, *The Middle East and North Africa*, vol. 1, 257–8.

Arabic version of the same article was even more vague, stating that the emir "knows (*ya'rifu*) the dominion of the authority (*hukm sultanat*) of France in Africa."[89]

In reality, the Tafna treaty was a treaty of mutual recognition, which guaranteed the rights of Muslims in French enclaves, as well as the rights of the French in the emir's territory (articles 5 and 11), and provided—for free—the circulation of individuals and commodities and the handing over of convicted criminals between the two parties (articles 10 and 12). It also established consular-style agents for the representation of each party in the other's territory (article 15). The treaty only subordinated the emir's power to French authority in loose and limited ways: it forced him to purchase weaponry and ammunition "in France" (article 7, but 'Abd al-Qadir soon interpreted this as a French promise to provide him with military equipment); it barred him from ceding coastal territory to a foreign power without French consent (article 13, which implicitly conceded such a right for the majority of the emir's territories); and it reserved maritime trade to French-held ports (article 14, but no provision was made to curtail smuggling).[90] General Bugeaud, the main French negotiator of the treaty, believed that France's territorial settlements should remain small and merely serve as an example that "will entice the Arabs, give them our tastes and encourage them to become attached to the soil." The treaty would enable France to achieve the "conquest" of Algeria, but "thanks to commerce, civilization, the softness of our habits (*moeurs*) and laws."[91]

In France, Tafna met with widespread approval. It seemed to fulfil the vision of "limited occupation" (*occupation restreinte*) that earned François Guizot, the leading liberal thinker and statesman, a "universal and marked movement of approval" the previous year in the Chamber of Deputies. In this speech, Guizot eschewed a "restless, bellicose" policy intent on "suddenly expanding, by trickery or by force, French domination, official French domination on all the parts, all the tribes of the former Regency's territory." France

89. For a comparison of the French and Arabic versions of the treaty see Danziger, *Abd al-Qadir*, 248–55.

90. On the treaty's commercial provisions, see Richard A. Roughton, "Economic Motives and French Imperialism: The 1837 Tafna Treaty as a Case Study," *Historian*, 47, 3 (1985).

91. Bugeaud to minister of war, 24 Apr. 1837, in *Documents relatifs au traité de la Tafna: 1837*, ed. Georges Yver (Algiers: J. Carbonnel, 1924), 19; see also Bugeaud to Comte Molé, Prime Minister, 29 May 1837, in Yver, *Documents*, 94–100.

should not abandon its coastal enclaves, he continued, but in the rest of the Regency it should strive "to keep good relations with indigenous inhabitants" and not encroach upon their "independence" and "sovereignty."[92] It was the same vision which inspired Loubon's idyllic prophecy, published in 1837 and discussed at the beginning of this chapter, and it was the Tafna treaty that led Alexis de Tocqueville to write his first—highly optimistic—articles on the future of Franco-Algerian relations.[93] Even Amédée Desjobert, these days remembered as a fierce critic of France's conquest after 1840, endorsed the Tafna agreement, because in 1837 he remained opposed to "the abandonment of our possession," lest it reduced "the influence that [France] may have on the civilization of the north of Africa." Desjobert was especially enthusiastic about the possibilities of collaboration with 'Abd al-Qadir, "the progressive man, the revolutionary man," whose ascendancy would guarantee French material and political interests at a minimal cost.[94]

The hope that France had found in 'Abd al-Qadir a reliable partner was extremely common. The emir was routinely described—in the instructions to the new French consul at his capital of Mascara, in administrative reports and political pamphlets, and even in the memoirs of the emir's French private secretary—as a "second" or "Algerian" Muhammad 'Ali.[95] The time spent by 'Abd al-Qadir in Egypt, travelling back and forth on a pilgrimage to Mecca between 1826 and 1828, was frequently invoked to suggest that the emir self-consciously sought to emulate the achievements of the Egyptian pasha. Such enthusiasm was no doubt in part the product of self-delusion. 'Adb al-Qadir is probably better understood as a pious Muslim pragmatist, intent on consolidating

92. Speech given on 10 June 1836, repr. in Guizot, *Histoire parlementaire*, vol. 2, 473–82.

93. "First Letter on Algeria (23 June 1837)" and "Second Letter on Algeria (22 August 1837)" in Tocqueville, *Writings on Empire*, 5–26.

94. Amédée Desjobert, *La question d'Alger: politique, colonisation, commerce* (Paris: Dufart, 1837), 306–7, 319; on Desjobert as an adversary of empire (after 1840), see Pitts, *A Turn to Empire*, 185–9.

95. *Correspondance du Capitaine Daumas, Consul à Mascara (1837–1839)*, ed. Georges Yver, (Algiers: Adolphe Jourdan, 1912), 561; no name of author, "Observations sur la traité du 30 mai avec Abd el-Kader et les avantages immenses qui pourraient résulter pour la France et l'Afrique, la civilisation et l'humanité," 3 Nov. 1837, ANOM, F80 1672; Desjobert, *La question d'Alger*, 324; Léon Roches [a Frenchman in the service of 'Abd al-Qadir in the 1830s, who later became a French diplomatic agent in the Far East], *Trente-deux ans à travers l'Islam*, 2 vols. (Paris: Firmin-Didot, 1884–1885), vol. 1, 64. On the popularity of Muhammad 'Ali in France, see Pierre Caquet, *The Orient, the Liberal Movement, and the Eastern Crisis of 1839–1841* (Basingstoke: Palgrave-MacMillan, 2016), 51–91.

his fragile grip over Algerian warring tribes, than as a Francophile modernizer or an empire builder in the mould of 'Ali.[96] But there is plenty of evidence to suggest that the French and 'Abd al-Qadir sincerely attempted to implement the Tafna agreement. French officials were delighted by the surge of commercial exchanges that followed the treaty, with a near 80 percent increase in exports from French-held ports between 1836 and 1838.[97] The French consul in Mascara was confident that peace would last, because 'Abd al-Qadir "senses that he can only grow under the shadow of France."[98] And French authorities went to great lengths to maintain good relations with the emir: they punctiliously delivered the weaponry promised at Tafna and let French deserters join his army; they returned slaves who had escaped from 'Abd al-Qadir's territory and tolerated the settlement of disputes between Muslims by his *caïds* within their own enclaves.[99]

Yet after only two and a half years, in November 1839, the war with 'Abd al-Qadir resumed. Why did the Tafna moment prove so short-lived? Colonialist historians used to blame the emir's treachery and secret ambition to eradicate French settlements.[100] More significant was France's failure to impose informal domination on Ahmad, bey of Constantine, in the east of the Regency. A first military expedition led by General Bertrand Clauzel, a survivor of the 1802 Saint-Domingue expedition and a notorious advocate of a more territorial conception of French domination in Algeria, ended in disaster in November 1836. Clauzel was dismissed and disgraced, but a desire to avenge his humiliation led to a second expedition that stormed Constantine in October 1837. The avowed goal of the expedition was not territorial domination. Prior to it, the French government envisaged the conclusion of an agreement with Ahmad that would be similar to the Tafna treaty.[101] However, even after the French capture of Constantine, Ahmad turned down French offers of peace, opting instead for continued resistance from further south in the prov-

96. Danziger, *Abd al-Qadir*.

97. The Intendant civil in Algiers to the minister of war, 29 July and 28 Oct.1837, ANOM, F80 1672; the figure is my calculation, based on Ministère de la Guerre, *Tableau de la situation des établissements français dans l'Algérie*, 20 vols. (Paris: 1838–1868), vols. i and ii (1837 and 1838).

98. Yver, *Correspondance du Capitaine Daumas*, 82.

99. Yver, *Correspondance du Capitaine Daumas*, 95–6, 100–1, 280–1; Yver, *Documents*, 487–8.

100. Schefer, *L'Algérie*, 317–19; on the controversy surrounding Tafna, see René Gallissot, "Présentation," in Emerit, *L'Algérie à l'époque d'Abd el-Kader*, 7–18.

101. The minister of war to Bugeaud, 25 June 1837, in Yver, *Documents*, 148–51.

ince. Efforts to persuade a Tunisian prince to replace Ahmad as bey also failed. With some reluctance, the Constantine province was placed under direct French rule.[102] This account, based on the official correspondence of French military leaders, probably underestimates their personal aspirations to territorial rule. But the fact that they felt the need to conceal them is suggestive of a strong official preference for informal domination.

The occupation of the northern Constantine province may be considered a mere amplification of the original French preference for colonial settlements in the east. However, it seriously undermined the Tafna agreement. In and of itself, it expanded the logic of violent coercion—even in the 1830s, French military occupation implied an increase in acts of depredations and often gratuitous cruelty at the expense of indigenous Algerians. The French claim to territorial domination and the collapse of Ahmad's rule also instigated a rivalry with 'Abd al-Qadir, who began to assert his own authority over indigenous tribes in the east. An official French map published in 1838, one of the first to designate the former Regency as "Algérie", portrays the difficult co-existence of these informal and territorial projects perfectly.[103] Using green-shaded borders, the map acknowledged the quasi sovereignty of 'Abd al-Qadir's emirate over nearly two thirds of the Algerian territory. But in pink-shaded borders it confirmed French rule over the Oran and Algiers enclaves, and registered the recent territorial claim to the eastern Constantine province—although effective French authority was almost inexistent in moutaineous Greater Kabylia and south of Constantine itself.[104]

Partitions are precarious equilibria. A series of territorial disputes, culminating in the pompously celebrated crossing of the Iron Gates pass in the Bibans mountains by French forces in October 1839, led 'Abd al-Qadir to resume hostilities the following month, with a surprise attack that devastated French settlements across the Mitidja plain near Algiers. The French should

102. On the proposed convention with Ahmad, modelled on the Tafna treaty, see Maréchal Valée, governor general, to Comte Molé, Prime Minister, 25 Oct. 1837, in *Correspondance du Maréchal Valée, gouverneur des possessions françaises dans le Nord de l'Afrique*, 4 vols., ed. Georges Yver (Paris: Larose, 1949–1957), vol. 1, 26–7; on the attempt to replace Ahmad by a relative of the bey of Tunis, see Molé to Valée, 27 Oct. 1837 and Valée to Molé, 8 Nov. 1837, in ibid., 44–6, 61–7.

103. On the emergence of the word *Algérie* in 1838–1839, see Blais, *Le mirage de la carte*, 72.

104. Auguste-Henri Dufour, *Algérie: dédié au Roi* (Paris: C. Simmoneau, 1838); image available on Bibliothèque Nationale de France, Gallica, https://gallica.bnf.fr/ark:/12148/btv1b530880833, accessed 10 February 2020.

almost certainly be held responsible for the new outbreak of war, because their efforts to assert their sovereignty in the east undermined the logic of Tafna and sapped the legitimacy of 'Abd al-Qadir in his own dominions. But their surprise at 'Abd al-Qadir's offensive suggests that they still hoped to maintain a system of informal dominance in central and western Algeria. They brought down their informal empire themselves, but somewhat unwittingly. The French were also surprised by their inability to repel 'Abd al-Qadir's attacks effectively. By the spring of 1840, their enclaves of Oran and Algiers were all but blockaded and were dependent on maritime supplies for their survival.

At this point the eruption of the Eastern crisis—Europe's most serious war scare since 1815, caused by the efforts of Muhammad 'Ali, France's Egyptian protégé, to expand his dominions at the expense of his Ottoman overlord—raised the stakes of French difficulties in Algeria.[105] In the event of war, British naval supremacy almost certainly implied cutting off French forces and settlers' maritime supplies. After Tafna, the value of French settlements' net imports of grain fell from 3.5 million francs in 1837 to 0.7 million in 1838, but following the renewal of war with 'Abd al-Qadir they leapt to 13.7 million in 1840.[106] War would have resulted in famine and an ignominious surrender to either 'Abd al-Qadir's forces or the British navy. The parliamentary commission that sanctioned the objective of formal conquest in 1842–1843 repeatedly conjured up memories of these dire straits to justify the extension of French rule. In the words of Gustave de Beaumont, a member of the commission, "the army and the population" needed to become "independent, thanks to cultivation, from the assistance of [metropolitan] France." Alexis de Tocqueville, another member of the commission, "fully support[ed]" the argument made by his close friend.[107]

The Eastern crisis also compounded the case for formal conquest because it resulted in a major humiliation for France. Forced to back down against a reconstituted coalition of the powers that had vanquished Napoleon, and compelled to let Anglo-Ottoman forces coerce Muhammad 'Ali into submis-

105. Schroeder, *The Transformation of European Politics*, 726–56; on the crisis's impact on French opinion, see Pierre Caquet, "The Napoleonic Legend and the War Scare of 1840," *International History Review*, 35, 4 (2013).

106. My calculations, based on *Tableau de la situation des établissements*, vols. ii, iii and iv (1838, 1839 and 1840).

107. Minutes of the "Commission de la colonisation de l'Algérie," 30 Jan. 1842, ANOM, F80 1128.

sion, the July Monarchy could ill afford a compromise in Algeria.[108] This consideration helps to explain the extraordinary transformation of Guizot and Bugeaud, two advocates of territorial restraint, into the chief artisans of a brutal war of conquest as, respectively, head of the French government and governor general in Algeria after 1840. Correspondence between the two men reveals the fact that they saw conquest as a necessary means to divert the bellicose instincts of the French and keep peace in Europe. Considering the conquest on its own terms, Bugeaud described it as a "senseless" enterprise.[109] Guizot also tended to view Algeria as a burden, referring to it as a justification for his otherwise great reluctance to condone projects of territorial expansion: "We already had enough on our hands with Algeria to conquer and colonize."[110]

The territorial turn of 1840 was strictly limited to Algerian circumstances and did not mark a broader adhesion to formal imperialism. In the eyes of the French political elite, the collapse of collaboration with ʿAbd al-Qadir left France with two alternatives: the abandonment of its imperial designs, or the complete occupation of the former Regency. Very few followed Desjobert in clamouring for the evacuation of French possessions.[111] The trajectory of Tocqueville, whose advocacy of colonialism has intrigued intellectual historians, was far more typical.[112] In 1837, he supported the Tafna agreement because he still believed that empire could be achieved by informal means: "by the mere fact of the superiority of its knowledge, a powerful and civilized people such as ours exercises an almost invincible influence on small and barbarous peoples."[113] His disturbing endorsement of violent conquest, in an essay written in 1841, may have reflected, in part, an intellectual disillusion with the capacity of extra-European peoples, especially of Muslim faith, for moral and material progress. Yet the immediate and, in his own words, "foremost" cause of his new conviction that France should employ even inhuman means to

---

108. Bertrand Goujon, *Monarchies postrévolutionnaires, 1814–1848* (Paris: Le Seuil, 2012), 331–42; Caquet, *The Orient*, 203–42; Sessions, *By Sword and Plow*, 67–124.

109. Bugeaud to Guizot, 27 Nov. 1841, repr. in Guizot, *Mémoires*, vol. 6, 396; see also Anthony T. Sullivan, *Thomas-Robert Bugeaud, France and Algeria, 1784–1849: Politics, Power, and the Good Society* (Hamden, CT: Archon books, 1983), 65–7.

110. Guizot, *Mémoires*, vol. 6, 274.

111. Desjobert's unusual stance may have been due to his hostility to empire, discussed in Pitts, *A Turn to Empire*, 185–9, but it probably also reflected the interests of his constituents in Le Havre, where Algeria was seen as favouring the interests of the rival port city of Marseille.

112. Pitts, *A Turn to Empire*, 189–239.

113. Tocqueville, "Second Letter on Algeria": 22.

conquer Algeria lay in France's recent international humiliation: France could not abandon Algeria "at a time such as our own, when she appears to be falling to the second rank and seems resigned to let the control of European affairs pass into other hands."[114]

Focusing on France's desire for informal domination and the way this unravelled can help us to understand the extraordinary escalation of French violence after 1840. The term "war," a study of violence in colonial Algeria concluded, should be reserved for the final conflict with 'Abd al-Qadir, which ended with his capture in December 1847.[115] The numbers of French soldiers stationed in North Africa between 1839 and 1846 doubled to more than one hundred thousand. It was during this time that the French army deployed a strategy of systematic devastation, and that the French administration devised new legal instruments to displace indigenous tribes and confiscate large tracts of land.[116] This escalation, or abrupt substitution by a very formal kind of empire, also confirms that informal domination should be considered an imperial project. However, the enormous costs of territorial rule would lead the Second Napoleonic Empire to explore once again the informal dimension of the French imperial repertoire.

Economic Failure

The French authorities considered the conquest of the Regency completed shortly after the surrender of 'Abd al-Qadir and after the Second Republic formally annexed Algeria in 1848, although Greater Kabylia—a region that straddled the Algiers and Constantine provinces—remained de facto independent until 1858. This military and political success, however, was not translated into a colonial or commercial success. Most French contemporaries lamented the immense costs of the Algerian enterprise to France, and (more rarely) those to Algeria's indigenous inhabitants. In the main, as suggested by

114. Tocqueville, "Essay on Algeria,": 59; on Tocqueville's dismay at France's climbdown during the 1840 crisis, see Mary Lawlor, *Alexis de Tocqueville in the Chamber of Deputies: His Views on Foreign and Colonial Policy* (Washington, DC: Catholic University of America Press, 1959), 43–66, and on the astonishment of John Stuart Mill at Tocqueville's bellicose views, see Georgios Varouxakis, *Victorian Political Thought on France and the French* (Basingstoke: Palgrave Macmillan, 2002), 142–7.

115. Gallois, *A History of Violence*, 158–71.

116. John Ruedy, *Land Policy in Colonial Algeria: The Origins of the Rural Public Domain* (Berkeley: University of California Press, 1967), 87–97.

TABLE 2.1. Algeria's fiscal deficit, 1850–1899

	Average annual net transfer (in millions of francs)	Colonial revenue as a share of expenditure (in %)
1850–1859	66	20
1860–1869	68	26
1870–1879	70	33
1880–1889	84	33
1890–1899	85	39

Source: Bobrie, "Finances publiques et conquête coloniale": 1228.

the data of official publications that sought to trumpet French success, these complaints were justified.

Even after the end of major military operations, Algeria remained a fiscal abyss. From about 80 million francs in the 1840s, net annual transfers to Algeria—French public expenditure in Algeria minus revenue levied in the colony—barely declined (see table 2.1). These transfers represented approximately 0.5 percent of France's national income, a figure comparable with France's development aid in the early twenty-first century, which stood at about 0.4 percent of GDP between 2012 and 2017.[117] The main beneficiaries were French companies, especially in the mining and railway sectors through subsidies and loan guarantees, and European settlers, who as an encouragement to colonization remained exempt from direct taxation until 1919. The proportion of expenditure covered by colonial revenue slowly improved, but as shown by table 2.1 it remained below 40 percent until the end of the century. This fiscal imbalance was in sharp contrast with the near fiscal self-sufficiency achieved by most British colonies in the mid-nineteenth century, or the much lower level of metropolitan subsidies to French colonies acquired after 1880.[118]

117. On net transfers to Algeria see François Bobrie, "Finances publiques et conquête coloniale: le coût budgétaire de l'expansion française entre 1850 et 1913," *Annales. Économies, sociétés, civilisations*, 31, 6 (1976); on development aid between 2012 and 2017, see OECD data on Official Development Aid, https://data.oecd.org/oda/net-oda.htm (accessed 28 December 2019).

118. Lance E. Davis and Robert A. Huttenback, *Mammon and the Pursuit of Empire: The Political Economy of British Imperialism, 1860–1912* (Cambridge: Cambridge University Press, 1986), 169. British colonies received disguised subsidies under the form of explicit or implicit guarantees on colonial loans, but the authorization given to the colonial government of Algeria to raise guaranteed loans after 1900 did not reduce the level of metropolitan transfers; see Jacques Bouveresse, *Un parlement colonial? Les délégations financières algériennes (1898–1945)* (Mont Saint-Aignan: Publications des universités de Rouen et du Havre, 2008). On the high costs of colonial

TABLE 2.2. Diachronic annual growth rate of the European settler population in Algeria (1831–1901) and Australia (1791–1861)

Algeria (Australia)	Algeria	Australia
1831–1841 (1791–1801)	27.2	7.5
1841–1851 (1801–1811)	13.9	7.2
1851–1861 (1811–1821)	3.9	11.6
1861–1872 (1821–1832)	2.2	8.1
1872–1881 (1832–1841)	4.9	11.4
1881–1891 (1841–1851)	2.5	7.1
1891–1901 (1851–1861)	1.9	10.3

Sources: Ministère de la guerre, Tableau des établissements, vol. 1 to vol. 10; Gouvernement général civil de l'Algérie, Annuaire statistique de l'Algérie. Année 1932 (Alger: E. Pfister, 1933), 32–33; Australian Bureau of Statistics, "Australian Historical Population Statistics," released 18 Sep. 2014, at http://www.abs.gov.au/population, accessed 1 Feb. 2017.

Despite France's extraordinary fiscal effort, the growth of the European settler population continued to be seen by contemporaries as mediocre. In an attempt to counter these perceptions, Jennifer Sessions has contended that, in reality "Algeria's settler population grew at rates quite comparable with those of other 'neo-Europes' in the early nineteenth century": for instance, after sixty years of colonization, Algeria in 1891 had approximately four hundred and eighty thousand European settlers, while Australia, where settlement began in 1788, had only four hundred thousand European settlers in 1850.[119] Such a diachronic comparison is ingenious, but fraught with methodological challenges: demographic change in settler colonies owed a lot to migration, and can a crossing from Marseille to Algiers by steamboat be compared with a voyage by sailboat from London to Sydney (in conditions of global maritime warfare until 1815)? Above all, the choice of a single year (1850 for Australia and 1891 for Algeria) conceals extremely different patterns of demographic growth, as shown by a systematic diachronic comparison (see table 2.2).

---

rule in Algeria, see François Crouzet and Jean-Pierre Dormois, "The Significance of the French Colonial Empire for French Economic Development (1815–1960)," Revista de historia económica, 16, 1 (1998) and on the low level of metropolitan subsidies to sub-Saharan African colonies, see Elise Huillery, "The Black Man's Burden: The Cost of Colonization of French West Africa," Journal of Economic History, 74, 1 (2014).

119. Sessions, By Sword and Plow, 290; James Belich gives a more measured comparative assessment of European settlement in Algeria as "spasmodic, but substantial" in Replenishing the Earth, 502–4.

If Algeria in the 1890s had a European population that was slightly superior to Australia's in the 1850s, it was due to an explosive rate of growth in the first two decades of French presence, aided by massive military intervention and various state-funded schemes to encourage colonial immigration. In the subsequent five decades, Australia's European population grew between two and a half and five times faster than Algeria's. This trend proved well entrenched, and after ninety years of colonization, Algeria's settler population in 1921 (721,000) was only a third of Australia's in 1891 (2,307,000). Settlement also progressed much faster in New Zealand, where the European population represented a mere fifth of Algeria's in 1851 (27,000 vs 131,000) and surpassed it by 32 percent in 1901 (773,000 vs 583,000).[120] Algerian demographic growth is all the more unimpressive in that, unlike in Australia and New Zealand, around half of the immigrants hailed not from the mother country, but from other European states, or even British colonies (Malta).[121]

Another stark difference with Anglo settler colonies, and a significant source of disappointment, was the small share of European immigrants who engaged in agricultural activities. According to the 1856 census, only 40 percent of the European civilian population either lived in rural areas or was engaged in agricultural activities.[122] Constantine, the focus of initial French agricultural colonization schemes and the largest province, not only had the smallest European population but also the lowest proportion of Europeans engaged in agriculture.[123] The share of Algeria's land owned by Europeans increased, especially after a law removed restrictions on the acquisition of indigenous land property in 1873, but property became concentrated in the hands of a small number of often absentee landowners and a growing proportion was farmed out to indigenous Algerians.[124] This failure is connected with the disappointment of another repellent but frequently voiced French hope that, as in Australia or the United States, European settlers would gradually replace the indigenous population throughout Algerian territory. By killing hundreds of

120. My calculations, based on *Tableau des établissements, Annuaire statistique de l'Algérie*, and Brian R. Mitchell, *International Historical Statistics. Africa, Asia and Oceania 1750–2005* (Basingstoke: Palgrave Macmillan, 2007), 14.

121. For a discussion of the political, social and environmental causes of the limited results of French settlement projects, see Claude Lützelschwab, *La Compagnie genevoise des colonies suisses de Sétif* (Bern: Peter Lang, 2006), 147–205.

122. *Tableau de la situation des établissements*, vol. 14 (1856–1857), 176–77.

123. *Tableau de la situation des établissements*, vol. 20 (1866), 5, 182.

124. Ageron, *Les Algériens musulmans*, vol. 1, 67–128 and vol. 2, 739–75.

France's first intentions to colonize were tied in with Algeria's commercial potential, especially as a provider of tropical primary materials. In this respect, results were particularly disappointing. Thanks to a high tariff on foreign imports introduced in 1843 and the scale of military operations during the conquest, Algeria became a significant outlet for French producers, especially of alcoholic beverages (22 percent of French exports to Algeria in 1849) in the 1840s.[127] Yet "official values," the sole available measure until 1847 (although it did not take into consideration price changes after 1826), probably overestimated Algeria's share of French exports. In any case, more reliable "real values," based on estimated current prices, show that Algeria's share rapidly declined after that, from 8 percent at the end of the war of conquest to 4 percent in the 1860s and 1870s (see figure 2.1).

Furthermore, economic historians now tend to view imports from the colonies as a better indicator of the colonial contribution to metropolitan development. After all, imports, especially of primary products unavailable in Europe, saved "ghost acres" of land that permitted the growth of more productive branches of activity.[128] Thanks to the removal of import duties on some Algerian agricultural products in 1851, the share of Algeria in French imports rose from 0.5 percent in 1850 to 3 percent in 1855, but fell back to 2–2.5 percent in

125. My calculations, indigenous Jews (naturalized in 1871) and their descendents excluded, based on Gouvernement général, *Annuaire statistique*, 32–3; on the demographic impact of the famine, see Djilali Sari, *Le désastre démographique* (Algiers: Société Nationale d'Édition et de Diffusion, 1982) and on the problems posed by the reliability of censuses for the indigenous population, see Kamel Kateb, *Européens, "indigènes" et juifs en Algérie (1830–1962)* (Paris: Institut National d'Etudes Démographiques, 2001), 97–117.

126. Anthony J. Christopher, "A South African Domesday Book: The First Union Census of 1911," *South African Geographical Journal*, 92, 1 (2010).

127. *Tableau de la situation des établissements*, vol. 8 (1844–1845), 315–16, and vol. 11 (1850–1851), 542; figure based on "real values," i.e., at estimated current prices.

128. See for instance Kenneth Pommeranz, *The Great Divergence: China, Europe and the Making of the World Economy* (Princeton, NJ: Princeton University Press, 2000).

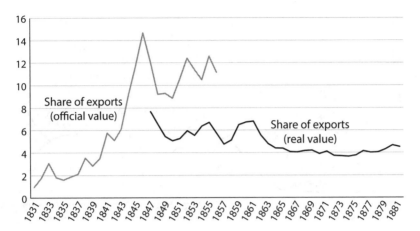

FIGURE 2.1. Share of exports to Algeria in France's total exports, in %, 1831–1881. *Source:* My calculations, excluding re-exports and based on Direction générale des Douanes, *Tableau décennal du commerce de la France avec ses colonies et les puissances étrangères, 1827–1896,* 13 vols. (Paris: 1838–1898). "Official values" were based on 1826 prices, while "real values," available only from 1847, were annual estimates.

the 1860s. The Ottoman Empire and even British India remained more important sources of French imports until the 1880s (see figure 2.2).

The type of products imported from Algeria proved to be an even greater disappointment for the French. Still in 1848, the minister of commerce, chairing the first of several commissions that prepared the law of 1851 on Algerian commercial legislation, asserted: "Algeria must, as much as possible, cultivate its own products." The commission's co-chair, Alexis de Tocqueville, then minister of foreign affairs, agreed, concluding that some form of trade barrier with Algeria remained necessary: "Customs assimilation, just as other types of assimilation, is unworkable." The director general of customs, another member of the commission, remained hopeful that Algeria would "one day" provide France with "the sixty million [of francs] of silk" and "the one hundred million of cotton which, every year, France needs to buy abroad."[129] Yet in the early 1860s (1862–1866), Algeria's staple exports were "animal remains" (31 percent, in "real value"), essentially raw wool and skins; "farinaceous products" (19 percent), mostly grain; and olive oil (5 percent). Despite generous subsidies and the surge in world prices due to the American Civil War, the share of raw cotton over the same five years remained insignificant, peaking at

129. Minutes of the "Commission mixte pour la révision du régime commercial de l'Algérie," 31 Oct. 1848, ANOM, 30 COL 47.

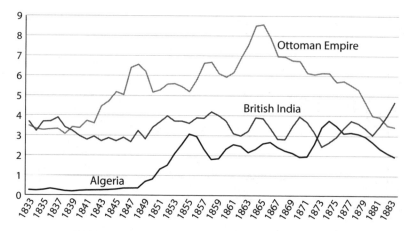

FIGURE 2.2. Share of imports from Algeria, the Ottoman Empire and British India in France's total imports, in %, 1833–1883. *Source:* My calculations, excluding merchandise to be re-exported and based on "official values" for imports between 1833 and 1848 and "real values" for imports between 1849 and 1883, with a three-year moving average, in Direction des Douanes, *Tableau décennal.*

1.5 percent of Algeria's exports in 1865.[130] One indigenous product, halfa grass, a plant used for the fabrication of high-quality paper, experienced an export boom from the late 1860s, but over 80 percent of Algeria's halfa exports between 1867 and 1884 were destined to Britain, aiding British rather than French industrialization.[131] Only in the 1890s would intensive cultivation of the vine enable colonial Algeria to find a profitable specialization in the world market, but this contradicted France's initial ambitions of encouraging the production of commodities that were unavailable in metropolitan France.

The Arab Kingdom, a Failed Revival of Informal Empire

The perception of formal rule in Algeria as an economic burden was widely shared under the Second Empire of Napoleon III, at least unofficially. When the British economist William Nassau Senior, in a private conversation in 1863, suggested that France might "make an Algeria" of French-invaded Mexico, the minister of foreign affairs, Édouard Drouyn de Lhuys, retorted that the gov-

130. *Tableau de la situation des établissements*, vols. 17–20 (1862, 1863, 1864 and 1865–1866); figures for "commerce général," which include re-exports, but these were negligible.

131. Gouvernement général civil de l'Algérie, *Statistique générale de l'Algérie. Années 1882 à 1884* (Alger: Association ouvrière, 1885), 222

ernment was "not mad enough to wish for a dependency" that would cost them another "two or three millions sterling a year"—or 50 to 75 million francs, approximately the amount of contemporary fiscal transfers to Algeria (see table 2.1).[132] Such unease with the enormous costs of France's colonial venture in North Africa played a significant role in the most thoroughgoing attempt at reforming the colony, often described as the "Arab Kingdom" policy of the 1860s. The phrase was popularized in a public letter by Napoleon III to the governor general in 1863. It served to denote not a renunciation of French domination, but a shift away from formal rule: "Algeria," Napoleon III wrote, "is not a colony properly speaking, but an Arab kingdom . . . I am the Emperor of the Arabs as well as the Emperor of the French."[133]

In practice, given the presence of an already sizeable European population (about two hundred thousand), the Arab Kingdom policy could not aim to establish an independent Algerian state under French tutelage. Instead, it sought to contain European immigration, confine Europeans to industrial activities, and promote the political and economic rights of indigenous Algerians so that they could contribute to the country's agricultural development. The main inspiration behind this policy was economic rather than humanitarian. It accompanied the free-trade revolution that had begun with the Anglo-French commercial treaty in 1860 and was completed by the relaxation of restrictions on the foreign trade of old colonies (Antilles, Réunion) in 1861 and Algeria in 1866. The idea of an Arab Kingdom horrified contemporary European settlers and was dismissed by the republican historiography of Algeria as a sinister plot to turn Arab masses into supporters of Bonapartist authoritarianism. Since the 1960s, historians have rehabilitated the humane intentions of "Arabophile" or "indigenophile" policies, championed by the Saint-Simonian Ismaÿl Urbain (1812–1884), but they have continued to insist upon their limited impact.[134]

132. Nassau William Senior, *Conversations with Distinguished Persons, During the Second Empire, from 1860 to 1863*, 2 vols. (London: Hurst and Blackett, 1880), vol. 2, 290–1

133. Napoleon III to Duc de Malakoff, Governor General of Algeria, 6 Feb. 1863, repr. in Napoléon III, *Œuvres de Napoléon III*, vol. 5, 189–193.

134. Annie Rey-Goldzeiguer, *Le Royaume arabe: la politique algérienne de Napoléon III, 1861–1870* (Algiers: Société nationale d'édition et de diffusion, 1977); Ageron, *Les Algériens musulmans*, vol. 1, 397–414; Henry Laurens, *Le royaume impossible: la France et la genèse du monde arabe* (Paris: Armand Colin, 1991), 70–74; Osama W. Abi-Mershed, *Apostles of Modernity: Saint-Simonians and the Civilizing Mission in Algeria* (Stanford, CA: Stanford University Press, 2010),

From this book's perspective, Urbain's Arab Kingdom project is significant because it can be interpreted as the revival of an informal model of empire.[135] Traditional historiography has neglected Urbain's role because his vision of an "Algeria for the Algerians" was at odds with what Algeria eventually became. His illegitimate birth and mixed racial ancestry might have contributed to this disregard. He was born in French Guyana, the son of Marie Gabrielle Appoline, who had one African grandparent and owned a small plantation, and a Marseille merchant, Urbain Brue, who let his son use his first name as a last name. Above all, Urbain's conversion to Islam and marriage to an indigenous Muslim woman made him an intolerable figure for colonialist *bien pensants*. Another reason his role has been overlooked might be the fact that many of his reports were signed by his superiors in the French administration, and he often used a pseudonym for his pamphlets or newspaper articles which are scattered in dozens of periodicals.[136] Nevertheless, he was well connected and proved to be an influential force in French Algeria from the late 1830s until the fall of the Second Empire in 1870.

Urbain adhered to Saint-Simonianism shortly after the 1830 Revolution and remained a lifelong and ardent promoter of economic growth. In 1833, he followed a Saint-Simonian mission to Egypt, where he taught French, learnt Arabic, and converted to Islam.[137] In a series of articles about Egypt in a French daily, he praised the modernizing policies of Muhammad 'Ali, especially the use of French engineers and skilled workers to direct public works, but he also lamented the pasha's mercantilist monopolies and warmongering. Several factors relating to his later advocacy of the Arab Kingdom dated from his stay in Egypt. He already believed that French possessions in the Maghreb should

159–200; Gavin Murray-Miller, "A Conflicted Sense of Nationality: Napoleon III's Arab Kingdom and the Paradoxes of French Multiculturalism," *French Colonial History*, 15, 1 (2014).

135. For another analysis which also contrasts the Bonapartist project in Algeria with republican conceptions of colonial sovereignty, see Gavin Murray-Miller, "Bonapartism in Algeria: Empire and Sovereignty before the Third Republic," *French History*, 32, 2 (2018).

136. For the identification of Urbain's authorship of certain writings and for a great deal of contextual information, this section relies on the thoroughly researched biography, in two volumes, by Michel Levallois, *Ismaÿl Urbain (1812–1884): une autre conquête de l'Algérie* (Paris: Maisonneuve et Larose, 2001) and *Ismaÿl Urbain: Royaume arabe ou Algérie franco-musulmane? 1848–1870* (Paris: Riveneuve, 2012).

137. Régnier, *Les Saint-simoniens en Egypte*, 124–9; see also Urbain's diary, in Ismaÿl Urbain, *Voyage d'Orient; suivi de poèmes de Ménilmontant et d'Égypte*, ed. Philippe Régnier (Paris: L'Harmattan, 1993).

be used to "ensure for ever to our nation a great ascendancy over all the Muslim peoples" and that French attempts to transform indigenous societies should be confined to their public, external aspects: "Muslim populations need to learn from us work, industry, administrative science, in short political and social life; but their private character, the family habits (*mœurs*), must be respected."[138]

The rapid progress of Urbain's career owed a great deal to the patronage of Michel Chevalier, the free-trade imperialist, who in 1837 had Urbain appointed as interpreter for Général Bugeaud in the Oran province and helped him to become the Algerian correspondent of the prestigious *Journal des Débats*. Urbain used his early articles in the *Débats* to defend the Tafna arrangement negotiated by Bugeaud with 'Abd al-Qadir: "The Arab nation," he wrote, was "now constituted under the authority of 'Abd al-Qadir" and there was "no future for our commercial establishment in Africa except in a sincere alliance with the Emir." France, he added, should accept "the free exercise of [the Arabs'] sovereignty," while its "small colonies" on the coast should merely "set an example of order and industry" to the indigenous population.[139] The collapse of Tafna led him to support war *à outrance* against 'Abd al-Qadir, although he dismissed colonization by European settlers as a "utopia" and advocated relying on indigenous Algerians themselves as "one of the principal colonizing elements". Following "the example of Egypt" would allow French commerce to prosper, while "a new [Algerian] people emerges and develops under France's tutelage."[140]

In the 1840s, Urbain became the interpreter and advisor of the Duc d'Aumale, a son of King Louis-Philippe who served as governor of the Constantine province in 1843–1847 and governor general of Algeria in the last months of the July Monarchy. Urbain figured next to Aumale in the centre of Horace Vernet's colossal propaganda painting (5 × 21 metres), *Capture of the Smala of Abd el-Kader* (1845), which celebrated a major French victory over the

138. "Souvenirs des Français en Egypte, " *Le Temps*, 19 Oct. 1836; on his assessment of Muhammad 'Ali's policies, see also "L'arrivée au Caire" and "Les prétendans à la succession de Mehemet-Ali. Ibrahim-Pacha et Abbas-Pacha, " *Le Temps*, 25 Dec. 1836 and 29 Jan. 1837.

139. "Lettre sur l'Afrique" and "Des Arabes, " *Journal des Débats*, 17 Nov. 1837 and 19 Dec. 1837.

140. [Ismaÿl] Urbain, "Du gouvernement et de l'administration des tribus arabes en Algérie," Oct. 1842, ANOM, F80 1674; modified versions of the report were published in *Revue de l'Orient et de l'Algérie*, 4, 2 (1847) , as a pamphlet under the title *Algérie. Du gouvernement des tribus. Chrétiens et musulmans, Français et Algériens* (Paris: Just-Bouvier, 1848), and *Tableau de la situation des établissements*, vol. 10 (1846–1847–1848–1849), 713–36.

FIGURE 2.3. Horace Vernet, *Capture of the Smala of Abd el-Kader* (1845), detail.
Source: Château de Versailles, MV2027; Photo: © RMN-Grand Palais. Reproduced by
permission of RMN-GP (Château de Versailles).

emir. Urbain is the only French soldier in the painting without his sword
drawn: instead, he holds a young Arab child in his arms and looks protectively
at a group of Arab women (to the right of the central figure of Aumale, who is
mounting an elegant white horse, as shown in figure 2.3). In the midst of the
violence, Vernet allegedly said, he wanted to include "a useful man."[141]

Urbain's influence declined after the fall of the July Monarchy in 1848, but
under the Second Empire he imposed himself as the leader of the Arabophile
party. As *chef de bureau* in Parisian ministries in charge of Algeria in the 1850s,
he helped steer through reforms of the indigenous judicial and educational
systems that increased the role of native judges and teachers.[142] In 1860, he
became a member of the Conseil du Gouvernement in Algiers, a legal and
advisory body with similar functions to the Conseil d'Etat in Paris. His pam-

141. Reported by Gustave d'Eichtal in a letter to Urbain, quoted in Levallois, *Ismaÿl Urbain*
(1812–1884), 487–8; on the commissioning and reception of Vernet's painting, see Sessions, *By*
Sword and Plow, 112–20.

142. See his defence of these and other reforms in Georges Voisin [Ismaÿl Urbain], *L'Algérie*
pour les Algériens (Paris: Michel Lévy frères, 1861).

phlet *L'Algérie française. Indigènes et immigrants*, published anonymously two years later, caused an outcry among settlers and their metropolitan supporters, especially after the letter of Napoleon III about the Arab Kingdom reproduced large sections of it verbatim in 1863.[143] Although Urbain's pamphlet condemned the immorality of France's treatment of indigenous Algerians, the crux of its argument lay in settlerism's economic unviability. "Administrative empiricists," he wrote to another leading Arabophile, Frédéric Lacroix, while he was working on the pamphlet, should make way to "political economists." "The great difficulties of the government of Algeria," he added a few weeks later, "are problems of political economy." A defence of the benefits of free trade in the original manuscript was removed from the published version, lest it offend metropolitan opinion, still hostile to the Anglo-French commercial treaty of 1860.[144]

L'Algérie française revived an economic critique of formal imperialism dating back to Raynal, and combined it with Saint-Simonian opinions on the aptitudes of different human races. Urbain did not call for the renunciation of French sovereignty, an unpalatable option after the war of conquest. Instead, he proposed the abandonment of European settler colonialism. Agricultural settlements, he argued, were a "rational" project in the days of "occupation restreinte" (in the 1830s), because they were only intended as a complement to "trading posts on the coast, in a cultivated area of limited extent," while the rest of Algeria under 'Abd al-Qadir's rule would remain under mere French "suzerainty." The conquest of the 1840s, however, had rendered this mode of colonization obsolete and turned the millions of indigenous Algerians now under French rule into "an intractable problem." Furthermore, agricultural colonization focused on commercial tropical crops may have been "logical" as long as France was still "under the yoke of the protectionist system," but with the adoption of free trade by the Second Empire, it had become an "anachronism."[145] Urbain proposed replacing the failing mercantilist conception of colonization with a "racial" division of labour. On the one hand, indigenous Muslims should be recognised as the sole "true farmers" in charge of

143. See the comparison of the two texts in Marcel Emerit, *Les Saint-Simoniens en Algérie* (Paris: Les belles lettres, 1941), 270–3.

144. Urbain to Lacroix, 11 Jan. and 25 Feb. 1862, quoted in Levallois, *Ismaÿl Urbain: Royaume arabe*, 311–14.

145. [Ismaÿl Urbain], *L'Algérie française. Indigènes et immigrants* (Paris: Challamel aîné, 1862), 15–25.

"agricultural colonization." On the other, Europeans should confine themselves to "industrial colonization," by which Urbain meant the importation of capital and skilled labour for the provision of credit, the construction of infrastructures, and the mining and food-processing industries.[146]

Urbain's project was an attack on old colonial ideas rather than empire. In a pamphlet defending Urbain's tract and the emperor's letter, Lacroix compared colonial Algeria to former French slave plantations in the Caribbean: "The negroes of Algeria have a white face, this is the only difference."[147] "You identified the sore point in your pamphlet," Urbain, whose mother had owned a small plantation in Guyana, commented on his friend's work: "Algeria in matters of prejudice is every bit as bad as the old French Antilles."[148] Yet if Urbain condemned the blind colour prejudice that underpinned mercantilist slavery, his views on race, Islam or imperial violence remained ambivalent, and subordinated to the priority he gave to economic development. Before France's second and definitive abolition of slavery in 1848, he criticized the zeal of French abolitionists and thought that the emancipation of Blacks should be reliant on the creation of a strict labour regime "to make them worthy of liberty, to make them appreciate hard work."[149] The motives behind his conversion to Islam appear to have been complex, combining a sincere admiration for past Arab achievements and Muslim spirituality with a more cynical desire to use Islam as a vehicle for the industrial transformation of the Muslim world: "next to the engineer, there must be an imam," for with "reflection" alone "one would obtain nothing" in the East.[150] Urbain kept his indigenous wife at arm's length, and after her death married a French Catholic woman in the Cathedral of Algiers in 1867. Perhaps most disturbingly, for all his criticisms of the treatment of indigenous Algerians by the French colonial regime, his writings remained almost completely silent about the atrocities committed by the French army during the war of 1839–1847, of which, as a military interpreter at the time, he could not have been unaware.[151]

146. Ibid., 30–46.

147. [Frédéric Lacroix], L'Algérie et la lettre de l'empereur (Paris: Firmin Didot & Challamel, 1863), 8.

148. Urbain to Lacroix, 8 Oct. 1863, quoted in Levallois, Ismaÿl Urbain: Royaume arabe, 437.

149. "L'habitation Éléonore," Le Temps, 15 Jan. 1837.

150. Urbain, Voyage d'Orient, 94; on Urbain's views on Islam, see also his "De la tolérance dans l'islamisme," Revue de Paris, 31, 4 (1856).

151. Urbain admitted that the French perpetrated a few "massacres" in the 1830s, but claimed that these were inspired by the "Turkish system" and that subsequently "this violence found no

For Urbain, the justification of empire lay in economic development, and formal rule was guilty of inefficiency rather than immorality. His ideas may therefore be construed as an attempt at the partial de-territorialization of French domination in North Africa by making it rely on European capital rather than settlers. This preference for the importation of French capital over immigration resembled the concept of "investment colonization" propounded a few years later by Paul Leroy-Beaulieu, and it foreshadowed the "association-ist" critique of republican "assimilationism" at the end of the century.[152] Urbain never advocated French withdrawal from Algeria. Instead, his ambition to turn France into an "instructor" of Algerian society recalls contemporary French projects of informal dominance in Egypt or Mexico.[153] France should imitate "what the vice-roys [pashas] of Egypt are doing," Lacroix's defence of Urbain's project concluded.[154] Harking back to the days of the Tafna arrange-ment, the influential press baron Emile de Girardin, another Arabophile, even advocated "erecting Algeria into a vice-royalty for life, to be entrusted to 'Abd al-Qadir as great vassal of a suzerain France"—the emir, exiled in Syria, had regained much of his popularity in French opinion.[155]

The significance of the Arab Kingdom policy is disputed. Due to the ill will of the French civilian colonial administration, which continued to favour the interests of European settlers, the confiscation of indigenous land was slowed rather than halted. Access to education for Muslim children remained limited, and very few indigenous Algerians availed themselves of the possibility of ac-quiring full French citizenship which was opened by the Senatus-Consulte

---

imitators," in *L'Algérie pour les Algériens*, 87; he also asserted that losses of European and Algerian lives had been the same since 1830, at 500,000 for each side, but his unsourced estimate for the European side seems to have included natural causes of death, and even so it is almost certainly an exaggeration (*L'Algérie française*, 47–8).

152. On "colonisation par les capitaux," see chapter 4 in this book; on assimilation and as-sociation, see Alice Conklin, *A Mission to Civilize: The Republican Idea of Empire in West Africa, 1895–1930* (Stanford, CA: Stanford University Press, 1997), 174–211, and R. F. Betts, *Assimilation and Association in French Colonial Theory, 1890–1914* (New York: Columbia University Press, 1961), 106–64.

153. [Urbain], *L'Algérie pour les Algériens*, 129–30.

154. [Lacroix], *L'Algérie*, 70.

155. *La Presse*, 23 July 1865, quoted in Levallois, *Ismaÿl Urbain: Royaume arabe*, 567; on the hopes that 'Abd al-Qadir would become the ruler of the Arab Kingdom, see Claude Vigoureux, "Napoleon III et Abd-el-Kader," *Napoleonica*, 4, 1 (2009).

(constitutional law) of 1865.[156] But these limitations were intentional. The Arab Kingdom was not designed to forge an independent Algerian nation-state or even establish full equality between Europeans and Muslims. For instance, since indigenous Algerians were chiefly destined to farm the land, mass schooling was not an Arabophile priority, and in Urbain's view at least, the main purpose of the 1865 Senatus Consulte was a provision that offered indigenous Algerians employment in the French regular army and administration, rather than access to full citizenship. Crucially, the goal of reducing immigration was achieved—although European births began to exceed deaths from 1860, the annual growth rate of the settler population was halved from 4 percent in the 1850s to 2 percent in the 1860s (see table 2.2). In the late 1860s, the Brazilian government started recruiting disappointed Algerian settlers for its own colonial projects in South America. Few settlers took up the invitation (just seventy-five in the Oran province in 1868), but the initiative suggests that the Arab Kingdom policy succeeded in giving Algeria a bad reputation for colonial emigration on a global scale.[157]

By the end of the 1860s, the Arab Kingdom was meeting with increasing skepticism, especially in metropolitan circles. Although the great famine of 1867–1868 was mainly due to droughts and swarms of locusts, European settlers attributed it to the alleged incapacity of indigenous cultivators and the regime's Arabophile policies. Republicans used these arguments as part of their efforts to undermine the Second Empire's legitimacy. Yet in 1869–1870, the Bonapartist regime made a last effort to adopt a separate constitution for Algeria, a project that was anathema to republicans and settlers who wanted Algerian provinces to be annexed as *départements*. In order to assuage republican opponents, the project of separate constitution included the creation of three representatives (for Oran, Algiers and Constantine) in the French parliament. However, it was also remarkable for the degree of autonomy it granted the colony, with extensive powers transferred to a new colonial assembly and

156. Didier Guignard, "Conservatoire ou révolutionnaire ? Le sénatus-consulte de 1863 appliqué au régime foncier d'Algérie," *Revue d'histoire du XIXe siècle*, 41 (2010); Abi-Mershed, *Apostles of Modernity*, 188–200; Patrick Weil, *Qu'est-ce qu'un français ? Histoire de la nationalité française depuis la Révolution* (Paris: Grasset, 2002), 225–7.

157. The prefect of the Bouches-du-Rhône to the minister of the interior, 29 Nov. 1871, in folder "Affaire Antoine Badin," which records efforts to discourage further emigration to Brazil from Oran in the early years of the Third Republic, in Archives départementales des Bouches-du-Rhône, 4M2147.

provincial councils.[158] The project generated heated debates about the extent
of the franchise at local elections. Urbain clamoured for it to be extended to
all indigenous Algerians who resided in "civilian territories" (the portions of
Algeria that were under civil rather than military law and administration), as
well as non-French settlers. This electoral body, with comparable numbers of
European and Muslim voters, would have undermined the settlers' political
supremacy, while linking indigenous electoral rights to residency in civilian
territories would have dissuaded settlers from demanding their extension and,
consequently, the application of French civil law to larger swathes of indigenous properties.[159]

For Urbain, however, the political enfranchisement of indigenous Algerians
was not intended to assimilate them into French culture, but on the contrary
to entrench the distinct identity of Algeria. Writing under a pseudonym in the
Bonapartist press, he maintained that Algeria should not become "a slavish
imitation of the France of the Gauls, the Romans and the Franks." Instead, it
should be considered as "an Algerian France, which will be simultaneously
French, Berber, Arab and European," or as "an annex of France, with its populations from all races, all origins, of diverse customs (*mœurs*) and varied idioms,
more or less amalgamated with French words, with a specific and appropriate
legislation." It would nonetheless remain "permeated with a French spirit" and
"closely affiliated with the public law we have been endowed with by modern
civilization."[160] The Second Empire's attempt to institutionally entrench the
Arab Kingdom met with formidable opposition. Even the committee in charge
of drafting the constitution opposed the enfranchisement of "the followers of
the Talmud or the Koran"—that is, both Jews and Muslims—at least for the

158. "Rapport à l'empereur—Constitution de l'Algérie," 5 May 1869, ANOM, F80 1703; Armand Béhic [secretary of the commission on Algeria's constitution], "Senatus-Consulte portant
organisation du gouvernement et de l'administration générale de l'Algérie. 2ᵉ rédaction,"
ANOM, F80 1704.

159. Ismaÿl Urbain, Report on "Organisation des conseils généraux électifs en Algérie," 16
June 1869, in minutes of the Conseil Général de Gouvernement, ANOM, GGA 3F60. According
to the results of the 1866 census, Europeans (French and other nationalities), made up
46 percent, 50 percent and 42 percent of the population of civilian territories in, respectively,
the Algiers, Oran and Constantine provinces; indigenous Muslims 49 percent, 40 percent and
52 percent; and indigenous Jews 5 percent, 10 percent and 6 percent (my calculations, based on
Tableau de la situation des établissements, vol. 20 [1866], 36, 38, 40).

160. Ferdinand Boudeville [Ismaÿl Urbain], "Conseils généraux électifs. 3e article," *Le Peuple
français*, 2 June 1870, quoted in Levallois, *Ismaÿl Urbain: Royaume arabe*, 812–14.

election of Algeria's representatives in metropolitan assemblies.[161] In parliamentary debates in Paris, the republican leader Jules Favre conjured up the horrifying prospect of an indigenous Algerian coming to sit among deputies in Paris "to defend the principles [of tribal property, polygamy, etc.] he defends on his soil," to approving exclamations of "Ah! Ah!" among left-wing deputies. Favre succeeded in getting a motion passed that called for annexation rather than a separate constitution.[162] In June 1870, the government adopted a compromise for the franchise at local Algerian elections, which would have increased indigenous representation but maintained European dominance.[163]

The advent of the Third Republic, following the collapse of the Bonapartist regime during the war declared in July against Prussia, turned the stalling of reforms into a debacle. Urbain resigned from the Algerian administration and moved to Marseille a few days after the proclamation of republican rule. Within a few months, a series of decrees by the provisional republican government granted most settlers' demands, including administrative assimilation and a considerable extension of civilian territories. In 1873, a new land law abolished the legal protections surrounding indigenous properties, and the 1870s witnessed a short but significant boom of the settler population (see table 2.2). In 1881, the *Code de l'indigénat* entrenched the legal inferiority of indigenous Muslims. Algeria's representatives in the metropolitan parliament (three in 1875, and six in 1881) became a vociferous and influential lobby in favour of European settlers. Hopes of turning Algeria into an autonomous and prosperous country under mere French influence were relegated to the margins of French political and intellectual life, at least until the mid-twentieth century.[164]

Joseph Loubon's dream of an Algeria supplying France with large quantities of tropical commodities and being under French tutelage rather than direct administration was therefore neither isolated nor hypocritical. It was widely shared among the French elites, and the July Monarchy made earnest attempts

161. Armand Béhic, "Régime politique," ANOM, F80 1703; see also minutes of the Commission de l'Algérie, 7 and 21 June 1869, ANOM, F80* 20141, fols. 32–3, 92–4.

162. *Annales du Sénat et du Corps Législatif. Session de 1870*, 6 vols. (Paris: Le Moniteur universel, 1870–1871), vol. 2, 537, 541 (9 Mar. 1870).

163. Rey-Goldzeiguer, *Le Royaume Arabe*, 660–70.

164. Ageron, *Les Algériens musulmans*, vol. 1, 414–29.

to turn it into reality until 1840. After Algerian military resistance was crushed, the Second Napoleonic Empire partly revived it, with its project of turning Algeria into an Arab Kingdom. How the dream came to be shattered is a complex story that allows for several complementary interpretations. It is reasonable to stress the role played by the army and the thirst for military glory and formal conquest, even at the price of extraordinary violence.[165] However, there were other factors: geopolitical circumstances (the predicament of the Ottoman Empire in the 1820s and the crisis of 1840 that left France humiliated on the international stage); indigenous resistance, which was greater than anticipated, led by Ahmad Bey in Constantine and by 'Abd al-Qadir in the rest of the country; and the environmental realities of North Africa, not least the low levels of humidity that rendered Algeria unsuitable for the cultivation of tropical crops and vulnerable to severe droughts.[166]

Placing emphasis on the initial intentions of the French and the complex causes of their unravelling is not a radical revision of existing accounts, but it does help to show that the actual course of Algerian colonization was not entirely deliberate. Even in Algeria, at least some French players pursued informal empire. It was only once this project had failed that France's political elite opted for formal conquest. Acknowledging these dynamics of thwarted ambition does not reduce French responsibility for the actual atrocities of the conquest or colonial rule. It is still remarkable that, when confronted with the alternatives of evacuation or bloody conquest, the French elite chose the latter. Instead, these dynamics confirm that informal domination formed an important part of the contemporary imperial repertoire, because when deemed expedient, it could turn into a highly visible and coercive sort of empire. The French preference for informal empire never completely excluded the use of formal means.

Still, claims that the conquest of Algeria marked the birth of modern French colonialism appear exaggerated. The focus on colonial settlements in early French schemes connecst this conquest with the Enlightened reimagining of

165. The sizeable French military and European settler colony constituted a significant "bridgehead," identified as a crucial factor in the transformation of informal into formal domination in John Darwin, "Imperialism and the Victorians: The Dynamics of Territorial Expansion," *English Historical Review*, 112, 447 (1997).

166. On the enduring French tendency to misconstrue Algeria's physical environment, see Diana K. Davis, *Resurrecting the Granary of Rome: Environmental History and French Colonial Expansion in North Africa* (Athens: Ohio University Press, 2007) and Caroline Ford, "Reforestation, Landscape Conservation, and the Anxieties of Empire in French Colonial Algeria," *American Historical Review*, 113, 2 (2008).

colonization in the late eighteenth century, rather than the late nineteenth-century style of territorial expansion that did not rely on colonial emigration.[167] The Third Republic extended certain instruments of domination to its new conquests that were elaborated in Algeria, such as the infamous *code de l'indigénat*, but nowhere did it seek to replicate the Algerian model of pseudo assimilation, with the creation of *départements* and representation in the French parliament.[168] Even in contiguous and culturally comparable Tunisia and Morocco it opted for a protectorate regime that drifted towards direct rule rather than annexation.[169] Algeria was a *sui generis* type of colonization, and between 1840 and 1880 the enormous costs and mediocre economic returns of the Algerian conquest did nothing to dispel the French preference for informal empire. Instead, those years witnessed an assertion of imperial status that relied primarily on informal means, beginning with an economic dynamism that enabled France to become the world's main provider of conspicuous commodities.

167. With the exception of the small penal colony of New Caledonia; see Isabelle Merle, *Expériences coloniales: la Nouvelle-Calédonie, 1853–1920* (Paris: Belin, 1995).

168. Olivier Le Cour Grandmaison, *De l'indigénat: anatomie d'un monstre juridique. Le droit colonial en Algérie et dans l'empire français* (Paris: Zones, 2010).

169. On the case of Tunisia, see Lewis, *Divided Rule*.

3

Champagne Capitalism

THE COMMODIFICATION OF LUXURY AND
THE FRENCH EMPIRE OF TASTE

IN 1867, the American traveller, writer and former consul in Reims, Robert Tomes, pointed to the extraordinary global dissemination of the taste for champagne wine as evidence that, contrary to Napoleon's famous jibe about Britons, it was the French who were "emphatically the shopkeepers of the world."[1] Fifteen years later, the publisher and journalist Henry Vizetelly drew an even more vivid, and somewhat sensationalist, picture of the global reach of French champagne. According to the founder of the *Illustrated London News*, not only did "the popping of champagne corks" conclude every successful *pronunciamento* in Latin America, but champagne had become a favourite of indigenous rulers "at the mouths of the unexplored rivers of Equatorial Africa," and of the Japanese, who were "so eager to welcome everything European"; even Ottoman, Egyptian and Persian grandees had overcome their religious scruples, so that the Middle East, "the first region to impart civilisation," had become "the last to receive its reflux in the shape of the sparkling wine." Both Tomes and Vizetelly, however, insisted that the main centre of champagne consumption was Britain. So common had champagne become at British public and private functions that Vizetelly feared, or affected to fear, that its disappearance would "threaten a collapse of our social system," and perhaps endanger Britain's global economic dominance, due to the crucial daily role it played in the City of London: "The amount of business . . . transacted by the aid of the wine is incalculable. Bargains in stocks and shares, tea

1. Robert Tomes, *The Champagne Country* (New York: Hurd and Houghton, 1867), 59–60.

and sugar, cotton and corn, hemp and iron, hides and tallow, broadcloth and shoddy, are clinched by its agency."[2]

From a few hundred thousand bottles before the Revolution of 1789, the output of champagne rose to eighteen million in 1869. Of these, more than four in five (88 percent in 1880) were exported, and Britain was indeed by far the largest foreign market: between 1860 and 1880 it always represented more than half of the foreign sales of Moët & Chandon, the largest producer of champagne.[3] Far from being exceptional, the global success of champagne wine spearheaded a commercial boom which saw France become the world's leading supplier of luxury and *demi-luxe* (semi-luxury) commodities between 1830 and 1870.[4] Thanks to a drastic reduction in transport costs and the lowering of tariffs in many parts of the world, the mid-nineteenth century witnessed a formidable acceleration of global economic integration. Victorian Britain is often perceived as one of the leading proponents and beneficiaries of what some historians have described as the onset of modern globalization.[5] Yet France also played a significant role in promoting global trade, and

2. Henry Vizetelly, *A History of Champagne, with Notes on the Other Sparkling Wines of France* (London: Vizetelly & Co, 1882), 78–9, 109–10; according to Tomes, the French market came a distant fifth, after those of Britain, British colonies, the United States and Russia, in Tomes, *The Champagne Country*, 91.

3. Claire Desbois-Thibault, *L'extraordinaire aventure du champagne: Moët et Chandon, une affaire de famille, 1792–1914* (Paris: Presses universitaires de France, 2003), 128–31; Kolleen M. Guy, *When Champagne Became French: Wine and the Making of a National Identity* (Baltimore, MD: Johns Hopkins University Press, 2003), esp. 15–17, 51. On the emergence of the champagne wine industry, see also Michel Etienne, *Veuve Clicquot Ponsardin: aux origines d'un grand vin de champagne* (Paris: Économica, 1994).

4. Patrick Verley, "Essor et déclin des industries du luxe et du demi-luxe au XIXe siècle" in *Le luxe en France: du siècle des "Lumières" à nos jours*, ed. Jacques Marseille (Paris: Association pour le développement de l'histoire économique, 1999), 107–23; see also Patrick Verley, *L'échelle du monde: essai sur l'industrialisation de l'Occident* (Paris: Gallimard, 1997), 543–615. Verley's work has superseded the more downcast analysis, which focused on the relative decline of French trade after 1880, by André Broder, "Le commerce extérieur: l'échec de la conquête d'une position internationale," in the influential *Histoire économique et sociale de la France*, eds. Fernand Braudel and Ernest Labrousse, 2nd edn., 5 vols. (Paris: Presses Universitaires de France, 1993), vol. 3: *1789-années 1880: l'avènement de l'ère industrielle*, 305–46.

5. Kevin H. O'Rourke and Jeffrey G. Williamson, "When Did Globalization Begin?," *European Review of Economic History*, 6, 1 (2002); Ronald Findlay and Kevin H. O'Rourke, *Power and Plenty: Trade, War, and the World Economy in the Second Millennium* (Princeton, NJ: Princeton University Press, 2007), 365–428.

between the late 1840s and the late 1860s its exports grew twice as fast as Britain's.[6]

Every empire requires an economic power base. Highlighting the extent of French economic success in the mid-nineteenth century therefore helps us to appreciate the sources of French imperial expansion. It also helps us to understand its original modalities. France's boom relied mainly on its specialization in the provision of conspicuous commodities for old and new elites. The allure of these commodities was closely tied to the anti-revolutionary undertones of French political regimes between 1800 and 1870—their global dissemination rested upon collaboration with foreign elites, rather than the expansion of French territorial rule. This cooperation took several forms, including a global partnership with Britain to secure supplies of raw materials and open foreign markets, the importation of foreign labour—especially in Paris, a city turned into the shop window of French luxury industries—to maximize France's competitive edge, and support for friendly regimes in the extra-European world (military intervention to create a Francophile monarchy in Mexico provides a hubristic example of this). French champagne capitalism was the power base of a sophisticated model of global *rayonnement* that combined soft cultural elements with the regular projection of military hardware across the world, or what may be termed an empire of taste.

This analysis draws on the so-called revisionist thesis about French economic growth in the nineteenth century, which showed that per capita incomes grew as fast in France as in Britain between 1815 and 1914, or perhaps even slightly faster.[7] Yet it diverges from it in two significant ways. First, while the revisionists praised France's model of growth as an alternative path of economic development, which was socially less disruptive than British-style

6. Between 1848 and 1868, and excluding re-exports, French exports grew 241 percent, and British exports 116 percent (my calculations, based on Direction des Douanes, *Tableau décennal* and Board of Trade, *Annual Statement of the Trade and Navigation of the United Kingdom with Foreign Countries and British Possessions*, 17 vols. [London: H.M.S.O., 1855–1871]); these, and unless otherwise stated all other annual trade figures in the chapter, are three-year averages, e.g., "1848" refers to the average of 1847, 1848 and 1849.

7. For a summary of the controversy, see François Crouzet "The Historiography of French Economic Growth in the Nineteenth Century," *Economic History Review*, 56, 2 (2003); the main statement of the revisionist thesis is Patrick O'Brien and Caglar Keyder, *Economic Growth in Britain and France, 1780–1914* (London: Allen and Unwin, 1978); on the French path of development as the product of political preferences, see Jeff Horn, *The Path Not Taken: French Industrialization in the Age of Revolution, 1750–1830* (Cambridge, MA: MIT Press, 2006).

industrialization, this chapter highlights the extent to which champagne capitalism was complementary with, and even dependent on, Britain's industrial development. Second, and in accordance with more recent scholarship that has underlined the deceleration of French growth at the end of the century, this chapter suggests that the floundering of France's model of development after 1870 was connected to its republican turn on the domestic stage and the embrace of formal imperialism abroad.[8] This reappraisal of the role of transnational factors in French development is also inspired by the recent surge of interest in global commodity chains and empires.[9] The most compelling study focuses on the "empire of cotton" in the nineteenth century, although cotton textiles represented a much lower share of French exports than British ones: 2 percent vs 35 percent of total exports in value around 1860.[10] This chapter, however, identifies the global chain of silk as being more revealing of the extent of France's integration in world economy and its imperial implications.[11] Like champagne, France's silk industry originated in aristocratic courtly consumption, was organized in small units of production, and enjoyed

8. Jean-Pierre Dormois, *L'économie française face à la concurrence britannique à la veille de 1914* (Paris: L'Harmattan, 1997).

9. On the concept's origins in world-system theory, see *Commodity Chains and Global Capitalism*, eds. Gary Gereffi, and Miguel Korzeniewicz (Westport, CT: Greenwood Press, 1994). On its more recent applications, see Steven C. Topik and Allen Wells, "Commodity Chains in a Global Economy," *A World Connecting, 1870–1945*, ed. Emily Rosenberg (Cambridge, MA: Harvard University Press, 2012), 593–812.

10. See Beckert, *Empire of Cotton.* The figures are for the share of cotton yarns and finished textiles; the figure for British exports is from James A. H. Imlah, *Economic Elements in the "Pax Britannica." Studies in British Foreign Trade in the Nineteenth Century* (Cambridge, MA: Harvard University Press, 1958), 104, and the figure for French exports is my calculation, based on Direction des Douanes, *Tableau décennal.*

11. Traditional economic histories of France have tended to neglect the silk industry. For instance, the reference work of Claude Fohlen on textile manufacturing excluded it from the scope of its investigations on the grounds that it was an "aberrant branch" of the French economy, since silk textiles were "a luxury product" with an "extremely narrow clientele," in *L'industrie textile au temps du Second Empire* (Paris: Plon, 1956), 51–2. The silk industry was heavily concentrated in the Lyon region, and the majority of studies are especially concerned with its impact on regional development; see especially Pierre Cayez, *Metiers Jacquard et hauts fourneaux: aux origines de l'industrie lyonnaise* (Lyon: Presses universitaires de Lyon, 1978) and *Crise et croissance de l'industrie lyonnaise* (Paris: CNRS, 1980). For a more global perspective on modern silk manufacturing, see Giovanni Frederico, *An Economic History of the Silk Industry, 1830–1930* (Cambridge: Cambridge University Press, 1997).

strong export-led growth until the 1870s.[12] Between 1820 and 1870, silk textiles were France's leading export, making up about 20 percent of total exports in value. Yet the industry became increasingly dependent on British-mediated imports of raw silk from China, while a vast and growing proportion of its customers were located beyond French borders, especially in the United States and in Britain and its empire.

Despite such interdependence, the French empire of taste was not a purely capitalistic enterprise. It pursued profit, but also power and prestige. As seen in this book's first chapter, the imperial overtones of French support for free trade were unmistakable in the writings of Abbé de Pradt and Michel Chevalier. This chapter explores further the cultural, political and economic origins of French specialization in the provision of luxury and semi-luxury commodities, in order to understand how it helped France regain imperial status after 1815. By reconciling economic modernity with the preservation of firm hierarchies, French conspicuous commodities exercised a special kind of fascination on foreign elites and facilitated collaboration with other imperial and indigenous powers. The act of turning economic gains into global political advantages was especially overt during the Second Napoleonic Empire, and the latter's downfall contributed to the eventual decline of the empire of taste after 1870.

The Acceleration of Globalization in France

France was a major beneficiary of the onset of modern globalization between the 1840s and the 1870s. French foreign trade had already experienced a sustained growth in the eighteenth century, especially between the end of the Seven Years' War and the outbreak of the 1789 Revolution. But this earlier era of commercial prosperity had relied on the re-exportation of sugar and other tropical goods from French colonies to the rest of continental Europe, rather than exporting commodities produced in France. Even though mainland France was not unaffected, these exchanges did not result in a marked special-

---

12. On the causes of the French silk industry's success after 1800 see Charles Sabel and Jonathan Zeitlin, "Historical Alternatives to Mass Production"; see also Alain Cottereau, "The Fate of Collective Manufactures in the Industrial World: The Silk Industries of Lyons and London, 1800–1850," in *World of Possibilities. Flexibility and Mass Production in Western Industrialization*, eds. Charles Sabel and Jonathan Zeitlin (Cambridge: Cambridge University Press, 1997), 75–152.

ization of the French economy.[13] In any case, this entrepôt trade was almost entirely wiped out by maritime warfare during the Revolution and the Continental Blockade (1806–1813).[14] The strenuous efforts made to revive it after 1815, including the toleration of an illicit but flourishing slave trade and attempts to restore French domination in Saint-Domingue, faltered in the mid-1820s due to the irruption of Cuba, the United States and Brazil as major producers of sugar, cotton and coffee, and a global decline in the price of tropical commodities.[15] As a result, French foreign trade stagnated in value and further shrank as a share of the national income. As the July Monarchy dismantled mercantilist legislation and global trade picked up after 1830, French commercial exchanges started to recover, with exports increasing 60 percent between 1831 and 1846. But the great acceleration took place in the mid-century, with exports more than trebling (+241 percent) between 1848 and 1868 (see figure 3.1).

The main cause of France's export boom was certainly the acceleration of global trade after 1850. But commercial exchanges increased more rapidly in France than in the rest of the world. In particular, they accelerated more than in Britain, in an age of legendary British commercial prosperity. As shown in figure 3.2, the ratio of French to British exports rose from about 50 percent in 1850 to about 90 percent in the mid-1860s. It then stabilized at about 70 percent until the mid-1870s, before plunging to about 45 percent in the mid-1880s.[16]

The economic reforms of the Second Empire, including the improvement of credit conditions through the creation of new joint stock banks, the acceleration of railway construction through state-guaranteed loans, and the adoption of more liberal trade policies symbolized by the 1860 commercial treaty

13. Guillaume Daudin, *Commerce et prospérité: la France au XVIIIe siècle* (Paris: Presses de l'université Paris-Sorbonne, 2005); Emma Rothschild, "Isolation and Economic Life in Eighteenth-Century France," *American Historical Review*, 119, 4 (2014).

14. François Crouzet, "Wars, Blockade, and Economic Change in Europe, 1792–1815," *Journal of Economic History*, 24, 4 (1964); Kevin H. O'Rourke, "The Worldwide Economic Impact of the French Revolutionary and Napoleonic Wars, 1793–1815," *Journal of Global History*, 1, 1 (2006).

15. David Todd, "Remembering and Restoring the Economic Old Regime: France and its Colonies, 1815–1830," in *War, Demobilization and Memory: The Legacy of War in the Era of Atlantic Revolutions*, eds. Alan Forrest, Karen Hagemann, and Michael Rowe (Basingstoke: Palgrave Macmillan, 2016), 203–19.

16. The adverse consequences of the American Civil War on British cotton exports can account only in part for the mid-1860s peak on figure 3.2, while the trough c. 1870 is chiefly due to the collapse of French exports during the Franco-Prussian war of 1870–1.

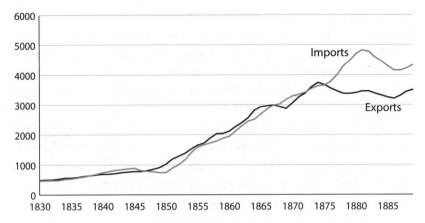

FIGURE 3.1. French exports and imports, in millions of francs, 1830–1889. *Source:* My calculations, excluding re-exports and merchandise to be re-exported, and based on "official values" for the years 1830 to 1849 and "real values" for the years 1850 to 1889, with a five-year moving average, in Direction des Douanes, *Tableau décennal*.

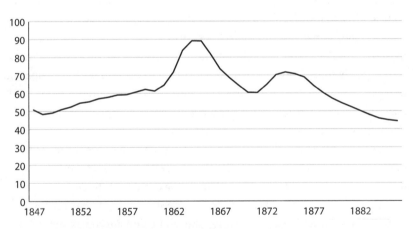

FIGURE 3.2. Ratio of French exports to British exports, in %, 1847–1886. *Source:* My calculations, excluding re-exports and based on "real values," with a three-year moving average, in Direction des Douanes, *Tableau décennal* and Board of Trade, *Annual Statement* (conversion rate: £1 = 25 francs).

with Britain, offer a conventional explanation of the extraordinary growth of French foreign trade, and they were certainly major contributory factors.[17] For

17. See for instance Roger Price, *The French Second Empire: An Anatomy of Political Power* (Cambridge: Cambridge University Press, 2001), 210–49, and Jean-Claude Yon, *Le Second Empire. Politique, société, culture* (Paris: Armand Colin, 2004), 102–23. The formidable rise of French

instance, the connection of Champagne's main towns, Epernay and Reims, to the national rail network in 1849 and 1854, respectively, was crucial to the growth of champagne exports because it reduced transportation costs and the risk of bottle breakage, which was greater with road transport (champagne could not be stored in barrels). The champagne industry was also a major beneficiary of the 1860 treaty, which drastically reduced British taxation on French wines and brandies.[18] Yet the abrupt stagnation of the value of French exports, and their relative decline in comparison with British exports from the mid-1870s, suggest that other factors were at play, since the new banks and railways did not disappear with the end of the Second Empire and France only embraced resolutely protectionist policies in the 1890s.

Both the above-global-trend growth of French exports until the 1870s and the below-trend stagnation until the 1890s may be attributed, in part, to France's specialization in luxury and semi-luxury industries. In prosperous times, such as the long upswing of the world economy from the late 1840s until the early 1870s, global expenditure on such commodities rose faster than incomes, while in more difficult times, as during the so-called Great Depression of 1873–1896, demand for them declined more rapidly than for essential commodities. As a result of the high-income elasticity of its main exports, France was arguably more sensitive than other industrial economies to the ups and downs of nineteenth-century globalization, and this sensitivity helps to explain the keenness of successive French governments, especially after 1850, to open up (or keep open) foreign markets.

Contemporary official statistics do not allow us to measure the overall proportion of luxurious or semi-luxurious commodities in French exports, in part due to a lack of detail (for instance, fine wines were not distinguished from ordinary wines), and fundamentally because it would require controversial assumptions on which commodities should be considered as superfluous luxuries and which as necessities. However, it is reasonable to assume that, on average, silk textiles were more luxurious than cotton textiles, and the divergent trends of these two commodities' exports is suggestive of the intense specialization of the French economy in this period (see figure 3.3). Note that

exports was also certainly connected to the succesful adaptation of more traditional commercial institutions, such as the tribunaux de commerce, to capitalist development; see Claire Lemercier, "Un modèle français de jugement des pairs. Les tribunaux de commerce, 1790–1880," unpublished Thèse d'habilitation (University of Paris 8, 2012).

18. Desbois-Thibault, L'extraordinaire aventure, 130; Nye, War, Wines, and Taxes, 101.

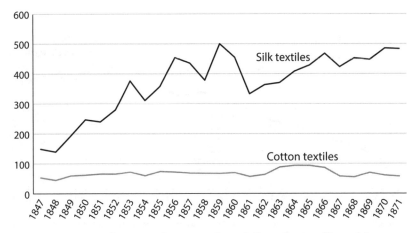

FIGURE 3.3. French exports of cotton textiles and silk textiles, in millions of francs, 1847–1871. *Source:* My calculations, excluding re-exports and based on "real values" in Direction des Douanes, *Tableau décennal.*

the divergence, with the export of silk textiles growing 230 percent and those of cotton textiles only 24 percent between 1849 and 1859, predated the disruption of cotton supplies by the American Civil War. If anything, the latter had a more significantly adverse effect on the export of silk textiles, because the war and the high tariffs adopted by the victorious North drastically curtailed one of the French industry's main foreign markets.

Due to the volume of its foreign sales (435 million francs in 1865), the silk industry made the largest contribution to France's export boom after 1850 in absolute terms. Export of wines and liquors (predominantly made up, one may presume, of the finer sorts) grew faster, from 88 million francs in 1849 to 319 million in 1865, and made the second largest absolute contribution. However, several smaller industries made an even larger relative contribution when their exports skyrocketed, and may be seen as the best representatives of French commercial dynamism. Two outstanding examples of this were the *articles de Paris* (marquetry and other ornamental knickknacks, an industry concentrated in the Paris region) and the new industry of *prêt-à-porter* (ready-made clothing, also over-represented in Paris), a by-product of the improvement of sewing machines and of the multiplication of *magasins de nouveauté* (fancy goods stores) from 1800 and department stores from 1850.[19] As shown

19. Philippe Perrot, *Fashioning the Bourgeoisie: A History of Clothing in the Nineteenth Century* (Princeton, NJ: Princeton University Press, 1994), 52–56, 66–79; Fiona Lesley Ffoulkes, "The

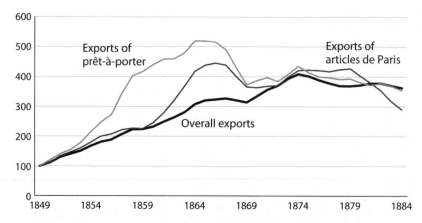

FIGURE 3.4. French exports of *articles de Paris* and *prêt-à-porter* clothes compared to overall
French exports, 1849–1884, with index 1849 = 100. *Source:* My calculations, excluding
re-exports and based on "real values," with a five-year moving average, in Direction des
Douanes, *Tableau décennal.*

in figure 3.4, while overall exports trebled between 1850 and the mid-1860s, exports of *articles de Paris* grew more than fourfold and exports of *prêt-à-porter* more than fivefold, reaching 200 million and 118 million francs respectively in 1865.

Arguably, these export industries made a crucial contribution to the relative prosperity of the Second Empire. Not only did exports grow much faster (241 percent) than the national income (64 percent) between 1848 and 1868, but export-oriented industries were closely associated with the introduction of new, sophisticated technologies and marketing techniques.[20] The success of the silk industry relied on a constant series of improvements on the Jacquard loom (invented in 1804 and based on a punch-card system which, in an age of information technology, seems hardly less modern than the spinning jenny), as much as on the traditional *savoir-faire* of the Lyonnais *canuts* (silk workers).[21] Even the growth of the wine industry was aided by new technologies, such as machines for the bottling of champagne, a delicate operation due

Métier of the Fashion Merchant (*Marchande de Modes*): Luxury and the Changing Parisian Clothing System, 1795 to 1855" (unpublished PhD dissertation, University of Southampton, 2017).

20. My calculations, using five-year moving averages, based on Direction des Douanes, *Tables décennales,* and Jean-Claude Toutain, "Le produit intérieur brut de la France, 1789–1990," *Economies et Sociétés. Série HEQ,* 11, 1 (1997).

21. Charles Ballot, *L'introduction du machinisme dans l'industrie française* (Lille: Marquant & Paris: Rieder, 1923), 369–82; Essinger, *Jacquard's Web,* 27–43.

to the effervescent nature of the wine. Such machinery saved little labour because it did not employ much energy (the champagne-bottling machine, for instance, was not steam powered, lest the fumes altered the wine's quality), but it increased per capita productivity and improved the quality of products.[22] Similarly, the rise of the *prêt-à-porter* industry owed a great deal to the introduction of the first sewing machines in the 1820s and their significant improvement by Isaac Singer in the 1850s. It was also a typically middle-class consumption product, sold at fixed or much-advertised discounted prices in larger establishments than traditional shops, to a bourgeois clientele, while the upper classes continued to purchase made-to-measure clothes.[23] The industry's rapid growth in France—much more rapid than in Britain, where the first department stores only opened in the 1870s—and its fast-rising export aptly illustrate the competitive advantages of mid-nineteenth-century French capitalism.[24]

This sophistication of French capitalism has long been recognised by cultural and social historians, but it has been strangely overlooked by economic historians. Even the upholders of the revisionist thesis in the historiography of French economic growth have tended to focus on the benefits of its archaic traits, such as limited rural migration to anarchic cities.[25] The main cause of this neglect was probably the stalling of French commercial dynamism after 1870, although it could also reflect a gender bias. The clientele of the dynamic sectors of the French industry was overwhelmingly female. The eighteenth-century silk industry had dressed aristocrats of both sexes, but its nineteenth-century customers were predominantly bourgeois women.[26] The Parisian

22. Desbois-Thibault, *L'extraordinaire aventure*, 140–5.

23. Perrot, *Fashioning the Bourgeoisie*, 66–79.

24. On the emergence of department stores in France, see Michael B. Miller, *The Bon Marché: Bourgeois Culture and the Department Store* (Princeton, NJ: Princeton University Press, 1981), and on their later spread in Britain see William Lancaster, *The Department Store: A Social History* (London: Leicester University Press, 1995).

25. O'Brien and Keyder, *Economic Growth*, 185–98.

26. On the gendering of patterns of consumption, see Jennifer M. Jones, *Sexing La Mode: Gender, Fashion and Commercial Culture in Old Regime France* (Oxford: Berg, 2004) for the pre-revolutionary era, and Leora Auslander, "The Gendering of Consumer Practices in Nineteenth-Century France," in *The Sex of Things: Gender and Consumption in Historical Perspective*, eds. Victoria de Grazia and Ellen Furlough (Berkeley: University of California Press, 1996), 79–112; on the feminization of silk textiles' consumption after 1800, see Natalie Rothstein "Silk: The Industrial Revolution and After" in *The Cambridge History of Western Textiles*, ed. David Jenkins, 2 vols. (Cambridge: Cambridge University Press, 2003), vol. 2, 790–808.

grands magasins were "a feminine universe par excellence."[27] Even champagne was described, at least in Britain, as a "favourite with the ladies," or "[the ladies'] wine par excellence."[28] Paris after 1815 dictated the colourful, varied and ever-changing fashion for women, but London set the increasingly sober and uniform standards for men.[29] Britain's economic achievements, primarily based on large-scale manufacturing, mineral extraction and shipping were more evidently connected to contemporary conceptions of masculinity and power. These perceptions have influenced a traditional economic historiography mostly written by men. Yet we need to consider the findings of social and cultural historians concerning the peculiar role played by luxury, fashion and taste, as it is crucial when it comes to understanding the domestic and global dynamics of French capitalism after 1800.

The Banality of Luxury

France's nineteenth-century specialization in the production of luxury and semi-luxury commodities had its roots in the Old Regime's economy of guild production and courtly consumption. For a long time, liberal and Marxist historians alike tended to denigrate the economic performance of the Bourbon regime. In their view, persistent feudal or mercantilist structures dragged down growth, while the 1789 Revolution seemed to be the natural outcome of economic weaknesses and contradictions.[30] Yet in recent decades, scholarship has drawn a rosier picture of French economic growth between 1715 and 1789. The Colbertian regime of regulations has been shown to remedy asymmetries of information in an age of commercial uncertainty, the economic privileges awarded by the Crown have been reinterpreted as providing a powerful stimu-

27. *Cathedrals of Consumption: The European Department Store*, eds. Geoffrey Crossick and Serge Jaumain (Aldershot: Ashgate, 1998), 2.

28. "London at dinner; or where to dine" (1858), quoted in Alfred Simon, *History of the Champagne Trade in England* (London: Wyman and sons, 1905), 106; Vizetelly, *A History of Champagne*, 111.

29. Perrot, *Fashioning the Bourgeoisie*, 25–33; Penelope Byrde, "Dress: The Industrial Revolution and After," in *Cambridge History of Western Textiles*, vol. 2, 882–909; Carlo Marco Belfanti, *Histoire culturelle de la mode* (Paris: Institut français de la mode, 2014), 227–48.

30. For a classic statement of this denigation, see Ernest Labrousse, *La crise de l'économie française à la fin de l'Ancien Régime et au début de la Révolution* (Paris: Presses Universitaires de France, 1943).

lus to industrial and export growth, and the formidable, if fragile, prosperity of French colonial trade has attracted renewed attention.[31]

Focusing on the case of French silk industry in the eighteenth century, William Sewell Jr. pushed this reappraisal further, locating an important aspect of "the rise and triumph of capitalism" in western Europe in Old Regime France—namely the emergence of a set of industrial and commercial techniques that aimed at "enhancing consumer desire." If this process began with genuinely luxurious commodities at the court of Versailles in the late seventeenth century, it extended to an ever wider range of "fashionable consumer goods" after 1700.[32] While stressing the significance of desire enhancement in contemporary economics to highlight the importance of this "particularly French" contribution to the history of modern capitalism, Sewell suggests that in the nineteenth century, the importance of fashion-driven production receded as "industrialization" shifted its emphasis towards "cutting costs and

31. François Crouzet, "Angleterre et France au XVIIIe siècle: analyse comparée de deux croissances économiques," *Annales. Économies, Sociétés, Civilisations*, 21, 2 (1966), trans. as "England and France in the Eighteenth Century: A Comparative Analysis of Two Economic Growths" in François Crouzet, *Britain Ascendant: Comparative Studies in Franco-British Economic History* (Cambridge: Cambridge University Press, 1990), 12–43; recent reappraisals of the Old Regime's economic performance include Philippe Minard, *La fortune du colbertisme: État et industrie dans la France des Lumières* (Paris: Fayard, 1998) and Jeff Horn, *Economic Development in Early Modern France: The Privilege of Liberty, 1650–1820* (Cambridge: Cambridge University Press, 2015); and, although also concerned with the limits of the Old Regime growth model, Paul Cheney, *Cul de Sac: Patrimony, Capitalism, and Slavery in French Saint-Domingue* (Chicago: University of Chicago Press, 2017).

32. Sewell, "The Empire of Fashion": 82, 84 and 87; on the dissemination of a taste for luxury and the emergence of "demi-luxe" or "populuxe," see Cissie Fairchilds, "The Production and Marketing of Populuxe Goods in Eighteenth-Century Paris," in *Consumption and the World of Goods*, eds. John Brewer and Roy Porter (London: Routledge, 1993), 228–48; Daniel Roche, *Histoire des choses banales: naissance de la consommation dans les sociétés traditionnnelles (XVIIe-XIXe siècle)* (Paris: Fayard, 1997); Carlo Poni, "Mode et innovation: les stratégies des marchands de soie à Lyon au XVIIIème siècle," *Revue d'histoire moderne et contemporaine*, 45, 3 (1998); Colin Jones and Rebecca Spang, "*Sans-culottes, sans café, sans tabac*: Shifting Realms of Necessity and Luxury in Eighteenth-Century France," in *Consumers and Luxury: Consumer Culture in Europe, 1650–1850*, eds. Maxine Berg and Helen Clifford (Manchester: Manchester University Press, 1999), 37–62; Michael Kwass, "Big Hair: A Wig History of Consumption in Eighteenth Century France," *American Historical Review*, 111, 3 (2006); Natacha Coquery, *Tenir boutique à Paris au XVIIIe siècle: Luxe et demi luxe* (Paris: Édition du Comité des travaux historiques et scientifiques, 2011).

multiplying output through technological development."[33] In this, Sewell is perhaps guilty of being overly conscientious in seeking to maintain an orthodox Marxist reading of economic development in the nineteenth century. As shown above, France's extraordinary commercial boom in the mid century was driven by the same type of fashionable industries, with silk textiles still occupying the first rank among them. It is therefore possible to argue that, far from receding after 1800, this French enhancement of consumer desire was in fact exported and globalized.

Indeed contemporaries, and not only nationalist French writers, frequently commented upon France's lead in the production of luxurious and fashionable commodities, and what appeared to be their peculiar ability to generate consumer desire. In 1868, for instance, *The Economist*'s editor, Walter Bagehot, even as he commended England's mastery of "the process of production," acknowledged France's superiority in the fabrication of "demand-producing articles," which "would not be bought if they did not make themselves coveted and admired." This was true, he claimed, in "the three great lines of human industry": "food, clothes, and houses," although in his view the French genius for generating new material desires was best illustrated by the *articles de Paris*, these "endless incidentals and *et ceteras* of ornamentation and civilisation, which can hardly be said to satisfy a previously-felt want, but create a desire for themselves by a choiceness in workmanship and a perfection in indescribable detail."[34] The more than creditable performance of French exhibiters, especially the producers of luxury goods, at the first universal exhibitions, reinforced this perception. The Crystal Palace exhibition of 1851 is often remembered as a celebration of Britain's dominance as the workshop of the world.[35] Yet 20 percent of the prizes awarded went to French exhibits (against 10 percent to exhibits from the Zollverein, or German customs union), most of which were by Parisian or Lyonnais producers of finer goods, helping to consolidate the image of French tasteful inventiveness beyond French borders.[36] It was

33. Sewell, "The Empire of Fashion," 117.

34. [Walter Bagehot], "One Difference between France and England," *The Economist*, 12 Sep. 1868.

35. Paul Young, "Mission Impossible: Globalization and the Great Exhibition," in *Britain, the Empire, and the World at the Great Exhibition of 1851*, eds. Jeffrey A. Auerbach and Peter H. Hoffenberg (Aldershot: Ashgate, 2008), 3–25.

36. British exhibitors obtained 40 percent of all the prizes, but two thirds of French exhibitors won prizes, against only a quarter of British exhibitors; Louis Bergeron, *Les industries du luxe en France* (Paris: Odile Jacob, 1998), 20.

largely in response to this perceived superiority of the French, especially in designs of silk and silverwork, that the South Kensington Museum, the ancestor of the Victoria & Albert Museum, was founded in 1852.[37] In the view of contemporary Britons, at least until the 1870s, it was not only Continental Europeans who should endeavour to catch up with British industrial prowess, but also Britons (and others) who should seek to emulate French excellence at producing desirable commodities.

French political economists highlighted the superior quality of French products at the Crystal Palace exhibition even more brazenly.[38] Adolphe Blanqui, a disciple of Jean-Baptiste Say, contended that "all the products, wherever they came from, looked common and provincial when compared to those of France." The "elegance, grace and *je ne sais quoi*" of commodities made in France amounted in his view to an "inexhaustible capital," comparable to England's coal mines. According to Blanqui, the exhibition of Lyon silk textiles ("plain cloths, cut or crimped velvets, taffeta, satins and *gros de Naples* [plain stout silks], crapes, plush, scarves, dobbies [patterned fabrics], brocades, church or palace cloths"), on the first floor of the Crystal Palace, made a particularly strong impression on the public: "This part of the Exhibition [was] very dangerous for husbands. From the morning to the evening, thousands of ecstatic women jot[ted] down in their notebooks" the names and addresses of French manufacturers.[39] Blanqui's boastful tone served the tactical purpose of assuaging the fears of French protectionist lobbies. But it also denoted his desire, shared by many other French economists who harboured misgivings about British-style mass industrialization and urbanization, to promote a distinct French economic model, based on "the gradual development of [France's] natural industries, that is to say, almost all the fabrications upon which a skilful hand and the purity of taste can exert their influence."[40]

37. Jeffrey A. Auerbach, *The Great Exhibition of 1851: A Nation on Display* (New Haven, CT: Yale University Press, 1999), 122; see also Tobin Andrews Sparling, *The Great Exhibition: A Question of Taste* (New Haven, CT: Yale Center for British Art, 1982), 28–29, and Anthony Burton, *Vision & Accident: The Story of the Victoria and Albert Museum* (London: Victoria & Albert Publications, 1999), 109–12.

38. Whitney Walton, *France at the Crystal Palace: Bourgeois Taste and Artisan Manufacture in the Nineteenth Century* (Berkeley: University of California Press, 1992).

39. Adolphe Blanqui, *Lettres sur l'exposition universelle de Londres* (Paris: Capelle, 1851), 36, 61–2, 109, 131–2.

40. Blanqui, *Lettres*, 283; on the growing influence of French fashion on women's fashion in Britain after 1850, see Penelope Byrde, *Nineteenth-Century Fashion* (London: Batsford, 1992),

In this view, the emulation of Britain's free-trade policies and more intense participation in global commercial exchanges were not destined to help France imitate the British pattern of development, but on the contrary to forge a distinct one, some features of which prefigured the economic model described by revisionist historians of nineteenth-century French growth.

With the benefit of hindsight, the notion that a factor as subjective and evanescent as "superior taste" should be considered a major asset in global competition may seem far-fetched, but it was widely shared among contemporaries. Even Jean-Baptiste Say, in the immediate aftermath of the Napoleonic Wars, asserted that British producers would soon be unable to sustain foreign competition, not only because of the heavy taxes rendered necessary by Britain's enormous public debt, but also as a result of a marked decline in British producers' taste: "the long separation of the English nation from the classical lands of Europe" during the wars had, he claimed, "altered its taste in the industrial arts"; "its vases, furniture and lamps" no longer had any "purity, lightness or elegance"; the English had "fallen back into this gothic and convoluted taste, into these heavy and complicated ornaments which do not represent anything"; and English "designs of fabrics" and "choice of colours" lagged behind "the progress of Europe."[41] Say's oddly assured tone in matters of taste probably derived from his professional experience as an apprentice in his father's Lyonnais silk merchant house and as salesman in a Parisian house before the Revolution.[42] Yet his tone was somewhat at odds with his hostility towards luxury, since good taste was determined by fashion, and luxury governed fashion.[43] This dichotomy would have been minimal in Say's day, when neoclassical canons of beauty dominated French art and craftsmanship, especially between the 1780s and 1820s; but it would become more apparent after 1850, when the exuberant Second Empire style of ornamentation echoed the *pompier* genre of French academic art.

In any case, Say's hostility towards luxury has been exaggerated. It may have been present in the moral treatise he published at the end of the republican

69–87, and, on the representative character of Blanqui's views, Walton, *France at the Crystal Palace*, 199–220.

41. Say, *De l'Angleterre*, 32–3.

42. Evert Schoorl, *Jean-Baptiste Say: Revolutionary, Entrepreneur, Economist* (London: Routledge, 2013), 5–6.

43. Jeremy Jennings, "The Debate about Luxury in Eighteenth- and Nineteenth-Century French Political Thought," *Journal of the History of Ideas*, 68, 1 (2007): 91–4.

1790s, *Olbie* (1800).[44] But it declined after 1820. Say's last major opus, the *Cours complet d'économie politique pratique* (1828–1829), continued to favour "reproductive" over "wasteful" consumption, an implicit condemnation of sumptuary expenditure.[45] However this work, which was designed to reach a wide audience, was full of practical advice about the everyday choices of consumers, revealing a more pragmatic side to Say's economic thinking. Say maintained that consumers should only aim to satisfy their "real" needs, but he admitted that real needs expanded with "the degrees of progress of society" and varied in the different classes. He therefore condemned the purchase of "a jewel" or "a sophisticated piece of furniture" by "mediocre fortunes," but condoned it for richer consumers, and he ranked *argenterie* (silver service) as a necessity, even though, in a recommendation that betrayed his approval of *demi-luxe*, he thought silver-plated preferable to sterling silver cutlery. More generally, Say advocated a pattern of consumption that favoured quality over low price, in line with the orientation of French industrial production: "One should, whatever one's means are, consume the best quality."[46]

The tacit reappraisal of the role of luxury, fashion and taste by Say, the leading French political economist, or by his disciple Blanqui, reflected an important ideological shift since the raging of a furious controversy on the merits and dangers of *le luxe* in the last decades of Old Regime France. The promotion of luxury (alongside public debt) as a mercantilist instrument of economic development in Jean-François Melon's influential *Essai politique sur le commerce* (1734) received the endorsement of Voltaire in *Le Mondain* (1736) and *La défense du Mondain* (1737). Yet it elicited a wide range of critical responses, grounded in a moral concern with the nefarious effects of luxury on patriotism and virtue or, as in the case of the *Économistes* or Physiocrats from the 1760s, in a more pragmatic fear that luxury was diverting capital towards unproductive expenditure.[47] François Quesnay, the leading Physiocrat, selected the example of the silk stocking industry to illustrate the alleged sterility

44. Jean-Baptiste Say, *Olbie, ou Essai sur les moyens de réformer les mœurs d'une nation* (Geneva: Institut Coppet, 2014; first published in Year VIII), esp. 50–1; on the significance of this writing in Say's thought, see Whatmore, *Republicanism*, 125–9.

45. Say, *Cours complet*, vol. 1, 333–4.

46. Say, *Cours Complet*, vol. 5, 64–78.

47. John Shovlin, *The Political Economy of Virtue: Luxury, Patriotism, and the Origins of the French Revolution* (Ithaca, NY: Cornell University Press, 2006); on the debate about luxury and its international ramifications, see also Christopher J. Berry, *The Idea of Luxury: A Conceptual and Historical Investigation* (Cambridge: Cambridge University Press, 1994), 126–76.

of manufacturing activities, by contrast with agriculture, which he saw as the fount of reproducible wealth.[48] This debate was not brought to an abrupt end with the Revolution.[49] Nevertheless, its intensity declined markedly. According to Google N-gram, the frequency of the word *luxe* in French-language publications declined by 95 percent between 1770 and 1800, and it was halved again between 1800 and 1820.[50] Even if Say remained, in principle, firmly against luxury, the leading French political economist was now mainly exasperated by the importance previously accorded to this question. In the *Cours complet*, he declared himself astonished by "the number of volumes" written "for and against luxury" until 1800, and expressed almost equal disdain for the "moral declamations" of the opponents of luxury (an implicit repudiation of his own stance in *Olbie*) as for the "specious arguments" of its defenders.[51]

Luxury was neither victorious nor vanquished in post-revolutionary debates, but it became banal and ceased to be controversial.[52] As many historians of the eighteenth-century controversy have contended, this tends to confirm that the anxiety generated by luxury was linked to its perceived subversion of formal, social distinctions, since the abolition of such distinctions by the Revolution rendered the concern void. Admittedly, the Revolution also dealt a severe blow to the luxury industries, especially during the Terror. Not only did their often aristocratic and clerical clientele diminish, due to executions, emigration and impoverishment, but in its most radical Montagnard phase the revolutionary government actively discouraged private sumptuary expenditure.[53] The silk industry was also adversely affected by the repression of a

48. *Gazette du Commerce*, 24 Dec. 1765; quoted in Anne-Marie Piuz, "La soie le luxe et le pouvoir dans les doctrines françaises (XVIe-XVIIIe siècles)," in *La seta in Europa sec. XII–XX*, ed. Simonetta Cavaciocchi (Florence: Le Monnier, 1993), 817–37: 833–4.

49. Jennings, "The Debate about Luxury": 83–5.

50. See decline of the Google Ngram frequency of "luxe" in French-language works, from c. 0.001 percent in 1765–1774 to c. 0.00005 percent in 1795–1804 to c. 0.000025 percent in 1815–1824; https://books.google.com/ngrams, accessed 27 Sep. 2017.

51. Say, *Cours complet*, vol. 1, 333.

52. Philippe Perrot, *Le Luxe. Une richesse entre faste et confort, XVIIIe-XIXe siècle* (Paris: Le Seuil, 1995), esp. 91–124.

53. Natacha Coquery, "Luxury and Revolution: Selling High-Status Garments in Revolutionary France," in *Selling Textiles in the Long Eighteenth Century: Comparative Perspectives from Western Europe*, eds. Jon Stobart and Bruno Blondé (Basingstoke: Palgrave MacMillan, 2014), 179–92.

Federalist insurrection in Lyon between August and October 1793 (the city's population shrank by 40 percent between 1790 and 1800), and by the loss of its substantial German and Italian markets as a result of continental warfare between 1792 and 1802.[54] The nascent champagne industry similarly suffered from a reduction of its domestic and foreign markets.[55]

Yet few moral and political qualms were expressed when French luxury industries experienced a strong resurgence after 1800. For instance, by the early 1810s the silk industry appeared to have recovered its 1790 level of output. The revival of Lyonnais silk manufacturing relied on traditional factors, including large orders from the re-established Catholic Church (1801) and the Napoleonic regime's court after the proclamation of the Empire (1804), and renewed access to its Germanic and Italian aristocratic clientele, thanks to Napoleon's military victories. Its rapid growth was also aided by the spread of the Jacquard loom, although the latter consisted in a combination of several Old Regime technologies rather than a radical innovation. While the dissolution of guilds during the Revolution had disrupted the production of silk textiles, the Lyon Chamber of Commerce, created in 1802, assumed many functions of the old "Fabrique," including the policing of relations between merchants, masters and their workers.[56] A much-trumpeted symbol of this successful amalgamation of economic modernity and traditional corporatist values was Joseph-Marie Jacquard's decision not to patent his loom, so that it could be more easily adopted by Lyonnais workshops—although he received a pension for life from municipal authorities and was more financially motivated than the legend, which took hold after his death in 1834, would suggest.[57]

The resurgence of silk and other luxury industries was therefore connected in multiple ways with efforts to roll back the most radical aspects of the Revolution. The new genre of elaborate silk-woven portraits—of Napoleon as First Consul, of Jacquard as a pious inventor, of Napoleon III as emperor of the French—was another spectacular manifestation of the close ties between this sector of the French economy and the revamped monarchical order that domi-

54. Cayez, *Métiers Jacquard et hauts fourneaux*, 78–96.

55. This decline was followed by a rapid resurgence after 1802; see Etienne, *Veuve Clicquot Ponsardin*, 87–126.

56. Cayez, *Metiers Jacquard et hauts fourneaux*, 96–141.

57. Ballot, *L'introduction du machinisme*, 374, 380–1.

nated French politics, under several guises, from 1800 until 1870.[58] And even as luxury became more banal, that did not stop it from remaining political.

Foundations of Neo-courtly Economic Growth

If the First Napoleonic Empire allowed French luxury and fashion industries to regain most of the ground lost in the 1790s, the decades which followed the return of peace in 1815 saw them expand their horizons beyond the French and European aristocracy to the fast growing ranks of the middle classes in Europe and neo-Europes, and even the elites of the extra-European world. Economic historians have often failed to emphasize the degree to which this commercial expansion continued to rely on courtly mechanisms, although it was increasingly the entire city of Paris that tended to assume the stimulating function traditionally played by the court. One of the reasons for this relative neglect is that a great proportion of the value added by producers of tasteful French commodities, through capitalization on French cultural prestige and effective marketing, is not easily captured by traditional positivist or statistical approaches. Such elusiveness is particularly pronounced in the case of several emerging service industries, from restaurants to prostitution, which, to a large extent, also relied on foreign demand, under the form of tourism. The foundations of this neo-courtly model of commercial growth were therefore both material, with new Parisian commercial infrastructures playing a crucial role, and immaterial, as they endeavoured to fulfil a wide array of consumer desires.

The special role played by Paris in the stimulation of desire led Gabriel Tarde, the author of the classical work of social psychology *The Laws of Imitation* (1890), to describe the French capital as an extreme example of the way the nineteenth century's new metropolises, aided by new transport and communication technologies, determined entire countries' ways of thinking and buying: "Paris lords it over the provinces, royally and orientally, more than the court ever did over the city. Every day, by telegraph or train, Paris dispatches its ready-made ideas, desires, conversations and revolutions, along with its ready-made clothing and furnishing." Stressing the enthrallment of French and

58. Camille Pernon, *Bonaparte réparateur*, 1802; Didier Petit et Cie, *Portrait de Joseph-Marie Jacquard*, 1839, based on the painted portrait by Jean-Claude Bonnefond (1834); and Maison Furnion, *Portrait de l'Empereur Napoléon III*, 1855, Lyon, Musée des Tissus, MT 2153, MT 25800, MT 42746, http://www.mtmad.fr (accessed 10 January 2019).

other European consumers by Paris in the nineteenth century may have the appearances of a *cliché*. Yet, as pointed out by Tarde, "the suggestive and imperative fascination" exercised by Paris was "so profound, so complete and so continuous that hardly anyone was astonished any more," and contemporaries (as well as writers of more recent works) have often tended to find an unsatisfactory explanation in an alleged Parisian predisposition for chic and glamour. The roots of this "chronic . . . magnetism," which turned even Parisian workers into "an aristocracy, much admired and much envied by peasants," were more complex and deserve to be investigated.[59]

The difficulty of understanding this phenomenon is compounded by the focus of historical scholarship on the later *grands magasins* which flourished under the Third Republic. But as pointed out by the interwar literary critic Walter Benjamin in his posthumous *Passagenwerk* (1982), the pioneering role of Paris in modern processes of commodification and commercialization predated Le Bon Marché by at least fifty years; hence Benjamin's interest in the arcaded and roofed commercial passages that proliferated in Paris under the Bourbon Restoration.[60] The first arcaded passage, *le passage des panoramas*, was in fact inaugurated in 1799, and tellingly it remained dedicated to the luxury and fashion trades for many decades. The name of the second passage, *du Caire*, inaugurated the same year, alluded to Bonaparte's conquest of Egypt, and the claim, frequently made by contemporaries, that its passages were modelled on Oriental bazaars, as well as the common use of Oriental decorative motifs, which were sometimes copied from the illustrations of the *Description de l'Egypte* (the major eventual by-product of Bonaparte's expedition, published between 1809 and 1828), helped give them an exotic, imperial flavour. The latter was often combined with spatial connections to Old Regime luxury, since most of the twenty-five passages opened between 1811 and 1839—by private entrepreneurs, but with the support of the Paris municipality—replaced churches and aristocratic hotels destroyed during the Revolution.[61]

59. Gabriel Tarde, *Les lois de l'imitation: étude sociologique* (Paris: Félix Alcan, 1890), 253–4.

60. Walter Benjamin, *The Arcades Project*, trans. Howard Eiland and Kevin McLaughlin (Cambridge, MA: Belknap Press, 1999), esp. 31–61.

61. Hazel Hahn, *Scenes of Parisian Modernity: Culture and Consumption in the Nineteenth Century* (Basingstoke: Palgrave Macmillan, 2009), 32–3; Jean-Claude Delorme and Anne-Marie Dubois, *Passages couverts parisiens*, 2nd edn (Paris: Parigramme, 2014), esp. 7–14, 37–8.

No less significant was the multiplication of *magasins de nouveautés* after 1800, specializing in fashionable clothes. These shops pioneered many of the marketing innovations often associated with the *grands magasins,* including elaborate window displays, spacious interiors, set prices, and a right to a full refund, not limited to damaged goods. After 1830, the *magasins de nouveautés* also grew rapidly in size, sometimes reaching enormous proportions, as in the case of À la Ville de Paris, opened in 1843 and intended to affirm, according to a notice in the press, France's "commercial preponderance in Europe."[62] Another advertisement claimed that the shop sold "everything that the textile industry produces," but that it showcased products "of the greatest luxury, opulent lace, cashmeres from the Indies, fabrics for furnishing, everything to make an opulent *corbeille* [the groom's gift basket to the bride]."[63] The scale of À la Ville de Paris, the artist Honoré Daumier suggested in a cartoon on new "monstrous" shops, would dazzle the "Foreigners in Paris," not unlike the pomp of the former Bourbon court, also designed to assert French supremacy and inspire awe across Europe.[64]

The conventional focus of the scholarship on Le Bon Marché and its grand opening in 1869 notwithstanding, Parisian department stores are best understood as the product of a continuous process.[65] This focus on continuity echoes the work of historical geographers, who have shown that even the wholesale "Haussmannization" of Parisian urban infrastructures after 1850 stemmed from decades of state and municipal planning: the era of Baron Haussmann, the mighty prefect of the Seine between 1853 and 1870, was not a rupture, but an acceleration of earlier efforts to turn Paris into the worthy

---

62. Hahn, *Scenes of Parisian Modernity,* 39.

63. Piedade Da Silveira, *Le magasin de nouveautés "À la ville de Paris"* (Fontenay-sous-Bois: Caisse de retraites des entreprises à commerces multiples, 1994), 17.

64. Honoré Daumier, "Les magasins de plus en plus monstres," *Le Charivari,* 18 Aug. 1844, part of Daumier's series "Les étrangers à Paris"; the cartoon, which shows a foreign bourgeois customer lost in the shop asking an assistant for directions, closely echoed a similar cartoon by Édouard de Beaumont , "Le magasin de la ville de Paris," published in *La Mode* in 1843; see Da Silveira, *Le magasin de nouveautés "A la ville de Paris,"* 3–4.

65. This focus owes much of course to the popularity of Emile Zola's novel, *Au Bonheur des Dames* (1883), about a fictitious *grand magasin* modelled on the Bon Marché. Le Bon Marché's main innovation was a more diverse range of merchandise, but textiles and clothes continued to make up the bulk of its sales until late in the nineteenth century; see Miller, *The Bon Marché,* 49–53.

(shop) window of France onto the world.[66] The roots of Paris's novel commercial infrastructures even predated the Revolution, since they lay in the wooden galleries of the Palais-Royal, commissioned by the Duc d'Orléans in 1784. From the Palais-Royal area, the new shopping infrastructures—*passages*, *magasins de nouveautés*, and eventually *grands magasins*—spread and radiated until they encompassed much of the western *beaux quartiers*.[67] This movement of expansion has sometimes been taken to demonstrate the loosening of the connection between the court and luxury trades.[68] But it can also be interpreted as the merging of the court into the city.

Arguably, this assumption of courtly functions by Paris began in the last decades of the Old Regime, as the Parisian salons, also governed by a rigorous if less formal etiquette, displaced Versailles as the setters of intellectual, artistic and clothing fashions.[69] The return of the court to Paris after the Revolution manifested the city's new dominance, but it also enabled the court to harness the city and regain a significant role in powering France's economy through lavish spending on urban infrastructures and festivities.[70] The absolutist courtly model, with its seat in Versailles, certainly shaped the course of French economic development in the early modern period. It could be said that the Bonapartist courtly model, by turning a large part of Paris into a court of sorts,

66. On urban planning under Napoleon, see Allan Potofsky, *Constructing Paris in the Age of Revolution* (Basingstoke: Palgrave MacMillan, 2009), 216–42, and under the July Monarchy, David Harvey, *Paris, Capital of Modernity* (New York: Routledge, 2003), 59–89; on the continuous trend underlying the transformation of commercial infrastructure, see Marie Gillet, "Innovation and Tradition in the Shopping Landscape of Paris and a Provincial City, 1800 to 1900," in *The Landscape of Consumption*, eds. Jan Hein Furnée and Clé Lesger (Basingstoke: Palgrave McMillan, 2014), 184–207. Another aspect of continuity was the commercial judicial infrastructures, which were very well suited to small and medium-sized French firms, especially in Paris; see Lemercier, "Un modèle de jugement des pairs," esp. 241–350 for a comparison with commercial justice in Britain and the United States.

67. Bernard Marrey, *Les grands magasins des origines à 1939* (Paris: Librarie Picard, 1979), 12–15.

68. Ffoulkes, "The *métier* of the Fashion Merchant," 165–86.

69. Antoine Lilti, *Le monde des salons: sociabilité et mondanité à Paris au XVIIIe siècle* (Paris: Fayard, 2005), esp. 137–43 on the role of the salons in delineating the *beaux quartiers*.

70. Philip Mansel, "Paris, Court City of the Nineteenth Century," *Court Historian*, 11 (2006); on lavish spending on art and craft works under Napoleon III, notably thanks to a civil list of more than 30 million francs a year, see Catherine Granger, *L'empereur et les arts. La liste civil de Napoléon III* (Paris: École des chartes, 2005).

multiplied those effects on patterns of consumption and production, so much so that France could serve as a global procurer of luxury.

Luxury entrepreneurs cultivated the monarchical flavour of their trade long after they ceased to depend on courtly patronage. Their propensity to choose names including "du roi," "de l'empereur" or the name of a specific dynasty for their shop or business, and often the relevant coats of arms on shops signs and invoices, even appears to have increased after 1830, with around five hundred shops bearing such a name in Paris by the end of the July Monarchy.[71] Until the 1820s, when the court and the aristocracy remained important clients of Parisian luxury trades, the names of new shops usually referred to the Orient, which was always evocative of luxury, or the title of a recent successful play, because the theatre stage and its actresses were a major influence on fashion.[72] Many of the new royal or imperial connections were of course as imaginary as the suggestion, in the advertising leaflet of César Birotteau in Honoré de Balzac's eponymous novel (1837), that the perfumer's latest cosmetic product, the *huile céphalique*, benefited from the patronage of King Charles X himself.[73] The recent champagne industry was also adept at stressing real or imaginary associations with the Old Regime. The mythical attribution of the invention of sparkling champagne to the late seventeenth-century Benedictine monk Dom Pierre Pérignon, whose monastery was dissolved and vandalized during the Revolution, dates from the 1820s. It was almost certainly designed to dispel memories of the stalwart support of the Champagne bourgeoisie for the Revolution and Napoleon's regime before 1815. But it endured through the

71. Mansel, "Paris, Court City": 17.

72. The Saint-Germain-des-Prés silk *nouveautés* shop Les Deux Magots de la Chine, founded at the end of the First Empire (and turned into the famous café, still in existence, Les Deux Magots in 1884), combined the two tactics, since its name alluded to a widely acclaimed play staged in 1813 as well as grotesque orientalizing figures on ornamental objects, or *magots*; see Piedade Da Silva, *Le magasin de nouveautés "Aux Deux Magots"* (Fontenay-sous-Bois: Caisse de retraites des entreprises à commerces multiples, 1993). On the persisting importance of aristocratic clientele for luxury shops in the 1820s, see Fiona Ffoulkes, "'Quality always distinguished itself': Louis Hyppolyte LeRoy and the Luxury Clothing Industry in Early Nineteenth-Century Paris," in *Consumers and Luxury*, eds. Berg and Clifford, 183–205.

73. *Histoire de la grandeur et de la décadence de César Birotteau* in Honoré de Balzac, *La Comédie Humaine*, 12 vols. (Paris: Gallimard, 1976–1981), vol. 6, 155–6; Balzac was sensitive to the change in contemporary marketing trends, since the name of Birotteau's earlier leading cosmetic product, the *double pâte des sultanes*, was evocative of Oriental luxury. On advertising in this novel, see Danielle Dupuis, "*César Birotteau*: de la publicité à la littérature," *L'année balzacienne*, 9, 1 (2008).

definitive fall of the Bourbons in 1830 and their Orléans cousins in 1848, probably due to the titillating contrast it drew with the frequent use of champagne in very secular contexts, especially in relation to seduction or debauchery.[74]

Champagne producers also cultivated a courtly or aristocratic image in the elaborate labels of champagne bottles, which were introduced in the mid-century as a means of reducing the sales of fraudulent champagne.[75] These labels almost always designated the bottle's contents as "imperial" or "royal," and frequently included monarchical symbols: the labels of bottles destined for Britain often included a lion and a unicorn, while those for domestic and other continental markets often depicted an eagle or a pair of bees, another element of Bonapartist heraldry.[76] The courtly undertones were sometimes more subtle, as in the case of a label deposited in 1859 for a "Cavalier" vintage of "Fleur de Sillery Grand Mousseux," complete with the depiction of a genteel seventeenth-century horseman, destined for the United States market.[77] Since self-identification with the royalist Cavaliers who had supported Charles I during the English Civil War and the castigation of New Englanders as Puritanical Roundheads were popular in the Antebellum American South, this label shows that French champagne producers were well informed about the political culture of their export markets.[78] Several labels of bottles destined for British India, including the vintages "Aux Indes Orientales" (1868) and "Gold Comet—Especially Adapted for India" (1873), suggest that champagne wine was consumed in sufficient quantity by Anglo-Indians to justify special *cuvées*.[79] They reinforce the sense that champagne was—or that its producers sought for it to be perceived as—a drink for dominant classes: European aristocrats and City bankers, but also American slave-owners and British colonial masters. Much like Parisian shops, champagne producers also used labels to

74. Guy, *When Champagne Became French*, 28–9.

75. Guy, *When Champagne Became French*, 17–19.

76. See the collection of champagne bottle labels deposited at the prefecture of the Marne, Châlons-en-Champagne, Archives Départementales de la Marne (henceforth ADM), 16 U 194; for an example of the use of monarchical and imperial symbols, see the label deposited by Henri Joseph Gaëtan Devenoge & Cie, wine merchants at Epernay, on 25 Nov. 1864 for the vintage "Gloria 1857," which depicted a Napoleonic eagle sitting atop the globe.

77. Label deposited by Henri Joseph Gaëtan Devenoge & Cie, 5 Nov. 1859, ADM, 16 U 194.

78. Susan S. Durant, "Cavalier Myth," in *The New Encyclopedia of Southern Culture*, 19 vols., eds. Charles R. Wilson, James G. Thomas Jr. and Ann J. Abadie (Chapel Hill: University of North Carolina Press, 2006), vol. 4: *Myth, Manners, and Memory*, 206–7.

79. Labels deposited by Devenoge & Cie, 26 July 1868 and 26 June 1877, ADM, 16 U 194.

highlight, whenever they could, their status as privileged providers of certain princely figures, including the Egyptian Khedive Isma'il (vintage "Souvenir d'Ouverture du Canal Maritime de Suez," 1869) or even, no doubt for bottles exclusively destined for export markets in the wake of the disastrous Franco-Prussian war, the German Kronprinz and future emperor Friedrich III (1876).[80]

Courtly commodification was not confined to silk *nouveautés* or champagne: it can be observed in countless other sectors of the French economy specialized in the provision of luxury or semi-luxury commodities and services. Examples range from cosmetics, especially perfumes, to jewellery, decorative bronzes, table silverware and crystal glasses.[81] In each case, the phenomenal growth of the industry's output (2,000 percent for perfumes between 1810 and 1862; 700 percent for bronzes between 1827 and 1860) was aided by significant technological innovations, such as the use of steam for the distillation of flower essences in the 1830s or electroplating for jewellery and silverware in the 1840s.[82] But it also relied on canny and relentless marketing. An anecdotal but telling example, given France's modern reputation as a land of succulent cheeses, of how this specialization transformed the French economy was the invention of Roquefort as a gourmet cheese. Until the early-nineteenth century, France's cheese output was very low by European standards and French cheeses had a poor reputation—until the 1820s, Parisian restaurants mostly served foreign cheeses, such as English Cheshire. The *philosophe* Denis Diderot is sometimes credited as having begun the reappraisal of Roquefort as "Europe's first cheese," for the sophistication of its methods of production as much as for its taste. But it only became popular with Parisian gourmets under the July Monarchy, and exports became a substantial outlet in the 1860s,

80. Labels deposited by Jean Roussillon & Cie, 14 Sep. 1869, and Devenoge & Cie, 25 Sep. 1876, ADM 16 U 194.

81. Most Parisian companies which prospered in the mid-nineteenth century were founded in the last decades of the Old Regime; see Alain Plessis, "Au temps du Second Empire, de l'entreprise de luxe au sommet des affaires," in *Le luxe en France*, ed. Marseille, 49–62, and Pierre Goubert, *Du luxe au confort* (Paris: Belin, 1988), 47–8; on the Old Regime roots of the French cosmetics industry, see Morag Martin, *Selling Beauty: Cosmetics, Commerce and French Society, 1750–1830* (Baltimore, MD: Johns Hopkins University Press, 2009).

82. Francis Démier, "Du luxe au demi-luxe, la réussite des bronziers parisiens au XIXe siècle," in *Le luxe en France*, ed. Marseille, 63–91; Eugénie Briot, *La fabrique des parfums. Naissance d'une industrie de luxe* (Paris: Vendémiaire, 2015), 80–1, 131–60; Bergeron, *Les industries du luxe*, 41–50.

especially, once again, to Britain—the destination of one third of Roquefort exports by 1882.[83]

A less flippant example, almost entirely disconnected from technological progress, was the affirmation of Paris as the world capital of commodified love and sex. The French state's exceptional tolerance—officially on grounds of public health—of prostitution, which ceased to be a criminal offence in 1810, contributed to what was probably a well-deserved reputation. The 1823 "Charter of Tolerance" of the Paris *prefecture de police* for brothels became the symbol of such leniency. But the number of brothels in France steadily declined after 1840, and only those specializing in rare practices or spectacular debauchery continued to prosper.[84] More significant was the growing social tolerance for venal love in Paris and other urban centres. The courtly origins of courtesans, or women kept by one or several lovers, are fairly obvious. The number of courtesans grew in the second half of the eighteenth century, with the Palais-Royal becoming Paris's hot spot for this elegant form of prostitution, as well as of most luxury trades, after 1780.[85] As with other luxurious commodities, the taste for venal or partly venal love spread from the aristocracy to the middle classes in the mid-nineteenth century. A gradient of names—*demi-mondaines, lionnes, cocottes, lorettes, grisettes,* and so on—served to denote different levels of involvement, from being a woman's principal economic activity to an occasional practice, and differences in the woman's social station and that of her partners. This world of venal love remained closely connected to several other aspects of the French specialization in luxury, from the popularity of champagne in brothels to the launching of new fashions—a speciality of *cocottes,* whose patrons were frequently entrepreneurs in the *nouveautés* business—to the ranks of *modistes* (shop assistants) and actresses, which is where the majority of *grisettes* and *lorettes* came from.[86]

83. Sylvie Fabre, *Le sacre du Roquefort: l'émergence d'une industrie agroalimentaire* (Rennes: Presses universitaires de Rennes and Tours: Presses universitaires François Rabelais de Tours, 2015), 79, 279.

84. Jill Harsin, *Policing Prostitution in Nineteenth-Century Paris* (Princeton, NJ: Princeton University Press, 1985).

85. Nina Kushner, *Erotic Exchanges: The World of Elite Prostitution in Eighteenth-Century Paris* (Ithaca, NY: Cornell University Press, 2013).

86. Alain Corbin, *Les filles de noce: misère sexuelle et prostitution, XIXe siècle,* 2nd edn (Paris: Flammarion, 2015), 235–86; see also Emmanuel Pierrat, *Les lorettes: Paris, capitale mondiale des plaisirs au XIXe siècle* (Paris: Le Passage, 2013) and, on fashion and prostitution, Françoise

However, the most compelling example of the commodification of French taste is probably the emergence of France as the country of gastronomy and restaurants in the early-nineteenth century. Much like other aspects of France's specialization in luxury or semi-luxury, the refinement and codification of cooking, combined with a desire to make this cuisine accessible to a wider-paying public, only dated from the second half of the eighteenth century. The first restaurants, in contrast with mere *tables d'hôtes*, opened in the Palais-Royal neighbourhood in the 1770s. They fared poorly during the Terror, but their numbers grew rapidly from the mid-1790s onwards, even though late into the nineteenth century they remained heavily concentrated in Paris. Grimod de la Reynière, a minor *philosophe* who was partial to practical jokes, popularized the ideal of the *gourmet* in his scandalous *Almanach des gourmands* during the Napoleonic Empire. Under the Bourbon Restoration, Jean Anthelme Brillat-Savarin's aphoristic *Physiology of Taste* (1825) made gastronomy respectable, and the chef Antoine Carême codified the new French cuisine in several works, culminating in his posthumous *L'art de la cuisine française au dix-neuvième siècle* (1833).[87] Good food, however, was far from being the sole interest of Grimod, Brillat-Savarin and Carême, who had previously been, respectively, the owner of a Lyon perfume and lace business, a liberal political economist, and an ardent supporter of the urban regeneration of Paris.[88] Similarly, when the restaurants' customers recounted their experience, they had surprisingly little to say about what they ate, and much more to say about the luxurious setting and licentious atmosphere of these quintessentially Parisian venues.[89] In gastronomy, as in many other French industries, what was commodified was much less material than in traditional accounts of the Industrial Revolution. And the much-vaunted Frenchness of these commodities

---

Tétart-Vittu, "Femmes du Monde et du demi-monde," in Musée de la mode de la Ville de Paris, *Sous l'empire des crinolines* (Paris: Paris musées, 2008), 30–7.

87. Rebecca L. Spang, *The Invention of the Restaurant: Paris and Modern Gastronomic Culture* (Cambridge, MA: Harvard University Press, 2000); Priscilla Parkhurst Ferguson, *Accounting for Taste: The Triumph of French Cuisine* (Chicago: University of Chicago Press, 2004), 49–82.

88. On Grimod's career in the luxury trade, see Giles MacDonogh, *A Palate in Revolution: Grimond de La Reynière* (London: Robin Clark, 1987), 37–8 and Ned Rival, *Grimod de la Reynière: le gourmand gentilhomme* (Paris: Le pré aux clercs, 1983), 85–93; on their enthusiasm for modern commerce, see Jean-Anthelme Brillat-Savarin, *Vues et projets d'économie politique* (Paris: Gignet et Michaud, 1801) and Marie-Antoine Carême, *Projet d'architecture pour l'embellissement de Paris*, 5 vols. (Paris: F. Didot père et fils, 1821–1826).

89. Spang, *The Invention of the Restaurant*, 197–8.

notwithstanding, their purchasers and consumers were, in rapidly increasing numbers, foreigners.

The Global Commodification of French Taste

The commodification of French taste has been studied extensively, but usually as an endogenous process designed to cultivate a sense of national identity, with the tacit complicity of the nation-state.[90] The chronological emphasis of most existing studies at the end of the nineteenth century may account for the domination of this interpretation, because the Third Republic was engaged in an overt and intensive project of nation-building.[91] However as noted above, the rapid expansion of French luxury and semi-luxury sectors took place in the middle rather than at the end of the nineteenth century. After the 1870s, these industries often saw their output stagnate or decline. *Fin-de-siècle* nationalist marketing should perhaps be viewed instead as an attempt to compensate for the decline of foreign demand, a trend which is also reflected in the adoption of a more protectionist commercial policy after 1890.[92] Above all, the prevailing focus on the later-nineteenth century obscures the cosmopolitan and conservative rather than national and republican origins of the commodification of French taste.

Taste, as well as colour, is mainly in the eye of the beholder. Any (tasteful) twenty-first-century observer who examines examples of nineteenth-century French fashion designs or decorative bronzes, or tries to imagine the somewhat stilted atmosphere of rooms overflowing with gilding and mirrors in nineteenth-century French restaurants, or who reads Carême's recipes (which almost invariably relied on rich sauces) is unlikely to feel seized by a frantic desire to purchase clothes or dine out. Similarly, the gaudiness of silk dresses with complex motifs and the overabundance of Orientalizing trinkets in the

---

90. Guy, *When Champagne Became French*, 10–39; for a broader attempt to trace the origins of French taste, although still confined to the late nineteenth century and France itself, see Lisa Tiersen, *Marianne in the Market: Envisioning Consumer Society in Fin-de-Siècle France* (Berkeley: University of California Press, 2001).

91. Eugen Weber, *Peasants into Frenchmen: The Modernization of Rural France, 1870–1914* (Stanford, CA: Stanford University Press, 1976).

92. On French protectionist policies as a means of maintaining French specialization rather than promoting new industries, see Léo Charles, "Protection, spécialisation et croissance économique pendant la première mondialisation en France et en Suisse (1850–1913)," (unpublished PhD thesis, University of Bordeaux, 2016).

background of contemporary women's portraits tend to befuddle modern viewers, even when the subject was a high-society woman who enjoyed the reputation of a queen of fashion, as in Dominique Ingres's masterful portrait of Marie-Clotilde Moitessier (née de Foucauld), the wife of a Second Empire Paris banker.[93] In fact, spending a lot of time looking at or thinking about nineteenth-century French luxury helps us understand the extent to which our current conception of what is tasteful or even luxurious relies on the rejection of mid-nineteenth-century French canons. This process of rejection began with criticisms of the Parisian artistic avant-garde in the second half of the century, intensified with intellectual movements such as the Frankfurt School in the early-twentieth century (Walter Benjamin's fascination with the modernity of nineteenth-century Paris was, to a large extent, a horrified fascination), and arguably triumphed after the 1970s, when French *haute cuisine* and *haute couture* lost the near monopoly they had exercised over good taste.

If France is still perceived today as a leading light of plastic and decorative arts in the nineteenth century, it is mainly due to the emergence of new experimental trends in the 1860s, though they only gained public recognition after 1880. The collection of the Museum of Orsay, one of the most popular grand museums opened in the twentieth century, comprises very few works by the representatives of French academic *beaux-arts*: only four paintings by Ingres, for instance, and three by Jean-Léon Gérôme, two of the most widely acclaimed painters of the years 1840 to 1870. By contrast, Orsay's collection includes forty-eight paintings by Gustave Courbet, thirty-four by Édouard Manet, eighty-six by Claude Monet, and eighty-one by Pierre-Auguste Renoir.[94] The Museum of Orsay and its success represents a revenge of sorts on the famous *salon des refusés*, held in 1863 alongside the official *salon* just across the Seine in the Palais de l'Industrie (built to host the 1855 universal exhibition), during which art critics and crowds heaped ridicule on the innovative approaches of Courbet, Manet and their followers. Yet the triumph of impressionism and other *avant-gardiste* trends during the Third Republic did not translate into commercial success for France's decorative and luxury

93. Dominique Ingres, *Madame Moitessier* (1856), National Gallery, London; the portrait can be viewed here: https://www.nationalgallery.org.uk/paintings/jean-auguste-dominique-i ngres-madame-moitessier (accessed 26 Mar. 2019). On the sitter and her portrait, see Aileen Ribeiro, *Ingres in Fashion* (New Haven, CT: Yale University Press, 1999), 163–9.

94. Catalogue of works of the Musée d'Orsay, http://www.musee-orsay.fr/fr/collections /catalogue-des-oeuvres/ (accessed 9 Nov. 2017).

industries.[95] On the contrary, it corresponded with the decline of France's specialization in the procurement of luxurious and semi-luxurious commodities. According to the statistics of foreign trade, it was the earlier, more flamboyant incarnation of French taste that conquered the global market.

The economic significance of this successful specialization between 1830 and 1870 should not be underestimated. The argument so far has focused on Paris, due to the fact that good taste was mainly fashioned in the capital city, and a large amount of luxury was consumed there by visiting foreigners and provincial Frenchmen or women, as well as Parisians. Yet this specialization affected many other parts of France. Not only did provincial consumers emulate Parisian fashion, but the prodigious rise in demand for these commodities radically transformed the economic conditions of many French regions. The prosperity of Lyon and Saint-Etienne relied increasingly on the fabrication of silk textiles, with the number of looms more than trebling between 1815 and 1847.[96] The economy of the Rhône valley was also upended by the spread of the mulberry tree (host of the silk worm, and therefore the source of raw silk), which displaced a previously widespread domestic system of cotton spinning.[97] Alsace's economy became increasingly dependent on the export of high-quality patterned cotton textiles, a specialty of Mulhouse, the population of which rose from six thousand in 1800 to fifty thousand in 1860.[98] The making of fine wines was a major source of economic growth in Champagne, Burgundy and the Bordelais, the harvesting of flowers (the main raw material for the production of perfumes) in Provence, and the integration of sheep breeding with industrial caves for the maturing of Roquefort in the Rouergue (Massif Central). Integration into the global market was not a purely Parisian phenomenon, and rapid economic change was far from limited to the growth of large-scale manufacturing or mining in northern or eastern France.

95. On the republican affinity of "the new painting" until the 1880s, see Philip Nord, *Impressionists and Politics: Art and Democracy in the Nineteenth Century* (London: Routledge, 2000), 11–35; on the Bonapartist government's attempts to harness the fine arts for political ends, see Patricia Mainardi, *Art and Politics of the Second Empire: The Universal Expositions of 1855 and 1867* (New Haven, CT: Yale University Press, 1987).

96. Cayez, *Métiers Jacquard*, 143–4.

97. Jean-François Klein, *Les maîtres du comptoir: Desgrand père et fils (1720–1878)* (Paris: Presses de l'Université Paris Sorbonne, 2013), 120–1, 227.

98. Georges Livet and Raymond Oberlé, *Histoire de Mulhouse des origines à nos jours* (Strasbourg: Edition des Dernières Nouvelles d'Alsace, 1977), 173; Michel Hau, *L'industrialisation de l'Alsace* (Strasbourg: Publications près les universités de Strasbourg, 1987), 75–91.

Nor was the commodification of French good taste a purely economic, apolitical phenomenon. Perhaps unsurprisingly, the promotion of luxury and support for France's specialization as provider of luxurious commodities to the rest of the world was connected in multiple ways to a preference for a monarchical and conservative, if not necessarily illiberal, settlement of post-revolutionary French politics. The political movement for free trade that emerged in the 1840s, culminating in the foundation of an Association pour la Liberté des Echanges in 1846, was far more conservative than the British Corn Law League of Richard Cobden. Frédéric Bastiat, the leader of this "French League," upheld radical views, but he abandoned the campaign when the banking and commercial interests that financed it prevented him from giving his propaganda "a sufficiently democratic direction."[99] The Lyonnais silk merchant-manufacturers enjoyed their well-earned reputation for pious Catholicism that was often combined with *légitimiste* support for the elder branch of the Bourbons. The Bordelais vineyard proprietors were also intensely royalist in the early years of the Bourbon Restoration, before becoming ardent supporters of a very conservative brand of Orléaniste liberalism in the mid-century. The champagne producers fervently supported the First and Second Napoleonic Empire. The Mulhouse manufacturers were almost all Protestant and upheld more progressive opinions, but they proved fiercely hostile to the ephemeral democratic Second Republic of 1848–1851.[100] Of course, protectionist cotton and wool manufacturers were hardly enthusiastic about democratic republicanism. But perhaps because they focused on the domestic market, they found it easier to accommodate and influence republican regimes. Adolphe Thiers, the liberal politician who best symbolizes this flexibility, presiding as he did over the foundation of the Third Republic after 1870, was closely connected to protectionist lobbies.[101]

The nineteenth-century politics of French luxury were not unlike Talleyrand's: they were malleable, in the sense that they were not tied to a particular faction, but not unprincipled, being based on a sincere abomination of popular

---

99. Todd, *Free Trade and Its Enemies*, 200–201; on the democratic undertones of Cobdenism, see Anthony Howe, *Free Trade and Liberal England* (Oxford: Clarendon Press, 1997).

100. On the politics of these regional bourgeoisies, see André-Jean Tudesq, *Les grands notables en France, 1840–1849. Étude historique d'une psychologie sociale*, 2 vols. (Paris: Presses Universitaires de France, 1964).

101. Todd, *Free Trade and Its Enemies*, 125–9, 223–4.

demagoguery and a dislike of the excesses of personal rule.[102] Talleyrand's own sophisticated taste for luxury is well known, and Carême's rise to fame as the inventor of *haute cuisine* owed a great deal to his nearly two-decade-long employment as the chef of Talleyrand's household. Talleyrand even experimented with culinary diplomacy when he loaned Carême to the British Prince Regent and the Russian Czar after the fall of Napoleon.[103] The once-popular notion that restaurants were invented by impoverished aristocrats has been shown to be a myth. But during the Revolution, restaurants were not unfairly perceived as nests of royalist conspiracies, and many chefs learnt their trade in aristocratic households. The phrase "gastro-liberalism," used to describe the main thrust of Brillat-Savarin's *Physiology of Taste*, captures well the political undertones of the exaltation of good taste in post-revolutionary France. It was liberal in the sense that it valued the pursuit of pleasure and individual freedom, especially economic freedom, but it was also wary of revolution, sometimes to the point of skepticism about the virtues of political liberty.[104] This gastro-liberalism may be construed as a practical version of the more sophisticated concern of contemporary liberal thinkers, from Benjamin Constant and François Guizot to Michel Chevalier, with the excesses of democracy. Alexis de Tocqueville, who upheld a more conciliatory attitude towards the progress of equality, worried instead about the corrupting effects of materialism and ostentation.[105] During his trip to America, he sometimes mocked the poor taste—in dress, food or music—of even educated New Yorkers, but it was the doomed Native Americans who, due to their elaborate make-up and ornamental jewellery, were dismissed as "les plus *fashionable*."[106]

102. Talleyrand served three constitutional monarchies, the moderate Republican Directory and the First Napoleon Empire, and it is difficult to imagine him refusing to serve Napoleon III; the only regime Talleyrand would not serve was the Montagnard Republic, and he broke with Napoleon in 1808.

103. Ferguson, *Accounting for Taste*, 56–7.

104. Spang, *The Invention of the Restaurant*, 118; on the counterrevolutionary undertones of gastronomy, see also Emma Spary, *Feeding France: New Sciences of Food, 1760–1815* (Cambridge: Cambridge University Press, 2014), 235–67.

105. André Jardin, *Alexis de Tocqueville* (Paris: Hachette, 1984), 353–67; on the Jansenist roots of his moral ideas, see Lucien Jaume, *Tocqueville. Les sources aristocratiques de la liberté* (Paris: Fayard, 2008), esp. 207–16.

106. Alexis de Tocqueville to his sister-in-law, Émilie de Tocqueville, 7 Sep. 1831, in Alexis de Tocqueville, *Œuvres complètes*, ed. Jean-Pierre Mayer et al., 18 vols. (Paris: Gallimard, 1951–2003), vol. 14, 132.

Such conservative undertones are important when one tries to understand the appeal of French good taste, outside as well as within France. Insofar as it was informed by political and social concerns, and notwithstanding the conventional perception of nineteenth-century France as a source of radical ideas, this taste for French commodities was anti-revolutionary. The proliferation of *demi-luxe* or *populuxe* commodities is sometimes cited as a form of democratization.[107] But most consumers of such commodities belonged to the middle classes, and *demi-luxe* essentially served to elevate the latter above the toiling masses, whose patterns of consumption remained dominated by necessity. In other words, French good taste helped to aristocratize emerging bourgeoisie at least as much as this bourgeoisie democratized consumption.[108] It is not coincidental that the global boom in French commodities between 1840 and 1870 corresponded with the rapid expansion of new dominant classes, of a bourgeois or neo-aristocratic type, in several parts of the world. The growing share of Britain (excluding its colonial possessions) as a destination for French export, from 11 percent in 1835 to 33 percent in 1865, reflected a surge in the numbers of middle-class British consumers. Conversely, the United States' share collapsed after the fall of the Cotton Kingdom, from 15 percent in the 1850s to 7.5 percent in the early 1870s. This decline of American demand was only partly compensated by the rise of new plantocracies, for instance in Egypt, whose share in French exports quintupled, thanks to the proceeds of a boom in cotton cultivation, from 0.4 to 2 percent between 1852 and 1864.[109]

The conspicuous nature of French commodities and their consumption as an instrument of social distinction also helps to explain the growing popularity of French language and culture in the nineteenth century, across Europe and beyond. Trade statistics do not capture these exports, but chapter 5 will show that cultural influence indirectly brought significant financial and commercial advantages to French economic agents. Moreover, changes in the sort of French cultural products enjoyed outside France are suggestive of what the sociologist Theodor Veblen would have called their invidious function,

107. See for instance Gilles Lipotevski, *L'empire de l'éphémère: la mode et son destin dans les sociétés modernes* (Paris: Gallimard, 1987).

108. On the conspicuous and other functions of luxury goods in the eighteenth century, see Kwass, "Big Hair": 657–8.

109. The share of two other slavocracies, Brazil and Cuba, in French exports, was larger in per capita terms than that of other Latin American countries, but declining in this period, from respectively 3.3 percent and 1.6 percent in 1852 to 2.6 and 0.9 percent in 1864 (my calculations, based on Direction des Douanes, *Tableau décennal*).

because they closely reflected the gradual transformation of European social structures. In the eighteenth century, most Europeans who learnt French and frequently consumed French cultural products were members of court-attending aristocracies.[110] But from the early 1800s, French, often Paris-based writers and artists began to export a new range of middle- rather than high-brow cultural products, accessible to a wider (bourgeois) audience, which was still far from being a universal (mass) audience. These products were often not even originally French. The novel, for instance, had first appeared in the Anglophone and Germanic worlds, but from the 1820s onwards, novelists such as Honoré de Balzac, Alexandre Dumas *père*, Eugène Sue and other masters of the suspenseful *roman-feuilleton* garnered a European-wide audience.[111] Equally typical of this new form of commodified cultural influence was the extraordinary popularity, beyond French borders, of new theatre genres, highly sentimental and often licentious. Success in Paris, which counted twice as many theatre seats per inhabitant as London in the 1850s, ensured production in a dozen French-language theatres in European capital cities, as well as in Constantinople and Alexandria. This was followed by the production of adapted translations in countless theatres throughout and beyond Europe.[112] *La Dame aux Camélias* (1852), the scandalous and melodramatic story of a Paris courtesan by Alexandre Dumas *fils*, toured the world's stages, reaching Melbourne, Australia, in an English-language, expurgated version in 1856.[113]

110. On the politics of the exportation of French culture before the Revolution, see Rahul Markovits, *Civiliser l'Europe: politiques du théâtre français au XVIIIe siècle* (Paris: Fayard, 2014).

111. On the ascent of French novels in Western and, to a lesser extent, global culture, see Franco Moretti, *Atlas of the European Novel, 1800–1900* (London: Verso, 1998), esp. 185–6, and Pascale Casanova, *La république mondiale des lettres* (Paris: Le Seuil, 1999). Even the Victorian British readers consumed French novels on a larger scale than previously thought; see Juliette Atkison, *French Novels and the Victorians* (Oxford: Oxford University Press, 2017). On French literary exports, and growing royalties for French authors thanks to the emergence of an international copyrights legislation after 1850, see Frédéric Barbier, "Les marchés étrangers de la librairie française," in *Histoire de l'édition française*, eds. Roger Chartier and Henri-Jean Martin, 4 vols. (Paris: Fayard, 1982–1986), vol. 3: *Le temps des éditeurs. Du romantisme à la Belle Époque*, 268–81.

112. Christophe Charle, *Théâtres en capitales: naissance de la société du spectacle à Paris, Berlin, Londres et Vienne, 1860–1914* (Paris: Albin Michel, 2008), 309–52.

113. Charles Sowerwine, "Échos de Paris aux Antipodes: le théâtre et l'opéra français à Melbourne (1850–1914)," in *Le théâtre français à l'étranger au XIXe siècle. Histoire d'une suprématie culturelle*, ed. Jean-Claude Yon (Paris: Nouveau Monde, 2008), 255–80.

A remarkable example of the commodification of French culture, suggestive of the role played by this process in the dissemination of French taste
among the world's bourgeoisie, is the refashioning of the *vaudeville* genre by
the then-prodigiously popular and now almost entirely forgotten playwright
Eugène Scribe. Between 1830 and 1860, a quarter of all the plays staged in
Naples were authored or co-authored by Scribe. Even in Britain, where the
influence of French theatre was not so keenly felt, two of his plays were translated or adapted more than a dozen times. The peak of Scribe's career was his
sojourn in London, where he was much feted by London society in May and
June of 1850. Scribe's particular genius was as commercial as it was artistic, and
it is suggestive that both his father and his brother were merchants of silk
nouveautés. The rise of *vaudeville* shows many similarities with the story of
other popular French commodities. Inspired by the still-courtly comedies of
Beaumarchais and Marivaux in the late eighteenth century, it became respectable thanks to the patronage of the Duchesse de Berry, wife and later mother
of the presumptive heir to Charles X, in the 1820s. Women were the main
(though not exclusive) consumers of Scribe's plays, leading the aesthete and
misogynist writer Jules Barbey d'Aurevilly to dismiss them as the literary
equivalents of "trinkets" and "shawls," while Scribe's disciple Ludovic Halévy
hailed *vaudeville* as another "article de Paris." Even Scribe's politics, which
combined a mild preference for liberal institutions with a profound distaste
for revolutionary radicalism, recall the gastro-liberalism of Brillat-Savarin and
the tactical suppleness of Talleyrand.[114]

Of course, foreign consumers of French material or immaterial semi-
luxurious commodities were not just passive recipients: they too played an active role in the shaping of French good (or good French) taste. As commodification became more reliant on foreign demand, its modalities were increasingly
shaped by foreign borrowing or preferences. One of the secrets of Scribe's
global success was his avid reading of foreign plays. The contents of Scribe's
enormous library suggest that Stendhal's analysis of the playwright's method
was essentially correct: "Mr Scribe picks up all the best crafted comedies from
Germany, Italy, England and Spain, and he draws from them small French plays
in a single act that can be staged in about three quarters of an hour."[115] Another
example of decisive foreign influence on what passed as French taste was the

114. Jean-Claude Yon, *Eugène Scribe: la fortune et la liberté* (Paris: Librairie Nizet, 2000), 21–2,
76, 237–49, 268–77.

115. Quoted in Yon, *Eugène Scribe*, 86.

creation of new, drier varieties of champagne, such as *brut* and *demi-sec* in the 1860s, to satisfy the preference of British and American consumers, while in France champagne was traditionally a sweetened dessert wine. Today *brut* and *demi-sec* are the most common varieties of champagne, but for a time they were only available on the British and American markets.[116] So much for the quintessential Frenchness of this and many other French commodities, and even commercial infrastructures, as arcaded passages and department stores were sometimes explicitly acknowledged to be modelled on Oriental bazaars.[117]

Another factor involving foreign agency in the global commodification of French taste was the rise of international tourism. Northern European and especially British aristocrats had gone on Grand Tours across France and Italy since the late seventeenth century, but after 1815 the more affluent sections of the British and other middle classes began to travel for leisure, albeit for shorter durations and in a less lavish style. France asserted itself as a favoured destination and Paris as a must-see.[118] As with international trade in material commodities, the two decades following 1850 witnessed an acceleration of the influx of British tourists on the continent, thanks to the spread of railways but also to the abolition of passport controls for British subjects entering France in 1861. In 1866, approximately one hundred and twenty thousand Britons, many of them tourists, visited France.[119] According to available estimates, France's net income from tourism rose tenfold between the 1820s and the 1860s, and in the latter decade it surpassed the trade surplus in goods.[120] Tourists

---

116. Desbois-Thibault, *L'extraordinaire aventure*, 135.

117. See section above on the neo-courtly foundations of French economic growth and, on the reciprocal influence of French and Middle-Eastern commercial infrastructures, Uri M. Kupferschmidt, *European Department Stores and Middle Eastern Consumers: The Orosdi-Back Saga* (Istanbul: Ottman Bank Archives and Research Centre, 2007), esp. 12–14.

118. On the beginning of international tourism in France, see Paul Gerbod, "Les touristes étrangers à Paris dans la première moitié du XIXe siècle," *Bulletin de la société de l'histoire de Paris et de l'Ile de France*, 110 (1983), and on British tourism in France in the mid-nineteenth century, see Paul Gerbod, *Voyages au pays des mangeurs de grenouilles. La France vue par les Britanniques du XVIIIe siècle à nos jours* (Paris: Albin Michel, 1991), 108–29. Thomas Cook began offering organized travel to Paris in the early 1860s; see Lynne Whitney, *Grand Tours and Cook's Tours: A History of Leisure Travel, 1750 to 1915* (London: Aurum Press, 1998), 146–50.

119. That year, French customs recorded 240,000 arrivals and departures of British subjects; cited in *Gagliani's New Paris Guide for 1867* (Paris: A. and W. Gagliani, 1867), 1–2.

120. Maurice Lévy-Leboyer, "La balance des paiements et l'exportation des capitaux français," in *La position internationale de la France. Aspects économiques et financiers*, ed. Maurice Lévy-Leboyer (Paris: EHESS, 1977), 75–142: 119–120.

were particularly important customers for the high end of the luxury sector, such as *haute couture*.[121] Tourists also contributed to French prosperity, we can presume, by bringing home a new or renewed taste for French commodities, which in turn sustained French exports. The good reputation of French taste was as much a product of foreign appreciation as of the inherent qualities of French commodities, making the French empire of taste, like most empires, a fundamentally transnational enterprise.

The Imperialism of the Empire of Taste

Few would deny that nineteenth-century France ruled over an empire of fashion (at least Western women's fashion) and governed the empire of taste in Europe and, increasingly, those parts of the world that were under European domination. These phrases recurred in contemporary discourses, as they do in modern historical scholarship. But many, including some of those who have used the phrase, would disagree that this system of economic and cultural domination should be considered an empire in the full, more political sense of the term, comparable to the earlier Roman or the contemporary British empire. The word "empire" in this instance is likely to be dismissed as a metaphor used to convey the crushing extent of French cultural domination. At best, some will suggest, this was a consolatory empire, essentially rhetorical, designed to assuage wounded national pride after the loss of real, territorial empires in 1763 or 1815. However, it is also very tempting to take the use of the word "empire" seriously, and highlight what was authentically imperial about French economic and cultural domination. Two imperial traits stand out. The first, given that all empires are collaborative yet hierarchical enterprises between different national or ethnic groups, is the contribution of numerous non-French auxiliaries to the dynamics of champagne capitalism; the second is the French state's overtly political utilization of champagne capitalism's successes, especially under Napoleon III, in a bid to assert French supremacy in some parts of the world, or merely to proclaim France's status as global overlord.

This is not to deny that the refined or tasteful empire of champagne capitalism played a consolatory role. In fact, it is striking how many possibly apoc-

---

121. Customers of *haute couture* houses in the 1860s were often "foreigners staying at a hotel," according to Françoise Tétart-Vittu, "The French-English Go Between: 'Le Modèle de Paris' or the Beginning of the Designer, 1820–1880," *Costume*, 26, 1 (1992): 42.

ryphal stories, which all showed the French luxury industries mitigating the humiliations of 1814–1815, were circulated in subsequent years. The most famous is the one attributing champagne's popularity in Russia to Veuve Clicquot's patriotic attempts to inebriate the Cossack regiments that invaded eastern France in 1814.[122] Another is the tale of the Prussian general Blücher, the victor, alongside the Duke of Wellington, of the battle of Waterloo in 1815, who allegedly lost most of his wealth—around 1.5 million francs—gambling in the fashionable brothels of the Palais-Royal in subsequent months.[123] Yet another is that of Talleyrand obtaining, during the negotiations of the First Treaty of Paris in 1814, the crucial recognition of French cheese as the best in Europe by ministers of the Allied powers.[124] More generally, the notion that the hundreds of thousands of foreign soldiers who occupied northern France between 1815 and 1818 acquired an indelible taste for fine French products, entertainment and women, was often repeated in later celebrations of the commercial success of French luxury or semi-luxury industries, and may contain a grain of truth.[125]

Foreigners were not only morally vanquished by the bedazzling array of pleasures produced by champagne capitalism. More and more frequently as the century went on, they also became active participants in the production of French commodities. An outstanding example is that of Charles Worth, an Englishman born in rural Lincolnshire, who has often been hailed, with some exaggeration, as the inventor of Parisian *haute couture*. In reality, Worth's main talent lay in his ability to commercialize high fashion on an industrial scale, with the help of his Swedish partner, Otto Bobergh, and his French wife, Marie Vernet. Founded in the early 1850s, by 1870 Worth's house counted 1,200 employees. The pace of Worth's ascent, from an apprenticeship with a draper near

122. For a contemporary iteration of this legend, see Victor Fiévet, *Madame Veuve Clicquot (née Ponsardin), son histoire et celle de sa famille* (Paris: Dentu, 1865), 60–1. In reality, exports of champagne to Russia started at the end of the eighteenth century and took off between 1802 and 1808; see Michel Etienne, *Veuve Clicquot*, 123–4.

123. The story is repeated in Russell T. Barnhart, "Gambling in Revolutionary Paris: The Palais Royal: 1789–1838," *Journal of Gambling Studies*, 8, 2 (1992): 161; in reality, and although he effectively spent a great deal of time gambling at the Palais-Royal, Blücher appears to have left the French capital with winnings amounting to 19,000 thalers, see Michael V. Leggiere, *Blücher: Scourge of Napoleon* (Norman: University of Oklahoma Press, 2014), 363.

124. Vabre, *Le sacre du Roquefort*, 52.

125. On memories of these years, see Christine Haynes, "Remembering and Forgetting the First Modern Occupations of France," *Journal of Modern History*, 88, 3 (2016).

London's Picadilly Circus, was unusual, but his foreign background less so.[126] At the same time as Worth reigned over high fashion, Cora Pearl, born in Devon under the name of Eliza Crouch, imposed herself as the queen of Parisian courtesans. Her conquests included the Duc de Morny, the illegitimate half-brother of Napoleon III and possible grandson of Talleyrand, and Prince Napoleon, a cousin of the emperor, two extremely influential figures of the regime. Pearl was closely identified with the era's moral turpitudes, and after the scandal caused by the attempted suicide of a ruined lover, she was expelled from France in 1873.[127] We can recognize several of her features, under a male but still British guise, in the character of Robert Jenkins in Alphonse Daudet's novel about the dubious *moeurs* of the 1860s, *Le Nabab* (1877): Jenkins, a "fashionable doctor" and Paris's "busiest man," owed his popularity with the regime's grandees to the aphrodisiac pills which he marketed as *perles* (pearls).[128]

Worth, Pearl and the imaginary Jenkins were archetypal rather than exceptional. There were nearly three times as many foreign residents in Paris as in London (119,000 versus 41,000) in the 1860s, and due to London's larger size (2.8 versus 2.1 million), their share in the city's population was four times as high (5.7 percent versus 1.4 percent).[129] The multi-authored *Paris-Guide* of 1867, with a preface by Victor Hugo, returned time and time again to this extensive foreign presence, what made Paris "the caravanserai of the world," ac-

126. Diana de Marly, *The History of Haute Couture* (London: Batsford, 1980), 14–23; the heroic account of Worth's invention of haute couture owes much to the family legend reported by Jean-Philippe Worth in his *A Century of Fashion* (Boston: Little, Brown & Co., 1928).

127. Wilfred H. Holden, *The Pearl from Plymouth* (London: British Technical and General Press, 1950), esp. 39–40 on Pearl's professional handling of accounting and business-like treatment of her lovers; see also Virginia Rounding, *Grandes Horizontales: The Lives and Legends of Marie Duplessis, Cora Pearl, La Païva and La Présidente* (London: Bloomsbury, 2003), 195–228.

128. Alphonse Daudet, *Le Nabab* (Paris: Charpentier, 1877), 1, and on the corrosive effects these pills had on the moral as well as the physical health of those who took them, see ch. 18 "Les perles Jenkins," 339–62; the character of Jenkins was also probably inspired by the "English physician" said to have provided the Duc de Morny with youth-preserving "blue pills," discussed in Rounding, *Grandes Horizontales*, 213.

129. *Census of England and Wales for the Year 1861. General Report* (London: Eyre and Spottiswoode, 1863), 39 and "T25—Recensement de 1866," part of "Données historiques de la Statistique générale de France," https://www.insee.fr (accessed 4 Jan. 2018); the figures are given for the Seine department (2.1 million inhabitants) rather than the city of Paris alone (1.8 million) because the census does not indicate the number of foreigners at townhall level.

cording to the Cuban-born and mixed-race Severiano de Heredia, and a "universal city" according to the Russian populist Alexander Herzen, two contributors.[130] "If one abruptly lifted the lid," Ludwig Bamberger, another contributor and German former radical turned banker, claimed, "you [Frenchmen] would see that it is Russians, Italians, Poles, Germans who sneak into this anthill [of Paris] and, borrowing your language and your appearance, make their business and yours, covering you with glory or opprobrium as the case may be." The most sought-after doctors in Paris, Bamberger noted, were German; and so were "the legions of street-sweepers," although most were pious Lutherans from the Grand-Duchy of Hesse, who cleaned the *boulevards* every morning to make them fit for another day of Parisian pleasure seeking.[131]

Even when they had no professional activity, foreign residents played a significant role in the Parisian and French economy as lavish consumers.[132] The rich, easy to swindle foreigner with generous spending habits was perhaps the most widespread cultural stereotype during those years, although he (it was rarely a she) was generally represented as British in the 1820s, Russian in the 1840s and North or Latin American after 1850. In 1866, foreign residents included nearly 10,000 Britons, who "were taking their revenge against the restrictions of the *etiquette* and social laws" of their country; around 4,500 Americans, who had abandoned their "republican" habits and "surpassed [all the Europeans] in luxury"; and also 35,000 Germans, 8,000 Italians, 6,000 Dutchmen, 4,000 Poles, 2,500 Spaniards, 1,500 Russians, 300 Romanians, 300 Ottomans, and 4,000 individuals of "various nationalities."[133] The latter group included growing numbers of rich Latin Americans, either students who were rumoured to buy their degrees from the Sorbonne, giving them more time to enjoy Parisian pleasures, or absentee proprietors who had relocated their household across the Atlantic. The lavish lifestyle of families such as the Mexican Erazzu, the Chilean Argos or the Cuban Alfonso, the *Paris-guide* commented, gave "a sense of the immense revenue yielded by slave plantations,

---

130. *Paris-Guide, par les principaux écrivains et artistes de la France*, 2 vols. (Paris: Librairie internationale, 1867), vol. 2, 1087, 1099.

131. Ludwig Bamberger, "La colonie allemande," *Paris-Guide*, vol. 2, 1017–42.

132. Foreign residents already played a significant role in the city's economy under the July Monarchy; see Philip Mansel, *Paris between Empires, 1814–1852* (London: John Murray, 2001), 361–2.

133. *Paris-guide*, vol. 2, 1028, 1052, 1074; the figures given by the guide were those of the 1866 census for the Seine department.

and large mining concerns or landholdings." Helping them gain access to the
court of Napoleon III also facilitated their political "intrigues," and the guide
drew a direct connection between this influence and France's attempt to establish a monarchical regime in Mexico after 1862.[134]

Foreign collaboration with the French empire of taste was not confined to
Paris. Even as he described the French as the true "shopkeepers of the world,"
Robert Tomes, the American consul in Reims, noted that the French lacked
"aptitude for great commerce." According to his account, French champagne
houses and other successful commercial enterprises were more often than not
managed by capitalists of abler nationalities: "While [the French] is the shopkeeper, the German, the Englishman and the American are the merchants."[135]
Recent research into the history of the champagne industry has, to a large
extent, borne out Tomes's contention. Most of the commercial agents who
played an important part in spreading the taste for champagne across Europe
and the world were German by birth. These agents often owed their position
to their command of foreign languages, and they frequently rose to become
the controlling partners in champagne firms, even founding their own: the
founders of Heidsieck, which dominated export to North America, and of
prestigious houses such as Mumm, Deutz, Krug or Bollinger, were all German
born.[136]

Another significant example of the role played by foreign collaboration in
the French empire of taste was the supply of raw materials to France's leading
export industry, silk textiles, by British trade. From 1800 until 1850, around
50 percent of the raw silks used by Lyonnais workshops still came from France,
thanks to the expansion of the cultivation of mulberry trees in the southeast,
while 40 percent were imported from Italy, and the remaining 10 percent from
the Levant. However, in the early 1850s, intensive cultivation in southern
France facilitated the spread of a disease of the silk worm, the *pébrine* or "pep-
per disease," which more than halved the French output of raw silks and soon
affected Italy and other Mediterranean producers. The booming Lyon silk
industry was rescued by imports of Chinese raw silks, but these relied heavily

134. Severiano de Heredia, "Les Hispano-Américains," *Paris-guide*, vol. 2, 1081–6.

135. Tomes, *The Champagne Country*, 91.

136. *Le champagne: une histoire franco-allemande*, eds. Claire Desbois-Thibault, Werner Paravicini and Jean-Pierre Poussou (Paris: PUPS, 2011), esp. 253–323.

on the commercial infrastructure of the British Empire.[137] Annual re-exports of Asian raw silks from Britain to France grew from 17 to 110 million francs between 1852 and 1862.[138] The same period also witnessed the first direct exports from Shanghai to Marseille, under the helm of budding commercial giant Jardine & Matheson. The Lyonnais firms involved in this direct trade, such as Desgrand père et fils or Arlès-Dufour & Cie, acted as mere consignees. What's more, even on the direct route to Marseille, the high insurance premium (up to 25 percent of the value of the fragile cargo) benefited London insurers (usually Lloyds underwriters), and the Chinese raw silks reached Marseille after a transshipment on fast Peninsular & Oriental ships in British Indian ports.[139]

France's reliance on British commerce for its supplies of raw silks was anything but exceptional. Between 1855 and 1865, British re-exportation to France, mostly of primary products, grew from 98 to 373 million francs (+281 percent), while the export of British-made products to France only increased from 130 to 240 million francs (+85 percent).[140] Conversely, over the same period, the export of French-made products to Britain rose from 345 million to just over one billion francs (+196 percent), while French re-exportation to Britain only grew from 160 million to 313 million francs (+95 percent).[141] In other words, what drove the formidable growth of Anglo-French trade was an exchange of French-made goods with re-exported British primary products, and the result was a rapidly increasing trade surplus for France (about 250 million francs in 1855 and about 750 million in 1865). These figures may be taken to reveal a

---

137. Cayez, *Crise et croissance*, 23–31; Debin Ma, "The Modern Silk Road: The Global Raw-Silk Market, 1850–1930," *Journal of Economic History*, 56, 2 (1996); on the eventual establishment of French commercial firms on the Chinese coast after 1870, in connection with the military conquest of northern Indochina, see Jean-François Klein, "Soyeux en mer de Chine. Stratégies des réseaux lyonnais en Extrême-Orient (1843–1906)" (unpublished PhD thesis, University of Lyon II, 2002), 321–616.

138. My calculations, based on *Annual statement*; the year book does not record these re-exports before 1852.

139. See correspondence of Jardine & Matheson (Hong Kong) with Desgrand père & fils (Lyon, Marseille), Arlès-Dufour (Lyon, Marseille) and Wilson & Co. (Lyon) between 1854 and 1863 in Cambridge University Library, Jardine & Matheson MSS (henceforth JM), C11/18–31; see for instance the first order of Desgrand for sixty-five bales of Jaysaam raw silk and twelve bales of thrown silk, in Jardine & Matheson to Desgrand père & fils, 25 Mar. 1854, JM, C11/18, fol. 448.

140. My calculations, based on *Annual Statement* (conversion rate: £1 = 25 francs).

141. My caculations, based on Direction des Douanes, *Tableau décennal*.

growing French dependency on British consumers and British (imperial) supplies of raw materials. But they can also be read—at least through the lens of the once-popular "dependency theory" which emphasizes the advantages of exporting manufactured goods—as showing how France drew far larger benefits from this exchange than Britain.[142] According to this interpretation, it was Britain who was becoming dependent on sophisticated French commodities and who was forced to give France access to its imperial resources in order to pay for them.

Yet rather than establishing the subordination of either country to one another, the Anglo-French commercial boom of the mid-nineteenth century revealed an extraordinary interdependency between the French empire of taste and the British naval and territorial empire. Careful consideration of this commercial boom also undermines the received wisdom that, while British trade in the nineteenth century was becoming increasingly global, French trade became focused on Europe.[143] This alleged Europeanization of French trade is disputable, at least until the 1870s, because it chiefly relies on the inclusion of Britain within "Europe" in trade statistics. French trade in the mid-nineteenth century was Anglicized rather than Europeanized. For instance, between 1830 and 1870, while the share of Britain in French exports trebled from around 10 percent to over 30 percent, that of the German customs union stagnated, hovering between 5 and 10 percent, even though the latter was one of Europe's fastest growing markets.[144] Anglicization should not be equated with Europeanization, because British trade played a mediating role between Europe and the rest of the world, as seen above with British supplies of extra-European raw materials to French industry. Unfortunately, contemporary British statistics do not enable us to estimate what proportion of imported French commodities was subsequently sold on overseas markets, but it is likely to have been substantial. A clue can be found in the statistics on "transshipment" (the transfer of merchandise from one ship to another, not included in the main trade statistics, because such goods were not cleared by customs):

142. On dependency theory, see Joseph Love, "The Origins of Dependency Theory," *Journal of Latin American Studies*, 22, 1 (1990), and in defence of its continued relevance, see David L. Blaney, "Reconceptualizing Autonomy: The Difference Dependency Theory Makes," *Review of International Political Economy*, 3, 3 (1996).

143. See for instance Paul Bairoch, *Commerce extérieur et développement économique de l'Europe au XIXe siècle* (Paris: Mouton and EHESS, 1976), 80–8.

144. My calculations, based on Direction des Douanes, *Tableau décennal*.

80 percent of goods transshipped in British ports in the early 1850s, and 50 percent in the early 1860s, originated from France before they were re-expedited to overseas markets.[145] British commercial infrastructure not only provided French producers with much-needed raw materials, but also facilitated, it seems, the global dissemination of French-produced commodities.

This commercial interdependence closely mirrored the alignment of British and French foreign policy, at least outside Europe. A good illustration of how a congruence of commercial interests could translate into an imperial partnership is found in the Anglo-French military alliance against China during the Arrow War, also known as the Second Opium War (1856–1860). The commercial motives of Britain's intervention—ensuring the opening of the Chinese market to Indian opium and other British-controlled commodities—has traditionally been contrasted with the more spiritual, official French war aim of bringing to a halt the persecution of Catholic missionaries. However, economically minded historians have shown that France's participation in the war was equally inspired by a desire to secure supplies of raw silk from southern China, as these were threatened by the progress of the Taiping rebellion.[146] A similar concern with supplies of raw silk informed the international, French-led intervention in Lebanon, officially designed to protect Ottoman Christians from Muslim persecutions, in 1860–1861.[147]

There were many other ways in which the French propensity for the commodification of luxury and pleasure were entwined with imperial activity, usually of the informal type. In order to provide the new emperor of Mexico with adequate munificence, but also to underline the profitable relationship that the French Second Empire wished to establish with the new Mexican monarchy, Napoleon III offered Maximilian I an extravagant silver table service of 4,938 pieces, including sixteen candelabra. The service was not sterling but silver-plated, as a way of showcasing the command of electroplating achieved

145. The official *Annual Statement* also indicates that the majority of transhipped goods (c. 90 percent) were "manufactures," but it gives no further details.

146. Robert Y. Eng, *Economic Imperialism in China: Silk Production and Exports, 1861–1932* (Berkeley: University of California, 1985), 23–7; J. Y. Wong, *Deadly Dreams: Opium, Imperialism, and the 'Arrow' War (1856–1860) in China* (Cambridge: Cambridge University Press, 1998), esp. 439–41.

147. Marcel Emerit, "La crise syrienne et l'expansion économique francaise en 1860," *Revue historique*, 207 (1952); Dominique Chevallier, "Lyon et la Syrie. Les bases d'une intervention," *Revue historique*, 224 (1960).

by Christofle, the leading French gold and silversmith company.[148] Another illustration of how commodification within France served imperial pursuits abroad was the popularity of Parisian *cocottes* with foreign dignitaries. The *police des moeurs*, in charge of supervising the *demi-monde*, kept detailed records on these relationships, which no doubt served diplomatic as well as policing ends. Most of these files were lost during the Commune of 1871, but we know from later records that the French police kept a particularly close eye on the sexual adventures of members of the Egyptian Khedivial household. They inform us, for instance, that Blanche Bertin, the daughter of a coachman, and Marthe Lemoulant, a former seamstress, were the mistresses of Eram Bey, the Khedive's steward; Louise Mayer, a former silk *nouveautés* shop assistant, was mistress to Mustapha Fazil, the Khedive's brother; Mathilde Leroy, who called herself the "comtesse de Bloëm de Sigmarengen," was mistress to Hussein Pasha, the Khedive's son and heir; and Hortense Schneider and Léa Silly, two leading Parisian actresses, were mistresses to Khedive Isma'il himself.[149] This information formed part of the broader cultural and economic web that placed Egypt under French informal domination until the 1870s.

The multifarious connections between French commodities and France's global imperial status were celebrated in grand style at the universal exhibition held in Paris in 1867. London's Great Exhibition of 1851 has been much studied as a celebration of British supremacy, but the principle of exhibiting artistic or industrial achievements was a French and, in some respects, courtly tradition. The Académie's *salons* for paintings since the late seventeenth century and national industrial exhibitions since the 1790s already served to project cultural and economic power beyond French borders.[150] The second universal

148. Bergeron, *Les industries du luxe*, 67–8.

149. Several of these women sojourned in Egypt for a time, as did a more famous Parisian beauty who also became the mistress of Ismaÿl in 1869–1870, Blanche d'Antigny; see *Le livre des courtisanes: archives secrètes de la police des moeurs*, ed. Gabrielle Houbre, (Paris: Tallandier, 2006), 59, 152–3, 158, 167, 347, 434–5, 564–6 and, on Blanche d'Antigny, Joanna Richardson, *The Courtesans: The Demi-Monde in Nineteenth-Century France* (London: Weidenfeld and Nicolson, 1967), 5–27.

150. On continuity with earlier national artistic and industrial exhibitions, see Édouard Vasseur, "Pourquoi organiser des Expositions universelles? Le 'succès' de l'Exposition universelle de 1867," *Histoire, Economic & Société*, 24, 4 (2005); more specifically, on the continuity of displays of silk textiles, see Anne Forray-Carlier and Florence Valantin, "La reconnaissance internationale: des Expositions des produits de l'industrie française aux Expositions universelles," in *L'art de la soie: Prelle, 1752–2002: des ateliers lyonnais aux palais parisiens*, eds. Anne Forray-

exhibition, held in Paris in 1855, built on this tradition as much as on the Crystal Palace exhibition. Two innovations revealed the organizers' desire to re-harness the concept of universal exhibition to make it more favourable to French political and commercial interests: first, the inclusion of a new section for fine art, with nearly three-quarters of these exhibits made by French artists; and second, the right for exhibitors of all sections to indicate the price of the products on display. In 1851, British organizers had forbidden price tags, lest they dim the internationalist and pacifist values the exhibition purported to promote. In 1855, by contrast, French organizers embraced the exhibition as an opportunity to intensify the global commodification of French taste. Contemporary maps show that a giant sales office, where customers could place orders, immediately faced the exit of the main exhibition hall.[151] Organizers of the third universal exhibition, held in London in 1862, felt obliged to retain the new features, and the aggressive commercialism of the displays met with the disapproval of many British observers. Although the number of visitors (six million) matched that of 1851, the event was not deemed a great success, and Britain never hosted another world fair.[152]

Michel Chevalier and the other organizers of the fourth exhibition in 1867 increased the commercialism of the event, while simultaneously turning it into a demonstration of French economic power. In some *Recollections*, the French-born British perfumer Eugene Rimmel expressed admiration for the scale of "the most brilliant, the most complete, the most original of those interesting displays called 'International Exhibitions'"; "never," he claimed, "had we before such an opportunity of studying [the various nations of the world's] every-day life in its most minute detail." But Rimmel, despite being a talented cosmetics marketer himself, was shocked by the relentless efforts of the organizers to turn a large profit, especially by leasing dozens of designated spaces for restaurants and refreshment stalls in the park that surrounded the exhibi-

---

Carlier, Florence Valantin, Philippe Verzier, et al. (Paris: Paris Musées et A.C.R. Éditions internationales, 2002), 99–160.

151. Barrie M. Racliffe, "Paris, 1855," in *Encyclopedia of World's Fairs and Expositions* (Jefferson, NC: McFarland, 2008), 21–6; "Plan de l'exposition de 1855," repr. in Sylvain Ageorges, *Sur les traces des expositions universelles* (Paris: Parigramme, 2006), 19; see also Benjamin, *The Arcades Project*, 189.

152. Thomas Prasch, "London, 1862," in *Encyclopedia of World's Fairs*, 27–32; on the resistance of British organizers to the commercialization of world exhibitions, see Louise Pubrick, "Introduction," in *The Great Exhibition of 1851: New Interdisciplinary Essays*, ed. Louise Pubrick (Manchester: Manchester University Press, 2001), esp. 15–17.

tion hall on the Champ de Mars: "The natural result of these exactions was, that the Exhibition assumed a *shoppy* [sic] appearance."[153] Despite or thanks to these contraptions, the 1867 exhibition met with the favour of the public, with more than eleven million visitors in six months.[154] An acclaimed innovation that would be retained in later exhibitions was the installation, in the park, of national pavilions. European pavilions tended to showcase Western technological prowess. The British pavilion, for instance, included a lighthouse made of iron that prefigured the Eiffel Tower of the 1889 exhibition. Most pavilions of extra-European nations were instead replicas of ancient wonders, with a predilection for parts of the world under strong French influence: the Egyptian section included a mock temple of Edfu, recently excavated by the Egyptologist Auguste Mariette, while military engineers who had returned from the Mexican expedition erected a replica of the Aztec temple of Xochicalco (see figure 3.5).[155]

Historians have sometimes dismissed the 1867 exhibition as the last extravaganza of a doomed regime.[156] It is true that the growth of Prussia's power after its victory over Austria in 1866 generated anxiety in France, and the execution of Maximilian I of Mexico on 19 June 1867 (during the exhibition) dealt a serious blow to French prestige. But few contemporaries anticipated the imminent collapse of Bonapartist rule, and the immediate effect of the extensive display of French luxurious commodities, with more than 1,200 square meters dedicated to French silk textiles, and 90 linear meters of cham-

153. Eugene Rimmel, *Recollections of the Paris Exhibition of 1867* (London: Chapman and Hall, 1867), 1–2; the condemnation of the excessive commercialism of the exhibition was excised from the French-language edition, *Souvenirs de l'exposition universelle* (Paris: Dentu, 1868), "Avant-propos," 1–4. On Rimmel's contribution to the perfume and cosmetics industry, see Geoffrey Jones, *Beauty Imagined: A History of the Global Beauty Industry* (Oxford: Oxford University Press, 2010), 18–20.

154. Édouard Vasseur, "L'exposition universelle de 1867 à Paris: analyse d'un phénomène français au XIXe siècle" (unpublished PhD dissertation, École des chartes 2005).

155. On the Egyptian temple, see Auguste Mariette, *Exposition universelle de 1867. Aperçu de l'histoire ancienne d'Égypte pour l'intelligence des monuments exposés dans le temple du parc égyptien* (Paris: Dentu, 1867); on the scientific expedition in Mexico, of which the temple at the 1867 exhibition was an outcome, see Paul N. Edison, "Conquest Unrequited: French Expeditionary Science in Mexico, 1864–1867," *French Historical Studies* 26, 3 (2003). See also photographs of the two temples, AN, CP F12 11893, items 719 ("Temple d'Edfou") and 758 ("Temple mexicain"), viewable online at https://www.siv.archives-nationales.culture.gouv.fr/siv/ (accessed 13 Feb. 2018).

156. See for instance Arthur Chandler, "The Paris Exposition Universelle, 1867: Empire of Autumn," *World's Fair*, 6, 2 (1986).

FIGURE 3.5. View of the Paris universal exhibition in 1867. This idealized view is from the hill of Chaillot on the right bank of the Seine. The "English quarter," on the lower right quarter of the park in this view, was celebrated as "the most brilliant and the richest in monuments" (*L'exposition universelle de 1867 illustrée*, 21 Oct. 1867); it included the replicas of ancient Egyptian and Aztec temples as well as a British iron lighthouse that prefigured the Eiffel Tower. *Source:* Eugène Cicéri and Philippe Benoist, *Vue officielle de l'exposition à vol d'oiseau* (Paris: Lemercier & Cie, 1867); image Library of Congress, LC-DIG-pga-00497.

pagne and other French wines, was one of reassurance about the economic foundations of French power.[157] "These [universal] exhibitions," the economist Henri Baudrillart asserted, in a work based on the lectures of political economy that he gave at the Collège de France, where he temporarily replaced Michel Chevalier in 1866–1867, were "one of the most powerful means of diffusion and propagation for luxury in the course of history," especially as "fully half of the visitors" (he claimed) were women, ever avid for "everything that shines and seduces."[158] The unprecedented flocking of 2.5 million tourists to

157. "Arrêté réglant l'admission et l'installation des exposants de la classe 31, fils et tissus de soies," 21 July 1866, AN, F12 3047; "Arrêté réglant l'admission et l'installation des exposants de la classe 73," 20 Aug. 1866, to which is attached a provisional layout including 720 bottles of "vins de champagne," AN, F12 3069.

158. Henri Baudrillart, *Histoire du luxe privé et public depuis l'antiquité jusqu'à nos jours*, 4 vols. (Paris: Hachette, 1880–1881), vol. 4, 591–4; on the original lectures, see vol. 1, i–ii.

the capital, equivalent to the addition of one hundred thousand prodigal consumers every day for six months, according to Baron Haussmann, also resulted in record sales or takings for the Parisian pleasure-industrial complex, from shops selling *articles de Paris* to theatres and prostitutes.[159] At no other point in the modern era was French dominance over a wide array of commodified pleasures, material or immaterial, so widely acknowledged, and never was Paris's status as the capital of a global empire of taste so uncontested. The relentless staging of further universal exhibitions by the Third Republic, in 1878, 1889 and 1900, during which exhibits from newly acquired formal colonies held pride of place, implicitly testified to the powerful impression made upon contemporaries by the exhibition of 1867, and the way in which it had helped to confer on France an imperial status that had been thrown in doubt after the travails of 1870–1871.[160]

After the collapse of the Second Empire, French commercial prosperity stalled. Exports of conspicuous commodities stagnated or declined, and in the 1880s, even France's tolerance for prostitution and the popularity of French plays and novels began to wane.[161] This coincidence tends to confirm that the earlier boom was, in part, a political phenomenon. The global appeal of French commodities owed a lot to the image of conservative, economic efficiency projected by successive French monarchies, and it no doubt benefited from the zeal displayed by these regimes, especially under Napoleon III, when it came to promoting French commercial interests from China to Mexico, by military means if necessary. Another adverse political factor was the Commune of Paris insurgency and its harsh repression in 1871.[162] Not only did it dent the image of Paris as the global capital of commodified pleasures, but the

159. "Rapport du préfet sénateur de la Seine [Baron Haussmann]," 5 Dec. 1867, AN, F12 2929; see also Volker Barth, "Paris, 1867," *Encyclopedia of World's Fairs*, 37–43, and, on prostitution during the exhibition, Corbin, *Les filles de noces*, 312.

160. Wolfram Kaiser, "Vive la France! Vive la République? The Cultural Construction of French Identity at the World Exhibitions in Paris 1855–1900," *National Identities*, 1, 3 (1999); see also *Les expositions universelles en France au XIXe siècle: techniques, publics, patrimoines*, eds. Anne-Laure Carré, Marie-Sophie Corcy and Christiane Demeulenaere-Douyère (Paris: CNRS, 2012).

161. Christine Machiels, *Les Féminismes et la prostitution, 1860–1960* (Rennes: Presses Universitaires de Rennes, 2016), 31–63; Charle, *Théâtres en capitales*, 26–8, 313–16.

162. On the global aspects of the Commune, see Quentin Deluermoz, *Commune(s), 1870–1871. Une traversée des mondes au XIXe siècle* (Paris: Le Seuil, 2020).

death or exile of thousands of skilled Parisian workers diminished the competitive edge of French luxury industries—a Communard later compared the economic impact of repression to that of the persecution and flight of Huguenots under Louis XIV.[163] Yet France's champagne-capitalist model of development was showing signs of weakness before 1870, and on balance it seems likely that the decisive factors of French commercial stagnation were external, rather than domestic: new competitors emerged for the production of semi-luxuries, especially Italy and the Austro-Hungarian empire, while the Great Depression of 1873 reduced sumptuary expenditure on a global scale. In any event, French commercial stagnation after the 1870s shows that champagne capitalism was a spectacular but fragile model of development, perhaps because it relied so much on reputation and other immaterial factors.

It is also tempting to think that the crumbling of the empire of taste's economic basis contributed to the resurgence of French territorial imperialism after 1880. Champagne capitalism was not conducive to territorial expansion, because the costs of informal domination were lower and the imposition of French sovereignty risked alienating the foreign collaborators who purchased French commodities. Conversely, the relative rise of industries oriented towards mass rather than conspicuous consumption under the Third Republic reduced the potential advantages of an informal strategy and increased those of formal rule. In practice, the acquisition of vast territories in sub-Saharan Africa, Madagascar and Indochina did little to help the ailing luxury and semi-luxury industries, because local elites purchased few French conspicuous commodities, and rapid colonial expansion did not prevent the near halving of France's share in total world exports between 1880 and 1914.[164] Yet the new colonies provided substantial outlets for French cotton and those other mass-consumption industries that were not competitive on the global market.[165] This shift from free-trade imperialism to global protectionism also helps us understand the deterioration of Anglo-French imperial relations between 1880 and 1900, as the two countries increasingly sought to export the same products on the same markets.

163. Prosper-Olivier Lissagaray, *Histoire de la Commune de 1871* (Paris: Dentu, 1896), 462.

164. Dormois, *L'économie française.*

165. Brunschwig, *Mythes et réalités;* Marseille, in *L'empire colonial,* nuanced Brunschwig's analysis, but even he concluded that colonial expansion chiefly benefited the least dynamic sectors of the French economy.

The French empire of taste may also provide a useful point of comparison with other capitalist imperial formations that relied on a sophisticated combination of economic, cultural and military power, such as the United States in the twentieth century. It is noteworthy that Coca Cola, one of the commodities most closely associated with modern American imperialism, was directly inspired by "Vin Mariani," a product typical of champagne capitalism: launched in the 1860s, this French red wine, infused with coca leaves, enjoyed a brief but global fad, thanks to relentless marketing. The Confederate veteran John Pemberton began selling his "French wine of coca" in Atlanta in 1882, before efforts by the state legislature to make Georgia a dry state imposed the adoption of a new name and a less energetic formula in 1884.[166] Modern American imperialism cannot be reduced to a French-style empire of taste refurbished for mass consumption, if only because it has proved to be more comprehensive and enduring. Yet the similarities between the nineteenth-century French and twentieth-century American imperial repertoires illustrate how, in the age of global capitalism, imperial domination can rely on the command of global commodity chains as well as territorial control, and how even the economic power base of modern empires rests on cultural, as well as material factors. The next chapter considers another economic feature of France's nineteenth-century informal empire that also lends itself to modern comparisons and can help further elucidate the role played by cultural affinities or sympathies: the large-scale exportation of capital, as a means of enabling asymmetric cooperation and levying imperial tributes.

---

166. Frederick Allen, *Secret Formula: How Brilliant Marketing and Relentless Salesmanship Made Coca-Cola the Best-Known Product in the World* (New York: Harper Business, 1994), 22–4; Mark Pendergrast *For God, Country, and Coca-Cola: The Unauthorized History of the Great American Soft Drink and the Company That Makes It* (New York, NY: Basic Books, 2000), 22–5.

4

Conquest by Money

THE GEOPOLITICS AND LOGISTICS OF
INVESTMENT COLONIZATION

IN ÉMILE ZOLA'S *L'Argent* (1891), a novel from the Rougon-Macquart cycle
set in the 1860s, the main protagonist, Aristide Saccard, founds a "Banque
universelle" with the twin aims of dethroning the Jewish domination of Parisian finance and accomplishing a "conquest . . . by . . . money" of the Middle
East: "That conquest of the East that Napoleon had failed to achieve with the
sword [when a French military expedition occupied Egypt and Syria between
1798 and 1801] would be accomplished by a financial company . . . Asia would
be conquered by force of millions, for a return of billions."[1] The main objective
of the *Banque universelle* was the economic regeneration of Asia Minor and
greater Syria, through railway construction, the mining of bullion and the development of credit in the Ottoman world. The system of domination
imagined by Saccard also relied on modern technology—Zola described it as
"a conquest by the twin forces of science and money"—and on religious inspiration: many backers of the *Banque universelle* were pious Catholics, who
furtively hoped that this financial conquest would pave the way for a grandiose
translation of the Holy See, endangered by Italian unification, from Rome to
Jerusalem.[2]

Unlike Anthony Trollope's *The Way We Live Now* (1875), the other great
novel on the surge of European foreign investment after 1850, which bears little
connection to contemporary British imperial ventures, *L'Argent* can be read as

---

1. Emile Zola, *L'Argent* (Paris: Gallimard, 1980), 120, 326.
2. Zola, *L'Argent*, 120-2.

a novel on informal empire.[3] Although Zola relied on the financial scandals of the 1880s for his descriptions of Saccard's manoeuvres at the Bourse or with the press, the novel, like the rest of the *Rougon-Macquart* series, remained first and foremost an attack on the Second Napoleonic Empire's policies and impact on French society.[4] Remarkably, *L'Argent* is also the only novel in the twenty-volume Rougon-Maquart cycle that deals with the Bonapartist regime's global ambitions. By contrast, Algeria is almost completely absent from Zola's "natural and social history" of the Second Empire.[5] It would seem that, for the great realist novelist, the mainspring of Bonapartist expansionism lay not in formal conquest or settler colonialism, but in the spectacular development of French finance after 1850. Tellingly, *L'Argent* alludes several times to the regime's greatest financial-imperial fiasco, the Mexican expedition of 1862–1867, which affected several hundreds of thousands of French savers.[6] At the same time, its focus on Saccard's scheme in the Middle East accurately reflected the concentration of French foreign investment in the Ottoman world, which absorbed a quarter of French exports of capital (two thirds of the capital exported beyond Europe) between 1850 and 1880, while the share of all French colonies including Algeria was only 5 percent.[7]

This chapter seeks to vindicate Zola's focus on finance as an instrument of domination in the middle of the century and retraces the origins of this imperialization of finance to the aftermath of the Napoleonic Wars. John A. Hobson's contention—that a surplus of savings, leading to the emergence of a large, organized financial sector, was "the taproot of imperialism"—has in-

3. The French-sounding name of the main crook in Trollope's book, "Melmotte," even suggests that the author wished to denounce such financial scams as an import from across the Channel; see Anthony Trollope, *The Way We Live Now* (London: Penguin, 2000), 30: "within the last two years [Augustus Melmotte] had arrived in London from Paris." The character's name also recalled that of the protagonist of Honoré de Balzac's fantastic novel on pacts with the devil and financial speculations, *Melmoth réconcilié* (1835).

4. See for instance Corinne Saminadayar-Perrin, "Fictions de la Bourse," *Cahiers naturalistes*, 78 (2004), and Adeline Wrona, "Mots à crédit: *L'Argent*, de Zola, ou la presse au cœur du marché de la confiance," *Romantisme*, 151 (2011).

5. William Gallois, *Zola: The History of Capitalism* (Oxford: P. Lang, 2000), 119–32.

6. Zola, *L'Argent*, 45, 147, 224.

7. Rondo Cameron, *France and the Economic Development of Europe, 1800–1914*, 2nd edn (London: Routledge, 2000), 88.

spired generations of historians and social scientists.[8] A recent and influential iteration of this thesis, Peter Cain and Anthony Hopkins's paradigm of "gentlemanly capitalism," has persuasively underlined the role of the City of London in shaping the course of British imperial expansion.[9] This chapter draws on Cain and Hopkins's elegant model of interaction between politics and finance, but with the important caveat that France's financial imperialism was not as gentlemanly as Britain's. Instead, the more active role of the government and the implication of hundreds of thousands of small investors gave this French version a ruthless and *déclassé* flavour. French foreign investments were more openly connected to imperial pursuits, mostly of an informal type, and more predatory, because French capitalists demanded high yields in return for loans to French client states. This type of financial imperialism was arguably more effective than Britain's at establishing political control by informal means, even if in the long term it often proved unsustainable.

A major difficulty when trying to appreciate the imperial dimension of international finance in the nineteenth century is the still-influential view, which owes much to Lenin's *Imperialism, the Highest Stage of Capitalism* (1917), that financial imperialism was a major cause of the First World War.[10] This approach has been discredited by historians who emphasized the preference of financiers for cooperation over conflict between European powers, or the role of contingent and peripheral factors, in the outbreak of the war.[11] Yet it retains some credibility in the case of French financial imperialism, because large-scale French lending to the Russian empire has long been recognised as a facilitating factor of the crucial Franco-Russian alliance.[12] But whatever the

8. John A. Hobson, *Imperialism: A Study* (New York: Cosimo, 2005; first edn 1902), 71–93.

9. Peter Cain and Anthony G. Hopkins, *British Imperialism, 1688–2015*, 2nd edn (Harlow: Pearsons, 2002).

10. On Lenin's influence and the confusions surrounding his analysis, see Eric Stokes, "Late Nineteenth-Century Colonial Expansion and the Attack on the Theory of Economic Imperialism: A Case of Mistaken Identity?," *Historical Journal*, 12, 2 (1969); see also Norman Etherington, *Theories of Imperialism: War, Conquest and Capital* (London: Croom Helm, 1984).

11. Niall Ferguson, *The Cash Nexus: Money and Power in the Modern World* (London: Penguin, 2001), 279–314, and more specifically on finance and politics before 1914, Niall Ferguson, *The House of Rothschild*, 2 vols. (London: Viking, 1999), vol. 2: *The World's Banker, 1849–1999*, 369–437; Christopher M. Clark, *The Sleepwalkers: How Europe Went to War in 1914* (London: Allen Lane, 2012), xxiv–xxix.

12. The *emprunts russes* (Russian loans) played a significant part in Lenin's original argument, although the Bolshevik leader had domestic political motives of his own for inveighing against a major prop of the Czarist regime; see Vladimir I. Lenin, *Imperialism: The Highest Stage of*

significance of this politico-financial relationship in the origins of the First World War, we must resist the teleological temptation to project this analysis onto earlier French exports of capital, especially outside Europe.[13] This chapter examines instead the logic and practicalities of such exports before the 1880s, from their emergence in the 1820s until they became commonplace, outpacing British exports of capital in the 1860s. If anything, it suggests that geopolitical and domestic political considerations played an even greater part in French exports of capital to the Americas and the Middle East than in *fin-de-siècle* Europe. But it also shows that a strategy aptly described by the economist Paul Leroy-Beaulieu as "investment colonization" was designed as an alternative rather than a prelude to formal conquest. This approach was intended to facilitate cooperation or at least avoid confrontation with other European imperial powers (and indigenous elites), casting further doubt on simplistic constructions of nineteenth-century capitalism as the root cause of territorial imperialism or major military conflagrations.

This financial dimension of French informal imperialism was closely connected to the intensive commodification of luxury, examined in the previous chapter. Economic theorists view capital as a factor of production, but cultural theorists would stress that in its most basic sense of money, it can also be understood as a high-end good, at once invisible and extremely invidious, that financial agents seek to commodify and sell.[14] Foreign loans also played an important part in France's commercial boom after 1850, as they often served to pay, directly or indirectly, for other countries' imports of French commodi-

---

Capitalism (London: Penguin, 2010; first Russian edition 1917), esp. 76–7. Yet the main study of French capital exports to Russia, Réné Girault, *Emprunts russes et investissements français en Russie, 1887–1914* (Paris: Armand Colin, 1973), tends to downplay the role of political factors; on the politics of French (and British) lending to the Russian empire, see Jennifer Siegel, *For Peace and Money: French and British Finance in the Service of Tsars and Commissars* (Oxford: Oxford University Press, 2014).

13. For a reappraisal of the reciprocal influence of finance and politics before the age of high imperialism, see Glenda Sluga, "'Who Holds the Balance of the World?' Bankers at the Congress of Vienna, and in International History," *American Historical Review*, 122, 5 (2017).

14. Arjun Appadurai, "Introduction: Commodities and the Politics of Value," in *The Social Life of Things: Commodities in Cultural Perspective*, ed. Arjun Appadurai, 2nd edn (Cambridge: Cambridge University Press, 2013), 3–63; on the social significance of money in turn-of-the-nineteenth-century France, see Rebecca Spang, *Stuff and Money in the Time of French Revolution* (Cambridge, MA: Harvard University Press 2015), esp. 1–18.

ties.[15] Examining the rationale and practical arrangements of French foreign lending in detail can therefore shed further light on the articulation of the military, economic and cultural foundations of French informal imperial power. After underlining the peculiar propensity of France to export its capital in the nineteenth century, the chapter shows how a strand of French political economy, from Talleyrand to Leroy-Beaulieu, overtly promoted loans to friendly foreign states as a way of exercising tutelage beyond national borders. It then turns to several prominent instances of French foreign lending—Haiti in the 1820s, the Ottoman Empire after 1850 and Mexico in the 1860s—to examine the logistics of French imperial finance and highlight the persistent primacy of political control rather than profit as the *ultima ratio* of French capital exports.

The Global Scale of French Foreign Lending

The great surge of European capital export after 1850 was a French affair, as well as a British one, at least until the 1870s. Contemporaries were well aware of the fact, as shown by the quotation of George Goschen, banker and later chancellor of the exchequer, that opens Cain and Hopkins's pivotal chapter on the role of financial services in powering British expansion: "English and French banking principles," Goschen stated in 1865, "are on a crusading tour throughout the world."[16] According to available estimates, between 1850 and 1869 France's total capital exports even slightly exceeded Britain's (13 billion francs versus 11 billion; see figure 4.1).[17] This French lead vanished after 1870. By 1914 Britain's

15. Luca Einaudi, *Money and Politics: European Monetary Unification and the International Gold Standard (1865–1873)* (Oxford: Oxford University Press, 2001), 43–5.

16. Cain and Hopkins, *British Imperialism*, 160–1, where Goschen's statement is erroneously described as "from the 1880s," although the article from which it was drawn, "Seven Per Cent," a very optimistic assessment of the capital export boom in the 1860s that included a discussion of "French ideas" about banking, was first published in *The Edinburgh Review* in January 1865; repr. in George Goschen, *Essays and Addresses on Economic Questions* (London: Arnold, 1905), 10–47.

17. Figures based on Lévy-Leboyer, "La balance des paiements" and A. H. Imlah, "British Balance of Payments and Export of Capital, 1816–1913," *Economic History Review*, 5, 2 (1952); conversion rate of £1 = 25 francs. Before 1850, Britain's exports appear to have been significantly larger than France's, but total amounts remained limited, with respectively 4.3 billion francs and 0.9 billion between 1820 and 1849; on the acceleration of cross-border flows of capital in the second half of the nineteenth century, see Kevin O'Rourke and Jeffrey G. Williamson, *Globalization*

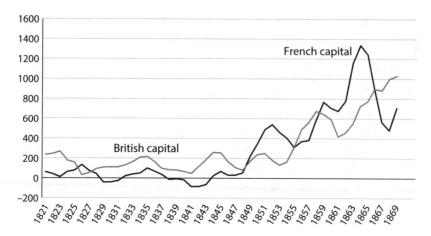

FIGURE 4.1. French and British exports of capital, in millions of francs, 1821–1869. *Source:* Based on Imlah, "British Balance of Payments" and Lévy-Leboyer, "La balance des paiements," using a three-year moving average and a conversion rate of £1 = 25 francs.

stock of foreign investment was approximately twice that of France, at 90 billion francs versus 45 billion.[18] Despite this relative decline, however, France continued to export far more capital than economic theory would predict, given its relatively low level of industrial development (capital exports should be inversely correlated with the potential returns of domestic investment), leading numerous observers, then and in subsequent decades, to puzzle over this seemingly irrational behaviour.[19]

---

and History: *The Evolution of a Nineteenth-Century Atlantic Economy* (Cambridge, MA: MIT Press, 1999), 207–49.

18. Herbert Feis, *Europe, the World's Banker, 1870–1914. An Account of European Foreign Investment and the Connection of World Finance with Diplomacy before the War* (New Haven, CT: Yale University Press, 1930), 23, 47. These often-cited figures have been endorsed by Charles P. Kindleberger, *A Financial History of Western Europe* (London: Allen & Unwin, 1984), 225, and O'Rourke and Williamson, *Globalization and History*, 211; but Donald C. M. Platt, *Britain's Investment Overseas on the Eve of the First World War: The Use and Abuse of Numbers* (London: Macmillan, 1986), 131–4, has argued that they probably overestimated Britain's stock of foreign investment and underestimated France's stock in 1914.

19. Critiques included Harry White, one of the architects of the International Monetary Fund, whose PhD thesis on French capital exports already underlined the need for regulation of the global circulation of capital; see Harry D. White, *The French International Accounts* (Cambridge, MA: Harvard University Press, 1936), esp. 279–83, 311–12; on White's role in the reshaping of the global financial system after the Second World War, see Benn Steil, *The Battle of*

The perception of nineteenth-century French foreign investments as being irrational was compounded by the eventual default of several major borrowing governments after the First World War, the Soviet Union's repudiation of Czarist Russia's foreign debt being the most famous example.[20] Yet recent econometric research has suggested that French investors, at least between 1880 and 1914, were as sensitive as their British or German counterparts to the perceived level of risk and anticipated returns.[21] The dismissal of the French propensity to export a large amount of capital as irrational is therefore unjustified, and overly informed by the benefit of hindsight: few, if any contemporaries could have predicted the scale, horror and enormous consequences of the Great War. Instead of condemning the French predilection for foreign investment, especially under the form of foreign state bonds, one should elucidate its main economic and political causes.

Two macroeconomic factors stand out. First, the French specialization in the provision of luxury or semi-luxury commodities, examined in the previous chapter, implied limited needs in physical capital, because these industries relied more on skilled labour and other immaterial factors such as the foreign appreciation of French quality; limited domestic investment opportunities meant that a greater share of savings was available to be exported. Second, France enjoyed a relatively high savings rate, not least thanks to a precocious decline in the birth rate that resulted in quasi demographic stagnation after 1850. Given that life expectancy remained slightly below average by contemporary western European standards, French households enjoyed a low

Bretton Woods: John Maynard Keynes, Harry Dexter White, and the Making of a New World Order (Princeton, NJ: Princeton University Press, 2013), 17–60.

20. In reality, due to wartime advances by the British Treasury, Britain's financial losses were equivalent to France's, but as France's were borne by larger numbers of bondholders the political repercussions were much greater; see Siegel, *For Peace and Money*, 2.

21. Antoine Parent and Christophe Rault, "The Influences Affecting French Assets Abroad Prior to 1914," *Journal of Economic History*, 64, 2 (2004); Rui Esteves, "The Belle Époque of International Finance: French Capital Exports 1880–1914," Department of Economics Discussion Paper Series, 534 (University of Oxford, 2011); Maxime Merli and Antoine Parent, "La diversification des portefeuilles français à la veille de 1914 ou l'image écornée du rentier français du 19e siècle," *Revue d'économie politique*, 121, 6 (2011). More generally, on the efficiency of the Parisian financial market throughout the century, see Pierre-Cyrille Hautcoeur and Angelo Riva, "The Paris Financial Market in the Nineteenth Century: Complementarities and Competition in Microstructures," *Economic History Review*, 65, 4 (2012).

dependency ratio and a greater capacity for saving.[22] These observations echo those made at the time by two influential commentators of economic life, the British journalist Walter Bagehot and the economist Paul Leroy-Beaulieu: both suggested that France's economic peculiarities, including the cultivation of consumer pleasure and a mania for financial investment, ultimately derived from the surplus of leisure time that came about as a result of having fewer children.[23] We can dispute the direction of causality, but France's exceptional propensity to export its savings appears to have been connected in multiple ways to other main features of its economic model.

Several micro institutional factors also contributed to the surge of French foreign investment in the mid-nineteenth century. For a long time, economic historians insisted on the underdevelopment of French financial institutions until the emergence of national deposit banks in the 1860s. Yet we now know that from at least the mid-eighteenth century, large swathes of the French population took out credit through the mediation of notaries, government keepers of legal records who also played a private role as lawyers, financial advisors and real-estate brokers. As lenders or as borrowers, millions of French men and women were therefore used to credit operations by the 1850s. Furthermore, the notaries' dominance of the domestic market in medium to long-term mortgages encouraged banks to look for other types of investment, beyond national borders if necessary. In their role as financial advisors, notaries may also have helped disseminate a new taste for foreign investment across the French population.[24] So did the *receveurs généraux*, another type of semi-

22. On the specificities of the French demographic regime as Malthusian rather than corresponding with an early demographic transition, see E. Anthony Wrigley, "The Fall of Marital Fertility in Nineteenth-Century France: Exemplar or Exception?," *European Journal of Population—Revue européenne de démographie*, 1, 1 and 2, 3; on the significance of this demographic regime for French model economic development in the nineteenth century, see Crouzet, "The Historiography of French Economic Growth": 237–8.

23. [Walter Bagehot], "One Difference between France and England," *The Economist*, 12 Sep. 1868; Paul Leroy-Beaulieu, "Le luxe. La fonction de la richesse: I Caractère et variété du Luxe. Son rôle économique," *Revue des Deux Mondes*, 126 (1894): 98–9. However, Leroy-Beaulieu later grew increasingly worried about the consequences of demographic stagnation for French power; see Georges Photios Tapinos, "Paul Leroy-Beaulieu et la question de la population. L'impératif démographique, limite du libéralisme économique," *Population*, 54, 1 (1999) and, on the complex reception of Malthus's ideas in France, Yves Charbit, *Du malthusianisme au populationnisme: les économistes français et la population* (Paris: Presses universitaires de France, 1981).

24. Philip T. Hoffman, Gilles Postel-Vinay and Jean-Laurent Rosenthal, *Dark Matter Credit: The Development of Peer-to-Peer Lending and Banking in France* (Princeton, NJ: Princeton Uni-

public, semi-private agents, who were charged with the collection of tax receipts but who also served as local bankers in the French provinces.[25] As we will see, *receveurs généraux* helped issue and market two important foreign imperial public loans—Haiti's in 1825 and Mexico's in 1865.

French familiarity with credit was enhanced by the application of some of the commodification processes to investment vehicles, examined in the previous chapter.[26] Efforts to commodify investment, and therefore, in a sense, capital itself, are best documented in the case of France's national public debt. Between 1830 and 1880, the number of individuals who owned *rentes* (government bonds), most of whom were French residents, rose from 125,000 to nearly one million, not least thanks to a gradual reduction of the minimum subscription required from investors, from one thousand francs in 1815 to three francs in 1870. By contrast, over the same period in Britain, the number of individuals who owned government bonds remained stable, at about two hundred thousand.[27] Reduction in the minimum subscription, combined with

---

versity Press, 2019), esp. 176–94 on the complementary nature of banks' and notaries' financial activities.

25. Pierre-François Pinaud, *Les receveurs généraux des finances, 1790–1865* (Geneva: Droz, 1990).

26. On the links between credit and commodification—for instance, of land and real estate—see Alexia Yates, "Mobilizing Land in Nineteenth-century France: The Double Life of Property and the Grounding of Modern Capitalism," *Critical Historical Studies*, 6, 2 (2019) and Alexia Yates, *Selling Paris: Property and Commercial Culture in the Fin-de-Siècle Capital* (Cambridge, MA: Harvard University Press, 2015). A link may also be drawn between the high French propensity to save and invest and the commodification of sex, since professional and semi-professional prostitutes (courtesans, *cocottes* and *grisettes*) were notoriously expert at avoiding childbearing, and a desire to limit family sizes was often cited as a justification for the exceptional tolerance of prostitution in France; see Corbin, *Les filles de noces*, 358–77. On the connections between sexuality and finance before 1800, see Clare Haru Crowston, *Credit, Fashion, Sex: Economies of Regard in Old Regime France* (Durham, NC: Duke University Press, 2013), esp. 139–94.

27. Estimates for 1830 in "État indiquant le classement par catégories des propriétaires des rentes françaises à 5 percent subsistantes au 1er janvier 1830," Savigny-le-Temple, Centre des Archives Économiques et Financières (henceforth CAEF), B 49463; estimates for 1880 in Zheng Kang and Thierno Seck, "Les épargnants et le marché financier," in *Le Marché financier français au XIXe siècle*, 2 vols., eds. Pierre Cyrille Hautcoeur and Georges Gallais Hamonno (Paris: Publications de la Sorbonne, 2007), vol. 1, 314–53: 335; on the reduction in the minimum subscription, see Jean-Marie Vaslin, "Le siècle d'or de la rente perpétuelle française," in *Le Marché financier français*, vol. 2, 117–207: 127 and Pierre-Cyrille Hautcoeur, "Les transformations du crédit en France au XIXe siècle," *Romantisme*, 151 (2011): 36.

attractive yields and marketing devices such as lottery bonds, would play an equally important part in spurring on the dissemination of foreign investment across new layers of the French population.[28]

The crucial role played by the national public debt in initiating ordinary savers to financial investment almost certainly contributed to their marked preference for foreign public debt, when they began to invest beyond national borders. After 1860, Paris became the world's main issuance market for foreign states' loans, by a significant margin.[29] This predilection of nineteenth-century French savers for foreign public debt was much decried by early twentieth-century commentators. Lenin described this French variant of his model as "usury imperialism" by contrast with British "colonial imperialism."[30] Condemning foreign public debt as a dangerous type of investment, owing to the absence of means of redress in case of default, John Maynard Keynes noted that loans to foreign states "reached their utmost limit of magnitude and of imprudence in [nineteenth-century] France."[31] Anglophone economic historians have also had harsh words to say about the proliferation of French lending to foreign states after 1850. Despite his distinguished contribution to the reappraisal of French economic dynamism in the nineteenth century, Rondo Cameron dismissed the French "government loan business" as "capital down the drain" on economic but also moral grounds, because French lending often "fed the flames of civil or international strife, destructive of life and wealth, or maintained in power corrupt and reactionary governments."[32] Brinley Thomas, a major historian of the mobility of capital in the nineteenth century, also expressed much disdain for the French exportation of capital,

28. Charles E. Freedman, "The Growth of the French Securities Market, 1815–1870," in *From the Ancien Régime to the Front Populaire: Essays in the History of Modern France in Honor of Shepard B. Clough*, ed. Charles K. Warner (New York: Columbia University Press, 1969), 75–92; David Todd and Alexia Yates, "Public Debt and Democratic Statecraft in Nineteenth-Century France," in *A World of Public Debts: A Political History*, eds. Nicolas Barreyre and Nicolas Delalande (Basingstoke: Palgrave Macmillan, forthcoming in December 2020).

29. According to a contemporary estimate by Alfred Neymarck, in 1900 the total nominal value of foreign governments' bonds listed in Paris reached 59 billion francs, against 25 billion of French *rentes* and 52 billion for securities issued by French or foreign corporations; Oskar Morgenstern, *International Financial Transactions and Business Cycles* (Princeton, NJ: Princeton University Press, 1959), 514.

30. Lenin, *Imperialism*, 27.

31. John M. Keynes, "Foreign Investments and National Advantages," *The London Nation*, 9 August 1924.

32. Cameron, *France and the Economic Development of Europe*, 404–24.

because as a result of government interference it almost exclusively sought "the attainment of national [political] objectives". This is a somewhat simplistic view—as seen above, French investors were as sensitive as others to market incentive—but not entirely erroneous, since the government frequently distorted these incentives.[33]

One influential account, written in English, painted a rosier picture of the French enthusiasm for foreign states' debt, but tellingly its author, Herbert Feis, was an advisor to the American State Department rather than a professional economist or economic historian. In his review of European finance before World War I, *Europe, the World's Banker* (1930), Feis even waxed lyrical about the global reach of French capital and drew explicit connections with other aspects of France's openness to the world and influence beyond its borders: "French finance had the same thriving cosmopolite activity as the rest of Paris business [in universities, the boulevards, etc.], the same tolerance and indulgence for difference and weakness, the same disposition to strike a bargain with these qualities." The Paris market, he believed, was unrivalled for "the diversity of its connections and transactions, its willingness to deal with all comers, its zest for strangeness." As a result, "for the borrowing representatives of the races of the continent, of the Latin-American states, of the whole circle of the Mediterranean coast ... Paris was the financial capital, as it was the intellectual and culinary one."[34]

Feis's favourable judgment was perhaps influenced by his own French-Alsatian background.[35] But it is more significant that *Europe, the World's Banker* was initially a report to the American State Department's Council on Foreign Relations in the early days of "dollar diplomacy."[36] Between the British model of foreign investment, focused on private and colonial ventures, and the French one that favoured the forging of transnational collaboration under the guidance of the government, Feis implicitly defended the latter, with some success in the long term, if one considers the political role of American foreign lending after the Second World War. His work evinced admiration for the ways

33. Brinley Thomas, "The Historical Record of International Capital Movements to 1913," in *Capital Movements and Economic Development*, ed. John H. Adler (London: Macmillan, 1967), 3–32: 11.

34. Feis, *Europe, the World's Banker*, 38–9.

35. "Herbert Feis," American National Biography Online, www.anb.org (accessed 12 Mar. 2018).

36. Emily S. Rosenberg, *Financial Missionaries to the World: The Politics and Culture of Dollar Diplomacy, 1900–1930* (Cambridge, MA: Harvard University Press, 1999).

in which the French government "guided and often controlled" outflows of capital through discreet administrative mechanisms, while mostly keeping a free hand in deciding whether to intervene when a borrowing government defaulted. The costs of such interventions, Feis noted, were often limited, as when the sending of a single French battleship in 1892 sufficed to force Haiti's government to resume servicing the debt it had initially contracted with France in 1825.[37]

France's model of economic development in the nineteenth century endowed it with an unusually large surplus of capital. Yet the remarkable alignment of France's capital exports with its geopolitical goals was not only the product of macro- or micro-economic factors. It was also connected with the political aspiration to informal empire.

Debt and Empire in French Political Economy

The notion that finance could serve to leverage power abroad was explicitly endorsed by several prominent French writers on political economy. Their enthusiasm for public indebtedness, national or foreign, was even one of the chief ways in which mainstream French economics differed from British classical political economy in the nineteenth century, especially after David Ricardo condemned both public borrowing and foreign investment as being detrimental to the national accumulation of capital.[38] The heralds of commercial globalization, under the slogan of "free trade," may have been British, but the cheerleaders of financial globalization were French.

This intellectual enthusiasm for public indebtedness in France after 1815 is all the more remarkable because, until the Revolution of 1789, French economists had denounced the risk of bankruptcy caused by the development of "public credit" with astonishing verve. For example, Victor Riquetti, Marquis de Mirabeau, one of the most widely-read authors of political economy in the last decades of the Old Regime, condemned "public credit" as causing "the

---

37. Feis, *Europe, the World's Banker*, 118–22, 148.

38. "It is by the profuse expenditure of Government, . . . and by loans, that the country is impoverished," in *The Works and Correspondence of David Ricardo*, 10 vols., ed. Piero Sraffa (Cambridge: Cambridge University Press, 1951–1973), vol. 1, 246–9; and "It can never be allowed that the emigration of Capital can be beneficial to a state," in *The Works and Correspondence*, vol. 3, 274. On the perpetuation of Ricardian orthodoxy in subsequent decades, see Nancy Churchman, *David Ricardo on Public Debt* (Basingstoke: Palgrave, 2001) and Takuo Dome, *The Political Economy of Public Finance in Britain 1767–1873* (London: Routledge, 2004).

desolation of the entire surface of the earth, because it amounted to whole nations selling themselves, their children and their posterity in the name of the public interest."[39] Such anxiety stemmed, in part, from memories of the collapse of John Law's "System" in the 1720s.[40] As shown by Michael Sonenscher, this fear of public credit can even be construed as the lynchpin of the reconfiguration of sovereignty and political legitimacy that took place during the Revolution itself.[41] But just as the other great economic anxiety of the Old Regime, about the pernicious effects of luxury, receded sharply in the aftermath of the Revolution, so did the fear of public credit. This is unsurprising because the two concerns were linked. Both reflected disquiet at the corrupting effects of artificial means of fostering prosperity, both were attacked by the same authors, especially the Physiocrats, and both were defended by the same writers, often admirers of Law, such as Jean-François Melon or René Louis Voyer d'Argenson.

However, the fear of public credit faded a little later than anxiety about luxury: in the 1820s, rather than under Napoleon.[42] The timing of this suggests that the new equanimity owed something to what contemporaries and many subsequent historians have described as the "miraculous" resurrection

39. Quoted in Michael Sonenscher, "The Nation's Debt and the Birth of the Modern Republic: The French Fiscal Deficit and the Politics of the Revolution of 1789," *History of Political Thought*, 18, 1 and 2 (1997): 90. On the fiscal context of these anxieties, see Kathryn Norberg, "The French Fiscal Crisis of 1788 and the Financial Origins of the Revolution of 1789," in *Fiscal Crises, Liberty, and Representative Government, 1450–1789*, eds. Philip T. Hoffman and Kathryn Norberg (Stanford, CA: Stanford University Press, 2002), 253–98, and Gail Bossenga, "Financial Origins of the French Revolution," in *From Deficit to Deluge: The Origins of the French Revolution*, eds. Thomas E. Kaiser and Dale K. Van Kley (Stanford, CA: Stanford University Press, 2011), 37–66.

40. Thomas E. Kaiser, "Money, Despotism, and Public Opinion in Early Eighteenth-Century France: John Law and the Debate on Royal Credit," *Journal of Modern History*, 63, 1 (1991); Rebecca Spang, "The Ghost of Law: Speculating on Money, Memory and Mississippi in the French Constituent Assembly," *Historical Reflections / Réflexions Historiques*, 31, 1 (2005); and Spang, *Stuff and Money*, 63, 79–82.

41. Sonenscher, "The Nation's Debt," and Michael Sonenscher, *Before the Deluge: Public Debt, Inequality, and the Intellectual Origins of the French Revolution* (Princeton, NJ: Princeton University Press, 2009).

42. On early efforts to rehabilitate public credit under Napoleon, see Tyson Leuchter, "The Illimitable Right: Debating the Meaning of Property and the *marché à terme* in Napoleonic France," *Modern Intellectual History*, 15, 1 (2018).

of France's public credit at the beginning of the Bourbon Restoration.[43] In order to pay the heavy indemnity (1.8 billion francs) imposed on France by the second Treaty of Paris in 1815, the restored monarchy borrowed very large sums, yet the quoted value of French *rentes* rose steadily. Foreign bankers, led by Barings, arranged France's first loans after the Napoleonic Wars, but after 1820 the French branch of the House of Rothschild, in collaboration with the rest of the Parisian *haute banque*, acquired a near monopoly on the issuance of French state bonds.[44] Tentatively under the July Monarchy and systematically under the Second Empire, the French government also began to sell bonds directly to the public. The economic benefits of such direct issuance were slight, for the costs of organizing large public subscriptions matched or exceeded bankers' fees. Yet the ensuing increase in the number of bondholders— at least sevenfold between the 1820s and the 1870s—accrued significant political benefits, each bondholder having a greater stake in domestic stability and French geopolitical ventures. By the end of the nineteenth century, and not even including the rapid growth of other forms of public indebtedness (guaranteed loans to railway companies, municipal debt, etc.), France had accumulated the world's largest national debt. Most of this debt was still owned by a few tens of thousands of investors, but the enormous number of bondholders testified to its popularity and legitimacy.[45]

The growing reliance of the French state on public debt contrasted with the decline in absolute terms of the British national debt (and its drastic decline

---

43. *1816 ou la genèse de la foi publique: la fondation de la Caisse des dépôts et consignations*, eds. Alya Aglan, Michel Margairaz and Philippe Verheyde (Geneva: Droz, 2006); Zheng Kang, "L'Etat constructeur du marché financier," in *Le marché financier*, vol.1, 159–93; Michel Lutfalla, "La rente, de Waterloo à Sedan," in *Histoire de la Dette Publique en France*, ed. Michel Lutfalla (Paris: Garnier, 2017), 81–104; Jerome Greenfield, *The Making of a Fiscal-Military State in Post-Revolutionary France* (Cambridge: Cambridge University Press, forthcoming), chapters 2 and 3.

44. Eugene N. White, "Making the French Pay: The Costs and Consequences of the Napoleonic Reparations," *European Review of Economic History*, 5, 3 (2001); Jerome Greenfield, "Financing a New Order: The Payment of Reparations by Restoration France, 1817–18," *French History*, 30, 3 (2016). On the Rothschilds' domination of the French national debt market, see Bertrand Gille, *Histoire de la maison Rothschild*, 2 vols. (Geneva: Droz, 1965–1967), vol. 1, 57–105, and Niall Ferguson, *The House of Rothschild*, vol. 1, 111–38.

45. Vaslin, "Le siècle d'or"; Richard Bonney, "The Apogee and Fall of the French Rentier Regime, 1801–1914," in *Paying for the Liberal State: The Rise of Public Finance in Nineteenth-Century Europe*, eds. José Luis Cardoso and Peter Lains (Cambridge: Cambridge University Press, 2010), 81–102.

in relation to the national income) between 1820 and 1910.[46] France's indebtedness was crucial to the funding of French military ventures, from the interventions in Spain and Greece under the Restoration, to the conquest of Algeria
under the July Monarchy, to campaigns in the Middle East, East Asia and Latin
America under the Second Empire, and to the conquest of a territorial empire
in Africa and Asia under the Third Republic. After Waterloo, France may be
said to have adopted the British model of fiscal-military state.[47] Yet it adapted
the original model in two significant ways: by considerably enlarging the
bondholding public, and by encouraging the purchase of the public debt of
client states by domestic bondholders. In many ways, this *rentier* expansionism
fulfilled the vision expounded in the previous century by Voyer d'Argenson of
a "democratic monarchy" (or "royal democracy"), reconciled with modern
commerce, backed up by a large investing public, and capable of projecting
power abroad.[48]

A major link in the revival of this eighteenth-century vision after 1815 was
the Prince de Talleyrand. As noted in the first chapter, Talleyrand, in his observations on the persistence of British ascendance in the young American
Republic during his exile there, already pointed to the role of British credit,
alongside cultural factors such as a common language, in the forging of "a connection difficult to break off" even after formal independence.[49] In his memoirs, Talleyrand confessed to a veritable passion for public finance, a subject
which he discovered as *agent général* (financial secretary) of the French clergy
in the 1780s and which subsequently remained, in his eyes, "so full of charm."
The same memoirs show that Talleyrand held the Physiocrats in limited es-
teem. Instead, his mentor was the cosmopolitan Protestant financier Isaac
Panchaud, "a man of genius," endowed with "the most ardent, the most exten-

---

46. Martin Daunton, *Trusting Leviathan: The Politics of Taxation in Britain, 1799–1914* (Cambridge: Cambridge University Press, 2001), 49, 109–35.

47. On the concept of fiscal-military state, see John Brewer, *The Sinews of Power: War, Money
and the English State, 1688–1783* (London: Unwin Hyman, 1989) and *The British Fiscal Military
States, 1660–c.1783*, eds. Aaron Graham and Patrick Walsh (London: Routlege, 2016). For a long-
term perspective on the French fiscal-military state, see Richard Bonney, "The Rise of the Fiscal
State in France, 1500–1914," *The Rise of Fiscal States: A Global History, 1500–1914*, eds. Bartolome
Yun-Casalilla and Patrick O'Brien (New York: Cambridge University Press, 2012), 93–110.

48. At the same time, Voyer d'Argenson was fiercely hostile to territorial expansion; see
Sonenscher, *Before the Deluge*, 160–5.

49. Talleyrand-Périgord, *Mémoire sur les relations commerciales*, 29.

sive and the most rigorous mind."[50] Another admirer of Law, Panchaud had published a spirited defence of public indebtedness in 1781 that propounded various institutional mechanisms—a *caisse d'escompte* (discounting bank) and a *caisse d'amortissement* (sinking fund)—to reduce the costs of public borrowing.[51] In Talleyrand's opinion, France lost its global struggle with Britain between 1793 and 1815 because the latter heeded Panchaud's advice.[52]

The Restoration's embracing of public credit after 1815 may be construed as the belated triumph of Panchaud's vision. One of the main architects of the new policy was Joseph-Dominique Louis, three times minister of finance between 1814 and 1819 and an old protégé of Talleyrand.[53] Yet the most spectacular effort to restore the legitimacy of credit as a sound system of public finance was the pamphlet entitled *Réflexions sur la réduction de la rente* (1824). This work was signed by the liberal banker Jacques Laffitte, but its actual author was probably the young journalist Adolphe Thiers, another protégé of Talleyrand.[54] In the first two volumes of his *Histoire de la Révolution française*, which rendered him famous in 1823, Thiers already lavished praise on the financial wisdom of the plan defended by the "bishop of Autun" [Talleyrand] to rescue the French monarchy from bankruptcy in 1790, and in 1826 he published an analysis of Law's system that lamented the failure of the Scottish financier's "unfortunate genius."[55]

The *Réflexions* caused a mini scandal among French liberals. First, the book appeared to endorse a contemporary project of the royalist government to

50. Talleyrand-Périgord, *Mémoires*, eds. Couchoud and Couchoud, 88–91.

51. Isaac Panchaud, *Réflexions sur l'état actuel du crédit de l'Angleterre et de la France* (Paris, 1781); on Panchaud's ideas, see Herbert Lüthy, *La banque protestante en France: de la Révocation de l'Édit de Nantes à la Révolution*, 2 vols., 3rd edn (Paris: EHESS, 1998), vol. 2, 390–1, 420–38, and Michel Lutfalla, "Économistes britanniques et français face à la question de l'amortissement: d'Isaac Panchaud aux lendemains de la loi de 1816," in *1816 ou la genèse de la foi publique*, eds. Aglan, Margairaz and Verheyde, 23–42.

52. Talleyrand-Périgord, *Mémoires*, eds. Couchoud and Couchoud, 91.

53. François Bonneville, "Le Baron Louis (1755–1837): Portait d'un financier au service de l'État," *Revue française de finances publiques*, 128 (2014); Yves Guénin, *Le baron Louis. 1755–1837* (Paris: Perrin, 1999), esp. 18–20 on Louis and Talleyrand's views on public finance.

54. Bertrand Gille, *La banque en France au 19e siècle. Recherches historiques* (Geneva: Droz, 1970), 111.

55. Adolphe Thiers, *Histoire de la Révolution française*, 10 vols. (Paris: Lecomte et Durey, 1823–1827), vol. 1, 211, 278; Adolphe Thiers, *Law, et de son système de finance* (Paris: Bureau de l'encyclopédie progressive, 1826), 79; see also Adolphe Thiers, *Histoire de Law* (Paris: Michel-Lévy, 1858).

impose a conversion of existing state bonds that would reduce their yield and therefore the income of bondholders. Self-interest reinforced the instinctive rejection of a royalist proposal, because the majority of bondholders were reputed to belong to the more commercially minded liberal party.[56] Second, liberal hostility was grounded in a principled opposition to the expansion of public credit. Jean-Baptiste Say, the leading liberal political economist, maintained in successive editions of his *Treatise on Political Economy* that capital borrowed by the state was always "dissipated and wasted."[57] In an implicit response to the *Réflexions*, Say added to the fifth edition of his *Treatise* (1826) a scathing attack on the growth of public credit enabled by cosmopolitan "financial companies" since 1815, with the result that "capital accumulated by industry and individual economy in all the corners of the world [was] pumped up and handed over to the great powers."[58]

While Say harked back to Physiocratic hostility towards public credit, Laffitte (or Thiers) heaped praise on the efforts of the late Old Regime to manage its public debt more effectively, and even on Law's System, a "system so simple, so grand, which displays so well the characteristics of a great progress in social machinery."[59] The key to the emulation of Britain's economic success, the author of the *Réflexions* contended, was a decline in the rate of interest that would facilitate both public and private borrowing. The *Réflexions* was not a mere resurrection of older ideas, because it pointed to the growing interconnectedness of financial centres since the end of the Napoleonic Wars, a phenomenon demonstrated by the contribution of foreign investors to the Bourbon Restoration's first loans—a new factor that infinitely expanded the amount of capital that states could borrow: "The bonds of all states," it claimed, now "belonged to capitalists from all states."[60]

56. At least until the following year, when the payment of a large indemnity, under the form of *rentes*, to those expropriated during the Revolution increased bondholding among royalist aristocrats; see Christian Rietsch, "Le 'milliard des émigrés' et la création de la rente 3%," in *Le Marché financier*, vol. 2, 209–60.

57. Say, *Traité d'économie politique. Édition variorum*, vol. 2, 1043.

58. Say, *Traité d'économie politique. Édition variorum*, vol. 2, 1055–61; see also the attack on the *Réflexions* by a Swiss radical admirer of Say, Jean-Jacob Fazy, "Examen et réfutation de l'ouvrage de M. Laffitte," in Jean-Jacob Fazy, *Opuscules financiers sur l'effet des privilèges, des emprunts publics et des conversions sur le crédit de l'industrie en France* (Paris: Naudin, 1826).

59. Jacques Laffitte, *Réflexions sur la réduction de la rente et sur l'état du crédit* (Paris: Bossange père, 1824), 24.

60. Ibid., 155–6.

Thiers's authorship of the *Réflexions* is not certain, but at least he wholeheartedly espoused its conclusions: in his correspondence with the editor of the German liberal daily the *Allgemeine Zeitung*, he described the book as "a work of genius."[61] Thiers's personal immorality and political cynicism often evoked the reprobation of his contemporaries. Alexis de Tocqueville, for instance, called him "the grandson of Machiavelli" (Talleyrand, Thiers's patron, was almost certainly the son in this putative genealogy).[62] His bloody repression of the Paris Commune has also tainted his memory in the eyes of progressive historians. Yet none of his private or public misdeeds should detract from his significance as a consistent advocate of the expansion of public credit in nineteenth-century France, from his probable authorship of the *Réflexions* to the success of the *emprunt Thiers* to finance the indemnity owed to Germany after the war of 1870–1871.[63] Just as William Ewart Gladstone came to embody the Victorian passion for fiscal rectitude, Thiers often appeared as the incarnation of the new French passion for public borrowing.[64] Such was Thiers's eloquence on financial matters, a British banker established in Paris for three decades later reminisced that he once "for more than four hours kept the audience [in the chamber of deputies] spellbound by the magic of his tongue." Indeed, according to the same banker, the only other European statesman who shared Thiers's "gift of dealing with abstruse financial problems and dry budget questions, in a way interesting to the general public" was "Mr Gladstone," although the two men upheld almost opposed principles.[65]

The prominent role played by Talleyrand and his protégés towards the rehabilitation of public credit is significant from the perspective of this book, because these statesmen were as interested in the projection of French power abroad as in the preservation of domestic stability. Furthermore, Laffitte or Thiers's *Réflexions* helped nurture the passion for public borrowing of the nascent Saint-Simonian movement, which would in turn exercise an extra-

61. Thiers to Johann Friedrich Cotta, 1 Aug. 1824, in Robert Marquant, *Thiers et le baron Cotta. Étude sur la collaboration de Thiers à la Gazette d'Augsbourg* (Paris: Presses Universitaires de France, 1959), 157–60.

62. Tocqueville to Louis de Kergolay, 5 Aug. 1836; quoted in Jaume, *Tocqueville*, 390.

63. Robert Schnerb, "La politique fiscale de Thiers," *Revue historique*, 201 and 202 (1949); Stephen Sawyer, "A Fiscal Revolution: Statecraft in France's Early Third Republic," *American Historical Review*, 121, 4 (2016).

64. Eugenio Biagini, *Liberty, Retrenchment and Reform: Popular Liberalism in the Age of Gladstone* (Cambridge: Cambridge University Press, 1992), 103–38.

65. Edward Blount, *Memoirs*, ed. S. J. Reid (London: Longmans & Co, 1902), 252.

ordinary influence in the corridors of power under the July Monarchy and the Second Empire. In a journal founded in 1825 and subsidized by Laffitte, Saint-Simonian writers highlighted the merits of Law's system and of investment in various forms of public debt, foreign as well as French.[66] Prosper Enfantin, the leader or "supreme father" of the Saint-Simonian sect, even proposed the gradual but complete substitution of taxation by public borrowing as a way of mobilizing the capital owned by the idle classes. Such a shift, he argued, would crown the transition from a feudal order to an industrial one, by "completely replacing the use of force with an act of confidence in the material relations between the government and the governed."[67] Similarly, the gigantic "Mediterranean System" of steamship lines, railways and roads imagined by Michel Chevalier, Enfantin's main disciple, would be mostly financed by public loans.[68]

After he formally rejected Saint-Simonianism in 1832, Chevalier renounced the sect's utopian objectives and phraseology, but he remained a fervent advocate of public borrowing for funding new infrastructures. The official purpose of his journey across North America—commissioned by Thiers, then minister of commerce and public works—between 1833 and 1835 was to examine the merits of the public financing of railway construction, practiced by American federated States, as a potential alternative to the British model of private financing, favoured by other French liberals.[69] A similar desire to increase the legitimacy of public debt probably explains why Thiers, during his second spell as prime minister in 1840, appointed Chevalier as professor of political economy at the Collège de France. The promotion of public borrowing became a recurring theme of Chevalier's lectures. The distrust of public credit, he conceded, may have been legitimate under the bellicose and secretive Old Regime. But the Revolution of 1789, backed up by that of 1830, made

66. P[rosper] Enfantin, "Des banquiers cosmopolites" and "Opuscules financiers," and J. Allier, "Crédit, discrédit, banquiers, industriels, industrie, producteur," Le Producteur, 2 (1826); and O[linde] R[odrigue], "Considérations sur le Système de Law," Le Producteur, 4 (1826). On Saint-Simonian ideas about finance, see Gilles Jacoud, Political Economy and Industrialism: Banks in Saint-Simonian Economic Thought (London: Routledge, 2010) and Clément Coste, "L'économique contre le politique: la dette, son amortissement et son financement chez de jeunes et vieux Saint-Simoniens (1825–1880)," Cahiers d'économie politique, 70, 1 (2016).

67. P[rosper] E[nfantin], "Du système des emprunts comparé à celui des impôts," Le Producteur, 3 (1826): 249.

68. Michel Chevalier, "Le système," 132.

69. Walch, Michel Chevalier, 37–8.

such suspicions groundless: the "hideous bankruptcy," "this monster against which Mirabeau [*fils*, who shared his father's views on public credit] formerly made his thunderous voice heard" in the Constituent Assembly, was "much less to be feared" now that France had a transparent budget that was subject to parliamentary scrutiny. Chevalier acknowledged the hostility of British economists to public indebtedness, but attributed it to the persistence of an "aristocratic" distrust of royal power among British liberals. This didn't apply to France's "democratic" July Monarchy, while the development of public credit would consolidate the regime by encouraging investment among all classes.[70]

This vibrant defence of public borrowing as a means of accelerating economic development may not seem that original in the twenty-first century, but in the 1840s it was iconoclastic. Chevalier's lectures were sneered at by orthodox economists.[71] A large fraction of the audience was made up of Saint-Simonians. Such a large number of former disciples attended Chevalier's inaugural lecture that Ismaÿl Urbain, who was also present, compared the event to "a resurrection of the dead."[72] The programme expounded upon by Chevalier—including the creation of national deposit banks and state guarantee on loans by railway companies—prefigured the policies that he and other former Saint-Simonians implemented under the Second Empire. Another probable attendee of the lectures was Lorenz von Stein, the German economist and sociologist, who as a student in Paris in the early 1840s took a special interest in Saint-Simonianism and socialist doctrines. Stein was a pivotal figure in the emergence of German *Kathersozialismus*, which exercised considerable influence on public policies as far as the United States and Japan in the second half of the nineteenth century.[73] The impact of Stein's engagement with France's earlier enthusiasm for public debt could be detected in his treatise on

70. Michel Chevalier, "Discours d'ouverture de l'année 1842–43," in *Cours d'économie politique*, 1st edn., 3 vols. (Paris: Capelle, 1842–1850), vol. 2, 1–24 (esp. 13–17); Michel Chevalier, "Discours d'ouverture de l'année 1843–44" and "Discours d'ouverture de l'année 1844–45," in *Cours d'économie politique*, 2nd edn., 3 vols. (Paris: Capelle, 1855–1866), vol.1, 63–107 (esp. 65, 95).

71. See for instance the hostile review in the *Journal des économistes*, 1 (1842): 204–8.

72. Levallois, *Ismaÿl Urbain. Une autre conquête*, 320–1.

73. Herbert Hax, *Vademecum zu einem Klassiker der Staatswissenschaft* (Düsseldorf: Verlag Wirtschaft und Finanzen, 1998); on the impact of German economic and social reformism in the United States, see Daniel T. Rodgers, *Atlantic Crossings: Social Politics in a Progressive Age* (Cambridge, MA: Belknap, 1998).

public finance (1860), which asserted the superiority of a "French [economic] literature" favourable to public indebtedness over an "English literature" that remained consistently hostile.[74]

This gradual rehabilitation of public indebtedness after the Napoleonic Wars is crucial when it comes to understanding Paul Leroy-Beaulieu's equanimity towards public borrowing, and the way it metamorphosed into enthusiasm for foreign investment as a new form of colonization. Leroy-Beaulieu did not employ the utopian language of the Saint-Simonians to defend public debt. Yet his own *Traité sur la sciences des finances* (1877) bore the mark of Chevalier (his father-in-law)'s influence, as well as that of the defence of public indebtedness by Stein and his disciples. Leroy-Beaulieu took pains to refute the work of Dudley Baxter, a British economist and statistician who, a few years earlier, had accused France's "Latin" temperament of being responsible for the rapid global expansion of public indebtedness after 1850: as "the leading Continental Nation, that set the fashion in finance and armaments, as well as in less important matters . . . [France's] example had a great effect upon neighbouring budgets."[75] Leroy-Beaulieu invoked the large public debt accumulated by several "Teutonic" nations in the past (Holland and Britain in the eighteenth century, the United States during the Civil War) to disprove Baxter's theory about "the alleged influence of race on the formation of the debts of different nations." Noting that only "primitive"—mostly African—states were completely without a public debt, Leroy-Beaulieu went further and asserted that contracting a public loan was generally "the first step taken by a nation on the path of civilization."[76]

Universal approval of public indebtedness, as a mark of a globally spreading civilization, was connected with the stalwart support of Leroy-Beaulieu and other French writers for the exportation of capital. Intellectual historians have noted a discrepancy between the hostility of British economists to capital export and the actual expansion of British foreign investment after 1850. Following Edward Gibbon Wakefield, John Stuart Mill made an exception with

74. Lorenz von Stein, *Lehrbuch der Finanzwissenschaft* (Leipzig: J. A. Brockhaus, 1860), 460–2; see also Carl-Ludwig Holtfrerich, "Public Debt in Post-1850 German Economic Thought vis-a-vis the Pre-1850 British Classical School," *German Economic Review*, 15, 1 (2013).

75. Robert Dudley Baxter, *National Debts* (London: Robert John Bush, 1871), 81.

76. Paul Leroy-Beaulieu, *Traité de la science des finances*, 2 vols. (Paris: Corbeil, 1877), vol. 2, 468–76.

regard to the exportation of capital to British settler colonies.[77] But it was Leroy-Beaulieu who generalized this principle, declaring capital export to be almost always beneficial, in *De la colonisation chez les peuples modernes*—a work written in the 1860s, in the midst of the French capital-export boom, even if it was only published in 1874. Leroy-Beaulieu invoked Wakefield and Stuart Mill's views, but consciously or not, he deformed them by extending their conclusions, which had been limited to Britain's settler colonies,to the entire world.[78]

Leroy-Beaulieu radicalized this vision in the second edition of *De la colonisation* (1882) and noted its special application to the case of France, a country rich in capital but with few emigrants due to its demographic stagnation: "The true sinews of colonization are investments much more than emigrants. France has capital in abundance; she lets it travel willingly; her trusting hands disseminate it to the four corners of the universe."[79] In the same edition, Leroy-Beaulieu highlighted the many political and economic advantages to be derived by France from the payment of a "tribute" by borrowing countries. Not least was the way in which capital export enabled the wider public to participate in and benefit from French expansion: "every person who saves some money, a small employee, a farmer, a worker, a spinster or a widow, can, while staying close to their fireplace and without any great knowledge of geography, powerfully contribute to colonization, to the exploitation of the globe."[80] Leroy-Beaulieu's *De la colonisation* has sometimes been cited as a blueprint for the Third Republic's territorial empire. Yet its originality, based on the reappraisal of public indebtedness since 1815, lay in this novel concept of "investment colonization" (*colonisation des capitaux*) as an alternative to territorial empire.

The Haitian Origins of French Capital Exports

French financial imperialism was far from a purely intellectual construct. The ideas of Laffitte, Thiers, Chevalier and Leroy-Beaulieu were also inspired by the rapid progress of the cross-border circulation of capital and its political

77. Donald Winch, *Classical Political Economy and Colonies* (London: G. Bell & Sons, 1965), 76–81, 140–1; Semmel, *The Rise of Free Trade Imperialism*, 85–91.

78. Leroy-Beaulieu, *De la colonisation*, 1st edn., 491–500.

79. Leroy-Beaulieu, *De la colonisation*, 2nd edn., vii.

80. Leroy-Beaulieu, *De la colonisation*, 2nd edn., 536–41.

implications after 1815. The influx of foreign capital into France in the aftermath of the Napoleonic Wars turned French *rentes* into Europe's "most international" security and helped establish Paris as a key centre of international finance by 1820.[81] Laffitte (or Thiers) contended that this new "intimacy" between financial places, especially Paris and London, extended the possibilities of state borrowing, while Leroy-Beaulieu lauded the opportunities for French finance created by this "internationality" of capital markets.[82] By the 1820s, Paris was already enjoying a significant role in the nascent global market in government bonds. This new type of investment was connected with hopes of establishing a novel style of European dominance in the Americas, as shown, in France's case, by the interest of the government and financiers in a loan to the republic of Haiti in 1825. The boom ended with a crash, but it laid the foundations of a more sustained increase in lending to foreign states after 1850.

The first capital export boom of the nineteenth century has often been described as a predominantly British affair, as the fledgling Spanish American republics issued all their loans in London. Yet this choice of London was largely determined by contingent geopolitical motives: the British government favoured the independence of the new republics, while Continental powers were hostile—Bourbon France especially so, due to its alliance with the Spanish Bourbons and lingering hopes of regaining control over its own breakaway colony of Saint-Domingue.[83] As the widespread circulation of Abbé du Pradt's publications shows (see chapter 1), the French public did not share its government's misgivings about the independence of Spanish America. Liberal opinion, at least, was favourable. The emissaries of the self-proclaimed independent American republics were feted in Parisian salons, and the contracts for the loans they were sent to negotiate were redacted in French, in French law, and signed on French soil. This choice of a French legal vehicle was in part opportunistic. It enabled the British agents in charge of issuing the loans to bypass the more stringent British legislation on usury (so that Spanish

---

81. Ranald C. Michie, *The Global Securities Market: A History* (Oxford: Oxford University Press, 2006), 63–5.

82. Laffitte, *Réflexions*, 86; Leroy-Beaulieu, *Traité*, vol. 2, 146–7.

83. Rafe Blaufarb, "The Western Question: The Geopolitics of Latin American Independence," *American Historical Review*, 112, 3 (2007); see also *Connections after Colonialism: Europe and Latin America*, eds. Matthew Brown and Gabriel Paquette (Tuscaloosa: University of Alabama Press, 2013).

American bonds could yield a nominal 6 percent or 7 percent, instead of the maximum 5 percent for British securities) and to avoid taxation of the interest paid on the loan by the British government.[84] But there is reason to think that France provided more than just a legal framework for the exportation of European capital to Latin America, and that the French public took a serious interest in Spanish American bonds as investment opportunities.

For instance, the first British lawsuit against an issuer of Spanish American bonds was brought by a French financier, Gabriel Doloret. In January 1823, eight months after the first 1 million pounds sterling (25 million francs) Colombian loan began to be marketed in London, Doloret asked for an injunction to ban the loan's British agents from further parting with the proceeds, until the Colombian government's consent to the loan could be ascertained. Doloret himself held Colombian bonds with a face value of three thousand pounds sterling. Incidental remarks in his bill of complaints suggest that the loan had attracted French as well as British investors: Colombian bonds, he asserted, had been "very generally circulated in London and Paris," "obtained credit in those cities" and the agents for the loan "continued to produce, issue, dispose of and circulate [the bonds] in the public money market of London, and also in that of Paris." In support of his request for an injunction, Doloret invoked the legal opinion of a French lawyer that the contract for the loan—"written . . . in the French language" and "entered into and signed and sealed" in Paris on 13 March 1822—was in reality "not binding" in French law.[85] The Chancery Court, judging in equity rather than Common Law, upheld Doloret's request against the agents of "the alleged and supposed Colombian government," although four months later "matters"

84. Frank G. Dawson, *The First Latin American Debt Crisis: The City of London and the 1822–25 Loan Bubble* (New Haven, CT: Yale University Press, 1990), 28; Michael P. Costeloe, *Bonds and Bondholders: British Investors and Mexico's Foreign Debt, 1824–1888* (Westport, CT: Praeger, 2003), 14–16; Maurice Lévy-Leboyer, *Les banques européennes et l'industrialisation internationale dans la première moitié du XIXe siècle* (Paris: Presses Universitaires de France, 1964), 464–88; Juan Flores, "Bonds and Brands: Foundations of Sovereign Debt Markets, 1820–1830," *Journal of Economic History*, 69, 3 (2009).

85. Pleadings for Gabriel Marie Doloret vs Charles Herring, William Graham, John Diston Powles, and Simon Bolivar, 16 and 17 Jan. 1823, Kew (London), The National Archives (henceforth TNA), C 13/2173/15 and C 13/2175/28; according to *The Times*, 20 Jan. 1823, Doloret's lawsuit was "well known, and the utmost anxiety to know the particulars [was] felt by thousands of persons" who had purchased Spanish American bonds.

between the plaintiff and the defendants were "accommodated" out of court and the injunction lifted.[86]

Doloret was a louche character. In 1818, he lost his position as *receveur general* in Amiens (Somme) after embezzling public funds.[87] Between 1824 and 1833, he was involved in at least three minor financial scandals: the forged endorsement of a bill of exchange transmitting 10,000 pounds sterling (250,000 francs) from London to Paris; the defrauding of a Parisian merchant, conned into believing that an associate of Doloret's owned vast plantations in Haiti, to the tune of 700,000 francs; and a failed attempt to raise a loan for the insurgent government of Don Carlos, the reactionary pretender to the Spanish throne.[88] There can be little doubt that Doloret's primary motive, with regards to the Colombian loan as well as other affairs, was his material interest. But his dabbling in post-Napoleonic cross-border finance and its colonial ramifications suggested an increasing French appetite for international investment, as was his claim—uncontested by the defending agents of the Colombian loan or the Chancery Court—that Spanish American bonds were commonly traded in Paris in as early as 1823. His involvement in the Colombian loan helps to explain the claim of Laffitte—or more likely, that of Thiers—in *Réflexions* that investors now lent "to all the governments," including the absolutist governments of Prussia and Russia, the "barbaric governments" of Spain and Portugal, and even "those whose colour has not yet been amnested by the whites of Europe," a probable allusion to Spanish American republics, which were often perceived as non-White countries.[89]

One French firm that purchased large quantities of Spanish American securities was the Banque Paravey & Cie, founded by Pierre-François Paravey in

---

86. Court of Chancery decrees, 20 Jan. 1823 and 1 Feb. 1823, TNA, C33/702, fols. 315, 400; 26 Mar. 1823 and 7 Apr. 1823, TNA, C33/703, fols. 702, 737; 1 May 1823, TNA, C33/704, fol. 1101.

87. Pinaud, *Les receveurs généraux*, 117.

88. On the bill of exchange, see *The Times*, 24, 28 and 30 June 1824, and Rothschild frères to N. M. Rothschild, 28 June 1824, The Rothschild Archive, London (henceforth TRA), XI/85/8A; on the swindling of a Parisian merchant, see *Plaidoyer de Maître Lavaux, dans le procès entre le Sieur Darrac et le Sieur Friedlein* (Paris: Porthmann, 1833), esp. 4, 20 and 30 for further biographical information on Doloret; and on the aborted attempt to issue a loan for the Carlist insurgents, see *Mémoire pour M. Tassin de Messilly prévenu d'avoir pratiqué des manœuvres et entretenu des intelligences avec Don Carlos* (Paris: Dezauche, 1834) and *Procès instruit contre MM Jauge, Tassin de Messilly, Gabriel Doloret etc. prévenus d'avoir favorisé l'entreprise de Don Carlos contre l'Espagne* (Paris: Dezauche, 1834).

89. Laffitte, *Réflexions*, 40–1.

1818.[90] Paravey was a veteran of revolutionary armies who became a merchant specialized in the importation (and possibly smuggling) of colonial goods into the French-occupied Rhineland in the early 1800s. After the collapse of the Napoleonic Empire, he relocated from Mainz to Paris, where he became the manager of a small bank. The bank's sole *commanditaire* (investor-partner), for one million francs, was the Duc de Dalberg, a Rhineland aristocrat who elected to remain French after 1814. Dalberg enjoyed numerous connections in the worlds of international politics and finance. In 1810, and in return for a loan, he obtained the passport that enabled Jakob (later James de) Rothschild to settle in France and eventually found the French branch of the Rothschild House.[91] Since serving as Baden's ambassador in Paris in 1803, Dalberg had also become an intimate friend of Talleyrand, who in turn invested one million francs in Paravey & Cie in 1822.

The only extant study of Paravey & Cie, now nearly fifty years old, linked its eventual demise to the relative backwardness of France's "financing of industrialization."[92] Greater hindsight, and Cain and Hopkins's insistence that, even in nineteenth-century Britain, the growth of modern finance owed at least as much to overseas ventures as to the rise of modern manufacturing, suggest rather that the Paravey bank's fortunes were tied to the rapid but brief resurgence of colonial trade in the early years of the Restoration; and that it was its involvement in the Haitian loan of 1825, part of France's efforts to reassert a measure of political and economic control over its former colony of Saint-Domingue, which caused its downfall.

At first, Paravey & Cie was very prosperous. It speculated on cotton, coffee and other *denrées coloniales* and took a controlling share in several sugar refineries. Its investments in Parisian real estate included a terrain destined for the construction of a new warehouse for tropical products. Inquiries made by Paravey about the insuring of ships against British capture suggest that the bank may have been involved in the illicit French slave trade of the 1820s.[93] Dalberg, and perhaps Talleyrand, also used their personal account with Paravey & Cie to purchase large quantities of Spanish American stocks issued in

---

90. Most of the information on Paravey & Cie in this and the following paragraphs is drawn from Karl-Georg Faber, "Aristokratie und Finanz. Das Pariser Bankhaus Paravey et Compagnie (1819–1828)," *Vierteljahrschrift für Sozial- und Wirtschaftsgeschichte*, 57, 2 (1970).

91. Gille, *Histoire de la Maison Rothschild*, vol. 1, 45.

92. Faber, "Aristokratie und Finanz": 206.

93. Paravey to N. M. Rothschild, 10 and 26 Apr. 1823, TRA, XI/38/200.

London. By February 1823, Dalberg's holdings included some Colombian bonds—the same security over which Doloret brought his lawsuit—with a considerable face value of fifty-three thousand pounds sterling (1.325 million francs).[94] Dalberg also speculated on Mexican, Brazilian, Russian, Spanish and Piedmontese bonds, as well as French *rentes*.[95]

Dalberg's investment decisions on the bond market were frequently determined by geopolitical considerations, and ultimately relied on his privileged access to political and diplomatic circles. For instance, in 1820 he cited informants in Madrid to justify his large purchases of Spanish bonds: "[Spain's] colonies," he had been assured, "for the most part will return to the mother country, or will take on a share of the [Spanish] debt."[96] His growing interest in Spanish American bonds was almost certainly connected to Abbé de Pradt's propaganda in favour of the independence of Spain's colonies. Dalberg, like Talleyrand, was personally acquainted with Pradt. In his memoirs, Talleyrand recalled how, in February 1814, the three men were surprised in his salon by the minister of police, who accused them (with some justice) of "conspiracy against the government [of Napoleon]."[97] And Dalberg read Pradt's prose: "send me without delay Mr de Pradt's latest pamphlet," he instructed Paravey, during a stay in Turin in 1820.[98] However, Paravey himself was reluctant to invest the bank's funds in foreign bonds, due to what he perceived as the greater dangers of such political investments: "Not only can governments borrow too much, poorly administer their finances, face unforeseen wars, experience internal commotions, but the value of public bonds can be significantly altered by a mere accident or a personal misfortune, or even a mistake of the public, which lets itself become misled so easily."[99]

---

94. Paravey to N. M. Rothschild, 5 Feb. 1823, TRA, XI/38/200.

95. Paravey to Dalberg, 22 Feb. 1820 (sale of French *rentes*), 11 Mar. 1820 (purchase of Russian bonds), 29 Apr. 1820 (sale of Piedmontese bonds), and 27 May 1820 (purchase of Spanish bonds), Worms Stadtarchiv (hereafter WS), Dalberg MSS,159/376/2; Paravey to Dalberg, 5 Feb. 1825 (purchase of Brazilian bonds), and 6 Feb. 1826 (purchase of Colombian bonds) WS, Dalberg MSS, 159/376/6; Paravey to Dalberg, 18 Oct. 1827 (purchase of Mexican bonds), WS, Dalberg MSS, 159/742.

96. Dalberg to Paravey, 8 July 1820, WS, Dalberg MSS, 159/376/2.

97. Talleyrand-Périgord, *Mémoires*, eds. Couchoud and Couchoud, 599.

98. Dalberg to Paravey, 10 June 1820, WS, Dalberg MSS, 159/376/2.

99. Paravey to Dalberg, 4 Nov. 1824, WS, Dalberg MSS, 159/376/7; see also Paravey to Dalberg, 23 May 1820, WS, Dalberg MSS, 159/376/2.

This caution did not dampen Paravey's extraordinary enthusiasm at the prospect of a Haitian loan.[100] When he found out, in August 1825, that Haiti had accepted the conditions laid out by France in return for the recognition of its independence, Paravey, who had just arrived in Le Havre to inspect a sugar refinery, only stayed to "change horses" and returned "immediately" to Paris. When he reached France's capital city, he still felt "shaken" and "excited."[101] He instructed his son to make immediate preparations for a trip to Haiti, where the young Paravey would seek investment opportunities for the bank. Yet the main cause of Paravey's prompt return to Paris was his desire to obtain a share of the loan that would serve to finance Haiti's indemnity to expropriated French colonists. Friends of his patrons in the government had informed him that an indemnity, financed by a loan to be raised on the Parisian market, was one of the conditions of the recognition of Haitian independence. Thanks to the same connections, Paravey obtained the right to issue 16 percent of the loan, as a part a syndicate of which the other members were Laffitte & Cie (36 percent), Rothschild frères (22 percent), and the Syndicat des receveurs généraux, a banking association of tax officials supervised by the finance ministry (26 percent).[102]

Why did Paravey throw his usual caution regarding foreign bonds to the winds? He was undoubtedly influenced by his patrons' speculations on the bond market and flattered to find himself "in such honourable company"— Laffitte and Rothschild formed the pinnacle of Parisian *haute banque*.[103] Furthermore, Paravey shared the widespread conviction that Saint-Domingue's prosperity could be revived. Haiti, he believed, could pay not only "7 to 8 million [francs] per year," or the amount necessary to service the loan, "but 25 million" if necessary: its public revenue amounted to 40 or 45 million francs, an "exceptional tax" could be levied on "the Haitians who became proprietors of the land thanks to the revolution," and there was always "the resource of the

100. On the enduring memories of Saint-Domingue wealth in post-revolutionary France, see Jean Hébrard, "Les deux vies de Michel Vincent, colon à Saint-Domingue (c. 1730–1804)," *Revue d'histoire moderne et contemporaine*, 57, 2 (2010), and Mary D. Lewis, "Legacies of French Slave-Ownership, or the Long Decolonization of Saint-Domingue," *History Workshop Journal*, 81, 1 (2017).

101. Paravey to Dalberg, 16 Aug. 1825, WS, Dalberg MSS, 159/376/8.

102. Paravey to Dalberg, 28 Aug. 1825, 1, 7, 16 and 24 Sep. 1825, and 2, 8, 12 and 19 Oct. 1825, WS, Dalberg MSS, 159/376/8; Paravey to Talleryand, 25 Oct. 1825, 1 and 5 Nov. 1825, WS, Dalberg MSS, 159/377/1.

103. Paravey to Talleyrand, 5 Nov. 1825, WS, Dalberg MSS, 377/1.

estates and Plantations that [could] be ceded [to French creditors] and leased [to Haitian debtors]."[104] Another crucial factor was the active promotion of the loan by the French state, which seemed to offer an implicit guarantee to investors. French officials were also optimistic about Haiti's commercial prospects, especially as an outlet for French commodities: Haitians were still one of the world's most "consumption-prone" populations, and they remained fond of Paris's "latest fashion" and "Bordeaux wines."[105] The loan, in the minds of French negotiators, would serve to restore commercial relations with Saint-Domingue, because it would have to be paid back in Haitian tropical commodities; it was an economic substitute for the political "suzerainty" that the Haitian government had consistently rejected since the beginning of negotiations.[106] Repeated interventions by Joseph de Villèle to broker the terms of the loan testify to its political nature: "The Haiti loan was concluded as I wanted it," the prime minister wrote in his diary on 4 November 1825.[107]

Despite being a self-professed defender of "liberal ideas" and "constitutional principles," Paravey sneered at the "philanthropic" considerations of some supporters of the recognition of Haitian independence.[108] His meetings

104. Paravey to Dalberg, 2 Oct. 1825, WS, Dalberg MSS, 159/376/8.

105. Ange Mackau, "Extrait du rapport de M. de Mackau sur sa mission à St Domingue," [1825], AAE, Correspondance Politique, Haiti, 1, fol. 26.

106. See untitled report on negotiations with the Haitian republic to the minister of the navy and colonies, June 1824, and "Rapport au Conseil [du Roi]," 1 Aug. 1824, on the French government's preference for "a right of suzerainty and protection" in return for the recognition of independence, or if not possible, "a treaty of alliance and commerce" sealed by "an indemnity of 100 million [francs]," CAOM, CC9A54. Paravey kept abreast of the discussions between the French and Haitian governments, reporting in the summer of 1824 that "the negotiation of St D[omingue]" was "still hanging over this question of suzerainty," in Paravey to Dalberg, 3 Aug. 1824, WS, Dalberg MSS, 159/376/7.

107. Quoted in Gille, La Maison Rothschild, vol. 1, 151–2; on the negotiations, see also Jean-François Brière, Haïti et la France, 161–6, and on the indemnity and its amount, see Frédérique Beauvois, "L'indemnité de Saint-Domingue: 'Dette d'indépendance' ou 'rançon de l'esclavage'?," French Colonial History, 10, 1 (2009), and Frédérique Beauvois, "Monnayer l'incalculable? L'indemnité de Saint-Domingue, entre approximations et bricolage," Revue historique, 655 (2010).

108. On Paravey's politics, see Paravey to Dalberg, 18 Dec. 1819, WS, Dalberg MSS, 159/376/1 and Paravey to Dalberg, 21 Dec. 1827, WS, Dalberg MSS, 159/742. Paravey's sneering at the "philantropic principles" of some advocates of the recognition of Haiti's independence, in Paravey to Dalberg, WS, Dalberg MSS, 159/376/8, was directed at Guillaume-Louis Ternaux, the woollen manufacturer, who condemned "all the prejudices of colour, all these distinctions between the varieties of the human species" in a pamphlet promoting the loan published in

with "the envoys of Haiti" during the negotiation of the loan also tempered his enthusiasm for the future of Franco-Haitian commercial relations. Without explicitly referring to their race, he described himself as "a little disgusted" by the idea of conducting business relations with "the new freedmen" and he "no longer [thought] about sending [his] son to Saint-Domingue."[109] In any event, its participation in the Haitian loan soon caused Paravey & Cie's downfall. The flotation of the loan at the Bourse in November 1825 coincided with a financial panic that began in London when there was an abrupt drop in the value of Spanish American stocks.[110] Paravey & Cie was unable to issue more than a small fraction of its share of the loan and, as a result, failed to honour its obligations with the syndicate. New terms were negotiated, but in March 1828 the bank's inability to make a payment to the syndicate precipitated its liquidation. In his last letter to Dalberg before committing suicide, Pierre-François Paravey lamented that "our only, really and reasonably doubtful affair is that of Haiti."[111] Talleyrand and Dalberg had personally guaranteed the bank's share in the Haitian loan, so they incurred very substantial losses—over two million francs— in addition to the funds they had invested in Paravey & Cie.[112] In subsequent years, Talleyrand repeatedly regretted how "this infamous affair," "this horrible affair," "the affair of Haiti," had left him in dire financial straits.[113]

Due to Haiti's economic decline, the recognition of its independence did not revive the legendary prosperity of trade with Saint-Domingue. French exports to the former colony rose, but continued to lag behind those of Britain and the United States. However, Haiti's new debt—many times renegotiated and only wiped out in the 1930s—eventually proved profitable for French in-

---

November 1825, *Considérations sur l'emprunt d'Haïti* (Paris: Les marchands de nouveautés, 1825), 18, and whose nephew Charles Ternaux served as the Haitian Republic's agent for the loan.

109. Paravey to Talleyrand, 11 Nov. 1825, WS, Dalberg MSS, 159/377/1.

110. Dawson, *The First Latin American Debt Crisis*, 110–37; Maurice Gontard, *La Bourse de Paris (1800–1830)* (Aix-en-Provence: Edisud, 2000), 206–9.

111. Paravey to Dalberg, 21 Mar. 1828, WS, Dalberg MSS, 159/742.

112. Untitled notarized act, between Talleyrand and Dalberg on the one hand, and Laffitte & Cie, Rothschild frères and the Syndicat des receveurs généraux on the other, 24 July 1828, WS, Dalberg MSS, 159/377/3; see also another copy of the same document in Centre des Archives du Monde du Travail, Roubaix (henceforth CAMT), 132 AQ 73, folder 1: "Emprunt d'Haïti et difficultés avec la maison Paravey."

113. Talleyrand to Dalberg, 26 Nov. 1828, 30 June 1829 and 13 Sep. 1829, in Ernst, *Talleyrand und der Herzog von Dalberg*, 62, 68, 80.

vestors and substantially increased France's political clout in Haiti.[114] Payments often took the form of Haitian commodities, especially coffee, and France became once again Haiti's largest export market.[115] Permanent negotiations over debt payments helped the French consul general in Port-au-Prince to play a significant role in national politics, and only after the United States' intervention of 1915 did American influence supersede France's.[116] Another significant, long-term benefit to France of the Haitian loan—and of an equally political loan, issued in Paris by Spain in 1824—was the creation of legal and administrative structures that later enabled Paris to rival London for the issuance of government bonds. It was to facilitate these loans that in November 1823 the French government repealed a ban dating from the 1780s on the quotation of foreign stocks at the Bourse.[117] Yet by subjecting every quotation to the joint authorization of the ministries of finance and foreign affairs, the government was able to influence the success or failure of such issues with French investors.[118]

The emergence of Paris, almost simultaneously with London, as an international market for government bonds was therefore closely connected with aspirations to informal dominance in the decolonizing Americas. Furthermore, after Haiti and Spain quickly defaulted on their loans, in 1828 French courts denied investors the right to seize Haitian or Spanish assets on French soil. The decisions were cloaked in a language of respect for the sovereignty of foreign states: "states are independent from each other," the government-appointed Paris prosecutor insisted, and French "civil law" could not be imposed on foreign governments.[119] The next chapter on extra-territorial juris-

---

114. For a reappraisal of the loan's ultimate benefits for France, see Thomas Piketty, *Capital et idéologie* (Paris: Le Seuil, 2019), 263–7.

115. Benoît Joachim: "Commerce et décolonisation: l'expérience franco-haïtienne au XIXe siècle," *Annales. Économies, Sociétés, Civilisations*, 27, 6 (1972).

116. Brière, *Haïti et la France*, 219–302; Benoit Joachim, *Les racines du sous-développement en Haïti* (Port-au-Prince: H. Deschamps, 1980); Jacques Blancpain, *Un siècle de relations financières entre Haïti et la France: 1825–1922* (Paris: L'Harmattan, 2001); Laurent Dubois, *Haiti: The Aftershocks of History* (New York: Metropolitan Books, 2012), 89–203.

117. The ban dated from 1785; see Gille, *La banque et le crédit*, 226–8 and Lüthy, *La Banque protestante*, vol. 3, 702–3.

118. Joseph de Villèle to Syndicat des agents de changes, 12 Nov. 1825 (copy), AAE, Contentieux, 752 SUP 145.

119. [Charles Ternaux and Joseph Gandolphe], *Procès pour la république d'Haïti* (Paris: Veuve Porthmann, 1828), 20, 25, in relation of the case Ternaux, Gandolphe & Cie vs Republic of Haiti, Paris tribunal, 25 Apr. 1828; on the same day, the Paris tribunal dismissed a claim against Spain

diction will show that in other circumstances, especially in relation to French economic interests in the Middle East and Asia, France's judiciary would show fewer qualms about intervening in foreign legal orders. In reality, the 1828 rulings conformed to the wishes of the French government, which in later years consistently instructed courts to ignore such requests for redress, because it wanted to remain sole judge of what sanctions should be taken against defaulting foreign states. [120] Investment in foreign public debt remained primarily construed as a political matter, rather than a legal or economic one.[121]

Conquest by Money in the Middle East

After the crash of the late 1820s, French (and British) foreign investment fell back to very low levels, which lasted around twenty years (see figure 4.1). Issues of foreign sovereign debt in Paris were rare, but investment in the national debt took on a more imperial flavour as the enormous costs of the conquest of Algeria (about 1.5 billion francs between 1830 and 1848) were a major factor behind its rapid growth under the July Monarchy.[122] The resurgence of French investment in foreign public debt after 1850 can therefore be connected to the

that had defaulted on a loan contracted in order to finance a military "expedition to America," in the case Blaguerie, Saget et Cie vs the Kingdom of Spain, in *Procès pour la république d'Haïti*, 3–6

120. On these efforts to maintain the 1828 jurisprudence, reiterated by the Cour de Cassation, the supreme civil law court, on 23 January 1849, see "Avis du Comité du Contentieux, question de l'incompétence des tribunaux," Apr. 1854, AAE, Contentieux, 752 SUP 111.

121. British courts also refused to take cognizance of investors' requests for redress in cases of foreign sovereign defaults, but unlike in France, the jurisprudence probably contributed to the reluctance of British investors to purchase foreign public debt; see, for instance, Robert Phillimore, *Commentaries upon International Law*, 4 vols., 3rd edn (London: Butterworth, 1879–1889) vol. 2, 9–11. On the connections between military interventions to enforce debt repayment, often termed "supersanctions," and imperialism, see Kris J. Mitchener and Marc Weidenmier, "Empire, Public Goods and the Roosevelt Corollary," *Journal of Economic History*, 65, 3 (2005), and Kris J. Mitchener and Marc Weidenmier, "Supersanctions and Debt Repayment," *Journal of International Money and Finance*, 29, 1 (2010).

122. Only two foreign loans, by Belgium and the Papal States, were issued in Paris in the 1830s; see Youssef Cassis, *Capitals of Capital: A History of International Financial Centres, 1780–2005* (Cambridge: Cambridge University Press, 2006), 30; on the fiscal costs of the Algerian conquest and the growth of France's national debt, see Jerome Greenfield, "The Price of Violence: Money, the French State and 'civilization' during the Conquest of Algeria, 1830–1850s," forthcoming in *French Historical Studies*.

economic disillusion with France's colonial venture in North Africa, discussed
in chapter 2, and the adoption of a more informal approach to global expansion under the Second Napoleonic Empire. During the reign of Napoleon III,
the growth of the national debt, facilitated by the creation of new national
deposit banks (Crédit Mobilier and Crédit Foncier in the 1850s, Crédit Lyonnais and Société Générale in the 1860s) continued unabated to fund new
urban and transport infrastructures, as well as military interventions.[123] Yet it
was accompanied by a surge of investment in the debt of foreign states, most
of them French allies or clients. The Bonapartist government encouraged this
channelling of French savings into foreign public debts for economic and political reasons. According to the influential minister Eugène Rouher (dubbed
the "vice-emperor" by contemporaries, and the model for the power-grabbing
politician Eugène Rougon, Aristide Saccard's brother, in Zola's *Rougon-
Macquart* series), this lending not only enabled France to levy "an enormous
tribute" on borrowing states, under the form of increased orders for French
commodities as well as debt payments, it also established over them a "suzerainty" comparable to British domination over Portugal and some Latin American states.[124]

This politico-economic logic informed French capital exports in Europe,
notably in the case of vast French purchases of Piedmontese and—after Italy's
unification in 1860—Italian bonds, designed to facilitate the replacement of
Austrian by French paramountcy in the peninsula.[125] Efforts to regain Continental supremacy by financial means culminated in the Latin Monetary
Union, which briefly turned large parts of Europe into a Franc zone of sorts in
the second half of the 1860s. But it was only in the most capital-poor countries,
such as Greece or Romania, that this policy resulted in a tangible increase of
French political influence that may be described as imperial.[126] In Italy's case,
the large share of the national debt owned by French investors did not prevent
the new kingdom from remaining neutral when the Franco-Prussian War

123. Greenfield, *The Making of a Fiscal-Military State*, ch. 6: "The Bonapartist State" and ch.
7: "The Revival of the Interventionist State."

124. See the report in Rouher's private papers, by Rouher himself or by one of his close advisors, "Des emprunts d'État," 23 May 1865, AN, 44 AP 20.

125. On French financial support for Italian unification, see Ferguson, *The House of Rothschild*, vol. 2, 89–115.

126. Einaudi, *Money and Politics*, 89–142; Marc Flandreau, "The Economics and Politics of
Monetary Unions: A Reassessment of the LMU, 1865–1871," *Financial History Review*, 7, 1
(2000).

erupted in 1870.[127] The imperial dimension of French lending to foreign states was more in evidence outside Europe, where it was combined with diplomatic pressures to put French civil servants in charge of local public finances—a strategy that prefigured the discreet but effective stranglehold exercised by a small number of British officials over China's public purse after they were entrusted with the management of the country's main source of tax receipts (the maritime customs).[128]

Bonapartist France's most successful attempt at establishing an imperial style of domination by financial means was without a doubt the surge of French investment in Ottoman and Egyptian public debts from the mid-1850s. In both cases, the rapid growth of public indebtedness led to bankruptcy in the mid-1870s and the formal supervision of local finances by ad hoc European-staffed administrative bodies: the Caisse de la Dette Publique (1878) in Egypt and the Administration de la Dette Publique (1881) in the Ottoman Empire.[129] Representatives of British and French bondholders enjoyed equal representation on these two bodies, but as the French representatives were more or less formally appointed by the French government, and French nationals owned a larger share of the public debt (especially in the case of the Ottoman Empire), they served as vehicles of French rather than British influence. Even after Britain's military occupation of Egypt in 1882, British administrators denounced the Caisse as a French "Imperium in Imperio" that seriously limited their capacity to implement fiscal reforms.[130]

Some historians have contested the imperialist character of such institutions, alleging that they were the unintended results of local fiscal mismanage-

127. AJP Taylor, *The Struggle for Mastery in Europe, 1848–1918* (Oxford: Clarendon Press, 1971), 209–10.

128. For a critical assessment of the literature on the Chinese customs and its British inspector general, Robert Hart, see Henk Vynckier and Chihyun Chang, "*Imperium in Imperio*: Robert Hart, the Chinese Maritime Customs Services, and Its (Self-)Representations," *Biography*, 37, 1 (2014); on British informal rule in China, see Jürgen Osterhammel, "Britain and China, 1842–1914," in *The Oxford History of the British Empire*, 5 vols., ed. Wm Roger Louis (Oxford: Oxford University Press, 1998–1999), vol. 4, 146–69.

129. On dual control and the Caisse de la Dette Publique in Egypt, see Malak Labib, "Crise de la dette publique et missions financières européennes en Egypte, 1878–1879," *Monde(s)*, 4, 2 (2013); on the Ottoman Administration de la Dette Publique, see Murat Birdal, *The Political Economy of Ottoman Public Debt* (London: Tauris, 2010) and V. Necla Geyikdaği, *Foreign Investment in the Ottoman Empire* (London: Tauris, 2011), esp. 29–52.

130. Alfred Milner, *England in Egypt*, 2nd ed. (London: Edward Arnold, 1894), 65, 413–14.

ment, or stressing the benefits of international control as shown by a sharp reduction in the interest rate demanded by foreign investors.[131] Yet as will be seen below in the case of the Ottoman Empire, French officials foresaw bankruptcy many years before it took place, but they continued to encourage the purchase of Ottoman bonds by French investors because they anticipated that it would ultimately increase France's influence: it was, again, a case of political calculation and short-term material gains for the debt issuers, trumping long-term economic rationality. Moreover, highlighting the benefits of international control does not disprove that the latter should be construed as imperial. Rather, it replicates an argument made in defence of formal empire, which also tended to result in better-balanced budgets and lower borrowing costs.[132] Analyses disputing the imperialist proclivities of foreign financial supervision also neglect the imperializing effects of purchasing of Middle Eastern bonds across western Europe, as the popularity of the so-called *valeurs à turban* ("turban-wearing stocks") gave a stake in France's geopolitical ambitions to hundreds of thousands of French households.

The Ottoman Empire's tendency to rely on European capital to finance its fiscal deficit originated in its inability to meet the fiscal demands of modern warfare during the Crimean War of 1854–1856. In order to bolster the finances of their allies against the Russian empire, in 1855 the British and French governments guaranteed an Ottoman public loan of 5 million pounds sterling (125 million francs), simultaneously issued in London and Paris. The guarantee ensured the loan's success with European investors—it was issued above par— but in return Britain and France obtained the appointment of commissioners who were charged with controlling Ottoman expenditure. Reflecting an already marked contrast in attitudes towards government interference with foreign investment, this Anglo-French guarantee was approved by a very slight majority in the House of Commons and unanimously by the French Corps Législatif.[133] The Ottoman Empire subsequently floated fourteen major loans on

---

131. On the domestic causes of the Ottoman Empire's bankruptcy, see Christopher Clay, *Gold for the Sultan: Western Bankers and Ottoman Finance, 1856–1881* (London: Tauris, 2000); on the advantages of international control, see Ali Coşkun Tunçer, *Sovereign Debt and International Financial Control: The Middle East and the Balkans, 1870–1914* (Houndsmill: Palgrave Macmillan, 2015), esp. 29–78 on Egypt and the Ottoman Empire.

132. Niall Ferguson and Moritz Schularick, "The Empire Effect: The Determinants of Country Risk in the First Age of Globalization, 1880–1913," *Journal of Economic History*, 66, 2 (2006).

133. A. du Velay, *Essai sur l'histoire financière de la Turquie depuis le règne du Sultan Mahmoud II jusqu'à nos jours* (Paris: A. Rousseau, 1903), 147–8; see the British government's reservations

European markets between 1858 and 1877, although the proceeds of each increasingly served to pay off the charges incurred by previous ones.[134] As early as 1865, Achille Fould, the French finance minister, warned that Turkey's "ever-growing debt" and its "unceasing loans" would end in bankruptcy, and he pleaded for the quotation of Ottoman bonds at the Paris Bourse to become forbidden: "The French government would be reneging on its responsibility if it let its nationals indefinitely commit themselves to enterprises with uncertain prospects."[135]

Fould, however, lost the argument to the French ambassador in Constantinople and the French minister of foreign affairs, who insisted that forbidding the quotation of Ottoman bonds would harm France's "material and political interests": not only would the blow to Ottoman credit disadvantage existing French bondholders and French banks that had made considerable short-term advances to the Ottoman Treasury, but it risked causing the downfall of an Ottoman ministry led by a defender of French interests, Grand Vizier Fuat Pasha.[136] Rouher, minister of State, went as far as to contend that "the public funds of states allied to France were *legally entitled*" to be traded at the Paris Bourse, and Napoleon III himself ordered that the quotation of Ottoman bonds continued to be authorized as a mark of France's "friendship" for the Ottoman government.[137] The prevailing view from Paris was therefore that even if an Ottoman bankruptcy was ultimately probable, lending should continue because it conformed to French geopolitical interests.

Another factor behind this leniency of the French government vis-à-vis Ottoman borrowing was the growing influence of the Banque Impériale

---

on the guarantee in the folder "Emprunt turc de 1855," especially Comte de Persigny, ambassador in London, to Comte Drouyn de Lhuys, minister of foreign affairs, 4 June 1855, in AAE, M&D, Turquie, 99.

134. Birdal, *The Political Economy*, 28.

135. Achille Fould, minister of finance, to Drouyn de Lhuis, draft letter, December 1865, and "Note" on the same issue, unsigned, 12 Dec. 1865, CAEF, B 0031280.

136. Marquis de Moustier, ambassador in Constantinople, to Drouyn de Lhuis, 14 June 1865, and Drouyn de Lhuis to Fould, 26 June 1865, CAEF, B 0031280.

137. Rouher's intervention is cited in a note by the Ottoman ambassador in Paris, communicated by the minister of foreign affairs to the minister of finance, 26 June 1865, CAEF, B 0031280 (emphasis in the original text); see also a note about a conversation between Rouher and Napoleon III (signature illegible, letterhead "Ministère d'État—Cabinet du Ministre"),13 Dec. 1865, CAEF, B 0031280.

Ottomane in Constantinople.[138] The financial establishment, founded in 1863 and enjoying some of the privileges of a central bank, had initially been a private British initiative. But French diplomats ensured that it was launched as a joint Anglo-French venture, and French investors led by the Crédit Mobilier gradually became the dominant shareholders.[139] The bank's first director in Constantinople between 1863 and 1867 was not only a Frenchman, but an inspector general of the French finance ministry, the Marquis Alexandre de Plœuc, who went on to serve as deputy governor of the Banque de France from 1867 until 1878.[140] Descended from an impecunious Breton noble family, Plœuc had climbed the ranks of the finance administration and specialized in the provision of expert advice to foreign governments. After short stints in the financial administrations of the Papal States and Greece, in 1859 he became a member of the Ottoman Treasury Council, with a "very large" indemnity paid by the Ottoman government, although he continued to report to the French finance and foreign affairs ministers.[141]

On the Ottoman Treasury Council, Plœuc fought off some of the reforms proposed by British advisors in order to increase Ottoman economic growth and revenue—such as changes to "the tax-base, the *waqfs* [religious foundations], the mines, the forests, the constitution of [private] property, the monetary system"—deeming them "inappropriate", as the Ottoman administration was too "corrupt" to implement them, and "dangerous", because major tax reforms almost always initially reduced yields, while the Ottoman Treasury was already (in 1861) "in the most absolute distress." Instead, Plœuc contended,

138. André Autheman, *La Banque Impériale Ottomane* (Paris: Comité pour l'histoire économique et financière de la France, 1996) and Edhem Eldem, *A History of the Ottoman Bank* (Istanbul: Ottoman Bank Historical Research Center, 1999); for a detailed account of the bank's early years, see Clay, *Gold for the Sultan*, 60–86; on the Banque Impériale's role in the growth of Western investment in the Ottoman world, see *East Meets West: Banking, Commerce and Investment in the Ottoman Empire*, ed. Philip L. Cottrell (Aldershot: Ashgate, 2008).

139. On the proliferation of Anglo-French joint financial ventures after 1850, especially in relation to foreign investment, see Philipp Cottrell "La cooperation financière franco-anglaise, 1850–1880," in Lévy-Leboyer, *La position internationale*, 177–86.

140. Alain Plessis, *Régents et gouverneurs de la Banque de France sous le Second Empire* (Geneva: Droz, 1985), 341–9; on the growing role played by inspectors of the finance ministry in French administrative and economic life, see Emmanuel Chadeau, *Les inspecteurs des finances au XIXe siècle (1850–1914). Profil social et rôle économique* (Paris: Economica, 1986), esp. 11–12 and 161 on Plœuc.

141. An unidentified member of the Personnel division of the ministry of finances (signature illegible) to Plœuc, 3 June 1859, AN, 272 AP 15.

Western powers should "advise or impose" the principles of "accountability" and "publicity" in order to effect a change in "the very form of the government." In practice, this meant increasing foreign control over Ottoman finances, including "an examination of the budgets and accounts by the Treasury Council upon which sit foreigners" and "French (or English) accountants next to native accountants in every ministry."[142]

After 1863, Plœuc helped turn the Banque Impériale Ottomane into an instrument of French influence in Constantinople. With his French correspondents at least, he always emphasized his attention to French interests: "future appointments should benefit the French element," Plœuc wrote about the bank's initial development.[143] A Levantine merchant described himself as an admirer of the bank, or "*bancomane*," and therefore a "*francomane*."[144] Plœuc met with some setbacks, as other banks—but most of them French, such as subsidiaries of the Société Générale and the Comptoir d'Escompte—competed with the Banque Impériale to manage the profitable issuance of new Ottoman loans. Yet the privileged bank displaced local financiers as the main provider of short-term advances to the Ottoman Treasury, giving it a special leverage on Ottoman high politics. It frequently received the support of the French ambassador in its almost incessant wrangling with Ottoman authorities over monetary and financial affairs. Even after Plœuc left Constantinope to become deputy governor of the Banque de France in 1867, he remained a key actor of Franco-Ottoman financial and political relations. He continued to receive a dizzying array of requests, ranging from Frenchmen seeking a position in the Ottoman administration to Ottoman officials looking for an apartment in Paris.[145] Administrators of the Banque Impériale still sought and followed the advice provided by "le marquis."[146] As we will see in the next chapter, Plœuc also orchestrated a campaign from Paris that nearly succeeded

142. Draft report to the minister [of foreign affairs], Sep. 1861, AN, 272 AP 14.

143. Plœuc to the Paris Committee of the Banque Impériale Ottomane, draft, no date [1863?], AN, 272 AP 15.

144. Garabed Caracacho, a Constantinople merchant, to Plœuc, 9 Apr. 1863, AN, 272 AP 15.

145. Isaac Péreire to Plœuc, 14 Mar. 1864, soliciting a position in Turkey for "Mr Gallois," a civil engineer, AN, 272 AP 14, and "Khalil" [probably Khalil Bey, the diplomat and art collector] to Plœuc, 12 Jan. 1866, about "a very pretty apartment" overlooking the fashionable Boulevard des Italiens in Paris, AN, 272 AP 15; see also numerous requests in the "Orient" folder, AN, 272 AP 14 and the "Notes diverses" folder, AN, 272 AP 16.

146. See for instance Émile Deveaux, deputy director of the Banque Impériale Ottomane, to Casimir Salvador, secretary of the Paris committee, 28 May 1869, CAMT, 207 AQ 53; on

in foiling Ottoman and Egyptian efforts to curtail European extraterritorial privileges in the 1870s.

Between 1867 and 1889, Plœuc's successors as director general of the Banque Impériale were British, but the influence of their French deputies became decisive, not least because French investors purchased most of the loans issued by the bank. These deputies, like Plœuc, had been and continued to think of themselves as serving the French government. For instance, by 1869 Émile Deveaux, another former inspector of the French finance ministry, had been remunerated by the Ottoman government for ten years, first as a member of the Treasury Council and then as an administrator of the Banque Impériale. Yet he was thrilled to be introduced to the Empress Eugénie, when she visited Constantinople en route to the inauguration of the Suez Canal, "with the other French *fonctionnaires*" who served in the Ottoman capital.[147] Deveaux's correspondence with French bankers and officials teemed with Orientalist remarks on the "ignorance" and "stubbornness" of his Turkish interlocutors.[148] One of his favoured means of negotiation with Ottoman ministers was "the protests of the two embassies [of Britain and France] which we can raise in case of need," and he wished that he and the bank had "gunboats at our disposal."[149]

Deveaux also continued to provide the French government with detailed and increasingly pessimistic analyses of Ottoman public finances.[150] His figures and arguments were reproduced in formal proposals by the French foreign affairs ministry for a regime of "financial control" by a committee made up of "a majority of Europeans," most of whom would be the administrators of the Banque Impériale. All Ottoman revenue would be paid "into the hands of the commissioners," who would also be able "to refuse the payment of any expenditure" not provided for in an official budget.[151] In other words, the French government proposed to place Ottoman public finances under European, French-led supervision. This echoed the views expressed by Plœuc as early as 1861 and foreshadowed the control exercised by the Administration de

Salvador, another former inspector of the finance ministry, see Nicolas Stoskopf, *Les patrons du Second Empire. Banquiers et financiers parisiens* (Paris: A. et J. Picard, 2002), 325.

147. Deveaux to Salvador, 15 Oct. 1869, CAMT, 207 AQ 53.

148. Deveaux to Salvador, 9 Oct. 1869, CAMT, 207 AQ 53.

149. Deveaux to Salvador, 5 Oct. and 16 Oct. 1868, CAMT, 207 AQ 53.

150. Émile Deveaux, "Note" (copy), enclosed in Melchior de Vögué, ambassador in Constantinople, to Charles de Rémusat, minister of foreign affairs, 10 Apr. 1872, CAEF, B 0031279.

151. Vögué to Louis Decazes, minister of foreign affairs, 19 Jan. 1874, CAEF, B 0031279.

la Dette Publique after 1881. The restriction of Ottoman financial sovereignty was not an accident, but the product of two decades of European and especially French pressures.

This growth of French financial clout in Constantinople owed a great deal to the popularity of Ottoman bonds with the French public. By the early 1870s, the *valeurs à turban* had become one of the most popular investments among small savers. "The number of [the Ottoman Empire's] creditors" in France, the author of a study on French "mœurs financières" wrote, was "immense," not only among the "semi-wealthy" (*demi-fortunes*) and "middle classes," but also "workers" and "servants." The same author suggested that this popularity was partly grounded in "sympathy" for France's allies and memories of French exploits in the region, from the Crusades to Napoleon's Egyptian expedition. However, he admitted that another significant factor was the stocks' "high yield."[152] Deveaux, who as administrator of the Banque Impériale had extensive experience of issuing these bonds, realistically stressed the high-yield factor: while in London large investors valued security more, "the sort of public [in France] that throws itself on foreign loans is exclusively attracted by the lure of high yields," hence its predilection for Ottoman bonds.[153] While sober prospectuses for the British public underlined the "securities" assigned to specific Ottoman loans, prospectuses for the French public stressed the "interest [of] more than *10* percent" or "nearly *12* percent" of Ottoman bonds.[154]

152. Alexis Bailleux de Marisy, "Mœurs financières de la France, IV: les valeurs orientales," *Revue des Deux Mondes*, 44 (1874): 650, 678. Ottoman bonds remained favoured by the less wealthy even after the Ottoman Empire's bankruptcy in 1876 and into the twentieth century; for instance in Bordeaux in 1911, these bonds made up 25 percent of all the financial assets of "foremen" and 11 percent of those of "artisans," but less than 2 percent of those of "rentiers" and 0.1 percent of those of "high civil servants"; see Adeline Daumard, *Les fortunes françaises au XIXe siècle. Enquête sur la répartition et la composition des capitaux privés à Paris, Lyon, Lille, Bordeaux et Toulouse* (Paris: Mouton, 1973), 522–3.

153. Deveaux to Vögué, 6 June 1871, CAEF, B 0031279.

154. Compare "Gouvernement impérial ottoman—Emprunt de 1873" (several prospectuses) and "Imperial Ottoman Six Per Cent Loan, 1873" in CAMT, 207 AQ 236; emphases in the original French prospectuses. Walter Bagehot discouraged British investors from purchasing the bonds of countries governed by "Oriental despotisms" because they lacked "good administration" and "continuous political morality," in "The danger of Lending to Semi-Civilised countries," *The Economist*, 23 Nov. 1867; repr. in *The Collected Works of Walter Bagehot*, vol. 9, 419–23.

At the beginning of the 1860s, the number of French investors in Ottoman bonds reached the tens of thousands.[155] By the early 1870s, there were almost certainly hundreds of thousands of them: "over two billions francs of Turkish funds have been sold in France, especially to small savers (*petits portefeuilles*)," a French ambassador asserted in order to justify yet another proposal to place Ottoman finances under Franco-European control.[156] When the Ottoman Empire finally ceased payments in 1876, angry petitions from French bond-holders demonstrate what a large number of Frenchmen and women partici-pated in this form of financial imperialism.[157] For instance, there were 465 signatories in Toulon (70,000 inhabitants in 1876) and thirteen signatories in the nearby small town of Tourves (2,200 inhabitants).[158] These are high fig-ures for Provence, a region that was not noted for its level of capitalist devel-opment, although the fact that Toulon was a major port may have increased local interest in overseas ventures. Adding up the claims made by the 465 Toulon petitioners, we can see that that the Toulonnais alone would have owned between 3.5 and 5 million francs of Ottoman bonds at a nominal value (2 to 3 million francs at purchase value). No doubt some petitioners exagger-ated their holdings, but the figure lends credence to the ambassador's esti-mate of 2 billion francs for the whole of France, and it suggests, if average holdings were similar in other regions, approximately two hundred thousand bondholders nationally.[159] Leroy-Beaulieu's vision of every French "small employee," "farmer," "worker," "spinster or a widow" as a potential participant in "investment colonization" was not a figment of his imagination, but reflected, in part, social reality.[160]

---

155. According to the Compagnie des agents de change (brokers' syndicate), there were 13,921 subscribers to the 1860 Ottoman loan; Syndic de la compagnie des agents de change to the minister of finances, 18 June 1861, CAEF, B 0032280.

156. Vögué to Decazes, 29 Dec. 1873, CAEF, B 0031279.

157. For an analysis of the impact of the bankruptcy on French banks and investors, see Jean Bouvier, *Le Crédit Lyonnais de 1863 à 1882. Les années de formation d'une banque de dépôts*, 2 vols. (Paris: SEVPEN, 1961), vol. 2, 682–731.

158. Comité toulonnais des porteurs français de la dette turque to the minister of foreign affairs, 18 Apr. 1878, AAE, Contentieux, 752 SUP 140.

159. On average Toulon petitioners claimed to own approximately 10,000 francs (at face value) of Ottoman bonds, but the range was wide, from dozens of petitioners who said they only held a single bond to Joséphine Martineng, who said she owned 122, and Pascal Pira, who said he owned 1,940; see Comité toulonnais, 18 Apr. 1878, AAE, Contentieux, 752 SUP 140.

160. Leroy-Beaulieu, *De la colonisation*, 2nd edn (1882), 537.

Petitions in the 1870s also show that the then-common perception of women as being particularly active participants in financial-imperial ventures contained an element of truth, despite legal restrictions on the purchase of financial assets by married women. In Toulon, 68 out of 465 signatories (15 percent) were women, and 52 of them described themselves as widows.[161] In Zola's *L'Argent*, women—especially a widow, the Princess of Orviedo, and a spinster, Caroline Hamelin—play a prominent role in the elaboration of Saccard's financial-imperial scheme, and pious Catholic women were the chief propagandists of the *Banque Universelle*: "Women above all were passionate," and "indoctrinated the men": "Promptly buy some *Universelle* stocks," they told them, "if you want us to love you."[162] Zola was particularly interested in the speculative proclivities of aristocratic women. But female buyers of Ottoman bonds included Françoise Fabre, who described herself as "single" and a "milliner" when she signed a petition about Ottoman bonds, along with five other residents of Lorgues (4,200 inhabitants), near Toulon, at the age of eighty-one in 1878. Fabre claimed to own one Ottoman bond of a nominal value of five hundred francs.[163] This was not her first financial operation—in 1867, describing herself as a "fruit seller," she had lent four hundred francs for six years, at 5 percent yearly interest, to a farmer in Lorgues.[164] Perhaps she had purchased her Ottoman bond in 1873, when she recouped the principal of that earlier loan. Her 1881 death certificate shows that she, too, was in fact a widow, of Jean-Baptiste Martel, a *revendeur* (retailer), and that she had two sons, a mason and a tailor, and a daughter, married to a butcher, all three residents of Lorgues.[165] Her only possessions when she died, in a single room that she rented, were a bed and a table, with a total estimated value of forty-two francs, and, found in the table's drawer, three French *rentes*, with a total face value of two thousand five hundred francs.[166] Fabre had somehow disposed of her Ot-

161. In addition, seventeen signatories did not give a first name or gave one (Dominique, Camille etc.) that could be either male or female; see Toulon petition, 18 Apr. 1878, AAE, Contentieux, 752 SUP 140.

162. Zola, *L'Argent*, 302–3.

163. The town's other petitioners—a retired notary, a doctor, two landowners, and a house painter—were all men; see Lorgues petition, 15 Apr. 1878, AAE, 752SUP/140.

164. Notarial record of "Fabre, Françoise, obligation par Evaque, Jean-Baptiste," 10 Jan. 1867, Draguignan, Archives Départementales du Var (henceforth ADV), 3 E 73/173.

165. Death certificate of Françoise Fabre, 21 Aug. 1881, ADV, 2 MI EC1945R1.

166. Inventory of the possessions of Françoise Fabre, 29 Aug. 1881, ADV, 3 E 73/202.

toman bond before the new Administration de la Dette Publique resumed payments in 1882.

How far-fetched is it to suggest that the small investor Françoise Fabre, widow Martel, was an imperialist? Evidently, her main motivation when she purchased an Ottoman bond was to make a financial gain, but this was also the main conscious objective of Deveaux or Plœuc.[167] Although the latter two engaged more directly with the Ottoman world, their financial and political schemes required the participation of many thousands of Fabres, who became creditors of the Sultan—as did, for instance, the self-conscious imperialist, Michel Chevalier, who purchased one thousand Ottoman bonds (nominal value: five hundred thousand francs) in 1865.[168] By encouraging collective petitions and individual protests, the Ottoman Empire's bankruptcy arguably increased consciousness of global affairs among the likes of Françoise Fabre. The bankruptcy may even have contributed to the royalist government's decisive electoral defeats in 1876 and 1877, when the "couches nouvelles" hailed by the republican leader Léon Gambetta overthrew the rule of "notables" for good.[169] In January 1878, the new republican government dismissed Plœuc, a prominent notable and a royalist MP between 1871 and 1876, from his functions at the Banque de France.[170]

On the whole, France's conquest of the Ottoman Empire by money was successful. The losses incurred by French investors should not be exaggerated. Not only did they receive handsome payments up until 1876, but from 1882 the Ottoman Empire resumed the servicing of its debt at a more reasonable rate. The preponderance of French investors in the public debt considerably increased French influence over Ottoman politics and economic life, until the 1908 "Young Turk" nationalist revolution, after which German interests became dominant.[171] The material benefits of this financial imperial venture, at

167. Plœuc estimated that his own wealth in stocks and cash increased from 370,000 francs in 1865 to 1.33 million in 1874, in "Valeurs mobilières et numéraires", AN, 272 AP 14.

168. See list of subscribers in "Emprunt 1865. Traités particuliers originaux," CAMT, 207 AQ 235.

169. Daniel Halévy, La fin des notables (Paris: Grasset, 1930); Furet, La Révolution, vol. 2, 461–3.

170. See press clipping on protests against "government interference in the management of the bank" at the shareholders' assembly of the Banque de France on 31 Jan. 1878, from Le Moniteur des tirages financiers [1 Feb. 1878], AN, 272 AP 14.

171. Jacques Thobie, Intérêts et impérialisme français dans l'empire ottoman (1895–1914) (Paris: Publications de la Sorbonne, 1977), esp. 279–315, 647–715; see also Michelle Raccagni, "The

least for well-informed investors, were larger than the costs, and the political advantages derived from it were enormous. The results of the conquest of Egypt by money were more ambivalent, due to the larger share of the country's debt being owned by British investors and the British military occupation after 1882. But there, too, there is ample evidence that massive French investment in the public debt and the semi-public Suez Canal company followed a political logic at least as much as a financial one.[172]

Financial Imperial Overreach in Mexico

The most ambitious and sophisticated scheme of conquest by money was probably the investment in Mexico's public debt during the Second Empire's expedition of 1862–1867. Few scholars would contest the imperialist nature of France's Mexican venture, because it entailed the country's military occupation by a French force of forty thousand and the creation of an ephemeral Mexican monarchy under Maximilian of Habsburg. Ever since François-René de Chateaubriand and other conservative thinkers had begun to call for the transformation of former Spanish American colonies into monarchies protected by France in the 1820s, there had been connections between this project and the development of French finance.[173] Thus, in 1828, as he was speculating on Mexican bonds, the Duc de Dalberg wrote a memorandum addressed to the French government that propounded an intervention designed to create a "constitutional monarchy" in Mexico, with a "French prince" or, if Britain objected, "a prince of Bavaria" on the new throne.[174] Financial considerations also played a decisive role in the immediate origins of the expedition, officially designed to compel Mexico to resume payments on earlier loans contracted

French Economic Interests in the Ottoman Empire," *International Journal of Middle East Studies*, 11, 3 (1980) and V. Necla Geyikdaği, "French Direct Investments in the Ottoman Empire before World War I," *Enterprise and Society*, 12, 3 (2011).

172. On the politics and economics of French foreign lending in Egypt, see David S. Landes, *Bankers and Pashas: International Finance and Economic Imperialism in Egypt*, 2nd edn (New York: Harper & Row, 1969); see also Gerald Arboit, "L'arme financière dans les relations internationales: l'affaire Ceruschi sous le Second Empire," *Revue d'histoire moderne et contemporaine*, 46, 3 (1999).

173. Shawcross, *France, Mexico and Informal Empire*, 44–152.

174. Duc de Dalberg, "Le Mexique vu du cabinet des Tuileries," 1828, WS, Dalberg MSS, 159/748.

in Europe.[175] Michel Chevalier, one of the expedition's main cheerleaders, also insisted in the significance of Mexican silver mines for the stability of French bimetallic monetary system, and therefore, ultimately, financial power.[176]

Yet from the perspective of this book, the most remarkable aspect of the Mexican venture was the attempt to ensconce French influence over the new monarchy, at minimal cost for the French treasury, by financial means. The Convention of Miramar, concluded by Maximilian before he set out for Mexico in April 1864, committed Mexico to refund France the costs of the expedition and settle the claims of French subjects against the previous Mexican regime, in large part through new loans raised in Europe.[177] A new Commission of Mexican Finances, with a seat in Paris and three commissioners (one Briton, one Frenchman, one Mexican), was to collect the proceeds of loans and give them back to Mexico's creditors.[178] In practice, the Commission became a branch of the French finances administration. The positions of British and Mexican commissioners remained vacant, and the French commissioner, Comte Charles de Germiny, a former governor of the Banque de France (and future administrator of the Banque Impériale Ottomane), was in sole command.[179] The Commission's offices were located on rue du Monthalbor, just behind the French ministry of finances, and its fifty-strong staff was drawn from the French fiscal administration and Parisian banks, although the rent and the salaries were charged to the Mexican government.[180] In addition, a state councillor, aided by two inspectors of the finance ministry, were sent to supervise the reorganization of Mexican public finances in Mexico City; the state councillor's emoluments were said to be an extravagant two hundred

175. On the use of the "Jecker bonds" as a pretext for France's intervention, see Steven C. Topik, "When Mexico Had the Blues: A Transatlantic Tale of Bonds, Bankers, and Nationalists, 1862–1910," *American Historical Review*, 105, 3 (2000): 717.

176. See chapter 1 for Chevalier's concerns, and on France's bimetallic system, Marc Flandreau, *L'or du monde: la France et la stabilité du système monétaire international, 1848–1873* (Paris: L'Harmattan, 1995).

177. In addition to an immediate payment of 66 million francs thanks to the proceeds of loans floated in Europe, Mexico was due to reimburse France through yearly cash payments of 25 million francs; Miramar convention, 10 Apr. 1864, articles 9, 10, 11, 12 and 14 CAEF, B 0032492.

178. See text of the five Miramar decrees of 10 and 11 April 1864, CAEF, B 0032492.

179. On Germiny, see *Les patrons du Second Empire. Banquiers et financiers*, 195–7.

180. The rent was 11,000 francs per year and the staff costs were "on average" 10,000 francs a month; see "Note concernant les opérations de crédit et les travaux de la commission des finances du Mexique à Paris," 3 Aug. 1865, fols. 8–10, 17, in CAEF, B 0032492.

thousand francs (eight thousand pounds sterling) a year, half at Mexico's expense.[181] An attempt was also made to found a privileged Banque Impériale du Mexique in Mexico City, whose statutes, drawn up by the Paris Commission, closely resembled those of the Constantinople bank, but geopolitical uncertainty eventually dissuaded French capitalists from providing the necessary capital.[182]

This management of Mexico's external debt from Paris represented an extraordinary grab for power. Although the Commission was set up at the Mexican government's expense, it mainly served French interests. Germiny did not hesitate to turn down Mexican instructions to execute payments that he disapproved of.[183] When the Commission ran short of cash, he proposed to suspend payments to its creditors, "except . . . the French Treasury, of course."[184] However, the Commission's main task was to supervise the issuing of new Mexican bonds. A first loan (nominal value: two hundred million francs), issued in London and Paris in the autumn of 1864, met with a lukewarm response from investors: only half of the bonds were subscribed. A second loan (two hundred and fifty million francs) issued in the spring of 1865, in collaboration with the Comptoir d'Escompte and with the active support of the French state, was an unmitigated success. A quarter to a third of the two loans' actual proceeds were directly remitted to the French Treasury, as a contribution to expedition costs.[185] In addition, 10 percent of the 1865 loan's proceeds were allocated to a sinking fund that exclusively purchased French state bonds.[186] A significant fraction (around 10 percent) of the total proceeds was also used to placate earlier British bondholders. Much less than half, and perhaps as little as 15 percent of the actual proceeds, were credited to Maximilian's

181. Émile de Kératry, *La créance Jecker, les indemnités française et les emprunts mexicains* (Paris: Librairie internationale, 1868), 121–3.

182. "Projet adressé à Mexico le 16 novembre [1864]," CAEF, B 0032492; on the negotiations about the project, see Geneviève Massa-Gille, "Les capitaux français et l'expédition du Mexique," *Revue d'histoire diplomatique*, 79, 3 (1965): 224–37.

183. See for instance Germiny to Joachim Velasquez de Leon, minister of State of the Emperor of Mexico, 16 Nov. 1864 (draft), and Germiny to General Almonte, Ambassador of Mexico in Paris, 6 June 1866 (copy), CAEF, B 0032492.

184. Germiny to Fould, 6 Nov. 1865 (draft), CAEF, B 0032492.

185. Germiny to Fould, 6 Nov. 1865 (draft), CAEF, B 0032492.

186. Germiny to Fould, 27 Apr. 1865 (copy), CAEF, B 0032492.

government, and even these figures remained subject to the Commission's control.[187]

The operations supervised by the Commission of Mexican Finances therefore turned France into Mexico's principal creditor, while financing a large share of the French war effort in Mexico—directly through remittances to the French Treasury, indirectly through the purchase of French *rentes*. The multiple advantages of this scheme explain why the Bonapartist regime lent such extraordinary support to the crucial second Mexican loan. In April 1865, as the end of the Civil War raised the threat of an American intervention in Mexican affairs, Rouher solemnly reassured potential bond buyers in a speech to the Corps Législatif: "France will continue to protect Mexico until its work there has been fully consolidated."[188] *Receveurs généraux* were instructed to assist the Comptoir d'Escompte in the selling of bonds. Not only were the nominal yields very attractive (around 12 percent), but a lottery awarding premiums of up to five hundred thousand francs was introduced to further stimulate interest.[189] Advertising in the press for other foreign bonds— especially Ottoman bonds—was banned in order to reduce competition for savings.[190]

As a result, the loan met with tremendous success, especially among small savers. By November 1865, Germiny estimated that "approximately three hundred thousand" Frenchmen and women owned Mexican bonds, and many of them were "investors of very limited means" (*très petites bourses*).[191] The more than two hundred inquiries and complaints received by the Commission du Mexique before 1866 show, in particular, how popular these bonds were among the provincial lower middle classes. Most of the letter writers were, in the words of Jacques Abeille, who was from the village of Bargemon in Provence, "people like [himself], shopkeepers, petty landowners, tradesmen,

187. Topik, "When Mexico Had the Blues": 719, claims that the Mexican government's share was even as low as 6 percent, but the figure was probably obtained as a proportion of the loan's nominal value rather than its actual proceeds.

188. Quoted in Eugène Forcade, "Chronique de la quinzaine," *Revue des Deux Mondes*, 56 (1865): 1064.

189. On lottery bonds, see Todd and Yates, "Public Debt and Democratic Statecraft."

190. Fould to Drouyn de Lhuis, 30 May 1865, CAEF, B 0031280.

191. Germiny to Fould, 6 Nov. 1865 (draft), CAEF, B 0032492; a pamphlet defending the interests of bondholders gave the same figure of 300,000 "families," in Louis Bellet, *La vérité sur les obligations mexicaines* (Paris: Guérin, 1867), 4.

artisans."[192] Nearly four in five resided in the provinces, in fifty different *départements*.[193] The only distinguished inquirer was the author of children's books, the Comtesse Sophie de Ségur, née Rospotchina, but the inquiry was on behalf of her maid, Constance Janssens, who had lost a bond certificate and, as a result, missed "22 francs and 60 centimes" (around eighteen shillings) in interest payments.[194]

As the United States imposed a withdrawal of the French expeditionary corps and republican forces gained ground against Maximilian's regime in 1866, the value of the bonds collapsed. It was this crash, claimed the Comte de Kératry, a former officer in Mexico who became a leading critique of the expedition, that turned the foreign policy disaster into a severe blow to the legitimacy of the Bonapartist regime: "From a French standpoint," the only remaining question was "that of the rights of bondholders," who were so numerous "in our provinces and our countryside."[195] The *procureurs généraux* who surveyed provincial opinion reported a surge of "anxiety" among bearers of Mexican bonds, who were "numerous, especially among the middle classes" (*procureur* of Amiens, in Picardy), or a "hue and cry" in favour of a conversion of the bonds into French *rentes* (*procureur* of Nancy, in Lorraine).[196] After Maximilian's execution and the repudiation of the loans by Mexico in 1867, the French government consented to indemnify Mexican bondholders in *rentes*, but at only a third of the bond's nominal value.[197]

Several scholars have recently encouraged us to reappraise the significance of France's Mexican venture in the 1860s. Rather than a bizarre aspiration of the sole Napoleon III, the expedition was the product of several decades of

192. Jacques Abeille to Comte de Germiny, 22 June 1865, in folder "Réclamations, emprunt de 1865," CAEF, B 0032494.

193. Only thirty-six inquiries were addressed by Paris residents, and several of the latter were brokers enquiring on behalf of clients who may also have resided outside Paris; eight inquiries were addressed by foreign residents (three from Britain, two from Austria, two from Belgium, and one from Switzerland) and three by men in active military service outside France. See the 206 "réclamations" and "demandes de renseignements" in CAEF, B 0032494.

194. Comtesse de Ségur to Commission du Mexique, 9 May 1865, in folder "Réclamations, emprunt de 1864 (1865)," CAEF, B 0032494.

195. Émile de Keratry, "Le Mexique et les chances de salut du nouvel empire," *Revue des Deux Mondes*, 65 (1866): 444.

196. Quoted in Massa-Gille, "Les capitaux français": 223–4.

197. On the dispute on the outstanding bonds between Mexico and France, which lasted until 1904, see Topik, "When Mexico Had the Blues."

thinking about the means of restoring French power in the New World, and it enjoyed a degree of support in conservative Mexican quarters.[198] Its eventual failure was the product of several contingent factors, including the outcome of the American Civil War. This reappraisal should extend to the financial dimension of the project—looking back with the benefit of hindsight can distort our judgement on past financial speculations.[199] Had the Mexican monarchy endured, the loans may have turned out to be a very reasonable investment and would be remembered as a cunning ploy to project French power at a very limited cost for the French Treasury. Even if we see the eventual failure of France's project in Mexico as inevitable, the financial infrastructure of the project should be considered a miscalculation rather a state-orchestrated scam. It constituted the most ambitious instance of the "conquest by money" approach, espoused with more success by the Bonapartist regime in other parts of the world. The costs, especially for the French government, were modest, but the potential gains—ascendancy in a country promised to become, in the view of many observers, a lynchpin of the global economy due to its mineral resources and strategic location between the Atlantic and Pacific worlds— were enormous.

The scheme's failure, even more so than the fall of Maximilian, was therefore a terrible blow to the Bonapartist regime's legitimacy. It has been persuasively described as marking a major "crisis" of the French fiscal-military state, which nurtured domestic political malaise at the end of the 1860s and, through the retrenchment it imposed on military spending, directly contributed to France's catastrophic defeat against Prussia in 1870–1871.[200] France's capital exports began to decline around 1865 (see figure 4.1) and following the collapse of the Second Napoleonic Empire they significantly lagged behind Britain's for twenty years (5.7 billion francs versus 30.3 billion between 1870 and 1889).[201] The Third Republic did not discourage the issuance of foreign stocks in Paris, and even rescinded a modest tax on such operations in 1873. But a law guaranteeing the freedom to issue stocks, French or foreign, in 1872 and the

198. Cunningham, *Mexico and the Foreign Policy of Napoleon III*; Shawcross, *France, Mexico and Informal Empire*.

199. Gary S. Shea, "Financial Market Analysis Can Go Mad (in the Search for Irrational Behaviour during the South Sea Bubble)," *Economic History Review*, 60, 4 (2007).

200. Jerome Greenfield, "The Mexican Expedition of 1862–1867 and the End of the Second Empire," *Historical Journal*, 63, 3 (2020).

201. Imlah, "British Balance of Payments;" Lévy-Leboyer, "La balance des paiements."

relaxation of newspaper censorship that culminated in the 1881 law on press freedom reduced the government's means of influencing savers. Its right to refuse the quotation of foreign stocks became controversial and fell into disuse.[202] In retrospect, the Second Empire's ability to direct foreign investment appears to have relied, to a significant extent, on its authoritarian nature.

French foreign investment revived after 1890, and French savers continued to show a marked preference for foreign public bonds over private stocks. Yet the imperial nature of this second surge of French capital exports is questionable. Despite the priority given by the Third Republic to colonial expansion, only a small share of these exports was destined to formal colonies (around 11 percent between 1882 and 1913). The Russian empire received a much larger proportion of French foreign investment over the same period (about 33 percent), largely under the form of bonds issued by the Czarist government.[203] As mentioned at the beginning of this chapter, the *emprunts russes* had an important geopolitical dimension, and their popularity among French investors no doubt benefited from the institutional credit infrastructure laid by the Second Empire. However, they neither aimed for nor resulted in a conquest of Russia by French money. It was the Russian rather than the French government that sought to manipulate the opinion of French savers—through the payment of bribes to the French press. [204] Yields on *emprunts russes* were reasonable and justified by Russia's strong economic growth until 1914.[205] After the Bolshevik repudiation of the Russian empire's external debt, the French government credibly refused to accept responsibility for this default.[206]

202. See proposals to abolish the authorization for the quotation of foreign stocks, by the minister of foreign affairs in 1873 and by the minister of finances in 1890, AAE, Contentieux, 752 SUP 145.

203. Cameron, *France and the Economic Development of Europe*, 486; for a critique of this low figure, see Marseille, *Empire colonial*, 121–32.

204. Between 1900 and 1913, the Russian diplomat Arthur Raffalovitch disbursed 6.5 million francs in subsidies to the French press; see Marc Martin, "Retour sur 'l'abominable vénalité de la presse française'," *Le temps des médias*, 6, 1 (2006).

205. Réné Girault, *Emprunts russes et investissements français en Russie*. The widespread holding of *emprunts russes* across French society also suggests that it was not as speculative an investment as Mexican or Ottoman bonds in the 1850s or 1860s. In Bordeaux in 1911, Russian bonds represented 5 percent of all the financial assets of "shop assistants," 7 percent of those of "employees," 13 percent of those of "artisans," but also 7 percent of those of "rentiers" and 2 percent of those of "high civil servants"; see Daumard, *Les fortunes françaises*, 522–3.

206. Siegel, *For Peace and Money*, 168–209.

This chapter has sought to nuance the widespread disapproval by historians, economists and even novelists such as Zola of France's extraordinary propensity to export its capital in the nineteenth century, seeing it as both irrational and immoral. From a political standpoint, French lending was not only rational but extremely astute, as it enabled France's government to channel the country's large surplus of saving into ventures that could further French ascendancy in regions that were seen to be significant from a strategic or economic point of view—the Caribbean when it was still perceived as a major source of primary products for Europe in the 1820s, and Central America and the Middle East after 1850, when they looked poised to become global commercial crossroads. These ventures frequently resulted in the bankruptcy of recipients of French capital and some losses for French investors. But sovereign foreign default cannot be systematically interpreted as a failure of French ambition, as it also often increased French influence on domestic politics. Nor should the economic costs of defaults for France be exaggerated. Investors' losses were often less than they seemed (due to the low purchase value of foreign bonds, the high yields accrued before the default, and the eventual resumption of payments), and they were made up for by other economic benefits, ranging from the fees raised by foreign loans' issuers to the privileged access to other economic opportunities that accompanied lending to a foreign government. Investors' losses may also be construed as an implicit and voluntary tax that served to finance French imperial ambitions. It was only in Mexico that a French scheme met with unmitigated disaster, but this failure was due to geopolitical rather than financial miscalculations, and the resulting blow to the Bonapartist regime's legitimacy suggests the contribution of more successful ventures to its earlier popularity.

The immorality of French financial imperialism is harder to deny than its irrationality. This chapter has shown that projects of financial tutelage were frequently informed by cynical calculations and racialist or orientalizing prejudices, as were many other aspects of French aspirations to informal empire. Yet the intensity of the moral indignation deployed by Zola and later chroniclers or historians also points to the enduring influence of a republican conception of virtue on representations of France and its past. In comparison to the inequities of formal French colonial rule in North or sub-Saharan Africa, the wrongs of French financial imperial ventures—pressure to service high yielding loans or French meddling in domestic political or administrative life—were relatively slight. The source of Zola and others' fierce indignation was more the corrupting effects of these financial ventures on metropolitan

French society. This republican concern with the morally degrading effects of transnational financial speculation could already be found in Say's criticisms of the emergence of an international market for state bonds in the 1820s. It culminated, after the resurgence of French foreign lending in the 1890s, in the famous and virulent attack of Lysis, the pseudonym of the radical republican journalist Eugène Le Tailleur, against what he dubbed a "Napoleonic organization" of capital exports that risked turning the Third Republic into a "financial monarchy."[207] These anxieties may or may not be deemed legitimate, but due to the republican sympathies of a majority of historians of modern France, they have exercised an excessive influence on the mixture of neglect and disgust that colours most accounts of nineteenth-century French lending to foreign states.

By contrast, this and the previous chapter have argued that the political economy of nineteenth-century France is better understood if it is viewed as a capitalist monarchy rather than a republic-in-waiting. Due to its reliance on the deployment of French informal power in several parts of the world, this capitalist monarchical model should also be considered intrinsically imperial. The recurring use of the words "tribute" and "suzerainty" by its most prominent advocates shows a high degree of imperial self-consciousness on the part of the French political elite. Through a specialization in the production of conspicuous commodities and the mass purchase of bonds issued by French client states, this cultural and economic empire transformed the lives of millions of French men and women. Focusing on the case of Egypt, France's most profitable informal colony until the 1870s, the next chapter will show that these economic relations should also be considered imperial because they were profoundly asymmetric, especially in the Middle East, where agents of French informal imperialism benefited from exorbitant extraterritorial legal privileges.

207. Lysis, *Contre l'oligarchie financière en France*, 11th edn (Paris: Albin Michel, 1914; first published in 1908), 11, 34; on the fierce controversy caused by Lysis's pamphlet, of which about thirty-five thousand copies were sold in the early twentieth century, see Charles E Freedman, *The Triumph of Corporate Capitalism in France, 1867–1914* (New York: University of Rochester Press, 1993), 58–82.

5

Agents of Informal Empire

FRENCH EXPATRIATES AND EXTRATERRITORIAL JURISDICTION IN EGYPT

FÉLIX CLÉMENT (1826–1888) was one of many now-forgotten French Orientalist painters. The son of a baker in the village of Donzère, just north of Provence, Clément won the Prix de Rome (the most illustrious prize for young French artists) in 1856, for a conventional religious painting. In 1862, at the invitation of François Bravay, a fellow southern Frenchman and confidant of the Egyptian vice-roy Sa'id, Clément went to Egypt. There, he became the friend and long-standing guest of Prince Halim, Sa'id's younger brother, in his palace of Shubra, near Cairo. Clément stayed at Shubra for six years, to teach Halim European-style painting and decorate his palace. But in 1868 the two men fell out, and Clément lodged a complaint with the French consulate, alleging that Halim had failed to compensate him adequately for the six years he spent at Shubra. Three other French artists residing in Egypt, appointed by the French consul in Cairo, determined that Halim ought to pay Clément 800,000 francs (32,000 pounds sterling): 338,500 francs for the thirteen completed portraits and twenty-five unfinished pictures left by Clément at Shubra, and the rest for his expenses and the losses represented by having spent six years of his life, "the time of his greatest ardour," in Egypt. Despite these flimsy grounds—his Egyptian years inspired some of Clément's most successful paintings, which he exhibited at official Parisian Salons throughout the 1860s—and the lack of evidence about Halim's alleged promises of payment, the French consulate, the ministry of foreign affairs and a Paris tribunal endorsed the claim. As Halim fled to Constantinople, Clément had to wait until

1878 before he received an indemnity from the Egyptian government, which had been reduced to three hundred thousand francs.[1]

The one-sided investigation of the "Affaire Clément" by French consular officials left several of its aspects in the dark, not least Halim's version of events. But the case illustrates well the combination of cultural, commercial and legal factors that underpinned French informal domination in Egypt, and above all the extraordinary reach of French jurisdiction into Egyptian economic life. The rapid increase of French exports of commodities and capital examined in the previous chapters does not prove beyond reasonable doubt that France exercised an imperial sort of domination, because it may also be interpreted as reflecting France's natural advantages in the global economy, such as a skilled labour force and abundant savings. Even the imperial language used by contemporaries to describe French economic accomplishments can be construed as rhetoric, designed to flatter the vanity of the French public. However, a concrete examination of how French commodities and capital came to occupy a preeminent place in certain markets shows that this success did not always derive from pure and perfect competition. On the contrary, it also relied on political pressures and the imposition of rules and practices that distorted economic exchanges, to the advantage of French merchants and financiers. The previous chapters mentioned several macro factors that permitted these distortions, from the use of gunboats to the opening of foreign markets and the channelling of investment into the public debt of friendly or client states. Shifting our focus to French activities in foreign markets helps us identify the micro cultural and legal factors that further distorted markets to the advantage of French agents.

The case of Egypt, an autonomous province of the Ottoman Empire, offers a particularly illuminating example of how French informal imperialism functioned on the ground between the 1820s and 1870s. Memories of Egypt's occupation in 1798–1801 helped nurture French ambitions. The monumental *Description de l'Égypte* (twenty-three volumes published between 1809 and

---

1. AAE, Contentieux, 253, folder "Affaire Clément," esp. the summary of the experts' conclusions in "Note pour le ministre," 16 June 1869. On Clément's life, see the (hagiographic) Maurice Champavier, *Félix Clément, peintre d'histoire* (Paris: Fischbacher, 1889), esp. 38–48 on his stay in Egypt. A portrait of a daughter of Muhammad 'Ali by Clément, wearing a fashionable French silk dress, is reproduced in Heikel Azza, *L'Égypte illustrée par les peintres du XIXe siècle* (Cairo: Max Group, 2000), 62; for other works by Clément inspired by Egypt, see Charlotte Fortier-Beaulieu and Hélène Moulin, *A.-Félix Clément: itinéraire d'un peintre drômois* (Valence: Musée de Valence, 1996).

1828), an early specimen of a new discourse on Western civilizational superiority over the Orient, testified to an intense interest amidst French intellectual circles.[2] Yet French influence in Egypt did not primarily derive from the Napoleonic expedition. For twenty years after his ascent as supreme ruler of Egypt in 1805, the country's pasha (governor), Muhammad 'Ali, cultivated good relations with Britain and favoured Italian military or medical experts. Egypt's rapprochement with France only began in the 1820s, in response to several geopolitical factors, not least Britain's greater determination than France in upholding the integrity of the Ottoman Empire and the authority of the Sultan, 'Ali's suzerain and sometimes adversary.[3] After a French military mission was invited to train the Egyptian army in 1825, spectacular gifts bore witness to the Franco-Egyptian special relationship: Egyptian presents included the giraffe which marched triumphantly from Marseille to Paris in 1827 and Luxor's obelisk in 1836, while among the French presents was a clock representing French technological prowess that was installed in Muhammad 'Ali's Cairo citadel in 1845.[4] Geopolitical collaboration was real, if not always successful. In 1829, the French government attempted to engineer an Egyptian intervention in the Algiers Regency.[5] In 1840, France risked war in Europe in a failed attempt to defend Muhammad 'Ali's conquests in the Levant.[6] Perhaps most revealing of the extent to which Egypt became enmeshed in the global web of French imperial ambitions was the bizarre Egyptian contribution of one battalion of Sudanese soldiers to the ill-fated Mexican expedition in the 1860s.[7]

2. Edward Said, *Orientalism* (London: Penguin, 2003; first published 1978), 84–7; on the reception of the *Description*, see Henry Laurens, "Le mythe de l'expédition d'Égypte en France et en Égypte aux XIXe et XXe siècles," in Henry Laurens, *Orientales*, 3 vols. (Paris: CNRS, 2004), vol. 1, 207–15.

3. On the replacement of Italian by French advisors and experts, see Mohamed Hamdi Abdou, "L'impact culturel de la France en Égypte au cours du XIXe siècle," unpublished PhD dissertation (University of Rennes II, 1988), 141–90.

4. On Egypt's gifts, see Erik Ringmar, "Audience for a Giraffe: European Expansionism and the Quest for the Exotic," *Journal of World History*, 17, 4 (2006), and Porterfield, *The Allure of Empire*, 13–41; on France's gift, installed in the citadel's neo-Ottoman mosque, see Muhammad Al-Asad, "The Mosque of Muhammad 'Ali in Cairo," *Muqarnas*, 9 (1992).

5. Henry Laurens, *Le royaume arabe*, 38–9.

6. On Muhammad 'Ali's popularity in France, see Caquet, *The Orient*, 51–92.

7. Richard Hill and Peter Hogg, *A Black Corps d'Élite: An Egyptian-Sudanese Conscript Battalion with the French Army in Mexico, 1863–1867, and its Survivors in Subsequent African History* (East Lansing: University of Michigan Press, 1995).

This Franco-Egyptian close relationship was not limited to symbolic ges-
tures or high politics. From the mid-1820s, hundreds of Egyptians, mostly
drawn from the ruling Turkish elite, came to study in Paris.[8] Thousands of
Frenchmen visited Egypt and, more and more often, settled there.[9] This flow
in both directions increased cultural and economic exchanges, but the Franco-
Egyptian relationship was increasingly asymmetric. The sojourns of educated
Egyptians in Paris contributed to the gradual replacement of Italian by French
as the main Egyptian medium of communication with Europe.[10] By contrast,
the thousands of Frenchmen and women expatriated in Egypt, who constitute
the main focus of this chapter, learnt little Arabic or Ottoman Turkish. Most
of these expatriates were not as eminent as the Egyptian dignitaries who visited Paris, but many of them were highly skilled and came to play an important
part in Egyptian economic life. French expatriates also benefited from a regime of jurisdictional extraterritoriality, initially grounded in the Capitulations
that were freely conceded by Ottoman authorities to European merchants, but
which, as this regime became inscribed in international law and singularly
expanded in Egypt after 1850, gave them serious advantages over their Egyptian and even European competitors.[11] Under the close supervision of French
consular bureaucracy, these immigrants became the agents and sometimes
profiteers of French informal rule in Egypt.

These institutional changes facilitated a decline of early modern patterns of
cross-cultural trade, which relied on the negotiated definition of a common
ground and often remained in the hand of small diasporic groups. After 1850,
European—especially French—merchants and financiers captured a rising

8. On Egyptian students in France, see Daniel L. Newman, "Introduction," in Rifa'a Rafi
'al-Tahtawi, *An Imam in Paris: Accounts of a Stay in France by an Egyptian Cleric (1826–1831)*, ed.
Daniel L. Newman (London: SAQI, 2011), 17–86; see also Anouar Louca, *Voyageurs et écrivains
égyptiens en France au XIXe siècle* (Paris: Didier, 1970), esp. 55–100.

9. The number of travel accounts in French rose from 27 between 1797 and 1839, to 37 between 1840 and 1859 and 62 between 1860 and 1879; see Friedrich Wolfzettel and Frank Estelmann, *L'Égypte après bien d'autres. Repertoire des récits de voyage en langue française en Égypte,
1794–1914* (Turin: Moncalieri, 2002), 35–174.

10. Ibrahim Abu-Lughod, *The Arab Rediscovery of Europe: A Study in Cultural Encounters*,
2nd edn (Princeton, NJ: Princeton University Press, 2011), esp. 43–9.

11. Byron Cannon, *Politics of Law and the Courts of Nineteenth-Century Egypt* (Salt Lake City:
University of Utah Press, 1988), 21–36; David Todd, "Beneath Sovereignty: Extraterritoriality
and Imperial Internationalism in Nineteenth-Century Egypt," *Law and History Review*, 36, 1
(2018).

and disproportionate share of fast-growing exchanges of commodities and capital with Egypt.[12] The object of this chapter is not to lament the iniquity of these new arrangements or the ensuing exploitation of Egypt, but to reappraise their significance as cultural and legal mechanisms of domination. It first examines the rise of French imperial expatriation in Egypt and the economic implications of French cultural dominance in Egyptian society. It then turns to the transformation of the capitulary regime, a traditional feature of the Ottoman plural legal system, into an imperial instrument that particularly benefited French nationals. Last, it analyses the crisis of the French-dominated system of extraterritoriality in the 1870s, which was solved by the internationalization of extraterritorial jurisdiction in 1876 and by British colonial occupation in 1882.

French Imperial Expatriates

In comparison with other European countries, nineteenth-century France experienced very low levels of overseas emigration. According to available estimates, twenty-seven times as many Britons (eleven million) and even twice as many Norwegians (eight hundred thousand) as Frenchmen or Frenchwomen (four hundred thousand) emigrated between 1815 and 1930.[13] However, these figures predominantly reflect the small French contribution to settlement emigration in North America and other Neo-Europes, the chief cause of which was the stagnation of France's population after 1830. Even in Algeria, France's main settlement colony, half of the settlers originated from other European countries.[14] Yet this low propensity to settle in Neo-Europes should not be equated with low global mobility.[15] No estimates are available, but tangential evidence, such as rising numbers of travel accounts, suggests

---

12. On extraterritoriality and the decline of traditional cross-cultural trade, see Philip D. Curtin, *Cross-Cultural Trade in World History* (Cambridge: Cambridge University Press, 1984), 230–54; on Mediterranean cross-cultural trade in the eighteenth century, see Francesca Trivellato, *The Familiarity of Strangers: The Sephardic Diaspora, Livorno, and Cross-Cultural Trade in the Early Modern Period* (New Haven, CT: Yale University Press, 2012).

13. Dudley Baines, *Emigration from Europe, 1815–1930* (Basingstoke: Macmillan, 1991), 3–4.

14. Émile Temine, "La migration européenne en Algérie au XIXe siècle: migration organisée ou migration tolérée," *Revue des mondes musulmans et de la Méditerrannée*, 43 (1987).

15. For a typology of mobility in the nineteenth century, see Valeska Huber, "Multiple Mobilities: Über den Umgang mit verschiedenen Mobilitätsformen um 1900," *Geschichte und Gesellschaft*, 36, 2 (2010); see also Sunil Amrith, "Empires, Diasporas, and Cultural Circulation,"

that, in the early modern period, the French were at least as inclined as other Europeans to travel and settle, although usually temporarily, in overseas countries.[16] The frequency of political exile, especially among the political and economic elite, and the conquest and loss of multiple territories by French armies, could only further encourage these forms of mobility between 1789 and 1815, and the fall of Napoleon did not bring them to a complete and abrupt end.[17] Settlerism may have been key to the constitution of the nineteenth-century British, predominantly formal empire.[18] Conversely, expatriation—a type of migration intended at least initially as temporary, often by urban workers who were rich in human or physical capital—played a significant role in French informal imperial expansion.[19]

Due to the lack of available (especially quantitative) sources, historians of migration have paid little attention to these transient population movements. Yet these European migrants were crucial facilitators of the channelling of commodities, capital and much else between the European and extra-European worlds, albeit on terms that were increasingly favourable to Europe.[20] On average these migrants were highly skilled, and their expertise could make a significant contribution to economic development or depredation, in areas under informal as well as formal European domination. Tellingly, one of the largest British expatriate communities outside Britain's formal empire was to be found in late nineteenth-century Argentina, a country long seen as the most salient case of British informal imperialism.[21] By all accounts,

---

in *Writing Imperial Histories*, ed. Andrew Thompson (Manchester: Manchester University Press, 2013), 216–39.

16. Daniel Roche, *Humeurs vagabondes. De la circulation des hommes et de l'utilité des voyages* (Paris: Fayard, 2003).

17. *Les noblesses françaises dans l'Europe de la Révolution*, éd. Philippe Bourdin (Rennes: Presses Universitaires de Rennes, 2010); Nathalie Petiteau, *Lendemains d'empire: les soldats de Napoléon dans la France du XIXe siècle* (Paris: La boutique de l'histoire, 2003), esp. 159–88.

18. Belich, *Replenishing the Earth*; Magee and Thompson, *Empire and Globalisation*, 64–116.

19. In relation to American informal imperialism, see Nancy L. Green, "Expatriation, Expatriates, and Expats: The American Transformation of a Concept," *American Historical Review*, 114, 2 (2009).

20. On British expatriation and empire, see *Settlers and Expatriates: Britons over the Seas*, ed. Robert Bickers (Oxford: Oxford University Press, 2010).

21. David Rock, "The British of Argentina," in *Settlers and Expatriates*, ed. Bickers, 18–44; on the economic life and lack of imperial consciousness of these expatriates, see Deborah Cohen, "Love and Money in the Informal Empire in Argentina," *Past & Present*, 245 (2019).

French nationals made up a large proportion of such expatriates in the nineteenth-century global economy, especially at major crossroads such as the Middle East, Central America and Asian treaty ports.[22] Egypt may be considered archetypal, due to the fact that, after 1850, it became home to the largest French expatriate community outside Europe and the Americas.

Demographic data about foreign communities in nineteenth-century Egypt is clouded in uncertainty, not only because of the unreliability of existing censuses, but also because the boundaries of national identity remained vague and fluctuating, perhaps even more so in the Levant than in the rest of the world: many European nationals were colonial subjects (e.g., British Maltese or French indigenous Algerian emigrants), while some individuals frequently changed nationality for opportunistic reasons.[23] Yet it is certain that the number of Europeans who resided in Egypt grew rapidly. A commonly cited estimate puts it at approximately 6,000 in 1840, 68,000 in 1870 and 111,000 in 1897.[24] The French were one of the fastest-growing foreign communities, with less than a thousand residents in 1850 and around 15,000 in the early 1870s.[25] The dozens of French experts invited by Muhammad ʿAli in the

22. On the greater leniency of French authorities towards emigration than has often been assumed, see François Weil, "L'État et l'émigration de France," in *Citoyenneté et émigration. Les politiques du départ*, eds. Nancy Green and François Weil (Paris, EHESS: 2006), 119–35. Studies of French expatriate communities include *Des Pyrénées à la Pampa: une histoire de l'émigration d'élites, XIXe-XXe siècles*, ed. Laurent Dornel (Pau: PUPPA, 2013) and Anne-Marie Planel, *Du comptoir à la colonie. Histoire de la communauté française de Tunisie, 1814–1883* (Paris: Riveneuve, 2015).

23. Elizabeth H. Shlala, "The De Rossetti Affair: Legal Pluralism and Levantine Identity at the Crossroads of Empires," *British Journal of Middle Eastern Studies*, 43, 1 (2016); and for the period after 1882, Will Hanley, *Identifying with Nationality: Europeans, Ottomans, and Egyptians in Alexandria* (New York: Columbia University Press, 2017), esp. 155–72.

24. Daniel Panzac "The Population of Egypt in the Nineteenth Century," *Asian and African Studies*, 21, 1 (1987): 26–9; *The Cambridge History of Egypt*, ed. M. W. Daly, 2 vols. (Cambridge: Cambridge University Press, 1998), vol. 2, 274.

25. My estimates; the figure for 1850 is based on reports listing the number of households headed by a French national or *protégé* (208 households in Alexandria, 31 December 1850) or the number of French nationals (211 individuals, including *protégés* and nine Algerian subjects, in Cairo, 31 Dec. 1848), in AAE, Affaires diverses politiques, 28/1 and 28/2; and the figure for the early 1870s is a compromise between the number of French residents in 1873 registered in the Cairo, Alexandria and Suez consulates (8,257; not including French residents in the new consular districts of Port-Said and Ismailia), in "Statistique des Français résidant à l'étranger d'après les documents transmis par les agens diplomatiques et consulaires," 1874, AAE, Affaires diverses politiques, 28//11 and an estimate of 17,500 French nationals, frequently cited during

late 1820s, and the Saint-Simonians who volunteered their services in the early 1830s—one of whom, Thomas (Ismaÿl) Urbain, later became the architect of the Arab Kingdom policy in Algeria, as seen in chapter 2—were succeeded by a larger flow of entrepreneurs, adventurers or skilled workers, attracted by the growth of the Egyptian cotton trade and the building of the Suez Canal and other infrastructures.[26]

The birth records of French nationals in France's Egyptian consulates—an indirect indication of the size of the French community—confirm that its growth mainly took place between 1855 and 1870 (see figure 5.1).[27] They also suggest that the French community's size declined after 1871, a trend which, according to Egyptian censuses, continued after 1882, even though the overall number of European residents kept growing: the number of French residents declined from 15,500 (17 percent of all foreign residents) in 1882 to 14,500 (9.5 percent) in 1907.[28] French expatriation therefore peaked when French political influence in Egypt was acknowledged to have been at its maximum, in the 1860s; and it decreased as the same influence began to wane in the 1870s.[29] The imposition of formal British rule in 1882 did not reverse the decline, although it did not accelerate it. This strong correlation between expatriation and political influence is suggestive of the links between temporary migration and informal empire.

The death records of French nationals represent a less reliable indicator of the expatriate community's size, because mortality fluctuates more than natality, but they do broadly confirm a pattern of strong demographic growth be-

the controversy on extra-territorial jurisdiction in the early 1870s, and endorsed by Jasper Y. Brinton, *The Mixed Courts of Egypt*, 2nd ed. (New Haven, CT: Yale University Press, 1968), 18.

26. Philippe Régnier, *Les Saint-Simoniens en Egypte* (Cairo: Banque de l'Union Européenne, 1989); *La France et l'Egypte à l'époque des vice-rois, 1805–1882*, eds. Daniel Panzac and André Raymond (Cairo: Institut français d'archéologie orientale, 2002), esp. 171–234.

27. All the figures below on births and deaths of French nationals in Egypt, in the years 1827 to 1882 included, are based on AAE, État civil, Alexandrie, vols. 1–15 (1792–1882); Le Caire, vols. 1–6 (1822–1882); Suez, vols. 1–4 (1861–1886); Port-Saïd, vols. 1–2 (1867–1882); and Ismaïlia, vol. 1 (1872–1889). I am very grateful to Sylvie Prudhon, from the Archives Diplomatiques, for her guidance on this material, to Arnaud Coulon, for his compiling of the data, and to the Leverhulme Trust for financing the work.

28. Samir Saul, *La France et l'Egypte de 1882 à 1914. Intérêts économiques et implications politiques* (Paris: Comité pour l'histoire économique et financière de la France, 1997), 516.

29. Agatha Ramm, "Great Britain and France in Egypt, 1876–1882," in *France and Britain in Africa: Imperial Rivalry and Colonial Rule*, eds. Prosser Gifford and Wm. Roger Louis (New Haven, CT: Yale University Press, 1971), 73–120.

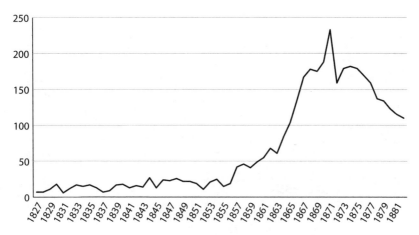

FIGURE 5.1. Births of French nationals and *protégés* recorded in French consulates in Egypt, 1827–1882. *Source:* My calculations, excluding under ten recorded births of colonial Algerian Muslim subjects, and based on AAE, État civil, Alexandrie, vols. 1–15 (1792–1882); Le Caire, vols. 1–6 (1822–1882); Suez, vols. 1–4 (1861–1886); Port-Saïd, vols. 1–2 (1867–1882); and Ismaïlia, vol. 1 (1872–1889).

tween 1855 and 1870, followed by rapid decline (figure 5.2). Death records also include useful information about the social background of French male expatriates, with an indication of the deceased's profession in 2,938 out of 3,309 adult male deaths recorded between 1827 and 1882.[30] A special case was the very large number (1,162, out of 2,938) of active French military members, whose deaths were recorded by Egyptian consulates. Most of them were presumably not residents in Egypt—at least 80 percent served in the navy—and should not be considered genuine expatriates. However, their numbers are a good reminder that the expansion of French influence took place under the shadow of gunboats, especially as the number of deceased active military plummeted after 1871, when this influence began to decline.[31]

The 1,768 French adult males other than active soldiers who died in Egypt between 1827 and 1888, and for whom a legible indication of profession is available, only offer a snapshot of this expatriate community, as many expatriates

30. This number of adult male deaths excludes those of ninety-eight Algerian subjects; deaths recorded without an indication of profession include forty-five "sans profession," four "travellers" and one "refugee."

31. 761 active sailors or naval officers were recorded as having died in Egypt between 1861 and 1870 and only 80 between 1871 and 1880.

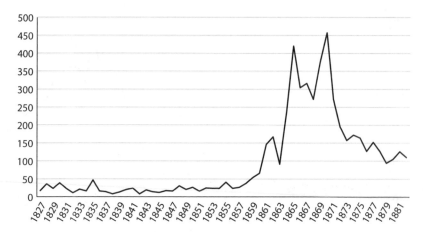

FIGURE 5.2. Deaths of nationals and *protégés* recorded in French consulates in Egypt, 1827–1882. *Source:* My calculations, excluding ninety-eight recorded deaths of colonial Algerian Muslim subjects, and based on AAE, État civil, Alexandrie, vols. 1–15 (1792–1882); Le Caire, vols. 1–6 (1822–1882); Suez, vols. 1–4 (1861–1886); Port-Saïd, vols. 1–2 (1867–1882); and Ismaïlia, vol. 1 (1872–1889).

returned to France before they died. Yet there is little reason to believe that this sample is not representative.[32] Existing scholarship on nineteenth-century cross-Mediterranean migrations tends to emphasize the "humble social status" of European migrants to North Africa, labelling them "Europe's human castoff."[33] Such generalizations may be acceptable in the case of, for instance, Maltese or southern Italian migrants to Tunisia, who usually moved as a result of strong demographic pressure and lack of economic opportunities at home. But they would not apply well to French migrants, at least not to those who migrated elsewhere than Algeria. The death-record data from France's Egyptian consulates suggests that, on average, French expatriates enjoyed a respectable social status and were often highly skilled. My own somewhat subjective classification suggests that out of the 1,768 French deceased males, 272 were highly skilled (including 65 merchants or bankers; 47 medical doctors; 37 lawyers or high civil servants; 33 engineers or architects; and 15 professors or scientists) and 1,058 were skilled (including 190 employees or

32. Death being a more random event than marriage or birth, the profession of the deceased provides at least a better indication of the composition of the French expatriate community than the profession of spouses or parents, also available in the État civil registers.

33. Julia A. Clancy-Smith, *Mediterraneans: North Africa and Europe in an Age of Migration, c. 1800–1900* (Berkeley: University of California Press, 2011), 3, 65.

agents; 137 mechanics; 58 accountants, brokers or *commis*; 48 tradesmen and entrepreneurs; 43 foremen; 43 artisans specialized in metals, and a wide array of shopkeepers such as 29 butchers, 28 bakers, 15 tailors and 11 *restaurateurs*). Only 391 were low skilled (including 87 workers and 49 cooks), of whom only five were agriculturalists (*agriculteurs, cultivateurs*). On average French expatriates in Egypt were much more skilled than metropolitan France's still largely agricultural workforce.[34]

France's consulates in Egypt between 1827 and 1882 recorded far fewer deaths of French adult female expatriates (696) than male (2,140, if active soldiers and sailors are excluded). The implied one-to-three female-to-male ratio is consistent with the character of this emigration, which is more transient than in settlement colonies. Unfortunately, records for the female deceased are less informative on their economic activities than those for the male deceased, with no indication of profession in 516 (74 percent) cases. What information there is, however, suggests that these Frenchwomen were not as skilled as the male emigrants, although still probably more skilled than women in metropolitan France, with only two highly skilled women (one merchant and one convent mother superior), 76 skilled (including 29 tradeswomen or *modistes*, 29 nuns, 10 teachers, but also one broker and one photographer) and 82 low skilled (including 29 seamstresses or laundresses, 26 servants and 12 cooks). Nevertheless, the average social status of female expatriates was almost certainly higher than this data suggests, because many deceased women were—or had been—married to men of respectable status. Tellingly, among the expatriate deceased there were almost as many female *rentières* (8) as male *rentiers* (9), an indication of relative economic success, although the small proportion of expatriates living off their investments points again to the transient nature of French migrations to Egypt: most hoped to live off their *rentes* back in metropolitan France.

The Colony's Influence

The overall numbers of European expatriates in Egypt may not seem large, but their effect on Egyptian economic life was enormous. The case of Édouard Dervieu, the main protagonist of David Landes's classic study *Bankers and Pashas*, may be considered exemplary if extreme. Descended from a family of Lyon silk merchants, which connects him to one of the most vibrant branches

---

34. *Histoire économique et sociale de la France*, eds. Braudel and Labrousse, vol. 3, 220–1.

of French champagne capitalism, Dervieu relocated from Marseille to Alexandria in the late 1850s. In Egypt he served as director of the largest French shipping company, Messageries imperiales. He soon abandoned his position to become the confidant and private banker of two Egyptian rulers, Sa'id (r. 1854–1863) and his nephew Isma'il (r. 1863–1879). Dervieu's financial advice helped foster the rapid growth of Egypt's national debt, which would result in the country's bankruptcy in 1876 and occupation by Britain in 1882. This was hardly the outcome hoped for by Dervieu, an ardent French nationalist.[35] Yet his career illustrates the extent to which expatriates, as key intermediaries between Egypt and Europe (in this instance European capital markets), helped transform Egyptian economics, society and politics after 1850.

Dervieu's career is also suggestive of the mutually reinforcing aspects of French influence. The secret of Dervieu's prodigious ascent was the close personal relationship he forged, first with with Sa'id and then with Isma'il, until the latter cut Dervieu loose in 1868. In his correspondence with Parisian bankers, Dervieu rarely failed to emphasize his "intimité" with Egyptian rulers, because his own creditworthiness depended upon it.[36] In his gripping study of Dervieu's rise and fall, Landes noted the crucial role of this intimacy, but considered it an exogenous, contingent factor.[37] Yet Dervieu's close personal relations with Egyptian rulers originated in his marriage to the daughter of Matthieu Koenig, a minor French Orientalist and the tutor of several sons of Muhammad 'Ali, including Sa'id.[38] Dervieu's privileged access to the Egyptian court should therefore be viewed as a by-product of earlier French migrations to Egypt and of the establishment of French cultural ascendancy in the

35. David S. Landes, *Bankers and Pashas. International Finance and Economic Imperialism in Egypt*, 2nd edn (New York: Harper & Row, 1969), 103–4, 165.

36. See, for instance, Édouard Dervieu to Alfred André, 20 May 1863, 20 Oct. 1863 and 26 Oct. 1863, Roubaix, Centre des Archives du Monde du Travail (henceforth CAMT), 44 AQ 11.

37. Landes, *Bankers and Pashas*, 319–20.

38. Marriage of Édouard André Dervieu, "agent des services maritimes des messageries imperiales," born in Marseille and aged 33, with Zoë Esther Koenig, born in Alexandria and aged 21, 5 May 1856, AAE, État civil, Alexandrie, 4/10. The bride's witnesses for the marriage contract were two French officials in the Egyptian government, while one of the groom's was the French consul general; see notarized contract in AAE, Chancellerie, 4, 30 Apr. 1856. While in Egypt, the couple had three children, in 1860, 1863 and 1866, in AAE, État civil, Alexandrie, 4/56, 5/67 and 6/222. Zoë's father, Matthieu Koenig, "secrétaire des commandements au gouvernement égyptiens," died aged 63 in 1865, in AAE, État civil, Alexandrie, 6/74. On Koenig, also a former chief of the translation office of the Egyptian minister of foreign affairs, see Newman, "Introduction," 43.

Ottoman province. Both Sa'id and Isma'il, partly educated in Paris as well as by French tutors in Egypt, were fluent in French. How else could Dervieu, who understood neither Ottoman Turkish nor Arabic, have risen to become Isma'il's "secrétaire particulier"?[39]

For French and other Francophone expatriates in Egypt, French cultural ascendancy, including the primacy of French as the language of business, was only a recent advantage. Until the early nineteenth century, the lingua franca of cross-cultural trade between Europe and the Ottoman world had been Italian, or a pidgin version of it.[40] In fact, one of the factors contributing to the strong position of French trade in the eighteenth-century Ottoman world had been the assistance offered to French merchants by consular interpreters, or dragomans, who thanks to a ten-year training at the École des jeunes de langue founded by Jean-Baptiste Colbert in the 1660s (eight years in Paris, followed by two years in Constantinople) were proficient in Ottoman Turkish, Arabic and sometimes also Persian.[41] In the 1790s, the disbanding of the school at the beginning of the Revolution, together with the dispersal of consular officials who were often hostile to the new regime, was identified by the ministry of external relations as a major cause of the abrupt decline of French political and economic influence in Ottoman lands. "The Turks," one memorandum lamented, "only speak and write Turkish. They would find speaking what they call a Christian language demeaning."[42] French diplomats, another report explained, often dealt with Ottoman officials "by means of the lingua franca," but as soon as "business becomes serious, the Pashas suddenly forget their bad Italian, and a dragoman who knows Turkish and Arabic becomes necessary."[43] Plans to revive the school were drawn up by the commercially minded minister Charles Delacroix, a former secretary of Turgot, and approved in 1797 by

39. Dervieu to André, 20 Oct. 1863, CAMT, 44 AQ 11.

40. Jocelyn Dakhlia, *Lingua Franca. Histoire d'une langue en Méditerranée* (Arles: Actes Sud, 2008).

41. Frédéric Hitzel, "L'École des Jeunes de langue d'Istanbul. Un modèle d'apprentissage des langues orientales," in *Langues et langages du commerce en Méditerranée et en Europe à l'époque moderne*, eds. Gilbert Buti, Michèle Janin-Thivos and Olivier Raveux (Aix-en-Provence: Presses de l'université de Provence, 2013), 23–31.

42. "Mémoire sur l'Ecole des Jeunes de langues," 6 Frimaire year 4 [26 Nov. 1795], AAE, M&D, Turquie, 164.

43. "Rapport au Directoire Exécutif," Fructidor year 5 [Aug.-Sep. 1797], AAE, M&D, Turquie, 165.

his successor Talleyrand, who was also one the main advocates of the military expedition to Egypt that took place the following year.[44]

In the nineteenth century, the revived École des jeunes de langue continued to train new dragomans, and British consular officials complained that, unlike their French counterparts, they had to hire less trustworthy Levantines as interpreters.[45] But their numbers did not keep up with the intensification of trade between Europe and the Ottoman world, undoubtedly because the spread of French in the Ottoman Empire made them less useful.[46] The rise of French was the product of multiple educational endeavours, ranging from the funding of military and medical instruction in French by Ottoman authorities, in Constantinople from the 1780s and Egypt from the 1820s, to the subsidizing of student missions in France, such as the Mission égyptienne, and the multiplication of French-language primary schools, funded by Catholic missionary orders or the Alliance Israélite Universelle, from five in 1850 to five hundred throughout the Ottoman world by the early twentieth century.[47] The first French-language Ottoman newspapers appeared in Smyrna in the 1820s and by the 1870s ten newspapers, fully or partly in French, were published in Constantinople alone; even newspapers for British subjects, such as the *Levant Herald* and *Levant Times*, were half written in French.[48] In the 1850s, fluency

44. Minute d'arrêté, "Restauration de l'École des Enfants de Langue," Fructidor year 5 [Aug.-Sep. 1797].

45. Frédéric Hitzel, "L'institution des Jeunes de langue de Constantinople au début du XIXᵉ siècle," in *De Samarcande à Istanbul: étapes orientales*, ed. Véronique Schiltz (Paris: CNRS, 2015), 203–219; on the superior reliability of French dragomans, see Edmund Hornby, supreme consular judge in Constantinople, to Lord Russell, foreign secretary, 17 Aug. 1859, TNA, FO 780/333.

46. See the correspondence between the school's administrator and the minister of foreign affairs; for instance, in 1853 only two students graduated from the school, and were appointed *élèves-drogmans*, in Desgranges aîné, the secretary-interpreter of the Emperor and school administrator to the minister of foreign affairs, 9 Aug. 1853, AAE, M&D, Turquie, 170, fol. 76.

47. Matthew Burrows, "'Mission civilisatrice': French Cultural Policy in the Middle-East, 1860- 1914," *Historical Journal*, 29, 1 (1986).

48. Gérard Groc and Ibrahim Caglar, *La presse française de Turquie de 1795 à nos jours. Histoire et catalogue* (Istanbul: Isis, 1985); Joëlle Pierre, "La presse française de Turquie, canal de transmission des idées de la Révolution," *Le Temps des médias*, 5, 2 (2005); see also the database "Presse francophone dans l'Empire Ottoman," http://heritage.bnf.fr/bibliothequesorient/fr/presse-ottomane-francophone (accessed 7 June 2018). The 1870s have been described as the "golden age" of book publishing in French in the Ottoman world, in Johann Strauss, "Le livre français d'Istanbul," *Revue des mondes musulmans et de la Méditerranée*, 87–88 (1999).

in French became a requirement in the upper echelons of Ottoman bureaucracy and in 1868 the school for imperial functionaries, the Galata Serai (Galatasaray), was re-founded as a Francophone *lycée*.[49] Fluency in French became
at least as common in the Egyptian bureaucracy, so much so that after Britain's
occupation in 1882 British officials were obliged to communicate among themselves and with their indigenous subordinates "in halting French."[50]

French was already the language of European aristocracies in the eighteenth
century. After 1820 its usage spread within Europe to the middle classes, in
parallel to the fast-growing consumption of French cultural products, and beyond Europe to old and new elites, especially in the Middle East.[51] When the
international lawyer James Lorimer, a staunch British imperialist and believer
in the superiority of the Anglo-Saxon race, proposed the constitution of a
world government in the late 1870s, with its seat in Constantinople, it appeared
to him a matter of course that the "organ of intercommunication amongst [its]
members" should be French, "the only language which almost all cultivated
Europeans speak"; Lorimer could only hope that one day English may "rank
pari passu with French" as a working language.[52] The status of French as a
global language should therefore be seen as a product of France's informal
empire. It predated territorial expansion under the Third Republic, and efforts
by the French state to promote the learning of French outside France after 1890

49. Carter Vaughn Findley, *Ottoman Civil Officialdom: A Social History* (Princeton, NJ:
Princeton University Press, 1989), 164–8, 170–2.

50. Milner, *England in Egypt*, 418; on fluency in French among Egyptian bureaucrats before
1882, see F. Robert Hunter, *Egypt under the Khedives, 1805–1879: From Household Government
to Modern Bureaucracy* (Pittsburgh, PA: University of Pittsburgh Press, 1984), 80–122; and on
the consumption of French (and Italian) theatre and opera in Cairo after 1860, see Adam
Mestyan, *Arab Patriotism: The Ideology and Culture of Power in Late Ottoman Egypt* (Princeton,
NJ: Princeton University Press, 2017), 84–119.

51. Although a great deal of attention has been given to the spread of the French language
within France at the beginning of the modern period—see for instance Michel de Certeau,
Dominique Julia and Jacques Revel, *Une politique de la langue. La Révolution française et les patois:
l'enquête de Grégoire* (Paris: Gallimard, 1975)—to my knowledge there is unfortunately no comprehensive study of international *francophonie* in the nineteenth century.

52. James Lorimer, *Of the Denationalisation of Constantinople and its Devotion to International
Purposes* (Edinburgh: Edmonston and Douglas, 1876), 23; James Lorimer, *The Institutes of the
Law of Nations*, 2 vols. (Edinburgh: Blackwood, 1883), vol. 2, 264–9. On Lorimer's politics, see
Martti Koskenniemi, "Race, Hierarchy and International Law: Lorimer's Legal Science," *Euro-
pean Journal of International Law*, 27, 2 (2016).

may be construed as an attempt to stymie its slow decline in comparison to German in Europe and English everywhere else.[53]

There were of course serious limitations to the allegedly universal spread of French in the nineteenth century. In Britain itself the elite may have accepted French's superior status and used it for their own ends of social exclusivity. In London Clubs and many restaurants, for instance, dinner menus were written exclusively in French until the early twentieth century.[54] But in the more democratic Anglo settler societies, French was much less widely used. Upon landing in the United States in 1831, Alexis de Tocqueville noted with surprise (and pleasure, because he wished to improve his English) that even among educated New Yorkers "nobody speaks [French]."[55] Another significant exception to French cultural domination was Asia beyond the Middle East. When Commodore Perry's fleet entered the Edo Bay in order to force the opening of Japan to world trade in 1853, a Japanese official on a guard boat held up for the American sailors to read "a scroll of paper . . . in the French language," instructing them to "go away, and not anchor at their peril." The reputation of French as the language of international diplomacy had reached isolationist Tokugawa Japan. Yet the subsequent parleys that saw Japanese officials give in to American demands were held in Dutch, the main language of Euro-Japanese trade since the seventeenth century.[56] East of Suez, French only prevailed in a few territorial outposts under French rule (and after 1885, Indochina), and English became the dominant language.[57] Tellingly, the Hong Kong office of Jardine & Matheson addressed the Lyonnais consignees

53. See for instance the connections between the state-subsidized Alliance française and the colonial lobby, in Janet Horne, "'To Spread the French Language Is to Extend the *Patrie*': The Colonial Mission of the Alliance Française," *French Historical Studies*, 40, 1 (2017).

54. Amy B. Trubek, *Haute Cuisine: How the French Invented the Culinary Profession* (Philadelphia: University of Pennsylvania Press, 2000), 46.

55. Alexis de Tocqueville to Louise de Tocqueville (his mother, née de Rosambo), 14 May 1831, in Tocqueville, *Œuvres complètes*, vol. 14, 83.

56. Francis Hawks, *Narrative of the Expedition of an American Squadron to the China Seas and Japan Performed in the Years 1852, 1853 and 1854 under the Command of Commodore M.C. Perry, United States Navy*, 4 vols. (Washington, DC: A.O.P. Nicholson, 1856), vol. 1, 234.

57. On the use of French in Asia beyond the Middle East, see Mathilde Kang, *Francophonie en Orient: Aux croisements France-Asie (1848–1940)* (Amsterdam: Amsterdam University Press, 2017).

of its Chinese raw silk in English and, with a touch of irritation, instructed its French correspondents to "always address us in the English language."[58]

Even in Egypt, French cultural dominance faced significant limits. French became the main medium of communication between European and Egyptian elites, but pidgin Italian continued to prevail between lower class Europeans and Egyptians until the early twentieth century.[59] And of course not every member of the Egyptian elite had an excellent command of French. In his memoirs, a French consul general in Alexandria reported his annoyance at having to use a dragoman in a negotiation with one of the principal Egyptian ministers in 1876. But the fact that the need for an interpreter should be considered exceptional is also evidence of the prevalent use of French in Franco-Egyptian interactions, while the consul's fear that his dragoman would fail to translate faithfully "his rather harsh words" confirms that this prevalence had imperial undertones.[60] There can be little doubt that, even confined to an elite level of cross-cultural interactions, this dominance provided native French speakers with substantial economic advantages, because elite Egyptian actors played a disproportionate part in commercial and financial transactions. There are several other instances of French economic success in Egypt based on cultural affinity, besides Dervieu's prodigious ascent. The adventurer who brought the painter Félix Clément to Egypt, François Bravay, was the son of a saucepan seller in Languedoc, but he gained the confidence of Sa'id by means of endless "*bons mots*, puns and racy jokes" in French.[61] Through generous contracts awarded by the Egyptian ruler, Bravay converted this cultural capital into a fortune amounting to several millions, but his success would have been unimaginable had Sa'id not been fluent in French.[62] The very favourable terms obtained by Ferdinand de Lesseps from Sa'id for the original concession of the Suez Canal in 1854 also had a cultural origin: they owed a great deal to the two men's old friendship, which itself originated from Muhammad 'Ali's desire for his son to frequently visit the household of Matthieu de Lesseps, the

58. Jardine & Matheson to Desgrand père et fils, 9 July 1855, JM, C11/19.

59. Will Hanley, "Foreignness and Localness in Alexandria, 1880–1914," unpublished PhD dissertation (Princeton University, 2007), 54.

60. Jules Alexis Des Michels, *Souvenirs de ma carrière* (Paris: Plon, Nourrit et Cie, 1901), 127.

61. Auriant [Alexandre Hadjivassiliou], *François Bravay, ou le nabab* (Paris: Mercure de France, 1943), 29–30.

62. Olivier Senlis, *François Bravay, le vrai Nabab* (Paris: DoD, 2017).

French consul in Alexandria between 1831 and 1838 and Ferdinand's father, in order to learn the French language and French manners.[63]

The ascendancy of French as the language of economic transactions extended beyond Egypt and tainted other Europeans, including Britons. A study of European finance in Constantinople noted that British financiers frequently employed "a strange mixture of English and French," as in the request of a banker to his London manager for "authority to racheter la première catégorie [buy back the first category]" of new consolidated Ottoman bonds.[64] Egyptian linguistic and cultural familiarity with France is the leitmotif of a work from the early 1880s by the journalist Pierre Giffard that listed the many contributions of French engineers, architects, merchants, financiers, lawyers and agronomists towards Egypt's economic development since the 1820s. The book was published a year after Britain's occupation, which Giffard contrasted with France's earlier "peaceful conquest" by French expatriates: "Egypt has been civilized, organized by Frenchmen, only by Frenchmen."[65] The book's jingoistic tone sometimes bordered on the ridiculous—Giffard was a master publicist, later to conceive of the Tour de France as a means of promoting his newspaper L'Auto. Yet the long list it gave of eminent French expatriates in Egypt, his descriptions of the "Haussmannisation" of Alexandria's urban landscape, the vignettes of Parisian-style arcaded shopping streets or "brasseries à femmes" in Cairo's new centre, or his remarks on the prevalence of French on urban street and shop signs, are suggestive of the breadth and intensity of Franco-Egyptian cultural-cum-economic connections before the 1880s.[66]

The benefits enjoyed by France or French expatriates as a result of their involvement in Egyptian economic life are as difficult to quantify as they are impossible to ignore. But we may see them, in part, reflected by the prodigious growth of French exports to Egypt during the cotton boom: +1,060 percent in twelve years, between 1852–1853 and 1864–1865, or around five times the

63. Pierre Crabitès, *Ismail the Maligned* (London: George Routledge & Sons, 1933), 3–4; François Charles-Roux, *L'Égypte de 1801 à 1882. Mohamed Aly et sa dynastie jusqu'à l'occupation anglaise* (Paris: Plon, 1936), 262–3. These works from the colonial era probably exaggerate Sa'id's naivety, but the origins of his personal acquaintance with Ferdinand de Lesseps are well attested; see also Zachary Karabell, *Parting the Desert: The Creation of the Suez Canal* (London: John Murray, 2003), 66–74.

64. Clay, *Gold for the Sultan*, 529.

65. Pierre Giffard, *Les Français en Égypte* (Paris: Havard, 1883), iv, 144.

66. Giffard, *Les Français*, 1–144.

growth of overall Egyptian imports over the same period (+206 percent).[67] Informal domination did not result in a monopoly. By 1864–1865, France's annual exports to Egypt, at 61.5 million francs, still lagged behind Britain's, which stood at 150.5 million. But British exporters benefited from the fact that Britain absorbed most of Egypt's cotton exports, and merchants were loath to let ships return from Liverpool to Alexandria on ballast.[68] That France's exports were growing nearly twice as fast as Britain's in these circumstances suggests a distortion that is tantamount to a preferential trade regime. It would be even more complicated to try and assess the distortive effects of French influence on foreign investment into Egypt, but it is significant that the stock of French capital invested in Egypt surpassed the stock of British capital by a margin of two to one, even after Britain's occupation in 1882, up until 1914.[69] Yet these distortions were only partially the direct product of cultural influence. They were also partially indirect, because they could result from the wilful manipulation of the Egyptian legal system by French officials and expatriates. The new regime of extraterritoriality that emerged in Egypt after 1840 benefited all the European migrants, but until the 1870s it benefited the French more than others.

A French Legal Borderland

Contemporaries frequently compared Egypt to the American Frontier. George S. Batchelder, a former judge at Saratoga Springs in the state of New York, who came to serve on the "mixed" (international) bench of the new Egyptian courts created in 1876, described the country as "a sort of California or 'Great West' for the adventurous and fortune-seeking elements of Southern Europe." Yet unlike in America, Batchelder noted, immigrants eschewed naturalization. Instead, "this enormous accession to the Egyptian population," thanks to the personal legal system that prevailed in the Ottoman world, remained under "the law of the fatherland." European consuls became small

67. For French exports, see *Tableau décennal*; for overall Egyptian imports, see "The World Trade Historical Database," http://www.uc3m.es/tradehist_db (accessed 7 Aug. 2018).

68. For British exports to Egypt, see *Annual Statement*; on Egyptian exports of cotton to Britain, see Roger Owen, *Cotton and the Egyptian Economy, 1820–1914: A Study in Trade and Development* (Oxford: Clarendon Press, 1969), 196–205 and Roger Owen, *The Middle East in the World Economy, 1800–1914*, 2nd edn (London: Tauris, 2002), 135–7.

69. Saul, *La France et l'Égypte*, 526–31.

"potentates," governing "their respective colonies."[70] This was especially true, a former American consul in Alexandria stated, of French consuls and their nationals: a French resident in Egypt "desires that the Consulate should take notice of almost every act in his life," while "the number of times that officer [the French consul general] is called upon to sign his name officially is almost incredible."[71] The legal hyperactivity of French consulates became one of the factors that enabled the French to benefit from a privileged status among expatriates, allowing France to enjoy what a British lawyer described as "semi-sovereignty" over Egypt by the early 1870s.[72]

How the French came to wield such legal influence in Egypt is a complex story. In part, it was due to the quickening pace of legal reform throughout the globe in the mid-nineteenth century. This legal reordering was inspired by Europe's new economic and political ascendancy, but it did not imply the imposition of European sovereignty. As shown by Lauren Benton, British statesmen and legal thinkers tended to favour the creation of autonomous territorial units, with Britain acting as the ultimate arbitrator of a global system of states.[73] Despite the prominent role played by the French legal model in nineteenth-century legal reforms both within and beyond Europe, the prevailing view among French politicians and law scholars has not been so extensively studied. What we know suggests that, although the French also supported legal reforms, they were particularly keen to use them as a way of maximizing France's political and economic influence, and that they upheld a more aggressive conception of extra-territoriality.[74] In other words, legal influence, alongside trade and culture, was to play a significant part in promoting

70. George S. Batchelder, "The International Court of Egypt," *Albany Law Journal*, 19 (1879): 290; the comparison recalls the image of the "Klondike on the Nile" in Landes, *Bankers and Pashas*, 69.

71. Charles Hale, "Consular Service and Society in Egypt," *Atlantic Monthly*, Sep. 1877, 280–90.

72. James Carlile MacCoan, *Consular Jurisdiction in Turkey and Egypt* (London: G. Norman, 1873), 42.

73. Benton, *Law and Colonial Culture*, 210–52; Lauren Benton and Lisa Ford, *Rage for Order: The British Empire and the Origins of International Law, 1800–1850* (Cambridge, MA: Harvard University Press, 2016), esp. 18–24. For a similar emphasis on the state-building effects of the spread of international law, see Richard S. Horowitz, "International Law and State Transformation in China, Siam and the Ottoman Empire during the Nineteenth Century," *Journal of World History*, 15, 4 (2004).

74. Todd, "Beneath Sovereignty": 116–21.

France's tutelage and establishing "a French empire of language, commerce and laws" in the vision expounded as early as 1800 by Talleyrand's friend, the diplomat Alexandre d'Hauterive.[75]

However, the emergence of French legal hegemony in Egypt was also the product of the country's very peculiar situation in the international legal order. On the one hand, it remained a province of the Ottoman Empire, a principle strengthened by the 1840 London convention that reasserted Constantinople's suzerainty after the Eastern crisis. As such, it was strongly affected by the wave of legal reforms that swept the Ottoman world in the Tanzimat era (1839– 1876).[76] On the other hand, the 1840 London convention confirmed the hereditary character of Muhammad 'Ali's rule, which entrenched the province's autonomy. Egyptian rulers could therefore give their own interpretation of Tanzimat reforms and build an empire of their own, focusing their efforts on the Sudan after they were forced to surrender Syria in 1840.[77] And at the same time, the relative weakening of Egypt after the Eastern crisis turned it into a privileged terrain for British, French and other European (Italian, Austrian) imperial ambitions in the Middle East. From being "allied" to France, Egypt became "protected" by it after 1840.[78] In other words, Egypt was an empire within an empire, and at the confluence of several informal empires. The outcome was extreme legal confusion, from which the French benefited considerably in the third quarter of the century.

A case in point was the expansion of extraterritorial jurisdiction in Egypt after 1850. European extraterritoriality originated from the strong form of legal pluralism that prevailed in the Ottoman world since the sixteenth century. Despite the name, the Ottoman Capitulations that granted small colonies of European merchants a degree of jurisdictional autonomy did not, until the early nineteenth century, manifest European superiority. Instead, they were negotiated and mutually advantageous arrangements, typical of cross-cultural trade before the modern era. European merchants enjoyed a degree of self-jurisdiction, but they were subjected to significant legal restrictions, including spatial segregation in Ottoman cities and a ban on the purchase of Ottoman real estate. In cases of mixed (European-Ottoman) legal disputes, Ottoman

75. Rothschild, "Language and Empire, c. 1800": 208.

76. Hanioğlu, A Brief History of the Late Ottoman Empire, 72–108.

77. Efraim Karsh and Inari Karsh, Empires of the Sand: The Struggle for Mastery in the Middle East, 1789–1923 (Cambridge, MA: Harvard University Press, 1999), 27–68.

78. Sabri, L'empire égyptien, 542–3.

jurisdiction prevailed.[79] However, plural legal systems tend to be fluid. After 1830, in return for western European diplomatic support against Russian expansionism, the Ottoman government consented to a reformulation of the Capitulations into significant privileges for western Europeans. The November 1838 Anglo-Ottoman treaty of Balta Liman removed a wide range of legal restrictions on British participation in Ottoman economic life and asserted the permanent character ("now and for ever") of the Capitulations.[80] In January 1839, France obtained a similar rewording of its own capitulatory arrangements.[81]

The scholarship on informal empire has frequently cited Balta Liman as an early instance of "free trade imperialism."[82] This is a valid assessment, but the significance of Balta Liman lay in the subordination of Ottoman municipal—especially economic—law to international law rather than the reduction of Ottoman tariffs, because the latter were already very low.[83] From concessions that could be revoked by the Ottoman Sultan, the Capitulations became an open-ended international commitment. The multilateral treaty of Paris that concluded the Crimean War (1853–1856), at the same time as it welcomed the Ottoman Empire in the European system of international law, confirmed the legal incorporation of the Capitulations into the international order. A vague promise was made to Ottoman representatives at the Paris Congress that capitulatory arrangements would later be repealed, in return for the continuation

79. Maurits H. van der Boogert, *The Capitulations and the Ottoman Legal System: Qadis, Consuls, and Beratcs in the Eighteenth Century* (Leiden: Brill, 2005); Karen Barkey, "Aspects of Legal Pluralism in the Ottoman Empire," in *Legal Pluralism and Empires, 1500–1850*, eds. Lauren Benton and Richard J. Ross (New York: New York University Press, 2013), 83–107.

80. See article 1 of the treaty in *A Complete Collection of the Treaties and Conventions, and Reciprocal Regulations, at Present Subsisting between Great Britain & Foreign Powers*, ed. Lewis Hertslet, 31 vols. (London: Butterworth, 1827–1940), vol. 5, 506–10; compare with article 4 of the previous Anglo-Ottoman treaty, concluded in 1809, in Hertslet, *A Complete Collection of the Treaties and Conventions*, vol. 2, 370–77.

81. *Recueil des traités de la France*, 23 vols., ed. Jules de Clercq (Paris, 1864–1907), vol. 4, 439–43, article 1; compare with articles 2 and 3 of the peace treaty of 1802, in Clercq, *Recueil*, vol. 1, 588–90.

82. See for instance Gallagher and Robinson, "The Imperialism of Free Trade": 11, and Reşat Kasaba, "Treaties and Friendships: British Imperialism, the Ottoman Empire, and China in the Nineteenth Century," *Journal of World History*, 4, 2 (1993).

83. Şevket Pamuk, *The Ottoman Empire and European Capitalism, 1820–1913* (Cambridge: Cambridge University Press, 1987), 28–31.

of domestic legal reforms.[84] But the promise was not kept, and it took the nationalist revolution led by Mustapha Kemal to wrest the abolition of the Capitulations from Western powers after the Ottoman Empire's dismemberment at the treaty of Lausanne in 1923.[85]

The evolution of the Capitulations shows that informal or free trade imperialism did not only consist in removing taxes on foreign trade. Instead, this type of imperial domination relied on a wider set of asymmetric legal arrangements, of which low tariffs were but one aspect. Balta Liman prefigured many similar treaties that established or expanded European extraterritorial jurisdiction, especially in the Middle East and East Asia. Such "unequal treaties"—so called because they mostly created obligations for the non-European party— were an important facet of the surge in international treaty making between 1830 and 1860.[86] They deserve to be considered imperial, because they incorporated extra-European countries in the nascent global legal order, but granted them an inferior status.[87]

This is not to say that legal transformations in the mid-century extra-European world only benefited the Europeans. In the Middle East, numerous Ottoman actors took advantage of legal innovations to develop their own businesses. The adoption of the corporation by some Levantine merchant families, as the legal vehicle for their transactions, is a compelling example.[88] But most of those who lost through these legal changes were still to be found among

84. Jennifer Pitts, "Boundaries of Victorian International Law," in *Victorian Visions of Global Order: Empire and International Relations in Nineteenth-Century Political Thought*, ed. Duncan Bell (Cambridge: Cambridge University Press, 2007), 72–3, and Davide Rodogno, *Against Massacre: Humanitarian Interventions in the Ottoman Empire, 1815–1914* (Princeton, NJ: Princeton University Press, 2012), 47–54.

85. Turan Kayaoglu, *Legal Imperialism: Sovereignty and Extraterritoriality in Japan, the Ottoman Empire and China* (Cambridge: Cambridge University Press, 2010), 104–48.

86. Edward Keene, "The Treaty-Making Revolution in the Nineteenth Century," *International History Review*, 34, 3 (2012).

87. On the connections between international law and empire building, see Jennifer Pitts, *Boundaries of the International: Law and Empire* (Cambridge, MA: Harvard University Press, 2018) and Martti Koskenniemi, *The Gentle Civilizer of Nations: The Rise and Fall of International Law, 1870–1960* (Cambridge: Cambridge University Press, 2004), esp. 11–97.

88. Kristen Alff, "Levantine Joint-Stock Companies, Trans-Mediterranean Partnerships, and Nineteenth-Century Capitalist Development," *Comparative Studies in Society and History*, 60, 1 (2018); on law and economic development in the Ottoman world, see Timur Kuran, *The Long Divergence: How Islamic Law Held Back the Middle East* (Princeton, NJ: Princeton University Press, 2011).

Ottoman, especially Muslim subjects, and there is some evidence that, after 1850, even the Levantine Christians or Jews who had acted as brokers of Euro-Ottoman trade for centuries began to lose ground to Western business ventures. Informal imperialism was developmental rather than purely predatory.[89] In this sense, too, it prefigured later formal colonialism. Yet it ensured that Europeans took the lion's share of growing wealth and income, at least in the mid-century Middle East.[90]

The reforms of the Tanzimat era were a response to Western legal encroachment, designed to curtail it. However, Ottoman codification was largely modelled on French legislation, especially insofar as it affected economic life. The 1850 Ottoman Code de Commerce, for instance, was almost a word-for-word translation of the 1807 French Code. This reliance on French models for legal reforms was almost certainly a major factor behind the spread of the French language and culture among the educated elite—in sharp contrast to the 1790s, when reports sent to the French ministry of foreign affairs designated Turkish "legal scholars" (*légistes*) as the chief cultivators of "this prejudice [against Western languages] at the court of the Grand Seigneur."[91] However, at the core of the Ottoman Empire, the adoption of French legal norms was combined with a sustained effort to contain Western extra-territorial jurisdiction. Ottoman jurisdiction in mixed European-Ottoman cases was vigorously asserted, and in the 1860s new regulations strictly limited the number of Ottoman subjects who could claim European legal protection.[92] The main European powers, Britain and France, willingly collaborated with reforms to reduce the numbers of *protégés*. The latter had ceased to be an indispensable economic intermediary, and

---

89. On this distinction, see Anthony Hopkins, "Back to the Future: From National History to Imperial History," *Past & Present*, 164 (1999): 206.

90. Owen, *The Middle East*, 287–93; Pamuk, *The Ottoman Empire*, 82–107.

91. "Mémoire sur l'Ecole des Jeunes de langues," 6 Frimaire year 4 [26 Nov. 1795], AAE, M&D, Turquie, 164.

92. Notably, the 1863 regulation on foreign consulates' *protégés* and the 1869 nationality law; see Will Hanley, "What Ottoman Nationality Was and Was Not," *Journal of the Ottoman and Turkish Studies Association*, 3, 2 (2016): 284–5, and Salahi Sonyel, "The Protégé System in the Ottoman Empire," *Journal of Islamic Studies*, 2, 1 (1991). Such extraterritorial jurisdictional protection should not be confused with limited consular assistance, as still exists today, or with the looser system of political protection that some European powers sought to assert over non-Muslim communities of the Ottoman Empire; see Rodogno, *Against Massacre*, 30. On the complex repertoire of imperial protection see *Protection and Empire: A Global History*, eds. Lauren Benton, Adam Clulow and Bain Attwood (Cambridge: Cambridge University Press, 2018).

Western merchants frequently demanded that their Levantine competitors no longer benefit from the good offices of British or French consulates.[93]

In Egypt, European legal intrusion was far more extensive. Even more so than at the heart of the Ottoman Empire, the role of indigenous *protégés* in cross-cultural trade, and their numbers relative to the size of the European population, declined. In the words of Lord Cromer, the arch-imperialist British proconsul in Egypt after 1882, if in the rest of the Ottoman world Europeans were "privileged," in Egypt they were "ultra-privileged."[94] At first the Egyptian government followed Constantinople's lead in resisting European legal encroachments. In 1845, new Egyptian mixed courts, the *Majālis al-Tujjār*, with foreign judges making up a minority of the bench, were set up to regulate cross-cultural economic exchanges.[95] However, from the mid-1850s, citing the bias and inefficiency of the *Majālis*, European consular courts started to claim jurisdiction over mixed cases when the defending party was their national. This practice went beyond the letter of the Capitulations. European lawyers justified it by invoking the old Roman maxim *actor sequitur forum rei*: the plaintiff must follow the forum of the thing in dispute. Although contemporaries did not explicitly refer to the maxim's imperial origins, it is noteworthy that it arose from a desire to protect Roman citizens from lawsuits before local courts in newly annexed provinces in the eastern Mediterranean in the first century BCE.[96]

It is unclear why the Egyptian government tolerated such an expansion of extra-territoriality. European sources tend to cite an Egyptian desire, especially

93. On Anglo-French cooperation with Ottoman authorities to reduce the numbers of protégés, see "Beneath Sovereignty": 113–14; however, consulates with few national residents, such as the United States', appear to have continued to grant jurisdictional protection on a more extensive scale; see Ziad Fahmy, "Jurisdictional Borderlands: Extraterritoriality and 'Legal Chameleons' in Precolonial Alexandria, 1840–1870," *Comparative Studies in Society and History*, 55, 2 (2013).

94. Earl of Cromer, *Modern Egypt*, 2 vols. (London: Macmillan, 1908), vol. 2, 428; on Cromer, see Roger Owen, *Lord Cromer: Victorian Imperialist, Edwardian Proconsul* (Oxford: Oxford University Press, 2004).

95. Omar Cheta, "Rule of Merchants: The Practice of Commerce and Law in Late Ottoman Egypt, 1841–1876," unpublished PhD dissertation (New York University, 2014), 31–53; Jan Goldberg, "On the Origins of Majālis al-Tujjār in Mid Nineteenth-Century Egypt," *Islamic Law and Society*, 6, 2 (1999).

96. Claudia Moatti, "Migration et droit dans l'empire romain," in *The Impact of Mobility and Migration in the Roman Empire*, eds. Elio Lo Cascio and Laurens E. Tacoma (Leiden: Brill, 2017), 222–45.

from the beginning of the reign of Sa'id (1854) onwards, to encourage the immigration of skilled Europeans and foreign capital imports. It is also possible that the Egyptian government sought to loosen the legal grip of central Ottoman authorities—the *Majālis*'s decisions could be appealed in Constantinople. In any event, this expansion of extra-territorial jurisdiction was not the result of British pressure. British consular officials initially protested against the usurpation of jurisdiction by their European counterparts, and the British courts of Alexandria and Cairo were the last European courts, in around 1860, to accept jurisdiction over mixed cases.[97] By contrast, French consular courts aggressively sought to extend their jurisdiction. The most spectacular manifestation of this strategy was the French court of Alexandria's successful assertion of its jurisdiction over the Suez Canal Company, although the latter's statutes stipulated that "external" litigation (between the Company and other parties) fell under Egyptian jurisdiction, while "internal" litigation (between investors) was reserved for French metropolitan courts.[98]

Throughout the Ottoman world, rising numbers of economically active European migrants resulted in a tremendous increase—and qualitative change—in consular judicial activity. In the mid-1870s, the French consul in Tunis looked back nostalgically to the days before 1850, when consular jurisdiction mainly consisted in an effort of conciliation between a few "honourable" merchants. But as French "colonies" dramatically expanded in the wake of the Crimean War, he lamented, "Consular courts have been flooded by a multitude of heretofore unheard of cases," the bulk of which were small unpaid debts.[99] The number of appeals of French consular decisions in the Levant heard by the Court of Aix-en-Provence (an appellate jurisdiction inherited from the Old Regime's Parlement de Provence) rose from ten over the years 1850–1851 to fifty-nine over the years 1863–1864. The growth of litigation in Egypt was the main cause of this rapid increase, with appeals of decision by the consular courts of Alexandria and Cairo rising from just one over the years 1850–1851 to thirty-six over 1863–1864.[100] In Alexandria, consular court busi-

97. See for instance MacCoan, *Consular Jurisdiction*, 21–2.

98. See article 16 of the terms of the revised concession, ratified by the Ottoman government, 22 Feb. 1866, in *Archives of Empire*, eds. Barbara Harlow and Mia Carter, 2 vols. (Durham, NC: Duke University Press, 2003), vol. 1, 634.

99. Théodore Roustan, consul general in Tunis, to Louis Decazes, minister of foreign affairs, 18 July 1876, AAE, 752 SUP 114.

100. Louis Féraud-Giraud, *De la juridiction française dans les échelles du Levant et de Barbarie*, 2nd ed., 2 vols. (Paris: A. Durand, 1866), vol. 1, iii–iv.

ness, as measured by the number of decisions made, increased fivefold in just five years, from forty-two in 1858 to 210 in 1862.[101]

Faced with an increase in consular judicial business on a similar scale, the British government responded by creating a new order of extra-territorial jurisdiction, with a supreme court in Constantinople hearing appeals of decisions made by British consular courts throughout the Ottoman world (and Persia and Morocco). This semi-professionalization of British consular justice was intended to provide Ottoman authorities with a model of judicial institutions which they could emulate, while managing the growth of litigation. The government's instructions made it clear that British "influence" should not extend beyond encouraging reform, and consular officials were discouraged from interfering directly with the Ottoman judiciary. By contrast, the French government shunned proposals for a substantial overhaul of consular justice and instead merely appointed new "juges-consuls" in the busiest consulates, such as Alexandria. This was partly due to the fact that regulations dating from the late eighteenth century defined the procedures to be followed and laws to be applied much better than in the more recent British system of consular justice; British consular officials, as late as the 1850s, still admitted to relying on French regulations for their procedures and Napoleonic codes for the substance of their decisions.[102] More generally, France in the mid-nineteenth century possessed a larger and more professional consular service than other European powers.[103] But the French decision not to reform consular justice

101. "Statistique des jugements rendus par les tribunaux consulaires de Constantinople et d'Alexandrie," n.d. [1863], AAE, 752 SUP 113.

102. On British and French reforms of consular justice after 1850, see Todd, "Beneath Sovereignty": 116–21.

103. Anne Mézin, "Les services consulaires français au XIXe siècle," in *Consuls et services consulaires au XIXe siècle. Die Welt der Konsulate im 19. Jahrhundert. Consulship in the 19th century*, eds. Jörg Ulbert and Lukian Prijac (Hamburg: DOBU, 2010), 47–61; Ferry de Goey, *Consuls and the Institutions of Global Capitalism, 1783–1914* (London: Routledge, 2015), 8–10; on the growth of the consular service, Maurice Degros, "Les créations de postes diplomatiques et consulaires français de 1815 à 1870," *Revue d'histoire diplomatique*, 100, 3–4 (1986). On the role of consuls in Mediterranean trade, see *De l'utilité commerciale des consuls. L'institution consulaire et les marchands dans le monde méditerranéen (XVIIe-XXe siècle)*, eds. Arnaud Bartolomei, Guillaume Calafat, Mathieu Grenet and Jörg Ulbert (Rome and Madrid: Ecole française de Rome and Casa Velasquez, 2018), esp. 55–62 and 173–98 on French consuls. The professionalization of the French diplomatic and consular services began in the last decades of the Old Regime and resumed from the late 1790s at the instigation of Talleyrand and Hauterive; see Alain Méninger, "D'Hauterive et la formation des diplomates," *Revue d'histoire diplomatique*, 89, 1 (1975) and

along British lines was also rooted in a conscious effort to maintain the status quo and expand extraterritorial jurisdiction, rather than encourage Ottoman legal reforms.

The contrast between British and French attitudes may have reflected, in part, the greater emphasis that French intellectual and political life placed on the distinction between the civilized West and the stagnant East. British officials often expressed greater optimism about the prospect of legal reforms in the Ottoman world than their French counterparts, who were wont to assert the incompatibility of Muslim culture with the rule of law: as will be seen, such "legal orientalism" would often be invoked by French adversaries of legal reform at the end of the 1860s.[104] Nonetheless, French enthusiasm for extraterritoriality was not purely ideological, it also drew on the substantial political and economic benefits that the French government, and many French nationals, derived from its extensive application, especially in Egypt.

The Imperial Profits of Extraterritoriality

Extraterritoriality should not be equated with imperial exploitation. In the Ottoman world, the personality of law and jurisdiction was only rarely perceived as a privilege until the early nineteenth century. Furthermore, it is difficult to prove that European consular courts were biased or iniquitous. One study of British extraterritorial justice in Japan has suggested that they were not.[105] Similarly, French courts in Egypt did not always find in favour of French defendants.[106] This is not to suggest that the political and economic advantages of imperial extraterritoriality, so vehemently denounced by nationalists in the Middle East and East Asia, were an illusion. On the contrary, they were tangible, but also, more often than not, they were

---

Virginie Martin, "Devenir diplomate en Révolution: naissance de la 'carrière diplomatique'?," *Revue d'histoire moderne et contemporaine*, 63, 3 (2016).

104. On this concept, see Teemu Ruskola, *Legal Orientalism: China, the United States and Modern Law* (Cambridge, MA: Harvard University Press, 2013).

105. Richard T. Chang, *The Justice of the Western Consular Courts in Nineteenth-Century Japan* (Westport, CT: Greenwood Press 1984); on extra-territoriality in Japan, see also Christopher Roberts, *The British Courts and Extra-Territoriality in Japan, 1859–1899* (Leiden: Brill, 2014).

106. See for instance a court decision on the eviction of a French tenant named Julian, who was also condemned to the payment of rent arrears and an indemnity of 500 francs to his landlord Burnoum Pacha, a "local subject;" Centre des Archives Diplomatiques de Nantes, PO/20/463, decision 89 (23 Apr. 1864).

subtle and multifaceted—indirect consequences, rather than the immediate product, of European jurisdiction.

First came the control that extraterritoriality enabled foreign governments to exercise over their expatriated nationals.[107] This was especially true in the case of French expatriates, over whom French consuls held extensive powers, including that of deporting any Frenchman "harmful to the general good" back to France, without having to provide justificatory grounds. Such an arbitrary power, arising from an edict of 1778 on consulates in the Levant, strengthened the consul general in Egypt's position in the French community and provided him with a bargaining chip in negotiations with the Egyptian government. For instance, in 1881 the French authorities deported a French journalist, Gustave Laffon, to France after he wrote an article in a French-language newspaper that incensed local opinion because it described Muhammad as a "false prophet." When Laffon contested the decision before the Conseil d'État the following year, the ministry of foreign affairs defended this exceptional power as "the corollary of the exemption from local jurisdiction from which French nationals benefit in the Échelles [Ottoman port-cities]". This argument contradicted traditional justifications of extraterritoriality as a means of preserving the rule of law for European immigrants, but the Conseil d'État concurred and dismissed Laffon's complaint as baseless.[108] The extensive powers of consuls in the Levant even elicited the concern of Alexis de Tocqueville during his brief tenure as minister of foreign affairs under the Second Republic, although his efforts at reform came to nothing.[109]

If French nationals in Egypt and the rest of the Ottoman world did not enjoy legal guarantees that were as extensive as in metropolitan France (the

107. On this aspect of extraterritoriality in the American case, see Eileen P. Scully, *Bargaining with the State from Afar: American Citizenship in Treaty Port China, 1844–1942* (New York: Columbia University Press, 2001).

108. See folder "Affaire Laffon," in AAE, Contentieux, 255, especially the draft of a letter by the minister of foreign affairs to the Conseil d'État, 11 Aug. 1882, and a copy of the *arrêt* (decision) of the Conseil d'État, 2 Dec. 1882. In all the documents, the journalist is only referred to by his initial 'G.' and his last name, but he was probably the Gustave Laffon who, with his wife Annette, registered the birth of a child in Egypt in 1873; see AAE, État civil, Alexandrie, 12/39.

109. See folder "Réforme des échelles de 1849," in AAE, 752 SUP 113; Tocqueville's concerns about the limited protection of expatriates' rights in the Levant echoed his complaint, in 1841, that individual liberty for European settlers in Algeria "does not even have those [guarantees] it is given in most of the absolute monarchies of the [European] continent", in "Essay on Algeria," 100.

same was true, until the 1870s, of French settlers in Algeria), it would be a gross exaggeration to view them as victims of extraterritoriality. An advantage rarely brought up explicitly by defenders of extraterritoriality, but which was closely associated with expatriates' subjection to an extraterritorial jurisdiction, was their nearly complete exemption from the direct taxes levied by Egyptian or Ottoman authorities. This fiscal privilege contributed to the growth of political hostility to foreigners in Egypt in the 1870s.[110] It also proved a major source of frustration for British administrators after they took over Egypt's government in 1882 and endeavoured to balance the Egyptian budget.[111] In the case of French expatriates, this substantial fiscal privilege recalls the status of settlers in Algeria, who were also exempted from direct taxes until the First World War.[112] Another significant advantage of extraterritoriality, mostly psychological, although it no doubt occasionally had economic consequences, was the sense of impunity it gave Europeans in their daily interactions with Egyptian nationals or public authorities.[113]

However, an advantage that has rarely been remarked upon in scholarship on extraterritoriality, but which lay behind the furious controversy over the Egyptian legal order in Egypt and Europe after 1865, was the growing propensity of Europeans to repudiate the jurisdiction of Egyptian courts, even in cases where the defendant was a local subject. This practice violated not only the text of the Capitulations, but also the *actor sequitur* interpretation of them that had prevailed in Egypt after 1850. Local courts such as the *Majālis al-Tujjār* were routinely derided as being ineffective or prejudiced against Europeans— especially when the defendant was part of the Egyptian-state apparatus— because despite these mixed commercial courts' active role in the country's economic life, the government could appoint and revoke the indigenous magistrates who sat on them. These complaints were not baseless, but they were almost certainly exaggerated.[114] In any case, they led European consuls to take up the grievances of those under their jurisdiction and pressure the Egyptian

110. Juan R. I. Cole, *Colonialism and Revolution in the Middle East: Social and Cultural Origins of 'Urabi's Movement* (Princeton, NJ: Princeton University Press, 1993), 85–97.

111. Cromer, *Modern Egypt*, vol. 2, 428–42; Milner, *England in Egypt*, 44–76.

112. Todd, "The *impôts arabes*," 137–8.

113. Nubar Pasha, *Mémoires*, ed. Mirrit Boutros Ghali (Beirut: Librairie du Liban, 1983), 151–2.

114. Cheta, "Rule of Merchants" reappraised the role of the *Majālis al-Tujjār*, but on their limits see Todd, "Beneath Sovereignty": 123.

government into granting indemnities, to compensate the plaintiffs for the faults allegedly committed by Egyptian officials.

This excrescence of the already expansive regime of extraterritoriality in Egypt was far from being an anecdotal phenomenon. According to the Armenian-born, French-speaking Egyptian statesman and champion of judicial reform Nubar Pasha, the indemnities wrested by consuls amounted to "a fantastical number of millions" and were a major contributory factor to the galloping Egyptian public debt. Nubar added that "most of [the 1,800 outstanding claims for indemnities] were French" and other contemporaries, especially the consuls of powers other than France, also decried the pressing of claims as having been practiced by French consuls on an extravagant scale.[115] These quasi-judicial interventions mirrored, at a local level, the arbitration of a dispute between the Egyptian government and the Suez Canal Company, by a committee appointed by the French ministry of foreign affairs and sitting in Paris: in compensation for modifying certain clauses of the initial Suez concession (a curtailment of the Company's land property rights and use of coerced Egyptian labour), the committee, mainly endorsing the Company's claims, awarded it an indemnity of 84 million francs (about 3.36 million pounds sterling) in 1864.[116] The permanent body that supervised this function of French consuls in Egypt (and many other legal aspects of French activities beyond territories under French sovereignty) was the Comité du Contentieux, created in 1835 and reorganized in 1853. Like the ad hoc committee that arbitrated in favour of the Suez Company in 1864, the Comité du Contentieux was made up of legal scholars, councillors of state and several former ministers of foreign affairs. This politico-legal body played an important part in shaping French involvement in the fast-growing array of nineteenth-century interna-

---

115. Nubar Pasha, *Mémoires*, 197; in a memorandum dated 1867, Nubar contended that dubious foreign claims had cost the Egyptian Treasury 2,880,000 pounds sterling (c. 72 million francs) since 1863, in "Note on the future regulation of the legal and judicial relations between the foreign and native population of Egypt," in *The Judicial Organization in Egypt and Its Reform*, ed. Charles Manby (London: Spottiswoode and co, 1868), 4. British consuls frequently complained about what Robert Colquhoun, consul general in Alexandria, castigated as "the claims against the government which would not for a moment bear being submitted to a proper tribunal" by the French and other European consulates; see Colquhoun to Russell, 12 Aug. 1861, TNA, FO78/1591.

116. Jason W. Yackee, "The First Investor-State Arbitration: The Suez Canal Company v. Egypt (1864)," *Journal of World Investment and Trade*, 17, 3 (2016); on the significance of this arbitration, see also Landes, *Bankers and Pashas*, 173–88.

tional and transnational legal arrangements, and its rich archives are extremely informative about the reach and limits of French legal interventionism in Egypt and the rest of the Ottoman world.[117]

The vast majority of Egyptian matters considered by the Comité du Contentieux were indemnity claims. These ranged from minor cases, such as the eight-year-long efforts (1869–1877) of French consular officials to ensure the payment of a two-thousand-franc annual pension to the heirs of a French employee of the Egyptian government, to the more extraordinary request for an eight-hundred-thousand-franc indemnity by the Orientalist painter Clément, discussed at the beginning of this chapter.[118] Another major claim was the "affaire du bazar" that resulted in the payment of a large indemnity (450,000 francs), by the Egyptian government in 1869, to be shared between eighteen small French merchant houses, in compensation for what the French consulate deemed the fraudulent bankruptcy of dozens of Arab vendors in Alexandria's main bazaar.[119] This intricate case incidentally revealed the important role assumed by French trade in supplying Egyptian bazaar stalls, lending credence to the writer Théophile Gautier's assertion, in 1870, that the "keffiehs, gandouras and Eastern cloths" sold in Egyptian bazaars were all "made in Lyon."[120] Nor was the penetration of French economic influence limited to Egyptian cities, the claims show: in 1874, six French merchants who had lent liberally to farmers in Lower Egypt during the cotton boom claimed for an indemnity of two million francs, in compensation for the Egyptian government's decision in 1865 to forestall the repossession of the land of hundreds of farmers' who had defaulted

117. On the origins of the Comité du Contentieux, see "Rapport au directeur des affaires politiques," 26 Dec. 1867, AAE, Contentieux, 752 SUP 118; and on its role and influence, see Jean Baillou, Charles Lucet and Jacques Vimont, Les Affaires Étrangères et le corps diplomatique français, 2 vols. (Paris: CNRS, 1984), vol. 1, 584–5, 647, 716–22 and vol. 2, 49–52, 104–6.

118. Folders "Affaire Napoléon Conseil" and "Affaire Clément," AAE, Contentieux, 752 SUP 253.

119. Folder "Affaire du bazar," AAE, Contentieux, 752 SUP 252.

120. Théophile Gautier, Voyage en Égypte, ed. Paolo Tortonese (Paris: La Boîte à Documents, 1991), 65. The lack of Oriental authenticity resulting from the Frenchness of commodities and amenities in Egypt became a leitmotif of contemporary travel accounts after 1860; see for instance a journalist who regretted the Egyptian efforts to "Haussmannize Cairo," and claimed, in an Alexandria theatre: "If it were not for the audience, I would believe myself to be in France"; in Lambert de Lacroix, L'Égypte, cinq minutes d'arrêt!!! (Paris: E. Lachaud, 1870), 40, 50.

on their *sanads* (high-yielding loans to cotton farmers, also referred to as "village bonds").[121]

In December 1868, Pierre Poujade, an old hand in the French consular service and consul general in Alexandria, drew up a summary of the twenty-nine claims he had successfully pressed on the Egyptian government since taking up his position eight months earlier. The combined claims earned French citizens in Egypt nine hundred thousand francs in indemnities (including the four hundred and fifty thousand francs bazaar indemnity) and over one hundred thousand francs in annual pensions; for a few claims, such as the confirmation of property rights, Poujade gave no monetary estimate of the gain. Such figures suggest that at the peak of French influence, the French community benefited from the indemnity business to the tune of 1.5 to 2 million francs a year, or approximately one hundred and fifty to two hundred francs per French citizen resident in Egypt (none of the beneficiaries were French *protégés* or French Algerian subjects).[122] Some of these claims may have been justified, but understandably British and Egyptian officials were inclined to decry French consular activism, seeing it as a racket. These tangible economic gains also help explain why French expatriates rarely contested the extensive powers of the consul general or sought to evade control by their consulate. It is probably not a coincidence that in several instances where the Comité du Contentieux instructed French consuls in Egypt not to press for a claim, these had been made by individuals who professed suspicious (republican until 1870, radical after 1870) political opinions.[123]

It is not possible to determine precisely what proportion of the commercial gains made by French expatriates in Egypt should be considered as the product of natural economic exchange, and what proportion was the product of French imperial influence. Not even all the claims pressed on the Egyptian

121. Folder "Affaire des bons des villages (sanads)," AAE, Contentieux, 752 SUP 256; the petitioners contended that had they been allowed to repossess the farms, they would have become "the proprietors of a vast extent of land in Egypt."

122. "Tableau des réclamations contre le gouvernement égyptien, terminées au 21 décembre 1868," n.d., AAE, Contentieux, 752 SUP 254, folder "Affaire Koenig."

123. See for the instance the case of Barthélémy Carbonel, whose claim for a 1.5 million francs indemnity by the Egyptian government was dismissed by the Comité du contentieux in 1869, reconsidered by the ministry of foreign affairs after the fall of the Second Empire in 1870, and eventually dismissed by the tribunal and appeals court of Paris in 1872 and 1873. Carbonel's republican lawyers included the future president (1879–1887) Jules Grévy; folder "Affaire Carbonel," AAE, Contentieux, 752 SUP 252.

government by French consular agents can be equated with instances of imperial exploitation, since it is probably true that property and other economic rights were enforced in a more haphazard fashion in Egypt than in western Europe in the mid-nineteenth century. But in many cases, the claims were grossly exaggerated, and the privileged access of French consuls to the corridors of Egyptian power gave French nationals an advantage over Ottoman subjects or their European rivals. It is therefore unsurprising that Egyptian efforts to curtail extraterritoriality after 1860 met with the support of Britain and several other European powers, and fierce opposition from the French government. When reform finally came in 1876, it contributed to a rapid decline in French influence.

The Crisis of French Extraterritoriality in Egypt

The publication in 1867 of an eloquent memorandum by Nubar Pasha on the abusive extension of capitulatory privileges marked the beginning of a sustained effort to roll back French judicial and political interference in Egyptian affairs. In Nubar's words, the anarchic expansion of extraterritoriality "not only [hindered] the country in developing its resources, from furnishing to European industry and capital all that it [was] ready to furnish, but [put] an obstacle in the way of its organisation, and [ruined] it both morally and materially."[124] However, it would be anachronistic to see this campaign as somehow representing the labour pains of Egyptian nationalism. Nubar himself was a Christian Armenian educated in Switzerland and France. He owed his rise in the Egyptian administration to family connections and his perfect command of French and Ottoman Turkish, but he spoke little Arabic and in his memoirs (written in French) expressed much condescension for native Egyptians.[125] His proposal to replace consular courts with mixed tribunals, staffed with European or European-trained judges, had been encouraged, if not first mooted, by British consular agents.[126] Nubar's principal assistant in his ten-year crusade for judicial reform, the republican lawyer Paul Maunoury, who had settled in Alexandria after the Bonapartist coup of 1851, was anything

---

124. Nubar, "Note on the future regulation," 5.

125. Nubar, *Mémoires*, 14–15 on his linguistic abilities, and 374 for an example of his contempt for Egypt's "natives."

126. Todd, "Beneath Sovereignty": 123.

but an anti-imperialist, and later as an MP in France would staunchly support Jules Ferry's policy of colonial expansion.

Instead, Nubar and his backers are better understood as the advocates of a more territorial conception of government, which would increase administrative efficiency and reduce the depredations caused by informal French meddling. In his memorandum, probably hoping to assuage French hostility to his proposed reform, Nubar even described it as "traced upon the judicial organization of [French colonial] Algeria."[127] Yet as seen in this book's second chapter, the French Bonapartist government preferred to modify French domination in Algeria along Egyptian lines, while resisting the proposed reform in Egypt by all possible means. The Greek and Italian governments, whose consular services also governed large colonies in Egypt, expressed reservations, but in his memoirs Nubar accurately pointed at the French minister of foreign affairs, Léonel de Moustier, a former ambassador in Constantinople, as the chief adversary of Egyptian judicial reform, based on the fact that its adoption would result in "the end of [French officials'] pressure, their daily interference with the most ordinary affairs of Egypt."[128]

In December 1867, a committee of professional diplomats and legal scholars appointed by Moustier rejected Nubar's project for being unsuited to Egypt's as yet "incomplete civilization," and defended the plurality of jurisdictions as befitting "the most diverse mixture of races, customs, habits, religious beliefs and social conditions" that prevailed in the country.[129] Gradually, however, France bowed to the pressure of other European powers led by Britain and of some French interests, not least Lesseps's Suez Canal Company, whose representatives were also concerned about the effects of European depredations on Egypt's stability and solvability. At an international conference held in Cairo in 1869, at the same time as the grandiose ceremonies for the inauguration of the Suez Canal, French delegates found themselves isolated by Nubar and Maunoury's manoeuvres. In 1870 the new liberal ministry, led by Émile

127. Nubar, "Note on the future regulation," 3, 12.

128. Nubar Pasha to Colonel Stanton, consul general in Alexandria, 23 Aug. 1867, TNA, FO 78/2742; see also Nubar, *Mémoires*, 320–2.

129. "Rapport par la commission instituée à l'effet d'examiner les propositions faites par le gouvernement égyptien pour réformer l'administration de la justice en Egypte," 3 Dec. 1867, AN 20020495/21; according to Nubar, *Mémoires*, 326, the report was drafted by Féraud-Giraud, a staunch Bonapartist magistrate in Aix-en-Provence, and the author of the main scholarly work on French extra-territorial jurisdiction in the Middle East, *De la juridiction française*, cited above (n. 100).

Ollivier, consented to a reform that was confined to civil litigation—although, as pointed out by Ollivier's opponents at the time, his appointment to the Egyptian government's commissioner of the Suez Canal, a well-paid sinecure, probably influenced France's concessions.[130] This probable bribe shows that Egypt retained significant agency, despite its semi-subjection to France, but it does not disprove the imperial nature of the Franco-Egyptian relationship—in most imperial formations, peripheries seek to influence the politics of the centre.

Even this partial climbdown elicited a furious reaction from various French interests. The most vociferous opponents were French residents in Egypt. They repeatedly petitioned for "the upholding of the Capitulations."[131] Yet one of the campaign's principal instigators was the Marquis Alexandre de Plœuc, the director of the Banque Impériale Ottomane until 1867, and by now a deputy governor of the Banque de France. Plœuc's private papers show that he played a very active, if veiled role in organizing propaganda against the proposed reform. For instance, he commissioned a French professor at the Galata Serai lycée in Constantinople to write a pamphlet in defence of extraterritoriality. The professor, a staunch royalist, needed little prompting. He believed that, paradoxically, modernizing reforms in Turkey and Egypt had rendered the Capitulations "indispensable and obligatory, had they not been a legacy of the [Bourbon] monarchy;" the Turks were "no less Turkish", and in addition they had lost "the virtues of this Asiatic race" and become "hypocritical."[132] Plœuc's papers also contain the corrected proofs of various newspaper articles, written by himself or his clients, against Egypt's judicial reform. One such article described Ollivier's acceptance of the reform as "the unbelievable abdication of the prestige acquired in five centuries in the East that France appears to make voluntarily."[133]

Turmoil in France during and after its defeat against Prussia in 1870–1871 delayed the adoption of the reform. In a very concrete illustration of the entanglement of Egypt within France's legal system, the new codes to be applied

---

130. Saul, *La France et l'Égypte*, 227.

131. See for instance the petition by French nationals residing in Alexandria to the French minister of foreign affairs, 3 Mar. 1870, AN, 272 AP 16, folder "Documents imprimés."

132. [Signature illegible] to Plœuc, 22 Sep. 1868, AN, 272 AP 14; on the scientific and political publications of several Galata Serai's teachers in those years, see Strauss, "Le livre français": 282–3.

133. Proofs of "À propos de la prétendue réforme judiciaire en Orient," AN, 272 AP 14.

by the reformed judiciary, having been printed in Paris, could not be sent to the Egyptian government until the Prussian army lifted the siege of the city in January 1871.[134] The first ministries of the Third Republic, dominated by a co-alition of *orléaniste* and *légitimiste* royalists, were hostile to the project. At a second international conference convened in Constantinople in 1872–1873, the head of the British delegation reported, his French counterpart did his utmost to sabotage "any genuine scheme of judicial reform"; "on more than one occa-sion, his intention to render the project of reform useless, and to neutralize the effectual working of the new Tribunals was plainly expressed."[135] The French government's hostility reflected the views of most French residents in Egypt, but also of a growing strand of opinion at home. The British ambassador in Paris admitted that Egypt's judicial reform was "distasteful to Frenchmen gen-erally." In addition to "a very pertinacious opposition in the official Depart-ments [of the administration]," the French government had "to contend with a strong national feeling in and out of the [National] Assembly."[136]

Now a royalist MP for Paris (1871–1876), where his successful defence of the Banque de France's gold reserves against the Communards had gained him a considerable popularity among bourgeois voters, Plœuc continued to or-chestrate the campaign against judicial reform.[137] He kept up an abundant correspondence with the French pamphleteers who were hostile to the reform in Egypt, such as Aristide Gavillot, an assessor at the French consular tribunal and a judge on the *Majlis* (mixed commercial court) in Cairo, who maintained that regular judicial institutions could not function in Muslim countries, due to the "hateful," "retrograde" and "barbaric" influence of the Koran. Plœuc was also connected to the Comte Maillard de Marafy, a lawyer specializing in in-ternational property rights, who asserted that "the dividing line drawn by Ca-pitulations and treaties between races deeply opposed by sentiments and in-

134. "Note. Affaire Maunoury," n.d. (probably 1881) in AAE, Contentieux, 752 SUP 255, folder "Maunoury. Honoraires pour son concours dans l'œuvre de la réforme judiciaire égyptienne."

135. Philip Francis, supreme consular judge, to Henry Elliot, ambassador in Constantinople, 3 Mar. 1873, TNA, FO 407/5; see also "Procès-verbaux et rapports de la commission" in Con-stantinople, enclosed in Elliot to Lord Granville, foreign secretary, 4 Mar. 1873, TNA, FO 407/5.

136. Lord Lyons, ambassador in Paris, to Lord Derby, foreign secretary, 22 May 1874, TNA, FO 407/5; Lyons to Thomas Lister, under-secretary at the foreign office, 5 Oct. 1874, TNA, FO 407/6.

137. See orbituary, "M. le marquis de Plœuc," *La France illustrée*, 10 Sep. 1887, clipping in AN, 272 AP 14.

stitutions must be preserved for many long years still, and probably for ever."[138] The signature at the bottom of several letters addressed to Plœuc has been obscured in black; some letters contain ciphered passages; others are marked "à brûler" (to be burnt).[139] The need for such conspiratorial methods suggests that the campaign was connected to illicit speculations in high-yielding Egyptian treasury bonds of the time, notably by the Crédit Foncier, a semi-public financial institution that was supervised by Plœuc's Banque de France.[140] Plœuc's papers contain several orders for such bonds, on his behalf and that of others.[141]

Plœuc's Egyptian correspondence also shows his involvement in a judicial attempt to derail the reform by establishing the direct jurisdiction of French metropolitan courts in Egypt. Until the early 1870s, French metropolitan courts had been reluctant to assume such jurisdiction, although they sometimes did so when all parties consented—a practice that further illustrated the reach of French legal and judicial influence.[142] Yet in 1873, two French residents in Egypt sought to have their claims against the Egyptian government settled by Parisian tribunals. These were Honoré Paget, the owner of an Alexandrian steam-powered laundry that was seized by the Egyptian administration in 1866, and Théophile Leveau, the owner of a paper pulp factory at Syra near Alexandria, that was allegedly ruined by the confiscation of three tons of natron (mineral sodium) in 1871. Their lawyer was the author of several anti-reform pamphlets, Maillard de Marafy, who argued in a memorandum that the Egyptian government was neither "sovereign" nor even "half-sovereign,"

138. Aristide Gavillot, *Essai sur les droits des Européens en Turquie et en Egypte. Les capitulations et la réforme judiciaire* (Paris: Dentu, 1875), 268–9; L. Maillard de Marafy, *La réforme judiciaire en Egypte devant l'Assemblée nationale*, 2nd edn (Paris: Imprimerie nouvelle, 1875), 61; on their connections with Plœuc, see Gavillot to Plœuc, 2 Dec. 1876 and 8 Jan. 1877, AN, 272 AP 14, and Maillard to Plœuc, 27 july 1869, AN, 272 AP 16.

139. See various letters in folder "Orient" and "Égypte. 1876" in AN, 272 AP 14, folder "1876" in AN, 272 AP 15, folder "Capitulations. Égypte" in AN, 272 AP 16, and "Égypte" in AN, 272 AP 17.

140. Jean Bouvier, "Les intérêts financiers et la question d'Égypte," *Revue historique*, 224 (1960): 80–1.

141. See for instance, about a contribution of 5,000 pounds sterling by Plœuc to an overall advance of 100,000 pounds sterling to the Egyptian government, a letter by the Paris committee of the Banque impériale ottomane to Plœuc, 9 Sep. 1872, in AN, 272 AP 14.

142. See for instance "M. Carbonnel contre le gouvernement égyptien—Fourniture de foins—Inexécution de conventions," *La Gazette des tribunaux*, 15 Nov. 1873, clipping in AAE, Contentieux, 752 SUP 252, folder "Affaire Carbonel".

because all the attributes of sovereignty remained in the hands of the Ottoman sultan. At the same time, he stated, as the sultan's sovereignty was purely nominal, civilized European courts should assume full jurisdiction over their nationals, and Egyptians—including the Egyptian government—should be sued before French courts.[143] European courts, Maillard and his acolytes contended, should fill what they saw as a sovereignty void.[144]

The French courts rejected Maillard's far-fetched reasoning. But at the National Assembly in December 1874, Plœuc defended petitions by the same claimants alongside a petition against the reform, made by French residents in Alexandria. Surprisingly, Plœuc's attack against the moderate government led by the Duc Decazes, who favoured a compromise along the lines of Ollivier's partial acquiescence to reform, met with the warm support of Léon Gambetta, the left-wing republican leader, who lamented "the despair of our nationals [in Egypt]."[145] Gambetta's backing of the royalist and Bonapartist factions that opposed judicial reform was most probably partially tactical and designed to embarrass Decazes's centrist ministry. Yet it may also have reflected Gambetta's preference, until 1880, for the politics of influence over those of territorial annexation.[146] In any case, the Gambettist newspapers' hostility towards reform jeopardized its adoption by the National Assembly. The British ambassador in Paris expected Decazes to lose the upcoming parliamentary vote and anticipated a major ministerial crisis.[147]

Further concessions by the Egyptian government and the fear of British supremacy caused by Benjamin Disraeli's purchase of the Khedive's shares in the Suez Canal Company in November 1875 eventually silenced French opposition to Egypt's judicial reform. In December 1875, France became the last

143. See documents on the two cases, and especially "Note de M. le Comte Maillard de Marafy sur les droits et obligations du vice-roi d'Égypte," part of "Mémoire judiciaire pour Honoré Paget," folder "Égypte," in AN 272 AP 17.

144. The argument bore some resemblance to the invocation of "territorium nullius" that served to justify colonial expansion after 1880; see Andrew Fitzmaurice, *Sovereignty, Property and Empire, 1500–2000* (Cambridge: Cambridge University Press, 2015), 271–90.

145. *Journal officiel de la République française*, 17 Dec. 1874, clipping in folder "Égypte" in AN 272 AP 17.

146. Only after 1878 did Gambetta gradually become a supporter of territorial expansion overseas; see Charles-Robert Ageron, "Gambetta et la reprise de l'expansion coloniale," *Outre-Mers*, 215 (1972).

147. Lord Lyons, ambassador in Paris, to Lord Derby, foreign secretary, 22 May 1874, TNA, FO 407/6.

of nineteen powers to ratify the international convention that established new territorial Egyptian-European courts, with a widespread jurisdiction over mixed civil—especially commercial—litigation. The convention was hardly a humiliation, because at France's insistence the scope of reform had been severely curtailed. Consular courts retained jurisdiction over criminal affairs and matters of personal status (nationality, marriage, inheritance, etc.), and French consular courts retained full jurisdiction over Catholic missions and missionaries. The codes to be applied by the new courts had been written in French, by a Frenchman (Maunoury, Nubar's ally), and were largely inspired by French law. Although the courts could also use Arabic or Italian, French soon imposed itself as their main working language.[148] Yet as highlighted by Nubar in his memoirs, the reform succeeded in considerably reducing French political influence over Egypt.[149]

End of French Ascendancy

The partial success of judicial reform preempted the transformation of the French presence in Egypt during the crisis, triggered by Egypt's bankruptcy in 1876 and ending with Britain's occupation in 1882. French influence did not disappear, but it became indirect and institutional, rather than political. The French language retained its place as the favoured elite means of communication, among Europeans and between Egyptians and Europeans, and French law continued to inspire far-reaching legal reforms. But gradually after 1876 and abruptly after 1882, French consular officials lost their capacity to affect political and administrative affairs. In other words, France ceased to exercise informal rule and Britain imposed a territorial solution to the Egyptian crisis, even if the British colonial government continued to employ several of the instruments forged in the era of French domination.

According to Ronald Robinson and John Gallagher—who neatly formulated the distinction between informal and formal empire over sixty-five years ago—the reason historians have written so much about the Egyptian crisis is because Britain's occupation of the country heralded the resurgence of a territorial style of British expansion, that resulted in the partition of the

148. See "Règlement d'organisation judiciaire" of the mixed courts and commentaries by by officials of the French ministry of justice, AN, 20020495/22, folder "Organisation des tribunaux mixtes."

149. Nubar, *Mémoires*, 456–9.

entire African continent between European powers over the next thirty years.[150] Anthony G. Hopkins (and Peter Cain) have contested Robinson and Gallagher's interpretation of occupation as a response to events beyond Britain's control and driven by strategic considerations, and pointed to their neglect of the objective economic interests that incited British policy makers to embark upon occupation.[151] This book is concerned with the dynamics of French rather than British expansion, and I do not wish to reignite what Hopkins already described, in 1986, as "a hundred years' war between rival armies of historians."[152] Yet this controversy has indirectly influenced the understanding of French imperial objectives, because both "armies" have tended to assign a role to France that fitted with their interpretation of British expansionism. For Robinson and Gallagher, Britain was "dragged" into Egypt by a desire to keep up with France's threats of intervention, even though at the eleventh hour its unreliable French ally pulled out of the planned joint operation.[153] By contrast, Hopkins and Cain maintained that France, suffering from imperial fatigue after the occupation of Tunisia in 1881, showed "restraint" and "did not want to be dragged into Egypt by Britain."[154]

Neither of these interpretations adequately explains why France, despite its old claim to preeminence in Egypt and frantic diplomacy at every stage of the crisis, ultimately decided not to intervene alongside Britain. A complementary interpretation, pointing to the paralysing effect of French political quarrels and the fear of war with Germany, is also unconvincing, because after 1882 persistent domestic and geopolitical tensions did not preclude the adoption of a resolute expansionist policy in sub-Saharan Africa, the Maghreb and Indochina.[155] I would like to outline an alternative interpretation: French diplomacy was active because it sought to salvage its informal dominion in Egypt, and even saw in the nationalist revolution, led by colonel 'Urabi, an opportunity to revive it,

150. Ronald Robinson and John Gallagher, *Africa and the Victorians: The Official Mind of Imperialism*, 2nd edn (London: MacMillan, 1981; first published in 1961), 76–121, 155–9.

151. Cain and Hopkins, *British Imperialism*, 2nd edn., 312–17.

152. Anthony G. Hopkins, "The Victorians and Africa: The British Occupation of Egypt in 1882," *Journal of African History*, 27, 2 (1986): 364.

153. Robinson and Gallagher, *Africa and the Victorians*, 120.

154. Cain and Hopkins, *British Imperialism*, 2nd edn., 317; see also Hopkins, "The Victorians": 376–9.

155. Robinson and Gallagher, *Africa and the Victorians*, 119; Agatha Ramm, "Great Britain and France," 107–10; Thomas and Toye, *Arguing about Empire*, 34–41.

but it shirked at military occupation because it did not aspire to formal colo-nization.[156] In other words, French policy in Egypt remained determined by a preference for informal empire, although its eventual floundering contrib-uted to France's shift to territorial expansionism in the 1880s.

There is neither the space here nor the need to examine in detail how this interpretation fits in with the countless twists and turns of the Egyptian ques-tion between 1876 and 1882. But three elements should show that it is at least a credible alternative. First, France's informal ascendancy was profoundly shaken in 1876. Not only did the new mixed or international courts strip French consular officials of one of their main means of influencing Egyptian affairs, but the country's bankruptcy—compounded by the new courts' im-mediate decision to uphold the claims of creditors against the Egyptian Trea-sury, regardless of the arrangements negotiated by French and other European diplomats—and the rapid decline in Egyptian prosperity affected France's economic interests more than those of other powers.[157] Large holdings of short-term Egyptian Treasury bonds by major banks, such as the Crédit Fon-cier and the Crédit Agricole, threatened the stability of the entire French fi-nancial system, while imports of semi-luxurious French commodities declined more sharply than those of other countries; even after the Egyptian economy started to recover in 1880, Austria-Hungary displaced France as the country's second supplier after Britain. The partial consolidation of the Egyptian na-tional debt in 1880 rescued French banks, but it also drastically reduced the share owned by French investors and augmented the share held by British bondholders.[158] The commercial, financial and legal foundations of French informal domination were all crumbling away, even before Britain's occupation.

Second, the gradual establishment, between 1876 and 1879, of an Anglo-French Dual Control or Condominium over the Egyptian government offered a new institutional basis for French influence, even if most contemporaries and

156. This interpretation draws in part on John Parsons, "France and the Egyptian Question, 1875–1894: A Study in Finance, Foreign Policy and Public Opinion," unpublished PhD disserta-tion (University of Cambridge, 1977).

157. Cannon, *Politics of Law*, 65–79.

158. On the decline of French holdings in Egypt's public debt, see Bouvier, "Les intérêts fi-nanciers": 100–101, Parsons, "France and the Egyptian Question," 20–29, 35–58, 73–5, 347–8, and Hopkins, "The Victorians and Africa,": 377, 379; on the relative decline of French exports to Egypt, see Parsons, "France and the Egyptian Question," 148–50, and Saul, *La France et l'Égypte*, 477–525.

historians agree that, in practice, it strengthened Britain's influence far more than France's. During the Dual Control, the French focused on securing as full as possible a repayment of Egyptian debt, out of concern for domestic financial stability and because of strong pressures from banking lobbies. They got what they wanted, but it was at the cost of political influence. By contrast, the British embraced France's former strategy of trading off financial gains for positions of influence in the Egyptian administration, with dozens of Britons appointed at senior level in Egyptian ministries. The Dual Control was a fig leaf for the evisceration of French power, and prior to 1882 Britain was already superseding France as the dominant informal empire in Egypt.[159]

Third, faced with this situation, France could neither wish for the continuation of Dual Control nor wish for its transformation into a joint occupation that was likely to aggravate the shift in favour of British domination. Instead, some French officials began to see in the advent of a new Egyptian regime, even one led by the nationalist 'Urabi, a chance to restore French informal dominance on new, more progressive foundations. It is worth stressing that British officials feared a French military invasion of Egypt less than a partnership between the French and 'Urabi, which would have risked undermining Britain's interests. "It looks," the British foreign secretary Lord Granville remarked in June 1882, "as if the French were about to cotton to Arabi ['Urabi]."[160] In July, the French government proposed a minor intervention, limited (unlike Britain's) to the Suez Canal area. The plan was designed to show France's special role in Egypt without alienating 'Urabi's nationalist government. In the French parliament, this project was voted down by an alliance between the radical Left and Right, which was very similar to that which opposed the reform of extraterritorial jurisdiction—while the royalists and Bonapartists still yearned for the old style of domination and friendship with the Khedives, radical republicans such as Georges Clémenceau openly espoused a new policy of "influence" based on collaboration with 'Urabi. All sides also anticipated a difficult and costly campaign against a French-trained Egyptian army, fired up by revolutionary nationalism. Among republicans, Gambetta was extremely isolated when he tried to dispel the illusions shared by most of his allies on the depth of Egyptian patriotic feelings: "Nationality cannot be invented,"

159. Ramm, "Great Britain and France," and Richard A. Atkins, "The Origins of the Anglo-French Condominium in Egypt, 1875–1876," *Historian*, 36 (1974).

160. Robinson and Gallagher, *Africa and the Victorians*, 109.

he claimed in a pronouncement that implicitly condemned the project of a republican informal empire as chimerical.[161]

France's abstention, therefore, manifested a peculiarly strong attachment to informal dominance in Egypt, rather than a genuine hostility to empire. Yet whatever hopes French adversaries of intervention harboured that Britain's army, which had not distinguished itself against the Zulus (1879) and the Boers (1880–1881), would run into serious difficulties were shattered by the British expeditionary force's quick and decisive victory at Tall al-Kabir on 13 September 1882.[162] The battle paved the way for Britain's occupation of Egypt and, by highlighting the growing technological gap between European and even the best-equipped African military forces, certainly contributed to the acceleration of European annexations in subsequent years.[163] "Ah! The laws of history, the march of civilization, the struggle for existence. Woe to the laggards who fall on the wayside," *Le Temps*, a leading moderate republican newspaper, commented.[164] But the battle also dealt a terrible blow, after the disappointments of Mexico and the Arab Kingdom in Algeria, to the efficacy of domination by informal means. The remarks made by *Le Temps* were ostensibly inspired by the fate of Egypt, but they could also be read as a warning about France's imperial future.

At the same time, the replacement of France's political ascendancy in Egypt with that of Britain helps to distinguish imperial from ordinary forms of influence—even after 1882, British colonial administrators drew upon the French model to refashion Egyptian institutions.[165] Not only did French remain the main language of the political and economic elite, including Britons

161. Parsons, "France and the Egyptian Question," 158–204; see 199–200 for the quotations from Clémenceau and Gambetta's speeches about the proposed intervention. On the roots of the Egyptian revolutionary movement, see Cole, *Colonialism and Revolution*, and Alexander Schölch, *Egypt for the Egyptians! The Sociopolitical Crisis in Egypt, 1878–1882* (London: Ithaca Press, 1981).

162. Egypt's army was modelled on France's and trained by French instructors, which may have contributed to an overestimation of its capacity to repel a European intervention; see Khaled Fahmy, *All the Pasha's Men: Mehmed Ali, His Army and the Making of Modern Egypt* (Cairo: American University in Cairo Press, 1997), esp. 79–81.

163. Daniel R. Headrick, *The Tools of Empire: Technology and European Imperialism in the Nineteenth Century* (New York: Oxford University Press, 1981), 115–26.

164. *Le Temps*, 14 Sep. 1882.

165. Robert Tignor, *Modernization and British Colonial Rule in Egypt, 1882–1914* (Princeton, NJ: Princeton University Press, 1966); on the continuities of reforms in Egypt before and after 1882, see Timothy Mitchell, *Colonising Egypt* (Berkeley: University of California Press, 1988).

in their dealings with other Europeans and native Egyptians, but the reach of French legal norms and procedures continued to expand. The 1876 judicial reform had been designed to reduce French interference with the everyday administration of the country, but the forms of the new mixed judiciary were exceptionally close to those of the administration of justice in metropolitan France: "Layout of the courtroom, dress and functions of prosecuting and judging magistrates, clerks, bailiffs, advocates, reading of the roll of cases, court proceedings, closing speeches, submissions by the prosecutor, deliberations, decisions or judgements, everything recalls our Courts and tribunals," a French lawyer commented. "If it were not for the dress of the judges [who had to wear the Ottoman fez, in addition to European black robes] and the occasional use of Italian, which recall that one is not in France, the illusion would be complete."[166]

In 1884, the British-led Egyptian administration inaugurated new native courts, closely modelled on the mixed tribunal and applying the codes drafted by Maunoury. Numerous Egyptian students continued to receive their legal training in France—in Paris or Aix-en-Provence, or at a new prestigious École française de droit du Caire. Even at the University of Cairo, law teachers were predominantly French professors, or British professors who had been trained in France or French Canada. Several studies have wondered at the paradoxical emergence, under British occupation, of a system of "Franco-Egyptian Law" in the late nineteenth century.[167] Yet this legal cultural influence did not translate into greater French political power. The French government instructed its appointees on mixed courts, the *caisse de la dette publique* and other partly internationalized Egyptian administrations to attempt to frustrate British initiatives. This obstructive policy irritated British officials and inspired Lord Cromer, Britain's proconsul, to inveigh against French "political egotism" and "the radical defects of internationalism, considered as a machinery for administration and legislation."[168] But it did not prevent British colonial rulers from eventually imposing their views. Alfred Milner, another high-ranking British

166. Paul Jozon, *Étude sur l'organisation des nouveaux tribunaux égyptiens* (Paris: Société de législation comparée, 1877), 473–4.

167. Leonard Wood, *Islamic Legal Revival: Reception of European Law and Transformations in Islamic Legal Thought in Egypt, 1875–1952* (Oxford: Oxford University Press, 2016), 153–99; Jan Goldberg, "Réception du droit français sous les Britanniques en Egypte: un paradoxe?," *Egypte. Monde arabe*, 34 (1998).

168. Cromer, *Modern Egypt*, vol. 2, 440.

administrator, was also exasperated by the "nauseating" manoeuvres of French officials, but he was confident that "the retarding and weakening effect of French hostility [was] steadily on the decrease," because France could not, "after all, defeat the main object of our policy by any action on the spot."[169] Hence the tolerance of British administrators for French legal and other instruments of domination, which were easier to recycle than reinvent.

We get a sense of the the limits of France's obstructionist policy in the confidential correspondence between the French ministry of justice and Alfred Vacher, a young French magistrate who served as deputy state prosecutor (1876–1879) and state prosecutor (1879–1887) for the new mixed Alexandria appeals court. A former state prosecutor at the criminal court of Dignes in upper Provence, he was considered "one of the best magistrates" of the Aix-en-Provence circuit, and in 1888 he became a judge at the prestigious Paris appeals court. Although employed by the Egyptian government, with an initial yearly salary of twenty-five thousand francs, Vacher described himself as a "forward sentinel" of French interests in Egypt. His letters recounted, in minute detail, his often petty attempts to thwart the progress of British, German and Italian influence in the mixed courts; for instance, he was not sure if the French chief clerk of the Alexandria court could be trusted, because he was Corsican and therefore suspected of harbouring Italian sympathies. Yet Vacher recorded few successes against "England's all-absorbing tendencies."[170] The profitable indemnity business also came to an end. Ironically, one of the last requests for an indemnity examined by the Comité du Contentieux came from the lawyer Maunoury, who felt he should have received more than five hundred and fifty thousand francs for his work in favour of Egypt's judicial reform. Pointing out that he compiled six legal codes for Egypt, when the French lawyer who wrote Haiti's civil code had received five hundred thousand francs from the Haitian government in the 1820s for a single volume, he demanded at least an additional eight hundred thousand francs—French legal imperial influence could be a lucrative business in myriad ways. But the French ministry of foreign affairs declined to press Maunoury's claim, entreating him instead to pursue it before the new courts he had helped to constitute.[171]

169. Milner, *England in Egypt*, 420–2.

170. See reports to the French ministry of justice, 26 May 1876, 12 July 1880 and 24 Feb. 1884, in "Rapports de M. Vacher, 1876–1884," AN, 20020495/22.

171. AAE, Contentieux, 255, folder "Maunoury. Honoraires pour son concours dans l'œuvre de la réforme judiciaire égyptienne," esp. "Note. Affaire Maunoury," n.d. (probably 1881). On

Britain's colonial administration therefore wrested French power from the trappings of France's semi-sovereignty after French consular officials and adventurers wrested indigenous autonomy away from official Egyptian and Ottoman institutions. France's hostility to British occupation crystallized after the mid-1880s, as its policy of "pinpricks" proved ineffective and Britain's domination became more entrenched.[172] Robinson and Gallagher were convinced that France's Egyptian grievance was the crucial factor behind its aggressive African expansionism in the 1880s.[173] Historians of Africa have often disagreed, pointing out that French expansion in West Africa began before Britain's occupation of Egypt, in the late 1870s.[174] Yet the two theses are not incompatible. Even if French expansionism in the Western Sudan had primarily local origins, the unravelling of France's informal domination in Egypt probably exacerbated it. Certainly according to French official propaganda the march to Fashoda, where the British and the French faced each other in 1898, was designed to force Britain out of Egypt; anti-British contemporary French cartoons included the pyramids and the sphinx in the background.[175] Rather than try to identify the single most important factor of the resurgence of French territorial imperialism, it would be preferable to focus on the more significant common ground reached by participants in this controversy. Henri Brunschwig, the French historian of Africa, asserted that, "everyone agrees . . . on France's responsibility" in initiating the partition of sub-Saharan Africa.[176]

the compilation of Haiti's Civil Code by a Parisian lawyer, Louis-Antoine Blanchet, in the 1820s, see Gélin Collot, "Le Code civil haïtien et son histoire," in *Du Code Noir au Code Civil*, ed. Jean-François Niort (Paris: L'Harmattan, 2005), 308.

172. Parsons, "France and the Egyptian Question," 271–90.

173. Robinson and Gallagher, *Africa and the Victorians*, esp. 163–75.

174. Colin W. Newbury and Alexander S. Kanya-Forstner, "French Policy and the Origins of the Scramble for West Africa," *Journal of African History*, 10, 2 (1969); see also Alexander S. Kanya-Forstner, *The Conquest of Western Sudan: A Study in French Military Imperialism* (London: Cambridge University Press, 1969). On the violence of the French conquest, see Bertrand Taithe, *The Killer Trail: A Colonial Scandal in the Heart of Africa* (Oxford: Oxford University Press, 2009).

175. G. N. Sanderson, "The Origins and Significance of the Anglo-French Confrontation at Fashoda, 1898," in *France and Britain in Africa*, eds. Gifford and Louis, 285–331; Darrell Bates, *The Fashoda Incident of 1898: Encounter on the Nile* (Oxford: Oxford University Press, 1984), esp. 1–10; reproduction of contemporary cartoon with Egyptian motifs in Thomas and Toye, *Arguing about Empire*, 79.

176. Henri Brunschwig, *Le partage de l'Afrique noire*, 2nd edn (Paris: Flammarion, 2009), 156; Brunschwig himself traced the origins of French colonial expansionism to the humiliation

This does not contradict this book's focus on the significance of the informal aspects of French imperialism. Robinson and Gallagher's least disputed and perhaps most important insight is that territorial conquest in the nineteenth century was rarely a goal in itself, but more often the consequence of a failure of informal empire. France's case fits this model very well. As seen in chapter 2, after 1840 it was already a crisis of informal empire that led the July Monarchy to embark on the full occupation of Algeria. After 1870, France's informal empire experienced an even more acute crisis, culminating in Britain's formal takeover of Egypt. This crisis, in turn, and in combination with the stagnation of French foreign trade and the rise of messianic republicanism, encouraged a shift towards a greater reliance on formal expansion—even if, under the veneer of sovereignty, French domination still often relied on semi-informal or indirect instruments of domination, such as the protectorate regime.

The notion that France established a novel and soft form of domination over Egypt in the nineteenth century is hardly new. The re-conquest of Egypt by means of "moral ascendancy" already featured as a typical platitude of contemporary political journalism in Honoré de Balzac's Lost Illusions (1837–1843).[177] Alphonse Daudet's once-popular novel Le nabab (1877), whose main character Bernard Jansoulet was modelled on François Bravay, the favourite of Sa'id and Isma'il, shows that this domination was commonly seen as a source of fabulous profit for ordinary French people, and imperial corruption in metropolitan France.[178] Had the master of French prose Gustave Flaubert completed his projected "great social novel" on "Harel Bey," an imaginary French emigrant to Egypt, we would have been left with an even more compelling literary testimony on the significance and limits of this imperial venture: this novel about "the modern Orient" was to examine "the struggle, or rather the merging of barbarity and civilization."[179] This chapter has shown that this

---

of the 1870–1871 war in *Mythes et réalités de l'impérialisme colonial français*. An alternative although not contradictory interpretation underlined the incoherence of French expansion; see Christopher M. Andrew, "The French Colonialist Movement during the Third Republic: The Unofficial Mind of Imperialism," *Transactions of the Royal Historical Society*, 26 (1976).

177. Honoré de Balzac, *Illusions perdues* (Paris: Gallimard, 1974), 270; the second part of the book, to which this passage belonged, was first published in 1839.

178. Jennifer Yee, *Colonial Comedy: Imperialism in the French Realist Novel* (Oxford: Oxford University Press, 2016), 97–100.

179. Gustave Flaubert, *Carnets de travails*, ed. Pierre-Marc de Biasi (Paris: Balland, 1988), 213 (second diary; probably 1862–1864) and 275–7 (nineteenth diary; 1862–3) for details of the

literary trope had some grounding in reality. France and Egypt forged a special if increasingly asymmetric relationship from the 1820s until the 1870s; tens of thousands of French men and women settled in Egypt, temporarily or permanently; and although only a few became fabulously rich, many took advantage of France's growing jurisdictional reach to gain profits that went far beyond natural economic exchange.

The collapse of French informal domination in around 1880 did not end these intensive Franco-Egyptian exchanges, but it did put them on a different footing, closer to normal market relations. French emigration and the export of commodities either stagnated or declined. Conversely, French private investment stock continued to increase, still surpassing British investment by a wide margin in 1914. French firms even tended to be larger and more capital-intensive than their British competitors. Typical of this new style of French economic success was the rise of Crédit Foncier d'Égypte, founded in 1880 and, thanks to its dominance of the land mortgage market, Egypt's largest bank by 1914.[180] Earlier French influence undoubtedly contributed to these successes. The introduction of land mortgages along the modalities of French commercial law was a major and controversial feature of legal reforms in the 1870s.[181] The relatively large share of Belgian capital in the stock of European investment in Egypt (14 percent in 1914, against approximately 30 percent for British capital) suggests that cultural factors such as *francophonie* were also still at play.[182] Yet since France was capital-rich and Egypt capital-poor, and returns on investment were no longer extortionate, this new pattern conformed better to natural economic exchange than the previous one.

In retrospect, Franco-Egyptian relations after 1880 further highlight the distorting effects of extraterritorial consular activism up until the 1870s. Extraterritoriality was more than a vague rhetoric of influence. Instead, it comes across as a concrete, if fluid and contested, mechanism of informal imperial power. It conferred privileges upon agents of informal empire and brought them tangible benefits. France's steadfast efforts to promote and defend extraterritoriality, in

---

novel's plot. Flaubert's project was also probably inspired by Bravay's career; see his comments on Daudet's *Le nabab*, in Flaubert to Edma Roger, 10 Nov. 1877, in Gustave Flaubert, *Correspondance*, ed. Jean Bruneau, 5 vols. (Paris: Gallimard, 1980–2007), vol. 5, 323–4.

180. On the rising share of French investors in Egypt's public debt after 1890, see Saul, *La France et l'Égypte*, 295–373, 529, and 547.

181. Herbert J. Liebesny, *The Law of the Near & Middle East: Readings, Cases, & Material* (Albany: State University of New York Press, 1975), 71–6.

182. Saul, *La France et l'Égypte*, 129–62, 529.

Egypt but also in the rest of the Ottoman world and in East Asia (and less successfully in Latin America), can be construed as the legal facet of velvet imperialism.[183] It is therefore not surprising that the global shift towards territoriality, or the worldwide rise of regimes of governance based on "the control of bordered political spaces" between 1860 and 1880, destabilized France's informal empire.[184] The decline of this empire and the resurgence of French formal imperialism did not only result from contingent factors. They also stemmed the changing modalities of global, economic and legal integration as they intensified in the last third of the nineteenth century.

183. On French extraterritoriality in East Asia, see Georges Soulié de Morant, *Exterritorialité et intérêts étrangers en Chine* (Paris: Greuthner, 1925), 126–227, and Pär Kristoffer Cassel, *Grounds of Judgment: Extraterritoriality and Imperial Power in Nineteenth-Century China and Japan* (Oxford: Oxford University Press, 2012), 54, 63–84; on French (and British) attempts to expand extraterritorial jurisdiction in Latin America, see Benton, *Law and Colonial Culture*, 235–9.

184. Charles S. Maier, "Consigning the Twentieth Century to History: Alternative Narratives for the Modern Era," *American Historical Review*, 105, 3 (2000): 808.

Conclusion

THE PENULTIMATE NOVEL of Émile Zola's Rougon-Maquart series, on the collapse of the Bonapartist Empire, is entitled *La Débâcle*. Although the narrative focuses on the disastrous 1870 campaign that ended with the defeat of Sedan, the book is full of allusions to the crumbling regime's taste for luxury, as in a description of Napoleon III, "this wretched emperor," en route to the eastern battlefields, "condemned to drag after him the irony of his imperial establishment, his lifeguards, coaches, horses, cooks, vanloads of silver utensils and champagne, all the pomp of his robe of state, embroidered with imperial bees."[1] The crushing military defeat in Zola's account appears as the outcome not only of incompetent strategy, but also of the corruption bred by Bonapartist *arrivisme* and materialism—in other words, of the moral downside to the political economy of champagne capitalism that was at the heart of mid-century French economic and imperial expansion.

France's imperial debacle was not confined to Europe. Zola's friend Édouard Manet offered an arresting representation of its global dimension in his *Execution of Maximilian* (1868–1869; see figure 6.1). Manet was notoriously averse to the historical and political genre so highly prized by French academic institutions. Indeed, his oeuvre is better remembered for its subtle but relentless critique of commodification and other aspects of modern urban—especially Parisian—life, and its decisive contribution to the emergence of modernist art.[2] This makes Manet's passionate incursion into *évènementiel* painting (the picture in figure 6.1 is the third and most complete of three large canvasses, in

---

1. Émile Zola, *La Débâcle* (Paris: Gallimard, 1984; first published in 1892), 85; trans. By L. W. Tancock, in *The Debacle* (Harmondsworth: Penguin, 1972).

2. Timothy James Clark, *The Painting of Modern Life: Paris in the Art of Manet and his Followers* (London: Thames and Hudson, 1984).

FIGURE 6.1. Édouard Manet, *The Execution of Emperor Maximilian*, third version (1868–1869). *Source:* Kunsthalle Mannheim, image from the collection *10,000 Meisterwerke der Malerei* (Berlin: The Yorck Project, 2005)

addition to a small oil painting and a lithograph, all made between 1867 and 1869) all the more beguiling, as if this event, a dramatic epilogue to France's failed effort to turn Mexico into a client state, could not be ignored. Manet was a staunch republican and his painting can be interpreted as a damning verdict on the Bonapartist aspiration to informal empire. The ironic detachment of the composition, the French-looking uniforms of the Mexican firing squad, and the uncanny resemblance of the figure on the right (a sergeant due to deliver the *coup de grâce* to Maximilian and his two generals) to the French emperor Napoleon III, combine to create a troubling confusion as to who is killing whom and which empire is collapsing. Despite the relaxation of censorship in the regime's last years, Manet was banned from commercializing the lithograph based on the painting, and none of the canvasses were displayed in France until 1905.[3]

Zola's sanctimonious tone may irritate modern readers, and Manet's complex successive works on Maximilian's execution lend themselves to multiple readings. But in conclusion I would like to endorse the former's view that French imperial collapse was the product of more than contingent circumstances, and the latter's suggestion that events such as the downfall of the Mexican empire should be relocated to the centre of historical accounts of French life in this period. Between 1867 and 1882, the French aspiration to imperial status by informal means met with an impressive succession of setbacks: the collapse of a French-sponsored Mexican monarchy, the unravelling of a policy of cooperation with indigenous elites in Algeria and Egypt, France's defeat by Prussia, and Germany's subsequent ascendancy in continental Europe. Each of these disasters has usually been treated by historians as a discrete episode, and the rout by Prussia as almost the sole cause of French decline. Yet France's defeat in 1870–1871 can be viewed as a symptom as well as a factor, especially if one pays due attention to the links between those events: the Mexican disaster resulted in a significant reduction of France's military expenditure, that contributed to Prussia's crushing victory, which in turn diminished French prestige in Egypt and triggered a revolt in Kabylia, that further discredited Bonapartist policy in Algeria. France's debacle was a global pheonomenon, comparable in scale to several previous or later imperial disintegrations.

Beyond relations of immediate cause and effect, what connected these catastrophic events was a sharp reduction in France's capacity to project its imperial power in the late 1860s. This diminution was as abrupt as the rise of informal clout after 1820 had been spectacular, because the structure of French imperial power was highly leveraged. France's soft cultural and ideological power served to amplify its hard economic and military power. Theorists of international relations categorize economic power as hard, but as seen

3. On Manet's absorption in the representation of Maximilian's execution, see Beth Archer Brombert, *Édouard Manet: Rebel in a Frock Coat* (Boston: Little, Brown, 1996), 211–15 and Michael Fried, *Manet's Modernism, or the Face of Painting in the 1860s* (Chicago: University of Chicago Press, 1996), 346–64; on the political significance of the painting, see John House, "Manet's Maximilian: History Painting, Censorship and Ambiguity," in *Manet: The Execution of Maximilian: Painting, Politics and Censorship*, ed. Juliet Wilson-Bareau (London: National Gallery Publications, 1992), 87–111, and Nord, *Impressionists and Politics*, 20–1, 31–4.

in chapters 3 and 4, in the case of mid-nineteenth-century France, even economic prosperity relied to a large extent on soft and immaterial foundations, such as the country's global image as the land of good taste, or complex transnational lending arrangements. Legal influence, as seen in chapter 5, was also the product of a sophisticated combination of hard and soft power. Leveraging enabled France to punch above its weight, as the hackneyed phrase puts it—or at least above the weight suggested by crude measures of power, such as military expenditure or steel and coal output.

However, as a result, the structure of French imperial power was highly vulnerable to deleveraging: almost literally, in the case of foreign lending to client states; inevitably, in the case of something as evanescent as good taste; and subtly, in the case of legal instruments, which could be voided by international agreements or foreign legal reforms. All empires are complex, due to the layering of sovereignty that characterizes their organization, but their very complexity usually increases their resilience. Major empires in world history, such as the Roman Empire or the Ottoman Empire, often experienced a slow decline before their ultimate downfall, or even, in the cases of Persia and China, a recurring resurgence. However, complexity arising out of leveraging, in politics as well as in finance, can result in a sudden unravelling. British informal domination in Argentina, China and the Middle-East collapsed suddenly—respectively in the 1930s, 1940s and 1950s—as did the very different informal empire of the Soviet Union at the end of the Cold War. The military, economic and cultural or ideological aspects of informal rule can reinforce one other, but the weakening of one element will also undermine the others and precipitate collapse.[4]

What caused the deleveraging of France's power and the unravelling of its informal empire is open to debate. Zola's emphasis on Bonapartist corruption echoed the classical republican trope of virtue as the mainspring of strong polities. Yet this vision reflected Zola's republican convictions rather than historical reality. Talleyrand's role as an early promoter of French informal imperialism should suffice to prove that virtue was never its moral mainspring. The fading of French informal power was relative, rather than absolute, and probably owed more to global transformations than to domestic decay. The emergence of the United States as a great power in the wake of the Civil War (1861–1865) and German unification were no doubt crucial factors. The former foiled French ambitions in Mexico, while the latter brought about the cataclysm of

---

4. Burbank and Cooper, *Empires in World History*, esp. 11–14, 305–6.

1870–1871. Yet we should not neglect the role played by the new providers of conspicuous commodities and services, whose emergence sapped French economic and cultural power after 1860. Vienna began to vie with Paris as Europe's capital of pleasure, the fast-growing Italian silk industry and producers of new synthetic fibers eroded the dominance of Lyon silk merchants for the most expensive textile products, and countless new decorative industries—located as far away as Punjab, in the case of "sindhworks", some orientalizing trinkets commercialized on a large scale in Europe from the 1860s—undercut *articles de Paris*.[5] The French model of development was easier to emulate than capital-intensive British-style industrialization, helping to explain why France experienced an even faster relative decline than Britain after 1870.

Military setbacks and economic weakening reduced the value of collaboration with France, further accelerating the waning of French global power. Modernizing elites began to look for alternative models of conservative modernity, such as Otto von Bismarck's Germany, while Britain's decision to occupy Egypt alone in 1882 demonstrated its diminished regard for the benefits of Anglo-French cooperation overseas—until the rise of German power facilitated its resurrection with the Entente Cordiale agreement in 1904. The upheaval of the Commune in 1871 and the rise of democratic republicanism in the 1870s certainly contributed to the reduced appeal of the French model among global elites. Yet this leftward tilt of France's politics can itself be interpreted as a consequence of the crisis of the French informal empire.[6] To account for the growing popularity and eventual triumph of republican opinions, historians have usually pointed to domestic and ideological factors, such as the greater moderation of republican leaders under the influence of positivist philosophy.[7] But we should also take into consideration the economic and geopolitical difficulties, even before the disasters of 1870–1871, that helped

5. Claude Markovits, *The Global World of Indian Merchants 1750–1947: Traders of Sindh from Bukhara to Panama* (Cambridge: Cambridge University Press, 2000), 110–55.

6. On the negative repercussions of the Commune for French influence, including in the Middle East and East Asia, see Quentin Deluermoz, "The Worlds of 1871," in *The Global History of Revolution*, ed. David Motadel (Cambridge: Cambridge University Press, forthcoming).

7. Claude Nicolet, *L'idée républicaine en France (1789–1914)* (Paris: Gallimard, 1994; first published in 1982); for a nuanced account of the rise of mass republicanism, see Quentin Deluermoz, *Le crépuscule des révolutions, 1848–1871* (Paris: Le Seuil, 2012), 290–306, and on the transnational origins of modern democratic ideas in France, see Stephen Sawyer, *Demos Assembled: Democracy and the International Origins of the Modern State* (Chicago: Chicago University Press, 2018).

enable the rise of mass republicanism. By all accounts, support for the Bonapartist regime held steady in the peasantry in the late 1860s, but it weakened among the millions of skilled workers, small entrepreneurs and *rentiers* whose position was endangered by the crisis of champagne capitalism. After 1880, the same social groups, still dissatisfied by their precarious economic situation, played an inflated role in the Boulanger and Dreyfus crises that threatened the stability of the new Third Republic.[8]

One should always beware the temptation of presentist interpretations, but economic historians identified an Atlantic-wide "backlash against globalization" in the last decades of the nineteenth century, long before today's debates about the resurgence of nationalism, protectionism or populism.[9] This book has argued that France was a greater beneficiary of nineteenth-century globalization than is generally acknowledged, but this left it especially vulnerable to the backlash of the late nineteenth century. From a global and imperial perspective, the final demise of monarchical institutions and the triumph of democratic republicanism in the 1870s can be seen as a response to this dissatisfaction. The politics of the Third Republic were very liberal, but its political economy marked a shift from global networks towards territoriality. This territorial turn was domestic, with its programme of intensive nationalization of metropolitan residents, and economic, with its return to protectionism.[10] But it was also imperial, with a formidable resurgence of formal expansion. Between 1870 and 1913 the area under French sovereignty, including metropolitan France, rose nearly tenfold, to more than 10 million square kilometers, as a result of successive annexations or protectorate treaties in sub-Saharan Africa, Madagascar, Indochina, Tunisia and Morocco. And yet what might look like an acceleration, especially on a map, was also a rupture. The logic of this land grabbing was profoundly different from the nodal and informal strategy examined in this book. The new territorial empire relied upon the control of resources and indigenous populations rather than the capture of commercial crossroads and the creation of economic opportunities for national expatriates.

8. Philip Nord, *The Politics of Resentment: Shopkeeper Protest in Nineteenth-Century Paris*, 2nd edn (New Brunswick, NJ: Transaction Publishers, 2005).

9. As early as the 1990s, for instance in O'Rourke and Williamson, *Globalization and History*, 93–117.

10. On the intensification of nation-building, see Weber, *Peasants into Frenchmen*, and on the gradual rise of import tariffs after 1870, see Charles, "Protection, spécialisation et croissance économique," 262–6, 269–72.

It depended less upon the persuasion of the elite, and more upon mass coercion. Its justificatory rhetoric was democratic, rather than anti-revolutionary.

This shift in preference was not absolute. Most empires are composites, based on informal and formal instruments of domination in varying proportions. The earlier preference for informal expansion did not preclude formal colonization in specific circumstances—as seen in this book, egregiously, in Algeria's case from 1840. Yet if we think of imperial domination as a spectrum of modalities, we can still agree that, after 1880, the territorial superseded the informal as the prevalent mode of French imperial expansion. This shift reflected a global reappraisal of territoriality between 1860 and 1880, perhaps accentuated in France's case by the Third Republic's desire to bolster its domestic legitimacy. By some measures, such as placing certain areas under territorial control, the new empire made France more global. Yet by others, such as the proportion of French exports in world trade, which nearly halved between 1880 and 1914, the new empire can also be seen as having served to conceal or assuage anxieties about global decline. This interpretation echoes the old emphasis on the economic irrationality of late nineteenth-century French territorial expansion.[11] But it suggests that the motive was a larger aspiration to attenuate the waning of French international *rayonnement* rather than a simple desire to avenge the military humiliation of 1870.

French imperial power retained significant informal features after 1880. Within the territorial empire, French officials frequently resorted to protectorate regimes that did not extend France's sovereignty but parcelled out that of indigenous polities, even if in practice such regimes tended to slide gradually towards greater assertion of territorial control.[12] The exacerbated racism that underpinned colonial expansion after 1880 may also owe something to the emphasis placed on the inherent differences between human races by several advocates of informal expansion, from the Abbé de Pradt to Michel Chevalier: in this we can detect an important element of continuity between the justification for informal and formal rule. Outside the colonial empire, high-end Parisian luxury retained its allure, because commercial decline mainly affected the semi-luxury industries, and the French language remained a global idiom, even if it lost ground to German in the realm of intellectual exchange. The French legal system remained influential, yet more often as a result of path dependency rather than direct emulation. French foreign lending experienced a re-

11. Brunschwig, *Mythes et réalités de l'impérialisme colonial français.*
12. Lewis, *Divided Sovereignty.*

surgence after 1890, but it could not catch up with British capital export again and it rarely resulted in anything resembling imperial domination. These instruments of informal power nonetheless enhanced France's capacity to influence world affairs, even if they no longer sufficed to confer upon it the imperial status craved for by the French elite and a substantial fraction of French opinion.

The new preference for territorial control after 1880 was later called into question. From around 1900, new associationist ideas began to challenge the Republican empire's official goal of assimilation.[13] The First World War and the collapse of global trade following the Great Depression tended to rehabilitate territorialist conceptions, as demonstrated by the popularity of the concepts of *mise en valeur* in the 1920s and *autarchie* in the 1930s. But the aftermath of the Second World War witnessed—alongside the brutal repression of nationalist movements, especially in Masagascar, Indochina and Algeria—the resurgence of a less territorial and quasi-federal conception of empire.[14] Whether the projects of a French Union in 1946 and Communauty in 1958 should be considered gimmicks or sincere attempts to found a democratic sort of empire remains open to debate. But it is significant that in relation to French sub-Saharan Africa, their failure resulted in neo-colonial dependency, rather than national self-governments. *Françafrique,* or the perpetuation of French domination south of the Sahara by a complex combination of military, economic and cultural means, stands, to this day, as a spectacularly effective kind of French informal empire.[15] It is even possible to see France's leading role in European integration as a parallel attempt to enhance its global status by soft and imperial means, albeit with a more limited success after the reassertion of German pre-eminence in Europe since the 1990s.[16] More generally, and just as on the domestic stage Gaullism borrowed from the French monarchical and

13. Conklin, *A Mission to Civilize,* 174–211; on later attempts to resuscitate indigenous polities under French tutelage that recalled the Arab Kingdom policy of the Second Empire, see also Eric Jennings, *Vichy in the Tropics: Pétain's National Revolution in Madagascar, Guadeloupe and Indochina* (Stanford, CA: Stanford University Press, 2002), 162–98.

14. Cooper, *Citizenship between Empire and Nation.*

15. For recent evaluations of French neo-colonialism, see Jean-Pierre Bat, *Le syndrome Foccart: La politique française en Afrique, de 1959 à nos jours* (Paris: Gallimard, 2012) and *Francophone Africa at Fifty,* eds. Tony Chafer and Alexander Keese (Manchester: Manchester University Press, 2013).

16. Michael Sutton, *France and the Construction of Europe, 1944–2007: The Geopolitical Imperative* (New York: Berghahn Books, 2007).

Bonapartist traditions, General De Gaulle's foreign policy of global *grandeur* had distinct undertones of informal imperialism.[17]

By and large, these French swings from the informal to the territorial and back again conformed to a global pattern. A growing worldwide concern with territoriality encouraged formal empire building by other powers, as well as France after 1870.[18] Conversely, an increasing sense of interdependency after 1950 favoured the deployment of soft power and informal ascendancy by both former major colonial powers, as well as the new American and Soviet super-powers.[19] Extant interpretations of the development of imperial formations often exaggerate the role of domestic factors and neglect that of global and external constraints, because they tend to rely on the accounts of empire build-ers who are keen to highlight their own agency. This book has instead sought to highlight the role of several of these constraints, from the pressures of the global market towards specialization in the provision of conspicuous com-modities and services to the necessity of collaborating with superior British imperial power and the local elite. Much remains to be done, however, to un-derstand these constraints on their own terms: what some contemporaries found so appealing about French culture and commodities in the mid-nineteenth century, why Britain tolerated this expansion of French power, and why so many foreign elites—in Europe, the Middle-East, Latin America and beyond—embraced cooperation with France remain intriguing questions, to which respective specialists may provide better answers than I ever could.

The crucial role played by global factors helps us to understand why em-pires tend to resemble one other at any given time, but it does not imply that all empires are the same. The main singularity of successive French imperial formations since 1789 was probably their assertiveness, relative to other Euro-pean countries' imperial ambitions and France's actual resources. This is well

17. Philip H. Gordon, *A Certain Idea of France: French Security Policy and the Gaullist Legacy* (Princeton, NJ: Princeton University Press, 1993) and Maurice Vaïsse, *La grandeur: politique étrangère du general De Gaulle, 1958–1969* (Paris: Fayard, 1998); see also the similarities between the Bonapartist and Gaullist aspirations to French moral ascendancy in the Arab World, in Gérald Arboit, *Aux sources de la politique arabe de la France. Le Second Empire au Machrek* (Paris: L'Harmattan, 2000).

18. Charles S. Maier, "Consigning the Twentieth Century to History"; see also Sven Beckert, "American Danger, United States Empire, Eurafrica and the Territorialization of Industrial Capi-talism," *American Historical Review*, 122, 4 (2017).

19. Wm. Roger Louis and Ronald Robinson, "The Imperialism of Decolonization," *Journal of Imperial and Commonwealth History*, 22, 3 (1994).

established in the cases of the Napoleonic and republican colonial empires, and this book has shown that between 1815 and 1880 France continued to pursue empire, albeit by informal means. France was not a nation-state that experienced aberrant imperial moments, but it was almost always a nation-state *and* an empire. This conclusion illustrates the principal analytical benefit of the concept of informal empire—in other words, the way it helps us discern fundamental continuities in the history of imperial formations. Its greatest limitation is a certain elusiveness. The attempt made in this book to capture its concrete workings through various lenses—intellectual, economic, cultural and legal—remains impressionistic. But if we can acknowledge blurriness, in the manner of a painting by Manet, we can thereby enrich our understanding of historical reality.

BIBLIOGRAPHY

Archives, France

National Archives

Archives des Affaires Étrangères, La Courneuve [AAE]
    Affaires diverses politiques (États des français à l'étranger)
    Chancellerie (Alexandrie)
    Contentieux (Dette publique; Égypte; Turquie)
    Correspondance consulaire et commerciale (Alger)
    Correspondance politique (Angleterre; Haiti)
    État civil (Alexandrie; Le Caire; Suez; Port-Saïd; Ismaïlia)
    Mémoires & Documents (Afrique; Algérie; Turquie)
    Personnel
Archives nationales, Pierrefitte-sur-Seine [AN]
    F 12 Ministry of Commerce
    45 AP Rouher MSS
    272 AP Ploeuc MSS
    20020495 (provisional), Ministry of Justice
Archives nationales d'outre mer, Aix-en-Provence [ANOM]
    GGA Gouvernement général de l'Algérie (Consulats de France, Correspondance générale)
    F80 Ministries of War and of the Interior, divisions relating to Algeria
    CC9 Correspondance à l'arrivée en provenance de Saint-Domingue
Bibliothèque nationale de France, Paris [BNF]
    Fonds français, Raynal MSS
Centre des archives diplomatiques de Nantes
    PO, Postes consulaires (Alexandrie)
Centre des archives du monde du travail, Roubaix [CAMT]
    44 AQ Neuflize MSS
    132 AQ Rothschild MSS
    207 AQ Banque Ottomane MSS
Centre des archives économiques et financères, Savigny-le-Temple [CAEF]
    Compagnie des Agents de change de Paris
    Commission des Finances du Mexique

Dette Publique (Gestion des emprunts français et étrangers)
Emprunts Ottomans

Local Archives

Archives départementales de la Marne, Châlons-en-Champagne [ADM]
    16 U Tribunal de Commerce
Archives départementales des Bouches-du-Rhône, Marseille
    4 M Police (Émigration)
Archives départementales des du Rhône, Lyon
    8 MP Commerce et Tourisme (Chambre de Commerce; Commerce extérieur)
Archives départementales du Var, Draguignan [ADV]
    3 E Actes notariés
    2 MI Registres de l'État civil

Archives, Germany

Stadtarchiv, Worms [WS]
Dalberg MSS

Archives, United Kingdom

Cambridge University Library
    Jardine & Matheson MSS
Hartley Library, Southampton
    Wellington MSS
The National Archives, Kew [TNA]
    Foreign Office Correspondence
    Court of Chancery
    Chancery: Entry Books of Decrees and Orders
The Rothschild Archive, London [TRA]
    XI/85 Business correspondence from de Rothschild frères
    XI/38/200 Paravey and Co.

Archives, United States of America

Historical Society of Pennsylvania, Philadelphia [HSP]
    Shaler MSS

United States National Archives, College Park, MD
    Record Group 59 Department of State Central Files

Newspapers and Magazines

Die Neue Zeit
Edinburgh Review
La Renommée
L'exposition universelle de 1867 illustrée
Le Journal des Débats
Le Journal des économistes
Le Temps
The Times

Visual Sources

Ciceri, Eugène and Philippe Benoist, *Vue officielle de l'exposition à vol d'oiseau*. Paris: Lemercier & Cie, 1867.

Daumier, Honoré. "Les magasins de plus en plus monstres," *Le Charivari*, 18 Aug. 1844.

Didier Petit et Cie. *Portrait de Joseph-Marie Jacquard*, 1839 (Lyon, Musée des Tissus).

Dufour, Auguste-Henri. *Algérie: dédié au Roi*. Paris: C. Simmoneau, 1838.

Gérôme, Jean-Léon. *The Reception of Siamese Ambassadors by the Emperor Napoleon III at the Palace of Fontainebleau*, 1864 (Château de Versailles).

Ingres, Dominique. *Madame Moitessier*, 1856 (London, National Gallery).

Maison Burlaton et Cie. *Portrait de l'empereur Napoléon*, 1855 (Lyon, Musée des Tissus).

———. *Portrait de l'empereur Napoléon III*, 1855 (Lyon, Musée des Tissus).

———. *Portrait de l'impératrice Eugénie*, 1855 (Lyon, Musée des Tissus).

Manet, Édouard. *The Execution of Maximilian*, third version, 1868–1869 (Mannheim Kunsthalle).

Pernon, Camille. *Bonaparte réparateur*, 1802 (Lyon, Musée des Tissus).

Vernet, Horace. *Capture of the Smala of Abd el-Kader*, 1845 (Château de Versailles).

Official Publications

Annales du Sénat et du Corps Législatif. Session de 1870, 6 vols. Paris: Le Moniteur universel, 1870–1871.

Board of Trade, *Annual Statement of the Trade and Navigation of the United Kingdom with Foreign Countries and British Possessions*, 17 vols. London: H.M.S.O., 1855–1871.

Clercq, Jules de, ed. *Recueil des traités de la France*, 23 vols. Paris: Amyot, 1864–1907.

Direction générale des Douanes, *Tableau décennal du commerce de la France avec ses colonies et les puissances étrangères, 1827–1896*, 13 vols. Paris: 1838–1898.

Documents officiels relatifs à la loi sur le régime douanier des colonies. Paris: Challamel, 1861.

Gouvernement général civil de l'Algérie, *Annuaire statistique de l'Algérie. Année 1932*. Algiers: E. Pfister, 1933.

Gouvernement général civil de l'Algérie, *Statistique générale de l'Algérie. Années 1882 à 1884*. Algiers: Association ouvrière, 1885.

Hertslet, Lewis, ed. *A Complete Collection of the Treaties and Conventions, and Reciprocal Regula-tions, at Present Subsisting between Great Britain & Foreign Powers*, 31 vols. London: Butter-worth, 1827–1940.

Ministère de la Guerre, *Tableau de la situation des établissements français dans l'Algerie*, 20 vols. Paris: 1838–1868.

Other Printed Primary Sources

Allart, Maurice. *Considérations sur la difficulté de coloniser la Régence d'Alger*. Paris: Selligue, 1830.

Allier, J. "Crédit, discrédit, banquiers, industriels, industrie, producteur," *Le Producteur*, 2 (1826).

Angell, Norman. *The Great Illusion: A Study of the Relation of Military Power to National Advan-tage*. Memphis, TN: Bottom of the Hill, 2012.

Anon. *Anti-Pradt, ou considérations générales sur les colonies et sur l'Amérique, pour servir d'antidote aux doctines métropolicides de M. l'archévêque de Malines*. Paris: Anthelme Boucher, 1822.

Avallon, Cousin d'. *Pradtiana, ou recueil des pensées, réflexions et opinions politiques de M. l'abbé de Pradt*. Paris: Plancher, 1820.

Azan, Paul. "Le rapport du comte de Clermont-Tonnerre, ministre de la guerre (1827)," *Revue africaine*, 338–339 (1929).

[Bagehot, Walter.] "One Difference between France and England," *The Economist*, 12 Sep. 1868.

——— "The New Mexican Empire," *The Economist*, 22 Aug 1863.

Balzac, Honoré de. *Illusions perdues*. Paris: Gallimard, 1974.

———. *La Comédie Humaine*, 12 vols. Paris: Gallimard, 1976–1981.

Batchelder, George S. "The International Court of Egypt," *Albany Law Journal*, 19 (1879).

Baudrillart, Henri. *Histoire du luxe privé et public depuis l'antiquité jusqu'à nos jours*, 4 vols. Paris: Hachette, 1880–1881.

Baxter, Robert Dudley. *National Debts*. London: Robert John Bush, 1871.

Bellet, Louis. *La vérité sur les obligations mexicaines*. Paris: Guérin, 1867.

Bianchi, Xavier. *Relation de l'arrivée dans la rade d'Alger du vaisseau de S. M. La Provence*. Paris: the author, 1830.

Blanqui, Adolphe. *Lettres sur l'exposition universelle de Londres*. Paris: Capelle, 1851.

Blount, Edward. *Memoirs*, ed. S. J. Reid. London: Longmans & Co, 1902.

Brillat-Savarin, Jean-Anthelme. *Vues et projets d'économie politique*. Paris: Gignet et Michaud, 1801.

Carême, Marie-Antoine. *Projet d'architecture pour l'embellissement de Paris*, 5 vols. Paris: F. Didot père et fils, 1821–1826.

Census of England and Wales for the Year 1861. General Report. London: Eyre and Spottiswoode, 1863.

Chevalier, Michel. *Cours d'économie politique*, 3 vols. Paris: Capelle, 1842–1850.

———. *Cours d'économie politique*, 2nd edn., 3 vols. Paris: Capelle, 1855–1866.

———. *De la Baisse probable de l'or des conséquences commerciales et sociales qu'elle peut avoir et des mesures qu'elle provoque*. Paris: Claye, 1857.

———. *Des mines d'argent et d'or du nouveau-monde*. Paris: Gerdès, 1846.

———. *Du droit international, de ses vicissitudes et de ses échecs dans le temps présent*. Paris: Claye, 1873.

———. *Du Mexique avant et pendant la conquête*. Paris: Fournier, 1845.

———. *Examen du système commercial connu sous le nom de système protecteur*. Paris: Guillaumin, 1852.

———. "La constitution de l'Angleterre," *Revue des Deux Mondes*, 72 (1867).

———. *La guerre et la crise européenne*. Paris: Claye, 1866.

———. *Le Mexique*. Paris: Maulde et Renou, 1851.

———. *Le Mexique ancien et moderne*. Paris: Hachette, 1863.

———. *Lettres sur l'Amérique du Nord*, 2 vols. Paris: Charles Gosselin, 1836.

———. "L'Europe et la Chine, l'occident et l'orient," *Revue des Deux Mondes*, 23 (1840).

———. *L'expédition du Mexique*. Paris: E. Dentu, 1862.

———. *L'exposition universelle de Londres considérée sous les rapports philosophique, technique, commercial et administratif au point de vue français*. Paris: Mathias, 1851.

———. *L'isthme de Panama. Examen historique et géographique des différentes directions suivant lesquelles on pourrait le percer et des moyens à y employer. Suivi d'un aperçu de l'isthme de Suez*. Paris: C. Gosselin, 1844.

———. *Politique européenne*. Paris: Le Globe, 1831.

———. *Question de l'or. Métaux précieux et monnaie*. Paris: Guillaumin, 1853.

Coëssin, Guillaume. *De l'esprit de conquête et de l'usurpation dans le système mercantile*. Paris: Le Normant, 1814.

Constant, Benjamin. *Mémoires sur les Cent Jours*, 2 vols. Paris: Béchet aîné, 1820.

———. *Political Writings*, ed. Biancamaria Fontana. Cambridge: Cambridge University Press, 1988.

———. *Recueil d'articles, 1825–1830*, ed. Ephraïm Harpaz, 2 vols. Paris: Honoré Champion, 1992.

———. *Recueil d'articles, 1829–1830*, ed. Ephraïm Harpaz. Paris: Honoré Champion, 1989.

———. *Recueil d'Articles. Le Mercure, La Minerve et La Renommée*, ed. Ephraïm Harpaz, 2 vols. Geneva: Droz, 1972.

Cromer, Earl of. *Modern Egypt*, 2 vols. London: Macmillan, 1908.

Daudet, Alphonse. *Le Nabab*. Paris: Charpentier, 1877.

Desjobert, Amédée. *La question d'Alger: politique, colonisation, commerce*. Paris: Dufart, 1837.

Des Michels, Jules Alexis. *Souvenirs de ma carrière*. Paris: Plon, Nourrit et Cie, 1901.

Dupin, Charles. *Observations sur la puissance de l'Angleterre et sur celle de la Russie*. Paris: Plassan, 1824.

Enfantin, P[rosper]. "Des banquiers cosmopolites," *Le Producteur*, 2 (1826).

E[nfantin], P[rosper]. "Du système des emprunts comparé à celui des impôts," *Le Producteur*, 3 (1826).

Enfantin, P[rosper]. "Opuscules financiers," *Le Producteur*, 2 (1826).

Ernst, Eberhard, ed. *Talleyrand und der Herzog von Dalberg: unveröffentlichte Briefe 1816–1832*. Frankfurt am Main: Lang, 1987.

Esquer, Gabriel, ed. *Correspondance du general Drouet d'Erlon*. Paris: Champion, 1926.

———, ed. *Correspondance du Maréchal Clauzel, gouverneur général des possessions françaises dans le nord de l'Afrique, 1835–1837*. 2 vols. Paris: Larose, 1948.

[Eyemery, Alexis et al.] *Dictionnaire des girouettes, ou nos contemporains peints par eux-mêmes*. Paris: Alexis Eymery, 1815.

Fauchat, Nicolas. *Observations sur les ouvrages de M. Pradt relatifs aux colonies.* Paris: E. Gide & A. Egron, 1817.

Fazy, Jean-Jacob. *Opuscules financiers sur l'effet des privilèges, des emprunts publics et des conversions sur le crédit de l'industrie en France.* Paris: Naudin, 1826.

Féraud-Giraud, Louis. *De la juridiction française dans les échelles du Levant et de Barbarie,* 2nd ed., 2 vols. Paris: A. Durand, 1866.

Fiévet, Victor. *Madame Veuve Clicquot (née Ponsardin), son histoire et celle de sa famille.* Paris: Dentu, 1865.

Flaubert, Gustave. *Carnets de travails,* ed. Pierre-Marc de Biasi. Paris: Balland, 1988.

———. *Correspondance,* ed. Jean Bruneau. 5 vols. Paris: Gallimard, 1980–2007.

Forcade, Eugène. "Chronique de la quinzaine," *Revue des Deux Mondes,* 56 (1865).

Gagliani's New Paris Guide for 1867. Paris: A. and W. Gagliani, 1867.

Gautier, Théophile. *Voyage en Égypte,* ed. Paolo Tortonese. Paris: La Boîte à Documents, 1991.

Gavillot, Aristide. *Essai sur les droits des Européens en Turquie et en Egypte. Les capitulations et la réforme judiciaire.* Paris: Dentu, 1875.

Giffard, Pierre. *Les Français en Égypte.* Paris: Havard, 1883.

Goschen, George. *Essays and Addresses on Economic Questions.* London: Arnold, 1905.

Guizot, François. *Histoire de la civilisation en Europe.* Paris: Robert Laffont, 1985.

———. *Histoire de la civilisation en France,* 2nd edn., 4 vols. Paris: Didier, 1840.

———. *Histoire parlementaire de France,* 5 vols. Paris: Michel Lévy, 1863–1864.

———. *Mémoires pour servir à l'histoire de mon temps,* 8 vols. Paris: Michel Lévy, 1858–1867.

Hale, Charles. "Consular Service and Society in Egypt," *Atlantic Monthly* (Sep. 1877).

Hawks, Francis. *Narrative of the Expedition of an American Squadron to the China Seas and Japan Performed in the Years 1852, 1853 and 1854 under the Command of Commodore M.C. Perry, United States Navy,* 4 vols. Washington, DC: A.O.P. Nicholson, 1856.

Hurewitz, Jacob C., ed. *The Middle East and North Africa in World Politics: A Documentary Record.* 2 vols. New Haven: Yale University Press, 1975–1979.

[Jonama y Bellsolá, Santiago.] *Lettres à M. l'abbé de Pradt, par un indigène de l'Amérique du Sud.* Paris: Rodriguez, 1818.

Jouffroy, Théodore. *Mélanges philosophiques,* 2nd edn. Paris: Ladrange, 1838.

Jozon, Paul. *Étude sur l'organisation des nouveaux tribunaux égyptiens.* Paris: Société de législation comparée, 1877.

Kératry, Émile de. *La créance Jecker, les indemnités française et les emprunts mexicains.* Paris: Librairie internationale, 1868.

———. "Le Mexique et les chances de salut du nouvel empire," *Revue des Deux Mondes,* 65 (1866).

Keynes, John M. "Foreign Investments and national advantages," *The London Nation,* 9 August 1924.

Laborde, Alexandre de. *Sur les véritables causes de la rupture avec Alger et sur l'expédition qui se prépare,* 2nd edn. Paris: Truchy, 1830.

[Lacroix, Frédéric.] *L'Algérie et la lettre de l'empereur.* Paris: Firmin Didot & Challamel, 1863.

Lacroix, Lambert de. *L'Égypte, cinq minutes d'arrêt!!!* Paris: E. Lachaud, 1870.

Lacuée-Saint-Just, Jean-Chrysostôme. *Économie politique. Des colonies: d'Alger, de sa possession, du système colonial.* Paris: Vve Béchet, 1830.

Laffitte, Jacques. *Réflexions sur la réduction de la rente et sur l'état du crédit.* Paris: Bossange père, 1824.

La Morinière, Joseph Noël de. *L'Amérique espagnole, ou Lettres civiques à M. de Pradt*. Paris: E. Gide, 1817.

Launay, Adrien. *Siam et les missionnaires français*. Tours: Alfred Mame, 1866.

Lenin, Vladimir I. *Imperialism: The Highest Stage of Capitalism*. London: Penguin, 2010.

Leroy-Beaulieu, Paul. *De la colonisation chez les peuples modernes*. Paris: Guillaumin, 1874.

———. *De la colonisation chez les peuples modernes*, 2nd edn. Paris: Guillaumin, 1882.

———. "Le luxe. La fonction de la richesse: I Caractère et variété du Luxe. Son rôle économique," *Revue des Deux Mondes*, 126 (1894).

———. *Les guerres contemporaines (1853–1866): recherches statistiques sur les pertes d'hommes et de capitaux*. Paris: Guillaumin, 1868.

———. "Les ressources de la France et de la Prusse," *Revue des Deux Mondes*, 89 (1870).

———. *Traité de la science des finances*, 2 vols. Paris: Corbeil, 1877.

Lissagaray, Prosper-Olivier. *Histoire de la Commune de 1871*. Paris: Dentu, 1896.

Lorimer, James. *Of the Denationalisation of Constantinople and its Devotion to International Purposes*. Edinburgh: Edmonston and Douglas, 1876.

———. *The Institutes of the Law of Nations*, 2 vols. Edinburgh: Blackwood, 1883.

Loubon, Joseph. *Alger en 1876*. Marseille: Feissat aîné et Demonchy, 1837.

Lysis, *Contre l'oligarchie financière en France*, 11th edn. Paris: Albin Michel, 1914.

MacCoan, James Carlile. *Consular Jurisdiction in Turkey and Egypt*. London: G. Norman, 1873.

Manby, Charles, ed. *The Judicial Organization in Egypt and its Reform*. London: Spottiswoode and co, 1868.

Marafy, L. Maillard de. *La réforme judiciaire en Egypte devant l'Assemblée nationale*, 2nd edn. Paris: Imprimerie nouvelle, 1875.

Mariette, Auguste. *Exposition universelle de 1867. Aperçu de l'histoire ancienne d'Égypte pour l'intelligence des monuments exposés dans le temple du parc égyptien*. Paris: Dentu, 1867.

Marisy, Alexis Bailleux de. "Mœurs financières de la France, IV: les valeurs orientales," *Revue des Deux Mondes*, 44 (1874).

Marquant, Robert. *Thiers et le baron Cotta. Étude sur la collaboration de Thiers à la Gazette d'Augsbourg*. Paris: Presses Universitaires de France, 1959.

Marx, Karl, and Frederick Engels, *Collected Works*, 50 vols. London: Lawrence and Wishart, 1975–2004.

Mémoire pour M. Tassin de Messilly prévenu d'avoir pratiqué des manœuvres et entretenu des intelligences avec Don Carlos. Paris: Dezauche, 1834.

Mérimée, Prosper. *Lettres à une inconnue*, 2 vols. Paris: Michel Lévy, 1874.

Michiels, Alfred. "La prise d'Alger, raconté par un captif," *Revue contemporaine*, 17 (1854).

Milner, Alfred. *England in Egypt*, 2nd edn. London: Edward Arnold, 1894.

Musso, Pierre, ed. *Le Saint-Simonisme, L'Europe et la Méditerranée*. Houilles: Manucius, 2008.

Napoléon III. *Œuvres de Napoléon III*, 5 vols. Paris: Amyot, 1854–1869.

Panchaud, Isaac. *Réflexions sur l'état actuel du crédit de l'Angleterre et de la France*. N.p., 1781.

Paris-Guide, par les principaux écrivains et artistes de la France, 2 vols. Paris: Librairie internationale, 1867.

Pasha, Nubar. *Mémoires*, ed. Mirrit Boutros Ghali. Beirut: Librairie du Liban, 1983.

Phillimore, Robert. *Commentaries upon International Law*, 4 vols. 3rd edn. London: Butterworth, 1879–1889.

Plaidoyer de Maître Lavaux, dans le procès entre le Sieur Darrac et le Sieur Friedlein. Paris: Porthmann, 1833.

Polignac, Jules de. *Etudes historiques, politiques et européennes*. Paris: Dentu, 1845.

[Pradt, Dominique de.] *Antidote au congrès de Rastadt*. London: the author, 1798.

Pradt, Dominique de. *The Colonies, and the Present American Revolutions*. London: Baldwin, Cradock and Joy, 1817.

———. *Congrès de Carlsbad*, 2 vols. Paris: F. Béchet aîné, 1819–1820.

———. *Congrès de Panama*. Paris: F. Béchet, 1825.

———. *The Congress of Vienna*. London: Samuel Leigh, 1816.

———. *De las Colonias, y de la revolución actual de la America*, 2 vols. Bordeaux: J. Pinard, 1817.

———. *De l'intervention armée pour la pacification de la Grèce*. Paris: Pichon-Béchet, 1828.

———. *Des colonies et de la révolution actuelle de l'Amérique*, 2 vols. Paris: F. Béchet and A. Egron, 1817.

———. *Des trois derniers mois de l'Amérique méridionale et du Brésil*. Paris: F. Béchet, 1817.

———. *Du congrès de Vienne*, 2 vols. Paris: Deterville and Delaunay, 1815.

———. *Examen du plan présenté aux Cortès pour la reconnaissance de l'indépendance de l'Amérique espagnole*. Paris: F. Béchet, 1822.

———. *La Prusse et sa neutralité*. London: the author, 1800.

———. *Les six derniers mois de l'Amérique et du Brésil*. Paris: F. Béchet, 1818.

———. *Les trois âges des colonies; ou, de leur état passé, présent et à venir*, 2 vols. Paris: Giguet, year X [1801].

———. *L'Europe et l'Amérique depuis le congrès d'Aix-la-Chapelle*, 2 vols. Paris: F. Béchet, 1821.

———. *L'Europe et l'Amérique en 1821*, 2 vols. Paris: F. Béchet, 1822.

———. *L'Europe et l'Amérique en 1822 et 1823*, 2 vols. Paris: F. Béchet, 1824.

———. *Parallèle de la puissance anglaise et russe relativement à l'Europe*. Paris: Béchet, 1823.

———. *Petit catéchisme à l'usage des français, sur les affaires de leur pays*. Paris: Béchet aîné, 1820.

———. *Pièces relatives à Saint-Domingue et à l'Amérique*. Paris: F. Béchet, 1818.

Prévost-Paradol, Anatole. *La France nouvelle*. Paris: Perrin, 2012.

Procès instruit contre MM Jauge, Tassin de Messilly, Gabriel Doloret etc. prévenus d'avoir favorisé l'entreprise de Don Carlos contre l'Espagne. Paris: Dezauche, 1834.

Procès-verbaux et rapports de la commission d'Afrique instituée par ordonnance du roi du 12 décembre 1833. Paris: Imprimerie royale, 1834.

Quérard, Joseph-Marie. *Une question d'histoire littéraire résolue. Réfutation du paradoxe bibliographique de M. R. Chantelauze: le comte Joseph de Maistre auteur de l'Antidote au Congrès de Rasdadt*. Paris: the author, 1859.

Raynal, Guillaume-Thomas. *Histoire philosophique et politique des établissements et du commerce des européens dans l'Afrique septentrionale*, ed. Jacques Peuchet, 2 vols. Paris, 1826.

———. *Histoire philosophique et politique des établissements et du commerce des Européens dans les deux Indes*, 6 vols. Amsterdam, 1772.

Rimmel, Eugene. *Recollections of the Paris Exhibition of 1867*. London: Chapman and Hall, 1867.

———. *Souvenirs de l'exposition universelle*. Paris: Dentu, 1868.

Roches, Léon. *Trente-deux ans à travers l'Islam*, 2 vols. Paris: Firmin-Didot, 1884–1885.

R[odrigue], O[linde]. "Considérations sur le Système de Law," *Le Producteur*, 4 (1826).

Say, Jean-Baptiste. *Cours complet d'économie politique pratique*, 6 vols. Paris: Rapilly, 1828–9.

———. *De l'Angleterre et des Anglais*. Paris: Arthus Bertrand, 1815.

———. *Essai historique sur les origines, les progrès et les résultats probables de la souveraineté des Anglais aux Indes*. Paris: Rignoux, 1824.

———. *Olbie, ou Essai sur les moyens de réformer les mœurs d'une nation*. Geneva: Institut Coppet, 2014.

———. *Traité d'économie politique. Édition variorum des six éditions (1803–1814–1817–1819–1826–1841)*, eds. Emmanuel Blanc, Pierre-Henri Goutte, Gilles Jacoud et al., 2 vols. Paris: Economica, 2006.

Senior, Nassau William. *Conversations with Distinguished Persons, During the Second Empire, from 1860 to 1863*, 2 vols. London: Hurst and Blackett, 1880.

Shaler, William. *Esquisse de l'État d'Alger, considéré sous les rapports politique, historique et civil*, trans. Xavier Bianchi. Paris: Ladvocat, 1830.

———. *Sketches of Algiers, Political, Historical, and Civil*. Boston, MA: Cummings, Hilliard and Company, 1826.

Sismondi, Jean-Charles Simonde de. *De l'expédition contre Alger*. Paris: Bureau de la Revue encyclopédique, 1830.

Sraffa, Piero, ed. *The Works and Correspondence of David Ricardo*, 10 vols. Cambridge: Cambridge University Press, 1951–1973.

Stein, Lorenz von. *Lehrbuch der Finanzwissenchaft*. Leipzig: J. A. Brockhaus, 1860.

St John-Stevas, Norman. *The Collected Works of Walter Bagehot*, 9 vols. London: The Economist, 1968.

Talleyrand-Périgord, Charles-Maurice de. *Essai sur les avantages à retirer de colonies nouvelles dans les circonstances présentes*. Paris: Baudouin, Year V [1797].

———. *Mémoires: 1754–1815*, eds. Paul-Louis Couchoud and Jean-Paul Couchoud, 2nd edn. Paris: Plon, 1982.

———. *Mémoires et correspondance du Prince de Talleyrand*, ed. Emmanuel de Waresquiel. Paris: Laffont 2007.

———. *Mémoire sur les relations commerciales des Etats-Unis avec l'Angleterre; suivi d'un essai sur les avantages à retirer de colonies nouvelles dans les circonstances présentes*. London: J. de Boffe, 1808.

Tarde, Gabriel. *Les lois de l'imitation: étude sociologique*. Paris: Félix Alcan, 1890.

[Ternaux, Charles, and Joseph Gandolphe], *Procès pour la république d'Haïti*. Paris: Veuve Porthmann, 1828.

Ternaux, Guillaume-Louis. *Considérations sur l'emprunt d'Haïti*. Paris: Les marchands de nouveautés, 1825.

Thiers, Adolphe. *Histoire de la Révolution française*, 10 vols. Paris: Lecomte et Durey, 1823–1827.

———. *Histoire de Law*. Paris: Michel-Lévy, 1858.

———. *Law, et de son système de finance*. Paris: Bureau de l'encyclopédie progressive, 1826.

Tocqueville, Alexis de. *Œuvres complètes*, ed. Jean-Pierre Mayer et al., 18 vols. (Paris: Gallimard, 1951–2003

———. *Writings on Empire and Slavery*, ed. Jennifer Pitts. Baltimore, MD: Johns Hopkins University Press, 2001.

Tomes, Robert. *The Champagne Country*. New York, NY: Hurd and Houghton, 1867.

Trollope, Anthony. *The Way We Live Now*. London: Penguin, 2000.

[Urbain, Ismaÿl.] *L'Algérie française. Indigènes et immigrants*. Paris: Challamel aîné, 1862.

Urbain, Ismaÿl. *Algérie. Du gouvernement des tribus. Chrétiens et musulmans, Français et Algériens*. Paris: Just-Bouvier, 1848.

———. "De la tolérance dans l'islamisme," *Revue de Paris*, 31, 4 (1856).

———. "Du gouvernement et de l'administration des tribus arabes en Algérie," *Revue de l'Orient et de l'Algérie*, 4, 2 (1847).

———. *Voyage d'Orient; suivi de poèmes de Ménilmontant et d'Égypte*, ed. Philippe Régnier. Paris: L'Harmattan, 1993.

Vizetelly, Henry. *A History of Champagne, with Notes on the Other Sparkling Wines of France*. London: Vizetelly & Co, 1882.

Voisin, Georges [Ismaÿl Urbain]. *L'Algérie pour les Algériens*. Paris: Michel Lévy frères, 1861.

Yver, Georges. *Correspondance du Capitaine Daumas, Consul à Mascara (1837–1839)*. Algiers: Adolphe Jourdan, 1912.

———. *Correspondance du Maréchal Valée, gouverneur des possessions françaises dans le Nord de l'Afrique*, 4 vols. Paris: Larose, 1949–1957.

———. *Documents relatifs au traité de la Tafna: 1837*. Algiers: J. Carbonnel, 1924.

Zola, Émile. *Au Bonheur des Dames* Paris: G. Charpentier, 1883.

———. *The Debacle*, trans. L. W. Tancock. Harmondsworth: Penguin, 1972.

———. *La Débâcle*. Paris: Gallimard, 1984.

———. *L'Argent*. Paris: Gallimard, 1980.

———. "Nos peintres au Champ-de-Mars," *La Situation*, 1 July 1867, repr. in Laurence des Cars, Dominique de Font-Réaulx and Édouard Papet, eds. *Jean-Léon Gérôme (1824–1904). L'histoire en spectacle*. Paris: Flammarion, 2010.

Secondary Sources

Abi-Mershed, Osama W. *Apostles of Modernity: Saint-Simonians and the Civilizing Mission in Algeria*. Stanford, CA: Stanford University Press, 2010.

Abu-Lughod, Ibrahim. *The Arab Rediscovery of Europe: A Study in Cultural Encounters*, 2nd edn. Princeton, NJ: Princeton University Press, 2011.

Abun-Nasr, Jamil M. *A History of the Maghrib in the Islamic Period*. Cambridge: Cambridge University Press, 1987.

Adelman, Jeremy. "An Age of Imperial Revolutions," *American Historical Review*, 113, 2 (2008).

———. "Introduction," in Jeremy Adelman, ed. *Empire and the Social Sciences: Global Histories of Knowledge*. New York: Bloomsbury, 2019.

———. *The Republic of Capital: Buenos Aires and the Legal Transformation of the Atlantic World*. Stanford: Stanford University Press, 1999.

———. *Sovereignty and Revolution in the Iberian Atlantic*. Princeton, NJ: Princeton University Press, 2006.

Ageorges, Sylvie. *Sur les traces des expositions universelles*. Paris: Parigramme, 2006.

Ageron, Charles-Robert. "Charles-André Julien (1891–1991)," *Revue française d'histoire d'outre-mer*, 79, 296 (1992).

——. "Gambetta et la reprise de l'expansion coloniale," *Outre-Mers*, 215 (1972).

——. *Histoire de l'Algérie contemporaine*, 8th edn. Paris: Presses Universitaires de France, 1983.

——. *Le gouvernement du general Berthezène à Alger en 1831*. Saint-Denis: Bouchène, 2005.

——. *Les Algériens musulmans et la France, 1871–1918*, 2nd edn., 2 vols. Saint-Denis: Bouchene, 2005.

——. *Modern Algeria: A History from 1830 to the Present*, trans. Michael Brett. London: Hurst & Co, 1991.

Aglan, Alya, Michel Margairaz and Philippe Verheyde, eds. *1816 ou la genèse de la foi publique: la fondation de la Caisse des dépôts et consignations*. Geneva: Droz, 2006.

Al-Asad, Muhammad. "The Mosque of Muhammad 'Ali in Cairo," *Muqarnas*, 9 (1992).

Aldrich, Robert. *Greater France: A History of French Overseas Expansion*. Basingstoke, UK: Palgrave, 1996.

Alff, Kristen. "Levantine Joint-Stock Companies, Trans-Mediterranean Partnerships, and Nineteenth-Century Capitalist Development," *Comparative Studies in Society and History*, 60, 1 (2018).

Allen, Frederick. *Secret Formula: How Brilliant Marketing and Relentless Salesmanship Made Coca-Cola the Best-Known Product in the World*. New York: Harper Business, 1994.

Amrith, Sunil. "Empires, Diasporas, and Cultural Circulation," in Andrew Thompson, ed. *Writing Imperial Histories*. Manchester: Manchester University Press, 2013.

Andrew, Christopher M. "The French Colonialist Movement during the Third Republic: The Unofficial Mind of Imperialism," *Transactions of the Royal Historical Society*, 26 (1976).

Appadurai, Arjun. "Introduction: Commodities and the Politics of Value," in Arjun Appadurai, ed. *The Social Life of Things: Commodities in Cultural Perspective*, 2nd edn. Cambridge: Cambridge University Press, 2013.

Arboit, Gabriel. "L'arme financière dans les relations internationales: l'affaire Ceruschi sous le Second Empire," *Revue d'histoire moderne et contemporaine*, 46, 3 (1999).

Arboit, Gérald. *Aux sources de la politique arabe de la France. Le Second Empire au Machrek*. Paris: L'Harmattan, 2000.

Armitage, David. *Foundations of Modern International Thought*. Cambridge: Cambridge University Press, 2013.

Armitage, David, and Sanjay Subrahmanyam, eds. *The Age of Revolutions in Global Context, c. 1760–1840*. Houndmills: Palgrave Macmillan, 2010.

Aron, Raymond. *Guerre et paix entre les nations*. Paris: Calman-Levy, 1962.

Arsan, Andrew. "'There is, in the Heart of Asia . . . an Entirely French Population': France, Mount Lebanon, and the Workings of Affective Empire in the Mediterranean, 1830–1920," in Patricia M. E. Lorcin and Todd Shepard, eds. *French Mediterraneans: Transnational and Imperial Histories*. Lincoln: University of Nebraska Press, 2016.

Atkins, Richard A. "The Origins of the Anglo-French Condominium in Egypt, 1875–1876," *Historian*, 36 (1974).

Atkinson, Juliette. *French Novels and the Victorians*. Oxford: Oxford University Press, 2017.

Auerbach, Jeffrey A. *The Great Exhibition of 1851: A Nation on Display*. New Haven, CT: Yale University Press, 1999.

Auriant [Alexandre Hadjivassiliou], *François Bravay, ou le nabab*. Paris: Mercure de France, 1943.

Auslander, Leona. "The Gendering of Consumer Practices in Nineteenth-Century France," in Victoria de Grazia and Ellen Furlough, eds. *The Sex of Things: Gender and Consumption in Historical Perspective*. Berkeley: University of California Press, 1996.

Autheman, André. *La Banque Impériale Ottomane*. Paris: Comité pour l'histoire économique et financière de la France, 1996.

Azza, Heikel. *L'Égypte illustrée par les peintres du XIXe siècle*. Cairo: Max Group, 2000.

Baillou, Jean, Charles Lucet and Jacques Vimont, *Les Affaires Étrangères et le corps diplomatique français*, 2 vols. Paris: CNRS, 1984.

Baines, Dudley. *Emigration from Europe, 1815–1930*. Basingstoke: Macmillan, 1991.

Bairoch, Paul. *Commerce extérieur et développement économique de l'Europe au XIXe siècle*. Paris: Mouton and EHESS, 1976.

Ballot, Charles. *L'introduction du machinisme dans l'industrie française*. Lille: Marquant & Paris: Rieder, 1923.

Bancarel, Gilles. *Raynal et ses réseaux*. Paris: Honoré Champion, 2011.

———. *Raynal ou le devoir de vérité*. Paris: Honoré Champion, 2004.

Barbier, Frédéric. "Les marchés étrangers de la librairie française," in Roger Chartier and Henri-Jean Martin, eds. *Histoire de l'édition française*, 4 vols. (Paris: Fayard, 1982–1986), vol. 3: *Le temps des éditeurs. Du romantisme à la Belle Époque*.

Barker, Nancy Nichols. *The French Experience in Mexico 1821–1861: A History of Constant Misunderstanding*. Chapel Hill: University of North Carolina Press, 1979.

Barkey, Karen. "Aspects of Legal Pluralism in the Ottoman Empire," in Lauren Benton and Richard J. Ross, eds. *Legal Pluralism and Empires, 1500–1850*. New York: New York University Press, 2013.

Barnhart, Russell T. "Gambling in Revolutionary Paris: The Palais Royal: 1789–1838," *Journal of Gambling Studies*, 8, 2 (1992).

Barth, Volker. "Paris, 1867," in *Encyclopedia of World's Fairs and Expositions*. Jefferson, NC: McFarland, 2008.

Bartolomei, Arnaud, Guillaume Calafat, Mathieu Grenet and Jörg Ulbert, eds. *De l'utilité commerciale des consuls. L'institution consulaire et les marchands dans le monde méditerranéen (XVIIe-XXe siècle)*. Rome and Madrid: École française de Rome and Casa Velasquez, 2018.

Bat, Jean-Pierre, *Le syndrome Foccart: La politique française en Afrique, de 1959 à nos jours*. Paris: Gallimard, 2012.

Bates, Darrell. *The Fashoda Incident of 1898: Encounter on the Nile*. Oxford: Oxford University Press, 1984.

Battesti, Michèle. *La marine de Napoléon III: une politique navale*, 2 vols. Chambéry and Vincennes: Université de Savoie and Service Historique de la Marine, 1997.

Bayly, Christopher A. *The Birth of the Modern World: Global Connections and Comparisons, 1780–1914*. Oxford: Blackwell, 2004.

———. "The First Age of Global Imperialism, c. 1760–1830," *Journal of Imperial and Commonwealth History*, 26, 2 (1998).

Beauvois, Frédérique. "L'indemnité de Saint-Domingue: 'Dette d'indépendance' ou 'rançon de l'esclavage'?," *French Colonial History*, 10, 1 (2009).

———. "Monnayer l'incalculable? L'indemnité de Saint-Domingue, entre approximations et bricolage," *Revue historique*, 655 (2010).

Beckert, Sven. "American Danger, United States Empire, Eurafrica and the Territorialization of Industrial Capitalism," *American Historical Review*, 122, 4 (2017).

———. *Empire of Cotton: A New History of Global Capitalism.* London: Allen Lane, 2014.

Belfanti, Carlo Marco. *Histoire culturelle de la mode.* Paris: Institut français de la mode, 2014.

Belich, James. *Replenishing the Earth: The Settler Revolution and the Rise of the Anglo-World, 1783–1939.* Oxford: Oxford University Press, 2009.

Bell, David. "Questioning the Global Turn: The Case of the French Revolution," *French Historical Studies*, 37, 1 (2014).

Bell, Duncan. *The Idea of Greater Britain: Empire and the Future of the World Order, 1860–1900.* Princeton, NJ: Princeton University Press, 2007.

———. *Reordering the World: Essays on Liberalism and Empire.* Princeton, NJ: Princeton University Press, 2016.

———. "What Is Liberalism?," *Political Theory*, 42, 6 (2014).

Bénichou, Pierre. *Le Temps des Prophètes. Doctrines de l'âge romantique.* Paris: Gallimard, 1977.

Benjamin, Walter. *The Arcades Project,* trans. Howard Eiland and Kevin McLaughlin. Cambridge, MA: Belknapp Press, 1999.

Benot, Yves. *Les Lumières, l'esclavage, la colonisation.* Paris: La découverte, 2005.

Benton, Lauren. *Law and Colonial Culture: Legal Regimes in World History, 1400–1900.* Cambridge: Cambridge University Press, 2002.

Benton, Lauren, Adam Clulow and Bain Attwood, eds. *Protection and Empire: A Global History.* Cambridge: Cambridge University Press, 2018.

Benton, Lauren, and Lisa Ford. *Rage for Order: The British Empire and the Origins of International Law, 1800–1850.* Cambridge, MA: Harvard University Press, 2016.

Bergeron, Louis. *Les industries du luxe en France.* Paris: Odile Jacob, 1998.

Bernard, Augustin. *L'Algérie* in Gabriel Hanotaux and Alfred Martineau, eds. *Histoire des colonies françaises et de l'expansion de la France dans le monde.* 6 vols. Paris: Société de l'histoire nationale et Librairie Plon, 1929–1934.

Berry, Christopher J. *The Idea of Luxury: A Conceptual and Historical Investigation.* Cambridge: Cambridge University Press, 1994.

Betts, R. F. *Assimilation and Association in French Colonial Theory, 1890–1914.* New York: Columbia University Press, 1961.

Bew, John. *Realpolitik: A History.* Oxford: Oxford University Press, 2016.

Biagini, Eugenio. *Liberty, Retrenchment and Reform: Popular Liberalism in the Age of Gladstone.* Cambridge: Cambridge University Press, 1992.

Bickers, Robert, ed. *Settlers and Expatriates: Britons over the Seas.* Oxford: Oxford University Press, 2010.

Birdal, Murat. *The Political Economy of Ottoman Public Debt.* London: Tauris, 2010.

Blais, Hélène. *Mirages de la carte: l'invention de l'Algérie coloniale.* Paris: Fayard, 2014.

———. "Qu'est-ce qu'Alger? Le débat colonial sous la Monarchie de Juillet," *Romantisme*, 139 (2008).

Blanchard, Pascal, Sandrine Lemaire and Nicolas Bancel, eds. *Culture coloniale en France: de la Révolution française à nos jours.* Paris: CNRS, 2008.

Blancpain, Jacques. *Un siècle de relations financières entre Haïti et la France: 1825–1922*. Paris: L'Harmattan, 2001.

Blaney, David L. "Reconceptualizing Autonomy: The Difference Dependency Theory Makes," *Review of International Political Economy*, 3, 3 (1996).

Blanning, Timothy. *The Origins of the French Revolutionary Wars*. London: Longman, 1986.

Blaufarb, Rafe. "The Western Question: The Geopolitics of Latin American Independence," *American Historical Review*, 112, 3 (2007).

Bobrie, François. "Finances publiques et conquête coloniale: le coût budgétaire de l'expansion française entre 1850 et 1913," *Annales. Économies, sociétés, civilisations*, 31, 6 (1976).

Bonneville, François. "Le Baron Louis (1755–1837): Portait d'un financier au service de l'État," *Revue française de finances publiques*, 128 (2014).

Bonney, Richard. "The Apogee and Fall of the French Rentier Regime, 1801–1914," in José Luis Cardoso and Peter Lains, eds. *Paying for the Liberal State: The Rise of Public Finance in Nineteenth-Century Europe*. Cambridge: Cambridge University Press, 2010.

Bonney, Richard. "The Rise of the Fiscal State in France, 1500–1914," in Bartolome Yun-Casalilla and Patrick O'Brien, eds. *The Rise of Fiscal States: A Global History, 1500–1914*. New York: Cambridge University Press, 2012.

Boogert, Maurits H van der. *The Capitulations and the Ottoman Legal System: Qadis, Consuls, and Beratıs in the Eighteenth Century*. Leiden: Brill, 2005.

Bornholt, Laura. "The Abbé de Pradt and the Monroe Doctrine," *Hispanic American Historical Review*, 24, 2 (1944).

Bossenga, Gail. "Financial Origins of the French Revolution," in Thomas E. Kaiser and Dale K. Van Kley, eds. *From Deficit to Deluge: The Origins of the French Revolution*. Stanford, CA: Stanford University Press, 2011.

Bouche, Denise, and Pierre Pluchon, *Histoire de la colonisation française*, 2 vols. Paris: Fayard, 1991.

Bouchène, Abderrahmane, Jean-Pierre Peyroulou, Ouanassa Siari Tengour and Sylvie Thénault, eds. *Histoire de l'Algérie à la période coloniale*. Paris: La Découverte, 2014.

Bourdin, Philippe, ed. *Les noblesses françaises dans l'Europe de la Révolution*. Rennes: Presses Universitaires de Rennes, 2010.

Bouveresse, Jacques. *Un parlement colonial? Les délégations financières algériennes (1898–1945)*. Mont Saint-Aignan: Publications des universités de Rouen et du Havre, 2008.

Bouvier, Jean. *Le Crédit Lyonnais de 1863 à 1882. Les années de formation d'une banque de dépôts*, 2 vols. Paris: SEVPEN, 1961.

———. "Les intérêts financiers et la question d'Égypte," *Revue historique*, 224 (1960).

Bouvier, Jean, and René Girault. *L'impérialisme à la française, 1914–1960*. Paris: La Découverte, 1986.

Bowden, Brett. *The Empire of Civilization: The Evolution of an Imperial Idea*. Chicago: University of Chicago Press, 2009.

Braudel, Fernand. "Gabriel Esquer (1876–1961)," *Annales. Économies, Sociétés, Civilisations*, 18, 3 (1963).

Braudel, Fernand, and Ernest Labrousse, eds. *Histoire économique et sociale de la France*, 2nd edn., 5 vols. Paris: Presses Universitaires de France, 1993.

Brewer, John. *The Sinews of Power: War, Money and the English State, 1688–1783*. London: Unwin Hyman, 1989.

Brière, Jean-François. *Haïti et la France, 1804–1848: le rêve brisé*. Paris: Karthala, 2008.

Brinton, Jasper Y. *The Mixed Courts of Egypt*, 2nd ed. New Haven, CT: Yale University Press, 1968.

Briot, Eugénie. *La fabrique des parfums. Naissance d'une industrie de luxe*. Paris: Véndémiaire, 2015.

Broder, André. "Le commerce extérieur: l'échec de la conquête d'une position internationale," in Fernand Braudel and Ernest Labrousse, eds. *Histoire économique et sociale de la France*, vol. 3: *1789-années 1880: l'avènement de l'ère industrielle*.

Brombert, Beth Archer. *Édouard Manet: Rebel in a Frock Coat*. Boston: Little, Brown, 1996.

Brower, Benjamin C. *A Desert Named Peace: The Violence of France's Empire in the Algerian Sahara, 1844–1902*. New York: Columbia University Press, 2009.

Brown, Matthew, ed. *Informal Empire in Latin America: Culture, Commerce and Capital*. Oxford: Blackwell, 2008.

Brown, Matthew, and Gabriel Paquette, eds. *Connections after Colonialism: Europe and Latin America*. Tuscaloosa: University of Alabama Press, 2013.

Brown, Nathan J. "Who Abolished Corvée Labour in Egypt and Why?," *Past & Present*, 144 (1994).

Brunschwig, Henri. *Le partage de l'Afrique noire*, 2nd edn. Paris: Flammarion, 2009.

———. *Mythes et réalités de l'impérialisme colonial français, 1871–1914*. Paris: Armand Colin, 1960.

Burbank, Jane, and Frederick Cooper, *Empires in World History: Power and the Politics of Difference*. Princeton, NJ: Princeton University Press, 2010.

Burrows, Matthew. "'Mission civilisatrice': French Cultural Policy in the Middle-East, 1860–1914," *Historical Journal*, 29, 1 (1986).

Burrows, Simon. *French Exile Journalism and European Politics*. Woodbridge: The Royal Historical Society, 2000.

Burton, Anthony. *Vision & Accident: The Story of the Victoria and Albert Museum*. London: Victoria & Albert Publications, 1999.

Byrde, Penelope. "Dress: The Industrial Revolution and After," in David Jenkins, ed. *The Cambridge History of Western Textiles*, 2 vols. Cambridge: Cambridge University Press, 2003, vol. 2.

———. *Nineteenth-Century Fashion*. London: Batsford, 1992.

Cahiers d'histoire, 7, 2 (1962). Special issue on Pradt.

Cain, Peter, and Anthony G. Hopkins, *British Imperialism, 1688–2015*, 2nd edn. Harlow: Pearsons, 2002.

Calafat, Guillaume. *Une mer jalousée: contribution à l'histoire de la souveraineté, Méditerranée, XVIIe siècle*. Paris: Le Seuil, 2019.

Collot, Gélin. "Le Code civil haïtien et son histoire," in Jean-François Niort, ed. *Du Code Noir au Code Civil*. Paris: L'Harmattan, 2005.

Cameron, Rondo. *France and the Economic Development of Europe, 1800–1914*, 2nd edn. London: Routledge, 2000.

Cannon, Byron. *Politics of Law and the Courts of Nineteenth-Century Egypt*. Salt Lake City: University of Utah Press, 1988.

Caquet, Pierre. "The Napoleonic Legend and the War Scare of 1840," *International History Review*, 35, 4 (2013).

————. *The Orient, the Liberal Movement, and the Eastern Crisis of 1839–1841*. Basingstoke: Palgrave-MacMillan, 2016.

Carlisle, Robert B. *The Proffered Crown: Saint-Simonianism and the Doctrine of Hope*. Baltimore, MD: Johns Hopkins University Press, 1987.

Carré, Anne-Laure, Marie-Sophie Corcy and Christiane Demeulenaere-Douyère, eds. *Les expositions universelles en France au XIXe siècle: techniques, publics, patrimoines*. Paris: CNRS, 2012.

Carroll, Christina. "Imperial Ideologies in the Second Empire: The Mexican Expedition and the *Royaume Arabe*," *French Historical Studies*, 42, 1 (2019).

Cars, Laurence des, Dominique de Font-Réaulx and Édouard Papet, eds. *Jean-Léon Gérôme (1824–1904). L'histoire en spectacle*. Paris: Flammarion, 2010.

Casanova, Pascale. *La république mondiale des lettres*. Paris: Le Seuil, 1999.

Cassel, Pär Kristoffer. *Grounds of Judgment: Extraterritoriality and Imperial Power in Nineteenth-Century China and Japan*. Oxford: Oxford University Press, 2012.

Cassis, Youssef. *Capitals of Capital: A History of International Financial Centres, 1780–2005*. Cambridge: Cambridge University Press, 2006.

Cayez, Pierre. *Crise et croissance de l'industrie lyonnaise*. Paris: CNRS, 1980.

————. *Metiers Jacquard et hauts fourneaux: aux origines de l'industrie lyonnaise*. Lyon: Presses universitaires de Lyon, 1978.

Certeau, Michel de, Dominique Julia and Jacques Revel, *Une politique de la langue. La Révolution française et les patois: l'enquête de Grégoire*. Paris: Gallimard, 1975.

Chadeau, Emmanuel. *Les inspecteurs des finances au XIXe siècle (1850–1914). Profil social et rôle économique*. Paris: Economica, 1986.

Chafer, Tony, and Alexander Keese, eds. *Francophone Africa at Fifty*. Manchester: Manchester University Press, 2013.

Champavier, Maurice. *Félix Clément, peintre d'histoire*. Paris: Fischbacher, 1889.

Chandler, Arthur. "The Paris Exposition Universelle, 1867: Empire of Autumn," *World's Fair*, 6, 2 (1986).

Chang, Richard T. *The Justice of the Western Consular Courts in Nineteenth-Century Japan*. Westport, CT: Greenwood Press, 1984.

Charbit, Yves. *Du malthusianisme au populationnisme: les économistes français et la population*. Paris: Presses universitaires de France, 1981.

Charle, Christophe. *Théâtres en capitales: naissance de la société du spectacle à Paris, Berlin, Londres et Vienne, 1860–1914*. Paris: Albin Michel, 2008.

Charles-Roux, François. *France et Afrique du Nord avant 1830. Les précurseurs de la conquête*. Paris: Félix Alcan, 1932.

Charles-Roux, François. *La production du coton en Egypte*. Paris: Armand Colin, 1908.

————. *L'Égypte de 1801 à 1882. Mohamed Aly et sa dynastie jusqu'à l'occupation anglaise*. Paris: Plon, 1936.

Cheney, Paul. *Cul de Sac: Patrimony, Capitalism, and Slavery in French Saint-Domingue*. Chicago: University of Chicago Press, 2017.

Chevallier, Dominique. "Lyon et la Syrie. Les bases d'une intervention," *Revue historique*, 224 (1960).

Christen, Carole, and François Vatin, eds. *Charles Dupin (1784–1873). Ingénieur, savant, économiste, pédagogue et parlementaire du Premier au Second Empire*. Rennes: Presses universitaires de Rennes, 2009.

Christopher, Anthony J. "A South African Domesday Book: The First Union Census of 1911," *South African Geographical Journal*, 92, 1 (2010).

Churchman, Nancy. *David Ricardo on Public Debt*. Basingstoke: Palgrave, 2001.

Clancy-Smith, Julia A. *Mediterraneans: North Africa and Europe in an Age of Migration, c. 1800–1900*. Berkeley: University of California Press, 2011.

Clark, Christopher. "After 1848: the European Revolution in Government," *Transactions of the Royal Historical Society*, 22 (2012).

———. *The Sleepwalkers: How Europe Went to War in 1914*. London: Allen Lane, 2012.

Clark, Timothy James. *The Painting of Modern Life: Paris in the Art of Manet and His Followers*. London: Thames and Hudson, 1984.

Clay, Christopher. *Gold for the Sultan: Western Bankers and Ottoman Finance, 1856–1881*. London: Tauris, 2000.

Cohen, Deborah. "Love and Money in the Informal Empire in Argentina," *Past & Present*, 245 (2019).

Cole, Juan R. I. *Colonialism and Revolution in the Middle East: Social and Cultural Origins of 'Urabi's Movement*. Princeton, NJ: Princeton University Press, 1993.

Coller, Ian. "The Republic of Marseille and the Making of Imperial France," in Philip Whalen and Patrick Young, eds. *Place and Locality in Modern France*. London: Bloomsbury, 2014.

Conklin, Alice. *A Mission to Civilize: The Republican Idea of Empire in West Africa, 1895–1930*. Stanford, CA: Stanford University Press, 1997.

Cooper, Duff. *Talleyrand*. London: Penguin, 2010.

Cooper, Frederick. "Alternatives to Empire: France and Africa after World War II," in Douglas Howland and Luise White, eds. *The State of Sovereignty: Territories, Laws, Populations*. Bloomington: Indiana University Press, 2009.

———. *Citizenship between Empire and Nation: Remaking France and French West Africa, 1945–1960*. Princeton, NJ: Princeton University Press, 2014.

Coquery, Natacha. "Luxury and Revolution: Selling High-Status Garments in Revolutionary France," in Jon Stobart and Bruno Blondé, eds. *Selling Textiles in the Long Eighteenth Century: Comparative Perspectives from Western Europe*. Basingstoke: Palgrave MacMillan, 2014.

———. *Tenir boutique à Paris au XVIIIe siècle: Luxe et demi luxe*. Paris: Édition du Comité des travaux historiques et scientifiques, 2011.

Coquery-Vidrovitch, Catherine, Jean Meyer, Jacques Thobie, et al., *Histoire de la France coloniale*, 2nd edn., 3 vols. Paris: A. Colin, 1996.

Corbin, Alain. *Les filles de noce: misère sexuelle et prostitution, XIXe siècle*, 2nd edn. Paris: Flammarion, 2015.

Coste, Clément. "L'économique contre le politique: la dette, son amortissement et son financement chez de jeunes et vieux Saint-Simoniens (1825–1880)," *Cahiers d'économie politique*, 70, 1 (2016).

Costeloe, Michael P. *Bonds and Bondholders: British Investors and Mexico's Foreign Debt, 1824–1888*. Westport, CT: Praeger, 2003.

Cottereau, Alain. "The Fate of Collective Manufactures in the Industrial World: The Silk Industries of Lyons and London, 1800–1850," in Charles Sabel and Jonathan Zeitlin, eds. *World of Possibilities: Flexibility and Mass Production in Western Industrialization*. Cambridge: Cambridge University Press, 1997.

Cottrell, Philip L., ed. *East Meets West: Banking, Commerce and Investment in the Ottoman Empire*. Aldershot: Ashgate, 2008.

———. "La cooperation financière franco-anglaise, 1850–1880," in Maurice Lévy-Leboyer, ed. *La position internationale de la France. Aspects économiques et financiers*. Paris: EHESS, 1977.

Courtney, Cecil P., and Jenny Mander, eds. *Raynal's Histoire des Deux Indes: Colonialism, Networks and Global Exchange*. Oxford: Voltaire Foundation, 2015.

Courtois, Alphonse. *Notice sur la vie et les travaux de Michel Chevalier*. Paris: Guillaumin, 1889.

Crabitès, Pierre. *Ismail the Maligned*. London: George Routledge & Sons, 1933.

Crossick Geoffrey, and Serge Jaumain, eds. *Cathedrals of Consumption: The European Department Store*. Aldershot: Ashgate, 1998.

Crouzet, François. "Angleterre et France au XVIIIe siècle: analyse comparée de deux croissances économiques," *Annales. Économies, Sociétés, Civilisations*, 21, 2 (1966).

———. *Britain Ascendant: Comparative Studies in Franco-British Economic History*. Cambridge: Cambridge University Press, 1990.

———. "The Historiography of French Economic Growth in the Nineteenth Century," *Economic History Review*, 56, 2 (2003).

———. "The Second Hundred Years War: Some Reflections," *French History*, 10, 4 (1996).

———. "Wars, Blockade, and Economic Change in Europe, 1792–1815," *Journal of Economic History*, 24, 4 (1964).

Crouzet, François, and Jean-Pierre Dormois, "The Significance of the French Colonial Empire for French Economic Development (1815–1960)," *Revista de historia económica*, 16, 1 (1998).

Crowston, Claire Haru. *Credit, Fashion, Sex: Economies of Regard in Old Regime France*. Durham, NC: Duke University Press, 2013.

Cubitt, Geoffrey. "The Political Uses of Seventeenth-Century English History in Bourbon Restoration France," *Historical Journal*, 50, 1 (2007).

Cunningham, Michelle. *Mexico and the Foreign Policy of Napoleon III*. Basingstoke: Palgrave, 2001.

Curtin, Philip D. *Cross-Cultural Trade in World History*. Cambridge: Cambridge University Press, 1984.

Dakhlia, Jocelyn. *Lingua Franca. Histoire d'une langue en Méditerranée*. Arles: Actes Sud, 2008.

Daly, M. W. ed., *The Cambridge History of Egypt*. 2 vols. Cambridge: Cambridge University Press, 1998.

Danziger, Raphael. *Abd al-Qadir and the Algerians: Resistance to the French and Internal Consolidation*. New York: Homes & Meier, 1977.

Darwin, John. "Imperialism and the Victorians: The Dynamics of Territorial Expansion," *English Historical Review*, 112, 447 (1997).

Darwin, John. *The Empire Project: The Rise and Fall of the British World-System, 1830–1970*. Cambridge: Cambridge University Press, 2009.

Da Silveira, Piedade. *Le magasin de nouveautés "A la ville de Paris"*. Fontenay-sous-Bois: Caisse de retraites des entreprises à commerces multiples, 1994.

———. *Le magasin de nouveautés "Aux Deux Magots"*. Fontenay-sous-Bois: Caisse de retraites des entreprises à commerces multiples, 1993.

Daudin, Guillaume. *Commerce et prospérité: la France au XVIIIe siècle*. Paris: Presses de l'université Paris-Sorbonne, 2005.

Daughton, J. P. "When Argentina Was 'French': Rethinking Cultural Politics and European Imperialism in Belle-Époque Buenos Aires," *Journal of Modern History*, 80, 4 (2008).

Daumard, Adeline. *Les fortunes françaises au XIXe siècle. Enquête sur la répartition et la composition des capitaux privés à Paris, Lyon, Lille, Bordeaux et Toulouse.* Paris: Mouton, 1973.

Daunton, Martin. *Trusting Leviathan: The Politics of Taxation in Britain, 1799–1914.* Cambridge: Cambridge University Press, 2001.

Davis, Diana K., *Resurrecting the Granary of Rome: Environmental History and French Colonial Expansion in North Africa.* Athens: Ohio University Press, 2007.

Davis, Lance E., and Robert A. Huttenback, *Mammon and the Pursuit of Empire: The Political Economy of British Imperialism, 1860–1912.* Cambridge: Cambridge University Press, 1986.

Dawson, Frank G. *The First Latin American Debt Crisis: The City of London and the 1822–25 Loan Bubble.* New Haven, CT: Yale University Press, 1990.

Degros, Maurice. "Les créations de postes diplomatiques et consulaires français de 1815 à 1870," *Revue d'histoire diplomatique,* 100, 3–4 (1986).

Dejung, Christof, David Motadel and Jürgen Osterhammel, eds. *The Global Bourgeoisie: The Rise of the Middle Classes in the Age of Empire.* Princeton, NJ: Princeton University Press, 2019.

Delorme, Jean-Calude, and Anne-Marie Dubois, *Passages couverts parisiens,* 2nd edn. Paris: Parigramme, 2014.

Deluermoz, Quentin. *Commune(s), 1870–1871. Une traversée des mondes au XIXe siècle.* Paris: Le Seuil, forthcoming in October 2020.

———. *Le crépuscule des revolutions, 1848–1871.* Paris: Le Seuil, 2012.

———. "The Worlds of 1871," in David Motadel, ed. *The Global History of Revolution.* Cambridge: Cambridge University Press, forthcoming.

Démier, Francis. *La France de la Restauration (1814–1830). L'impossible retour du passé.* Paris: Gallimard, 2012.

Démier, Francis. "Du luxe au demi-luxe, la réussite des bronziers parisiens au XIXe siècle," in Jacques Marseille, ed. *Le luxe en France: du siècle des "Lumières" à nos jours.* Paris: Association pour le développement de l'histoire économique, 1999.

Desan, Suzanne, Lynn Hunt and William Nelson, eds. *The French Revolution in Global Perspective.* Ithaca, NY: Cornell University Press, 2013.

Desbois-Thibault, Claire. *L'extraordinaire aventure du Champagne: Moët et Chandon, une affaire de famille, 1792–1914.* Paris: Presses Universitaires de France, 2003.

Desbois-Thibault, Claire, Werner Paravicini and Jean-Pierre Poussou, eds. *Le champagne: une histoire franco-allemande.* Paris: PUPS, 2011.

Dome, Takuo. *The Political Economy of Public Finance in Britain 1767–1873.* London: Routledge, 2004.

Dormois, Jean-Pierre. *L'économie française face à la concurrence britannique à la veille de 1914.* Paris: L'Harmattan, 1997.

Dornel, Laurent, ed. *Des Pyrénées à la Pampa: une histoire de l'émigration d'élites, XIXe-XXe siècles.* Pau: PUPPA, 2013.

Dousset, Émile. *Abbé de Pradt, grand aumônier de Napoléon, 1759–1837.* Rennes: Nouvelles éditions latines, 1959.

Doyle, Michael. *Empires.* Ithaca, NY: Cornell University Press, 1986.

Drayton, Richard. *Nature's Government: Science, Imperial Britain and the Improvement of the World.* New Haven, CT: Yale University Press, 2000.

Drescher, Seymour. "British Way, French Way: Opinion Building and Revolution in the Second French Slave Emancipation," *American Historical Review,* 96, 3 (1991).

Drolet, Michael. "Carrying the Banner of the Bourgeoisie: Democracy, Self and the Philosophical Foundations to François Guizot's Historical and Political Thought," *History of Political Thought*, 32, 4 (2011).

———. "Industry, Class and Society: A Historiographic Reinterpretation of Michel Chevalier," *English Historical Review*, 123, 504 (2008).

———. "A Nineteenth-Century Mediterranean Union: Michel Chevalier's *Système de la Méditerranée*," *Mediterranean Historical Review*, 30, 2 (2015).

Dubois, Laurent. *Avengers of the New World: The Story of the Haitian Revolution*. Cambridge, MA: Belknap, 2004.

———. *Haiti: The Aftershocks of History*. New York: Metropolitan Books, 2012.

Dugast, Alain. *La tentation mexicaine en France au XIXe siècle: L'image du Mexique et l'Intervention française*, 2 vols. Paris: L'Harmattan, 2008.

Dunham, Arthur L. *The Anglo-French Treaty of Commerce and the Industrial Revolution in France*. Ann Arbor: University of Michigan Press, 1930.

Dupuis, Danielle. "*César Birotteau*: de la publicité à la littérature," *L'année balzacienne*, 9, 1 (2008).

Durant, Susan S. "Cavalier Myth," in Charles R. Wilson, James G. Thomas Jr. and Ann J. Abadie, eds. *The New Encyclopedia of Southern Culture*, 19 vols. Chapel Hill: University of North Carolina Press, 2006, vol 4: *Myth, Manners and Memory*.

Duroselle, Jean-Baptiste. "Michel Chevalier et le libre-échange avant 1860," *Bulletin de la société d'histoire moderne*, 5 (1956).

———. *Tout empire périra: une vision théorique des relations internationales*. Paris: Université Paris 1, 1982.

Dwyer, Philip G. *Talleyrand*. London: Routledge, 2016.

Edison, Paul N. "Conquest Unrequited: French Expeditionary Science in Mexico, 1864–1867," *French Historical Studies*, 26, 3 (2003).

Einaudi, Luca. *Money and Politics: European Monetary Unification and the International Gold Standard (1865–1873)*. Oxford: Oxford University Press, 2001.

Eldem, Edhem. *A History of the Ottoman Bank*. Istanbul: Ottoman Bank Historical Research Center, 1999.

Emerit, Marcel. "La crise syrienne et l'expansion économique francaise en 1860," *Revue historique*, 207 (1952).

———. *L'Algérie à l'époque d'Abd el-Kader*. Paris: Bouchène, 2002.

———. *Les Saint-Simoniens en Algérie*. Paris: Les belles lettres, 1941.

Eng, Robert Y. *Economic Imperialism in China: Silk Production and Exports, 1861–1932*. Berkeley: University of California, 1985.

Esquer, Gabriel. *Les commencements d'un empire. La prise d'Alger. 1830*. Algiers: L'Afrique latine, 1923.

Essinger, James. *Jacquard's Web: How a Hand-loom Led to the Birth of the Information Age*. Oxford: Oxford University Press, 2004.

Esteves, Rui. "The Belle Époque of International Finance: French Capital Exports 1880–1914," Department of Economics Discussion Paper Series, 534, University of Oxford, 2011.

Etherington, Norman. *Theories of Imperialism: War, Conquest and Capital*. London: Croom Helm, 1984.

Etienne, Michel. *Veuve Clicquot Ponsardin: aux origines d'un grand vin de Champagne*. Paris: Économica, 1994.

Faber, Karl-Georg. "Aristokratie und Finanz. Das Pariser Bankhaus Paravey et Compagnie (1819–1828)," *Vierteljahrschrift für Sozial- und Wirtschaftsgeschichte*, 57, 2 (1970).

Fabre, Sylvie. *Le sacre du Roquefort: l'émergence d'une industrie agroalimentaire*. Rennes: Presses universitaires de Rennes and Tours: Presses universitaires François Rabelais de Tours, 2015.

Fahmy, Khaled. *All the Pasha's Men: Mehmed Ali, His Army and the Making of Modern Egypt*. Cairo: American University in Cairo Press, 1997.

———. "The Era of Muhammad 'Ali Pasha," in M. W. Daly, ed., *The Cambridge History of Egypt*. 2 vols. Cambridge: Cambridge University Press, 1998.

Fahmy, Ziad. "Jurisdictional Borderlands: Extraterritoriality and 'Legal Chameleons' in Precolonial Alexandria, 1840–1870," *Comparative Studies in Society and History*, 55, 2 (2013).

Fairchilds, Cissie. "The Production and Marketing of Populuxe Goods in Eighteenth-Century Paris," in John Brewer and Roy Porter, eds. *Consumption and the World of Goods*. London: Routledge, 1993.

Favier, Hervé. "Un émule de Talleyrand: l'abbé de Pradt sous l'oeil de la police (1816)," *Revue d'histoire diplomatique*, 93, 1–2 (1979).

Febvre, Lucien. "Civilisation: évolution d'un mot et d'un groupe d'idées," in Lucien Febvre et al., *Civilisation: le mot et l'idée*. Paris: La renaissance du livre, 1930.

Feis, Herbert. *Europe, the World's Banker, 1870–1914: An Account of European Foreign Investment and the Connection of World Finance with Diplomacy before the War*. New Haven, CT: Yale University Press, 1930.

Féraud, Laurent. *La Calle et documents pour servir à l'histoire des anciennes concessions françaises d'Afrique*. Algiers: Aillaud et Cie, 1877.

———. "La prise d'Alger en 1830 d'après un écrivain musulman," *Recueil des notices et mémoires de la Société archéologique de Constantine*, 3 (1865).

Ferguson, Niall. *The Cash Nexus: Money and Power in the Modern World*. London: Penguin, 2001.

———. *Empire: How Britain Made the Modern World*. London: Allen Lane, 2003.

———. *The House of Rothschild*, 2 vols. London: Viking, 1999.

Ferguson, Niall, and Moritz Schularick, "The Empire Effect: The Determinants of Country Risk in the First Age of Globalization, 1880–1913," *Journal of Economic History*, 66, 2 (2006).

Ferguson, Priscilla Pankhurst. *Accounting for Taste: The Triumph of French Cuisine*. Chicago: University of Chicago Press, 2004.

Ffoulkes, Fiona. "'Quality always distinguished itself': Louis Hyppolyte LeRoy and the Luxury Clothing Industry in Early Nineteenth-Century Paris," in Maxine Berg and Helen Clifford, eds. *Consumers and Luxury: Consumer Culture in Europe, 1650–1850*. Manchester: Manchester University Press, 1999.

Findlay, Ronald, and Kevin H. O'Rourke. *Power and Plenty: Trade, War, and the World Economy in the Second Millennium*. Princeton, NJ: Princeton University Press, 2007.

Findley, Carter Vaughn. *Ottoman Civil Officialdom: A Social History*. Princeton, NJ: Princeton University Press, 1989.

Fitzmaurice, Andrew. *Sovereignty, Property and Empire, 1500–2000*. Cambridge: Cambridge University Press, 2015.

Flandreau, Marc. "The Economics and Politics of Monetary Unions: A Reassessment of the LMU, 1865–1871," *Financial History Review*, 7, 1 (2000).

———. *L'or du monde: la France et la stabilité du système monétaire internationale, 1848–1873*. Paris: L'Harmattan, 1995.

Flandreau, Marc, and Juan Flores, "Bonds and Brands: Foundations of Sovereign Debt Markets, 1820–1830," *Journal of Economic History*, 69, 3 (2009).

Fohlen, Claude. *L'industrie textile au temps du Second Empire*. Paris: Plon, 1956.

Fontana, Biancamaria. *Benjamin Constant and the Post-Revolutionary Mind*. New Haven, CT: Yale University Press, 1991.

Ford, Caroline. "Reforestation, Landscape Conservation, and the Anxieties of Empire in French Colonial Algeria," *American Historical Review*, 113, 2 (2008).

Forray-Carlier, Anne, and Florence Valantin, "La reconnaissance internationale: des Expositions des produits de l'industrie française aux Expositions universelles," in Anne Forray-Carlier, Florence Valantin, Philippe Verzier, et al., eds. *L'art de la soie: Prelle, 1752–2002: des ateliers lyonnais aux palais parisiens*. Paris: Paris Musées et A.C.R. Éditions internationales, 2002.

Forsyth, Murray. "The Old European States-System: Gentz versus Hauterive," *Historical Journal*, 23, 3 (1980).

Fortier-Beaulieu, Charlotte, and Hélène Moulin, *A.-Félix Clément: itinéraire d'un peintre drômois*. Valence: Musée de Valence, 1996.

Fox, Edward J. *History in Geographic Perspective: The Other France*. New York: Norton, 1971.

Frederico, Giovanni. *An Economic History of the Silk Industry, 1830–1930*. Cambridge: Cambridge University Press, 1997.

Freedman, Charles E. "The Growth of the French Securities Market, 1815–1870," in Charles K. Warner, ed. *From the Ancien Régime to the Front Populaire: Essays in the History of Modern France in Honor of Shepard B. Clough*. New York: Columbia University Press, 1969.

———. *The Triumph of Corporate Capitalism in France, 1867–1914*. New York: University of Rochester Press, 1993.

Fried, Michael. *Manet's Modernism, or the Face of Painting in the 1860s*. Chicago: University of Chicago Press, 1996.

Furet, François. *La Révolution*, 2 vols. Paris: Hachette, 1988.

Gaffield, Julia, ed. *The Haitian Declaration of Independence: Creation, Context, and Legacy*. Charlottesville: University of Virginia Press, 2016.

Gainot, Bernard. "*La Décade* et la 'colonisation nouvelle'," *Annales historiques de la Révolution française*, 339 (2005).

Gallagher, John, and Ronald Robinson. "The Imperialism of Free Trade," *Economic History Review*, 2nd ser., 6 (1953).

Gallissot, René. "Présentation," in Marcel Emerit, *L'Algérie à l'époque d'Abd el-Kader*. Paris: Bouchène, 2002.

Gallois, William. "Genocide in Nineteenth-Century Algeria," *Journal of Genocide Research*, 15, 1 (2013).

———. *A History of Violence in the Early Algerian Colony*. Basingstoke: Palgrave Macmillan, 2013.

———. *Zola: The History of Capitalism*. Oxford: P. Lang, 2000.

Gardner, Lloyd, ed. *Redefining the Past: Essays in Diplomatic History in Honor of William Appleman Williams*. Corvallis: Oregon State University Press, 1986.

Gelber, Harry. *Battle for Beijing: Franco-British Conflict in China, 1858–1860*. Basingstoke: Palgrave Macmillan, 2016.

Gerbod, Paul. "Les touristes étrangers à Paris dans la première moitié du XIXe siècle," *Bulletin de la société de l'histoire de Paris et de l'Ile de France*, 110 (1983).

———. *Voyages au pays des mangeurs de grenouilles. La France vue par les Britanniques du XVIIIe siècle à nos jours*. Paris: Albin Michel, 1991.

Gereffi, Gary, and Miguel Korzeniewicz, eds. *Commodity Chains and Global Capitalism*. Westport, CT: Greenwood Press, 1994.

Geyikdaği, V. Necla. *Foreign Investment in the Ottoman Empire*. London: Tauris, 2011.

———. "French Direct Investments in the Ottoman Empire before World War I," *Enterprise and Society*, 12, 3 (2011).

Gille, Bertrand. *Histoire de la maison Rothschild*, 2 vols. Geneva: Droz, 1965–1967.

———. *La banque en France au 19e siècle. Recherches historiques*. Geneva: Droz, 1970.

Gillet, Marie. "Innovation and Tradition in the Shopping Landscape of Paris and a Provincial City, 1800 to 1900," in Jan Hein Furnée and Clé Lesger, eds. *The Landscape of Consumption*. Basingstoke: Palgrave McMillan, 2014.

Girard, Philippe R. *The Slaves Who Defeated Napoleon*. Tuscaloosa: University of Alabama Press, 2011.

Girardet, Raoul. *L'idée coloniale en France de 1871 à 1962*. Paris: Hachette, 2005.

Girault, René. *Emprunts russes et investissements français en Russie, 1887–1914*. Paris: Armand Colin, 1973.

Go, Julian. *Patterns of Empire: The British and American Empires, 1688 to the Present*. Cambridge: Cambridge University Press, 2011.

Godfroy, Marion. *Kourou, 1763: le dernier rêve de l'Amérique française*. Paris: Vendémiaire, 2011.

Goey, Ferry de. *Consuls and the Institutions of Global Capitalism, 1783–1914*. London: Routledge, 2015.

Goldberg, Jan. "On the Origins of Majālis al-Tujjār in Mid-Nineteenth Century Egypt," *Islamic Law and Society*, 6, 2 (1999).

———. "Réception du droit français sous les Britanniques en Egypte: un paradoxe?," *Egypte. Monde arabe*, 34 (1998).

Goldstein, Jan E. "Toward an Empirical History of Moral Thinking: The Case of Racial Theory in Mid-Nineteenth-Century France," *American Historical Review*, 120, 1 (2015).

Gollwitzer, Heinz. "Der Abbé de Pradt als weltpolitischer Denker," *Saeculum*, 22 (1971).

———. *Geschichte des Weltpolitischen Denkens*, 2 vols. Göttingen: Vandenhoeck & Ruprecht, 1972–1982.

Gontard, Maurice. *La Bourse de Paris (1800–1830)*. Aix-en-Provence: Edisud, 2000.

Gordon, Philip H. *A Certain Idea of France: French Security Policy and the Gaullist Legacy*. Princeton, NJ: Princeton University Press, 1993.

Goubert, Pierre. *Du luxe au confort*. Paris: Belin, 1988.

Goujon, Bertrand. *Monarchies postrévolutionnaires, 1814–1848*. Paris: Le Seuil, 2012.

Graham, Aaron, and Patrick Walsh, eds. *The British Fiscal Military States, 1660–c. 1783*. London: Routledge, 2016.

Granger, Catherine. *L'empereur et les arts. La liste civile de Napoléon III*. Paris: École des chartes, 2005.

Grazia, Victoria de. *Irresistible Empire: America's Advance through Twentieth-Century Europe*. Cambridge MA: Belknap Press, 2005.

Green, Nancy L. "Expatriation, Expatriates, and Expats: The American Transformation of a Concept," *American Historical Review*, 114, 2 (2009).

———. "French History and the Transnational Turn," *French Historical Studies* 37, 4 (2014).

Greenfield, Jerome. "Financing a New Order: The Payment of Reparations by Restoration France, 1817–18," *French History*, 30, 3 (2016).

———. *The Making of a Fiscal-Military State in Post-Revolutionary France.* Cambridge: Cambridge University Press, forthcoming.

———. "The Mexican Expedition of 1862–1867 and the End of the French Second Empire," *Historical Journal*, 63, 3 (2020).

———. "The Price of Violence: Money, the French State and 'Civilization' during the Conquest of Algeria, 1830–1850s," *French Historical Studies*, forthcoming.

Groc, Gérard, and Ibrahim Caglar, *La presse française de Turquie de 1795 à nos jours. Histoire et catalogue.* Istanbul: Isis, 1985.

Groffier-Kilbansky, Ethel. *Un encyclopédiste réformateur. Jacques Peuchet (1758–1830).* Laval, Canada: Presses universitaires de Laval, 2009.

Guénin, Yves. *Le baron Louis. 1755–1837.* Paris: Perrin, 1999.

Guignard, Didier. "Conservatoire ou révolutionnaire? Le sénatus-consulte de 1863 appliqué au régime foncier d'Algérie," *Revue d'histoire du XIXe siècle*, 41 (2010).

Guiral, Pierre. *Marseille et l'Algérie.* Gap: Ophrys, 1956.

———. *Prévost-Paradol: 1829–1870: pensée et action d'un libéral sous le Second Empire.* Paris: Presses Universitaires de France, 1955.

Gunn, John A. W. *When the French Tried to Be British: Party, Opposition and the Quest for Civil Disagreement, 1814–1848.* Montreal: McGill-Queen's University Press, 2009.

Guy, Kolleen M. *When Champagne Became French: Wine and the Making of a National Identity.* Baltimore, MD: Johns Hopkins University Press, 2003

Guyot, Raymond. *La première entente cordiale.* Paris: Rieder, 1926.

Hahn, Hazel. *Scenes of Parisian Modernity: Culture and Consumption in the Nineteenth Century.* Basingstoke: Palgrave Macmillan, 2009.

Halévy, Daniel. *La fin des notables.* Paris: Grasset, 1930.

Hamilton, C. I. *Anglo-French Naval Rivalry, 1840–1870.* Oxford: Clarendon Press, 1993.

Hanioğlu, Şükrü M. *A Brief History of the Late Ottoman Empire.* Princeton, NJ: Princeton University Press, 2008.

Hanley, Will. *Identifying with Nationality: Europeans, Ottomans, and Egyptians in Alexandria.* New York: Columbia University Press, 2017.

———. "What Ottoman Nationality Was and Was Not," *Journal of the Ottoman and Turkish Studies Association*, 3, 2 (2016).

Hannoum, Abdelmajid. *Violent Modernity: France in Algeria.* Cambridge, MA: Harvard University Press, 2010.

Harlow, Barbara, and Mia Carter, eds. *Archives of Empire*, 2 vols. Durham, NC: Duke University Press, 2003.

Harsanyi, Doina Pasca. *Lessons from America: Liberal French Nobles in Exile, 1793–1798.* University Park: University of Pennsylavania Press, 2010.

Harsin, Jill. *Policing Prostitution in Nineteenth-Century Paris.* Princeton, NJ: Princeton University Press, 1985.

Harvey, David. *Paris, Capital of Modernity.* New York: Routledge, 2003.

Hau, Michel. *L'industrialisation de l'Alsace.* Strasbourg: Publications près les universités de Strasbourg, 1987.

Hautcoeur, Pierre-Cyrille. "Les transformations du crédit en France au XIXe siècle," *Romantisme*, 151 (2011).

Hautcoeur, Pierre-Cyrille, and Angelo Riva, "The Paris Financial Market in the Nineteenth Century: Complementarities and Competition in Microstructures," *Economic History Review*, 65, 4 (2012).

Hax, Herbert. *Vademecum zu einem Klassiker der Staatswissenschaft*. Düsseldorf: Verlag Wirtschaft und Finanzen, 1998.

Haynes, Christine. "Remembering and Forgetting the First Modern Occupations of France," *Journal of Modern History*, 88, 3 (2016).

Hazareesingh, Sudhir. *From Subject to Citizen: The Second Empire and the Emergence of Modern French Democracy*. Princeton, NJ: Princeton University Press, 1998.

———. *The Legend of Napoleon*. London: Granta, 2005.

Headrick, Daniel R. *Power over Peoples: Technology, Environments, and Western Imperialism, 1400 to the Present*. Princeton, NJ: Princeton University Press, 2010.

———. *The Tools of Empire: Technology and European Imperialism in the Nineteenth Century*. New York: Oxford University Press, 1981.

Hébrard, Jean. "Les deux vies de Michel Vincent, colon à Saint-Domingue (c. 1730–1804)," *Revue d'histoire moderne et contemporaine*, 57, 2 (2010).

Henry, Jean-Robert. "Le centenaire de l'Algérie, triomphe éphémère de la pensée algérianiste," in Abderrahmane Bouchène et al., eds. *Histoire de l'Algérie à la période coloniale*. Paris: La Découverte, 2014.

Hill, Richard, and Peter Hogg. *A Black Corps d'Élite: An Egyptian-Sudanese Conscript Battalion with the French Army in Mexico, 1863–1867, and Its Survivors in Subsequent African History*. East Lansing: University of Michigan Press, 1995.

Hilton, Boyd. *A Mad, Bad, and Dangerous People? England, 1783–1846*. Oxford: Clarendon Press, 2006.

Hitzel, Frédéric. "L'École des Jeunes de langue d'Istanbul. Un modèle d'apprentissage des langues orientales," in Gilbert Buti, Michèle Janin-Thivos and Olivier Raveux, eds. *Langues et langages du commerce en Méditerranée et en Europe à l'époque moderne*. Aix-en-Provence: Presses de l'université de Provence, 2013.

———. "L'institution des Jeunes de langue de Constantinople au début du XIXe siècle," in Véronique Schiltz, ed. *De Samarcande à Istanbul: étapes orientales*. Paris: CNRS, 2015.

Hobson, John A. *Imperialism: A Study*. New York: Cosimo, 2005.

Hoffman, Philip T., Gilles Postel-Vinay and Jean-Laurent Rosenthal, *Dark Matter Credit: The Development of Peer-to-Peer Lending and Banking in France*. Princeton, NJ: Princeton University Press, 2019

Holden, Wilfred H. *The Pearl from Plymouth*. London: British Technical and General Press, 1950.

Holmes, Stephen. *Benjamin Constant and the Making of Modern Liberalism*. New Haven, CT: Yale University Press, 1984.

Holtfrerich, Carl-Ludwig. "Public Debt in Post-1850 German Economic Thought vis-a-vis the Pre-1850 British Classical School," *German Economic Review*, 15, 1 (2013).

Hobsbawm, Eric. *The Age of Revolution, 1789–1848*. London: Abacus, 2005.

Hopkins, Anthony G. *American Empire: A Global History*. Princeton, NJ: Princeton University Press, 2018.

————. "Back to the Future: From National History to Imperial History," *Past & Present*, 164 (1999).

————. "Informal Empire in Argentina: An Alternative View," *Journal of Latin American Studies*, 26, 2 (1994).

————. "The Victorians and Africa: The British Occupation of Egypt in 1882," *Journal of African History*, 27, 2 (1986).

Horn, Jeff. *Economic Development in Early Modern France: The Privilege of Liberty, 1650–1820*. Cambridge: Cambridge University Press, 2015.

————. *The Path Not Taken: French Industrialization in the Age of Revolution, 1750–1830*. Cambridge, MA: MIT Press, 2006.

Horne, Janet. "'To Spread the French Language Is to Extend the *Patrie*': The Colonial Mission of the Alliance Française," *French Historical Studies*, 40, 1 (2017).

Horowitz, Richard S. "International Law and State Transformation in China, Siam and the Ottoman Empire during the Nineteenth Century," *Journal of World History*, 15, 4 (2004).

Houbre, Gabrielle, ed. *Le livre des courtisanes: archives secrètes de la police des moeurs*. Paris: Tallandier, 2006.

House, John. "Manet's Maximilian: History Painting, Censorship and Ambiguity," in Juliet Wilson-Bareau, ed. *Manet: The Execution of Maximilian: Painting, Politics and Censorship*. London: National Gallery Publications, 1992.

Howe, Anthony. *Free Trade and Liberal England*. Oxford: Clarendon Press, 1997.

Huber, Valeska. "Multiple Mobilities: Über den Umgang mit verschiedenen Mobilitätsformen um 1900," *Geschichte und Geselleschaft*, 36, 2 (2010).

Huillery, Elise. "The Black Man's Burden: The Cost of Colonization of West Africa," *Journal of Economic History*, 74, 1 (2014).

Hunter, F. Robert. *Egypt under the Khedives, 1805–1879: From Household Government to Modern Bureaucracy*. Pittsburgh, PA: University of Pittsburgh Press, 1984.

Imlah, Albert H. "British Balance of Payments and Export of Capital, 1816–1913," *Economic History Review*, 5, 2 (1952).

————. *Economic Elements in the "Pax Britannica." Studies in British Foreign Trade in the Nineteenth Century*. Cambridge, MA: Harvard University Press, 1958.

Issawi, Charles. *An Economic History of the Middle East and North Africa*. New York: Columbia University Press, 1982.

Jacoud, Gilles. *Political Economy and Industrialism: Banks in Saint-Simonian Economic Thought*. London: Routledge, 2010.

Jansen, Marius B. *The Making of Modern Japan*. Cambridge MA: Belknap Press, 2000.

Jardin, André. *Alexis de Tocqueville*. Paris: Hachette, 1984.

Jaume, Lucien. *Tocqueville. Les sources aristocratiques de la liberté*. Paris: Fayard, 2008.

Jennings, Eric. *Vichy in the Tropics: Pétain's National Revolution in Madagascar, Guadeloupe and Indochina*. Stanford, CA: Stanford University Press, 2002.

Jennings, Jeremy. "The Debate about Luxury in Eighteenth- and Nineteenth-Century French Political Thought," *Journal of the History of Ideas*, 68, 1 (2007).

Joachim, Benoît. "Commerce et décolonisation: l'expérience franco-haïtienne au XIXe siècle," *Annales. Économies, Sociétés, Civilisations*, 27, 6 (1972).

————. *Les racines du sous-développement en Haïti*. Port-au-Prince: H. Deschamps, 1980.

Johnson, Walter. *River of Dark Dreams: Slavery and Empire in the Cotton Kingdom.* Cambridge, MA: Belknap, 2013.

Jones, Colin, and Rebecca Spang, "*Sans-culottes, sans café, sans tabac:* Shifting Realms of Necessity and Luxury in Eighteenth-Century France," in Maxine Berg and Helen Clifford, eds. *Consumers and Luxury: Consumer Culture in Europe, 1650–1850.* Manchester: Manchester University Press, 1999.

Jones, Geoffrey. *Beauty Imagined: A History of the Global Beauty Industry.* Oxford: Oxford University Press, 2010.

Jones, Howard. "Wrapping the World in Fire: The Interventionist Crisis in the Civil War," in Don. H. Doyle, ed. *American Civil Wars: The United States, Latin America, Europe, and the Crisis of the 1860s.* Chapel Hill: University of North Carolina Press, 2017.

Jones, Jennifer M. *Sexing La Mode: Gender, Fashion and Commercial Culture in Old Regime France.* Oxford: Berg, 2004.

Jouvenel, Bertrand de. "L'abbé de Pradt et l'Europe constitutionnelle," *Commentaire,* 7, 3 (1979).

Julien, Charles-André. *La question d'Alger devant les chambres sous la Restauration.* Algiers: J. Carbonel, 1922.

———. *L'avenir d'Alger et l'opposition des libéraux et des économistes en 1830.* Oran: Fouque, 1922.

———. *L'opposition et la guerre d'Alger à la veille de la conquête.* Oran: Fouque: 1921.

Julien, Charles-André, and Charles-Robert Ageron, *Histoire de l'Algérie contemporaine,* 2 vols. Paris: Presses Universitaires de France, 1964–1979.

Kaiser, Thomas E. "Money, Despotism, and Public Opinion in Early Eighteenth-Century France: John Law and the Debate on Royal Credit," *Journal of Modern History,* 63, 1 (1991).

Kaiser, Wolfram. "Vive la France! Vive la République? The Cultural Construction of French Identity at the World Exhibitions in Paris 1855–1900," *National Identities,* 1, 3 (1999).

Kale, Steven. "Gobineau, Racism, and Legitimism: A Royalist Heretic in Nineteenth-Century France," *Modern Intellectual History,* 7, 1 (2010).

Kalman, Julie. *Orientalizing the Jew: Religion, Culture and Imperialism in Nineteenth-Century France.* Bloomington: Indiana University Press, 2017.

Kang, Mathilde. *Francophonie en Orient: Aux croisements France-Asie (1848–1940).* Amsterdam: Amsterdam University Press, 2017.

Kang, Zheng. "L'Etat constructeur du marché financier," in Pierre Cyrille Hautcoeur and Georges Gallais Hamonno, eds. *Le Marché financier français au XIXe siècle,* 2 vols. Paris: Publications de la Sorbonne, 2007, vol. 1.

Kang, Zheng, and Thierno Seck, "Les épargnants et le marché financier," in Pierre Cyrille Hautcoeur and Georges Gallais Hamonno, eds. *Le Marché financier français au XIXe siècle,* 2 vols. Paris: Publications de la Sorbonne, 2007, vol. 1.

Kanya-Forstner, Alexander S. *The Conquest of Western Sudan: A Study in French Military Imperialism.* London: Cambridge University Press, 1969.

Karabell, Zachary. *Parting the Desert: The Creation of the Suez Canal.* London: John Murray, 2003.

Karsh, Efraim, and Inari Karsh, *Empires of the Sand: The Struggle for Mastery in the Middle East, 1789–1923.* Cambridge, MA: Harvard University Press, 1999.

Kasaba, Reşat. "Treaties and Friendships: British Imperialism, the Ottoman Empire, and China in the Nineteenth Century," *Journal of World History,* 4, 2 (1993).

Kateb, Kamel. *Européens, "indigènes" et juifs en Algérie (1830–1962)*. Paris: Institut National d'Etudes Démographiques, 2001.

Kayaoglu, Turan. *Legal Imperialism: Sovereignty and Extraterritoriality in Japan, the Ottoman Empire and China*. Cambridge: Cambridge University Press, 2010.

Keene, Edward. "The Treaty-Making Revolution in the Nineteenth Century," *International History Review*, 34, 3 (2012).

Kelly, Linda. *Talleyrand in London*. London: Tauris, 2017.

Kielstra, Paul Michael. *The Politics of Slave Trade Suppression in Britain and France, 1814–1848: Diplomacy, Morality and Economics*. Houndmills: MacMillan, 2000.

Kindleberger, Charles P. *A Financial History of Western Europe*. London: Allen & Unwin, 1984.

Klein, Jean-François. *Les maîtres du comptoir: Desgrand père et fils (1720–1878)*. Paris: Presses de l'Université Paris Sorbonne, 2013.

Knight, Ian. *With His Face to the Foe: The Life and Death of Louis Napoleon, the Prince Impérial, Zululand 1879*. Staplehurst: Spellmount, 2001.

Koebner, Richard, and Helmut Dan Schmidt. *The Story and Significance of Imperialism: A Political Word, 1840–1960*. Cambridge: Cambridge University Press, 1965.

Kontler, László. "Varieties of Old Regime Europe: Thoughts and Details on the Reception of Burke's *Reflections* in Germany," in Martin Fitzpatrick and Peter Jones, eds. *The Reception of Burke in Europe*. London: Bloomsbury, 2017.

Koskenniemi, Martti. "Race, Hierarchy and International Law: Lorimer's Legal Science," *European Journal of International Law*, 27, 2 (2016).

———. *The Gentle Civilizer of Nations: The Rise and Fall of International Law, 1870–1960*. Cambridge: Cambridge University Press, 2004.

Kramer, Paul. "How Not to Write the History of U.S. Empire," *Diplomatic History*, 42, 5 (2018).

———. "Power and Connection: Histories of the United States in the World," *American Historical Review*, 116, 5 (2011).

Kumar, Krishnan. *Visions of Empire: How Five Imperial Regimes Shaped the World*. Princeton, NJ: Princeton University Press, 2017.

Kupferschmidt, Uri M. *European Department Stores and Middle Eastern Consumers: The Orosdi-Back Saga*. Istanbul: Ottoman Bank Archives and Research Centre, 2007.

Kuran, Timur. *The Long Divergence: How Islamic Law Held Back the Middle East*. Princeton, NJ: Princeton University Press, 2011.

Kushner, Nina. *Erotic Exchanges: The World of Elite Prostitution in Eighteenth-Century Paris*. Ithaca, NY: Cornell University Press, 2013.

Kwass, Michael. "Big Hair: A Wig History of Consumption in Eighteenth-Century France," *American Historical Review*, 111, 3 (2006).

Labib, Malak. "Crise de la dette publique et missions financières européennes en Egypte, 1878–1879," *Monde(s)*, 4, 2 (2013).

Labrousse, Ernest. *La crise de l'économie française à la fin de l'Ancien Régime et au début de la Révolution*. Paris: Presses Universitaires de France, 1943.

Lafont-Couturier, Hélène, ed. *Gérôme et Goupil. Art & entreprise*. Paris: Réunion des musées nationaux and Bordeaux: Musée Goupil, 2000.

Lake, Marilyn, and Henry Reynolds. *Drawing the Global Colour Line: White Men's Countries and the Challenge of Racial Equality*. Cambridge: Cambridge University Press, 2008.

Lancaster, William. *The Department Store: A Social History*. London: Leicester University Press, 1995.

Landes, David S. *Bankers and Pashas: International Finance and Economic Imperialism in Egypt*, 2nd edn. New York: Harper & Row, 1969.

Laniol, Vincent. "Langue et relations internationales: le monopole perdu de la langue française à la Conférence de la Paix de 1919," in Denis Rolland, ed., *Histoire culturelle des relations internationales. Carrefour méthodologique*. Paris: L'Harmattan, 2004.

Laurens, Henry. "Le mythe de l'expédition d'Égypte en France et en Égypte aux XIXe et XXe siècles," in Henry Laurens, *Orientales*, 3 vols. Paris: CNRS, 2004.

———. *Le royaume impossible: la France et la genèse du monde arabe*. Paris: Armand Colin, 1991.

Lauzanne, Bernard, ed. *L'aventure coloniale de la France*, 5 vols. Paris: Denoël, 1987–97.

Lawlor, Mary. *Alexis de Tocqueville in the Chamber of Deputies: His Views on Foreign and Colonial Policy*. Washington, DC: Catholic University of America Press, 1959.

Le Bas, Dominique. "La venue de l'ambassade siamoise en France," *Aséanie. Sciences humaines en Asie du Sud-Est*, 3 (1999).

Lebel, Germaine. "Gabriel Esquer," *Bibliothèque de l'École des chartes*, 119, 1 (1961).

Le Cour Grandmaison, Olivier. *Coloniser, exterminer: sur la guerre et l'État colonial*. Paris: Fayard, 2005.

———. *De l'indigénat: anatomie d'un monstre juridique. Le droit colonial en Algérie et dans l'empire français*. Paris: Zones, 2010.

Leggiere, Michael V. *Blücher: Scourge of Napoleon*. Norman: University of Oklahoma Press, 2014.

Leonhardt, Holm A. *Kartelltheorie und Internationale Beziehungen. Theoriegeschichtliche Studien*. Hildesheim: Olms, 2009.

Leuchter, Tyson. "The Illimitable Right: Debating the Meaning of Property and the *marché à terme* in Napoleonic France," *Modern Intellectual History*, 15, 1 (2018).

Levallois, Michel. *Ismaÿl Urbain (1812–1884): une autre conquête de l'Algérie*. Paris: Maisonneuve et Larose, 2001.

———. *Ismaÿl Urbain: Royaume arabe ou Algérie franco-musulmane? 1848–1870*. Paris: Riveneuve, 2012.

Lévy-Leboyer, Maurice. "La balance des paiements et l'exportation des capitaux français," in Maurice Lévy-Leboyer, ed. *La position internationale de la France. Aspects économiques et financiers*. Paris: EHESS, 1977.

———. *Les banques européennes et l'industrialisation internationale dans la première moitié du XIXe siècle*. Paris: Presses Universitaires de France, 1964.

Lewis, Mary. *Divided Rule: Sovereignty and Empire in French Tunisia, 1881–1938*. Berkeley: University of California Press, 2014.

———. "Legacies of French Slave-Ownership, or the Long Decolonization of Saint-Domingue," *History Workshop Journal*, 81, 1 (2017).

Liebesny, Herbert J. *The Law of the Near & Middle East: Readings, Cases, & Material*. Albany: State University of New York Press, 1975.

Lignereux, Aurélien. *L'Empire des Français, 1799–1815*. Paris: Le Seuil, 2012.

Lilti, Antoine. *Le monde des salons: sociabilité et mondanité à Paris au XVIIIe siècle*. Paris: Fayard, 2005.

Lipotevski, Gilles. *L'empire de l'éphémère: la mode et son destin dans les sociétés modernes*. Paris: Gallimard, 1987.

Livet, Georges, and Raymond Oberlé, *Histoire de Mulhouse des origines à nos jours*. Strasbourg: Edition des Dernières Nouvelles d'Alsace, 1977.

Lochore, Reuel. *History of the Idea of Civilization in France, 1830–1870*. Bonn: Röhrscheid, 1935.

Lorcin, Patricia. *Imperial identities: Stereotyping, Prejudice and Race in Colonial Algeria*. London: Tauris, 1995.

Louca, Anouar. *Voyageurs et écrivains égyptiens en France au XIXe siècle*. Paris: Didier, 1970.

Louis, Wm Roger, and Ronald Robinson, "The Imperialism of Decolonization," *Journal of Imperial and Commonwealth History*, 22, 3 (1994).

Love, Joseph. "The Origins of Dependency Theory," *Journal of Latin American Studies*, 22, 1 (1990).

Lutfalla, Michel. "Économistes britanniques et français face à la question de l'amortissement: d'Isaac Panchaud aux lendemains de la loi de 1816," in Aglan, Margairaz and Verheyde, eds. *1816 ou la genèse de la foi publique*.

———. "La rente, de Waterloo à Sedan," in Michel Lutfalla, ed. *Histoire de la Dette Publique en France*. Paris: Garnier, 2017.

Lüthy, Herbert. *La banque protestante en France: de la Révocation de l'Édit de Nantes à la Révolution*, 2 vols. 3rd edn. Paris: EHESS, 1998.

Lützelschwab, Claude. *La Compagnie genevoise des colonies suisses de Sétif*. Bern: Peter Lang, 2006.

Ma, Debin. "The Modern Silk Road: The Global Raw-Silk Market, 1850–1930," *Journal of Economic History*, 56, 2 (1996).

MacDonogh, Giles. *A Palate in Revolution: Grimond de La Reynière*. London: Robin Clark, 1987.

Machiels, Christine. *Les Féminismes et la prostitution, 1860–1960*. Rennes: Presses Universitaires de Rennes, 2016.

Magee, Gary B., and Andrew S. Thompson, *Empire and Globalisation: Networks of People, Goods and Capital in the British World, c. 1850–1914*. Cambridge: Cambridge University Press, 2010.

Maier, Charles S. "Consigning the Twentieth Century to History: Alternative Narratives for the Modern Era," *American Historical Review*, 105, 3 (2000).

Mainardi, Patricia. *Art and Politics of the Second Empire: The Universal Expositions of 1855 and 1867*. New Haven, CT: Yale University Press, 1987.

Mansel, Philip. *Paris between Empires, 1814–1852*. London: John Murray, 2001.

———. "Paris, Court City of the Nineteenth Century," *Court Historian*, 11 (2006).

Marçot, Jean-Louis. *Comment est née l'Algérie française (1830–1850)*. Paris: La différence, 2012.

Markovits, Claude. *The Global World of Indian Merchants 1750–1947: Traders of Sindh from Bukhara to Panama*. Cambridge: Cambridge University Press, 2000.

Markovits, Rahul. *Civiliser l'Europe: politiques du théâtre français au XVIIIe siècle*. Paris: Fayard, 2014.

Marly, Diana de. *The History of Haute Couture*. London: Batsford, 1980.

Marrey, Bernard. *Les grands magasins des origines à 1939*. Paris: Librarie Picard, 1979.

Marseille, Jacques. *Empire colonial et capitalisme français: histoire d'un divorce*, 2nd edn. Paris: Albin Michel, 2005.

Marsh, Peter T. *Bargaining on Europe: Britain and the First Common Market*. New Haven, CT: Yale University Press, 1999.

Martin, Marc. "Retour sur 'l'abominable vénalité de la presse française,'" *Le temps des médias*, 6, 1 (2006).

Martin, Meredith. "History Repeats Itself in Jean-Léon Gérôme's Reception of the Siamese Ambassadors," *Art Bulletin*, 99, 1 (2017).

Martin, Morag. *Selling Beauty: Cosmetics, Commerce and French Society, 1750–1830*. Baltimore, MD: Johns Hopkins University Press, 2009.

Martin, Virginie. "Devenir diplomate en Révolution: naissance de la 'carrière diplomatique'?," *Revue d'histoire moderne et contemporaine*, 63, 3 (2016).

Marzagalli, Silvia. *Bordeaux et les Etats-Unis, 1776–1815: politique et stratégies négociantes dans la genèse d'un réseau commercial*. Geneva: Droz, 2015.

Massa-Gille, Geneviève. "Les capitaux français et l'expédition du Mexique," *Revue d'histoire diplomatique*, 79, 3 (1965).

Masson, Paul. *A la veille d'une conquête: concessions et compagnies d'Afrique (1800–1830)*. Paris: Imprimerie nationale, 1909.

Mauduit, Xavier, and Corinne Ergasse. *Flamboyant Second Empire! Et la France entra dans la modernité*. Paris: Armand Colin, 2016.

Maunier, René. "Un économiste oublié: Peuchet (1758–1830)," *Revue d'histoire des doctrines économiques et sociales*, 4 (1911).

Mehta, Uday Singh. *Liberalism and Empire: A Study in Nineteenth-Century British Liberal Thought*. Chicago: University of Chicago Press, 1999.

Méninger, Alain. "D'Hauterive et la formation des diplomates," *Revue d'histoire diplomatique*, 89, 1 (1975).

Merle, Isabelle. *Expériences coloniales: la Nouvelle-Calédonie, 1853–1920*. Paris: Belin, 1995.

Merli, Maxime, and Antoine Parent, "La diversification des portefeuilles français à la veille de 1914 ou l'image écornée du rentier français du 19e siècle," *Revue d'économie politique*, 121, 6 (2011).

Mestyan, Adam. *Arab Patriotism: The Ideology and Culture of Power in Late Ottoman Egypt*. Princeton, NJ: Princeton University Press, 2017.

Mézin, Anne. *Les Consuls de France au siècle des Lumières*. Paris: Direction des archives et de la documentation du ministère des affaires étrangères, 1997.

———. "Les services consulaires français au XIXe siècle," in Jörg Ulbert and Lukian Prijac, eds. *Consuls et services consulaires au XIXe siècle. Die Welt der Konsulate im 19. Jahrhundert. Consulship in the 19th century*. Hamburg: DOBU, 2010.

Michie, Ranald C. *The Global Securities Market: A History*. Oxford: Oxford University Press, 2006.

Miller, Michael B. *The Bon Marché: Bourgeois Culture and the Department Store*. Princeton, NJ: Princeton University Press, 1981.

Minard, Philippe. *La fortune du colbertisme: État et industrie dans la France des Lumières*. Paris: Fayard, 1998.

Mitchell, Brian, R. *International Historical Statistics. Africa, Asia and Oceania 1750–2005*. Basingstoke: Palgrave Macmillan, 2007.

Mitchell, Timothy. *Colonising Egypt*. Berkeley: University of California Press, 1988.

Mitchener, Kris J., and Marc Weidenmier. "Empire, Public Goods and the Roosevelt Corollary," *Journal of Economic History*, 65, 3 (2005).

———. "Supersanctions and Debt Repayment," *Journal of International Money and Finance*, 29, 1 (2010).

Moatti, Claudia. "Migration et droit dans l'empire romain," in Elio Lo Cascio and Laurens E. Tacoma, eds. *The Impact of Mobility and Migration in the Roman Empire*. Leiden: Brill, 2017.

Morant, Georges Soulié de. *Exterritorialité et intérêts étrangers en Chine*. Paris: Greuthner, 1925.

Moretti, Franco. *Atlas of the European Novel, 1800–1900*. London: Verso, 1998.

Morgenstern, Oskar. *International Financial Transactions and Business Cycles*. Princeton, NJ: Princeton University Press, 1959.

Murphy, Agnes. *The Ideology of French Imperialism, 1871–1881*. Washington, DC: Catholic University of America Press, 1948.

Murray-Miller, Gavin. "Bonapartism in Algeria: Empire and Sovereignty before the Third Republic," *French History*, 32, 2 (2018).

———. "A Conflicted Sense of Nationality: Napoleon III's Arab Kingdom and the Paradoxes of French Multiculturalism," *French Colonial History*, 15, 1 (2014).

Musso, Pierre. *Télécommunications et philosophie des réseaux. La postérité paradoxale de Saint-Simon*. Paris: Presses Universitaires de France, 1997.

Muthu, Sankar. *Enlightenment against Empire*. Princeton, NJ: Princeton University Press, 2003.

Needell, Jeffrey. *The Conservatives, the State, and Slavery in the Brazilian Monarchy, 1831–1871*. Stanford, CA: Stanford University Press, 2006.

———. *A Tropical Belle Époque: Elite Culture and Society in Turn-of-the-Century Rio de Janeiro*. Cambridge: Cambridge University Press, 1987.

Newbury, Colin W., and Alexander S. Kanya-Forstner, "French Policy and the Origins of the Scramble for West Africa," *Journal of African History*, 10, 2 (1969).

Newman, Daniel L. "Introduction," in Rifaʿa Rafi ʿal-Tahtawi, *An Imam in Paris: Accounts of a Stay in France by an Egyptian Cleric (1826–1831)*, ed. Daniel L. Newman. London: SAQI, 2011.

Nichols, Roy F. "Diplomacy in Barbary," *Pennsylvania Magazine of History*, 74, 1 (1950).

———. "William Shaler: New England Apostle of Rational Liberty," *New England Quarterly*, 9, 1 (1936).

Nicolet, Claude. *L'idée républicaine en France (1789–1914)*. Paris: Gallimard, 1994.

Nochlin, Linda. *The Politics of Vision: Essays on Nineteenth-Century Art and Society*. New York: Harper & Row, 1989.

Norberg, Kathryn. "The French Fiscal Crisis of 1788 and the Financial Origins of the Revolution of 1789," in Philip T. Hoffman and Kathryn Norberg, eds. *Fiscal Crises, Liberty, and Representative Government, 1450–1789*. Stanford, CA: Stanford University Press, 2002.

Nord, Philip. *Impressionists and Politics: Art and Democracy in the Nineteenth Century*. London: Routledge, 2000.

———. *The Politics of Resentment: Shopkeeper Protest in Nineteenth-Century Paris*, 2nd edn. New Brunswick, NJ: Transaction Publishers, 2005.

Nye, Joseph. *Soft Power: The Means to Success in World Politics*. New York: Public Affairs, 2004.

Nye, John V. *War, Wine, and Taxes: The Political Economy of Anglo-French Trade, 1689–1900*. Princeton, NJ: Princeton University Press, 2007.

O'Brien, Patrick, and Caglar Keyder, *Economic Growth in Britain and France, 1780–1914*. London: Allen and Unwin, 1978.

O'Rourke, Kevin H. "The Worldwide Economic Impact of the French Revolutionary and Napoleonic Wars, 1793–1815," *Journal of Global History*, 1, 1 (2006).

O'Rourke, Kevin, and Jeffrey G. Williamson, *Globalization and History: The Evolution of a Nineteenth-Century Atlantic Economy*. Cambridge, MA: MIT Press, 1999.

———. "When Did Globalization Begin?" *European Review of Economic History*, 6, 1 (2002).

Osterhammel, Jürgen. "Britain and China, 1842–1914," in Wm Roger Louis, ed. *The Oxford History of the British Empire*, 5 vols. Oxford: Oxford University Press, 1998–1999.

———. "Semi-Colonialism and Informal Empire in Twentieth-Century China: Towards a Framework of Analysis," in Wolfgang J. Mommsen and Jürgen Osterhammel, eds. *Imperialism and After: Continuities and Discontinuities*. London: Allen & Unwin, 1986.

———. *The Transformation of the World: A Global History of the Nineteenth Century*. Princeton, NJ: Princeton University Press, 2014.

Owen, Roger. *Cotton and the Egyptian Economy, 1820–1914: A Study in Trade and Development*. Oxford: Clarendon, 1969.

———. *Lord Cromer: Victorian Imperialist, Edwardian Proconsul*. Oxford: Oxford University Press, 2004

———. *The Middle East in the World Economy, 1800–1914*, 2nd edn. London: Tauris, 2002.

Pagden, Anthony. *Lords of All the World: Ideologies of Empire in Spain, Britain and France, c. 1500–1800*. New Haven, CT: Yale University Press, 1995.

Pamuk, Şevket. *The Ottoman Empire and European Capitalism, 1820–1913*. Cambridge: Cambridge University Press, 1987.

Panzac, Daniel. "The Population of Egypt in the Nineteenth Century," *Asian and African Studies*, 21, 1 (1987).

Panzac, Daniel, and André Raymond, eds. *La France et l'Egypte à l'époque des vice-rois, 1805–1882*. Cairo: Institut français d'archéologie orientale, 2002.

Paquette, Gabriel. "The Dissolution of the Spanish Atlantic Monarchy," *Historical Journal*, 52, 1 (2009).

Parent, Antoine, and Christophe Rault, "The Influences Affecting French Assets Abroad Prior to 1914," *Journal of Economic History*, 64, 2 (2004).

Parry, Jonathan. "The Impact of Napoleon III on British Politics, 1851–1880," *Transactions of the Royal Historical Society*, 11 (2001).

———. *The Politics of Patriotism: English Liberalism, National Identity and Europe, 1830–1886*. Cambridge: Cambridge University Press, 2006.

Pendergrast, Mark. *For God, Country, and Coca-Cola: The Unauthorized History of the Great American Soft Drink and the Company That Makes It*. New York: Basic Books, 2000.

Perrot, Philippe. *Fashioning the Bourgeoisie: A History of Clothing in the Nineteenth Century*. Princeton, NJ: Princeton University Press, 1994.

———. *Le Luxe. Une richesse entre faste et confort, XVIIIe-XIXe siècle*. Paris: Le Seuil, 1995.

Pervillé, Guy. "In memoriam. Charles-André Julien (1891–1991)," *Outre-Mers. Revue d'histoire*, 360–361 (2008).

Petiteau, Nathalie. *Lendemains d'empire: les soldats de Napoléon dans la France du XIXe siècle*. Paris: La boutique de l'histoire, 2003.

Picon, Antoine. *Les Saint-Simoniens: raison, imaginaire, utopie*. Paris: Belin, 2002.

Pierrat, Emmanuel. *Les lorettes: Paris, capitale mondiale des plaisirs au XIXe siècle*. Paris: Le Passage, 2013.

Pierre, Joëlle. "La presse française de Turquie, canal de transmission des idées de la Révolution," *Le Temps des médias*, 5, 2 (2005).

Piketty, Thomas. *Capital et idéologie*. Paris: Le Seuil, 2019.

Pinaud, Pierre-François. *Les receveurs généraux des finances, 1790–1865*. Geneva: Droz, 1990.

Piquet, Caroline. *Histoire du Canal de Suez*. Paris: Perrin, 2009.

Pitts, Jennifer. *Boundaries of the International: Law and Empire*. Cambridge, MA: Harvard University Press, 2018.

———. "Boundaries of Victorian International Law," in Duncan Bell, ed. *Victorian Visions of Global Order: Empire and International Relations in Nineteenth-Century-Political Thought*. Cambridge: Cambridge University Press, 2007.

———. "Republicanism, Liberalism, and Empire in Post-Revolutionary France," in Sankar Muthu, ed. *Empire and Modern Political Thought*. Cambridge: Cambridge University Press, 2012.

———. *A Turn to Empire: The Rise of Imperial Liberalism in Britain and France*. Princeton, NJ: Princeton University Press, 2005.

Piuz, Anne-Marie. "La soie, le luxe et le pouvoir dans les doctrines françaises (XVIe-XVIIIe siècles)," in Simonetta Cavaciocchi, ed. *La seta in Europa sec. XII-XX*. Florence: Le Monnier, 1993.

Planel, Anne-Marie. *Du comptoir à la colonie. Histoire de la communauté française de Tunisie, 1814–1883*. Paris: Riveneuve, 2015.

Plassart, Anna. "'Un impérialiste libéral?' Jean-Baptiste Say on Colonies and the Extra-European World," *French Historical Studies*, 32, 2 (2009).

Platt, Donald C. M. *Britain's Investment Overseas on the Eve of the First World War: The Use and Abuse of Numbers*. London: Macmillan, 1986.

Plessis, Alain. "Au temps du Second Empire, de l'entreprise de luxe au sommet des affaires," in Jacques Marseille, ed. *Le luxe en France: du siècle des "Lumières" à nos jours*. Paris: Association pour le développement de l'histoire économique, 1999.

———. *Régents et gouverneurs de la Banque de France sous le Second Empire*. Geneva: Droz, 1985.

Pommeranz, Kenneth. *The Great Divergence: China, Europe and the Making of the World Economy*. Princeton, NJ: Princeton University Press, 2000.

Poni, Carlo. "Mode et innovation: les stratégies des marchands de soie à Lyon au XVIIIe siècle," *Revue d'histoire moderne et contemporaine*, 45, 3 (1998).

Porterfield, Todd. *The Allure of Empire: Art in the Service of French Imperialism, 1798–1836*. Princeton, NJ: Princeton University Press, 1998.

Potofsky, Allan. *Constructing Paris in the Age of Revolution*. Basingstoke: Palgrave MacMillan, 2009.

Prasch, Thomas "London, 1862," in *Encyclopedia of World's Fairs and Expositions*. Jefferson, NC: McFarland, 2008.

Price, Roger. *The Second French Empire: An Anatomy of Political Power*. Cambridge: Cambridge University Press, 2001.

Pubrick, Louise. "Introduction," in Louise Pubrick, ed. *The Great Exhibition of 1851: New Interdisciplinary Essays*. Manchester: Manchester University Press, 2001.

Raccagni, Michelle. "The French Economic Interests in the Ottoman Empire," *International Journal of Middle East Studies*, 11, 3 (1980).

Ramm, Agatha. "Great Britain and France in Egypt, 1876–1882," in Prosser Gifford and Wm. Roger Louis, eds. *France and Britain in Africa: Imperial Rivalry and Colonial Rule*. New Haven, CT: Yale University Press, 1971.

Ratcliffe, Barrie M. "Paris, 1855," in *Encyclopedia of World's Fairs and Expositions*. Jefferson, NC: McFarland, 2008.

Raymond, André. "Une conscience de notre siècle: Charles-André Julien, 1891–1991," *Revue du monde musulman et de la Méditerranée*, 59, 1 (1991).

Régnier, Philippe. *Les Saint-simoniens en Egypte*. Cairo: Banque de l'Union Européenne, 1989.

Revue de Synthèse, 129, 1 (2008). Special issue on "Civilisations. Retour sur le mot et les idées."

Rey-Goldzeiguer, Annie. *Le Royaume arabe: la politique algérienne de Napoléon III, 1861–1870*. Algiers: Société nationale d'édition et de diffusion, 1977.

Ribeiro, Aileen. *Ingres in Fashion*. New Haven, CT: Yale University Press, 1999.

Riberette, Pierre. "Un réformateur du XIXe siècle et ses disciples: François-Guillaume Coëssin," in John Bartier and Jacques Valette, eds. *1848, les utopismes sociaux. Utopie et action à la veille des journées de février*. Paris: CDU-SEDES, 1981.

Richardson, Joanna. *The Courtesans: The Demi-Monde in Nineteenth-Century France*. London: Weidenfeld and Nicolson, 1967.

Riello, Giorgio. *Cotton: The Fabric That Made the Modern World*. Cambridge: Cambridge University Press, 2013.

Rietsch, Christian. "Le 'milliard des émigrés' et la création de la rente 3 percent," in Pierre Cyrille Hautcoeur and Georges Gallais Hamonno, eds. *Le Marché financier français au XIXe siècle*, 2 vols. Paris: Publications de la Sorbonne, 2007, vol. 2.

Ringmar, Erik. "Audience for a Giraffe: European Expansionism and the Quest for the Exotic," *Journal of World History*, 17, 4 (2006).

Rival, Ned. *Grimod de la Reynière: le gourmand gentilhomme*. Paris: Le pré aux clercs, 1983.

Roberts, Christopher. *The British Courts and Extra-Territoriality in Japan, 1859–1899*. Leiden: Brill, 2014.

Robinson, Moncure. "Obituary Notice of Michel Chevalier," *Proceedings of the American Philosophical Society*, 19 (1880).

Robinson, Ronald. "The Excentric Idea of Empire, with or without Colonies," in Wolfgang J. Mommsen and Jürgen Osterhammel, eds. *Imperialism and After: Continuities and Discontinuities*. London: Allen & Unwin, 1986.

Robinson, Ronald. "Non-European Foundations of European Imperialism: Sketch for a Theory of Collaboration," in Roger Owen and Bob Sutcliffe, eds. *Studies in the Theory of Imperialism*. London: Longman, 1972.

Robinson, Ronald, and John Gallagher, *Africa and the Victorians: The Official Mind of Imperialism*, 2nd edn. London: MacMillan, 1981.

Roche, Daniel. *Histoire des choses banales: naissance de la consommation dans les sociétés traditionnnelles (XVIIe-XIX siècle)*. Paris: Fayard, 1997.

———. *Humeurs vagabondes. De la circulation des hommes et de l'utilité des voyages*. Paris: Fayard, 2003.

Rock, David. "The British of Argentina," in Robert Bickers, ed. *Settlers and Expatriates: Britons over the Seas*. Oxford: Oxford University Press, 2010.

Rodgers, Daniel T. *Atlantic Crossings: Social Politics in a Progressive Age*. Cambridge, MA: Belknap, 1998.

Rodogno, Davide. *Against Massacre: Humanitarian Interventions in the Ottoman Empire, 1815–1914*. Princeton, NJ: Princeton University Press, 2012.

Røge, Pernille. *Économistes and the Reinvention of Empire: France in the Americas and Africa, c. 1750–1802*. Cambridge: Cambridge University Press, 2019.

Roger Louis, Wm, ed. *Imperialism: The Robinson and Gallagher Controversy*. New York: New Viewpoints, 1976.

Rosanvallon, Pierre. *La monarchie impossible: les Chartes de 1814 et 1830*. Paris: Fayard, 1994.

———. *Le moment Guizot*. Paris: Gallimard, 1985.

Rosenberg, Emily S. *Financial Missionaries to the World: The Politics and Culture of Dollar Diplomacy, 1900–1930*. Cambridge, MA: Harvard University Press, 1999.

Rosenblatt, Helena. *Liberal Values: Benjamin Constant and the Politics of Religion*. Cambridge: Cambridge University Press, 2008.

Rosenstock, Morton. "The House of Bacri and Busnach: A Chapter from Algeria's Commercial History," *Jewish Social Studies*, 14, 4 (1952).

Rothschild, Emma. *Economic Sentiments: Adam Smith, Condorcet and the Enlightenment*. Cambridge, MA: Harvard University Press, 2001.

———. "A Horrible Tragedy in the French Atlantic," *Past & Present*, 192 (2006).

———. *An Infinite History: The Story of a Family in France over Three Centuries*. Princeton, NJ: Princeton University Press, forthcoming in January 2021.

———. "Isolation and Economic Life in Eighteenth-Century France," *American Historical Review*, 119, 4 (2014).

———. "Language and Empire, c. 1800," *Historical Research*, 78 (2005).

Rothstein, Natalie. "Silk: The Industrial Revolution and After," in David Jenkins, ed. *The Cambridge History of Western Textiles*, 2 vols. Cambridge: Cambridge University Press, 2003, vol. 2

Roughton, Richard A. "Economic Motives and French Imperialism: The 1837 Tafna Treaty as a Case Study," *Historian*, 47, 3 (1985).

Rounding, Virginia. *Grandes Horizontales: The Lives and Legends of Marie Duplessis, Cora Pearl, La Païva and La Présidente*. London: Bloomsbury, 2003.

Ruedy, John. *Land Policy in Colonial Algeria: The Origins of the Rural Public Domain*. Berkeley: University of California Press, 1967.

Ruggiu, François-Joseph. "India and the Reshaping of French Colonial Policy (1759–1789)," *Itinerario*, 35, 2 (2011).

Ruskola, Teemu. *Legal Orientalism: China, the United States and Modern Law*. Cambridge, MA: Harvard University Press, 2013.

Saada, Emmanuelle. *Les enfants de la colonie: Les métis de l'empire français entre sujétion et citoyenneté*. Paris: La Découverte, 2007.

Sabel, Charles, and Jonathan Zeitlin. "Historical Alternatives to Mass Production: Politics, Markets and Technology in Nineteenth-Century Industrialization," *Past & Present*, 108 (1985).

Sabri, Muhammad. *L'empire égyptien sous Mohammed Ali et la question d'Orient (1811–1849)*. Paris: P. Geuthner, 1930.

Said, Edward. *Orientalism*. London: Penguin, 2003.

Saminadayar-Perrin, Corinne. "Fictions de la Bourse," *Cahiers naturalistes*, 78 (2004).

Sanderson, G. N. "The Origins and Significance of the Anglo-French Confrontation at Fashoda, 1898," in Prosser Gifford and Wm. Roger Louis, eds. *France and Britain in Africa: Imperial Rivalry and Colonial Rule*. New Haven, CT: Yale University Press, 1971.

Sari, Djilali. *Le désastre démographique*. Algiers: Société Nationale d'Édition et de Diffusion, 1982.

Sartori, Andrew. *Liberalism in Empire: An Alternative History*. Oakland: University of California Press, 2014.

Saul, Samir. *La France et l'Egypte de 1882 à 1914. Intérêts économiques et implications politiques*. Paris: Comité pour l'histoire économique et financière de la France, 1997.

Sawyer, Stephen. "Ces nations façonnées par les empires et la globalisation. Réécrire le récit national du XIXe siècle aujourd'hui," *Annales. Histoire, Sciences Sociales*, 69, 1 (2014).

———. *Demos Assembled: Democracy and the International Origins of the Modern State, 1840–1880*. Chicago: University of Chicago Press, 2018.

———. "A Fiscal Revolution: Statecraft in France's Early Third Republic," *American Historical Review*, 121, 4 (2016).

Schefer, Christian. *La grande pensée de Napoléon III: les origines de l'expédition du Mexique*. Paris: M. Riviére, 1939.

———. *L'Algérie et l'évolution de la colonisation française*. Paris: Honoré Champion, 1928.

Schnerb, Robert. "La politique fiscale de Thiers," *Revue historique*, 201 and 202 (1949).

Schölch, Alexander. *Egypt for the Egyptians! The Sociopolitical Crisis in Egypt, 1878–1882*. London: Ithaca Press, 1981.

Schoorl, Evert. *Jean-Baptiste Say: Revolutionary, Entrepreneur, Economist*. London: Routledge, 2013.

Schreier, Joshua. *Arabs of the Jewish Faith: The Civilizing Mission in Colonial Algeria*. New Brunswick, NJ: Rutgers Press, 2010.

Schroeder, Paul W. *The Transformation of European Politics, 1763–1848*. Oxford: Oxford University Press, 1994.

Schüller, Karin. *Die deutsche Rezeption haitianischer Geschichte in der ersten Hälfte des 19. Jahrhunderts. Ein Beitrag zum deutschen Bild vom Schwarzen*. Cologne: Böhlau, 1992.

———. "From Liberalism to Racism: German Historians, Journalists, and the Haitian Revolution from the Late Eighteenth to the Early Twentieth Centuries," in David P. Geggus, ed. *The Impact of the Haitian Revolution in the Atlantic World*. Columbia: University of South Carolina Press, 2001.

Scully, Eileen P. *Bargaining with the State from Afar: American Citizenship in Treaty Port China, 1844–1942*. New York: Columbia University Press, 2001.

Semmel, Bernard. *The Rise of Free Trade Imperialism: Classical Political Economy, the Empire of Free Trade and Imperialism, 1750–1850*. Cambridge: Cambridge University Press, 1970.

Senlis, Olivier. *François Bravay, le vrai Nabab*. Paris: DoD, 2017.

Sessions, Jennifer. *By Sword and Plow: France and the Conquest of Algeria*. Ithaca, NY: Cornell University Press, 2011.

Sewell, William H. "The Empire of Fashion and the Rise of Capitalism in Eighteenth-Century France," *Past & Present*, 206 (2010).

Shawcross, Edward. *France, Mexico and Informal Empire in Latin America, 1820–1867: Equilibrium in the New World*. Basingstoke: Palgrave MacMillan, 2018.

Shea, Gary S. "Financial Market Analysis Can Go Mad (in the Search for Irrational Behaviour during the South Sea Bubble)," *Economic History Review*, 60, 4 (2007).

Shepard, Todd. *The Invention of Decolonization: The Algerian War and the Remaking of France*. Ithaca, NY: Cornell University Press, 2006.

Shlala, Elizabeth H. "The De Rossetti Affair: Legal Pluralism and Levantine Identity at the Crossroads of Empires," *British Journal of Middle Eastern Studies*, 43, 1 (2016).

Shovlin, John. *The Political Economy of Virtue: Luxury, Patriotism, and the Origins of the French Revolution*. Ithaca, NY: Cornell University Press, 2006.

Shovlin, John, *Trading with the Enemy: Britain, France, and the Eighteenth-Century Quest for a Global Order*. New Haven, CT: Yale University Press, forthcoming in June 2021.

Shuval, Tal. "The Peripheralization of the Ottoman Algerian Elite," in Christine Woodhead, ed. *The Ottoman World*. London: Routledge, 2012.

Siedentop, Larry. "Introduction," in François Guizot, *The History of Civilization in Europe*. London: Penguin, 1997.

Siegel, Jennifer. *For Peace and Money: French and British Finance in the Service of Tsars and Commissars*. Oxford: Oxford University Press, 2014.

Simms, Brendan, and David J. B. Trim, eds. *Humanitarian Intervention: A History*. Cambridge: Cambridge University Press, 2011.

Simon, Alfred. *History of the Champagne Trade in England*. London: Wyman and sons, 1905.

Singaravélou, Pierre. *Professer l'Empire: "les sciences coloniales" en France sous la IIIe République*. Paris: Publications de la Sorbonne, 2011.

Sluga, Glenda. "'Who Holds the Balance of the World?' Bankers at the Congress of Vienna, and in International History," *American Historical Review*, 122, 5 (2017).

Sonenscher, Michael. *Before the Deluge: Public Debt, Inequality, and the Intellectual Origins of the French Revolution*. Princeton, NJ: Princeton University Press, 2009.

———. "The Nation's Debt and the Birth of the Modern Republic: The French Fiscal Deficit and the Politics of the Revolution of 1789," *History of Political Thought*, 18, 1 and 2 (1997).

Sonyel, Salahi. "The Protégé System in the Ottoman Empire," *Journal of Islamic Studies*, 2, 1 (1991).

Sowerwine, Charles. "Échos de Paris aux Antipodes: le théâtre et l'opéra français à Melbourne (1850–1914)," in Jean-Claude Yon, ed. *Le théâtre français à l'étranger au XIXe siècle. Histoire d'une suprématie culturelle*. Paris: Nouveau Monde, 2008.

Spang, Rebecca L. "The Ghost of Law: Speculating on Money, Memory and Mississippi in the French Constituent Assembly," *Historical Reflections / Réflexions Historiques*, 31, 1 (2005).

———. *The Invention of the Restaurant: Paris and Modern Gastronomic Culture*. Cambridge, MA: Harvard University Press, 2000.

———. *Stuff and Money in the Time of French Revolution*. Cambridge, MA: Harvard University Press 2015.

Sparling, Tobin Andrews. *The Great Exhibition: A Question of Taste*. New Haven, CT: Yale Centre for British Art, 1982.

Spary, Emma. *Feeding France: New Sciences of Food, 1760–1815*. Cambridge: Cambridge University Press, 2014.

Staum, Martin S. *Labeling People: French Scholars on Society, Race, and Empire, 1815–1848*. Montreal: McGill-Queen's University Press, 2003.

Stedman Jones, Gareth. "National Bankruptcy and Social Revolution: European Observers on Britain, 1813–1844," in Donald Winch and Patrick K. O'Brien, eds. *The Political Economy of British Historical Experience 1688–1914*. Oxford: Oxford University Press, 2002.

Steil, Benn. *The Battle of Bretton Woods: John Maynard Keynes, Harry Dexter White, and the Making of a New World Order*. Princeton, NJ: Princeton University Press, 2013.

Steiner, Philippe. "J.-B. Say et les colonies ou comment se débarrasser d'un héritage intempestif," *Cahiers d'économie politique*, 27–28 (1996).

Stokes, Eric. "Late Nineteenth-Century Colonial Expansion and the Attack on the Theory of Economic Imperialism: A Case of Mistaken Identity?," *Historical Journal*, 12, 2 (1969).

Stoler, Ann. L. "On Degrees of Imperial Sovereignty," *Public Culture* 18, 1 (2006).

Stone, Bailey. *Reinterpreting the French Revolution: A Global-Historical Perspective*. Cambridge: Cambridge University Press, 2002.

Stoskopf, Nicolas, *Les patrons du Second Empire. Banquiers et financiers parisiens*. Paris: A. et J. Picard, 2002.

Strauss, Johann. "Le livre français d'Istanbul," *Revue des mondes musulmans et de la Méditerranée*, 87–88 (1999).

Sullivan, Anthony T. *Thomas-Robert Bugeaud, France and Algeria, 1784–1849: Politics, Power, and the Good Society*. Hamden, CT: Archon Books, 1983.

Sutton, Michael, *France and the Construction of Europe, 1944–2007: The Geopolitical Imperative*. New York: Berghahn Books, 2007.

Taithe, Bertrand. *The Killer Trail: A Colonial Scandal in the Heart of Africa*. Oxford: Oxford University Press, 2009.

Tapinos, Georges Photios. "Paul Leroy-Beaulieu et la question de la population. L'impératif démographique, limite du libéralisme économique," *Population*, 54, 1 (1999).

Taricone, Fiorenza. *Il Sansimoniano Michel Chevalier: Industrialismo e liberalismo*. Florence: Centro editoriale toscano, 2006.

Tarrade, Jean. *Le commerce colonial de la France à la fin de l'Ancien Régime: l'évolution du régime de l'Exclusif, 1763–1789*, 2 vols. Paris: Presses Universitaires de France, 1972.

Taylor, A.J.P. *The Struggle for Mastery in Europe, 1848–1918*. Oxford: Clarendon Press, 1954.

Taylor, Miles. "The 1848 Revolutions and the British Empire," *Past & Present*, 166 (2000).

Temine, Émile. "La migration européenne en Algérie au XIXe siècle: migration organisée ou migration tolérée," *Revue des mondes musulmans et de la Méditerrannée*, 43 (1987).

Tétart-Vittu, Françoise. "Femmes du Monde et du demi-monde," in Musée de la mode de la Ville de Paris, *Sous l'empire des crinolines*. Paris: Paris musées, 2008.

———. "The French-English Go Between: 'Le Modèle de Paris' or the Beginning of the Designer, 1820–1880," *Costume*, 26, 1 (1992).

Theis, Laurent. *François Guizot*. Paris: Fayard, 2008.

———. *Guizot, la traversée d'un siècle*. Paris: CNRS, 2014.

Thobie, Jacques. *Intérêts et impérialisme français dans l'empire ottoman (1895–1914)*. Paris: Publications de la Sorbonne, 1977.

———. *La France impériale, 1880–1914*. Paris: Megrelis, 1982.

Thomas, Brinley. "The Historical Record of International Capital Movements to 1913," in John H. Adler, ed. *Capital Movements and Economic Development*. London: Macmillan, 1967.

Thomas, Martin, and Richard Toye, *Arguing about Empire: Imperial Rhetoric in Britain and France, 1882–1956*. Oxford: Oxford University Press, 2017.

Thompson, Andrew. "Informal Empire? An Exploration in the History of Anglo-Argentine Relations, 1810–1914," *Journal of Latin American Studies*, 24, 2 (1992).

Thomson, Ann. *Barbary and Enlightenment: European Attitudes towards the Maghreb in the Eighteenth Century*. Leiden: Brill, 1987.

———. "Colonialism, Race and Slavery in Raynal's *Histoire des Deux Indes*," *Global Intellectual History*, 2, 3 (2017).

————. "Raynal, Venture de Paradis et la Barbarie," *Dix-huitième Siècle*, 15 (1983).

Tiersen, Lisa. *Marianne in the Market: Envisioning Consumer Society in Fin-de-Siècle France.* Berkeley: University of California Press, 2001.

Tignor, Robert. *Modernization and British Colonial Rule in Egypt, 1882–1914.* Princeton, NJ: Princeton University Press, 1966.

Todd, David. "Beneath Sovereignty: Extraterritoriality and Imperial Internationalism in Nineteenth-Century Egypt," *Law and History Review*, 36, 1 (2018).

————. *Free Trade and Its Enemies in France, 1814–1851.* Cambridge: Cambridge University Press, 2015.

————. "A French Imperial Meridian, 1814–1870," *Past & Present*, 210 (2011).

————. "The *impôts arabes*: French Imperialism and Land Taxation in Colonial Algeria, 1830–1939," in John Tiley, ed. *Studies in the History of Tax Law*, vol. 3. Oxford: Hart, 2009.

————. "Remembering and Restoring the Economic Old Regime: France and Its Colonies, 1815–1830," in Alan Forrest, Karen Hagemann, and Michael Rowe, eds. *War, Demobilization and Memory: The Legacy of War in the Era of Atlantic Revolutions.* Basingstoke: Palgrave Macmillan, 2016.

————. "Retour sur l'expédition d'Alger: les faux-semblants d'un tournant colonialiste français," *Monde(s)*, 10, 3 (2016).

————. "Transnational Projects of Empire in France, c. 1815–c. 1870," *Modern Intellectual History*, 12, 2 (2015).

Todd, David, and Alexia Yates, "Public Debt and Democratic Statecraft in Nineteenth-Century France," in Nicolas Barreyre and Nicolas Delalande, eds. *A World of Public Debts: A Political History.* Basingstoke: Palgrave Macmillan, forthcoming in December 2020.

Topik, Steven C. "When Mexico Had the Blues: A Transatlantic Tale of Bonds, Bankers, and Nationalists, 1862–1910," *American Historical Review*, 105, 3 (2000).

Topik, Steven C., and Allen Wells, "Commodity Chains in a Global Economy," in Emily Rosenberg, ed. *A World Connecting, 1870–1945.* Cambridge, MA: Harvard University Press, 2012.

Toutain, Jean-Claude. "Le produit intérieur brut de la France, 1789–1990," *Economies et Sociétés. Série HEQ*, 11, 1 (1997).

Trivellato, Francesca. *The Familiarity of Strangers: The Sephardic Diaspora, Livorno, and Cross-Cultural Trade in the Early Modern Period.* New Haven, CT: Yale University Press, 2012.

Trubek, Amy B. *Haute Cuisine: How the French Invented the Culinary Profession.* Philadelphia: University of Pennsylvania Press, 2000.

Tudesq, André-Jean. *Les grands notables en France, 1840–1849. Étude historique d'une psychologie sociale*, 2 vols. Paris: Presses Universitaires de France, 1964.

Tunçer, Ali Coşkun. *Sovereign Debt and International Financial Control: The Middle East and the Balkans, 1870–1914.* Houndsmill: Palgrave Macmillan, 2015.

Vaïsse, Maurice. *La grandeur: politique étrangère du general De Gaulle, 1958–1969.* Paris: Fayard, 1998.

Varouxakis, Georgios. *Victorian Political Thought on France and the French.* Basingstoke: Palgrave, 2002.

Vaslin, Jean-Marie. "Le siècle d'or de la rente perpétuelle française," in Pierre Cyrille Hautcoeur and Georges Gallais Hamonno, eds. *Le Marché financier français au XIXe siècle*, 2 vols. Paris: Publications de la Sorbonne, 2007, vol. 2.

Vasseur, Édouard. "Pourquoi organiser des Expositions universelles? Le 'succès' de l'Exposition universelle de 1867," *Histoire, Economie & Société*, 24, 4 (2005).

Velay, A. du. *Essai sur l'histoire financière de la Turquie depuis le règne du Sultan Mahmoud II jusqu'à nos jours*. Paris: A. Rousseau, 1903.

Verley, Patrick. "Essor et déclin des industries du luxe et du demi-luxe au XIXe siècle," in Jacques Marseille, ed. *Le luxe en France: du siècle des "Lumières" à nos jours*. Paris: Association pour le développement de l'histoire économique, 1999.

———. *L'échelle du monde: essai sur l'industrialisation de l'Occident*. Paris: Gallimard, 1997.

Vigoureux, Claude. "Napoleon III et Abd-el-Kader," *Napoleonica*, 4, 1 (2009).

Vitalis, Robert. *White World Order, Black Power Politics: The Birth of American International Relations*. Ithaca, NY: Cornell University Press, 2015.

Vynckier, Henk, and Chihyun Chang, "*Imperium in Imperio*: Robert Hart, the Chinese Maritime Customs Services, and Its (Self-)Representations," *Biography*, 37, 1 (2014).

Walch, Jean. *Michel Chevalier, économiste saint-simonien*. Paris: Vrin, 1975.

Walt, Stephen M. *The Origins of Alliances*. Ithaca, NY: Cornell University Press, 1987.

Walton, Whitney. *France at the Crystal Palace: Bourgeois Taste and Artisan Manufacture in the Nineteenth Century*. Berkeley: University of California Press, 1992.

Waresquiel, Emmanuel de. *Talleyrand: le prince immobile*. Paris: Fayard, 2003.

Warshaw, Dan. *Paul Leroy-Beaulieu and Established Liberalism in France*. Dekalb: Northern Illinois University Press, 1991.

Weber, Eugen. *Peasants into Frenchmen: The Modernization of Rural France, 1870–1914*. Stanford, CA: Stanford University Press, 1976.

Weil, François. "L'État et l'émigration de France," in Nancy Green and François Weil, eds. *Citoyenneté et émigration. Les politiques du départ*. Paris, EHESS: 2006.

Weil, Patrick. *Qu'est-ce qu'un français? Histoire de la nationalité française depuis la Révolution*. Paris: Grasset, 2002.

Weiss, Gillian. *Captives and Corsairs: France and Slavery in the Early Modern Mediterranean*. Stanford, CA: Stanford University Press, 2011.

Whatmore, Richard. *Republicanism and the French Revolution: An Intellectual History of Jean-Baptiste Say's Political Economy*. Oxford: Oxford University Press, 2000.

White, Eugene N. "Making the French Pay: The Costs and Consequences of the Napoleonic Reparations," *European Review of Economic History*, 5, 3 (2001).

White, Harry D. *The French International Accounts*. Cambridge, MA: Harvard University Press, 1936.

White, Owen, and J. P. Daughton, eds. *In God's Empire: French Missionaries and the Modern World*. Oxford: Oxford University Press, 2012.

Whitney, Lynne. *Grand Tours and Cook's Tours: A History of Leisure Travel, 1750 to 1915*. London: Aurum Press, 1998.

Wilder, Gary. *The French Imperial Nation-State: Négritude and Colonial Humanism between the Two World Wars*. Chicago: University of Chicago Press, 2005.

Williams, William Appleman. *The Tragedy of American Diplomacy*. Cleveland: World Publishing, 1959.

Wilson III, Ernest J. "Hard Power, Soft Power, Smart Power," *Annals of the American Academy of Political and Social Science*, 616 (2008).

Winch, Donald. *Classical Political Economy and Colonies*. London: G. Bell & Sons, 1965.

Wolfzettel, Friedrich, and Frank Estelmann, *L'Égypte après bien d'autres. Repertoire des récits de voyage en langue française en Égypte, 1794–1914*. Turin: Moncalieri, 2002.

Wong, J. Y. *Deadly Dreams: Opium, Imperialism and the 'Arrow' War (1856–60) in China*. Cambridge: Cambridge University Press, 1998.

Worth, Jean-Philippe. *A Century of Fashion*. Boston: Little, Brown & Co., 1928.

Wood, Dennis. *Benjamin Constant: A Biography*. London: Routledge, 1993.

Wood, Leonard. *Islamic Legal Revival: Reception of European Law and Transformations in Islamic Legal Thought in Egypt, 1875–1952*. Oxford: Oxford University Press, 2016.

Wrigley, E. Anthony. "The Fall of Marital Fertility in Nineteenth-Century France: Exemplar or Exception?," *European Journal of Population—Revue européenne de démographie*, 1, 1 and 2, 3.

Wrona, Adeline. "Mots à crédit: *L'Argent*, de Zola, ou la presse au cœur du marché de la confiance," *Romantisme*, 151 (2011).

Yackee, Jason W. "The First Investor-State Arbitration: The Suez Canal Company v. Egypt (1864)," *Journal of World Investment and Trade*, 17, 3 (2016).

Yacono, Xavier. "Gabriel Esquer (1876–1961)," *Revue africaine*, 105 (1961).

Yates, Alexia. "Mobilizing Land in Nineteenth-Century France: The Double Life of Property and the Grounding of Modern Capitalism." *Critical Historical Studies*, 6, 2 (2019).

———. *Selling Paris: Property and Commercial Culture in the Fin-de-Siècle Capital*. Cambridge, MA: Harvard University Press, 2015.

Yaycioglu, Ali. *Partners of the Empire: The Crisis of the Ottoman Order in the Age of Revolutions*. Stanford, CA: Stanford University Press, 2016.

Yee, Jennifer. *Colonial Comedy: Imperialism in the French Realist Novel*. Oxford: Oxford University Press, 2016.

Yon, Jean-Claude. *Eugène Scribe: la fortune et la liberté*. Paris: Librairie Nizet, 2000.

———. *Le Second Empire. Politique, société, culture*. Paris: Armand Colin, 2004.

Young, Paul. "Mission Impossible: Globalization and the Great Exhibition," in Jeffrey A. Auerbach and Peter H. Hoffenberg, eds. *Britain, the Empire, and the World at the Great Exhibition of 1851*. Aldershot: Ashgate, 2008.

Unpublished Papers and Dissertations

Abdou, Mohamed Hamdi. "L'impact culturel de la France en Égypte au cours du XIXe siècle," unpublished PhD dissertation (University of Rennes II, 1988).

Charles, Léo. "Protection, spécialisation et croissance économique pendant la première mondialisation en France et en Suisse (1850–1913)," unpublished PhD thesis (University of Bordeaux, 2016).

Cheta, Omar. "Rule of Merchants: The Practice of Commerce and Law in Late Ottoman Egypt, 1841–1876," unpublished PhD dissertation (New York University, 2014).

Donath, Christian. "Persuasion's Empire: French Imperial Reformism, 1763–1801," unpublished Ph.D. dissertation (University of California San Diego, 2012).

Ffoulkes, Fiona Lesley. "The *Métier* of the Fashion Merchant (*Marchande de Modes*): Luxury and the Changing Parisian Clothing System, 1795 to 1855," unpublished PhD dissertation (University of Southampton, 2017).

Hanley, Will. "Foreignness and Localness in Alexandria, 1880–1914," unpublished PhD dissertation (Princeton University, 2007).

Klein, Jean-François. "Soyeux en mer de Chine. Stratégies des réseaux lyonnais en Extrême-Orient (1843–1906)" unpublished PhD thesis (University of Lyon II, 2002).

Lejeune, Claire. "L'abbé de Pradt (1759–1837)," unpublished PhD dissertation (University of Paris 4, 1996).

Lemercier, Claire. "Un modèle français de jugement des pairs. Les tribunaux de commerce, 1790–1880," unpublished Thèse d'habilitation (University of Paris 8, 2012).

Parsons, John. "France and the Egyptian Question, 1875–1894: A Study in Finance, Foreign Policy and Public Opinion," unpublished PhD dissertation (University of Cambridge, 1977).

Vasseur, Édouard. "L'exposition universelle de 1867 à Paris: analyse d'un phénomène français au XIXe siècle" unpublished PhD dissertation (École des chartes 2005).

Winch, Donald. "The Political Economy of Empire," given at the Institute of Historical Research, London, 5 November 2014.

Websites

American National Biography Online. www.anb.org

Australian Bureau of Statistics. http://www.abs.gov.au/population

Bibliothèque nationale de France, presse ottomane francophone. http://heritage.bnf.fr/bibliothequesorient/fr/presse-ottomane-francophone

Collections of the Château de Versailles. www.collections.chateauversailles.fr

Collections of the Musée d'Orsay, Paris. http://www.musee-orsay.fr/fr/collections/catalogue-des-oeuvres/

Collections of the National Gallery, London. https://www.nationalgallery.org.uk/paintings/

Federico-Tena World Trade Historical Database. http://www.uc3m.es/tradehist_db

Google Books, Ngram. https://books.google.com/ngrams

Institut national de la statistique et des études économiques. https://www.insee.fr

Kunsthalle, Mannheim. https://www.kuma.art

Musée des Tissus, Lyon. http://www.mtmad.fr

Navigocorpus database on shipping and maritime trade. http://navigocorpus.org

Organisation for Economic Cooperation and Development, data. https://data.oecd.org/oda/net-oda.htm

INDEX

'Abd al-Qadir: capture of, 104; coercion of, 22; collaboration with, 22, 96–100; compared to Muhammad 'Ali, 99; and *occupation restreinte*, 77, 115; proposed viceroy for Arab Kingdom, 117; quasi sovereignty of, 101; resistance of, 121; resumption of hostilities by, 101–2; smuggling of weapons to, 18–19; and Tafna treaty, 97–98, 99, 100, 102, 113; violence against, 73; war with, 102, 104

Aberdeen, Lord, 92

abolition of slavery: Britain and, 20; Chevalier on, 56; gradual, 56; first (1794), 9; in Haiti, 9, 35, 37, 43; Pradt on, 35, 41, 56; and Raynal's *Histoire*, 40n46,81; second (1848), 116; Urbain on, 116

access to power, 71

Adams, John Quincy, 28

Administration de la Dette Publique Ottomane, 208, 213–14, 217

Ageron, Charles-Robert, 75, 76

agriculture, as reproducible wealth, 140

Ahmad, bey of Constantine, 97, 100–101, 121

À la Ville de Paris (shop), 144

Algeria: 'Abd al-Qadir and, 22, 96–100; annexation of, 74, 104, 118, 119, 120; and Christian slavery, 78, 79, 91; civilian territories in, 120; and colonization, 55, 95; in comparison to Caribbean plantations, 116; conquest of, 57, 102–3, 206; and cotton, 86–87, 92; distinct identity of, 119; electoral rights in, 119–20; exports of, 108–110; famine in, 66, 108, 118; and fiscal

imbalance, 73, 105; as French foothold in North Africa, 66, 67, 78, 80, 82, 90; independence of, 9, 111, 118; land property law in, 68n141; Leroy-Beaulieu on, 68; nationalist movement in, 284; and *occupation restreinte*, 77, 98, 115; public debt of, 189; separate constitution for, 118–20; settlers in, 66, 106–8, 256; violence in, 2, 73; weapons smuggling in, 18–19. *See also* Algiers Regency; Arab Kingdom

Algiers (city): and agricultural settlements, 86, 89, 96, 115–16; French enclave in, 101, 102

Algiers Regency: and Christian slavery, 78, 79, 91; and the Concessions d'Afrique, 85–87; and the *créances Bacri*, 84, 85, 88, 89; Deval and, 75, 78, 83, 86, 88–89, 90; and Egyptian intervention attempt, 90–91, 229; French blockade of, 78, 90; French invasion of, 78, 89, 90, 92–93; French occupation of, 95, 98–99, 103; and La Calle fortification, 86–89; and Polignac, 90–91, 93; Shaler on, 82–84; and privateering, 78, 79, 81, 90, 91; and Tafna treaty, 97–103, 113; and territorial disputes, 101–2. *See also* Algeria

'Ali, Muhammad: and Algiers Regency, 90–91, 229; expansionism of, 102, 229; and France, 20, 112, 233–34; and Luxor Obelisk, 5, 229; modernizing policies of, 112; and relations with Britain and Italy, 229

Allgemeine Zeitung (newspaper), 192

Almanach des gourmands (Reynière), 150

Alsace, 153

American Civil War: effect of on US exports, 109, 128n16, 131, 156; French and British cooperation during, 18; and French occupation of Mexico, 221, 223, 224n205

Amis des Noirs, 35

Angell, Norman, 68n139

Anglo-French collaboration, 19–20, 57, 125, 251–52, 281; Arrow War (Second Opium War), 167; Banque Impériale Ottomane, 210–12; commercial treaty of 1860, 111, 115, 129–30; Dual Control of Egypt, 268–69; Greek War of Independence (1821), 78; and Ottoman public debt, 209–12

Anglo-French rivalry, 52–53, 95, 173, 273

Anglo-French trade, 165–66

Anglophilia, 45–46, 48, 50–51

"Anglo-Saxon race," 64, 67, 241

Anglo-Turkish war, 78

Anglo-Zulu war (1879), 19

Antidote au congrès de Rasdtadt (Pradt), 33, 34, 36, 40

Anti-Pradt, 40

Appoline, Marie Gabrielle, 112

Arabic language, 230, 239, 260, 266

Arab Kingdom: inequality between Europeans and Muslims in, 117–18; as a move towards informal empire, 111–12; Napoleon III on, 111, 115; political enfranchisement in, 119–20; and the Second Empire, 77, 111, 118, 119–20; 121; significance of, 117–18; Urbain on, 77, 111–12, 115–16. *See also* Algeria

Arab Kingdom policy, 66, 234

Arabophiles, 111, 114–15, 117, 118

Argentina, 18, 73, 232, 280

Arrow War (Second Opium War), 18, 63, 167

articles de Paris, 131–32, 136, 172, 281

Arzew, 96

Association pour la Liberté des Echanges, 154

Au Bonheur des Dames (Zola), 144n65

Aumale, Duc d', 113

Aurevilly, Jules Barbey d', 158

Australia, 73, 106–7

Bacri, house of, 84–85

Bagehot, Walter, 58–59, 65, 214n154; on French commodities, 136; on French demographics and investment, 182

Balzac, Honoré de, 146, 274

Bamberger, Ludwig, 163

Bankers and Pashas (Landes), 237

banking lobbies, 269

banking principles, 179

bankruptcy: of Egypt, 238, 266, 268; of French monarchy, 190; of Ottoman Empire, 209, 210, 214n152, 215, 217; and public debt, 193–94, 208; of recipients of French capital, 225; risk of, 186–87

banks and banking: Commission of Mexican Finances, 219; and credit operations, 182; and Egyptian debt, 268; and free trade movement, 154; joint stock banks, 60, 128; and loans to Ottoman Treasury, 210, 212; national deposit banks, 182, 194, 207. *See also* foreign investment

Banque Impériale du Mexique, 220

Banque Impériale Ottomane, 210–12

Banque Paravey & Cie, 199–202

Barbary Coast, 87–88, 94

Barbary States, 35–36, 79, 80–81

Bastiat, Frédéric, 154

Batchelder, George S., 245

Baudrillart, Henri, 171

Baxter, Dudley, 195

Bayly, Christopher, 76

bazaars: as architectural inspiration, 143, 159; and French goods, 258

Beaumont, Gustave de, 102

Belgium: foreign investment by, 206n122, 222n193, 275; French intervention and influence in, 33–34, 51–52, 95

Berry, Duchesse de, 158

beys, 97

bimetallism, 64, 219

birth rate, 181–82

Bismarck, Otto von, 281

Blanqui, Adolphe, 137

Blücher, Gebhard, 161

Bobergh, Otto, 161

Bolivar, Simon, 41, 43, 44

Bona, 85, 88, 96

Bonaparte. *See* Napoleon I

Bonaparte, Louis-Napoleon. *See* Napoleon III

Bordelais, 153, 154

Bourbon Restoration, and Algeria, 78, 82–83, 89–90, 93; and Charter of 1814, 45; and colonialism, 84–90, 200; and foreign investors, 191; and luxury goods, 143, 150, 154; public credit during, 187–88, 189, 190, 191; and Saint-Domingue, 43, 200; and Spanish America, 40, 197. *See also* France; July Monarchy

bourgeoisie, 13, 15, 133, 156, 158

Bourse, 176, 204, 205, 210

Brahmanism, 50

brands, 146–47, 148

Bravay, François, 227, 243, 274

Brazil: as commodity producer, 128; recruitment of Algerian settlers by, 118; and slavery, 21, 156n109

Bright, John, 62

Brillat-Savarin, Jean Anthelme, 150, 155

Britain: abolition of slavery by, 20; as arbitrator of global legal order, 246; and capital exports, 179–80, 195–96; as colonizer of North Africa, 82–83; constitution of, 44, 58–59; and Continental Blockade, 31, 128; exports of, 125n6, 204, 245; foreign investment by, 179–80; and the French language, 242, 244; judicial activity of, 252, 253; and lack of taste, 138; and masculinity, 134; national debt of, 188–89, 194, 195, 197–98; naval supremacy of, 17, 19, 44–45, 79, 102; and Portugal, 207; power of compared to Europe, 47; and *protégés*, 250, 251; and settler colonies, 10, 73, 107, 195–96, 232; and trade with America, 32, 35, 41; and transshipment of goods, 166–67

　　—and China: customs management, 208; Arrow War (Second Opium War), 18, 63, 167; informal British domination, 280; Opium War,

53; raw silk trade, 127, 164–65, 167

　　—and Egypt, 229, 256: Anglo-French Dual Control, 268–69; British occupation, 208, 268–69, 270, 281

　　—and France, 17–18, 18–20, 46–47, 70; French exports, 156; proposed merger, 52–53; Opium Wars, 53, 63, 167; trade partnership, 164–67. *See also* Anglo-French collaborations; Anglo-French rivalry

Brougham, Henry, 33

Brue, Urbain, 112

Bugeaud, Général, 77, 98, 103, 113

Bugia, 96

Burgundy, 153

Burke, Edmund, *Reflections on the Revolution in France*, 31, 34

Cain, Peter, 177

Caisse de la Dette Publique, 208

Cambodia, 20

Cameron, Rondo, 184

Canada, 33

canals, interoceanic, 63–64

capital exports: of Britain, 7–8, 179–80, 195–96, 283–84; into Egypt, 179–80, 195–96; of France, 7–8, 15, 179–80, 184–85, 226, 283–84. *See also* foreign investment; public credit; public debt

capitalism: and consumer desire, 135–36; and French global influence, 22, 125, 283; gentlemanly, 176–77; and imperialism, 13, 16, 160, 173, 174, 178; industrial, 28; and middle-class consumption, 133; and monarchy, 16, 226; and Saint-Simonianism, 28, 52, 112, 193, 194. *See also* champagne capitalism

Capitulations, 230, 247–49, 256, 262

Capture of the Smala of Abd el-Kader (1845) (Vernet), 113–14

Carême, Antoine, 150, 155

Caribbean, 36; European oversight in, 36, 56; French colonies in, 32, 80; slave plantations in, 116. *See also* Cuba; Haiti

Catholic Church: missionaries of, 167; and the silk industry, 140, 141, 154

Catholic vs Protestant political forms, 59

censorship, 224, 278–79

champagne: and bottling machines, 132–33; British consumption of, 123–24; and brothels, 149; as a drink for social elites, 147–48; as a drink for women, 134; dry varieties of, 159; exports of, 124, 130; and German entrepreneurs, 164; global reach of, 123–24; historical anecdotes about, 146–47, 161; labels and vintages of, 146–48; Moët & Chandon as exporter of, 124; at universal exhibition of 1867, 170

Champagne (province): 130, 146, 153

champagne capitalism: *articles de Paris* as symbol of, 131–32, 136, 172, 281; and conspicuous commodities, 13, 125, 130, 134, 135–36, 139, 148, 156–57, 181; and courtly commodification, 145–148, 149, 150, 154; and economic development, 125, 126, 134, 137, 153; and exports, 131–32, 134–35, 165–67; 172; and French influence, 22, 125, 283; foreign collaborators of, 125, 161–64; and gastronomy, 150–51, 155; and global trade expansion, 124–25, 128–130, 138, 154; and silk industry, 126; and taste, 127, 139, 142–43; and technology, 132–33; and tourism, 159–60; at universal exhibitions, 136–37, 168–72; and urban planning, 144; Zola on, 277. *See also* champagne; prostitution; shopping; silk, raw; silk textiles

champagne industry, 141, 146, 154, 164

Charles I (England), 147

Charles X, 45, 91–92, 146, 158

Chateaubriand, François-René de, 49–50, 218

cheese, 148–49, 161

Chevalier, Auguste, 58

Chevalier, Cordelia, 67

Chevalier, Michel: on abolition, 56; on bimetallism, 64, 219; at Collège de France, 171, 193, 194; and Constant's ideas, 69–70; on excesses of democracy, 60, 155; on expansionism, 56; and fourth universal exhibition, 169; and free trade, 29, 58–65, 127; on globalization, 30; influence of, 68, 70–71; on infrastructure and finance, 193–94; *Lettres sur l'Amérique du Nord*, 54–57; and Orientalism, 28, 53; Ottoman Empire investments of, 217; as patron of Urbain, 113; and racism, 55–56, 59, 65, 70, 283; as Saint-Simonian, 28, 52–53, 63; and "System of the Mediterranean," 53, 193; on transport infrastructure, 53, 54, 56, 63, 193, 194; travels in North America of, 54, 63, 65, 70, 193

China: British domination in, 208, 280; isolationism of, 61–62; Opium War, 53; Second Opium War, 18, 63, 167; as a source of raw silk, 127, 164–65, 167

Christianity, 49–50, 51, 143

civilization, concept of, 26, 27, 38, 48–51

Clauzel, Bertrand, 100

Clémenceau, Georges, 269

Clément, Félix, 227, 258

Clermont-Tonnere, Comte de, 91

Cobden, Richard, 62, 154

Coca Cola, 174

Code de l'indigénat, 120, 122

coffee, 128, 200, 205

Colbert, Jean-Baptiste, 239

Colbertian regulations, 134–35

Cold War geopolitics, 47

collaboration, 20–21, 96–97

Colombian bonds, 198–99, 201

colonial expansion vs intra-European war, 69

"colonial order," 36n35

colonies: and Anglo settlerism, 10, 73, 107, 195–96, 242; bias towards mother country of, 33; as bridgeheads, 121n167; demographic growth of, 106–7; fiscal balance of, 105; imports from, 108–9; independence of, 34–35; loss of, 30;

replacement of, 32, 80; restrictions on trade of, 32–33, 37, 60–61, 80, 189; slavery in, 33; Spanish, 27–28, 29, 40–43, 44, 201

colonies of exploitation, 69

"colonisation nouvelle," 80, 83

colonization: of Algeria, 55, 95; economists on, 94; foreign investment as, 195, 196, 215; industrial, 116; investment, 15, 117, 178, 210–15; lack of commitment to, 78; mercantilist, 68; Slavic Orthodox, 55

Comité du Contentieux, 257–58, 259, 272

Comment les dogmes finissent (Jouffroy), 50

Commission of Mexican Finances, 219, 221

commodification: of champagne, 147–48; and fashion, 131–33; and gastronomy, 150–51; and shopping, 143–45; and tourism, 159–60; of women, 14

commodities: foreign lending and sales of, 205, 207; debts as, 183; Haiti as outlet for, 203; luxury and *demi-luxe*, 13, 124, 125, 130, 139, 181, 281; paintings as, 6

Commune of 1871, 168, 172–73

Compagnie d'Afrique, 79, 85–86

Concessions d'Afrique, 85–86

Congress of Vienna (1815), 41

conquest: of Algeria, 4–5, 19, 57, 90, 98–99, 103, 104, 122, 206–7; under Bourbon Restoration, 89, 93; of Egypt, 143, 218, 274; formal vs informal, 10, 22, 68, 77, 80, 89, 93, 96, 102, 121, 273–4; hostility to, 25–26, 37, 44, 50, 55, 69, 70, 77, 90; of Indochina, 165n137; investment colonization as an alternative to, 178; under July Monarchy, 78, 95–96; of Mexico, 218; reconquest of Saint-Domingue, 75; under Third Republic, 122, 189; violence of, 2, 73, 77, 104, 121; war of, 103, 104, 115, 121; Zola on, 175–76

Conseil d'État, 60, 114, 255

Conseil du Gouvernement, 114

Conseil Supérieur du Commerce et des Colonies, 87

Constant, Benjamin: on conquest of Algiers, 93–94; and celebration of commerce, 69–70; and condemnation of conquest, 25, 37, 44; on excesses of democracy, 155; and French constitution, 25–26; on liberty, 60; *On the Spirit of Conquest*, 25–26, 37, 50; Pradt on, 37–38; on South American republics, 44; and support of coups, 58; and Talleyrand, 37

Constantine province: agriculture in, 107; colonial settlement in, 85; dispute over, 77, 96–97; French conquest of, 100–101; population of, 119n161

Constantinople: banking in, 210–11, 212, 214, 220, 244; dragoman training in, 239, 240; visit of Empress Eugénie to, 213; French language in, 240; and legal reforms, 251, 253, 262–63; as seat of possible world government, 241; suzerainty over Egypt of, 247; theatres in, 157

constitution: of Algeria, 118–20; of Britain, 39, 44, 58; of France, 25–26, 58–59, 75

consulates in Egypt, legal function of, 245–46, 251–55, 266

Continental Blockade, 31, 128

Convention of Miramar, 219

Corn Law League, 154

Corn Laws, 61

Coronation of Napoleon (1807) (David), 6, 12

corporations, 249

corvée, 20–21

cotton, 13, 126: cultivation in Algeria of, 73, 86–87, 92, 109; cultivation in Egypt of, 87, 156, 234, 244–45, 258–59; cultivation in the United States of, 87, 128; displacement of by silk in French industry, 130–31, 153; effects of American Civil War on, 109–10, 128n16, 131, 156; market for, 154, 173, 200; and slave labour, 13–14

counter-revolutionary modernity, 10–11

coup of 2 December 1851, 57–58

coup of 18 Brumaire, 58

coup of 18 Fructidor, 58

Courbet, Gustave, 152

Cours complet (Say), 140

créances Bacri, 84–85, 88, 89

Crédit Foncier d'Égypte, 275

Crédit Mobilier, 211
créole, 42
Crimean War, 18, 209, 248
Cromer, Lord, 251, 271
Crouch, Eliza, 162
Crusades, 52
Crystal Palace exhibition of 1851. *See* Great Exhibition of 1851
Cuba, 128
customs duties, 7, 43, 62, 109, 208

Dalberg, Duc de, 200–201, 204, 218
Daudet, Alphonse, 162, 274
Daumier, Honoré, 144
David, Louis, 6, 12
Decazes, Duc, 265
De la colonisation chez les peuples modernes (Leroy-Beaulieu), 67–69, 196
Delacroix, Charles, 239–40
De l'Angleterre et des Anglais (Say), 46
De l'esprit de conquête. See *On the Spirit of Conquest* (Constant)
De l'état de la France à la fin de l'an VIII (Hauterive), 31, 36
demographic stagnation, 17, 181–82, 196
department stores, 131, 133, 134, 144–45
dependency theory, 166
Dervieu, Édouard, 237–239, 243
Des colonies et de la révolution actuelle de l'Amérique (Pradt), 40–42, 43
Desjobert, Amédée, 99, 103
Desmichels Convention (Treaty of 26 February 1834), 97
Deval, Pierre: 78, 83, 86; and fly swatter incident, 75, 88; and La Calle fortifications, 88–89
Deveaux, Émile, 213
Disraeli, Benjamin, 265
dollar diplomacy, 185
Doloret, Gabriel, 198–99
dragomans, 239, 240, 243
Du congrès de Vienne (Pradt), 37–38, 40
Dupin, Charles, 48
Dutch language, 242

East Asia, 189
École des jeunes de langue, 239–40
economic development, 125–26, 139
economic freedom, 60, 155
economic growth: champagne capitalism as engine of, 125–26, 138, 153; neo-courtly model and, 14–15, 142–43; of Ottoman Empire, 211; before the Revolution, 134–35; of Russia, 224; Saint-Simonianism and, 112
economic integration, 16, 62
economic regulation, 61
Egypt: Anglo-French Dual Control of, 268–69; army of, 269, 270n162; British exports to, 245; British occupation of, 234, 238, 241, 270, 271–73, 281; Caisse de la Dette Publique in, 208; census of, 234; compared to American Frontier, 245; cultivation of cotton in, 87, 156, 234, 244–45, 258–59; European population in, 233–34; exports of, 244–45; and extraterritoriality, 245; financial conquest of, 218; French expatriates in, 230, 233–37; French exports to, 156, 244–45; French influence in, 55, 274–75, 279; French investment in, 208; French language in, 239, 241; French occupation of, 21–22, 27n8, 63, 78, 143; indemnity claims against, 264–65; judicial reform in, 260–66, 271–72; legal system of, 245–46, 247–49, 251–52, 256; and *Majālis al-Tujjār*, 251, 252, 256; *protégés* in, 251; public finances of, 238, 256, 257, 264, 266, 268, 275; relations of with Britain, 229; relations of with Italy, 229; sovereignty of, 264–65; Sudan and, 247; Suez Canal and, 21n69, 63, 213, 243, 257, 261, 262; and Syria, 247; Talleyrand's support for invasion of, 80–81
emancipation, 56, 116
emigration: to Algeria, 118; to Canada, 42; to Egypt, 234, 237, 275; French, compared to other European, 231; Revolutionary, 140; of Saint-Simonians, 55; settler, 15, 17, 231, 233 (*see also* settler colonies); to Spanish America, 42

empire of taste. *See* champagne capitalism

empires: and capitalism, 16, 126; and colonies of exploitation, 69; liberal vs despotic, 47; financial consequences of, 209; and indigenous collaboration, 17; informal, 23, 121, 247, 283 (*see also* champagne capitalism); main features of, 160, 174, 283, 285; and racism, 70; and repertoires of rules, 3

emprunts russes, 224

Enfantin, Prosper, 193

English Constitution (Bagehot), 59

English language, 242–43

Entente Cordiale agreement (1904), 51, 57, 281

Esquer, Gabriel, 74, 76

Essai politique sur le commerce (Melon), 139

Eugénie (empress), 5–6

Eurocentrism, 26–27, 50–51, 67–68

Europe, prevention of war in, 53, 61, 103

Europe, the World's Banker (Feis), 185–86

European civilization: celebration of, 44–45, 70; coinage of phrase, 26–27; endangered by European wars, 66–67; rhetoric of, 48–49

European racial supremacy (White European), 28, 35, 37, 42–43, 67–68

Exclusif, 60–61

Execution of Maximilian (Manet), 277–79

executive power, 58–59

expatriates, British, 232

expatriates, French: consular control of, 255; in Egypt, 230, 233–37, 244, 259; rights of, 246, 255–56

exports

—Britain: 125n6, 204, 245; capital exports, 7–8, 179–80, 195–96, 283–84; to Haiti, 204; raw silk, 127, 164–65; transshipment, 166–67

—France: 125n6, 129, 134–35; capital exports, 7–8, 15, 179–80, 184–85, 226, 283–84; to Egypt, 244–45; to Haiti, 204

extraterritorial jurisdiction: defence of, 253–54; 262; in Egypt, 247–48, 251–52, 256, 264–65; expatriates and, 230, 256; and French metropolitan courts, 264; and informal imperial power, 246–47, 254, 275–76; internationalization of, 231; limits of, 205; mixed cases, 250, 251, 252, 261; in Ottoman Empire, 250, 255; in Siam, 7; and taxation, 256

famine, 107–8, 118

fashion: *cocottes*, 149; *haute coduture*, 160, 161–62; Paris vs London, 134; *prêt-a-porter*, 131–32, 133; and tourism, 159–60

Fashoda, 18, 273

Favre, Jules, 120

Feis, Herbert, 185–86

financial centers, 191, 197

"First Common Market," 62–63

First Restoration, 34

First World War: and decline of French language, 8; and financial losses, 181; financial imperialism as cause of, 177–78, 185; and territoriality, 284

fiscal-military state, 189

foreign investment: Anglo-French collaboration and, 209–10; ban on, 205; as colonization, 195, 196, 215; dangers of, 180–81, 184–85, 201; determinants of, 15, 182, 184–85; in Egypt, 245, 275; *emprunts russes*, 177n22, 224; encouraged by Bonapartist government, 207; French and British models of, 185–86; French savers and, 15, 215, 221–22, 224; high-yield bonds, 214; Italian bonds, 207; lottery bonds, 184, 221; Mexican bonds, 219, 220, 221–22; Ottoman bonds, 210, 214–15, 221; Piedmontese bonds, 207; political considerations and, 206, 207; in Russia, 177n22, 224; Spanish American bonds, 198–99; as taxation, 225; women and, 216–17. *See also* capital exports; public credit; public debt

Fould, Achille, 210

Fox, Edward W., 4

France: as arbiter of taste, 136–37; and Belgium, 51–52; Britain, relations with, 17–18, 18–20, 46–47, 70 (*see also under* Britain); capital exports of, 7–8, 15, 179–80, 184–85, 226, 283–84; and *Code de Commerce* (1807), 250; desirability of collaboration with, 281; Egypt, asymmetry of relationship with, 230; exports of, 7, 125n6, 129, 173, 204, 283; and financial losses from First World War, 181; humiliation of, 103–4; influence of on European civilization, 48–51; legal system of, 271–72, 283; as model for Ottoman reforms, 250; national debt of, 188–89, 206, 207; as protector of Latin nations, 64–65; *protégés* of, 57, 233n25, 235, 236, 250–51, 259; and slavery, 20–21. *See also* Bourbon Restoration; July Monarchy; Old Regime; Second Empire; Third Republic

Franco-Prussian war, 66, 69; effects of, 22, 128n16, 262–63, 279; Italian neutrality during, 207–8

Franco-Russian alliance, 177

freedom of industry, 60

freedom of the press, 224

freedom of trade, 60

free trade: conservative support for, 154; liberals and, 29, 48; opinions on, 62; Say's views on, 46–47; Second Empire's adoption of, 115–16

free trade imperialism, 33, 68; and asymmetric legal arrangements, 249; in Siam, 7; treaty of Balta Liman as symbol of, 248, 249

free trade treaties, 60, 62

French Communauty, 284

French Directory, 58–59, 155n102

French Guyana, 112

French language, 156–57; in Egypt, 239, 240–41, 266, 270–71; as lingua franca, 8, 241–42, 283; in Ottoman Empire, 240–41, 250

French Union, 284

French West Indies, 35

Friedrich III (Germany), 148

Fuat Pasha, Grand Vizier, 210

Galata Serai (Galatasaray), 241, 262

Gambetta, Léon, 217, 265, 269–70

gastro-liberalism, 155, 158

gastronomy, 150–51

Gaulle, Charles de, 285

Gavillot, Aristide, 263

Génie du Christianisme (Chateaubriand), 49–50

genocide, 73

Gentz, Friedrich von, 31

German unification, 280–81

Germany, 67, 192, 284

Germiny, Charles de, 219, 221

Gérôme, Jean-Léon, 5–7, 12, 20, 152

Giffard, Pierre, 244

Girardin, Emile de, 117

Gladstone, William Ewart, 192

globalization: backlash against, 282; consciousness of, 29–30, 39–40, 124–25; and international trade, 16, 124–25, 127–30, 186

Glorious Revolution (1689), 44

Gobineau, Arthur de, 70

gold rushes, 64

gold-silver bimetallic standard, 64, 219

Goschen, George, 179

grain imports, 102

Gran Columbia, 44

grands magasins, 134, 143–44, 145

Grand Tours, 159

Grazia, Victoria de, 22

Great Depression (1873), 130, 173

Great Depression (1930s), 284

Greater Kabylia, 101, 104, 279

Great Exhibition of 1851 (London), 62, 136–37, 168–69

Greece: French financial influence in, 207; independence of, 18, 47, 78; intervention in, 189

Grimod de la Reynière, Laurent, 150

Grotius, Hugo, 38

guilds, 141

Guizot, François: on Algeria, 77; on civilization, 50–51; and doctrine of limited occupation, 98–99; on excesses of democracy, 155; *Histoire de la Révolution d'Angleterre*, 44; and Leroy-Beaulieu, 67; and support for war of conquest, 103

gunboat diplomacy, 7, 22, 61, 70, 186, 235. *See also* naval blockades

Guyana, 79

Habsburgs, 64, 66

Haiti: alliance of with Bolivar, 43; civil code for, 272; debt of, 186, 200, 202; exports from, 205; exports to, 203, 204; gunboat diplomacy and, 22; independence of, 36–37, 202; and plantations, 116, 202–3; revolution in, 9, 41 *See also* Saint-Domingue

Halévy, Ludovic, 158

halfa grass, 110

Halim, Prince, 227

hard power vs soft power, 2, 279–80

Haussmann, Baron Georges-Eugène, 144, 172

Haussmannization, 144, 244, 258n120

haute banque, 202

haute couture, 152, 160, 161–62

Hauterive, Alexandre d': and Continental Blockade, 31–32; on "French empire of language, commerce, and laws", 247; *De l'état de la France à la fin de l'an VIII*, 31, 36

Heredia, Severiano de, 163

Herzen, Alexander, 163

Histoire de la Révolution d'Angleterre (Guizot), 44

Histoire des Deux Indes (Raynal), 30–31, 35, 40; projects of colonial settlements in, 79; posthumous edition (Peuchet), 81–82

History of India (Mill), 46–47

Hobson, John A., 15, 176–77

Holland, public debt of, 195

Hong Kong,, 242–43

Hopkins, Anthony, 177

House of Rothschild, 188, 200

Hugo, Victor, 162

Huguenots, 173

Humboldt, Alexander von, 56

Hundred Days, 25–26

Hussein Dey, 75, 78, 88, 89; and Concessions d'Afrique, 85–86

Iberian America (Spanish and Portuguese America), independence in, 30, 38, 40, 42–43. *See also* Spanish American republics

Illustrated London News, 123

immigration: in Algeria, 66, 80, 107, 111, 118; in Mexico, 55, 65

Imperialism, the Highest Stage of Capitalism (Lenin), 177

import duties and tariffs, 45, 62, 108–9; in Algeria, 108; during American Civil War, 131; and global economic integration, 124; of Ottoman Empire, 248, 249

imports: from Algeria, 73, 108–10; British mediated, 127, 164–65; from Egypt, 244–45; of foreign capital 22n72; of France, 110, 129. *See also* capital exports; exports

impressionism, 152–53

incomes, per capita, 125

indemnities: Clément's claim for, 227–28; and Comité du Contentieux, 257–59, 272; from Egyptian government, 227–28, 257–259; from France to former *émigrés*, 191n56; after Franco-Prussian War, 192; from Haiti to expropriated French colonists, 43, 202, 203n106; Maunoury's claim for, 272; Mexican bondholders' claim for, 222; from Ottoman government to Plœuc, 211; at Treaty of Paris (1815), 188; to Suez Canal Company, 257

India, 17, 42, 109

indigenous populations: Algerians, 114–15; displacement of, 104, 107–8; Muslims, legal inferiority of, 120

indigo, 91

Indochina, 282, 284

industrialization, 135–36, 137

industries, luxury and *demi-luxe*, 13, 124, 125, 130, 181. *See also* commodification influence, global projection of, 3, 21–23, 55, 66–67, 185, 209, 225. *See also* champagne capitalism; commodification; foreign investment; public debt

informal dominance, 117, 270

informal empire: Arab Kingdom as a move towards, 112–13; collapse of, 274, 280–81; features of, 22–23; military glory and, 21–22; nation-state and, 9, 286

infrastructure: commercial, 13, 142, 145, 159, 165, 167; in Egypt, 234; funding of, 193, 207, 223; and Haussmannization, 144; transport, 53–54, 56, 63, 193, 194, 207, 234

Ingres, Dominique, 152

insurance premiums, 165

interdependency, 285

interest rates, 191, 208–9

intermarriage, 56

International Relations Theory, 19

investment colonization, 15, 117, 178, 210–15

investments: government bonds, 183–84; legal framework for, 60–61

Iron Gates pass, 101

Islam, 46, 50, 112

Ismai'il, Khedive, 148, 238–39

isolationism, 61–62, 242

Italian language, 239, 243, 271

Italy, 164, 207–8, 229

Jacquard, Joseph-Marie, 141

Jacquard loom, 14, 132, 141

Jecker, Jean-Baptiste, 64

Jefferson, Thomas, 39

Jews: in Algeria, 84–85; enfranchisement of, 119–20; French citizenship given to, 73

joint stock banks, 60, 128

Jouffroy, Théodore, 50

Journal des Débats, 113

Julien, Charles-André, 75, 76

July Monarchy, 51; and Algerian conquest, 90, 206; and colonization, 78; foreign policy of, 57; and future of Algiers Regency, 95; and mercantilist legislation, 128; and public debt, 188, 189, 194; Saint-Simonians and,

192–93. *See also* Bourbon Restoration; France; Second Empire

Jumel, Louis Alexis, 87

Kabyle people, 84

Kabylia, 101, 104, 279

Kathersozialismus, 194

Kautsky, Karl, 16

Kemal, Mustapha, 249

Keynes, John Maynard, 184

Koenig, Matthieu, 238

Laborde, Alexandre de, 93

labour, division of, 62

La Calle (el Kala), 85–86, 87–89, 92

Lacroix, Frédéric, 115, 116

La Dame aux Camélias (Dumas *fils*), 157

La défense du Mondain (Voltaire), 139

Laffitte, Jacques, 95, 190, 191; on interconnected financiale centers, 197; on lending to all governments, 199; as patron of Saint-Simonians, 193

Laffitte & Cie, 202

Laffon, Gustave, 255

La France nouvelle (Prévost-Paradol), 6667

laissez-faire economics, 61

L'Algérie française. Indigènes et immigrants (Urbain), 115

Landes, David, 237, 238

land mortgages, 275

La Prusse et sa neutralité (Pradt), 36–37

La Revue encyclopédique (periodical), 94

L'Argent (Zola), 175–76

Larnaurdie, Abbé, 7

L'art de la cuisine française au dix-neuvième siècle (Carême), 150

Latin America, public debt and military intervention in, 189

Latin Monetary Union, 207

L'Auto (newspaper), 244

Law, John, 187, 190, 191, 193

Laws of Imitation (Tarde), 142–43

Lebanon, 18, 167

Le Bon Marché, 134, 144

legal reform: in Algeria, 114; effects of international agreements on, 280; in Egypt, 246–47, 257, 260–66, 271; and Egyptian judicial reform, 257, 261, 271; and land mortgages, 275; in the Levant, 255; in Ottoman Empire, 249–250, 254

legal system: in Egypt, 245–46, 247–49, 251, 252, 260–66, 271; in France, 271–72, 283; in Ottoman Empire, 251, 253; Roman, 251

Le Globe (journal), 52

Le Journal des Débats (newspaper), 54, 56

Le Mondain (Voltaire), 139

Le Nabab (Daudet), 162

Lenin, 16, 177, 184

Leroy-Beaulieu, Paul, 67–69; on capital exports, 196; on French demographics and investment, 182; influence of, 71; on interconnected financial centers, 197; on investment colonization, 15, 117, 178, 215; on public debt, 195

Les commencements d'un empire (Esquer), 74

Les guerres contemporaines (Leroy-Beaulieu), 67–68

Lesseps, Ferdinand de, 243

Lesseps, Matthieu de, 243–44

Les trois âges des colonies (Pradt), 36, 41, 42

Le Tailleur, Eugène, 226

Le Temps (newspaper), 44

Lettres sur l'Amérique du Nord (Chevalier), 54–57

Levant, the, 164, 229, 252

Levant Herald (newspaper), 240

Levant Times (newspaper), 240

Lhuys, Edouard Drouyn de, 110–11

liberalism, 39, 58–59

liberals: on colonization, 89–90, 93; entry of term into lexicon, 29; and opposition to public credit, 191; views on Algiers Regency of, 95

liberty, civil vs political, 60

life expectancy, 181–82

Liverpool, Lord, 44

loans: defaults on, 205–6; colonial, 105n120; foreign, 178–79

London: and British imperial expansion, 177; conference of 1830–1831, 34; convention of 1840, 247; exhibitions in, 62, 168, 169; financial market of, 197, 198, 199, 204, 205, 209, 214, 220; foreign residents in, 162; French language in, 242; and high insurance premiums, 165; men's fashion in, 134; as possible seat of Anglo-French parliament, 52; Scribe's sojourn in, 158; Talleyrand as ambassador in, 34, 51, 95; theatres in, 157

Lorimer, James, 241

Loubon, Joseph, 72, 120

Louis, Joseph-Dominique, 190

Louis XIV, 12, 173

Louis XVI, 34

Louisiana, 33

Louis-Napoléon (son of Napoleon III), 19

Louis-Philippe, 44

Louverture, Toussaint, 32, 41

Luxor Obelisk, 5, 229

luxury: banality of, 140–41; commodification of, 178–79; demand for, 12–13; eighteenth-century attitudes towards, 139–40; pernicious effects of, 187

Lyon, 153

Lyon Chamber of Commerce, 141

Lysis, 226

Mackau, Ange de, 43–44

Madagascar, 57, 282, 284

magasins de nouveautés, 131, 144, 145

Maillard de Marafy, Comte de, 263, 264–65

Maistre, Joseph de, 34

Majālis al-Tujjār, 251, 252, 256

Manet, Édouard, 152, 277–79

Marx, Karl, 50, 82

Massif Central, 153

Maunoury, Paul, 260–61, 272

Maximilian of Habsburg, 64, 66, 167–68, 218, 279; execution of, 170, 222

Mediterranean: British hegemony in, 20, 79; Chevalier's "System of the Mediterranean," 53; and cotton cultivation, 87; in *La nouvelle France* (Prévost-Paradol), 67

Melon, Jean-François, 139, 187

Merrivale, Herman, 68

Metternich, Klemens von, 92

Mexico: and American Civil War, 221, 223, 224n205; Chevalier's trip to, 54–55, 63, 64, 65; execution of monarch of, 66, 170, 277–78; expedition to, 218–19; financial conquest of, 223; French and Britain cooperation over, 18; French invasion of, 22, 63, 218; and interoceanic canal, 63; loans to, 179, 183, 218–222; monarchy of, 64–65, 125, 163–64, 218–19, 223; racial makeup of, 65; silver production in, 64, 219; withdrawal of French forces from, 222

Middle East: British domination of, 280; champagne consumption in, 123; financial conquest of, 208–218; French military interventions in, 189

migration, 106, 133, 232, 234, 236–37

military glory, 21–22, 75, 91, 96, 121

Mill, John Stuart, 50, 68, 195–96

Mill, James, *History of India*, 46–47

Milner, Alfred, 271–72

Mirabeau (*fils*), 194

Mississippi Valley, 87

Mitidja plain, 101

Moët & Chandon, 124

moeurs, 98, 113, 119, 162; *police des moeurs*, 168

Moitessier, Marie-Clotilde, 152

monarchical regimes, 11; bicameral, 45; capitalism and, 15–16; constitutional, 39, 155n102, 218; democratic, 189; financial, 226

Monet, Claude, 152

monetary standards, 64, 219

money: as high-end good, 178; money market, 198; Zola on, 175. *See also* capital exports; foreign investment; public credit; public debt

Mongkut (Rama IV), 5, 20

Montagnard Republic, 140, 155n102

Morellet, Abbé, 81

Morny, Duc de, 162

Morocco, 67, 253; protectorate regime in, 122, 282. *See also* Barbary States

mortgages, 182, 275

Mostaganem, 96

Moustier, Léonel de, 261

Mulhouse, 153, 154

Museum of Orsay, 152

Muslims: and business development, 249–50; enfranchisement of, 117–18, 119–20; enhanced rights of, 98, 100; indigenous, 107–8, 115–16, 120; legal inferiority of, 73, 120; and rule of law, 254, 263; Tocqueville on, 103; Urbain and, 112, 113, 115–16

Napoleon, Prince, 162

Napoleon I: British hegemony as a result of the downfall of, 20, 102; conspiracy against, 201; Constant and , 25–26, 37; and Consulate of 1799–1804, 11; and Continental Blockade, 31; *Coronation of Napoleon* (David), 6, 12; cult of, 5; and efforts to ensure durable peace in Europe, 31; in Egypt, 27n8, 143, 214; and Hundred Days, 25–26; silk portrait of, 14, 141; and the silk industry, 141; urban planning under, 144–45

Napoleon III: Arab Kingdom instigated by, 111, 115; authoritarian regime of, 21; and champagne capitalism, 160; coup of, 58, 59, 60; court of, 12–13, 145, 163–64; gift of to Maximilian I, 167–68; half-brother of, 162; and Mexico, 65; and national debt, 207; and promotion of commercial interests, 167–68, 172; on quotation of Ottoman bonds, 210; and Saint-Simonians, 63; Siamese ambassadors' visit to, 5–6; silk portrait of, 14, 141; and Suez Canal, 63; and treaty of 1860, 62

national debt: effects of Algerian conquest on, 206; of Britain, 188–89; and domestic stability, 188; of Egypt, 238; vs foreign debt, 184–85; of France, 188, 206, 207

national deposit banks, 182, 194, 207
nationalism: in Egypt, 260, 267, 269; in
    Ottoman Empire, 217, 249; resurgence of,
    282, 284
national pavilions, at world fairs, 170, 171
nation-state: Arab Kingdom as, 118; France
    as, 4, 9, 286; and markets, 16
naval blockades: of Algeria, 78, 83, 90, 102;
    of Haiti, 43; of Rio de la Plata, 18. *See also*
    gunboat diplomacy
neo-colonial dependency, 41, 284
neo-Europes, 106, 142, 231
Neuville, Guillaume Hyde de, 83
New France, 54, 66–67
newspapers: censorship of, 224; French-
    language, in Ottoman Empire, 240, 255;
    Russian bribes to, 224
New Zealand, 107
North Africa: Britain as colonizer of, 82–83;
    Chevalier on, 55n97; colonial settlements
    in, 27; commodities of, 91; economic
    disillusionment with, 206–7; environmen-
    tal realities of, 121; European migrants to,
    236; French domination in, 63, 66–67, 73,
    80, 84, 96–97, 117; French soldiers in,
    97, 101, 104; *Histoire des Deux Indes* on,
    81; Leroy-Beaulieu on, 68; Ottoman
    dominance of, 80; precariousness of
    settlements in, 77; Raynal on, 80; Talley-
    rand on, 80, 86. *See also* Algeria; Algiers
    Regency; Barbary States; Egypt; Morocco
notaries, 182
nouveautés, 146n72, 148, 149, 158, 168
novels, French, 157, 172
Nubar Pasha, 257, 260–61

occupation restreinte (limited occupation), 77
Olbie (Say), 138–39, 140
Old Regime: and capitalism, 135; diplomatic
    and consular services of, 253n103; guild
    production under, 134; and luxury, 139,
    143, 146, 148n81, 187; Parlement de
    Provence under, 252; Parisian salons
    under, 145; and public credit, 186–87; and

public debt, 139, 191, 193; royalists'
    attitude towards, 90; technology under,
    141
Ollivier, Émile, 261–62, 265
On the Spirit of Conquest (Constant), 25–26,
    27–28
Opium Wars, 18, 53, 63, 167
Oran: and Brazil, 118; European population
    of, 119n161; as French enclave, 96, 97, 101,
    102; Général Bugeaud in, 113
oriental despotism, 59
orientalism, 1, 7, 83, 213, 228–229, 238, 258;
    legal, 254
Osterhammel, Jürgen, 22
Ottoman Empire: Administration de la
    Dette Publique in, 208, 213–14, 217;
    bankruptcy of, 209–10, 217; Banque
    Impériale Ottomane and French
    influence in, 212; Capitulations accorded
    by, 230, 247–49, 256, 262; Code de
    Commerce (1850) of, 250; and Crimean
    War (1853–1856), 209; French imports in,
    109; French investment in, 176, 208, 209;
    French language in, 250; Greek
    independence from, 18, 47, 78; legal
    reform and *protégés* in, 250–51; legal
    system of, 251, 253; and public debt,
    208–10, 213–14; suzerainty of, 229, 247;
    Tanzimat era in, 247, 250; tariffs of, 248,
    249; and threat posed by Europe, 78;
    Young Turk revolution in, 217
Ottoman Treasury, short-term advances to,
    212
Ottoman Treasury Council, 211

pacifism, 67–68, 169
paintings: *beaux-arts* and, 152; *Capture of the
    Smala of Abd el-Kader* (Vernet), 113–14;
    changing tastes in, 152–53; *Execution of
    Maximilian* (Manet), 277–79; impres-
    sionist, 152; at Museum of Orsay, 152; *The
    Reception of Siamese Ambassadors*
    (Gérôme), 5, 6–7, 20; at *salon des refusés*,
    152; *salons* of, 168, 227

Palais de l'Industrie, 152

Palais-Royal, 145, 149, 150, 161

Palmerston, Henry, 65

Panchaud, Isaac, 189–90

Parallèle de la puissance anglaise et russe (Pradt), 47, 48

paramountcy, 17, 77, 207

Paravey, Pierre-François, 199–200, 204

Paris: Conseil d'État in, 114; courtly functions of, 13, 142–43, 145–48; exhibitions in, 14, 169–72; as financial center, 64, 181n21, 184–85, 197, 198, 199, 205–6; foreign presence in, 125, 161–63; as international market for government bonds, 205; parliament in, 120; prostitution in, 142, 149, 161, 172, 183n26; resident foreigners in, 163–64; restaurants in, 150–51; as taste-maker, 142, 172; tourism in, 159–60; Treaty of Paris (1783), 54; Treaty of Paris (1814), 43, 161; Treaty of Paris (1815), 188; Treaty of Paris (1856), 248. See also *articles de Paris*; champagne capitalism; fashion; shopping

Paris Commune, 168, 172–73, 192, 281

Paris-Guide (1867), 162–63, 164

parliamentary bodies: British style of, 58–59; budget scrutiny of, 194; Chevalier on, 59, 64; colonial representation in, 119–20, 122; commission on Algiers Regency emanating from, 95–96, 102; Crown's power vs, 89–90; economic efficiency of, 59; of Gran Columbia, 44; increased power of, 59; and vote against intervention in Egypt, 269

passage des panoramas, 143

passage du Caire, 143

passages, arcaded, 13, 143, 145, 159

passport controls, 159

patronage, 63, 113, 146, 158

patterns of consumption, gendering of, 133–34

Peace Conference (1919), 8

Pearl, Cora, 162

Peel, Robert, 61

Pemberton, John, 174

perfumes, 148, 153

Perier, Casimir, 95

Pérignon, Dom Pierre, 146

Perry, Matthew, 242

Petit catéchisme (Pradt), 39

Peuchet, Jacques, 81–82, 84

Physiocrats, 79, 189; on diversion of capital, 139–40; on public credit, 187, 191

Physiology of Taste (Brillat-Savarin), 150, 155

piracy, 35–36, 78, 79, 81, 90, 91

Plœuc, Alexandre de, 211–12; dismissal of, 217; and judicial reform in Egypt, 262, 263–64, 265

police des moeurs, 168

Polignac, Jules de, 90–92, 93

political exile, 232; 'Abd al-Qadir in, 117; of Commune insurgents, 172–73; Talleyrand in, 15, 32, 33–34, 189

population stagnancy, 17, 181–82, 196, 231

portraits, silk-woven, 14, 141–42

Portugal, 199, 207

Poujade, Pierre, 259

Pradt, Abbé Dominique de: as archbishop of Malines, 33–34; on British protectorate, 47–48; and conspiracy against Napoleon, 201; Constant's influence on, 69–70; on free trade, 29, 127; on Haitian independence, 43–44; on independence of Spain's colonies, 27–28, 29, 41–43, 44, 201; publications of, 38–39, 70–71; on slavery and racism, 35–36, 41–42, 283; Talleyrand and, 27, 33–34, 201

—works by: *Antidote au congrès de Rasdtadt*, 33, 34, 36, 40; *Des colonies et de la révolution actuelle de l'Amérique*, 40–42, 43; *Du congrès de Vienne*, 37–38, 40; *La Prusse et sa neutralité*, 36–37; *Les trois âges des colonies*, 36, 41, 42; *Parallèle de la puissance anglaise et russe*, 47, 48; *Petit catéchisme*, 39

Pradtiana, 38, 39

prêt-a-porter, 131–32, 133

Prévost-Paradol, Anatole, 66–67
privateering, 35–36, 78, 79, 81, 90, 91
prostitution, 142, 149, 161, 168, 172, 183n26
protectionism: as anachronistic, 61, 115; of
  cotton and wool manufacturers, 154; and
  deterioration of Anglo-French relations,
  173; economic decline and, 151; free trade
  vs, 115, 173; under Third Republic, 13, 130,
  154, 282; universal exhibition used
  against, 137
protectorate: of Britain, 47–48; over Mexico,
  64–65; over Morocco and Tunisia, 122;
  under Third Republic, 282, 283
protégés, 57, 233n25, 235, 236, 250–51, 259
Protestantism, 54
Protestant vs Catholic political forms, 59, 154
Provence, 94, 153, 215, 221, 227, 272
Prussia: absolutist government of, 199;
  defeat of Habsburg Monarchy by, 66;
  growth in power of, 31, 66, 170;
  investments in government bonds of,
  199. See also Franco-Prussian war
public credit: under Bourbon Restoration,
  187–88, 189, 190, 191; Chevalier on,
  193–94; disdain for, 186–87; Talleyrand's
  enthusiasm for, 189; Thiers and, 190, 192.
  See also capital exports; foreign
  investment; public debt
public debt: of Britain, 138, 188; British
  investment in other countries', 19n63,
  206n121; civilization and, 195; domestic
  stability and, 188; of Egypt, 257, 264, 268,
  275; foreign, 184–85, 186, 206–7, 228;
  global market for, 197; increasing
  number of investors in, 183, 189; and
  infrastructure, 193; and institutions, 190,
  193, 194–95; and Law's System, 191, 193;
  of Mexico, 218; of Old Regime, 191; of
  Ottoman Empire, 208, 217, 218; and
  promotion of luxury, 139; and military
  ventures, 189; reliance on, 188; Saint-
  Simonian enthusiasm for, 193; taxation
  vs, 193. See also capital exports; foreign
  investment; public credit

Questnay, François, 139–40

racial determinism, 65
racism, 35–36; of Chevalier, 55–56, 59, 65,
  70, 283; and European racial supremacy
  (White European), 28, 35, 37, 42–43, 67–68;
  and legal orientalism, 254; of Lorimer,
  241; and orientalism, 1, 7, 83, 213, 228–229,
  238, 258; of Paravey, 203–4; of Pradt,
  35–36, 41–42, 283; Saint-Simonianism
  and, 55–56, 115–16; and segregation, 73.
  See also slavery
railways: in Asia Minor and greater Syria,
  175; and champagne exports, 130; investment in, 19n63; in North America, 54;
  public vs private financing of, 193; spread
  of, 159; state-guaranteed loans for, 60,
  105, 128, 188, 194; in "System of the
  Mediterranean," 53, 193; and tourism, 159
Rama IV (King Mongkut), 5, 20
raw materials, 32–33, 61, 62, 73, 125, 153, 164,
  166–67
Raynal, Guillaume: colonial projects of,
  79–80, 81, 89; Histoire des Deux Indes,
  30–31, 35, 40; Histoire, posthumous
  edition, 81, 82; as instigator of slave
  insurrection, 35
rayonnement, 22, 125, 283
Reception of Siamese Ambassadors (1864)
  (Gérôme), 5–7, 12, 20
receveurs généraux, 182–83, 199, 202, 204n112,
  221
re-exportation, 127–28, 164–65
Reflections on the Revolution in France
  (Burke), 31, 34
Réflexions sur la réduction de la rente, 190–92,
  199
Renoir, Pierre-Auguste, 152
rentes: dissemination of, 183–84; of
  expatriates in Egypt, 237; and growth of
  international finance, 197, 201; indemnity
  paid in, 191n56; purchase of by Mexico,
  221–22; quoted value of, 188
rentier, 189, 214n152, 224n205, 282

republican government: Algeria under, 111, 117, 118, 120; annexation by, 118, 120; assimilationism of, 117, 284; Chevalier on, 59, 64–65; colonialism of, 75–76, 274; and commodification of taste, 151; as democratic, 10, 11, 13; and dismissal of Plœuc, 217; and domestic markets, 154; economic downturn and advent of, 126; and Esquer, 74–75; and Gambetta, 217, 265, 269–70; Leroy-Beaulieu on, 69; and Manet, 278; vs monarchy, 64, 65, 13, 15–16, 69, 154; political economy of, 45–46, 138–39, 225–226; principles of, 280; rise of, 274, 281–82; Say and, 138–39, 226; of the United States, 64, 222; Zola, 280. *See also* monarchical regimes

restaurants: gastronomy and, 150–51; at fourth universal exhibition, 169–70

Restoration. *See* Bourbon Restoration

Revolution (1789–1799), 10; disbanding of language school under, 239; economic effects of, 134, 186–87, 193; and luxury goods, 124, 140–41; and military glory, 90; origins and repercussions of, 34–35, 39; Third Republic as result of, 11, 12; West Indies and, 80

Revolution (1830), 52, 77, 78, 95, 112, 193

Revolutions (1848), 11

Revue des Deux Mondes (periodical), 56

Rhineland, 200

Ricardo, David, 61, 186

Rimmel, Eugene, 169–70

Rio de la Plata, 18

Riquetti de Mirabeau, Victor, 186–87

Roman empire, 251, 280

Romania, 207

Roquefort cheese, 148–149, 153

Rossi, Pelegrino, 61n115

Rothschild, Jakob (James de), 200

Rothschild frères, 202

Rouher, Eugène, 207, 210, 221

Russia: bribery of French press by, 224; champagne in, 161; Crimean War of 1854–1856 against, 18, 209; Egypt and,
248; expansion in Asia by, 67, 248; foreign debt of, 181, 224; foreign investment in, 177–178, 199, 224; Ottoman Empire and, 18, 47, 78, 209, 248; power of, 47; rise of, 31; and Slavic Orthodox colonization, 55

Russo-Turkish wars, 78

Sa'id (pasha): becomes pasha, 251–52; and Bravay, 227, 243, 274; and Dervieu, 238–39; fluency in French of, 239, 243–44; and Halim (younger brother), 227; and immigration of skilled Europeans, 252; Paris education of, 239; and Suez Canal, 243–44

Saint-Domingue: as being de facto independent, 32; Chevalier on, 56; compared to Algiers, 94; efforts to regain control over, 36–37, 75, 81, 100, 128, 197, 200; independence of, 36, 43; insurrection of, 9, 35, 43, 56; leadership of, 32; loan by, 202–3, 204; Paravay and, 203–4; Pradt on, 56; racial warfare in, 36; Raynal and, 81; resumption of commercial relations with, 202–3; slavery in, 36; Talleyrand on, 80–81 *See also* Haiti

Saint-Etienne, 153

Saint-Simon, Henri de, 52

Saint-Simonianism: and admiration for Law's system, 192–93; Algeria and, 55; as creed of industrial capitalism, 28; and free love, 52; influence of, 52; and pseudo-scientific ideas of race, 55–56, 115–16; and public borrowing, 192–93, 195; and socialist doctrines, 194; and Suez Canal, 63; and taxes, 193

Saint-Simonians: Chevalier, 52, 193; in Egypt, 55, 234; Enfantin, 193; influence of under Second Empire, 192–93, 194; Leroy-Beaulieu and, 195; Napoleon III and, 62–63; Stein and, 194–95; Urbain and, 111, 112–13, 115, 234. *See also* Chevalier

salon des refusés, 152

salons: of paintings, 168, 227; as setters of fashion, 145; Spanish American emissaries feted in, 197–98 savings: abundance of, 15, 228; and commodification of sex, 183n26; competition for, 221, 224; imperialism and, 176–77; of small savers, 60, 196, 214–15, 221; as source of capital exports, 7–8, 176, 181–82, 184, 207, 225

Say, Jean-Baptiste: Anglophilia of, 45–47; on Britain's lack of taste, 138; on free trade, 46, 61; on luxury, 138–39, 140; as professor of political economy, 56–57; on public credit, 191, 226; on quality, 139; on settler colonies, 94; *Treatise on Political Economy*, 94, 191

Scribe, Eugène, 158

Second Empire: Algerian policy of, 77, 104, 110, 119, 121; Arabophile party under, 114; authoritarian nature of, 224; bonds sold by, 188; champagne producers' support for, 154; Chevalier and economic policies of, 28; commercial treaties of, 63; economic reforms under, 128–129, 224; end of, 112, 127, 130, 172, 223; exports during, 131–32; and free trade, 115–16; and funding of military ventures, 189; and growth of national debt, 207; liberal reforms under, 59; Mexican expedition of, 176, 218–19, 221, 223; and Mexico, 167–68; powers of parliamentary assemblies under, 59; and Prussia, 66, 223; republicans on Algerian policy of, 118; Saint-Simonians, influence on, 192–93, 194; style of, 138; Zola on, 176

Second Opium War (Arrow War), 18, 63, 167

Second World War, 185–86, 284

Senatus Consulte of 1865, 117–18

Senegal, 68

Senior, Nassau William, 110

settlements, agricultural, 86, 89, 96, 115–16

settlements, colonial: and costs of territorial rule, 70; female-to-male ratio in, 237; Guizot on, 57; in North Africa, 27, 77, 80, 92; in North America, 54, 56, 231, 232. *See also* Algeria

settlements, military, 91

settler colonies: Anglo, 10, 73, 107, 195–96, 242; as bridgeheads, 121n167; demographic growth of, 106–7

settlerism, 68, 96, 115, 232

Seven Years' War, 30, 79

Sewell, William, Jr., 135–36

sewing machines, 133

Shaler, William, 81–84, 88

shopping: at À la Ville de Paris, 144; in bazaars, 143, 159, 258; in *grands magasins*, 134, 143–44, 145; at Le Bon Marché, 134, 143; in *magasins de nouveautés*, 131, 144, 145; in arcaded passages, 13, 143, 145, 159; and *prêt-a-porter*, 131–32, 133

Siam, 5–7, 11, 20, 63

silk, raw: British imports of, 127; trade of, 127, 164–65, 167, 242–43

silk *nouveautés*, 146n72, 148, 158

silk portraits, 14, 141–42

silk stockings, 139–40

silk textiles: bourgeois women and, 133–34; *canuts* and fabrication of, 132; cotton textiles vs, 130–31; effect of Federalist insurrection on, 140–41; at exhibitions, 137, 170; French exports of, 14, 126–27, 131–32; global chain of, 126–27; Italian industry of, 281; and Jacquard looms, 14, 132, 141; Lyonnais merchants of, 132, 138, 141, 154, 281; as product of Lyon and Saint-Etienne, 153; and velvet, 14

silk worm, 153; disease of, 164

silver ore, 64, 219

Singer, Isaac, 133

Sismondi, Jean-Charles Simonde de, 94

Sketches of Algiers (Shaler), 82, 83–84

slavery: abolition of, 35–37, 41; Christian, 78, 79, 91; in colonies, 33, 36n35; Constant against, 37; Dupin on, 48; economists against, 94; indifference to, 20–21; Pradt on, 35, 36, 41–42

slave trade, 18, 128, 200

soft power vs hard power, 2, 279–80

Sonenscher, Michael, 187

Sorbonne, 50, 163

South Africa, 108

South Kensington Museum, 137

Soviet Union, 181, 224, 280

Spain: independence of colonies of, 27–28, 29, 40–43, 44, 201; military intervention in, 189; public debt of, 199, 201, 205

Spanish America, independence of, 30, 38, 40, 42–43

Spanish American republics: British loans to, 197–98; and lawsuit regarding Columbian bonds, 198–99; speculation on bonds of, 199–201

spinning jennies, 14, 132

Staël, Germaine de, 37

stagnation, economic: of French exports, 130, 173, 274; Ottoman government and, 79–80

Stein, Lorenz von, 194–95

Stendhal, 158

stock panics, 204, 206

stocks, 223, 224

Stuarts, the, 44

sub-Saharan Africa, 105n120, 173, 225, 267, 273, 282, 284

Sudan, 247, 273

Suez Canal: building of, 234; concession for, 243; and corvée labor, 21n69; inauguration of, 213, 261; military intervention near, 269; Ollivier as commissioner of, 262

Suez Canal Company, 63, 218, 257; in dispute with Egyptian government, 257; Disraeli's purchase of shares in, 265; in favour of judicial reform, 261; French jurisdiction over, 252

sugar, 91, 123–24, 127, 128, 200

suzerainty: over 'Abd al-Qadir, 115, 117; use of the word, 226; economic substitute for, 203; foreign debt and, 207; of the Ottoman Empire over Muhammad 'Ali, 229, 247

Syndicat des receveurs généraux, 202

synthetic fibers, 281

Syria, 247

"System of the Mediterranean," 53, 193

Tafna treaty, 97–103, 113, 117

Taiping rebellion, 167

Tall al-Kabir, 270

Talleyrand-Périgord, Charles-Maurice de, 27–28, 29; accused of conspiracy against Napoleon, 201; on Africa, 81, 86–87; as ambassador in London, 51–52, 95; and appointment of Deval, 86; on British credit in America, 189; on colonies in warm countries, 80; Constant and, 37; on Continental Blockade, 31–32; on credit and quasi-colonial domination, 15; and culinary diplomacy, 155; and Dalberg, 200, 201, 204; and defusing of Anglo-French tensions, 95; and Delacroix, 239–40; as early promoter of informal imperialism, 280; on Egypt, 80, 240; as exile to United States, 15, 32, 33–34, 189; on French cheese, 161; and French diplomatic and consular services, 253n103; as hostile to democratic republicanism, 15; as investor in Banque Paravey & Cie, 200–201; and language school, 239–40; and Louis, 190; luxury and, 154–55; on Panchaud, 189–90; possible grandson of, 162; Pradt and, 33–34, 201; on public finance, 189–90, 192; and purchase of Haitian bonds, 204; and representative government, 58; and settlement of Belgian question, 51–52; in support of coups, 58; and Thiers, 190; on trade with former colonies and voluntary monopolies, 32–33, 37, 80, 189

Tanzimat reforms, 247, 250

Tarde, Gabriel, 142–43

tariffs, 45, 108–9; in Algeria, 108; American, 131; global reduction of, 124; as obstacle to global domination, 62; of Ottoman Empire, 248, 249

taste: changing conceptions of, 151–53; as defining quality, 137, 138; foreign influence on, 158–59; occupation of France as formative of, 161; politics of, 154–56; tourism and, 159–60 taxation: by 'Abd al-Qadir, 97; in Britain, 130, 138, 197–98; of expatriates, 256; of foreign trade, 249; public borrowing vs, 193; of settlers, 105

technology: of electroplating, 148, 167–68; and export-oriented industries, 132–33; of Jacquard looms, 14, 132, 141; of spinning jennies, 14, 132; of steam distillation, 148

Ternaux, Guillaume-Louis, 203n108

territorial conquest. See On the Spirit of Conquest

territorial control, 2, 4, 5, 66–68; costs of, 69–70; and map of "Algérie," 101; rivalry over, 17–18

territoriality, 1, 282–83, 285

theatrical productions, 157–58

Thiers, Adolphe: and Chevalier's trip to US, 193; eloquence of, 192; and financing of war indemnity, 192; Histoire de la Révolution française, 190; on legitimacy of public debt, 193; on lending to governments, 199; and protectionism, 154; and Réflexions sur la réduction de la rente, 190, 191, 192, 197, 199

Third Republic: Algerian decrees of, 120; capital exports during, 223–24, 226; colonial empire of, 5, 9–10, 67–69, 74–75; crises of, 282; influence of Leroy-Beaulieu on, 67–69; impressionism and, 152–53; and judicial reform in Egypt, 263; mass consumption under, 173; nation-building under, 151; and the Revolution, 11, 12; public debt and military intervention of, 189; territorial expansion of, 282–83; universal exhibitions during, 172

Thomas, Brinley, 184–85

Tocqueville, Alexis de, 50; on Algeria, 99, 102, 103–4, 109; on atrocities, 77; and concern over consular power, 255; on French language in the US, 242; on materialism, 155; and study of American prisons, 54; on Thiers, 192; on trade barriers, 109

Tokugawa Japan, 242

Tomes, Robert, 123, 164

tourism, 159–60

trade liberalization, 62

trade surplus, 159, 165–66

Traité sur la science des finances (Leroy-Beaulieu), 195

"Travaux Publics," 60

treaties: commercial, 60, 62, 111, 115, 129–30; asymmetric, 63, 249

Treatise on Political Economy (Say), 94, 191

Treaty of 26 February 1834, 97

treaty of Balta Liman, 248, 249

treaty of Lausanne (1923), 249

Treaty of Paris (1783), 54

Treaty of Paris (1814), 43, 161

Treaty of Paris (1815), 188

Treaty of Paris (1856), 248

Tripoli, Regency of, 79–80

"Trois Glorieuses," 45

Trollope, Anthony, 175

Tunis, Regency of, 79–80

Tunisia, 67, 122, 282

Turkey, 38, 75, 210, 262

Turkish language, 239

United States: as capitalist imperial formation, 174; champagne consumption in, 147; Civil War in, 18, 66, 221, 222, 223, 280; as commodity producer, 128; Egypt compared to frontier of, 245; exports of, to Haiti, 204; and foreign investment, 185–86; French exports to, 156; French language in, 242; as irresistible empire, 22–23; public debt of, 195; smart power of, 2; and trade with Britain, 32, 35, 41; war of independence of, 34

Universal Exhibition of 1855 (Paris), 168–69

Universal Exhibition of 1862 (London), 169

Universal Exhibition of 1867 (Paris), 168, 169–70, 171

'Urabi, Ahmed, 267, 269

Urbain, Ismaÿl (Thomas): on Algeria for Algerians, 112, 113, 119; and Arab Kingdom, 77, 112–13, 234; as Arabophile, 111, 114–15, 117, 118; in *Capture of the Smala of Abd el-Kader* (1845) (Vernet), 113–14; and Chevalier, 113, 194; on economic development, 116–17; in Marseille, 120; in Egypt, 234; on industrial colonization, 116; racial ambivalence of, 116; as Saint-Simonian, 111, 112–13, 115, 234; and Senatus Consulte of 1865, 117–18; as translator for Duc D'Aumale, 113
urban planning, 144–45
Uruguay, 18
usury, 197–98

Vacher, Alfred, 272
vaudeville, 158
Veblen, Theodor, 156–57
Venezuela, 41
Vernet, Horace, 113–14
Vernet, Marie, 161
Versailles, 145
Veuve Cliquot, 161
Vienna, 281
Villèle, Joseph de, 203
Vizetelly, Henry, 123
Voltaire, 139
Voyer d'Argenson, René Louis, 187, 189

Wakefield, Edward Gibbon, 68, 195
wars: Anglo-French cooperation and, 18; American Civil War, 109, 128n16, 131, 156, 221, 223, 224n205; Anglo-Turkish war, 78; Anglo-Zulu war, 19; Arrow War (Second Opium War), 63, 167; Crimean War, 209, 248; effect of on silk industry, 141; Franco-Prussian war, 22, 66, 69, 128n16, 207–8, 262–63, 279; Greek War of Independence, 78; losses due to, 67–68; Opium Wars, 53, 63, 167; Russo-Turkish wars, 78; Seven Years' War, 30, 79; US war of independence, 34; World War I, 8, 177–78, 181, 185, 284; World War II, 185–86, 284
Waterloo, 18, 52, 189
Way We Live Now, The (Trollope), 175
weaponry, 89n59, 98, 100
West Africa, 273
Western Sudan, 273
West Indies, 30, 35, 80
Westphalian order, 31, 36
wines: Algerian exports of, 73; British taxes on, 130; consumed in Haiti, 203; French exports of, 131; growing production of, 153; Mariani, 174; at universal exhibition of 1867, 170–71. *See also* champagne
world fairs/universal exhibitions, 136–37, 169–70, 172
World War I. *See* First World War
World War II. *See* Second World War
Worth, Charles, 161–62

Zola, Emile: *Au Bonheur des Dames*, 144n65; on *Banque Universelle*, 216; on Bonapartist corruption, 280; on Gérôme, 6–7; on immorality of financial speculation, 225–26; *La Débâcle*, 277; *L'Argent*, 175–76, 216; as author of Rougon-Macquart series, 175, 207, 277; on women and investment, 216
Zoroastrianism, 46

A NOTE ON THE TYPE

This book has been composed in Arno, an Old-style serif typeface in the classic Venetian tradition, designed by Robert Slimbach at Adobe.